America's
TEST KITCHEN

ALSO BY THE EDITORS AT AMERICA'S TEST KITCHEN

The New Family Cookbook

The Complete Cooking for Two Cookbook

The America's Test Kitchen Cooking School Cookbook

The Cook's Illustrated Meat Book

The Cook's Illustrated Baking Book

The Science of Good Cooking

The Cook's Illustrated Cookbook

Pressure Cooker Perfection

The America's Test Kitchen Menu Cookbook

The America's Test Kitchen Quick Family Cookbook

The America's Test Kitchen Healthy Family Cookbook

The America's Test Kitchen Family Baking Book

THE AMERICA'S TEST KITCHEN LIBRARY SERIES

The Make-Ahead Cook

The How Can It Be Gluten Free Cookbook

Slow Cooker Revolution Volume 2: The Easy-Prep Edition

The Six-Ingredient Solution

Comfort Food Makeovers

The America's Test Kitchen D.I.Y. Cookbook

Pasta Revolution

Simple Weeknight Favorites

Slow Cooker Revolution

The Best Simple Recipes

THE TV COMPANION SERIES

The Complete Cook's Country TV Show Cookbook

The Complete America's Test Kitchen TV Show Cookbook 2001–2015

America's Test Kitchen: The TV Companion Cookbook (2002–2009 and 2011–2015 Editions)

THE COOK'S COUNTRY SERIES

From Our Grandmothers' Kitchens

Cook's Country Blue Ribbon Desserts

Cook's Country Best Potluck Recipes

Cook's Country Best Lost Suppers

Cook's Country Best Grilling Recipes

The Cook's Country Cookbook

America's Best Lost Recipes

AMERICA'S TEST KITCHEN ANNUALS

The Best of America's Test Kitchen (2007–2014 Editions)

Cooking for Two (2010–2013 Editions)

Light & Healthy (2010–2012 Editions)

THE BEST RECIPE SERIES

The New Best Recipe

More Best Recipes

The Best One-Dish Suppers

Soups, Stews & Chilis

The Best Skillet Recipes

The Best Slow & Easy Recipes

The Best Chicken Recipes

The Best International Recipe

The Best Make-Ahead Recipe

The Best 30-Minute Recipe

The Best Light Recipe

The Cook's Illustrated Guide to Grilling and Barbecue

Best American Side Dishes

Cover & Bake

Baking Illustrated

Italian Classics

American Classics

FOR A FULL LISTING OF ALL OUR BOOKS OR TO ORDER TITLES

CooksIllustrated.com

AmericasTestKitchen.com

or call 800-611-0759

THE BEST OF

America's
TEST KITCHEN

THE YEAR'S BEST RECIPES,
EQUIPMENT REVIEWS, AND TASTINGS

2015

BY THE EDITORS AT
AMERICA'S TEST KITCHEN

AMERICA'S TEST KITCHEN
17 Station Street, Brookline, MA 02445

THE BEST OF AMERICA'S TEST KITCHEN 2015
The Year's Best Recipes, Equipment Reviews, and Tastings

1st Edition

Hardcover: $35 US
ISBN-13: 978-1-936493-92-0 ISBN-10: 1-936493-92-6
ISSN: 1940-3925

Manufactured in the United States of America

10 9 8 7 6 5 4 3 2 1

Distributed by America's Test Kitchen
17 Station Street, Brookline, MA 02445

EDITORIAL DIRECTOR: Jack Bishop
EDITORIAL DIRECTOR, BOOKS: Elizabeth Carduff
EXECUTIVE EDITOR: Lori Galvin
ASSISTANT EDITOR: Melissa Herrick
EDITORIAL ASSISTANTS: Rachel Greenhaus and Samantha Ronan
DESIGN DIRECTOR: Amy Klee
ART DIRECTOR, BOOKS: Greg Galvan
ASSOCIATE ART DIRECTOR, BOOKS: Taylor Argenzio
DESIGNER: Jen Kanavos Hoffman
PHOTOGRAPHY DIRECTOR: Julie Cote
FRONT COVER PHOTOGRAPH: Carl Tremblay
STAFF PHOTOGRAPHER: Daniel J. van Ackere
ADDITIONAL PHOTOGRAPHY BY: Keller + Keller, Carl Tremblay, and Steve Klise
FOOD STYLING: Catrine Kelty and Marie Piraino
PHOTOSHOOT KITCHEN TEAM:
    ASSOCIATE EDITOR: Chris O'Connor
    TEST COOK: Daniel Cellucci
    ASSISTANT TEST COOK: Cecelia Jenkins
ILLUSTRATOR: John Burgoyne
PRODUCTION DIRECTOR: Guy Rochford
SENIOR PRODUCTION MANAGER: Jessica Quirk
SENIOR PROJECT MANAGER: Alice Carpenter
PRODUCTION AND TRAFFIC COORDINATOR: Britt Dresser
WORKFLOW AND DIGITAL ASSET MANAGER: Andrew Mannone
SENIOR COLOR AND IMAGING SPECIALIST: Lauren Pettapiece
PRODUCTION AND IMAGING SPECIALISTS: Heather Dube and Lauren Robbins
PROOFREADER: Elizabeth Emery
COPY EDITOR: Cheryl Redmond
INDEXER: Elizabeth Parson

PICTURED ON THE FRONT COVER: French Apple Tart (page 269)

CONTENTS

STARTERS AND SALADS

BLACK OLIVE TAPENADE

✓ WHY THIS RECIPE WORKS: Tapenade, the piquant olive spread from Provence, can wake up the most tired taste buds whether slathered on bruschetta, used as a dip for crudités, or whisked into a vinaigrette for a flavor boost. In developing our own version, we found that most recipes produced spreads with unbalanced flavor. For the best olive character in our spread, we used a ratio of 3 parts bright, fruity, brine-cured olives to 1 part earthy, rich, salt-cured olives. To ensure that the olives took center stage, we used a judicious hand with supporting ingredients like capers, anchovies, garlic, mustard, and olive oil. Finally, to temper saltiness and provide a creamy texture, we incorporated a quick homemade butter of untoasted pine nuts.

When I'm not snacking on olives by the handful, I'm often turning them into tapenade. The cured fruits form the base of this rich, pungent Provençal paste, which typically includes capers, anchovies, garlic, and a few glugs of olive oil. Because all those ingredients are pantry staples, tapenade is my first thought when I need a bruschetta topping, a no-cook sauce for boiled potatoes or pasta, or a vinaigrette picker-upper. Best of all, the hands-on work required for this soft spread is practically nil: a few seconds in the food processor and you're done.

But despite its ease and countless applications, good tapenade is hard to come by. It should spotlight the olives but also round out their assertiveness with rich, savory, and subtly sharp background flavors; however, just about every jarred condiment I've tasted and every recipe I've followed has been flawed. The tapenades are either too sharp, too fishy, or too salty—sometimes all three—not to mention greasy. I was convinced that the secret to producing bold but balanced tapenade was in the details. I'd have to fine-tune each component.

My supermarket's olive aisle was an obvious, if confusing, place to start. I wasn't just choosing among olive varieties; more significantly, I was choosing among harvesting and curing methods, which largely determine the differences that we see and taste in olives. The most traditional tapenades are made from black olives, and partly to help narrow the field, I decided to stick with these. Other than flavorless lye-cured canned black olives, I still had two styles to choose from: brine-cured and salt-cured (often referred to as oil-cured—a misnomer). I scooped up a couple of varieties within the two curing categories and processed 2 cups of

each olive in a bare-bones recipe, hoping that these basic tapenades would make apparent the best olive for the job. A dozen batches later, tasters weighed in. No one olive made a perfect spread: Though tasters favored the bright tanginess of kalamatas over the other brine-cured black olives, niçoise and Sicilian, the tapenade was one-dimensional. With their earthy richness, salt-cured black olives had complexity in spades (not to mention creamy texture), but that quality was overwhelmed by their heavy saltiness and bitterness.

Since one style of olive wasn't going to cut it, I started mixing and matching kalamatas and salt-cured olives until I figured out the right balance for complex flavor: 3 parts brine-cured olives to 1 part earthier, more intense salt-cured ones.

Satisfied with my olive base, I sifted through a stack of tapenade recipes for suggested amounts of capers, anchovies, garlic, and oil, as well as any other potential additions. Those sources—and several more tests—confirmed that I'd been right with 3 tablespoons of capers. (Tapenade actually takes its name from *tapeno*, the Provençal word for caper, but the briny buds almost always play a supporting role.) I minced and added a second anchovy to amp up the spread's background meatiness and stepped down the oil to ¼ cup, heeding my tasters' complaints about greasiness. I also switched from processing the oil with the rest of the ingredients to stirring it into the puree by hand, since whirring the oil causes its bitter-tasting polyphenols to separate and disperse throughout the mixture.

Slowly the strong flavors were evening out, and yet the ingredients hadn't quite coalesced into the superior result that I'd hoped for. My tapenade was still bluntly salty, and something was missing. I tried other additions, some off-the-wall: citrus zest and juice, brandy, mustard and mustard powder, cooked egg yolk, yeast extract—even canned tuna. My traditionalist tasters rejected all but the Dijon. Its subtle kick was a keeper.

Saltiness was another matter, since almost every ingredient was loaded with sodium. Rinsing the capers and anchovies helped, but not enough. What I needed was a buffer, and fat immediately came to mind since we know that it has a dulling effect on our taste receptors. My tapenade couldn't hold more oil, so I went back to my research for other clues and found an unlikely idea in a Romanian recipe: butter. I figured butter would temper the salt without separating out and turning the olive paste greasy. (Unlike oil, butter remains

BLACK OLIVE TAPENADE VINAIGRETTE

TAPPING INTO TWO KINDS OF OLIVES

The two common olive-curing methods affect the flavor of the fruit (and our tapenade) very differently.

BRINE-CURED: TANGY

Brine-cured black olives (made with mature fruit) undergo natural fermentation over a period of months in a strong salt brine, much like naturally fermented pickles. During fermentation, sugars in the fruit convert into acetic and lactic acid, providing the characteristic sour flavor.

SALT-CURED: EARTHY

Salt-cured black olives (often misleadingly labeled oil-cured) are packed in salt when fully ripe, left to dehydrate and soften over a month or two, and then briefly plumped in oil. The intensely flavored results have soft flesh, little acidity, and a good bit of their original bitterness.

A NUTTY SOLUTION TO SALTINESS

Given that tapenade is built on olives, capers, and anchovies, it can be tricky to keep the spread's saltiness in check. We adjusted ingredient ratios and rinsed away excess salt before we found our real fix in an Italian pesto–inspired trick: grinding pine nuts into paste. The mild flavored (untoasted) nuts, which, like the other tapenade ingredients, are a staple in Mediterranean cuisine, temper the saltiness without adding much distracting flavor of their own.

emulsified in the tapenade.) Indeed, when I added a few tablespoons to my tapenade, the spread's soft, silky texture was convincing, and the sodium was mellower. But the butter's dairy flavor just wasn't the right fit.

But butter wasn't a bad idea, I thought as I spied several kinds of nut butters in the pantry. They, too, had plenty of emulsified fat, so I processed my next batches with unsalted peanut, almond, and cashew butters. These tapenades looked great—rich, soft, and not at all oily—and the salt was in check. But I hadn't solved the flavor problem; in fact, the nuts' flavors were more distracting than the flavor of regular butter.

Just then I spotted a fellow cook tossing pine nuts into a food processor to make pesto, and the gears in my head started turning: Why couldn't I do the same and simply process these mild nuts (untoasted to keep their flavor quiet) into a butter before adding the rest of

my ingredients? Grinding ⅓ cup of them into a sticky, smooth butter took all of 30 seconds, and just as I'd hoped, they blended seamlessly into the background.

This was the tapenade I'd envisioned: robust, rich, just salty enough, and faintly sharp with garlic and mustard. I thought I'd keep the stuff on hand, just in case I needed a quick vinaigrette or an impromptu spread for bruschetta (tapenade keeps well for up to two weeks), but the way my colleagues kept snacking on it I knew it wouldn't last long.

—DAN SOUZA, *Cook's Illustrated*

Black Olive Tapenade

MAKES ABOUT 1½ CUPS

The tapenade must be refrigerated for at least 18 hours before serving. It's important to use untoasted pine nuts in this recipe so that they provide creaminess but little flavor of their own. We prefer the rich flavor of kalamata olives, but any high-quality brine-cured black olive, such as niçoise, Sicilian, or Greek, can be substituted. Do not substitute brine-cured olives for the salt-cured olives. Serve the tapenade as a spread with sliced crusty bread or as a dip with raw vegetables.

- ⅓ cup pine nuts
- 1½ cups pitted kalamata olives
- ½ cup pitted salt-cured black olives
- 3 tablespoons capers, rinsed
- 2 anchovy fillets, rinsed and patted dry
- 2 teaspoons Dijon mustard
- ½ garlic clove, minced
- ¼ cup extra-virgin olive oil

1. In food processor fitted with metal blade, process pine nuts until reduced to paste that clings to walls and avoids blade, about 20 seconds. Scrape down bowl to redistribute paste and process until paste again clings to walls and avoids blade, about 5 seconds. Repeat scraping and processing once more (pine nuts should form mostly smooth, tahini-like paste).

2. Scrape down bowl to redistribute paste and add olives, capers, anchovies, mustard, and garlic. Pulse until finely chopped, about 15 pulses, scraping down bowl halfway through pulsing. Transfer mixture to medium bowl and stir in oil until well combined.

3. Transfer to container, cover, and refrigerate for at least 18 hours or up to 2 weeks. Bring to room temperature and stir thoroughly before serving.

VARIATION

Black Olive Tapenade Vinaigrette
MAKES ABOUT ½ CUP

Serve on salad greens or with grilled swordfish, halibut, or sea bass.

    3 tablespoons Black Olive Tapenade
    4 teaspoons lemon juice
    ½ teaspoon honey
    3 tablespoons extra-virgin olive oil

Whisk tapenade, lemon juice, and honey together in medium bowl. Slowly whisk in oil until combined.

CHEDDAR OLIVES

✓ **WHY THIS RECIPE WORKS:** Pimento-stuffed olives wrapped in cheesy biscuit dough could be perfect party appetizers, but the dough needed some fine-tuning. Too much cheese and butter made the dough melt in the oven, and too little left it dry and crumbly with barely any cheese flavor. To find a happy medium, we used 7 tablespoons of butter and 2 cups of cheese, which made a tender dough that held its shape when baked. Worcestershire, paprika, and cayenne gave our surprise-inside party snacks an extra kick.

Recently, a coworker told me about a recipe for cheddar olives—pimento-stuffed cocktail olives swaddled in nuggets of cheesy biscuit dough—that his mom used to make. As soon as I heard about them, I had a feeling they would have the cheesy, pickle-y pluck to rival the usual pigs-in-a-blanket and mini-quiche party fare. After testing a few recipes, I saw clearly that while the idea was clever, the reality wasn't. At least not yet.

The cheesiest, most tender, and most delicious of the doughs liquefied in the oven, leaving the olives on top of greasy (but admittedly tasty) lumps of dough. The tidiest-looking cheddar olives stayed neatly tucked inside the dough after baking, but this dough was so dry and tough that some tasters peeled it off before eating the olives. Getting cheddar olives to be either tasty or neat was no problem. But could I have both?

With two sticks of butter and 4 cups of cheese in the dough, the problem with the tasty but messy recipe from the first round was too much fat. As for the dry yet neat dough, it contained less than a quarter of the cheese and butter and was held together by an egg, so neither its resilience nor its unappetizing texture was surprising. I decided to take a moderate approach: I used 7 (rather than 2 or 16) tablespoons of butter and 2 (rather than 1 or 4) cups of shredded cheese, plus one egg. That fixed the grease problem and helped the dough hold its shape yet still keep decent cheese flavor. But I still wasn't happy with how the dough adhered to the olives—some of the soft dough slid off during baking, leaving me with partially naked olives. Popping the cheddar olives in the fridge for an hour turned out to be an easy fix, firming up the dough enough for it to stand up to the heat of the oven. The chilling time also prevented the butter from leaking out when I baked the olives. Although the mini appetizers were turning out well using regular-size olives, I decided to try out a few different sizes to see if I could cram more olive flavor into the cheesy dough. A few simple tests revealed that my first instinct had been correct—the cheddar olives made with colossal or queen olives were simply too big, and detracted from the bite-size appeal. I stuck with regular-size olives.

Having gotten the major issues under control, I circled back to try some of the seasonings I'd seen in other recipes. After a few tests, I found that a teaspoon of Worcestershire sauce, along with some paprika and cayenne, gave the flavor of the dough a leg up. Move over, cocktail franks and mini quiches, and make room for salty, cheesy, just-try-to-stop-at-one cheddar olives.

—SARAH GABRIEL, *Cook's Country*

Cheddar Olives
MAKES 40 WRAPPED OLIVES

Use regular-size, not colossal or queen, cocktail olives. The cheddar olives must chill for at least 1 hour before baking. They taste best within a few hours of baking.

40	pimento-stuffed green olives, rinsed
1	cup (5 ounces) all-purpose flour
¾	teaspoon paprika
½	teaspoon pepper
⅛	teaspoon cayenne pepper
8	ounces extra-sharp cheddar cheese, shredded (2 cups)
7	tablespoons unsalted butter, cut into 7 pieces
1	large egg, lightly beaten
1	tablespoon water
1	teaspoon Worcestershire sauce

1. Spread olives on dish towel and roll around to dry. Pulse flour, paprika, pepper, and cayenne in food processor until combined, about 3 pulses. Add cheddar and butter and pulse until mixture resembles coarse crumbs, about 12 pulses. Add egg, water, and Worcestershire and process until dough ball forms, about 20 seconds.

2. Working with 2 teaspoons dough and 1 olive at a time, pat dough into 2-inch circle; place olive in center of dough; form dough around olive; and roll cheddar olive between your hands to make uniform ball. Place cheddar olives on large platter, cover tightly with plastic wrap, and refrigerate for 1 hour or up to 24 hours (or freeze to bake later).

3. Adjust oven racks to upper-middle and lower-middle positions and heat oven to 350 degrees. Line 2 rimmed baking sheets with parchment paper. Space cheddar olives evenly on prepared sheets. Bake until bottoms are well browned and tops are golden, 16 to 18 minutes (if baking from frozen, increase cooking time to about 25 minutes), switching and rotating sheets halfway through baking. Transfer cheddar olives to wire rack and let cool, about 30 minutes, before serving.

NOTES FROM THE TEST KITCHEN

SHAPING CHEDDAR OLIVES

After you've patted 2 teaspoons of dough into a circle, place olive in center and encase it with dough.

SOCCA

✔ WHY THIS RECIPE WORKS: In southern France, savory flatbreads called *socca* are a popular street food prepared from a simple, thin batter made with chickpea flour. Traditionally, the pancake-like batter is poured into a cast-iron skillet and baked in a wood-burning oven. To modify the cooking method for the home kitchen, we used the stovetop and a nonstick skillet. Making smaller flatbreads ensured that they cooked through quickly, plus it gave them a higher ratio of crunchy crust to soft interior.

Socca, savory chickpea flatbreads, may have originated in Italy, but they became truly popular as a street food in southern France. Socca boast crisp edges with a tender interior and an earthy, nutty flavor—cut into wedges, they make the perfect finger food to accompany a glass of wine before dinner. With so few ingredients—chickpea flour, water, olive oil, salt, and pepper—their simplicity poses undeniable appeal.

But there is a catch: Traditionally, the batter is poured into a cast-iron skillet and baked in a large, often wood-burning, oven, which gives the socca a smoky flavor and a crunchy, blistered top. But without a wood-burning oven, how could I modify the process to work in a home kitchen? And chickpea flour? That's not a flour most cooks generally keep on hand. Would it be worth seeking out this unusual ingredient?

To start, I tested cooking methods. One of the first recipes I tried was a modified version of the traditional recipe. It called for pouring the batter into a preheated cast-iron skillet and then baking the socca in the oven. I wasn't fond of this technique—pouring the batter into a hot skillet and then transferring the heavy pan back into the oven was cumbersome, and the socca turned out dry and limp instead of crisp and tender. Another recipe I tried called for three eggs to be added to the traditional ingredients, for a hybrid socca-crêpe. This recipe produced a batter that was thick and heavy, and the socca turned out almost rubbery. I ditched the eggs, deciding to stick with the traditional ingredients as my base.

After testing various oven methods, however, I still couldn't get the socca to crisp up. For the next test, I shifted my attention from the oven to the stovetop, and traded the cast-iron skillet for a nonstick skillet of a similar size. Feeling optimistic, I drizzled some oil in the pan and poured in the batter. But this iteration turned out even worse than the oven-baked versions—the direct heat of the stove cooked only the bottom of the flatbread, leaving the top sticky and raw. And flipping the hefty round of dough proved difficult and impractical. Luckily, there was an easy solution: For the next batch, I decided to divide the batter to make several smaller flatbreads. I switched to a smaller skillet and used only ½ cup batter for each flatbread. This made the socca easy to flip, allowed them to cook through, and as an added bonus, it also gave the flatbreads even more crisp outer crust.

Since socca contain so few ingredients, every element affected the flavor, which left little room for error. But still, I wondered if a more commonly available flour could be substituted for the chickpea flour. I made a batch with whole-wheat flour, which wasn't bad, but the flavor was nothing like traditional socca. I decided it was worth seeking out chickpea flour, which can be found in small packages in natural food stores and well-stocked supermarkets, or online directly from the manufacturer. Olive oil added another layer of flavor—to a point. Too much oil left the socca greasy, since the chickpea flour could only absorb so much liquid. Three tablespoons of oil was the perfect amount for 1½ cups of flour. After several tests, I determined that an equal amount of flour and water gave the batter the pancake-like consistency I wanted.

Finally, the batter and the technique had come together to make perfect socca—soft and tender inside, with appealingly crisp crusts. But when I stacked them on a plate to cool, my hard-won crunchy crust quickly steamed and became soft and soggy. A quick fix made short work of this problem: I stored the cooked socca on a wire rack in a warm oven, which allowed air to circulate around the flatbreads and kept the crunchy crusts intact. Since the socca cooked quickly, having the oven preheated also provided a "landing zone" where the socca stayed warm until they were ready to serve.

Since I now had socca which cooked up quickly and easily, I created two variations on these simple flatbreads. The first adds ground coriander and lemon zest for a bit of flavorful zing. The second, inspired by a recipe I tested early in the process, stirs in sweet caramelized onions and fragrant fresh rosemary for a heartier socca. Drizzled with good olive oil, socca will be a regular addition to my hors d'oeuvres selection.

—STEPHANIE PIXLEY, *America's Test Kitchen Books*

Socca (Chickpea Flatbreads)
MAKES 5 FLATBREADS; SERVES 4 TO 6

The flavor and consistency of chickpea flour is essential to this recipe. Look for chickpea flour (also sold as garbanzo bean flour) in well-stocked supermarkets or online. Chickpea flour should be stored in an airtight container in the refrigerator or freezer. Serve socca warm, drizzled with olive oil and sprinkled with coarse salt and freshly ground pepper.

1½ cups (6¾ ounces) chickpea (garbanzo bean) flour
½ teaspoon salt
½ teaspoon pepper
1½ cups water
6 tablespoons plus 1 teaspoon extra-virgin olive oil

1. Adjust oven rack to middle position and heat oven to 200 degrees. Set wire rack in rimmed baking sheet and place in oven. Whisk chickpea flour, salt, and pepper together in bowl. Slowly whisk in water and 3 tablespoons oil until combined and smooth.

2. Heat 2 teaspoons oil in 8-inch nonstick skillet over medium-high heat until shimmering. Add ½ cup batter to skillet, tilting pan to coat bottom evenly. Reduce heat to medium and cook until crisp at edges and golden brown on bottom, 3 to 5 minutes. Flip socca and continue to cook until second side is browned, 2 to 3 minutes. Transfer to wire rack in preheated oven. Repeat with remaining batter and oil. Cut each socca into wedges and serve.

VARIATIONS
Coriander-Lemon Socca

Add 1 teaspoon ground coriander and ½ teaspoon grated lemon zest to chickpea flour in step 1.

Caramelized Onion and Rosemary Socca

Heat 1 tablespoon olive oil in 8-inch nonstick skillet over medium-high heat until shimmering. Add ½ onion, sliced thin, reduce heat to medium, and cook, stirring often, until onion is softened and browned, about 10 minutes. Add 1½ teaspoons chopped fresh rosemary and cook until fragrant, about 30 seconds. Transfer to bowl and let cool slightly, then stir into chickpea flour batter. Wipe skillet clean and use in step 2.

MARYLAND CRAB FLUFF

MARYLAND CRAB FLUFF

✓ **WHY THIS RECIPE WORKS:** Battered and deep-fried crab cakes, called crab fluff, are a Baltimore specialty. For a twist on this regional favorite, we stirred a tempura-like batter right into our crab cake mixture, replacing some of the flour with crushed saltines for a lighter texture. This method was neater than dipping soft crab cakes into thin batter, and made a more cohesive crab fluff "fritter." We added extra flavor with scallions, Dijon mustard, and hot sauce.

While crab cakes are special occasion fare for most of us, along the crab-rich Maryland coast, many crab houses and fry shacks serve a more blue-collar, and possibly even more delicious, version: crab fluff. Crab fluff are battered and deep-fried Maryland crab cakes that usually come in a plastic basket with fries, coleslaw, and tartar sauce. Crispy fried crab cakes? Sign us up.

We hit our cookbook library and gathered recipes for crab fluff. Every version started with a basic crab cake: lump crab meat, an egg or two, a little mayo, some seasonings, and a minimal amount of saltine crumbs. But the batters were very different, ranging from heavy, pancakelike batters based on milk and flour; to beer batters resembling fried-fish batter; to light tempura batters made with flour, baking powder, and seltzer.

When we tasted the different versions, we preferred the lightness of the tempura-like batter. But there were problems: The recipes called for huge crab cakes, so they took a long time to cook and were a bit greasy. Also, trying to dip a soft crab cake into a thin batter proved a serious challenge, as the cakes fell apart and the batter dripped all over the counter on the way to the frying pot.

Our first fix, cutting the size of each crab cake in half, from ½ cup to ¼ cup (we used a dry measuring cup to portion the cakes before battering), was an easy one. This allowed the cakes to fry faster and "cleaner," with less grease absorption. To make them easier and less messy to put together, we started thinking about the elements of crab fluff—the crab cake and the batter—as a whole instead of two separate entities: It seemed a little crazy, but what if we mixed the batter (the flour, baking powder, and seltzer) right into the crab cake ingredients (the crabmeat, saltines, egg, mayo, and seasonings) instead of dipping the cakes into the batter? We could tell in our first test that this idea had promise—the "raw" fluff were now much easier and neater to transfer to the hot oil, and they were nicely cohesive when

cooked—but they were a little gummy and heavy. In the end, we cut the flour back from 1½ cups to ½ cup and upped the crushed saltines, going from six crackers to 10.

This recipe, which had shifted to something more like crab-fluff fritters, was almost there. After testing several times, it turned out that refrigerating the mix for at least 30 minutes before we portioned and fried it helped the mixture hold together. Spraying the dry measuring cup used to portion the fluff with vegetable oil spray meant that they slid out cleanly and safely into the hot oil. To give the fluff more flavor, we added sliced scallions, a little Dijon, and a tablespoon of hot sauce.

Crab fluff might not be fancy fare in Maryland, but these crisp, briny, sweet, almost delicate little cakes are so delicious that they'd suit any occasion at our houses.

—DIANE UNGER AND
CAROLYNN PURPURA MACKAY, *Cook's Country*

Maryland Crab Fluff
MAKES 12

You can buy jumbo lump crabmeat fresh or pasteurized; the latter is slightly cheaper. Our favorite pasteurized crabmeat is Phillips Premium Crab Jumbo. Serve fluff with cocktail or tartar sauce.

- 10 square or 11 round saltines, crushed fine
- ½ cup all-purpose flour
- 1½ teaspoons Old Bay seasoning
- ½ teaspoon baking powder
- ⅛ teaspoon cayenne pepper
- ½ cup seltzer
- 2 scallions, sliced thin
- 1 large egg plus 1 large yolk
- 2 tablespoons mayonnaise
- 1 tablespoon Dijon mustard
- 1 tablespoon hot sauce
- 1 pound jumbo lump crabmeat, picked over for shells and pressed dry between paper towels
- 2 quarts peanut or vegetable oil

1. Whisk crushed saltines, flour, Old Bay, baking powder, and cayenne together in large bowl. Whisk seltzer, scallions, egg and yolk, mayonnaise, mustard, and hot sauce into saltine mixture until combined. Gently fold crabmeat into batter until well combined. Cover and refrigerate for at least 30 minutes or up to 2 hours.

SAFE PORTIONING INTO HOT OIL

First chill the batter so it's not too loose. Next, coat a ¼-cup dry measure with vegetable oil spray, scoop the batter, and gently nudge each fluff into the oil with a spoon.

2. Set wire rack in rimmed baking sheet and line half of rack with triple layer of paper towels. Add oil to large Dutch oven until it measures about 1½ inches deep and heat over medium-high heat to 350 degrees.

3. Spray ¼-cup dry measure with vegetable oil spray. Place 6 packed scoops of crab mixture in hot oil, using spoon to help dislodge batter from dry measure. Adjust burner, if necessary, to maintain oil temperature between 325 and 350 degrees. Fry until deep golden brown and hot throughout, about 5 minutes. Transfer crab fluff to paper towel–lined side of rack and let drain for 1 minute, then move to unlined side of rack. Return oil to 350 degrees and repeat with remaining crab mixture. Serve.

SLOW-COOKER GARLICKY SHRIMP

✓ WHY THIS RECIPE WORKS: The gentle heat of the slow cooker is perfect for producing tender shrimp without fear of overcooking, so we set out to create a slow-cooker version of the tapas classic *gambas al ajillo,* or garlicky shrimp. In tapas restaurants, the shrimp are often served with crusty bread to soak up their flavorful oil. To adapt the recipe, we cooked sliced garlic and spices in olive oil right in the slow cooker. Only 30 minutes was enough to soften the raw flavor of the garlic and allow the spices' flavors to bloom. Once the oil was sufficiently flavored, we stirred in the shrimp. A quick poach in the garlicky oil was all it took to cook and season the shrimp and make this tapas favorite table-ready.

If there is one thing that can command attention in a Spanish tapas restaurant, it's the heady aroma wafting up from a dish of *gambas al ajillo*—little shrimp sizzling in a pool of olive oil and garlic. One bite will confirm that the garlic shares equal billing with the shrimp; when properly prepared, the shrimp is wonderfully sweet and tender and infused with deep garlic flavor. In restaurants, the dish is prepared by heating olive oil and aromatics in an earthenware ramekin before adding a small handful of shrimp. The shrimp are completely submerged in the oil, which infuses them with flavor and protects them from overcooking. At a tapas restaurant, where your table is overflowing with other dishes, it's easy to be content with a few small shrimp. Back at home, where most cooks are going to prepare only a single appetizer, the dish needs to be more substantial, meaning either bigger shrimp or more small ones. And using more shrimp meant using a lot more oil—too much to serve as a dipping oil. How could I increase the number of shrimp without wasting several cups of oil?

The test kitchen has developed recipes for garlicky shrimp before, but this time, I wanted to use the slow cooker. Delicate, quick-cooking shrimp are surprisingly well suited to the slow cooker's gentle heat. But I still needed to wrestle with two problems: how to coax the most flavor from a few simple ingredients, and how to avoid overcooking the shrimp while still infusing them with as much flavor as possible.

I knew that the shrimp themselves would only need a short time in the slow cooker to cook through. I decided to use large shrimp, since they take a bit longer to cook than their smaller cousins, giving them maximum time to absorb flavor from the garlic oil. I also peeled the shrimp, so the flesh could quickly pick up flavor. Even without the shell, the coating of oil would protect the delicate shrimp. I found that completely submerging the shrimp in oil was not necessary, since the shrimp would be sufficiently protected with just a thin layer. Just ¾ cup of oil was enough to coat 2 pounds of shrimp and provide enough extra oil to dip pieces of crusty bread into when serving.

Dumping all the ingredients into the slow cooker at the same time, while the simplest method, was a no-go: When perfectly cooked, the shrimp turned out bland and uninteresting, but letting them spend more time in the aromatic oil resulted in overcooking. I needed to

SLOW-COOKER GARLICKY SHRIMP

get more flavor faster. I knew that allicin, the chemical responsible for garlic's flavor, is highly soluble in oil. Allicin is produced when garlic is cut or crushed, but it quickly degrades into less flavorful compounds when exposed to air. Once in oil, however, the compound is protected from air and dissolves into the oil, imparting lots of flavor. With this in mind, I decided to develop flavor in the oil first, before using it to cook the shrimp.

Because of the slow cooker's moist heat environment, I knew that I would need to use lots of garlic so that the flavor did not become muted. I cooked the oil for 30 minutes with the aromatics to infuse flavor and bloom the spices. Tasters liked the addition of smoked paprika, which added a warmth and roundness to the oil. When the oil's flavor had developed, I stirred in 2 pounds of shrimp. After a few test runs, I settled on 20 to 40 minutes (depending on the size of slow cooker) as the perfect amount of time to cook the shrimp.

Just 50 minutes and ¾ cup of oil later, I had enough perfect, flavorful, garlicky shrimp to feed a crowd. The only problem now: making sure to save room for dinner.

—STEPHANIE PIXLEY, *America's Test Kitchen Books*

Slow-Cooker Garlicky Shrimp

SERVES 8 TO 10

This recipe is designed to work with 3½- to 7-quart slow cookers. While we prefer the deeper flavor of smoked paprika in this recipe, you can substitute sweet paprika. Serve with crusty bread for dipping in the infused oil.

- ¾ cup extra-virgin olive oil
- 6 garlic cloves, sliced thin
- 1 teaspoon smoked paprika
  Salt and pepper
- ¼ teaspoon red pepper flakes
- 2 pounds large shrimp (26 to 30 per pound), peeled and deveined
- 1 tablespoon minced fresh parsley

1A. FOR A 3½- TO 5-QUART SLOW COOKER: Combine oil, garlic, paprika, 1 teaspoon salt, ¼ teaspoon pepper, and pepper flakes in slow cooker, cover, and cook until flavors meld, about 30 minutes on high. Stir in shrimp, cover, and cook on high until opaque throughout, about 40 minutes, stirring halfway through cooking.

1B. FOR A 5½- TO 7-QUART SLOW COOKER: Combine oil, garlic, paprika, 1 teaspoon salt, ¼ teaspoon pepper, and pepper flakes in slow cooker, cover, and cook until flavors meld, about 30 minutes on high. Stir in shrimp, cover, and cook on high until opaque throughout, about 20 minutes, stirring halfway through cooking.

2. Transfer shrimp and oil mixture to serving dish. Sprinkle with parsley and serve.

GREEN BEAN SALAD

✅ **WHY THIS RECIPE WORKS:** For a ready-when-you-are salad that could easily be made ahead of time, we turned to crisp-tender green beans. Blanching the beans with a brief stint in boiling water followed by a cold shock in an ice bath ensured that the beans stayed bright green and retained their crisp texture even in the acidic dressing. Sliced radishes and toasted almonds gave the salad spice and crunch, and a lemony, mustard-laced dressing provided zing.

Christmas, Easter, Fourth of July, Thanksgiving—no matter the holiday, in my house green beans are on the table. So I thought that it would be nice to come up with a recipe that I could serve cold or at room temperature to relieve some of the pressure of delivering everything hot to the table at the same time.

A little research unearthed endless possibilities. As a starting point, I chose a diverse bunch of recipes—some called for cooking and chilling the beans, while others called for serving them raw and letting them soften in an acidic vinaigrette. Some recipes instructed the cook to leave the green beans whole, while the rest employed every manner of chopping, shredding, and fancy slicing. Seasonings ran the gamut from ginger and soy sauce to sage and rosemary. After an afternoon of cooking, I lined up an array of differing dishes for me and my tasters to try.

When it came to the cooking method (or lack thereof), beans that were boiled and immediately dressed turned muddy and drab after sitting in the acidic dressing. That was OK with me because I was secretly rooting for the raw beans—less work for the cook is never a bad thing on a holiday (or any day). But the raw beans didn't soften sufficiently in the dressing unless they were cut into paper-thin shreds; after I meticulously and laboriously sliced 2 pounds of beans, I knew that this procedure was a nonstarter. I opted instead for boiling and then shocking the beans, which means plunging them into ice water to immediately halt the cooking to preserve texture and color. Working with a handful of beans at a time and cutting them into 1½-inch pieces proved fast and efficient. As for the cooking, a few tests revealed that 6 minutes in boiling water, followed by the ice-water dunk to halt the cooking, produced crisp-tender beans that could soak up the flavorful dressing.

As for the dressing, I cast about for fresh, bright flavors that would suit the beans. A combination of lemon juice and zest, shallot, mustard, garlic, and olive oil proved just the thing. For herbs, I tried several before landing on dill. When it came to supporting players, sliced radishes brought color and peppery spice, while toasted almonds provided contrasting crunch.

I let the dressed salad sit for 30 minutes to give the flavors time to meld while I readied the rest of the meal; the forgiving timing of my bean salad was a real plus. I scattered on the nuts just before serving so they'd retain their crunch. At last, my green beans were well seasoned, nicely cooked, bright, and beautiful. Scrawled one test cook on her final tasting sheet: "Delicious. Don't change a thing."

—REBECCAH MARSTERS, *Cook's Country*

Green Bean Salad

SERVES 8

If you don't own a salad spinner, lay the green beans on a clean dish towel to dry in step 1. Our favorite Dijon is Grey Poupon Dijon Mustard. You can use parsley instead of the dill.

- 2 **pounds green beans, trimmed and cut into 1½-inch lengths**
- **Salt and pepper**
- 1 **teaspoon grated lemon zest plus 3 tablespoons juice**
- 1 **shallot, minced**
- 1 **tablespoon Dijon mustard**
- 1 **garlic clove, minced**
- ¼ **cup extra-virgin olive oil**
- 8 **radishes, trimmed and sliced thin**
- 3 **tablespoons minced fresh dill**
- ½ **cup sliced almonds, toasted**

1. Bring 4 quarts water to boil in large pot. Fill large bowl halfway with ice and water. Add green beans and 1 tablespoon salt to boiling water and cook until crisp-tender, about 6 minutes. Drain green beans and place in ice bath to cool. Drain again, transfer to salad spinner, and spin dry. (Blanched, shocked, and dried green beans can be refrigerated for up to 2 days.)

2. Whisk lemon zest and juice, shallot, mustard, garlic, and 1½ teaspoons salt together in large bowl. Slowly whisk in oil until incorporated. Toss radishes, dill, and green beans with vinaigrette and let sit for 30 minutes or up to 2 hours, stirring occasionally. Stir almonds into salad. Season with salt and pepper to taste. Serve.

BRUSSELS SPROUT SALAD

WHY THIS RECIPE WORKS: To make Brussels sprouts shine in a salad, we needed to get rid of some of their vegetal rawness. Rather than cooking the sprouts, we marinated them in an acidic vinaigrette made with lemon juice and Dijon mustard. The flavorful dressing softened and seasoned the sprouts. Adding toasted pine nuts and shredded Pecorino Romano to our salad just before serving added a layer of crunch and nutty richness.

BRUSSELS SPROUT SALAD

It wasn't that long ago that Brussels sprouts ranked high on the list of America's most hated vegetables. The picture began to change when roasting came into vogue; this technique produced Brussels sprouts so caramelized, so tender, and so downright delicious that it turned loathers into lovers. Recently, another preparation has been making the rounds that I think has a good shot at converting any remaining skeptics: Brussels sprout salad.

Instead of calling for roasting the sprouts at high heat to make them taste great, this recipe requires no heat whatsoever: The Brussels sprouts are raw. This isn't as weird as it sounds. Brussels sprouts are very much like miniature cabbages, and we think nothing of eating cabbage raw; coleslaw, anyone? To make Brussels sprout salad, you thinly slice the sprouts and then, depending on which recipe you are following, toss them with variously flavored vinaigrettes. Recipes I looked at called for apple cider vinegar, balsamic vinegar, and Dijon mustard, to name a few. The salads are dressed up with equally variable add-ins, such as bacon, pomegranate seeds, sunflower seeds, dried cranberries, walnuts, feta cheese, Parmesan . . . the list goes on. Brussels sprouts, it was clear, can accommodate many flavors and textures.

In the kitchen, I lined up packages of Brussels sprouts and got to work slicing, whisking, tasting, and judging. The consensus? We liked them all pretty well. I could see that some of my work would be simply picking and choosing among options. That said, every recipe I made shared one not insignificant flaw: The Brussels sprouts themselves tasted underseasoned, and they were raw in a bad way; I felt rabbity munching on them. Before I fixed that, however, I'd settle on a dressing. A bright, lemony vinaigrette—with a touch of Dijon—seemed to give the most balance to the earthy Brussels sprouts.

To both soften and season the Brussels sprouts, I sliced them, tossed them with salt, and put them in a colander so that the water drawn out by the salt could drain away. I stole this idea from our test kitchen coleslaw method. But as I was waiting, it occurred to me that I could simplify. I made the salad again, this time without salting; I simply let the salad marinate in its lemony vinaigrette. The marinating proved just as effective, and it let me skip a step. A test of intervals of time revealed that the sprouts needed 30 minutes to become properly seasoned and softened.

With the method down and the dressing decided, I tested different flavor combinations. Many test salads later, my tasters and I agreed on a combination of minced shallot, minced garlic, toasted pine nuts, and Pecorino Romano—the last two added just before serving. I found that finely grating the Pecorino caused it to clump into pasty bits, but shredded Pecorino worked much better, incorporating seamlessly into the other ingredients. With this salad, I think that unfairly maligned Brussels sprouts may have shed their reputation for good.

—CAROLYNN PURPURA MACKAY, *Cook's Country*

Brussels Sprout Salad

SERVES 8

Slice the sprouts as thin as possible. Shred the Pecorino Romano on the large holes of a box grater.

- 3 **tablespoons lemon juice**
- 2 **tablespoons Dijon mustard**
- 1 **small shallot, minced**
- 1 **garlic clove, minced**
  Salt and pepper
- 6 **tablespoons extra-virgin olive oil**
- 2 **pounds Brussels sprouts, trimmed, halved, and sliced very thin**
- 3 **ounces Pecorino Romano cheese, shredded (1 cup)**
- ½ **cup pine nuts, toasted**

NOTES FROM THE TEST KITCHEN

HOW TO SLICE BRUSSELS SPROUTS
You can use the slicing disk of your food processor or slice the sprouts with a chef's knife. Follow these steps to do the latter safely and quickly.

1. TRIM: Trim stem end of each sprout and then cut each sprout in half through cut end.

2. SLICE: With flat surface on cutting board, thinly slice each half.

1. Whisk lemon juice, mustard, shallot, garlic, and ½ teaspoon salt together in large bowl. Slowly whisk in oil until incorporated. Toss Brussels sprouts with vinaigrette and let sit for at least 30 minutes or up to 2 hours.

2. Fold in Pecorino and pine nuts. Season with salt and pepper to taste. Serve.

VARIATION

Brussels Sprout Salad with Cheddar, Hazelnuts, and Apple

Substitute 1 cup shredded sharp cheddar for Pecorino and ½ cup hazelnuts, toasted, skinned, and chopped, for pine nuts. Add 1 Granny Smith apple, cored and cut into ½-inch pieces.

BROWN RICE SALAD

✓ WHY THIS RECIPE WORKS: For this versatile side dish, we wanted to highlight the hearty nuttiness of brown rice in a flavorful, bright salad. Of course, the key to perfect rice salad is perfect rice, which we achieved using the pasta method. Boiling the rice in an abundance of water allowed the grains to absorb water evenly from all sides, and the high temperature of the water cooked the rice in only 25 minutes. Sprinkling the rice with an acid (such as citrus juice or vinegar) while it was still warm boosted its flavor. We came up with four bold-flavored combinations that complemented and brightened the earthy rice in this new crowd-pleasing favorite.

Summertime invariably brings an endless stream of pasta salads. I don't have anything against a well-made pasta salad—but this year, I want to shake things up a bit. A rice salad would be a nice change of pace, except that the rice (which is typically white) usually offers little more personality than the pasta. Brown rice seems a lot more intriguing. It retains the bran and most of the germ that are removed to produce white rice—elements that give brown rice a nutty flavor and pleasantly chewy texture. Sounds perfect for a hearty, flavorful rice salad, yes?

Unfortunately, no. The recipes I tried demonstrated the usual problems with brown rice—it is gummy or tough (and sometimes both) and takes forever to cook.

The dressings were also off the mark, often so dull or heavy that they weighed down rather than enlivened the salad. I set out to correct both problems.

The test kitchen actually has an oven method for cooking brown rice that consistently turns out perfectly separate grains. However, on hot summer days, I like to avoid turning on the oven. Furthermore, this method takes a full hour. I wanted to find a faster but equally reliable cooking method.

First I needed to choose my rice. Temporarily using our tried-and-true oven method, I tested standard long-, medium-, and short-grain brown rice, preferring the longer variety since its grains were less starchy and sticky than the shorter types. I also tried two specialty long-grain rices—brown jasmine and brown basmati. Basmati took top honors for its mildly sweet, aromatic flavor.

I then cycled through my options for shortcutting the cooking time. I rejected the use of a rice cooker, as not everyone has this appliance. The microwave delivered, cooking 1½ cups of rice in a mere 25 minutes. Yet after testing countless combinations of full and partial power, covered or not, stirring or not, different ratios of rice to liquid—you name it—I couldn't get the rice to cook evenly every time.

On to the stovetop. I already knew that the standard procedure of starting the rice in cold water (using twice as much water as rice) and simmering until the liquid was fully absorbed wouldn't lead to evenly cooked results, so I skipped this approach. Instead, I tried steaming the rice in a strainer perched over simmering water. As it turned out, this method required the same amount of time as a cold-water start (about 50 minutes), and the rice was still not uniformly tender—plus the tiny grains stuck to the strainer. I wondered if using the pilaf method of sautéing the rice in fat and aromatics before adding water would offer any benefits, but it didn't: The cooking time was the same, the rice texture was still uneven, and the flavor imparted by the aromatics wasn't noticeable in the finished salad.

I had seen a few recipes that called for boiling the rice in an abundance of water and then draining off the liquid as you would for pasta; these recipes claimed that this produced more evenly cooked rice. If boiling had at least that advantage, I'd be making progress. I brought 3 quarts of water to a rolling boil, added salt and 1½ cups of rice, and started testing for tenderness after 40 minutes. I was surprised to find the rice so tender that it was falling apart. I threw it out and started a new batch, this time checking at the 20-minute mark. To my delight, the rice was nearly done at that point and fully tender about 5 minutes later. But would it be evenly cooked? I drained the rice, spread it on a baking sheet to cool, and tried several samples. The grains were pleasantly chewy, separate, and uniformly cooked. I had hit the jackpot. But I wanted to know why.

One reason that the rice cooked faster in boiling water was simply that the water was hotter—212 degrees versus around 204 degrees when it simmers during the absorption method. But after a chat with our science editor, I realized the significant impact of the greater volume of water: Simply put, the more boiling water in the pot the more energy it has to transfer to the food. What's more, with an abundance of water, each grain of rice can absorb liquid from all sides, cooking faster and more evenly.

Next, I wanted to pair the nutty rice with bold flavors and contrasting textures. One winning combination featured asparagus, almonds, and goat cheese. Another incorporated the kick of a jalapeño chile with cherry tomatoes, velvety avocado, tender-crisp scallions, and lime juice. Yet another combined earthy mushrooms and walnuts with sweet fennel, and a final variation paired sweet bell peppers with salty olives and buttery Manchego.

I also found that I had to enlist especially bright, lively vinaigrettes to balance the rice's earthiness. A standard vinaigrette contains just 1 part acid to 3 or 4—sometimes even 5—parts oil. I tinkered with this ratio, adding more acid until I reached a nearly 1:1 ratio, 2 tablespoons acid to 2½ tablespoons oil, which finally satisfied my tasters. I also learned to keep the quantity of dressing minimal: About ¼ cup for the entire salad allowed the nuttiness of the rice and the bold flavors of the mix-ins to shine through.

I also ran one final test in which I doubled back to the cooked rice itself. Borrowing an idea from several of the test kitchen's potato salad recipes, immediately after spreading the rice on a baking sheet to cool for about 15 minutes, I sprinkled it with 2 teaspoons of acid (vinegar or citrus juice). As it does with warm potatoes, the acid was absorbed into the rice, boosting the grain's flavor.

With hearty, lively flavors and substantial—but not heavy—textures, these quick salads may just steal the show at your next summer cookout.

—ADAM RIED, *Cook's Illustrated*

Brown Rice for Salad

MAKES ABOUT 5 CUPS

We like the flavor of brown basmati rice, but any long-grain brown rice is acceptable. Use the same vinegar or citrus juice called for in the salad you plan to make.

- 1½ cups long-grain brown rice
- 2 teaspoons salt
- 2 teaspoons vinegar or citrus juice

Bring 3 quarts water to boil in large pot. Add rice and salt; cook, stirring occasionally, until rice is tender, 22 to 25 minutes. Drain rice, transfer to parchment paper–lined rimmed baking sheet, and spread into even layer. Drizzle rice with vinegar or citrus juice and let cool completely, about 15 minutes.

Brown Rice Salad with Asparagus, Goat Cheese, and Lemon

SERVES 6 TO 8

Look for asparagus that is bright green and firm.

- 1 tablespoon vegetable oil
- 1 pound asparagus, trimmed
  Salt and pepper
- 2½ tablespoons extra-virgin olive oil
- 1 shallot, minced
- 1 teaspoon grated lemon zest plus 2 tablespoons juice
- 1 recipe Brown Rice for Salad
- 4 ounces goat cheese, crumbled (1 cup)
- ½ cup slivered almonds, toasted
- ¼ cup chopped fresh parsley

1. Heat vegetable oil in 12-inch skillet over medium-high heat until shimmering. Add half of asparagus with tips pointed in 1 direction and remaining asparagus with tips pointed in opposite direction. Using tongs, arrange spears in even layer (they will not quite fit into single layer); cover and cook until bright green and still

THE BENEFITS OF BOILING BROWN RICE

When rice is cooked on the stovetop via the absorption method, the grains absorb almost all of the small amount of liquid that's in the pot early on in the cooking process. This can lead to uneven results, since only the grains that fully hydrate at the start will completely soften, while the grains that didn't initially absorb enough liquid will remain firm.

We found that boiling brown rice in an abundance of water not only cooked it more evenly but also shaved a good 25 minutes off the usual 50 minutes needed for the absorption method (i.e., simmering the rice in a set amount of liquid). With a large volume of boiling water in the pot (which is drained off when the rice is done), the liquid can penetrate the grains evenly from all sides, so their starches gelatinize more uniformly as well as more quickly. Boiling the rice (versus simmering it) also speeds up cooking because boiling water contains more energy than simmering water. All in all, boiling is an excellent way to cook brown rice.

---

crisp, 2 to 5 minutes. Uncover, increase heat to high, season with salt and pepper, and continue to cook until tender and well browned on 1 side, 5 to 7 minutes, using tongs to occasionally move spears from center to edge of pan to ensure all are browned. Transfer to plate and let cool completely. Cut into 1-inch pieces.

2. Whisk olive oil, shallot, lemon zest and juice, ½ teaspoon salt, and ½ teaspoon pepper together in bowl. Transfer cooled rice to large bowl. Add asparagus, all but 2 tablespoons goat cheese, and dressing; toss to combine. Let stand for 10 minutes.

3. Add ⅓ cup almonds and 3 tablespoons parsley; toss to combine. Season with salt and pepper to taste. Sprinkle with remaining almonds, reserved 2 tablespoons goat cheese, and remaining 1 tablespoon parsley; serve.

Brown Rice Salad with Jalapeño, Tomatoes, and Avocado
SERVES 6 TO 8

To make this salad spicier, add the reserved chile seeds.

- 2½ tablespoons extra-virgin olive oil
- 2 teaspoons honey
- 2 garlic cloves, minced
- 1 teaspoon grated lime zest plus 2 tablespoons juice
- ½ teaspoon ground cumin
- Salt and pepper
- 1 recipe Brown Rice for Salad
- 10 ounces cherry tomatoes, halved
- 1 avocado, halved, pitted, and cut into ½-inch pieces
- 1 jalapeño chile, stemmed, seeds reserved, and minced
- 5 scallions, sliced thin
- ¼ cup minced fresh cilantro

1. Whisk oil, honey, garlic, lime zest and juice, cumin, ½ teaspoon salt, and ½ teaspoon pepper together in bowl. Transfer cooled rice to large bowl. Add tomatoes, avocado, jalapeño, and dressing; toss to combine. Let stand for 10 minutes.

2. Add ¼ cup scallions and cilantro; toss to combine. Season with salt and pepper to taste. Sprinkle with remaining scallions and serve.

Brown Rice Salad with Fennel, Mushrooms, and Walnuts
SERVES 6 TO 8

Cremini mushrooms can be substituted for the white mushrooms.

- 4 teaspoons vegetable oil
- 1 pound white mushrooms, trimmed and quartered
- Salt and pepper
- 1 large fennel bulb, stalks discarded, bulb halved, cored, and sliced thin
- 2½ tablespoons extra-virgin olive oil
- 2 tablespoons white wine vinegar
- 1 shallot, minced
- 1 recipe Brown Rice for Salad
- ⅔ cup walnuts, toasted and chopped coarse
- 2 tablespoons minced fresh tarragon
- 2 tablespoons minced fresh parsley

1. Heat 2 teaspoons vegetable oil in 12-inch skillet over medium-high heat until shimmering. Add mushrooms and ½ teaspoon salt; cook, stirring occasionally, until pan is dry and mushrooms are browned, 6 to 8 minutes. Transfer mushrooms to large plate and let cool completely. Heat remaining 2 teaspoons vegetable oil in now-empty skillet until shimmering. Add fennel and ¼ teaspoon salt; cook, stirring occasionally, until just browned and crisp-tender, 3 to 4 minutes. Transfer to plate with mushrooms.

2. Whisk olive oil, vinegar, shallot, ½ teaspoon salt, and ½ teaspoon pepper together in bowl. Transfer cooled rice to large bowl. Add vegetables and dressing; toss to combine. Let stand for 10 minutes.

3. Add ½ cup walnuts, tarragon, and 1 tablespoon parsley; toss to combine. Season with salt and pepper to taste. Sprinkle with remaining walnuts and remaining 1 tablespoon parsley; serve.

Brown Rice Salad with Red Bell Peppers, Olives, and Manchego

SERVES 6 TO 8

Manchego is a rich, buttery Spanish cheese.

- 1 tablespoon vegetable oil
- 2 red bell peppers, stemmed, seeded, and cut into ¾-inch pieces
  Salt and pepper
- 2½ tablespoons extra-virgin olive oil
- 2 tablespoons sherry vinegar
- 2 teaspoons grated orange zest
- 2 garlic cloves, minced
- ½ teaspoon paprika
- 1 recipe Brown Rice for Salad
- 2 celery ribs, cut into ½-inch pieces
- 3 ounces Manchego cheese, cut into ¼-inch pieces (¾ cup)
- ⅔ cup pitted green olives, chopped
- ¼ cup minced fresh parsley

1. Heat vegetable oil in 12-inch skillet over medium-high heat until shimmering. Add bell peppers and ½ teaspoon salt; cook, without stirring, until just softened and starting to brown, 3 to 4 minutes. Transfer to large plate and let cool completely.

2. Whisk olive oil, vinegar, orange zest, garlic, paprika, ½ teaspoon salt, and ½ teaspoon pepper together in bowl. Transfer cooled rice to large bowl. Add bell peppers, celery, Manchego, olives, and dressing; toss to combine. Let stand for 10 minutes.

3. Add 3 tablespoons parsley and toss to combine. Season with salt and pepper to taste. Sprinkle with remaining 1 tablespoon parsley and serve.

STRAWBERRY PRETZEL SALAD

✔ **WHY THIS RECIPE WORKS:** This tri-layer Midwestern specialty doesn't resemble salad all that much, but after one bite, its sweet-salty, creamy-crunchy combination grabbed our attention. We knew we could make this slightly offbeat potluck favorite shine with some home-made elements. We used pretzel sticks, which crushed more evenly than classically shaped pretzels, to create a sturdy crust. We replaced the whipped topping called for in most recipes with real cream, which we whipped into softened cream cheese with some sugar for a tangy, not-too-sweet middle layer. The top layer, which is tradi-tionally made from artificial-tasting boxed Jell-O, got a flavor upgrade from plain gelatin flavored with real pureed strawberry juice and extra sliced berries.

In my family, it's just not a holiday unless Mom's pretzel salad is on the table. She lines a 13 by 9-inch baking pan with a mix of crushed pretzels, sugar, and melted butter and bakes it into a crust; she spreads it with a combination of sweetened cream cheese and whipped topping; and then she covers it all with a layer of strawberry Jell-O mixed with syrupy berries. The ingredients would make you think it's for dessert, but it's actually eaten with dinner. Confused? So were my colleagues. But this unlikely yet beloved dish holds a place of honor at backyard barbecues, potlucks, and holiday dinners all over the Midwest. And with good reason—the stuff is deliciously salty and sweet and creamy and crunchy.

All recipes for the salad are very similar; I made several with small variations, layering components and letting the salads chill. After a few hours, I called over my colleagues. They were pleasantly surprised. "That's actually pretty good," one conceded. But I'd still need to repair some flaws: crumbly crusts; bouncy, fake-tasting Jell-O tops; and enough sugar to open a candy store. Also, the store-bought whipped topping would have to go. Yes, these changes might mean extra kitchen work, but a fresher, fruitier pretzel salad sounded appealing. (Sorry, Mom.)

The crust was easy to fix—it was a simple matter of using pretzel sticks instead of classically shaped pretzels. The sticks crushed evenly, making for a sturdier crust.

STRAWBERRY PRETZEL SALAD

That done, I moved up a layer, replacing the Cool Whip with homemade whipped cream. I folded it into cream cheese that I'd beaten with sugar in a stand mixer. While this substitution worked nicely, the mixture was still too sweet and the process bothersome. Over several tests, I decreased the sugar from 1 cup to just ½ cup, and in an attempt to simplify the procedure, I tried slowly pouring the cream into the mixer with the cream cheese and sugar instead of whipping it separately. To my surprise, the mixture whipped up fine. I spread it over the cooled pretzel crust, chilled it, and tried a bite. Honest-to-goodness cream versus artificial whipped dairy topping? No contest.

For the gelatin layer, I hoped to ditch the artificially flavored boxed Jell-O and overly sweet frozen berries in syrup and pack in as much real strawberry flavor as I could. To do so, I'd make homemade Jell-O. After some experimentation, I had my game plan: Puree berries, strain to extract strawberry juice, heat liquid with sugar, and thicken with gelatin. By the time I was done, I was whizzing 2 entire pounds of frozen (for year-round consistency), thawed berries in the food processor and setting things to a relaxed wiggle with just 4½ teaspoons of gelatin. Instead of the strawberries in syrup, I folded in another full pound of sliced berries. Now I controlled the sweetness level—1½ cups of sugar proved to be enough. I chilled the strawberry topping for 30 minutes before layering it on the salad. Otherwise, as I learned from hard-won experience, it melted the cream and soaked the crust.

I checked all my modifications in a final pretzel salad and then called over tasters to judge it, though truthfully, the opinion I most cared about was my own. I chewed attentively and gave myself a pat on the back. The sweet-salty, creamy-crunchy contrasts mirrored my mom's version. The intense strawberry flavor and soft homemade cream were my own.

—NICK IVERSON, *Cook's Country*

Strawberry Pretzel Salad
SERVES 10 TO 12

For a sturdier crust, use (thinner) pretzel sticks not (fatter) rods. Thaw the strawberries in the refrigerator the night before you begin the recipe. You'll puree 2 pounds of the strawberries and slice the remaining 1 pound.

6½	ounces pretzel sticks
2¼	cups (15¾ ounces) sugar
12	tablespoons unsalted butter, melted and cooled
8	ounces cream cheese
1	cup heavy cream
3	pounds (10½ cups) frozen strawberries, thawed
¼	teaspoon salt
4½	teaspoons unflavored gelatin
½	cup cold water

1. Adjust oven rack to middle position and heat oven to 400 degrees. Spray 13 by 9-inch baking pan with vegetable oil spray. Pulse pretzels and ¼ cup sugar in food processor until coarsely ground, about 15 pulses. Add melted butter and pulse until combined, about 10 pulses. Transfer pretzel mixture to prepared pan. Using bottom of measuring cup, press crumbs into bottom of pan. Bake until crust is fragrant and beginning to brown, about 10 minutes, rotating pan halfway through baking. Set aside crust and let it cool slightly, about 20 minutes.

2. Using stand mixer fitted with whisk, whip cream cheese and ½ cup sugar on medium speed until light and fluffy, about 2 minutes. Increase speed to medium-high and, with mixer still running, slowly add cream in steady stream. Continue to whip until soft peaks form, scraping down bowl as needed, about 1 minute longer. Spread whipped cream cheese mixture evenly over cooled crust. Refrigerate until set, about 30 minutes.

3. Meanwhile, process 2 pounds strawberries in now-empty food processor until pureed, about 30 seconds. Strain mixture through fine-mesh strainer set over medium saucepan, using underside of small ladle to push puree through strainer. Add remaining 1½ cups sugar and salt to strawberry puree in saucepan and cook over medium-high heat, whisking occasionally, until bubbles begin to appear around sides of pan and sugar is dissolved, about 5 minutes; remove from heat.

4. Sprinkle gelatin over water in large bowl and let sit until gelatin softens, about 5 minutes. Whisk strawberry puree into gelatin. Slice remaining strawberries and stir into strawberry-gelatin mixture. Refrigerate until gelatin thickens slightly and starts to cling to sides of bowl, about 30 minutes. Carefully pour gelatin mixture evenly over whipped cream cheese layer. Refrigerate salad until gelatin is fully set, at least 4 hours or up to 24 hours. Serve.

SOUPS AND STEWS

CARROT-GINGER SOUP

WHY THIS RECIPE WORKS: Sometimes the simplest recipes get overcomplicated as more and more versions appear. Case in point: carrot-ginger soup, whose flavors often get elbowed out with the addition of other vegetables, fruits, or dairy. For a fresh, clean-tasting soup, we decided to go back to the basics. With a combination of cooked carrots and carrot juice, we were able to get well-rounded, fresh carrot flavor. Using a mixture of grated fresh ginger and crystallized ginger gave us a bright, refreshing ginger flavor with a moderate kick of heat. Finally, for a smooth texture without the fuss of straining, we added a touch of baking soda to help break down the carrots and ginger, producing a perfectly silky, creamy result. To keep the flavors straightforward and simple, we finished with some basic garnishes which provided texture and tang.

The coupling of sweet carrots and pungent ginger has the potential to produce an elegant, flavorful soup. It's troubling, then, that I've been unable to truly taste either ingredient in most of the versions I've tried. That's due primarily to the hapless addition of other vegetables, fruits, or dairy—all of which mask flavors. Another irritating problem is a grainy consistency; I like my pureed soups to be perfectly smooth and creamy. Could I bring this soup to its full potential, producing a version with a smooth, silken texture and pure, clean flavors?

I started by making a bare-bones version, sweating minced onion and garlic in butter and then adding peeled, sliced carrots, fresh grated ginger, and vegetable broth. I simmered the mixture until the carrots were tender and then gave it a whirl in the blender. Unfortunately, the carrot flavor seemed muddled. And while the soup had a fiery kick, it had not even a hint of the fresh, bright flavor associated with ginger. What's more, even though they'd been cooking away for 20 minutes and seemed sufficiently tender, the carrots hadn't completely broken down, so the soup was riddled with fibrous bits. Not a promising start.

First up for repair: flavor. For unadulterated carrot flavor, it made sense to ditch the broth in favor of plain water, which I augmented with a couple of complementary sprigs of fresh thyme. This was a vast improvement, eliminating the blurred vegetable backing of my first batch. Next, trying for an even more concentrated, caramelized taste, I whipped up two more soups—one with roasted carrots and another with slices sautéed in butter until caramelized. Unfortunately, neither method added quite the right flavor. Roasting brought an undesirable earthiness and sautéing yielded a soup that tasted like sweet potatoes.

But these tests made me realize that what was really missing in my soup was ultrafresh carrot flavor. That in turn made the solution seem obvious: Just use raw carrots—in the form of carrot juice. After a few tries, I settled on swapping ¾ cup of carrot juice for some of the water and stirring in another ¾ cup (along with a tablespoon of cider vinegar for sweet tang) right before serving for vibrancy. Between the earthy, sweet cooked carrots and the bright, raw carrot juice, this was an extremely well-balanced soup.

On to the ginger. My soup had the peppery heat associated with the root but almost none of its vibrant fruitiness. I rounded up the different forms of ginger—fresh juice, fresh grated, powdered, and crystallized—and started sampling. Grated fresh ginger and crystallized ginger were the best of the bunch, with the former supplying spiciness and the latter delivering the almost citrusy freshness that ginger is prized for.

Using a combination of fresh and candied ginger would be the way to go. I sautéed 1 tablespoon of finely grated fresh ginger and ¼ cup of minced crystallized ginger (plus 1 teaspoon of sugar to counter their spiciness) with the other aromatics and then continued with my recipe. In the finished soup, the duo struck an ideal balance of flavor and heat.

For the silkiest possible consistency, I tried cooking the carrots longer, until they were mushy and breaking apart. After I pureed it, the soup was better but still not as smooth as I wanted (I planned to avoid straining). It only made sense to turn to one of the test kitchen's secret weapons: baking soda. We have used it on numerous occasions to break down the cell walls of a vegetable as it cooks in water. Sure enough, with just ½ teaspoon of baking soda and 20 minutes of simmering, the soup was smoother than any I'd ever had. In fact, it was not only smooth but downright velvety—all without the need for lengthy cooking or fussy straining.

As finishing touches, a sprinkle of fresh chives and a dollop of sour cream provided subtle onion flavor and mild tang to play off of the sweet carrots. A few crispy, buttery croutons for textural contrast and my retooled classic was complete.

—SARAH MULLINS, *Cook's Illustrated*

SERVES 6

A food processor can be used to slice the carrots. In addition to sour cream and chives, serve the soup with Buttery Croutons (recipe follows).

2 tablespoons unsalted butter

2 onions, chopped fine

¼ cup minced crystallized ginger

1 tablespoon grated fresh ginger

2 garlic cloves, peeled and smashed

Salt and pepper

1 teaspoon sugar

2 pounds carrots, peeled and sliced ¼ inch thick

4 cups water

1½ cups carrot juice

2 sprigs fresh thyme

½ teaspoon baking soda

1 tablespoon cider vinegar

Chopped chives

Sour cream

1. Melt butter in large saucepan over medium heat. Add onions, crystallized ginger, fresh ginger, garlic, 2 teaspoons salt, and sugar; cook, stirring frequently, until onions are softened but not browned, about 5 minutes.

2. Increase heat to high; add carrots, water, ¾ cup carrot juice, thyme sprigs, and baking soda and bring to simmer. Reduce heat to medium-low and simmer, covered, until carrots are very tender, 20 to 25 minutes.

3. Discard thyme sprigs. Working in batches, process soup in blender until smooth, 1 to 2 minutes. Return soup to clean pot and stir in vinegar and remaining ¾ cup carrot juice. Return to simmer over medium heat and season with salt and pepper to taste. Serve with sprinkle of chives and dollop of sour cream.

Buttery Croutons

MAKES ABOUT 2 CUPS

3 tablespoons unsalted butter

1 tablespoon olive oil

3 large slices hearty white sandwich bread, cut into ½-inch cubes

Salt

Heat butter and oil in 12-inch skillet over medium heat. When foaming subsides, add bread cubes and cook, stirring frequently, until golden brown, about 10 minutes. Transfer croutons to paper towel–lined plate and season with salt to taste.

CREAMY CAULIFLOWER SOUP

✓ **WHY THIS RECIPE WORKS:** For a creamy cauliflower soup without cream, we relied on cauliflower's low insoluble fiber content to produce a velvety smooth puree. To ensure that cauliflower flavor remained at the forefront, we cooked the cauliflower in water (instead of broth), skipped the spice rack entirely, and bolstered the soup with sautéed onion and leek. We added the cauliflower to the simmering water in two stages so that we got the grassy flavor of just-cooked cauliflower and the sweeter, nuttier flavor of longer-cooked cauliflower. Finally, we fried florets in butter until both browned and used each as a separate, richly flavored garnish.

If you judged cauliflower by typical cauliflower soups, you might think of it as a characterless white vegetable with no flavor of its own. This is because most classic cauliflower soups go overboard on the heavy cream; thicken with flour; or incorporate ingredients like bacon, tomatoes, or curry powder, whose potent flavors smother this vegetable's more delicate ones. But if you've ever experienced the full spectrum of cauliflower's flavors, which can range from bright and cabbagelike to nutty and even sweet, you know cauliflower to be imminently worthy of being the real focal point of the recipe. I set out to create a soup that was creamy without being stodgy and that highlighted, rather than covered up, the flavors of this often mistreated vegetable.

I started by stripping down the soup to just cauliflower and water. I cut a 2-pound head of cauliflower into ½-inch-thick slices (slices cook more evenly than florets, which are hard to cut into same-size pieces) and simmered the vegetable in salted water for 15 minutes before pureeing it in a blender. I was immediately struck by its texture. The soup was supremely silky and smooth. I couldn't detect any of the graininess that would be evident in a puree of, say, cooked peas, or any

CREAMY CAULIFLOWER SOUP

of the glueyness you'd get when pureeing potatoes. I called a few colleagues over to try it, and they were just as astonished. How could a soup with no cream be so creamy?

As I began to do research, I learned that how much a vegetable breaks down when it is cooked and pureed depends largely on one thing: fiber. Vegetables have two kinds: soluble and insoluble. When subjected to heat and liquid, soluble fiber readily breaks down and dissolves, providing viscosity, while insoluble fiber remains stable even when pureed. Cream's lubricating effect goes a long way toward mitigating the graininess of insoluble fiber, which is why cream is so often included in pureed vegetable soups. Cauliflower, however, is remarkably low in overall fiber—and especially in insoluble fiber, with just ½ gram per ½-cup serving. (This is about one-third as much insoluble fiber as found in green peas.) No wonder cauliflower could be blended to an ultrasmooth creamy consistency—no cream needed.

Next I looked for additions that would complement the cauliflower flavor rather than compete with or overwhelm it. I started by swapping in chicken and vegetable broth for the water. Each added more flavor, but I found that this wasn't necessarily a good thing. The chicken broth was too dominant, while the vegetable broth just muddied the flavor. I stuck with water alone and headed to the allium bin.

I tested onion, shallot, leek, and garlic, which I softened in the pot with some butter before I added the cauliflower. Onion provided pleasant background sweetness, while leek lent a welcome grassiness, so I chose both.

I was wondering what to try next when I stumbled upon a cauliflower soup recipe from chef and restaurateur Thomas Keller that calls for cooking the vegetable for almost an hour. The recipe (from his book *Ad Hoc at Home*) also calls for a lot of cream, so when I tried the soup, it was hard to tell what impact longer cooking was having. But my curiosity was piqued, so I tried simmering the cauliflower in my working recipe for 30 minutes (twice as long as I had been simmering it up to this point). Even when I added back a little water to the pot to make up for the liquid that had evaporated over the longer cooking time, I was surprised by how much sweeter and nuttier-tasting this vegetable had become. Was it possible that mere cooking time could so greatly affect flavor?

I ran a simple experiment: I simmered six batches of cauliflower, each in 2 cups of water, cooking the first batch for 10 minutes and each subsequent batch for 10 minutes more so that the last pot cooked for 60 minutes. I called over my colleagues to sample all the batches side by side. The cauliflower that had cooked for 10 minutes had a pronounced grassy, cabbagelike flavor that reminded some tasters of cooked broccoli. By 20 minutes, this sulfurous bite was starting to fade, and by 30 minutes, it had transformed into a sweet nuttiness, which the cauliflower held on to through 40 minutes of cooking. Further cooking, however, led to a vegetable so tasteless that it was hard to identify it as cauliflower at all. Intrigued, I contacted our science editor.

It turns out that cauliflower, like all cruciferous vegetables, contains a host of odorless compounds that convert into volatile aromatic ones, first during cutting and then during cooking. One such compound is carbon disulfide, which becomes a gas at cooking temperatures. Anyone who's walked into a kitchen where cauliflower is on the stove is familiar with its sulfurous, cabbagelike scent. For the first 15 minutes of cooking, the concentration of carbon disulfide is relatively high. Over time it dissipates, allowing the sweeter, nuttier flavors of other compounds known as thioureas to be formed and come to the fore. But by the hour mark, both types of compounds have disappeared so that the vegetable has almost no flavor at all.

So at what point in the cooking process does cauliflower taste best? Most tasters remarked that they liked the punchy, cabbagey flavor of the cauliflower cooked for 10 and 20 minutes as well as the nuttier, cleaner, sweeter flavor of 30-minute-cooked cauliflower. Could I get all these flavors in my soup? For my next batch, I sliced the head into ½-inch-thick slices as usual and simmered half (along with the tougher core, which is edible so long as it's cooked until tender) for 30 minutes, adding the remaining half of the cauliflower after 15 minutes. It was a simple adjustment to the recipe, but the results were dramatic. Not only did this soup taste more intrinsically of cauliflower than any of its predecessors but its flavors were also more complex. It was at once grassy, pleasantly sulfurous, sweet, and nutty. I turned my focus to a few final touches.

I've always been a big fan of the intense nuttiness of roasted cauliflower and wondered if there was a way to bring some of that intensity to the soup. I cut a cup of ½-inch florets from the cauliflower before slicing up the rest for the soup. I melted a few more tablespoons of butter in a small skillet and fried the florets to a golden-brown color. Tossed with a little sherry vinegar and sprinkled over the soup, they served as the ideal complement to my clean-tasting puree. But during frying, the cauliflower wasn't the only thing that was cooking—the butter also turned a rich golden brown. This gave me an idea. Why not cook the florets in extra butter and use a drizzle of it as a second garnish? Just a teaspoon or two of browned butter brought richness to each bowl of soup. A shower of minced chives and some fresh black pepper finished the job.

I like to think I'm the kind of cook whose recipes often get accolades from those who try them, but my tasters' raves went beyond anything I'd ever experienced for such a simple recipe—a soup by which cauliflower should be proud to be judged.

—DAN SOUZA, *Cook's Illustrated*

Creamy Cauliflower Soup

SERVES 4 TO 6

White wine vinegar may be substituted for the sherry vinegar. Be sure to thoroughly trim the cauliflower's core of green leaves and leaf stems, which can be fibrous and contribute to a grainy texture in the soup.

1	head cauliflower (2 pounds)
8	tablespoons unsalted butter, cut into 8 pieces
1	leek, white and light green parts only, halved lengthwise, sliced thin, and washed thoroughly
1	small onion, halved and sliced thin
	Salt and pepper
4½–5	cups water
½	teaspoon sherry vinegar
3	tablespoons minced fresh chives

1. Pull off outer leaves of cauliflower and trim stem. Using paring knife, cut around core to remove; thinly slice core and reserve. Cut heaping 1 cup of ½-inch florets from head of cauliflower; set aside. Cut remaining cauliflower crosswise into ½-inch-thick slices.

2. Melt 3 tablespoons butter in large saucepan over medium-low heat. Add leek, onion, and 1½ teaspoons salt; cook, stirring frequently, until leek and onion are softened but not browned, about 7 minutes.

3. Increase heat to medium-high; add 4½ cups water, sliced core, and half of sliced cauliflower; and bring to simmer. Reduce heat to medium-low and simmer

NOTES FROM THE TEST KITCHEN

CREAMY BY NATURE

Most soups made from pureed vegetables contain cream for a simple reason: to mitigate the effects of insoluble fiber. All vegetables have both soluble and insoluble fiber, but only the soluble kind fully breaks down during cooking, which contributes viscosity to the soup. Insoluble fiber remains intact, and the best that the blades of a blender can do is break it down into smaller bits. But cauliflower has a leg up on other vegetables. It's very low in overall fiber—and only half of it is insoluble. This means that cauliflower is easily pureed into a silky-smooth soup with no cream at all.

VARY COOKING TIME TO COAX OUT CAULIFLOWER'S DIFFERENT FLAVORS

While developing our recipe for cauliflower soup, we discovered that cauliflower's flavor changes dramatically depending on how long you cook it. Shorter cooking times bring out its cabbagelike flavors, while longer cooking times turn it nuttier and sweet. Too much cooking drives off all its flavor. To bring the full spectrum of possible flavors into our soup, we cooked some of the cauliflower for 15 minutes and the remainder for 30 minutes.

gently for 15 minutes. Add remaining sliced cauliflower, return to simmer, and continue to cook until cauliflower is tender and crumbles easily, 15 to 20 minutes longer.

4. While soup simmers, melt remaining 5 tablespoons butter in 8-inch skillet over medium heat. Add reserved florets and cook, stirring frequently, until florets are golden brown and butter is browned and imparts nutty aroma, 6 to 8 minutes. Remove skillet from heat and use slotted spoon to transfer florets to small bowl. Toss florets with vinegar and season with salt to taste. Pour browned butter in skillet into small bowl and reserve for garnishing.

5. Process soup in blender until smooth, about 45 seconds. Rinse out pan. Return pureed soup to pan and return to simmer over medium heat, adjusting consistency with remaining water as needed (soup should have thick, velvety texture but should be thin enough to settle with flat surface after being stirred) and seasoning with salt to taste. Serve, garnishing individual bowls with browned florets, drizzle of browned butter, and chives and seasoning with pepper to taste.

SLOW-COOKER SPICY CHIPOTLE CHICKEN SOUP

✓ **WHY THIS RECIPE WORKS:** The hearty Mexican soup called *caldo Tlalpeño* features a spicy, tomatoey broth with bites of tender shredded chicken and chickpeas. We'd been wanting to create a slow-cooker chicken soup with big flavor and this seemed like just the recipe. We started with a little onion, garlic, and tomato paste, which we jump-started in the microwave to mellow the alliums and save the hassle of sautéing. Canned chipotle chiles— dried, smoked jalapeños in a tangy adobo sauce—provided smokiness and heat. We stirred this mixture into the slow cooker along with chicken broth to make a delicious spicy broth. As the chicken gently cooked in this flavorful liquid, it was slowly infused with the broth's bold flavor. Creamy canned chickpeas added bulk, and some bright cilantro and a couple of fresh tomatoes, chopped and stirred in at the end, nicely balanced the spicy soup.

There are few things that ward off the bitter chill of winter better than a bowl of hot, homemade chicken soup. The test kitchen has lots of chicken-based soup recipes designed for slow-cooking, but during one particularly frigid stretch of winter, I decided to look south of the border for inspiration to make a spicier, heartier chicken soup.

Caldo Tlalpeño is a smoky, spicy Mexican soup of chicken, chickpeas, and chipotle chiles. While the exact origin of the soup's name is unknown—some insist it references the smoky barbecue popular in the Mexico City suburb of Tlalpan—its flavor, spice, and spirit are unmistakably Mexican. Plus, long-cooked dishes are a hallmark of Mexican cooking, making this soup a good candidate for the slow cooker. While it's true that Mexican food derives much of its complexity from hard-to-find ingredients, I knew that with some thoughtful testing I could bring an authentic, but still manageable, version of this Mexican *caldo* north of the border.

Caldo Tlalpeño could rightfully be called chipotle soup, as it is the flavor, smoke, and spice of this chile that gives the soup its personality. While many traditional recipes called for charring, seeding, and soaking dried chipotle chiles, I was happily surprised to see that just as many used the canned alternative. Using canned chipotle chiles saves the labor-intensive steps involved in preparing dried chiles, and they offer impressive smoky flavor, heat, and depth. From past test kitchen experiments, I knew that they would hold up well to slow cooking.

As for the chicken, a few initial tests revealed that tasters preferred the light, clean taste of breast meat over richer dark meat. I opted to use bone-in, skin-on breasts; although they require a bit more prep work at the end of cooking, the delicate white meat is protected from overcooking by the skin and bones. As the chicken picked up flavor from the spicy broth, the broth also picked up flavor from the skin and bones of the chicken, and since I wasn't making homemade broth (the nuances would be lost in the smokiness of the chipotle chiles), I wanted to get as much chicken flavor as possible into the soup. I quickly shredded the chicken at the end of cooking for tender, flavorful pieces of meat in every bite.

Borrowing a trick from past test kitchen slow-cooker soups, I microwaved the onions, garlic, tomato paste, and oil before adding them to the slow cooker. The benefit of this step was twofold: I didn't have to spend time at the stove while the aromatics cooked, and the heat of the microwave bloomed the flavors of the alliums, making sure that I didn't end up with raw-tasting garlic or onions in my finished soup. A little bit of tomato paste gave the soup rich, savory flavor without watering it down.

This soup was coming together quickly and easily, and I wanted to keep it that way. Canned chickpeas seemed like a quick, convenient route, but would they hold up to the long cooking time? A test proved that the answer was yes. My streamlined soup was almost finished, but it still lacked bright, fresh notes to counter the warm smokiness. After some consideration, I decided to add another layer of tomato flavor. Fresh tomatoes, which I chopped and stirred in toward the end of cooking, held on to just enough of their acidity to provide a cool freshness, and some cilantro added just before serving offered up the final touch I needed to bring everything together.

Whenever winter seems like it'll never end, this south-of-the-border-inspired soup, garnished with fresh avocado, Monterey Jack cheese, lime wedges, and sour cream, will take you straight to warm, sunny Mexico.

—ASHLEY MOORE, *America's Test Kitchen Books*

Slow-Cooker Spicy Chipotle Chicken and Chickpea Soup

SERVES 8

This recipe is designed to work with 5½- to 7-quart slow cookers. Serve with sour cream, shredded Monterey Jack cheese, diced avocado, and/or lime wedges.

- 2 onions, chopped
- 4 teaspoons minced chipotle chile
- 1 tablespoon minced garlic
- 1 tablespoon tomato paste
- 1 tablespoon vegetable oil
- 8 cups chicken broth
- 2 (15-ounce) cans chickpeas, rinsed
- 3 (12-ounce) bone-in split chicken breasts, trimmed
  Salt and pepper
- 2 tomatoes, cored and chopped
- ½ cup minced fresh cilantro

1. Microwave onions, chipotle, garlic, tomato paste, and oil in bowl, stirring occasionally, until onions are softened, about 5 minutes; transfer to slow cooker. Stir in broth and chickpeas. Season chicken with salt and pepper and nestle into slow cooker. Cover and cook until chicken is tender, 3 to 4 hours on low.

NOTES FROM THE TEST KITCHEN

CHIPOTLE CHILES IN ADOBO
Chipotle chiles are jalapeños that have been ripened until red, then smoked and dried. They are sold as is, ground to a powder, or packed in a tomato-based sauce. We prefer the latter because the chiles are already reconstituted by the sauce, making them easier to use. Most recipes don't require an entire can, but these chiles will keep for 2 weeks in the refrigerator, or they can be frozen. To freeze, puree the chiles and quick-freeze teaspoonfuls on a plastic wrap–covered plate. Once the teaspoons of chiles are hard, peel them off the plastic and transfer them to a zipper-lock freezer bag. The chiles can be stored this way for up to 2 months. Thaw what you need before use.

2. Transfer chicken to cutting board, let cool slightly, then shred into bite-size pieces, discarding skin and bones. Using large spoon, skim excess fat from surface of soup.

3. Stir in shredded chicken and tomatoes and let sit until heated through, about 5 minutes. Stir in cilantro and season with salt and pepper to taste. Serve.

HEARTY CREAM OF CHICKEN SOUP

✅ WHY THIS RECIPE WORKS: Cream of chicken soup is a classic that should be in everyone's repertoire. For a flavorful base to our cream of chicken soup, we built a roux from rendered chicken skin. The rich fond created by the skin gave the soup depth without a work-intensive double-simmered broth. To prevent the white breast meat from overcooking, we simmered it in the broth for about 20 minutes, then removed it while the broth continued to cook, extracting maximum flavor from the skins. Chopped potatoes and carrots added substance and body.

I keep a freezer full of homemade stock, I once hosted a soup-only potluck, and I've made most every creamy soup in the book, from cream of broccoli to corn chowder. So it's safe to say that I'm a soup person. How is it, then, that cream of chicken soup has eluded me? I've eaten plenty of casseroles made with the canned version, but I've never had this soup as, well, soup.

I chose a half-dozen recipes to test alongside the canned version, just to be thorough. Recipes called for various thickeners (cream, roux, cornstarch) and chicken cuts (whole birds, just thighs or legs, just breasts). The simplest recipe called for simmering a chicken breast in store-bought broth, shredding the chicken, and then stirring it back into the broth with cream; I wasn't surprised that this soup was wan. The most complicated recipe was a two-day process calling for a double stock (you make stock and then make a second stock using the first stock in place of water); as you'd expect, this soup was rich and flavorful. The canned soup was awful—no wonder no one just heats and eats it.

HEARTY CREAM OF CHICKEN SOUP

I knew I wouldn't employ a double stock here; I needed a faster, simpler path to flavorful soup. It was clear that a roux was the easiest and best thickening method. I also decided that I wanted this soup to be more substantial. To that end, I added chopped potatoes and carrots, along with leeks, which we like in soups for their mild sweetness. Reducing a little sherry proved an easy path to enhanced depth. Lastly, we preferred the texture of shredded white meat in the soup, so I'd proceed with breasts.

For my next test, I browned two bone-in, skin-on chicken breasts and set them aside while I sautéed the leeks in butter, stirred in flour, added the sherry, and cooked it down a bit. I whisked in chicken broth and added diced potatoes and the browned chicken. I brought the soup to a boil and then simmered it until the chicken was cooked (about 20 minutes). I took out the chicken, shredded it, and returned it to the simmering pot about 20 minutes later with some heavy cream. This soup was decent, but the chicken flavor wasn't great.

Since I wanted rich chicken flavor, I knew that I couldn't give up on the browning of the chicken: The fond (the browned bits on the bottom of the pot) that searing creates is incredibly flavorful. And I knew that I couldn't leave the browned chicken in the pot the entire time because it would overcook. As I was reviewing my recipe, I got a crazy idea: Could I take the skin off of the chicken and brown it alone to create fond? I gave it a try, using the skin from two breasts. Eyeing the chicken fat in the pot, I decided to use it to help build the roux. I left the skin in the pot, added butter, and sautéed the leeks in the tasty fats. Then I proceeded as before, eventually adding the breasts and simmering them until they registered 160 degrees.

I pulled the meat out to rest but continued to simmer the skin in the broth to extract extra flavor. When the

meat cooled, I shredded it, removed the skin from the pot, stirred the cream and chicken into the soup, and collected my colleagues. We dipped in spoons, sipped, and agreed: Cream of chicken soup can be fast, hearty, and satisfying, after all.

—SARAH GABRIEL, *Cook's Country*

Hearty Cream of Chicken Soup

SERVES 6

Our favorite store-bought chicken broth is Swanson Chicken Stock.

- 2 (12-ounce) bone-in split chicken breasts, skin removed and reserved, trimmed
  Salt and pepper
- 1 tablespoon water
- 1 pound leeks, white and light green parts only, halved lengthwise, sliced ¼ inch thick, and washed thoroughly (2½ cups)
- 2 tablespoons unsalted butter
- ½ cup all-purpose flour
- ⅓ cup dry sherry
- 8 cups chicken broth
- 12 ounces Yukon Gold potatoes, peeled and cut into ¾-inch pieces
- 3 carrots, peeled and cut into ½-inch pieces
- 3 sprigs fresh thyme
- 1 bay leaf
- ½ cup heavy cream
- 3 tablespoons minced fresh chives

1. Season chicken with salt and pepper. Place water and chicken skin in Dutch oven and cook over medium-low heat with lid slightly ajar until enough fat has rendered from skin to coat bottom of pot, about 7 minutes.

2. Uncover pot, increase heat to medium, and continue to cook until skin has browned, about 3 minutes, flipping skin halfway through cooking. Add leeks and butter and cook until leeks are just softened, about 3 minutes. Stir in flour and cook for 1 minute. Stir in sherry and cook until evaporated, about 1 minute.

3. Slowly whisk in broth until incorporated. Add potatoes, carrots, thyme sprigs, bay leaf, and chicken and bring to boil. Reduce heat to medium-low and simmer,

---

NOTES FROM THE TEST KITCHEN

BUILDING CHICKEN FLAVOR
We brown just the chicken skin to create flavorful fond. Then we leave the browned skin in the pot while the soup simmers to extract all its flavor.

uncovered, until chicken registers 160 degrees, 20 to 25 minutes.

4. Transfer chicken to plate and let cool for 20 minutes. While chicken cools, continue to simmer soup for 20 minutes. Using shallow spoon, skim grease and foam from surface of soup. Discard chicken bones and shred meat into 1-inch pieces. Discard chicken skin, thyme sprigs, and bay leaf. Off heat, stir in cream and chicken. Season with salt and pepper to taste. Sprinkle individual portions with chives and serve.

VIETNAMESE BEEF PHO

☑ WHY THIS RECIPE WORKS: Traditional versions of this Vietnamese beef and noodle soup call for simmering beef bones for hours to make a deeply flavorful broth. We wanted to make this soup suitable for the home cook, which meant that beef bones were out of the question. Instead, we simmered ground beef in spiced store-bought broth, which gave us the complexity and depth we were after in a fraction of the time. To serve the soup, we poured our broth over thinly sliced strip steak and gathered a variety of essential garnishes, such as lime wedges, hoisin and chile sauces, and bean sprouts.

I can't think of an Asian cuisine that doesn't lay claim to a brothy noodle soup, but I also can't think of one that's as universally popular as *pho bo*. This Vietnamese beef and noodle soup's biggest selling point is its killer broth—a beefy, fragrant, faintly sweet concoction produced by simmering beef bones and water for hours with aromatics like ginger and onions and warm spices like cinnamon and star anise. Notably, those bones are often the only form of meat added to the cooking liquid; actual pieces of beef aren't introduced until serving, when the broth is strained and ladled onto very thin slices of raw steak (typically sirloin) and thin rice noodles in large individual serving bowls. Fresh herbs and a few aromatic vegetables are presented as garnishes. Pouring hot broth over the contents cooks the meat just enough and softens the noodles and vegetables. Condiments such as salty-sweet hoisin sauce, chili sauce, and fish sauce and lime wedges are passed at the table for individual flavor tinkering.

Those exotic yet approachable flavors are what fuel my frequent cravings for this dish, but like most soups built on long-simmered stocks, it's not something I've ever attempted at home. Who has the time to spend a day eking out a full-flavored beef stock, much less running around town trying to track down hard-to-find beef bones? But if I could devise an equally intense, complex-tasting broth in less time (and with easier-to-find ingredients), pho would surely become my ultimate beef and noodle soup to make at home.

Ditching the bones was an obvious first move, but finding an equally beefy substitute wasn't so simple. The easiest shortcut, I figured, would be to doctor store-bought beef broth with typical pho flavors. I threw together a working recipe based on that: 14 cups of beef broth (since pho is a one-bowl meal, this amount of liquid feeds four to six people), a handful of quartered onions, peeled and thinly sliced ginger, a cinnamon stick, six each star anise pods and whole cloves, a couple of teaspoons of salt, and a teaspoon of black peppercorns, all simmered for about 1½ hours. To say the result was a failure would be an understatement. The soup tasted exactly like what it was: spiced-up commercial broth. I tried adding a little fish sauce and sugar to the cooking liquid, and both were keepers—easy additions that rounded out the salty-sweet profile I was after. But the broth needed more help, so I made another batch in which I charred the onions and ginger under the broiler before adding them to the cooking liquid—a traditional technique for building savory depth in pho. Alas, the flavor boost was too subtle to warrant the extra step and certainly didn't compensate for the lack of meat. Pho made without beef bones was turning out to be more challenging than I'd thought.

But at that point it dawned on me that doing without beef bones didn't mean I had to do without beef altogether. My reference point was the test kitchen's trick for making an ultrameaty sauce for steak without going to the trouble of sourcing and roasting bones for the base. Instead, we build rich, meaty flavor in a hurry by simmering some ground beef with the cooking liquid and then discarding the solids. We discovered that ground meat works well because its muscle fibers are broken up in the grinding process and, therefore, release meaty flavor very quickly.

VIETNAMESE BEEF PHO

Feeling hopeful, I pulled together another batch of broth, but this time I added 2 pounds of ground beef along with the commercial broth, aromatics, and spices. While that simmered, I used a sharp knife to peel ⅛-inch-thick slices off of a 1-pound piece of beef sirloin (a placeholder until I did further testing with other cuts). I also soaked strands of thin dried rice noodles in warm water and then briefly boiled them. Soaking helped them slough off excess starch and made them soften evenly and quickly in the boiling water. Then I loaded up individual bowls with the noodles and meat, as well as chopped cilantro and thin-sliced raw onion and scallions, before pouring hot broth over each serving.

The good news was that this broth was in a different league compared with my previous attempts: It was remarkably more savory and full-bodied, thanks to the ground beef. The downsides were that the ground beef had released "scum" into the liquid that turned it cloudy; the liquid retained a touch of that commercial broth tinniness and vegetal flavor; and, frankly, I wasn't thrilled about throwing away 2 pounds of beef. But fortifying the broth with ground meat had improved its flavor so dramatically that I couldn't resist pursuing the technique further.

As someone who's made her fair share of stock when cooking in restaurants, I was familiar with that pesky layer of scum, which forms any time you boil meat or bones. Traditional stock recipes, pho included, call for blanching the bones before adding them to the cooking liquid, a step that washes away much of their surface proteins and fat, which form the scum. I gave it a try with the ground beef and was glad to see that the technique was effective: Covering the meat with water, bringing it up to a boil for 2 minutes, and then quickly draining and rinsing it (to remove clingy bits of protein and fat) before adding it to the beef broth made for a clearer, cleaner-tasting beef stock. Of course, it's not as easy to strain bits of ground meat as it is large beef bones, so I broke the 2-pound mass of meat into 1-inch chunks that weren't hard to fish out of the water. Swapping out a couple of cups of the broth for an equal amount of water took care of the tinny, vegetal notes without noticeably dampening the beefy flavor.

Making do with less beef broth also tempted my frugal side: Could I get away with less ground beef, too? Indeed, making my broth with 1½ pounds and 1 pound of ground beef, respectively, proved that the latter put up plenty of meaty flavor—and that the flavor payoff for 1 pound of meat was worth the sacrifice.

I had to admit that this broth had a lot going for it: all the flavor and complexity of real-deal beef broth without the fuss. My only hang-up was the 1½-hour simmer. For this pho to be part of my regular dinner rotation, not just a special-occasion dish, I'd need to hurry it along, so I tried skimping on the simmer time. To my delight, after testing various times, I discovered that the beef flavor peaked around the 45-minute mark—a change that put this soup on the table for a weeknight meal.

Some pho shops throw tough cuts like brisket and tripe into their long-simmered broths and offer them as garnishing options, but thin slices of raw, relatively tender steak are the most common and would do fine for my purposes. The question was which cut exactly, so I tried all the options I could think of: tenderloin, rib eye, strip steak, tri-tip, blade steak, flank, and eye of round. Tenderloin was favored for its supple texture, and its uniform cylindrical shape made thin-slicing it a breeze. But its prohibitive price meant that it was ill-matched for this humble soup. Plus, it offered nothing in the way of beefy flavor. Strip steak, tri-tip, and blade steak all offered good beefiness and reasonable tenderness at a fraction of the price. I chose to work with strip since it is usually the easiest to find. To make the steak less challenging to slice thin, I employed the test kitchen's favorite trick for prepping stir-fry meat: briefly freezing the whole steak, which firms it up enough for the blade to make clean cuts. As a bonus, freezing also ensured that the steak didn't overcook when it came in contact with the hot broth.

I also pared down the list of tableside garnishes and condiments to the essentials. The must-haves—bean sprouts for crunch, basil (preferably Thai basil, though Italian basil will work), lime wedges, hoisin and chile sauces, and additional fish sauce—balanced the straightforward meatiness and mellow sweetness of the broth with heat, acidity, and freshness.

As I ladled the fragrant broth into serving bowls, my colleagues and I remarked at how easily and quickly the complex flavors of pho had come together and how this seemingly exotic dish suddenly felt much closer to home.

—ERIN MCMURRER, *Cook's Illustrated*

NOTES FROM THE TEST KITCHEN

BEST ROUTE TO CLEAR STOCK

Boiling ground beef (or, more traditionally, beef bones) for stock coaxes out great beef flavor but also soluble proteins and melted fat that render the liquid cloudy and leave a layer of scum on its surface. Frequently skimming away those impurities as the liquid cooks is one way to clear up the stock, but it's a tedious chore and it never completely clarifies the stock. Blanching and rinsing the meat before adding it to the cooking liquid is a far more efficient method. The brief (2-minute) boil thoroughly agitates the meat so that its proteins and fat slough off but doesn't cook it long enough to wash away much flavor. A quick rinse rids the surface of any stubborn clingy bits.

BEEF SO THIN THAT IT COOKS IN THE BOWL

Traditionally, the steak for pho is sliced very thin and placed raw in the serving bowl. (It cooks, but ideally remains slightly rare, in the hot broth.)

To cut thin slices against the grain, freeze the meat until it's very firm. Then stand the meat on its cut end and, using a sharp, thin blade, point the tip downward and push the blade down and away from you in one stroke.

Vietnamese Beef Pho

SERVES 4 TO 6

Our favorite store-bought beef broth is Rachael Ray Stock-in-a-Box All-Natural Beef Flavored Stock. An equal weight of tri-tip steak or blade steak can be substituted for the strip steak; make sure to trim all connective tissue and fat. Look for noodles that are about ⅛ inch wide; these are often labeled "small." Don't use Thai Kitchen Stir-Fry Rice Noodles; they are too thick and don't adequately soak up the broth.

1	pound 85 percent lean ground beef
2	onions, quartered through root end
12	cups beef broth
2	cups water, plus extra as needed
¼	cup fish sauce, plus extra for seasoning
1	(4-inch) piece ginger, sliced into thin rounds
1	cinnamon stick
2	tablespoons sugar, plus extra for seasoning
6	star anise pods
6	whole cloves

	Salt
1	teaspoon black peppercorns
1	(1-pound) boneless strip steak, trimmed and halved
14–16	ounces (⅛-inch-wide) rice noodles
⅓	cup chopped fresh cilantro
3	scallions, sliced thin (optional)
	Bean sprouts
	Sprigs fresh Thai or Italian basil
	Lime wedges
	Hoisin sauce
	Sriracha sauce

1. Break ground beef into rough 1-inch chunks and drop in Dutch oven. Add water to cover by 1 inch. Bring mixture to boil over high heat. Boil for 2 minutes, stirring once or twice. Drain ground beef in colander and rinse well under running water. Wash out pot and return ground beef to pot.

2. Place 6 onion quarters in pot with ground beef. Slice remaining 2 onion quarters as thin as possible and set aside for garnish. Add broth, 2 cups water, fish sauce, ginger, cinnamon, sugar, star anise, cloves, 2 teaspoons salt, and peppercorns to pot and bring to boil over high heat. Reduce heat to medium-low and simmer, partially covered, for 45 minutes.

3. Pour broth through colander set in large bowl. Discard solids. Strain broth through fine-mesh strainer lined with triple thickness of cheesecloth; add water as needed to equal 11 cups. Return broth to pot and season with extra sugar and salt (broth should taste overseasoned). Cover and keep warm over low heat.

4. While broth simmers, place steak on large plate and freeze until very firm, 35 to 45 minutes. Once firm, cut against grain into ⅛-inch-thick slices. Return steak to plate and refrigerate until needed.

5. Place noodles in large container and cover with hot tap water. Soak until noodles are pliable, 10 to 15 minutes; drain noodles. Meanwhile, bring 4 quarts water to boil in large pot. Add drained noodles and cook until almost tender, 30 to 60 seconds. Drain immediately and divide noodles among individual bowls.

6. Bring broth to rolling boil over high heat. Divide steak among individual bowls, shingling slices on top of noodles. Pile reserved onion slices on top of steak slices and sprinkle with cilantro and scallions, if using. Ladle hot broth into each bowl. Serve immediately, passing bean sprouts, basil sprigs, lime wedges, hoisin, Sriracha, and extra fish sauce separately.

HEARTY VEGETABLE CHOWDER

✔ WHY THIS RECIPE WORKS: Many versions of vegetable chowder overwhelm the subtle flavors of the vegetables by using too much cream, or rely on exotic add-ins to build flavor. For our version of a hearty, flavorful vegetable chowder, we stuck to a classic flavor profile. The time-tested combination of carrot, celery, leek, and thyme provided a flavorful base, which we supplemented with smoky bacon and savory chicken broth. Starch released from vigorously stirring potatoes into the chowder created a silky texture, and trading cream for half-and-half provided creaminess without muting the vegetables' flavor. Some minced chives and lemon juice added notes of freshness.

Chowders exemplify the straightforward, hearty, satisfying nature of New England's best dishes. Lobster, corn, and clam are the three best-known chowders, but I've also been intrigued by recipes for vegetable chowder.

Most read pretty much the same: Sweat onions, carrots, and celery in butter or pork fat (from bacon or salt pork); add flour to thicken; stir in broth; add your root vegetables of choice; simmer until tender; and finish with heavy cream. I followed a handful of recipes, and after many hours of peeling, dicing, stirring, and simmering, I asked my coworkers to evaluate the results. The different vegetable and flavor combinations helped us get a handle on what we wanted: We opted for a classic onion, carrot, celery, and thyme flavor base. Yukon Gold potatoes gave the chowder satisfying bulk and heft and held their shape in the chowder without breaking down too much. Bacon bested salt pork for its smoky depth. Chicken broth underpinned the chowder nicely with good savory taste. With simplicity and clarity of flavor in mind, we decided to leave it at that.

Now I was ready to address the issue of floury and stodgy chowder. I knew that the fault lay with the roux, the combination of flour and butter that thickens most chowders. I tried replacing the roux with a slurry of cornstarch and broth, but the chowder still lacked the light, clean flavor I was after. Then I remembered a soup trick I'd learned in culinary school: adding cubed potatoes to the sweating aromatics and stirring vigorously. The constant stirring helps release the potatoes' sticky starch, which results in satiny smooth pureed soup. I'd borrow the technique, stirring the potatoes and then pureeing some of the vegetables in my chowder to thicken it.

Before trying the method, I switched to russet potatoes so I could take advantage of their higher starch content, and I substituted leeks for the onions for their silky quality when pureed. Now I began a new pot of chowder. After the leeks, carrots, and celery started to soften, I added the cubed russets and stirred constantly. Within 2 minutes, the potatoes were leaching a sticky starch that made all the vegetables tacky. I poured in the broth and simmered the whole lot for about 20 minutes. Once the vegetables were tender, I removed a few cups of the soup to puree and then stirred the puree back into the chowder. (Subsequent tests showed that 1 cup of the veggies and 2 cups of the broth were ideal amounts.)

We liked the soup's consistency, but my tasters refused to believe that the stirring had anything to do with it. To prove it, I made two more batches, constantly stirring the potatoes in one and not at all in the other. The no-stir batch was watery and gritty, the other smooth and velvety. Our science editor explained that starch was released from the damaged potato cells because the potatoes had been cut into small cubes, which my stirring broke down further.

Most chowders are finished with heavy cream, but the cream muted the vegetable flavor. We preferred half-and-half. I was wrapping up, enjoying a last bowl, when it struck me that my chowder could use a finishing boost. I stirred in minced chives for a little freshness and added an enlivening squeeze of lemon. The vegetables were tender, the chowder creamy, substantial, bright—refined, even. How very New England.

—NICK IVERSON, *Cook's Country*

Hearty Vegetable Chowder

SERVES 4 TO 6

If your blender lid has a vent, open it (and cover with a towel) when blending so the steam can escape.

- **6** slices bacon, chopped
- **1** pound leeks, white and light green parts only, halved lengthwise, sliced thin, and washed thoroughly
- **4** carrots, peeled, halved lengthwise, and cut into 1-inch pieces

2 celery ribs, halved lengthwise and
   cut into ½-inch pieces

1 teaspoon minced fresh thyme
   Salt and pepper

1½ pounds russet potatoes, peeled and
   cut into 1-inch pieces

2 garlic cloves, minced

4 cups chicken broth

1 bay leaf

½ cup half-and-half

1 tablespoon minced fresh chives

1 teaspoon lemon juice

1. Cook bacon in Dutch oven over medium heat until fat has rendered and bacon is nearly crisp, 7 to 9 minutes. Add leeks, carrots, celery, thyme, and 1 teaspoon salt and cook until leeks are translucent, about 8 minutes. Add potatoes and cook, stirring constantly, until starch begins to release and coat vegetables, about 2 minutes. Add garlic and cook until fragrant, about 30 seconds. Add broth and bay leaf and bring to boil.

2. Reduce heat to low, cover, and simmer, stirring occasionally, until vegetables are tender, about 20 minutes. Discard bay leaf. Transfer 1 cup of vegetables (using slotted spoon) and 2 cups of soup broth to blender; process until smooth, about 1 minute. Stir processed soup back into pot. Stir in half-and-half, chives, and lemon juice and gently rewarm soup. Season with salt and pepper to taste. Serve.

NOTES FROM THE TEST KITCHEN

ELIMINATE THE GUESSWORK
The best chowders have a smooth, creamy base punctuated by chunks of vegetables. We achieved this by pureeing precisely measured amounts of vegetables and liquid and using the puree to thicken the chowder.

CONTROL THE TEXTURE
Pureeing 1 cup of softened vegetables and 2 cups of liquid gives our chowder a creamy base.

BEST CHICKEN STEW

✓ **WHY THIS RECIPE WORKS:** In order to make a chicken stew that could satisfy like its beef brethren, we looked to two different chicken parts: We seared well-exercised wings to provide rich chicken flavor and plenty of thickening gelatin, and then we gently simmered small chunks of boneless chicken thighs for tender bites throughout the stew. To boost meatiness, we used a combination of bacon, soy sauce, and anchovy paste (whose fishy character was imperceptible in our stew). Finally, we took full advantage of the concentrating effect of reduction by cooking down wine, broth, and aromatics at the start and simmering the stew uncovered during its stay in the oven.

Living in a nation of chicken lovers, I'm always surprised at how rarely I find chicken stew on a menu or in a cookbook. We have great chicken pot pies, plenty of chicken casseroles, and some of the best chicken noodle soups going, but in the stew category we seem almost exclusively drawn to beef. The few chicken stews I have seen are either too fussy or too fancy, derivatives of French fricassee or coq au vin, or seem more soup than stew, with none of the complexity and depth I expect from the latter. It was time to make an adjustment to the American canon. I'd develop a chicken stew recipe that would satisfy like the beef kind—one with succulent bites of chicken, tender vegetables, and a truly robust gravy.

Since my clear goal was to develop a beef stew–caliber chicken stew, that's exactly where I started. Beef is practically designed for stew. Chuck roast (cut from the shoulder) can be easily cubed into even pieces, seared hard to develop a rich-tasting crust, and simmered for hours until fall-apart tender, all the while remaining juicy. This treatment is made possible by the meat's tough network of connective tissue, which slowly converts into lubricating gelatin during cooking. This turns the beef tender while the gravy is infused with rich beefiness and body—a culinary win-win.

How could I make chicken behave like beef? Well, I couldn't—not really: Today's chicken is butchered very young so even its thighs and drumsticks have little time to develop much connective tissue. But obviously the fattier, richer-tasting dark meat was my best choice. I could start by subbing boneless, skinless thighs for the

BEST CHICKEN STEW

meat in a basic beef stew recipe, shortening the cooking time drastically for the quicker-cooking chicken. I didn't expect perfection, but perhaps I'd have a good jumping-off point from which I could tweak and adjust as needed.

I heated a couple of tablespoons of oil in a large Dutch oven and seared 2 pounds of halved thighs. After they browned, I transferred them to a bowl. In the then-empty pot I softened some basic aromatics in butter and then sprinkled in flour to create a roux for thickening. Next I stirred in store-bought chicken broth, the browned chicken, and chunks of red potatoes and carrots. After an hour of gentle simmering, the vegetables were soft and the chicken was tender. The stew looked pretty good. But its appearance was deceiving: One bite revealed a weak-flavored gravy. Not to mention that the chicken, though not desiccated, showed a disappointing lack of juiciness. In fact, the vegetables were just about the only redeeming things in the pot.

I had a radical thought: What if, instead of trying to preserve some of its flavor and juiciness—which didn't work anyway—I cooked the life out of the chicken so that at least it would enrich the gravy? After the chicken had given it all up to the pot, I would discard it and cook more chicken in the stewing liquid just until tender. It didn't make sense to treat thighs or even drumsticks this way. But wings are another story. They actually have a decent amount of collagen, and because they're more about skin and bones than about meat, discarding them after they'd enriched the gravy wouldn't seem wasteful. (Wings are fun to pick at during a football game, but shredding them individually after cooking and stirring the meat into a stew would be a hassle that most cooks would prefer to avoid.)

I split a pound of wings at their joints to ensure that they'd lie flat and brown evenly, allowing me to maximize the flavorful Maillard reaction. After browning the wings on both sides, I removed them and built a gravy with aromatics, a roux, and chicken broth just as I had before. I then added the browned wings back to the pot along with potato and carrot pieces. I covered the pot and let everything simmer in a 325-degree oven for about 30 minutes.

Next I stirred in the halved boneless, skinless chicken thighs (I skipped searing this time to prevent them from drying out) and returned the pot to the oven until they were fork-tender, about 45 minutes longer.

When I removed the wings from the pot, they literally fell apart in my tongs, a sure sign that much of their connective tissue had been converted into gelatin. I also tasted the meat to see what flavor it might have left to give. The answer: not very much, meaning that I'd effectively extracted it into the gravy. Indeed, the stew had improved dramatically. The thighs were tender and juicy and the gravy was more chicken-y and velvety. It wasn't beef-stew good, but I was making progress.

Next I focused on really ramping up flavor. While good chicken soup is all about attaining pure chicken flavor, stew requires more depth and complexity—the kind of richness that can stave off winter's harshest chill. Browning the wings was a step in the right direction, but I needed a lot more reinforcement. My first move was to the fridge, where I rounded up some big flavor boosters: bacon, soy sauce, and anchovy paste. A few strips of bacon, crisped in the pot before I browned the wings in the rendered fat, lent porky depth and just a hint of smoke. Soy sauce and anchovy paste may sound like strange additions to an all-American chicken stew, but their inclusion was strategically sound. When ingredients rich in glutamates (such as soy sauce) are combined with those rich in free nucleotides (like anchovies), flavor-boosting synergy is achieved. The nucleotides affect our tastebuds so that our perception of meaty-tasting glutamates is amplified by up to 30 times.

I added 2 teaspoons of anchovy paste with the aromatics—onion, celery, garlic, and thyme—and a tablespoon of soy sauce along with the broth. Just as I'd hoped, things took an immediate turn to the more savory—without tasting salty or fishy. My colleagues were finally going for seconds and admitting that they'd consider eating a bowl of my chicken stew over beef stew. I was feeling pretty good, but I knew that I could take things further.

When I used to work in restaurants, one of the most important tools in my repertoire was the technique of reduction. Whether I was dealing with a stock, broth, sauce, or stew, I could always count on reduction to evaporate water and concentrate flavors. In that vein, I tried cooking my stew uncovered to gain a bit more intensity. The flavors concentrated, plus I got an extra boost of browning on the surface of the stew and around the rim of the pot. Deglazing the sides of the pot by wetting them with a bit of gravy and scraping it into the stew with a spatula produced a considerable flavor boost. Reduction was proving its value once again and I wondered if I could put it to even better use.

I started another batch. This time after the aromatics turned a fragrant golden brown, I stirred in a cup of the broth along with the soy sauce and a cup of white wine and brought everything to a boil. It took about 12 minutes for the liquid to fully evaporate, at which point the aromatics started to sizzle again and I proceeded to prepare the roux, add the rest of the broth, and continue with the recipe. A little over an hour later, I proudly presented my tasters with the results. The reduction had not only concentrated flavors but also mellowed everything for a rounder-tasting, soul-satisfying stew.

Having done essentially all the work upfront, all I had to do to finish the stew was remove the wings, add a splash of fresh white wine for some bright acidity, and sprinkle the pot with some chopped fresh parsley. This was truly a stew worthy of the name; the proof was in the pot, no beef necessary.

—DAN SOUZA, *Cook's Illustrated*

Best Chicken Stew

SERVES 6 TO 8

Anchovy paste helps deepen the meaty flavors of the soup, though the fishy character is imperceptible. Two mashed anchovy fillets (rinsed and dried before mashing) can be used instead of the anchovy paste. Use small red potatoes measuring 1½ inches in diameter.

- 2 **pounds boneless, skinless chicken thighs,**
  halved crosswise and trimmed
  Kosher salt and pepper
- 3 **slices bacon, chopped**
- 1 **pound chicken wings, halved at joint**
- 1 **onion, chopped fine**
- 1 **celery rib, minced**
- 2 **garlic cloves, minced**
- 2 **teaspoons anchovy paste**
- 1 **teaspoon minced fresh thyme**
- 5 **cups chicken broth**
- 1 **cup dry white wine, plus extra for seasoning**

BUILDING A RICH, FLAVORFUL GRAVY

1. START WITH BACON AND WINGS: Brown chopped bacon, then sear halved wings in rendered fat to develop meaty depth. Set bacon and wings aside.

2. ENHANCE FLAVOR BASE: Sauté aromatics, thyme, and anchovy paste in fat to create rich fond. Add chicken broth, wine, and soy sauce, then boil until liquid evaporates.

3. COOK GRAVY: Cook reserved bacon and wings (with potatoes and carrots) in more broth. This extracts flavor from meats and body-enhancing collagen from wings (later discarded).

THIS IS FOND, TOO

We often use liquid to release the browned bits, or fond, that remain on the bottom of the pan after meat has been sautéed or pan-seared; this enables us to easily stir the fond into the dish. These bits are packed with the complex flavors that are created by the Maillard reaction and can greatly enhance the flavor of a braise or a sauce. We found that leaving the lid off our chicken stew as it cooked in the oven led to the development of fond on the sides of the Dutch oven as well.

To take advantage of this flavor-packed substance, we deglazed the sides by wetting them with a bit of gravy and scraping it into the stew with a spatula. The result? A considerable flavor boost.

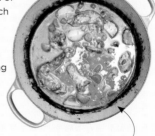

Scrape the dark ring into the stew.

1   tablespoon soy sauce

3   tablespoons unsalted butter, cut into 3 pieces

⅓   cup all-purpose flour

1   pound small red potatoes, unpeeled, quartered

4   carrots, peeled and cut into ½-inch pieces

2   tablespoons chopped fresh parsley

1. Adjust oven rack to lower-middle position and heat oven to 325 degrees. Arrange chicken thighs on baking sheet and lightly season both sides with salt and pepper; cover with plastic wrap and set aside.

2. Cook bacon in large Dutch oven over medium-low heat, stirring occasionally, until fat renders and bacon browns, 6 to 8 minutes. Using slotted spoon, transfer bacon to medium bowl. Add chicken wings to pot, increase heat to medium, and cook until well browned on both sides, 10 to 12 minutes; transfer wings to bowl with bacon.

3. Add onion, celery, garlic, anchovy paste, and thyme to fat in pot; cook, stirring occasionally, until dark fond forms on pan bottom, 2 to 4 minutes. Increase heat to high; stir in 1 cup broth, wine, and soy sauce, scraping up any browned bits; and bring to boil. Cook, stirring occasionally, until liquid evaporates and vegetables begin to sizzle again, 12 to 15 minutes. Add butter and stir to melt; sprinkle flour over vegetables and stir to combine. Gradually whisk in remaining 4 cups broth until smooth. Stir in wings and bacon, potatoes, and carrots; bring to simmer. Transfer to oven and cook, uncovered, for 30 minutes, stirring once halfway through cooking.

4. Remove pot from oven. Use wooden spoon to draw gravy up sides of pot and scrape browned fond into stew. Place over high heat, add thighs, and bring to simmer. Return pot to oven, uncovered, and continue to cook, stirring occasionally, until chicken offers no resistance when poked with fork and vegetables are tender, about 45 minutes longer. (Stew can be refrigerated for up to 2 days.)

5. Discard wings and season stew with up to 2 tablespoons extra wine. Season with salt and pepper to taste, sprinkle with parsley, and serve.

CHINESE BRAISED BEEF

✔ **WHY THIS RECIPE WORKS:** Chinese braised beef (also called red-cooked beef) is a slow-braised dish in which a thick, ultraflavorful, stew-like sauce envelops tender pieces of beef. We wanted to maintain the deeply complex flavors of the original but simplify the recipe for the home kitchen. We decided to use readily available boneless beef short ribs in place of traditional shank of beef. To streamline the classic cooking method, we opted to skip blanching the meat, and we moved the pot from the stovetop to the even heat of the oven. A pair of thickeners—gelatin and cornstarch—added body to the sauce. Five-spice powder provided characteristic flavor without the bother of whole spices, and a combination of hoisin sauce and molasses contributed an underlying sweetness that completed the dish.

Every culture has its own version of slow-cooked, satisfying, warm-you-from-the-inside-out comfort food, and Chinese red-cooked beef is a prime example of the genre. And while the dish shares some of the same homey appeal of American beef stew, it delivers something more intriguing: chunks of tender meat moistened in a modest amount of sauce that makes up for what it lacks in volume with its potent flavor. Furthermore, unlike American stews, red-cooked beef doesn't have add-ins like carrots or potatoes. Instead, it focuses exclusively on the beef and the sauce, the latter of which is redolent with flavorings like ginger, cinnamon, star anise, Sichuan peppercorns, and cardamom. The meal is typically rounded out with plenty of steamed vegetables and rice, which provide a neutral background for the intense sauce.

I learned quickly not to get hung up on the name. "Red-cooked" (or *hong shao*) comes from the notion that a protein (beef, pork, poultry, or fish) simmered in a lightly sweetened broth of soy sauce and spices takes on a ruddy hue, but every version that I've seen has a deep, rich brown color.

There are two approaches to red cooking. The first means braising the food in plenty of liquid and saving that liquid to be used repeatedly for the same purpose, imparting deeper flavor with each use. As appealing as that sounded, it wasn't really practical for an American home cook. I centered my attentions on the second approach, in which the meat is braised in liquid and then removed from the pot, after which the braising liquid is reduced to an intensely flavored, demi-glace-like consistency.

All the recipes in this style that I'd rounded up started out the same way: Cube a large cut of beef (shank is the most traditional), blanch the cubes in water (a step that's said to remove impurities), and then set them aside while you make the braising liquid. The most basic of these stocks called for simply combining water with soy sauce, a bit of sugar, rice wine (or sherry), ginger, scallions, garlic, and one or two spices. But even when such stocks were reduced, I found that they didn't have the layers of flavor that are key to the dish. On the other hand, more-elaborate recipes that incorporated caramelized sugar, pungent fermented condiments such as chili bean paste, and lengthy lists of whole spices were beautifully nuanced. My challenge, then, would be maintaining the complex, interesting flavor profile of this comfort food while making it as fuss-free as possible—no trips to an Asian market required.

To determine which cut of beef would be best, I blanched several braising cuts in boiling water (I'd revisit whether this step was really necessary later) and then simmered them in separate pots of water flavored with soy sauce, sugar, scallions, garlic, sherry, fresh ginger, and cinnamon sticks (likewise, I'd figure out the full spectrum of spices that I'd want to use when I was farther along). The shank worked beautifully. It was amazingly tender and moist, and it imparted a silky fullness to the sauce. But since shank is hard to find in American supermarkets, I set it as the benchmark to be matched and made my way through a list of alternatives.

Brisket was tender but dry. Chuck roast and blade steak were tender and rich but required a lot of trimming before going into the pot. In the end, I opted for boneless short ribs, which had enough fat and collagen to cook up moist but required minimal prep before I put them in the pot. True, short ribs didn't produce a sauce with the richness of that made with shank, but I would address that later. On the upside: Short ribs cooked in about half the time of shank. After bringing the pot to a simmer, I moved the bulk of the cooking to the oven, where the meat could simmer without constant monitoring. I left the meat in large pieces to make it easier to remove from the pot when it came time to strain out the aromatics and reduce my sauce,

and I simply used a pair of forks to pull apart the tender meat into bite-size chunks before I added them to the reduced sauce.

About that blanching step: Briefly cooking the meat in boiling water removes free proteins from the surface, which produces a clearer stock—but since I was reducing the stock to a concentrated, opaque sauce, I realized that this probably wasn't important. One test confirmed that blanching not only made no difference in the appearance of my red-cooked beef but didn't affect its flavor or texture either, so I happily eliminated that step.

And what about browning? In the West we are very influenced by French cooking, which often means browning meat to deepen its flavor. However, I decided that this wasn't necessary here. While browning could provide a moderate boost to the meatiness of the dish, short ribs are plenty beefy, and in the case of red cooking, the complex, potently flavored sauce would (or should) overshadow it. Which brought me to my next task: Improving the somewhat one-dimensional flavor of the sauce.

To balance the saltiness of the soy sauce and impart a subtle sweetness, thus far I had been using white sugar. Brown sugar added a little more depth, but I was still intrigued by recipes that incorporated caramelized sugar. For my next batch, I cooked ¼ cup sugar with a bit of water until it turned dark brown, then I added the other ingredients to the pot. Its slight bitterness contributed interesting new flavor notes. Could I get the same effect without the extra step? When I tried substituting 2 tablespoons of molasses straight out of the jar for the sugar, I was pleased to find that it provided a similarly bittersweet flavor. Some thick hoisin sauce introduced complementary sweetness and flavor and a bit of body, too.

Now for the spices. Though tasters had loved the versions I had made that called for a slew of whole spices, were they really necessary? Some recipes used just one spice—preground five-spice powder. It was here that I suffered a crisis of conscience. I had ditched the blanching step and opted for molasses over caramelized sugar (with, it must be said, no detrimental effect in either case), but surely substituting a ground mixture of spices was going a step too far.

Not at all. In fact, I found that with just 1½ teaspoons of five-spice powder (I did splurge on a fresh bottle to ensure maximum complexity), the flavors in the braise really came together, shifting from a subtle infusion to a more developed and powerful punch. A bit of heat was the only thing missing, so I added 1 teaspoon of red pepper flakes.

Now the sauce had all the deep, nuanced flavor that I was after, but the consistency was wrong. Because you know what you get when you boil down a water-based stock? Very flavorful water.

I wanted a sauce that would cling to the meat and rice rather than flow to the bottom of the bowl, and this wasn't it. I tried flour—the most common thickener in recipes for Western-style beef stews—but it produced a gravy rather than the lacquer-like glaze I wanted. Cornstarch wasn't quite right here either: It gave the sauce that slick texture often found in a stir-fry sauce, which seemed a bit lightweight for this application. What I really wanted was that rich glazelike texture I had gotten when I had braised the beef shanks for 4 hours. When I considered that it was the meat's collagen that really made that version such a success, the answer was obvious: Add gelatin.

I admit that I went a bit overboard at first: 2 tablespoons of gelatin gave the sauce a tacky consistency. Backing down to 1½ tablespoons, added at the beginning of

cooking, and introducing a mere teaspoon of cornstarch to finish produced a sauce that coated the meat nicely without forming a gel.

With its tender meat and satisfying heartiness, this version of red-cooked beef had all the appeal of an American-style stew, but the warmth of the sweet spices and the deep savory flavor of the soy sauce made it a welcome change from my usual cool-weather offerings. Best of all, with fussy steps like blanching meat and caramelizing sugar eliminated, this dish had come together with an ease that made it comfort food in every sense of the phrase.

—ANDREA GEARY, *Cook's Illustrated*

Chinese Braised Beef

SERVES 6

With its generous amount of soy sauce, this dish is meant to taste salty, which is why we pair it with plain white rice. A simple steamed vegetable like bok choy or broccoli completes the meal. Boneless beef short ribs require little trimming, but you can also use a 4-pound chuck roast. Trim the roast of large pieces of fat and sinew, cut it across the grain into 1-inch-thick slabs, and cut the slabs into 4 by 2-inch pieces.

1½	tablespoons unflavored gelatin
2½	cups plus 1 tablespoon water
½	cup dry sherry
⅓	cup soy sauce
2	tablespoons hoisin sauce
2	tablespoons molasses
3	scallions, white and green parts separated, green part sliced thin on bias
1	(2-inch) piece ginger, peeled, halved lengthwise, and crushed
4	garlic cloves, peeled and smashed
1½	teaspoons five-spice powder
1	teaspoon red pepper flakes
3	pounds boneless beef short ribs, trimmed and cut into 4-inch lengths
1	teaspoon cornstarch

1. Sprinkle gelatin over 2½ cups water in Dutch oven and let sit until gelatin softens, about 5 minutes. Adjust oven rack to middle position and heat oven to 300 degrees.

NOTES FROM THE TEST KITCHEN

BEEF SHANK—EVEN BETTER THAN SHORT RIBS

Shank is the very lean, sinewy cut from the lower leg of the steer. In the United States, it's often used to make low-fat ground beef. This is a shame because with a few hours of braising, it becomes meltingly tender, and its liquefied connective tissue imparts a silky richness to a sauce that requires little, if any, defatting. If you can find beef shank and have an extra hour or two, it's the best (and most economical) choice for red-cooked beef (and most braising recipes). You'll find shank sold both long cut and cross cut (with or without the bone). If using cross cut, decrease the gelatin to 2¼ teaspoons and increase the cook time in step 2 to 4 hours. If using long cut, cut it crossways into 1-inch-thick slabs, omit the gelatin, and increase the cook time in step 2 to 5 hours.

LONG-CUT SHANK
Lots of connective tissue; cooks in 5 hours.

CROSS-CUT SHANK
Less connective tissue; cooks in 4 hours.

2. Heat softened gelatin over medium-high heat, stirring occasionally, until melted, 2 to 3 minutes. Stir in sherry, soy sauce, hoisin, molasses, scallion whites, ginger, garlic, five-spice powder, and pepper flakes. Stir in beef and bring to simmer. Remove pot from heat. Cover tightly with sheet of heavy-duty aluminum foil, then lid. Transfer to oven and cook until beef is tender, 2 to 2½ hours, stirring halfway through cooking.

3. Using slotted spoon, transfer beef to cutting board. Strain sauce through fine-mesh strainer into fat separator. Wipe out pot with paper towels. Allow liquid to settle for 5 minutes, then return defatted liquid to pot. Cook liquid over medium-high heat, stirring occasionally, until thickened and reduced to 1 cup, 20 to 25 minutes.

4. While sauce reduces, use 2 forks to break beef into 1½-inch pieces. Whisk cornstarch and remaining 1 tablespoon water together in small bowl.

5. Reduce heat to medium-low, whisk cornstarch mixture into reduced sauce, and cook until sauce is slightly thickened, about 1 minute. Return beef to sauce and stir to coat. Cover and cook, stirring occasionally, until beef is heated through, about 5 minutes. Sprinkle scallion greens over top. Serve.

CALDO VERDE

WHY THIS RECIPE WORKS: Caldo verde is a traditional Portuguese soup of shredded greens, potatoes, and sausage. In our version, we pureed some of the potatoes with olive oil to make a thick, cohesive, silky-smooth base. Replacing some of the water with chicken broth added depth of flavor and a splash of white wine vinegar at the end of cooking provided brightness. Increasing the amount of potato and sausage turned this simple first course into a hearty and filling meal.

My fondness for caldo verde started in my friend Sam Paterson's kitchen. He grew up in a Portuguese community in Gloucester, Massachusetts, where this soup of sausage, potato, and hearty greens was a staple in many households, and he often invited me to dinner when his grandmother was serving her version. After sautéing onion and garlic in extra-virgin olive oil, she added cubed russet potatoes and a couple of quarts of water, brought the pot to a boil, and let the soup simmer until the potatoes were tender. As that was cooking, she browned pieces of smoky, garlicky linguiça sausage in a skillet and finely shredded a large bunch of kale as a stand-in for *couve tronchuda*, the traditional greens used for the dish. After about 10 minutes, she gave the pot a stir to break down the potatoes and introduce body to the broth; then she added the sautéed sausage and kale. The greens softened during the last few minutes of cooking and gave the soup its generally verdant appearance—and its name.

What I like best about this dish is that, while the flavors are rich, it's not a heavy soup. In fact, my friend's family serves it as a starter. Without changing the soup's essentially light character, I wanted to create a slightly heartier result—something that could function as a main course.

To start, I replaced the hard-to-find Portuguese linguiça sausage with widely available Spanish-style chorizo, which boasts a similar garlicky profile. I also sautéed the sausage right in the Dutch oven—no need to dirty a skillet. The ¼ cup of extra-virgin olive oil that many recipes suggest for cooking the sausage seemed excessive, so I reduced it to just 1 tablespoon. One more tweak: I split the water with an equal amount of chicken broth for deeper flavor.

While the soup simmered, I dealt with the greens. The problem with shredded kale, I'd noticed, was that the wilted strips dangle from the spoon, making the soup messy to eat. I also wondered if kale was really the best option: Several caldo verde recipes that I found call for collards to replace the traditional couve. One side-by-side test settled things: My tasters preferred the collards, which offered a delicate sweetness and a meatier bite. Chopping the leaves into bite-size pieces made them more spoon-friendly.

So far, my caldo verde was shaping up nicely, save for the broth itself, which was too thin. I also didn't love how three separate layers developed as the soup sat: a thin film of flavorful chorizo oil on top, broth beneath it, and a bed of grainy potato bits on the bottom of the pot. I wanted something with creamier, more even body.

Until now I'd been vigorously stirring the broth once the potatoes had softened so that they broke down. But it was becoming clear that using this mixing method

CALDO VERDE

would never produce the smooth body I wanted: I realized that I should just puree some of the softened potatoes into the liquid. This way, the broth would thicken up and become uniformly silky. I blitzed ¾ cup of the russets with an equal amount of broth in a blender. The resulting puree was definitely smooth-textured. The problem was that by the time the soup was simmering with the greens and the sausage, the unpureed potato pieces (which I wanted to remain intact) were completely blown out. Switching to lower-starch Yukon Golds, which hold their shape even during long cooking, was the easy solution.

And yet the broth was not quite as silky as I wanted it to be, which made me think of those 3 extra table-spoons of oil that I'd vetoed early on in my testing. Maybe emulsifying that fat in the broth would be just what the soup needed. I drizzled the oil into the blender with the softened potatoes and broth, and as I'd hoped, a brief whirl left me with a uniform, velvety puree. I added the greens to the broth and then stirred in the chorizo a few minutes later. When the greens were tender, I poured my potato-oil emulsion into the soup along with a bit of white wine vinegar to brighten the pot.

Here was just the hearty soup I wanted, with all the flavors that I loved in the classic.

—LAN LAM, *Cook's Illustrated*

NOTES FROM THE TEST KITCHEN

SPANISH-STYLE CHORIZO

Spanish chorizo, which comes in links, is generally sold cured and fully cooked. It's made from chopped pork and pork fat and seasoned with smoked paprika, garlic, and herbs. Its "jerkylike" texture reminded some tasters of pepperoni; its "pungent smoke" and "vinegary aftertaste" are all its own. Don't substitute Mexican chorizo for Spanish or vice versa; they are not interchangeable.

Caldo Verde
SERVES 6 TO 8

We prefer collard greens, but kale can be substituted. Serve this soup with hearty bread and, for added rich-ness, a final drizzle of extra-virgin olive oil.

- ¼ cup extra-virgin olive oil
- 12 ounces Spanish-style chorizo sausage, cut into ½-inch pieces
- 1 onion, chopped fine
- 4 garlic cloves, minced
  Salt and pepper
- ¼ teaspoon red pepper flakes
- 2 pounds Yukon Gold potatoes, peeled and cut into ¾-inch pieces
- 4 cups chicken broth
- 4 cups water
- 1 pound collard greens, stemmed and cut into 1-inch pieces
- 2 teaspoons white wine vinegar

1. Heat 1 tablespoon oil in Dutch oven over medium-high heat until shimmering. Add chorizo and cook, stirring occasionally, until lightly browned, 4 to 5 minutes. Transfer chorizo to bowl and set aside. Reduce heat to medium and add onion, garlic, 1¼ teaspoons salt, and pepper flakes and season with pepper to taste. Cook, stirring frequently, until onion is translucent, 2 to 3 minutes. Add potatoes, broth, and water; increase heat to high and bring to boil. Reduce heat to medium-low and simmer, uncovered, until potatoes are just tender, 8 to 10 minutes.

2. Transfer ¾ cup solids and ¾ cup broth to blender jar. Add collard greens to pot and simmer for 10 minutes. Stir in chorizo and continue to simmer until greens are tender, 8 to 10 minutes longer.

3. Add remaining 3 tablespoons oil to soup in blender and process until very smooth and homogeneous, about 1 minute. Remove pot from heat and stir pureed soup mixture and vinegar into soup. Season with salt and pepper to taste, and serve. (Soup can be refrigerated for up to 2 days.)

COLORADO GREEN CHILI

✔ WHY THIS RECIPE WORKS: This popular southwestern dish boasts rich bites of pork in a sauce dominated by green chiles. Only distantly related to its beefy cousins, Colorado green chili can be eaten as a stew or used as a saucy topping. For our version, we used a combination of readily-available Anaheim and jalapeño chiles. To achieve the mild vegetal taste and rich flavor that we liked, we used canned, diced tomatoes and more than 2 pounds of chiles, along with 3 pounds of boneless pork butt. Pureeing half of the chiles and chopping the other half by hand created a not-too-thick texture. To reduce the hands-on time, we started the pork with water in a covered pan, which rendered the fat, and then cooked the chili in the even heat of the oven to avoid having to stir constantly. Adding the jalapeños just before serving gave the chili a fresh hit of heat.

Most Americans have at least a glancing familiarity with Texas and New Mexico chilis, but not nearly so many realize that Denver, Colorado, also has a delicious chili tradition. Moderately spiced, this pork-based version is a relatively simple stew, but it has a complex and wonderful taste, thanks in part to the roasted green chiles from Hatch, New Mexico, that it contains. Denverites eat it as a main dish with flour tortillas or as a sauce of sorts, smothering everything from burgers to eggs to burritos.

Most recipes follow the same basic format: Roast green chiles until blistered and then peel, seed, and chop. Add the chiles to sautéed onions, garlic, and browned pork. Include cumin for spice. Pour in broth or water, stir in tomatoes, and thicken with masa harina (corn flour) or all-purpose flour. The Colorado chili simmers for an hour or three, and it's done when the meat is tender and the flavors have melded.

But because the ingredient amounts range, so do the resulting chilis, as I discovered when we tasted several versions. The ingredients produced chilis from thick to thin, hot to mild, muddy green to bright orange. The assortment did help us pin down what we liked: cohesive flavors, medium heat, and a noticeable vegetal taste. As the cook, I also wanted a comparatively easy recipe. Since none of these recipes met my full list of requirements, I combined their best features, putting together a recipe from canned, diced tomatoes, lots of garlic and cumin, and more than 2 pounds of chiles to 3 pounds of meat. Hatch green chiles are readily available in the Southwest. Don't live there? Then you have to mail-order them. To avoid that, for now I'd use Anaheims; I'd test more rigorously later.

My first order of business, though, was to decide on the best cut of pork. I compared loin, tenderloin, boneless country-style ribs, and boneless butt and settled on the last because its rich marbling suits this long-braised dish. I cut the meat into 1-inch cubes, which I browned to develop crust and add depth to the chili. I had to do this in three batches to avoid overcrowding the pot, tediously turning the cubes to brown all sides. To streamline, I borrowed a method that the test kitchen developed for stews. We cram a skillet with cubed beef, add water, and cover the pan. After several minutes, we uncover it, let the water evaporate, stir the beef, and let it brown in its own fat. A test with the pork pieces yielded similar results: even browning and flavorful fond. This method wasn't fast, but it was more hands-off than the traditional approach.

Turning to the chiles, although the Anaheims tasted bright and vegetal, just like the Hatch chiles, they lacked heat. I tested canned hot green chiles, poblanos, and jalapeños (all are easy to find throughout the United States) in combination with the Anaheims. The jalapeños fared best, so I tried them every which way with the Anaheims. Eventually, I had a game plan: Roast both types of chiles whole under the broiler, set aside the jalapeños, puree half of the Anaheims, dice the remainder, and add both to the chili pot with the broth to braise alongside the other ingredients, introducing complexity and background heat. Meanwhile, I chopped and seeded the jalapeños (reserving the seeds to add later for more heat, if needed), and just before serving the dish, I stirred them into the pot. The jalapeños gave the stew a fresh, hot vigor.

Unfortunately, prepping the chiles was a hassle. I had to flip them all partway through cooking, plus once they were cool, they were slippery and sticky, making them difficult to peel and even harder to seed. In culinary school I'd learned a great trick for roasting bell peppers. We sliced off the top and the bottom, made a cut down the side, removed the seeds and membranes, and then flattened the bell pepper; the flat surface broiled evenly, skin side up, and the skin subsequently came off easily. I successfully modified the technique for the Anaheims, and now I had to flip only the three jalapeños (which I continued to roast whole, to soften just slightly).

Colorado green chili should be thick enough to top a burger yet thin enough to eat on its own. I tested many possible thickeners: the usual masa harina and flour but also, in an effort to mimic masa harina's flavor, crushed tortilla chips and pulverized corn tortillas. Flour was easy and convenient and worked perfectly—well, almost. Without frequent stirring, the thickened stew burned and stuck to the pot. I moved the pot to a low (325-degree) oven, where it could cook more evenly. This hands-off method produced very tender pork in just an hour or so, sans scorching. Additionally, I ran the diced tomatoes through the food processor so that they'd blend into the chili better.

I put a final batch of chili through its paces—as a topping, under a fried egg, and as a stew sopped up with tortillas—and it lived up to its Rocky Mountain hype. My only disappointment? How quickly it disappeared.

—CHRISTIE MORRISON, *Cook's Country*

Colorado Green Chili

SERVES 6

The chiles can be roasted and refrigerated up to 24 hours in advance. Serve as a stew with tortillas; or use the chili as a topping for burgers, burritos, or eggs.

- 3 pounds boneless pork butt roast, trimmed and cut into 1-inch pieces
- ½ cup water
- Salt
- 2 pounds (10 to 12) Anaheim chiles, stemmed, halved lengthwise, and seeded
- 3 jalapeño chiles
- 1 (14.5-ounce) can diced tomatoes
- 1 tablespoon vegetable oil
- 2 onions, chopped fine
- 8 garlic cloves, minced
- 1 tablespoon ground cumin
- ¼ cup all-purpose flour
- 4 cups chicken broth
- Cayenne pepper
- Lime wedges

1. Combine pork, water, and ½ teaspoon salt in Dutch oven over medium heat. Cover and cook for 20 minutes, stirring occasionally. Uncover, increase heat to medium-high, and continue to cook, stirring frequently, until liquid evaporates and pork browns in its own fat, 15 to 20 minutes. Transfer pork to bowl and set aside.

2. Meanwhile, adjust 1 oven rack to lowest position and second rack 6 inches from broiler element. Heat broiler. Line rimmed baking sheet with aluminum foil and spray with vegetable oil spray. Arrange Anaheims, skin side up, and jalapeños in single layer on prepared sheet. Place sheet on upper rack and broil until chiles are mostly blackened and soft, 15 to 20 minutes, rotating sheet and flipping only jalapeños halfway through broiling. Place Anaheims in large bowl and cover with plastic wrap; let cool for 5 minutes. Set aside jalapeños. Heat oven to 325 degrees.

3. Remove skins from Anaheims. Chop half of Anaheims into ½-inch pieces and transfer to bowl. Process remaining Anaheims in food processor until smooth, about 10 seconds; transfer to bowl with chopped Anaheims. Pulse tomatoes and their juice in now-empty food processor until coarsely ground, about 4 pulses.

4. Heat oil in now-empty Dutch oven over medium heat until shimmering. Add onions and cook until lightly browned, 5 to 7 minutes. Stir in garlic and cumin and cook until fragrant, about 30 seconds. Stir in flour and cook for 1 minute. Stir in broth, Anaheims, tomatoes, and pork with any accumulated juices and bring to simmer, scraping up any browned bits. Cover pot, transfer to lower oven rack, and cook until pork is tender, 1 to 1¼ hours.

5. Without peeling, stem and seed jalapeños and reserve seeds. Finely chop jalapeños and stir into chili. Season chili with salt, cayenne, and reserved jalapeño seeds to taste. Serve with lime wedges.

NOTES FROM THE TEST KITCHEN

EASIER ROASTED CHILES
Roasting chiles whole and then seeding them—the usual procedure—makes a mess; the wet seeds stick to everything. We halve and seed the raw Anaheims, which is neater and lets us skip the usual flipping step. We leave the jalapeños whole; they soften but don't deeply roast.

READY FOR ROASTING
Arrange the chiles head to foot for the best fit.

CHAPTER 3

VEGETABLES AND SIDE DISHES

SLOW-COOKER ITALIAN BRAISED GREEN BEANS

✔ **WHY THIS RECIPE WORKS:** Slowly braising green beans makes for tender, creamy beans infused with lots of flavor. The Italian take on this method calls for adding tomatoes, garlic, and onion for a robustly flavored side dish. To adapt this recipe for the slow cooker, we microwaved the aromatics to bloom their flavors and jump-start their cooking. We found that a can of crushed tomatoes provided a bold tomato presence and guaranteed a sauce with the right consistency. For meaty richness and smoky notes, we included two strips of bacon; microwaving them with the aromatics helped to render some of their fat so we didn't need to add any oil. We then removed the spent bacon slices at the end of the cooking time.

Braised green beans are a far cry from their quick-sautéed or steamed cousins. Slowly braising green beans turns them incredibly tender, with an almost creamy texture, and infuses them with big flavor. To avoid having to babysit the beans for an hour or two, I decided to put the even heat of the slow cooker to work.

Ideally, braised green beans should be velvety-soft and tender—almost creamy—without disintegrating. Before I started cooking, I studied past test kitchen techniques for braising green beans. The pods of green beans are composed primarily of cellulose and pectin, polysaccharides that are the main building blocks of most plant cell walls. The tough fibers of cellulose are impossible to dissolve, but when pectin breaks down during cooking, water is able to enter the fibers, over time swelling and softening them. Pectin is affected by pH and will break down more slowly in an acidic environment. With this information in mind, I knew that the addition of an acidic element would be important to the texture of the final dish, since it would prevent the green beans from becoming a mushy mess.

Armed with the facts, I headed into the kitchen. First, I needed to decide how to flavor my beans. Some of our favorite versions of this dish take inspiration from Italy, using onion, garlic, and tomatoes to create a flavorful braising liquid. This iteration was appealing not only for the bold flavors it would create, but also because it has a built-in acidic element: tomatoes.

To develop a base for my recipe, I sautéed some garlic and onions, which I added to the slow cooker along with a can of crushed tomatoes. I mixed in the green beans, turned on the slow cooker, and tasted them at 1-hour intervals. The texture of the green beans was perfect after 8 to 9 hours on low heat—the beans were tender and creamy but still intact.

Next, I needed to tweak the aromatics to infuse the beans with big flavor—while crisp-tender, quick-sautéed green beans are good with just a sprinkle of lemon juice and herbs, the braised green beans begged for something richer and heartier. The onions and garlic were a must, but I ditched the sauté pan in favor of the microwave—a technique the test kitchen has used in slow-cooker recipes before. In just a few minutes, the microwave jump-started the cooking of the aromatics and deepened their flavor. For some Italian-inspired herbal flavor, I added a bit of dried thyme to the garlic and onions. I decided a touch of heat would offset some of the richness, so I also threw some red pepper flakes into the mixture. Satisfied with the aromatics, I turned my attention to the tomatoes. I made batches of green beans with canned diced tomatoes, canned crushed tomatoes, and tomato paste. In the end, the crushed tomatoes were the clear winner: They gave the sauce a smooth consistency with just enough body.

My green beans were well on their way, but something was still missing. I remembered that Southern-style recipes for braised green beans use ham hocks or bacon to infuse the beans with meaty flavor. I'm not one to turn down an opportunity to use bacon, so I gave it a try. Just two slices of bacon microwaved with the aromatics gave the dish just enough smoky, meaty richness, plus the rendered fat eliminated the need for extra oil. I took the bacon out after cooking the beans so that it didn't overwhelm the other flavors. When I tasted this version, I knew I had gotten it right: The beans were richly flavored, creamy-tender, and, best of all, nearly effortless.

—ASHLEY MOORE, *America's Test Kitchen Books*

Slow-Cooker Italian-Style Braised Green Beans

SERVES 4 TO 6

This recipe is designed to work with 5½- to 7-quart slow cookers.

- 1 onion, chopped
- 2 slices bacon
- 3 garlic cloves, minced
  Salt and pepper
- ½ teaspoon dried thyme
- ⅛ teaspoon red pepper flakes
- 1 (28-ounce) can crushed tomatoes
- 2 pounds green beans, trimmed

1. Microwave onion, bacon, garlic, ½ teaspoon salt, thyme, and pepper flakes in bowl, stirring occasionally, until onion is softened, about 5 minutes; transfer to slow cooker. Stir in tomatoes, then add green beans and toss to coat. Cover and cook until green beans are tender, 8 to 9 hours on low or 5 to 6 hours on high.

2. Discard bacon. Season with salt and pepper to taste. Serve. (Green beans can be held on warm or low setting for up to 2 hours.)

NOTES FROM THE TEST KITCHEN

TRIMMING GREEN BEANS QUICKLY

Instead of trimming the ends from one green bean at a time, line up the beans on a cutting board and trim all the ends with just one slice.

MINCING GARLIC

Here in the test kitchen, we go through large quantities of minced garlic every day, so we like the convenience and speed a garlic press offers. A good garlic press (our favorite is the **Kuhn Rikon Stainless Steel Epicurean Garlic Press**) can break down cloves more finely and evenly than an average cook using a knife, which means better distribution of garlic flavor throughout any given dish.

GRILLED CORN WITH FLAVORED BUTTER

✔ **WHY THIS RECIPE WORKS:** Grilled corn is a go-to summer treat, but we wanted a way to spice it up—literally. To incorporate flavorful herbs and spices into the corn, we found that a two-step approach worked best. First, we brushed the ears with vegetable oil and seared them over a hot grill fire. When the corn had a nice char, we moved the ears to a disposable pan on the grill and added a dollop of butter seasoned with herbs and other aromatic ingredients. The butter infused every kernel with extra flavor, and the disposable pan made the process simple and prevented butter-induced flare-ups on the grill.

A whole year goes by while I wait for that perfect matchup: fresh summer corn and the lick of the grill flame. Fire does something magical to the kernels, toasting them and deepening their natural sweetness. When it's corn season, I toss ears on the grill a couple of times a week, so I wanted to find a way to incorporate herbs, spices, and other seasonings with the usual smear of butter.

Whipping up a flavored butter is easy, but getting it to penetrate the corn is a different story: Simply slathering grilled corn with compound butter fails to infuse flavor into the kernels. I'd have to apply the butter before or during cooking. I considered two methods of preparing the ears: entirely shucked or partially shucked (peeling away all but the inner layers of husk). I tried the latter first, mixing softened butter with fresh chopped basil, parsley, and grated lemon zest, and then smearing it onto the ears and reassembling the husks.

The result was one hot mess—literally. Once on the blazing fire, the butter leaked out of the husks and dripped—and dripped and dripped—into the grill until an inferno singed the entire setup.

As for the naked-ear method, I knew that to avoid flare-ups, I'd have to use a less aggressive fire. I smeared more basil butter onto a batch and set it on a moderate grill. No flare-ups—good. But the butter still trickled off before it could season the kernels, which picked up no char at all.

To char the corn as quickly as possible, I would have to at least start it over a hot fire. I also had to find a way to keep the butter on the corn. For my next try, I brushed the kernels with vegetable oil to prevent them from drying out and placed the corn on the hot grill. After it charred, I scooped basil butter onto several pieces of foil and topped each dollop with a hot ear of corn. Using my faux flameproof "husks," I was able to wrap up each ear tightly—that butter was going nowhere. I returned the shrouded corn to the grill until I could hear the butter sizzling. Once I unwrapped the corn, I got an instant whiff of aromatic basil and lemon and toasty corn. But opening the hobo packs was dangerous—proven by the molten butter running down my arm.

I switched gears, ditching the foil packets for a disposable pan. After searing the corn, I placed it in the pan along with the herb butter. I sealed the pan with foil, put it on the grill, and after a few minutes heard that sweet sizzling sound. To make sure that the corn was well coated, I shook the pan a few times—consider it my personal homage to Jiffy Pop.

For variations on the basil mixture, I stuck to "summery" flavors. One combo blended sweet honey and spicy red pepper flakes; another with smoky chipotle, cilantro, and tangy orange zest gave a nod to Latin flavors; a "barbecue" butter boasted bold Cajun flavors; and a fourth, spicy butter got extra flavor from Old Bay seasoning. As it turns out, you can improve on hot, buttered grilled corn.

—BRIDGET LANCASTER, *Cook's Country*

Grilled Corn with Flavored Butter

SERVES 4 TO 6

Use a disposable aluminum roasting pan that is at least 2¾ inches deep.

- 1 recipe flavored butter (recipes follow)
- 1 (13 by 9-inch) disposable aluminum roasting pan
- 8 ears corn, husks and silk removed
- 2 tablespoons vegetable oil
  Salt and pepper

1. Place flavored butter in disposable pan. Brush corn evenly with oil and season with salt and pepper.

2. Grill corn over hot fire, turning occasionally, until lightly charred on all sides, 5 to 9 minutes. Transfer corn to pan and cover tightly with aluminum foil.

3. Place pan on grill and cook, shaking pan frequently, until butter is sizzling, about 3 minutes. Remove pan from grill and carefully remove foil, allowing steam to escape away from you. Serve corn, spooning any butter in pan over individual ears.

Basil and Lemon Butter

Serve with lemon wedges, if desired. We like to use a rasp grater for zesting citrus.

- 6 tablespoons unsalted butter, softened
- 2 tablespoons chopped fresh basil
- 1 tablespoon minced fresh parsley
- 1 teaspoon finely grated lemon zest
- ½ teaspoon salt
- ¼ teaspoon pepper

Combine all ingredients in small bowl.

Honey Butter

This butter also works well with cornbread.

- 6 tablespoons unsalted butter, softened
- 2 tablespoons honey
- ½ teaspoon salt
- ¼ teaspoon red pepper flakes

Combine all ingredients in small bowl.

Latin-Spiced Butter

Serve with orange wedges, if desired. We like to use a rasp grater for zesting citrus.

- 6 tablespoons unsalted butter, softened
- 2 tablespoons minced fresh cilantro
- 1 tablespoon minced fresh parsley
- 1 teaspoon minced canned chipotle chile in adobo sauce
- ½ teaspoon finely grated orange zest
- ½ teaspoon salt

Combine all ingredients in small bowl.

New Orleans "Barbecue" Butter

- 6 tablespoons unsalted butter, softened
- 1 garlic clove, minced
- 1 tablespoon Worcestershire sauce

GRILLED CORN WITH BASIL AND LEMON BUTTER

1 teaspoon tomato paste
½ teaspoon minced fresh rosemary
½ teaspoon minced fresh thyme
½ teaspoon cayenne pepper

Combine all ingredients in small bowl.

Spicy Old Bay Butter

Serve with lemon wedges, if desired.

6 tablespoons unsalted butter, softened
1 tablespoon hot sauce
1 tablespoon minced fresh parsley
1½ teaspoons Old Bay seasoning
1 teaspoon finely grated lemon zest

Combine all ingredients in small bowl.

SPINACH GRATIN

✓ **WHY THIS RECIPE WORKS:** Spinach gratin makes a perfect holiday side, but preparing enough fresh spinach for a crowd is impractical at best, and frozen spinach makes a stringy and unimpressive gratin. To solve this problem, we combined fresh curly-leaf spinach and frozen whole-leaf spinach (which we chopped ourselves to achieve more evenly sized pieces). To make a rich, silky sauce, we replaced the milk with half-and-half and used Gruyère cheese along with mustard, cayenne, nutmeg, and garlic to boost the flavor. A topping of homemade bread crumbs and more cheese made an appealing, crunchy crust, and a final addition of lemon zest and parsley after baking gave our gratin just the right amount of freshness and zing.

Among the meat and rich starches on my holiday table, a green vegetable dish is always welcome. My favorite is spinach gratin. For a large crowd, though, I'm caught between a rock and a hard place. I can either use frozen spinach, which makes for a stringy and listless casserole, or gird myself to face washing, stemming, chopping, wilting, and squeezing dry an enormous pile of fresh spinach; like all greens,

spinach wilts to a fraction of its original volume when it's cooked. That prep is tedious, to say the least, plus even my biggest pot can't fit the amount of fresh spinach needed to serve eight. This year, I hoped to develop a recipe for a spinach gratin with a rich and creamy base; a crisp, buttery top; and great cheesy flavor—without the bother.

It occurred to me that the test kitchen's creamed spinach, a similar recipe minus the cheese and topping, would make a good starting point. We briefly wilt two 10-ounce bags of spinach, enough to feed four, and then squeeze the spinach dry; the recipe uses curly-leaf spinach because baby spinach can quickly cook into spinach slime. It calls for building a standard white sauce by sautéing chopped onion in butter, adding spices and flour (for thickening), whisking in milk, and then stirring in the wilted spinach.

To transform creamed spinach into spinach gratin for a holiday crowd, I'd need to add cheese, glamorize and double the recipe, plus develop a topping. But as soon as I upped the quantities, I had, predictably, too much spinach to comfortably handle. And when I tried the recipe with frozen chopped spinach, the results were, as I'd guessed, stringy and anemic. (Even though frozen chopped spinach is mechanically cut, in our experience many of the pieces are actually too small, and the box includes the stringy stems.) Eventually, after several tests, I managed to eliminate the stringiness in a counterintuitive way: I used frozen whole-leaf spinach, which I chopped myself. The hand chopping fixed the texture, and although it added a few steps, it was still easier than prepping a mountain of fresh spinach.

Unfortunately, my gratin still didn't taste remotely fresh. Hoping for fresh taste and frozen convenience, I tried combining fresh and frozen spinach. After several more tests, I found that I was able to quickly wilt 8 ounces of fresh curly-leaf spinach right in the white sauce. Off heat, I added four 10-ounce boxes of frozen whole-leaf spinach, which I'd thawed, squeezed dry, and chopped fine. I scraped the mixture into a 13 by 9-inch dish and baked it. Happily, the modest amount of fresh spinach had an outsize impact.

For an elegant, holiday-appropriate sauce, I used Gruyère cheese and half-and-half—lots of it. I boosted the flavor with mustard, cayenne, nutmeg, and plenty of garlic. For the gratin topping, I combined fresh bread crumbs with melted butter and more cheese. A mere 15 minutes in the oven browned the crumbs nicely without cooking the spinach down to sludge.

But while the half-and-half added luxuriant richness, now the gratin lacked zip. After a little thought, I mixed together chopped parsley and lemon zest and sprinkled my gratin gremolata over the casserole. Just the thing.

—DIANE UNGER, *Cook's Country*

Spinach Gratin

SERVES 8 TO 10

Thaw the frozen spinach in the refrigerator overnight. Before using, squeeze it as dry as you can using a dish towel.

  2 **slices hearty white sandwich bread,**
       torn into 1-inch pieces
  8 **tablespoons unsalted butter**
  8 **ounces Gruyère cheese, shredded (2 cups)**
       Salt and pepper
  1 **onion, chopped fine**
  4 **garlic cloves, minced**
  ⅛ **teaspoon cayenne pepper**
  2 **tablespoons all-purpose flour**
  4 **cups half-and-half**
  8 **ounces curly-leaf spinach, stemmed and**
       chopped coarse
  1 **tablespoon Dijon mustard**
  ⅛ **teaspoon ground nutmeg**
  2½ **pounds frozen whole-leaf-spinach, thawed,**
       squeezed dry, and chopped fine
  ½ **cup minced fresh parsley**
  1 **teaspoon grated lemon zest, plus lemon wedges**
       for serving

1. Adjust oven rack to upper-middle position and heat oven to 425 degrees. Pulse bread in food processor to fine crumbs, about 10 pulses; transfer to bowl. Melt 3 tablespoons butter in microwave, about 30 seconds. Stir melted butter, ½ cup Gruyère, ½ teaspoon salt, and ½ teaspoon pepper into crumbs; set aside.

NOTES FROM THE TEST KITCHEN

USE A COMBINATION OF FRESH AND FROZEN
To prepare the amount of fresh spinach you'd need to serve spinach gratin to a crowd, you'd be washing, stemming, steaming, and squeezing four 10-ounce bags of fresh spinach—more than would fit in our Dutch oven. Instead, our recipe uses just 8 ounces of fresh spinach plus 2½ pounds of frozen.

TOO MUCH OF A GOOD THING
To make the gratin from all fresh spinach, you'd need the amount shown here.

2. Melt remaining 5 tablespoons butter in Dutch oven over medium heat. Add onion and cook until lightly browned, 7 to 9 minutes. Stir in garlic and cayenne and cook until fragrant, about 30 seconds. Stir in flour and cook for 1 minute. Slowly whisk in half-and-half and bring to simmer. Cook, whisking occasionally, until slightly thickened and reduced to about 3½ cups, about 10 minutes.

3. Stir in curly-leaf spinach and cook until just wilted, about 30 seconds. Off heat, stir in mustard, nutmeg, 1½ teaspoons salt, 1 teaspoon pepper, and remaining 1½ cups Gruyère until cheese is melted. Stir in thawed frozen spinach until thoroughly combined. Season with salt and pepper to taste. Transfer mixture to 13 by 9-inch baking dish.

4. Sprinkle crumb mixture evenly over spinach mixture. Bake until bubbling around edges and crumbs are golden brown, 15 to 17 minutes. Transfer to wire rack. Combine parsley and lemon zest in bowl; sprinkle over gratin. Let cool for 10 minutes. Serve with lemon wedges.

TO MAKE AHEAD: Crumb mixture can be covered and refrigerated for up to 24 hours. Spinach mixture can be cooled and refrigerated for up to 24 hours. When ready to serve, bake gratin until hot throughout, 15 to 20 minutes, then proceed with step 4.

ROASTED BALSAMIC-GLAZED MUSHROOMS

✅ **WHY THIS RECIPE WORKS:** Balsamic-glazed mushrooms are a steakhouse treat—we wanted to enjoy them at home and make enough for everyone around the table. To do so, we turned to the oven to avoid the tedious task of sautéing the mushrooms in batches. Since mushrooms release a lot of liquid, we cut them in half, salted them, and gave them a head start in the microwave. Draining the liquid, combined with preheating the baking sheet, allowed the mushrooms to brown quickly in the oven without drying out. We created a silky, luscious glaze with balsamic vinegar, butter, brown sugar, garlic, and thyme.

What can't you glaze with balsamic vinegar? Steak, fish, chicken, squash, root vegetables, and even fruit often get this sweet-tart shellacking. Balsamic-glazed mushrooms are a popular steakhouse side; I wanted to create a recipe for home cooks that would yield meaty mushrooms with a glossy, balanced balsamic glaze. Oh, and one more thing: With the holidays approaching, I'd need enough for eight people.

Since quantity was part of my goal and I didn't want to break the bank, I'd develop this recipe using inexpensive white button mushrooms. I also knew that I'd use the oven to avoid tedious batch cooking of the 4 pounds of mushrooms I'd need to feed eight. The oven recipes I found called for either tossing white mushrooms with a vinegar mixture and then roasting them on a baking sheet or roasting the mushrooms "naked" and subsequently tossing them with vinegar that had been reduced on the stovetop.

NOTES FROM THE TEST KITCHEN

WASHING MUSHROOMS

In the wild, mushrooms grow in damp forests, so it makes no sense to proclaim that one should "never wash mushrooms." You just want to avoid overdoing it. In the test kitchen, we place whole mushrooms in a colander, rinse them gently under cool running water, and then immediately pat them dry with towels. Because water beads up on the exterior of mushrooms, washing whole specimens is fine. Cut mushrooms are another story. The exposed flesh will soak up water like a sponge, so clean mushrooms before slicing them.

Both approaches had problems. Mushrooms are watery on their own so adding vinegar at the start meant that it took nearly 2 hours to reduce the liquids to a glaze, leaving the mushrooms tasting boiled. Roasting the mushrooms in the oven while reducing the vinegar in a saucepan seemed like a better idea, but it required an extra pan, and the glaze didn't adhere well and tasted like an afterthought. Cooking already-reduced glaze on the mushrooms improved adhesion, but the concentrated vinegar scorched easily. I'd stick with the one-pan oven approach and try to strike a balance between boiling the mushrooms and scorching the vinegar; I'd roast the mushrooms partway and then add the vinegar.

I tried roasting 4 pounds of halved mushrooms in a 500-degree oven for a half-hour before pouring on the balsamic so it could reduce while the mushrooms finished cooking. No go—the mushroom liquid flooded the pan, making the mushrooms spongy from the steam before I even had the chance to add the vinegar. I had to get rid of the moisture before roasting.

The test kitchen often uses salt to draw moisture out of vegetables before cooking, so I tossed the mushrooms in salt. But after 30 minutes, only a few drops of liquid had beaded on the surface. I tried cooking them covered with foil for 15 minutes; they released their liquid quickly, but it took forever to evaporate. What about the microwave? Thankfully, it did the trick; after about 15 minutes in the microwave, covered, salted, and halved, my mushrooms released about 2 cups of liquid.

I drained them in a colander, coated them with oil, and roasted them. The mushrooms had browned after 30 minutes, so I poured on the balsamic vinegar and returned the pan to the oven. After about 10 minutes, the vinegar had reduced to a glaze that coated the well-browned mushrooms. But beneath the glaze, the mushrooms had a tough, leathery surface. As they browned, they had dried out.

The fix here was simple: Preheat the baking sheet while I preheated the oven. The hot baking sheet jump-started browning, reducing the cooking time, so the mushrooms had less time to dry out. I added the vinegar and cooked the mushrooms for about 10 minutes longer, stirring halfway through to prevent scorching. Unfortunately, the vinegar tasted one-dimensional and slightly harsh. Ultimately, the combined force of butter, brown sugar, garlic, vinegar, and thyme added dimension, balanced the acidity, and heightened the glaze's shine. These mushrooms—finally—are as good as any you'd get in a steakhouse. Even better, my version makes enough to feed a small crowd.

—SARAH GABRIEL, *Cook's Country*

Roasted Balsamic-Glazed Mushrooms

SERVES 8

Buy mushrooms with caps about 1½ inches in diameter; use any smaller mushrooms whole. Once you add the vinegar, watch carefully so the mushrooms don't burn. If your microwave can't fit the mushrooms in one batch, microwave them in two batches, decreasing the microwave time to 10 minutes per batch.

- 4 pounds white mushrooms, trimmed and halved
- 1 tablespoon salt
- 3 tablespoons olive oil
- ¾ cup balsamic vinegar
- 3 garlic cloves, minced
- 1 teaspoon packed brown sugar
- ¾ teaspoon pepper
- 2 tablespoons unsalted butter, cut into 4 pieces
- 1 teaspoon minced fresh thyme

1. Adjust oven rack to lowest position, place rimmed baking sheet on rack, and heat oven to 500 degrees. Combine mushrooms and salt in large bowl. Cover with large plate and microwave until mushrooms release 1¾ to 2 cups liquid, 14 to 16 minutes, stirring halfway through microwaving. Strain mushrooms in colander and let sit for 5 minutes to drain completely. Return mushrooms to now-empty bowl, add oil, and stir to coat.

2. Transfer mushrooms to preheated sheet and roast until browned and liquid has evaporated, 22 to 25 minutes, stirring halfway through cooking. Whisk vinegar, garlic, sugar, and pepper together in 2-cup liquid measuring cup. Remove mushrooms from oven, pour vinegar mixture over mushrooms, and stir to coat. Return mushrooms to oven and roast until vinegar is reduced to glaze, 9 to 12 minutes, stirring halfway through cooking. Place mushrooms in serving bowl and stir in butter and thyme. Serve.

ROASTED BUTTERNUT SQUASH

✓ **WHY THIS RECIPE WORKS:** Taking a cue from famed chef Yotam Ottolenghi, we sought to create a savory recipe for roasted butternut squash that was simple and presentation-worthy. We chose to peel the squash thoroughly to remove not only the tough outer skin but also the rugged fibrous layer of white flesh just beneath, ensuring supremely tender squash. To encourage the squash slices to caramelize, we used a hot 425-degree oven, placed the squash on the lowest oven rack, and increased the baking time to evaporate the water. We also swapped in melted butter for olive oil to promote the flavorful Maillard reaction. Finally, we selected a mix of toppings that added crunch, creaminess, brightness, and visual appeal.

When it comes to preparing winter squash, I'm as guilty of taking the familiar route as the next person. I sprinkle the halves with some brown sugar, dot them with butter, and slide them into a hot oven. Or I cube the squash and toss it with oil before roasting to help it develop a bit more color and flavorful caramelization. Comforting, yes, but not all that inspiring.

A recipe in London-based chef Yotam Ottolenghi's book *Plenty* introduced me to a new squash universe. He slices the squash (skin and all) into thin half-moons to create more surface area for browning. And rather than add more sweetness, he tosses the roasted squash with savory ingredients, from chiles and lime to toasted nuts and spiced yogurt, which serve as a foil to the squash's natural sweetness. I decided to bring this approach into the test kitchen and put my own spin on it.

My tasters were equally smitten with Ottolenghi's approach, but while they liked the toppings, most found the texture of the roasted squash skin unappealing, and they noted that the squash wasn't especially caramelized.

My first move was to lose the skin. I could have bought prepeeled squash, but we've found that the flavor of whole squash that you peel yourself is superior. As for the roasting method, Ottolenghi uses a relatively hot oven but a short cooking time of 15 minutes—sufficient to tenderize but not long enough for caramelization. I found that when the squash slices were roasted on the middle oven rack, they turned a light golden brown in about 40 minutes—but only on the side in contact with

ROASTED BUTTERNUT SQUASH WITH RADICCHIO AND PARMESAN

the baking sheet. For deeper caramelization on both sides, the solution was simple. I moved the sheet to the lowest oven rack, where it would absorb even more heat from the main heating element on the oven's floor. I then flipped the squash (and rotated the baking sheet) partway through roasting so that both sides could caramelize.

So far, so good, but I had another idea. I had been tossing the squash with olive oil before roasting. But melted butter produced better browning, thanks to its milk proteins that undergo the Maillard reaction, leading to more complex flavors and aromas. These slices emerged perfectly caramelized, wonderfully sweet, and tender—until I got to the edge of each slice. Despite my having removed the skin, the outer edge of each slice was tough.

The reason is this: Below the skin sits a white layer of flesh laced with greenish fibers, and I discovered that this rugged matrix resists turning tender, even with prolonged cooking. The fix? A few more swipes with my vegetable peeler revealed a pumpkin-orange interior that baked up tender from the center to the outer edge of each slice.

My last step was to come up with toppings that provided a mix of contrasting textures and bold flavors—including one with brown butter, hazelnuts, lemon juice, and chives. You may not immediately recognize these dishes as the familiar roasted butternut squash, but actually, that's the point.

—DAN SOUZA, *Cook's Illustrated*

Roasted Butternut Squash with Browned Butter and Hazelnuts

SERVES 4 TO 6

For plain roasted squash omit the topping. This dish can be served warm or at room temperature. For the best texture it's important to remove the fibrous flesh just below the squash's skin.

SQUASH

- 1 large (2½- to 3-pound) butternut squash
- 3 tablespoons unsalted butter, melted
- ½ teaspoon salt
- ½ teaspoon pepper

TOPPING

- 3 tablespoons unsalted butter, cut into 3 pieces
- ⅓ cup hazelnuts, toasted, skinned, and chopped coarse
- 1 tablespoon water

- 1 tablespoon lemon juice
  Pinch salt
- 1 tablespoon minced fresh chives

1. FOR THE SQUASH: Adjust oven rack to lowest position and heat oven to 425 degrees. Using sharp vegetable peeler or chef's knife, remove skin and fibrous threads from squash just below skin (peel until squash is completely orange with no white flesh remaining, roughly ⅛ inch deep). Halve squash lengthwise and scrape out seeds. Place squash, cut side down, on cutting board and slice crosswise ½ inch thick.

2. Toss squash with melted butter, salt, and pepper until evenly coated. Arrange squash on rimmed baking sheet in single layer. Roast squash until sides touching sheet toward back of oven are well browned, 25 to 30 minutes. Rotate sheet and continue to bake until sides touching sheet toward back of oven are well browned, 6 to 10 minutes. Remove squash from oven and use metal spatula to flip each piece. Continue to roast until squash is very tender and sides touching sheet are browned, 10 to 15 minutes longer.

3. FOR THE TOPPING: While squash roasts, melt butter with hazelnuts in 8-inch skillet over medium-low heat. Cook, stirring frequently, until butter and hazelnuts are brown and fragrant, about 2 minutes. Immediately remove skillet from heat and stir in water (butter will foam and sizzle). Let cool for 1 minute; stir in lemon juice and salt.

4. Transfer squash to large serving platter. Drizzle butter mixture evenly over squash. Sprinkle with chives and serve.

VARIATIONS

Roasted Butternut Squash with Radicchio and Parmesan

Omit topping. Whisk 1 tablespoon sherry vinegar, ½ teaspoon mayonnaise, and pinch salt together in small bowl; gradually whisk in 2 tablespoons extra-virgin olive oil until smooth. Before serving, drizzle vinaigrette over squash and sprinkle with ½ cup coarsely shredded radicchio; ½ ounce Parmesan cheese, shaved into thin strips; and 3 tablespoons toasted pine nuts.

Roasted Butternut Squash with Goat Cheese, Pecans, and Maple

Omit topping. Stir 2 tablespoons maple syrup and pinch cayenne pepper together in small bowl. Before serving, drizzle maple mixture over squash and sprinkle with ⅓ cup crumbled goat cheese; ⅓ cup pecans, toasted and chopped coarse; and 2 teaspoons fresh thyme leaves.

Roasted Butternut Squash with Tahini and Feta

Omit topping. Whisk 1 tablespoon tahini, 1 tablespoon extra-virgin olive oil, 1½ teaspoons lemon juice, 1 teaspoon honey, and pinch salt together in small bowl. Before serving, drizzle tahini mixture over squash and sprinkle with ¼ cup finely crumbled feta cheese; ¼ cup shelled pistachios, toasted and chopped fine; and 2 tablespoons chopped fresh mint.

MELTING POTATOES

✔ **WHY THIS RECIPE WORKS:** With their crisp edges, creamy centers, and rich, buttery sauce, melting potatoes (also known as fondant potatoes in the U.K.) make an impressive and rich side dish for a holiday table. But in order to feed a holiday crowd, we needed to make a lot of potatoes. This ruled out stovetop methods, which would require us to cook the potatoes in batches. We opted for an oven-braise method. Turning up the heat of the oven and flipping the potato slices partway through cooking gave the potatoes a perfectly browned crust. A mere 1½ cups of broth was enough to braise the potatoes and create a thick, rich sauce to drizzle over the rounds before serving.

In the test kitchen, it's rare to come across a potato recipe that we don't know backward and forward. Enter melting potatoes. I had heard them described as potatoes with crisp edges and creamy centers in a supremely buttery sauce. When I went looking for recipes, I discovered that this dish is popular in the United Kingdom, where it's known as fondant potatoes. I followed the six recipes that I'd gathered, and while none quite hit the mark, it was obvious that melting potatoes were indeed too good to languish in obscurity in the United States.

Most melting potato recipes instruct you to square off the ends of the spuds and cut them crosswise into disks, though a few call for wedges. The potatoes are then pan-fried in either oil or melted butter and braised to tenderness in broth. I followed this procedure in my initial test and then, based on the results, made a few decisions: I'd cut the potatoes into disks—the wedge cut called to mind steak fries and wasn't elegant enough for the holidays. I'd use Yukon Golds since russets were mealy and red potatoes were too small. I also opted for butter over oil for, well, buttery flavor.

Next I confronted my big problem. I wanted to make enough potatoes to serve six to eight people at the holiday table, but there was no way that a single skillet could brown the necessary 3 pounds. Since messing with multiple batches meant holding warm potatoes, pan frying was out. Roasting was the obvious choice, but could I achieve that deeply browned crust without the direct heat of the stovetop?

I cut the potatoes into 1-inch-thick disks, tossed them with melted butter, and laid them in a single layer in a 13 by 9-inch baking pan. I roasted them at 425 degrees until the bottoms began to color, about 20 minutes, and then flipped the potatoes. After they had spent 20 more minutes in the oven, I added about 2 cups of broth to the pan, to come about halfway up the sides of the potatoes, and then returned them to the oven to cook through. While these potatoes got some color, they were far from crisp. In pursuit of the crispiness of pan-fried potatoes, I tried roasting them longer. A wrong turn—these potatoes were dried out and leathery. So what about roasting them at higher heat? I cranked the oven to 500 degrees. One side was beautifully browned, but the side that was face down to start was still a wimpy pale gold. I tried flipping the slices a second time, just before adding the broth. This method produced two beautifully bronzed sides.

As for the broth, I found that the potatoes needed just 1½ cups to braise. During cooking, the broth reduced and thickened from the potato starches, leaving just enough to drizzle over the gorgeously browned, buttery disks.

—CHRISTIE MORRISON, *Cook's Country*

MELTING POTATOES

SERVES 6 TO 8

Use potatoes at least 1½ inches in diameter. Do not use a glass baking dish, which could shatter.

- 3 pounds Yukon Gold potatoes, peeled
- 6 tablespoons unsalted butter, melted
- 1 tablespoon minced fresh thyme
- 1 teaspoon salt
- ½ teaspoon pepper
- 1½ cups chicken broth
- 2 garlic cloves, lightly crushed and peeled

1. Adjust oven rack to upper-middle position and heat oven to 500 degrees. Square off ends of potatoes and cut crosswise into 1-inch-thick disks. Toss potatoes with butter, thyme, salt, and pepper. Arrange potatoes in single layer in 13 by 9-inch baking pan.

2. Roast potatoes until bottoms are beginning to brown around edges, about 15 minutes. Remove pan from oven. Using flat metal spatula and tongs, loosen potatoes from bottom of pan and flip. Continue to roast until browned on second side, about 15 minutes longer.

3. Remove pan from oven, flip potatoes once more, and add broth and garlic. Roast until potatoes are tender and sauce has reduced slightly, about 15 minutes. Baste potatoes with sauce before serving.

SWEET POTATO FRIES

✓ **WHY THIS RECIPE WORKS:** Too often, sweet potato fries simply don't do justice to their namesake vegetable. We wanted thick-cut sweet potato fries with crispy exteriors and creamy, sweet interiors. Taking a cue from commercial frozen fries, which rely on a starchy coating to encourage crispness, we dunked the potato wedges in a slurry of water and cornstarch. Blanching the potatoes with salt and baking soda before dipping them in the slurry helped the coating stick to the potatoes, giving the fries a super-crunchy crust that stayed crispy. To keep the fries from sticking to the pan, we used a nonstick skillet, which had the added benefit of allowing us to use less oil. For a finishing touch to complement the natural sweetness of the fries, we made a spicy Belgian-style dipping sauce.

Though they're both called potatoes, white potatoes and sweet potatoes couldn't be more different. Sweet potatoes come from a completely different plant family than white potatoes like russets and contain far less starch, more water, and a lot more sugar. As a result, they cook very differently—a fact that is nowhere more apparent than when making fries: It's very hard to make sweet potato fries that rival classic French fries made from russets.

Sweet potato fries are typically soggy or burnt—and often they hit both marks at once. Occasionally a restaurant manages to deliver crispy sweet potato fries, but they never taste much like the tuber. These fries are usually not even house-made: They're frozen fries purchased from a food processing plant. Furthermore, they're frequently cut too thin for my liking, offering little in the way of a supercreamy, sweet-tasting interior—in my opinion, the biggest selling point of this vegetable. Fueled by a serious hunger for good thick-cut sweet potato fries, I ordered 50 pounds of the orange spuds and got to work.

While commercial frozen sweet potato fries lack flavor, I have to respect their ability to turn (and stay) supercrispy. How do they do it? When I compared the ingredient lists of a few products, I found a common theme: starch. A starchy coating on these frozen fries makes all the difference. This discovery didn't come entirely by surprise. After all, it's the high-starch composition of russet potatoes that makes them so suited to frying, and we use starchy coatings to give all kinds of low-starch foods (like chicken) a crispy fried exterior. Meanwhile, sweet potatoes don't just contain less starch than white potatoes do; a little research informed me that they also contain an enzyme that, when heated, converts some of the starch in the sweet potatoes into sugars. All this translates into a serious handicap in the world of deep frying.

So would adding a starchy coating to my fries be the fix that allowed them to crisp up? I rounded up a group of easy-to-find starches—potato starch, cornstarch, arrowroot, and all-purpose flour (while not a pure starch, it's often used for coating foods when deep-frying)—and ran a test to compare. After heating 2 quarts of vegetable oil in a large Dutch oven to 350 degrees, I dusted four batches of ¾-inch-wide peeled sweet potato wedges (which I'd cut in half crosswise for a more manageable shape) with each type of starch and fried them until tender and, in theory, crispy.

What a disappointment. None of the starches formed anything resembling a crispy crust: They clung meekly to the sweet potatoes as a dry, flaky, dusty coating. It turns out that cut sweet potatoes—unlike, say, chicken—don't exude much moisture. Instead, almost all the water that they contain stays trapped within their cell walls. Why is liquid so important in a coating when frying? In hot oil the food's surface moisture quickly turns into steam, and as the steam escapes the food, the outer starchy coating dries out and crisps. The escaping steam leaves behind small holes, and oil fills those holes, helping create a crispy brown crust. These little holes also break up the texture of the coating so that it's crunchy when bitten into rather than hard or leathery—think of a porous Nestlé Crunch bar versus a dense, hard bar of solid chocolate.

Given that, the solution seemed easy: I simply added some water to each of the starches, creating thin slurries that I could dip the wedges into before frying. This was a promising step forward. All the fries emerged with at least a modicum of crust. In the end, cornstarch won out, producing the best crust, with a nicely crisped texture.

But there were still some issues to deal with. For one, my fries looked more like sweet potato tempura—the fried coating was wispy and puffed away from the wedges. In addition, the coating, while crispy right out of the oil, had a tendency to quickly turn soft and soggy. And finally, the interiors of the sweet potatoes were more chalky than smooth, creamy, and sweet.

Thinking that I should switch gears, I turned my focus away from the coating and toward achieving the perfect creamy interior. The cause of the problem was quite clear: The short time that it took to dry and crisp the slurry on the outside wasn't sufficient to cook the thick wedges all the way through.

My first thought was to go the classic French fry route and treat my uncoated wedges to a quick blanch in lower-temperature (around 250-degree) oil before dipping them in the slurry and frying them again at the proper higher temperature to crisp the coating. I gave it a try, and while it resulted in a big difference for the interior texture—which turned soft and sweet—the oil slick on the outside of the blanched fries made it hard to get good slurry coverage. So I switched to blanching in water rather than in oil, simmering the wedges in a

couple of quarts of salted water until their exteriors were tender but their very centers remained slightly firm. (Blanched any further, my fries tended to break apart when mixed with the slurry.) Then I proceeded with the coating and frying as before. This adjustment made a big difference. Without an oily barrier, the slurry clung evenly to each blanched wedge. Plus, adding the salt created better-tasting interiors. This was the best batch yet.

It was time to return to the issues with the coating—namely, it was too thin (and thus prone to sog out) and didn't cling to the fries very well. Was there a way to thicken the coating and at the same time make it adhere better to the wedges? In the past, we've found that adding baking soda to the cooking water for white potatoes breaks down their exteriors, turning them pasty and starchy while their interiors remain firm. In many cases this would be a bad thing, but I wondered if using baking soda here would be a plus, creating a tacky exterior that the slurry would bind to more firmly.

I gave it a shot, adding 1 teaspoon of baking soda to the blanching water. After about 5 minutes of simmering, the water turned orange and the potatoes' exteriors were mushy, just as I'd expected. Once I'd folded these spuds into the slurry, a thick, gloppy orange paste coated the wedges. It looked promising—and it delivered. These wedges had a substantial, crispy coating that clung close to the potatoes, and my fries remained crispy for a long time out of the oil. What's more, they had visual appeal, with great orange color both inside and out. Finally I'd made exactly the fries that I'd been after.

My last move was to try to simplify and foolproof the frying process. My supersticky coating mixture meant that now my fries were pretty likely to stick to one another, as well as to the bottom of the pot. To eliminate the bottom-sticking issue, I opted for nonstick cookware. At first a skillet seemed like an odd choice, but I found that I could drop the oil from 2 quarts to just 3 cups and still keep the wedges fully submerged.

To limit how much the fries stuck to one another, I added them to the pan individually with tongs to ensure that there was good spacing around them—a simple step, considering I was using thick-cut wedges rather than shoestring fries. Any fries that did manage to stick together were easily pried apart with tongs or two forks either during or after frying.

While many restaurants serve ketchup with their sweet potato fries, I always find the combination

MAKING GOOD ON SWEET POTATO FRIES

Here's how we turned sweet potatoes into impressively crispy fries with perfect creamy interiors.

1. BLANCH: Blanching the wedges helps ensure that their interiors fully cook and turn creamy when fried. Adding baking soda to the water makes them tacky on the outside.

2. COAT: The cornstarch coating stays put thanks in part to the parcooked wedges' tacky exteriors, and it crisps up beautifully in the hot oil.

3. FRY: Frying the wedges in a nonstick skillet instead of a Dutch oven prevents them from sticking to the bottom of the pan. The change in vessel also allows us to use far less oil.

SWEET POTATO FRIES GONE WRONG

The typical sweet potato fry is cut thin, which means too little creamy sweet potato interior. Cutting our fries into wedges was a good fix, but their shape wasn't the only hurdle. Because sweet potatoes are low in starch—and a portion of what starches they do possess converts into sugars when heated—most sweet potato fries end up limp or burnt. Giving our sweet potato fries a starchy coating ensures a crust with a crispy texture.

LIMP, BURNT LOSERS
Low-starch sweet potatoes often burn before they crisp up.

cloyingly sweet. Instead, I took a cue from the Belgians and whipped up a creamy, spicy mayonnaise-based sauce. Into the mayonnaise base I stirred spicy Asian chili-garlic sauce and white vinegar.

Supercrispy, ultracreamy, and complete with a spicy sauce, these thick-cut sweet potato fries would be the reason I would save my russets for baking and mashing.

—DAN SOUZA, *Cook's Illustrated*

Thick-Cut Sweet Potato Fries

SERVES 4 TO 6

If your sweet potatoes are shorter than 4 inches in length, do not cut the wedges crosswise. We prefer peanut oil for frying, but vegetable oil may be used instead. Leftover frying oil may be saved for further use; strain the cooled oil into an airtight container and store it in a cool, dark place for up to one month or in the freezer for up to two months. We like these fries with our Spicy Fry Sauce (recipe follows), but they are also good served plain.

½ cup cornstarch
  Kosher salt
1 teaspoon baking soda
3 pounds sweet potatoes, peeled and cut into ¾-inch-thick wedges, wedges cut in half crosswise
3 cups peanut oil

1. Adjust oven rack to middle position and heat oven to 200 degrees. Set wire rack in rimmed baking sheet. Whisk cornstarch and ½ cup cold water together in large bowl.

2. Bring 2 quarts water, ¼ cup salt, and baking soda to boil in Dutch oven. Add potatoes and return to boil. Reduce heat to simmer and cook until exteriors turn slightly mushy (centers will remain firm), 3 to 5 minutes. Whisk cornstarch slurry to recombine. Using wire skimmer or slotted spoon, transfer potatoes to bowl with slurry.

3. Using rubber spatula, fold potatoes with slurry until slurry turns light orange, thickens to paste, and clings to potatoes.

4. Heat oil in 12-inch nonstick skillet over high heat to 325 degrees. Using tongs, carefully add one third of potatoes to oil, making sure that potatoes aren't touching one another. Fry until crispy and lightly browned,

7 to 10 minutes, using tongs to flip potatoes halfway through frying (adjust heat as necessary to maintain oil temperature between 280 and 300 degrees). Using wire skimmer or slotted spoon, transfer fries to prepared wire rack (fries that stick together can be separated with tongs or forks). Season with salt to taste and transfer to oven to keep warm. Return oil to 325 degrees and repeat in 2 more batches with remaining potatoes. Serve immediately.

Spicy Fry Sauce
MAKES ABOUT ½ CUP

For a less spicy version, use only 2 teaspoons of Asian chili-garlic sauce. The sauce can be made up to four days in advance and stored, covered, in the refrigerator.

- **6 tablespoons mayonnaise**
- **1 tablespoon Asian chili-garlic sauce**
- **2 teaspoons distilled white vinegar**

Whisk all ingredients together in small bowl.

RICE AND PASTA PILAF

 WHY THIS RECIPE WORKS: Typically, rice pilaf combines rice with pieces of vermicelli that have been toasted in butter to add richness and a nutty flavor. In order to produce rice that was as tender and fluffy as the pasta, we needed both elements to cook at the same rate. Jumpstarting the rice by soaking it in hot water for a mere 10 minutes softened its outer coating and let it absorb water quickly. Once the pasta and rice were cooked perfectly, we let the pilaf stand in the pot for 10 minutes with a towel under the lid to absorb steam. A handful of fresh parsley lent brightness to the finished pilaf.

For some, rice and pasta pilaf conjures up images of streetcars ascending steep hills to the tune of that familiar TV jingle. But for me, it's not the "San Francisco Treat" that comes to mind but Sunday dinners at my Armenian grandmother's. As it turns out, the two memories are not so disparate: Rice-A-Roni owes its existence to a fateful meeting in 1940s San Francisco. Lois DeDomenico, daughter of Italian immigrants, learned to make rice and pasta pilaf from her Armenian landlady, Pailadzo Captanian. The dish became a staple of the DeDomenico household and would eventually inspire Lois's husband, Tom, whose family owned a pasta factory, to develop a commercial version. They named the product after its two main ingredients—rice and macaroni (pasta)—and the rest is history.

The original dish is a simple affair: A fistful of pasta (usually vermicelli) is broken into short pieces and toasted in butter. Finely chopped onion and/or minced garlic is added next, followed by basmati rice. Once the grains are coated in fat, chicken broth is poured in. After simmering, the pilaf is often allowed to sit covered with a dish towel under the lid to absorb steam—a trick that yields superfluffy results. In a well-executed version, the rice and pasta are tender and separate, boasting rich depth from the butter and nuttiness from the toasted noodles.

Sadly, I never learned my grandmother's recipe, and the cookbook versions I tried fell short. Some featured mushy, overcooked vermicelli; in others, the rice was the problem, either sticking together in a mass or cooking up firm. Using both garlic and onion (shredded on a box grater so that it would add flavor but not a distracting texture), I patched together a recipe and mostly resolved the under- or overcooked rice problem simply by nailing the appropriate amount of liquid: 2½ cups to 1½ cups rice and ½ cup pasta.

But even with this ratio, my pilaf was plagued by a thin layer of somewhat raw, crunchy rice just beneath the pasta, which always floated to the top of the pot during simmering. What's more, the pasta was too soft and mushy. The quicker-cooking vermicelli seemed to absorb broth more rapidly than the rice, thereby denying the rice that surrounded it sufficient liquid to cook through. My theory was confirmed when I reduced the water by ¼ cup and deliberately left the pasta out of a batch: The rice cooked up tender as could be.

Adding more broth would make the dish soggy. Stirring during cooking helped, but it wasn't a reliable fix: Plenty of grains still emerged underdone.

I needed every last grain of rice to absorb the broth at the same rate as the pasta did. I considered removing

RICE AND PASTA PILAF WITH POMEGRANATE AND WALNUTS

the toasted vermicelli from the pot, starting the rice, and then adding back the pasta when the rice was nearly tender, but that seemed unwieldy. Then I came up with a more viable solution: soaking. Starches absorb water at relatively low temperatures, so I guessed that I could hydrate, or sort of parcook, the rice in hot tap water ahead of time. Sure enough, when I saturated the grains in hot water for 15 minutes before continuing with the recipe, the finished rice and pasta both had an ideal tender texture.

With my foolproof approach at hand, I developed a classic herbed variation as well as versions incorporating spices, sweet ingredients, and nuts. I now had a nutty, buttery, perfectly cooked side dish that brought me right back to my grandmother's kitchen.

—ANDREW JANJIGIAN, *Cook's Illustrated*

Rice and Pasta Pilaf

SERVES 4 TO 6

We prefer basmati rice in this recipe, but other types of long-grain rice will work.

- 1½ **cups basmati rice**
- 3 **tablespoons unsalted butter**
- 2 **ounces vermicelli, broken into 1-inch pieces**
- 1 **onion, grated**
- 1 **garlic clove, minced**
- 2½ **cups chicken broth**
- 1¼ **teaspoons salt**
- 3 **tablespoons minced fresh parsley**

1. Place rice in medium bowl and cover with hot tap water by 2 inches; let stand for 15 minutes.

2. Using your hands, gently swish grains to release excess starch. Carefully pour off water, leaving rice in bowl. Repeat adding and pouring off water 4 to 5 times, until water runs almost clear. Drain rice in fine-mesh strainer.

3. Melt butter in saucepan over medium heat. Add pasta and cook, stirring occasionally, until browned, about 3 minutes. Add onion and garlic and cook, stirring occasionally, until onion is softened but not browned, about 4 minutes. Add rice and cook, stirring occasionally, until edges of rice begin to turn translucent, about 3 minutes. Add broth and salt and bring to boil. Reduce heat to low, cover, and cook until all liquid is absorbed, about 10 minutes. Off heat, remove

lid, fold dish towel in half, and place over pan; replace lid. Let stand for 10 minutes. Fluff rice with fork, stir in parsley, and serve.

VARIATIONS

Rice and Pasta Pilaf with Herbs and Yogurt

Stir ¼ cup plain whole-milk yogurt, ¼ cup minced fresh dill, and ¼ cup minced fresh chives into pilaf with parsley.

Rice and Pasta Pilaf with Golden Raisins and Almonds

Place ½ cup golden raisins in small bowl and cover with boiling water. Let stand until plump, about 5 minutes. Drain and set aside. Stir 2 bay leaves and 1 teaspoon ground cardamom into rice with broth. Discard bay leaves and stir raisins and ½ cup slivered almonds, toasted and chopped coarse, into pilaf with parsley.

Rice and Pasta Pilaf with Pomegranate and Walnuts

Omit onion and garlic. Add 2 tablespoons grated fresh ginger to pan with rice. Stir ½ teaspoon ground cumin into rice with broth. Omit parsley and stir ½ cup walnuts, toasted and chopped coarse; ½ cup pomegranate seeds; ½ cup chopped fresh cilantro; and 1 tablespoon lemon juice into fluffed rice.

QUINOA PILAF WITH HERBS AND LEMON

WHY THIS RECIPE WORKS: Most recipes for quinoa pilaf turn out woefully overcooked because they call for nearly twice as much liquid as they should. We cut the water back to ensure tender grains with a satisfying bite, and gave it a stir partway through cooking to ensure the grains cooked evenly. We let the quinoa rest for several minutes before fluffing to help further improve the texture. We also toasted the quinoa in a dry skillet before simmering to develop its natural nutty flavor, and finished our pilaf with a judicious amount of boldly flavored ingredients.

In the span of a decade, quinoa, a seed with humble South American roots, has gone from obscurity to mass consumption in America. I've always assumed its rapid ascent is mainly due to awareness of its health benefits (it's a nearly complete protein that's rich in fiber). While in theory the cooked grain (almost no one calls quinoa a seed) has an appealingly nutty flavor and crunchy texture, in practice it more often turns into a mushy mess with washed-out flavor and an underlying bitterness.

Pilaf recipes that call for cooking the grain with onion and other flavorings don't help matters. If it's blown out and mushy, quinoa pilaf is no better than the plain boiled grain on its own. I was determined to develop a foolproof approach to quinoa pilaf that I'd want to make not because it was healthy but because it tasted great.

My first clue into what might go wrong with the usual quinoa pilaf surfaced as soon as I gathered up recipes to try. All called for softening onion in butter or oil, adding quinoa to the pan and toasting it in the same fat, then pouring in liquid, and simmering covered until the grains were cooked through and the liquid was absorbed. Almost without exception, these recipes used a 2:1 ratio of liquid to quinoa. Could that be the problem?

To find out, I put together a basic working recipe: Soften finely chopped onion in butter in a saucepan, stir in quinoa and water, cover, and cook until tender. I then tested a range of water-to-quinoa ratios and found that, while 2 to 1 might be the common rule, 1 to 1 was nearly perfect. To allow for evaporation, I tweaked this ratio just slightly, using a bit more water than quinoa (1¾ cups water to 1½ cups quinoa). After about 20 minutes of covered simmering, the quinoa was tender, with a satisfying bite.

Or at least most of it was. There was a ½-inch ring of overcooked seeds around the pot's circumference. The heat of the pot was cooking the outer grains faster than the interior ones. To even things out, my first thought was to stir the quinoa halfway through cooking, but I feared that I would turn my pilaf into a starchy mess, as so easily happens with rice. But I needn't have worried. A few gentle stirs at the midway point gave me perfectly cooked quinoa, with no ill effects. Why? While quinoa is quite starchy—more so than long-grain white rice—it also contains twice the protein of white rice. That protein is key, as it essentially traps the starch in place so you can stir it without creating a gummy mess.

The texture of the quinoa improved further when I let it rest, covered, for 10 minutes before fluffing. This allowed the grains to finish cooking gently and firm up, making them less prone to clump.

It was time to think about the toasting step. While the majority of quinoa on the market has been debittered, some bitter-tasting compounds (called saponins) remain on the exterior. We have found that toasting quinoa in fat can exacerbate this bitterness, so I opted to dry-toast the grains in the pan before sautéing the onion. After about 5 minutes in the pan, the quinoa smelled like popcorn. This batch was nutty and rich-tasting, without any bitterness.

Finally, I turned to seasonings. For a simple take, I finished the quinoa with herbs and lemon juice. Next, I looked to quinoa's birthplace for a combination with chile, queso fresco, lime juice, and peanuts. And to highlight quinoa's versatility, I developed a Mediterranean-inspired recipe with apricots, pistachios, and aged gouda. I always kept a judicious hand with additions, ensuring that my quinoa stayed in the spotlight—right where it belonged.

—DAN SOUZA, *Cook's Illustrated*

Quinoa Pilaf with Herbs and Lemon
SERVES 4 TO 6

If you buy unwashed quinoa, rinse the grains in a fine-mesh strainer, drain them, and then spread them on a rimmed baking sheet lined with a dish towel and let them dry for 15 minutes before proceeding with the recipe. Any soft herbs, such as cilantro, parsley, chives, mint, and tarragon, can be used.

1½	cups prewashed quinoa
2	tablespoons unsalted butter, cut into 2 pieces
1	small onion, chopped fine
¾	teaspoon salt
1¾	cups water
3	tablespoons chopped fresh herbs
1	tablespoon lemon juice

1. Toast quinoa in medium saucepan over medium-high heat, stirring frequently, until quinoa is very fragrant and makes continuous popping sound, 5 to 7 minutes. Transfer quinoa to bowl and set aside.

2. Return now-empty pan to medium-low heat and melt butter. Add onion and salt; cook, stirring frequently, until onion is softened and light golden, 5 to 7 minutes.

3. Increase heat to medium-high, stir in water and quinoa, and bring to simmer. Cover, reduce heat to low, and simmer until grains are just tender and liquid is absorbed, 18 to 20 minutes, stirring once halfway through cooking. Remove pan from heat and let sit, covered, for 10 minutes. Fluff quinoa with fork, stir in herbs and lemon juice, and serve.

VARIATIONS

Quinoa Pilaf with Chipotle, Queso Fresco, and Peanuts

Add 1 teaspoon chipotle chile powder and ¼ teaspoon ground cumin with onion and salt. Substitute ½ cup crumbled queso fresco; ½ cup roasted unsalted peanuts, chopped coarse; and 2 thinly sliced scallions for herbs. Substitute 4 teaspoons lime juice for lemon juice.

Quinoa Pilaf with Apricots, Aged Gouda, and Pistachios

Add ½ teaspoon grated lemon zest, ½ teaspoon ground coriander, ¼ teaspoon ground cumin, and ⅛ teaspoon pepper with onion and salt. Stir in ½ cup dried apricots, chopped coarse, before letting quinoa sit for 10 minutes in step 3. Substitute ½ cup shredded aged gouda; ½ cup shelled pistachios, toasted and chopped coarse; and 2 tablespoons chopped fresh mint for herbs.

NOTES FROM THE TEST KITCHEN

THE MANY COLORS OF QUINOA

In just the past few years, quinoa has moved beyond the shelves of natural food stores and can be found at most supermarkets. And while at one time you typically saw only white (or golden) quinoa, you'll notice that red and black (or a mixture of the three) are also increasingly available. White quinoa has the largest seeds of the three varieties. It has a nutty, vegetal flavor with a hint of bitterness; white quinoa is also the softest of the three types. Medium-sized red quinoa offers a heartier crunch and more prominent nuttiness. Black quinoa is the smallest of the three and has the thickest seed coat. Red and white quinoa can be used interchangeably in our pilaf recipes. We think black quinoa is best used in recipes tailored for its distinctive texture and flavor.

WHITE QUINOA

RED QUINOA

BLACK QUINOA

EXTRA-CRISPY SKILLET STUFFING

☑ **WHY THIS RECIPE WORKS:** We love the crispy part of Thanksgiving stuffing, but baking stuffing in a casserole dish results in a minimal amount of crunchy crust. To increase the crunch ratio, we used toasted cubes of French bread, which held up to the moisture in the stuffing and didn't turn soggy. To help the stuffing brown all over, we switched out the casserole dish for a skillet, which gave us the option of browning the stuffing from the bottom up. After sautéing the vegetables and browning the bottom of the stuffing, we moved the whole skillet into the oven to brown the top. Brushing the top with extra butter further encouraged flavorful browning.

To make classic Thanksgiving stuffing, you sauté onions and celery in a skillet with herbs, moisten dried bread cubes with broth and possibly eggs, combine everything, and bake the mixture in a casserole dish (unless you're stuffing the turkey). My family always fights over the crispy top crust, so this year I wondered if I could double the effect by baking the stuffing right in the skillet. My theory was that the heat from below (from contact with the hot skillet) coupled with the heat from above (from the hot oven) would produce twice the delicious crust.

I found some recipes that tried this. But by and large they failed to deliver the serious crunch and moist, but not soggy, interior that I envisioned. Still, I put together a recipe drawing on their more successful parts and our collective test kitchen expertise. After I dried white bread cubes in a 300-degree oven for nearly an hour, I mixed them in a bowl with the chicken broth, eggs, and sautéed vegetables and then let the mixture sit to saturate the bread. I melted a generous lump of butter in a 12-inch nonstick skillet (the same one I'd used for sautéing the vegetables) and piled in the stuffing, patting it down to an even layer. I brushed the top with extra butter to encourage more browning, and therefore crunch, and I baked it in a 350-degree oven.

When I pulled the skillet out some 50 minutes later, the stuffing had an impressive golden top. But disappointment lurked below. The bottom crust wasn't particularly crispy, and the middle was wet mush. I tried

EXTRA-CRISPY SKILLET STUFFING

using less broth, but I'd merely traded one evil (slimy bread in the center) for another (dry, chewy bread). Was the bread itself the problem? I tested my recipe using challah, whole wheat, supermarket Italian, and a baguette. The baguette held up well, plus its high ratio of crust to crumb helped with the crunch. And it gave me an idea. Instead of drying the bread in a low oven—standard test kitchen procedure—what if I toasted the bread? Might the whole loaf be more like the hard crust of the baguette and thus better withstand moisture? I toasted the cubes in a 450-degree oven until they were golden, which took less than 15 minutes. Then I made the stuffing in the skillet as before.

Better, but the bottom crust still wasn't crunchy enough. To get it going, once I'd packed the stuffing into the skillet, I kept the burner on low, basically frying the stuffing. I checked the bottom crust every so often by lifting it up with a spatula. When it was brown, after not quite 10 minutes, I stuck the skillet in the still very hot oven to encourage yet more browning on top of the stuffing. It came out perfectly. If, like me, you prefer the crusty portion of stuffing, then this is the recipe for you.

—CRISTIN WALSH, *Cook's Country*

Extra-Crispy Skillet Stuffing

SERVES 8

If your nonstick skillet doesn't have a metal handle, wrap the handle in a double layer of foil before placing it in the oven.

1½	pounds baguette, cut into ½-inch cubes (18 cups)
3¾	cups chicken broth
4	large eggs, lightly beaten
8	tablespoons unsalted butter
2	onions, chopped fine
3	celery ribs, minced
1½	teaspoons salt
1½	tablespoons minced fresh thyme
1½	tablespoons minced fresh sage
3	garlic cloves, minced
¾	teaspoon pepper

1. Adjust oven rack to upper-middle position and heat oven to 450 degrees. Arrange bread evenly on rimmed baking sheet and bake until light golden brown, 12 to 15 minutes, stirring halfway through. Let bread cool completely.

2. Whisk broth and eggs together in large bowl. Stir bread into broth mixture until evenly coated. Set aside, stirring occasionally, to saturate bread.

3. Melt 2 tablespoons butter in skillet over medium heat. Add onions, celery, and salt and cook until browned, 10 to 12 minutes. Stir in thyme, sage, garlic, and pepper and cook until fragrant, about 30 seconds. Stir onion mixture into bread mixture.

4. Melt 3 tablespoons butter in now-empty skillet over low heat. Add stuffing to skillet, pressing down firmly into even layer with spatula (skillet will be very full). Cook until bottom of stuffing is browned around edges when lifted with spatula, 7 to 10 minutes.

5. Melt remaining 3 tablespoons butter in microwave and brush evenly over top of stuffing. Transfer skillet to oven and bake until center of stuffing is hot and top is golden brown, about 20 minutes, rotating skillet halfway through baking. Let cool for 10 minutes. Serve.

NOTES FROM THE TEST KITCHEN

BROWNING = FLAVOR AND CRUNCH

For the ultimate crunch, we don't merely dry the bread; we toast it at high heat. To further develop its crust, we fry the stuffing in butter on the stovetop, without stirring. Then we brush the top with melted butter and put the skillet in a hot oven so the top can develop a similarly brown, crunchy crust.

GOOD COLOR
These toasted bread cubes are unusually dark for stuffing.

GREAT CRUNCH
Our method makes stuffing that is crispy on the top and on the bottom.

PASTA, PIZZA, AND MORE

SUMMER PASTA PUTTANSESCA

SUMMER PASTA PUTTANESCA

✓ **WHY THIS RECIPE WORKS:** When we make pasta puttanesca with fresh tomatoes, we want the tomatoes to share equal billing with the pungently flavorful olives and anchovies typical of this robust sauce. For a puttanesca that would make the most of a bumper crop of fresh tomatoes, we opted to use grape or cherry tomatoes, which are both excellent in summer and among the best varieties of tomatoes available year-round. To retain the fresh tomato flavor, we pureed the tomatoes and strained the juices, which we cooked down briefly to thicken the sauce. We added the tomato pulp back in at the end of cooking so we wouldn't lose the fresh tomato flavor. We traded the traditional long pasta for frilly campanelle, which held on to the coarse sauce and gave our dish a summery flair.

At the end of summer, I inevitably find myself with a glut of beautiful garden tomatoes, both small and large. As a result, I'm always searching for ways to use them beyond salads. Puttanesca, that most boisterous of classic Italian sauces (legend has it that it was invented by Neapolitan prostitutes on break between customers), is one of my favorite tomato-based sauces. I love the clash of flavors that it presents: Spicy pepper flakes, pungent garlic, and salty anchovies, olives, and capers meet up with clean-tasting fresh herbs and tangy-sweet tomatoes. Putting my harvest to use in this quick sauce appealed to both my pragmatic instincts and my stomach. Doing so would also address the generic "cooked" quality that stems from using canned tomatoes, the usual choice for this dish. I wasn't aiming for a no-cook sauce, but I did want a fresher puttanesca—one that retained the fruits' clean-tasting sweetness alongside the richer, more assertive flavors that are the essence of this dish.

My first step was trying several varieties of tomato in a basic puttanesca: minced garlic and anchovies (anchovy paste, for convenience), red pepper flakes, chopped black olives, and capers, all sautéed in olive oil. I quickly learned that this was not the place for larger tomatoes, which are typically full of juice. In order to keep that liquid from watering down my sauce, I had to reduce it—and when I did, its fresh flavor all but disappeared. Lesson learned: Use a low-moisture variety that wouldn't need much cooking. That decision pointed me to grape (or cherry) tomatoes; once

halved, they need very little simmering time to reduce to a sauce-like consistency. Availability was on my side, too: Not only is my garden full of these tomatoes by summer's end but they're also consistently decent in supermarkets year-round.

Of course there was a downside: The larger ratio of skin to flesh meant that my sauce was full of chewy skins. Peeling large tomatoes had been easy; after a quick dunk in boiling water, the skins slipped right off. But I wasn't about to fussily skin dozens of tiny tomatoes. Instead, I gave them a quick blitz in a blender, which pulverized the skins completely.

Unfortunately, doing so also caused them to shed more moisture—not as much as an equal quantity of big tomatoes but enough that it seemed I would have to revert to a longer simmering time. I had a better idea: What if I drained the pureed tomatoes in a strainer before adding them to the sauce? That way, I could use the pulp and discard the exuded liquid.

But just as I was about to discard the tomato juice, I realized my faulty thinking. The majority of tomato flavor resides in the juice, jelly, and seeds, so I'd essentially be throwing away the best part. The better approach was to briefly simmer the juice to concentrate its flavor. Once it had reduced to ⅓ cup, I added the uncooked pulp along with the olives and capers. When the sauce was heated through, the bulk of the tomatoes had softened but still tasted fresh.

Now I could concentrate on taming puttanesca's rowdier ingredients: the olives and the capers. I tested common varieties of high-quality black olives. Salt-cured were too salty, but brine-cured kalamata and Gaeta, both of which were fruity and pleasantly crisp-tender, were equally excellent choices. I chopped them coarsely—any finer and the sauce turned a muddy brown. I did finely chop the capers, however, so that their briny punch hit every bite. A smidgen of dried oregano introduced complexity; ½ cup of minced parsley offered freshness.

I instituted one final adjustment: Finding myself out of the standard spaghetti or linguine, I reached for campanelle. Surprisingly, we all preferred the compact size and convoluted twists of this pasta, since it did a better job of trapping the coarse sauce. I also liked that aesthetically it hinted at a summertime pasta salad, giving the dish an overall fresher appeal.

—ANDREW JANJIGIAN, *Cook's Illustrated*

Summer Pasta Puttanesca

SERVES 4

We prefer to make this dish with campanelle, but fusilli and orecchiette also work. Three very finely mashed anchovy fillets (rinsed and dried before mashing) can be used instead of anchovy paste. Buy a good-quality black olive, such as kalamata, Gaeta, or Alfonso.

- 3 tablespoons extra-virgin olive oil
- 4 garlic cloves, minced
- 1 tablespoon anchovy paste
- ¼ teaspoon red pepper flakes
- ¼ teaspoon dried oregano
- 1½ pounds grape or cherry tomatoes
- 1 pound campanelle
- Salt
- ½ cup pitted kalamata olives, chopped coarse
- 3 tablespoons capers, rinsed and minced
- ½ cup minced fresh parsley

1. Combine oil, garlic, anchovy paste, pepper flakes, and oregano in bowl. Process tomatoes in blender until finely chopped but not pureed, 15 to 45 seconds. Transfer to fine-mesh strainer set in large bowl and let drain for 5 minutes, occasionally pressing gently on solids with rubber spatula to extract liquid (this should yield about ¾ cup). Reserve tomato liquid in bowl and tomato pulp in strainer.

2. Bring 4 quarts water to boil in large pot. Add pasta and 1 tablespoon salt and cook, stirring often, until al dente. Reserve 1 cup cooking water, then drain pasta and return it to pot.

3. While pasta is cooking, cook garlic-anchovy mixture in 12-inch skillet over medium heat, stirring frequently, until garlic is fragrant but not brown, 2 to 3 minutes. Add tomato liquid and simmer until reduced to ⅓ cup, 2 to 3 minutes. Add tomato pulp, olives, and capers; cook until just heated through, 2 to 3 minutes. Stir in parsley.

4. Pour sauce over pasta and toss to combine, adding reserved cooking water as needed to adjust consistency. Season with salt to taste. Serve immediately.

FUSILLI WITH RICOTTA AND SPINACH

✔ **WHY THIS RECIPE WORKS:** Pasta like manicotti and tortellini are often stuffed with a creamy mixture of ricotta and fresh spinach. The combination is irresistible, but making fresh stuffed pasta is a work-intensive project. We decided to turn this dish inside out for a weeknight meal that would make the most of these classic flavors. In order to keep the ricotta texture and flavor distinct (and to prevent the graininess that comes from heating ricotta), we opted to add most of it in dollops over the finished dish rather than fold it into the sauce. To keep the spinach bright and green (and eliminate the tedious task of blanching and squeezing it dry), we cooked it very briefly in the pot along with the pasta. For complexity and balance, we added lots of minced garlic, cayenne, nutmeg, lemon juice and zest, and Parmesan cheese to our sauce.

Every so often I come across a recipe that teams simple boiled pasta with spinach and ricotta as a sort of quick "deconstructed" version of stuffed shells, manicotti, tortellini, or ravioli. Since the labor involved in cooking a stuffed pasta dish makes it the sort of project that most of us reserve for special occasions, a no-fuss dish resulting from simply tossing the same ingredients together has a lot of appeal.

But when I gave a few recipes of this sort a try, my enthusiasm faded. The authors all seemed to forget that the stuffed pasta is only one component of the dish: Ravioli and the like are typically served with a bright marinara, a meaty ragu, or even a nutty browned butter. When you take these contrasting flavors away, the dish

---

loses complexity, and the richness of the ricotta hijacks the mild spinach and pasta. My goal was to modify this quick dinner so that it was flavorful enough to stand on its own, with no need for an accompanying sauce to jazz it up. Most of the recipes that I found employ one of two basic methods: The first calls for buzzing raw spinach and ricotta in a food processor along with bold ingredients like garlic, Parmesan, and toasted nuts to create a "pesto." The uncooked puree is then tossed with hot pasta just prior to serving. The second approach requires sautéing chopped, blanched spinach in aromatics and then stirring in the ricotta. The mixture is cooked just long enough to create a uniform sauce. The problem with the first method was that the pesto tasted neither of mineral-y spinach nor of milky ricotta. Pureed together, the two components seemed to cancel each other out. The result of the latter method also tasted somewhat wan, but I could at least discern the ingredients, so that's where I began my testing.

First I set out to tackle the sauce's gritty, chalky texture. Heat causes the curds in ricotta to release water and coagulate, rendering the sauce grainy. I tried cooking the cheese as briefly as possible in order to prevent this from happening, but the effect doesn't take much heat to induce, and I had to at least bring the sauce to a simmer before dressing the pasta.

Some recipes suggested that adding a little cream would minimize grittiness (the fat in the cream coats the milk proteins in the cheese to slow down coagulation), but in order to prevent curdling entirely, I had to either add an excessive amount of cream or dial down the ricotta to the point that its presence was lost completely. Then I had a better idea. Since I really wanted to taste pure ricotta, what if I simply withheld most of the cheese and dolloped it onto the finished dish? This would prevent the sauce from turning grainy, while keeping the ricotta presence distinct.

To bring out the best from the cheese, I seasoned it with extra-virgin olive oil, salt, and pepper. And to make sure it didn't go onto the pasta cold, I let it sit out on the counter to warm up to room temperature while the pasta cooked. It worked perfectly: After combining a small amount of ricotta with cream and using it to dress the pasta, I spooned the remaining seasoned ricotta on top of the dish. Instead of a dilute amount of cheese in each bite, tasters got concentrated hits here and there, much as they would when eating filled pasta.

With the ricotta sorted out, I turned my attention to the spinach. I wanted to use baby spinach since it requires almost no prep prior to cooking. Figuring that it was worth trying the most straightforward approach to cooking it, too, I simply threw the coarsely chopped leaves into the pot with the pasta (curly fusilli nicely trapped the sauce) once it was al dente. This worked like a charm: In just 30 seconds, the spinach was wilted yet still brilliant green.

To make the flavors pop, I opted for a healthy dose of sautéed garlic mixed into the ricotta and cream mixture, along with sprinklings of nutmeg and cayenne for an underlying warmth. A generous dusting of grated Parmesan cheese provided additional depth, and lemon zest and lemon juice introduced welcome brightness. Finally, in order to produce a nice, velvety texture, I employed a dead-simple trick we've used in the past: Let the dressed pasta sit for a few minutes, stirring it occasionally, to draw out some of the pasta's starches. Together, these elements combined to give me a dish that was as easy to make as it was delicious.

—ANDREW JANJIGIAN, *Cook's Illustrated*

Fusilli with Ricotta and Spinach
SERVES 4 TO 6
We like fusilli for this recipe since its corkscrew shape does a nice job of trapping the sauce, but penne and campanelle also work well.

11 ounces (1⅓ cups) whole-milk ricotta cheese
3 tablespoons extra-virgin olive oil
   Salt and pepper

1   **pound fusilli**

1   **pound (16 cups) baby spinach, chopped coarse**

4   **garlic cloves, minced**

¼   **teaspoon ground nutmeg**

⅛   **teaspoon cayenne pepper**

¼   **cup heavy cream**

1   **teaspoon grated lemon zest plus 2 teaspoons juice**

1   **ounce Parmesan cheese, grated (½ cup), plus extra for serving**

1. Whisk 1 cup ricotta, 1 tablespoon oil, ¼ teaspoon pepper, and ⅛ teaspoon salt in medium bowl until smooth; set aside.

2. Bring 4 quarts water to boil in large pot. Add pasta and 1 tablespoon salt and cook, stirring often, until al dente. Reserve 1 cup cooking water. Stir spinach into pot with pasta and cook until wilted, about 30 seconds. Drain pasta and spinach and return them to pot.

3. While pasta cooks, heat remaining 2 tablespoons oil, garlic, nutmeg, and cayenne in medium saucepan over medium heat until fragrant, about 1 minute. Remove pan from heat and whisk in remaining ⅓ cup ricotta, cream, lemon zest and juice, and ¾ teaspoon salt until smooth.

4. Add ricotta-cream mixture and Parmesan to pasta and toss to combine. Let pasta rest, tossing frequently, until sauce has thickened slightly and coats pasta, 2 to 4 minutes, adjusting consistency with reserved cooking water as needed. Transfer pasta to serving platter, dot evenly with reserved ricotta mixture, and serve, passing extra Parmesan separately.

PASTA WITH PESTO AND POTATOES

✔ WHY THIS RECIPE WORKS: The idea of serving two starches together might seem unusual, but this dish from Liguria is the traditional way to serve classic basil pesto. The starch from red potatoes enriched the pesto, transforming it into a creamy sauce with good body. Tender green beans added color, flavor, and just enough contrasting texture. Although some traditional recipes called for cooking the potatoes, green beans, and pasta together in the same pot, we found that cooking them separately was the only way to ensure that each element was cooked perfectly.

I'm oblivious when it comes to trends, but even I know that carbohydrates are out of fashion. That's why the notion of putting pasta and potatoes in the same dish initially struck me as just plain wrong. But I was intrigued to learn that the preferred way to serve pesto in Liguria, Italy—the birthplace of the basil sauce—involved just that combination. Wondering what the Italians knew that I didn't, I found a handful of recipes and gave them a whirl.

For pasta, I chose short, thick double helix–shaped gemelli, which I knew would hold the sauce nicely. I ground one batch of basil leaves, garlic, and toasted pine nuts with a mortar and pestle as tradition dictated and buzzed another in a food processor before stirring in olive oil and grated Parmesan cheese. I then cooked batches of pasta, potatoes (peeled and cut into a variety of shapes), and green beans (cut into bite-size lengths) together in single pots of boiling salted water, staggering the addition of ingredients and hoping they would all finish cooking simultaneously. Finally, I tossed each dish's ingredients with pesto and some cooking water.

Some variations were dull and heavy, but I was surprised that many boasted a creamy lightness. Why? It all came down to how the potatoes were treated. The most successful recipes called for cutting the potatoes into chunks and then, once cooked, vigorously mixing them with the pesto, pasta, and green beans. The agitation sloughed off their corners, which dissolved into the dish, pulling the pesto and cooking water together to form a simple sauce.

But the recipe still needed work. The sauce was grainy and the sharp, raw garlic dominated. Timing was another issue: The green beans could be jarringly crisp and the pasta way too soft—or vice versa. As for that mortar and pestle—I'd opt for the convenience of the food processor.

I knew that the potatoes were the key to the sauce, and I wondered if my choice of russets was the reason for the slightly rough texture. Sure enough, when I substituted waxy red potatoes for russets, the graininess disappeared. Why? Waxy red potatoes contain about 25 percent less starch than russet potatoes do. When waxy potatoes are boiled, they absorb less water and their cells swell less and do not separate and burst as those in russet potatoes do. As a result, waxy potatoes produce a smooth, creamy texture, while russets can be mealy and grainy.

Now to address the timing problem. The traditional method of staggering the addition of ingredients to the pot doesn't allow for much variation in the size or

PASTA WITH PESTO, POTATOES, AND GREEN BEANS

quality of each, making it difficult to cook each element perfectly. But cooking each ingredient sequentially took too long, and boiling them simultaneously in separate pots dirtied too many dishes. By recycling my pine nut–toasting skillet to steam the beans and by fully cooking the potatoes in the water before the pasta went in, I was able to cook everything separately using only two pots. While the pasta bubbled, I made the pesto.

To mellow the garlic cloves, I toasted them skin on with the pine nuts. I drained the pasta and then returned everything to the pot, along with the pesto and 1¼ cups of cooking water. That sounds like a lot of cooking water, but the potato starch needs more water in which to disperse.

Finally, I stirred with a rubber spatula until the magic sauce formed. Two tablespoons of butter made it even silkier, and a splash of lemon juice brought all the flavors into focus. This simple classic taught me what the Ligurians have known all along: Fashion has its place, and the dinner plate isn't it.

—ANDREA GEARY, *Cook's Illustrated*

Pasta with Pesto, Potatoes, and Green Beans

SERVES 6

If gemelli is unavailable, penne or rigatoni make a good substitute. Use large red potatoes measuring 3 inches or more in diameter.

- ¼ cup pine nuts
- 3 garlic cloves, unpeeled
- 1 pound large red potatoes, peeled and cut into ½-inch pieces
- Salt and pepper
- 12 ounces green beans, trimmed and cut into 1½-inch lengths
- 2 cups fresh basil leaves
- 1 ounce Parmesan cheese, grated (½ cup)
- 7 tablespoons extra-virgin olive oil
- 1 pound gemelli
- 2 tablespoons unsalted butter, cut into ½-inch pieces and chilled
- 1 tablespoon lemon juice

1. Toast pine nuts and garlic in 10-inch skillet over medium heat, stirring frequently, until pine nuts are golden and fragrant and garlic darkens slightly, 3 to 5 minutes. Transfer to bowl and let cool. Peel garlic and chop coarsely.

NOTES FROM THE TEST KITCHEN

KEEPING PASTA WARMER LONGER

Pasta cools off quickly. Here's a tip to keep it warmer for longer.

Drain the cooked pasta in a colander set in a large serving bowl. In addition to heating the bowl, the starchy pasta water can easily be reserved for use in the sauce.

GRATING HARD CHEESE

When grating Parmesan and other hard cheeses, we use a rasp-style grater because it produces lighter, fluffier shreds of cheese that melt seamlessly into pasta dishes and sauces.

2. Bring 3 quarts water to boil in large pot. Add potatoes and 1 tablespoon salt and cook until potatoes are tender but still hold their shape, 9 to 12 minutes. Using slotted spoon, transfer potatoes to rimmed baking sheet. (Do not discard water.)

3. Meanwhile, bring ½ cup water and ¼ teaspoon salt to boil in now-empty skillet over medium heat. Add green beans, cover, and cook until tender, 5 to 8 minutes. Drain green beans and transfer to sheet with potatoes.

4. Process basil, Parmesan, oil, pine nuts, garlic, and ½ teaspoon salt in food processor until smooth, about 1 minute.

5. Add pasta to water in large pot and cook, stirring often, until al dente. Set colander in large bowl. Drain pasta in colander, reserving cooking water in bowl. Return pasta to pot. Add butter, lemon juice, potatoes and green beans, pesto, 1¼ cups reserved cooking water, and ½ teaspoon pepper and stir vigorously with rubber spatula until sauce takes on creamy appearance. Add additional cooking water as needed to adjust consistency and season with salt and pepper to taste. Serve immediately.

PASTA WITH CAULIFLOWER AND BACON

✔ **WHY THIS RECIPE WORKS:** Nutty cauliflower, meaty bacon and crisp bread crumbs often team up into a winning pasta dish on restaurant menus, but making this dish at home can be a fussy affair. To cut back on the number of pans this dish usually requires, we browned the cauliflower in the same skillet that we had used to cook the bacon and panko crumbs. By employing a risotto method and cooking our pasta in a small amount of water, we were able to skip the draining step and make a creamy sauce using the pasta starch. Topping our pasta with bacon-flavored bread crumbs added another layer of flavor and ensured that the crumbs stayed crisp. Parsley and lemon juice added freshness to the finished dish.

In restaurants, the combination of pasta, cauliflower, bacon, and bread crumbs can be transformed into a dish far greater than the sum of its parts: lush and creamy, a wonderfully balanced combination of nutty florets, meaty bacon, and crunchy crumbs. At home, however, the promise of the dish is often overshadowed by the sinkful of dirty pots and pans left after cooking. This is because most times, the cauliflower and bread crumbs are roasted or toasted in different pans in the oven, while the bacon is crisped in a skillet and a pot of water is set to boil for the pasta. Four pans for what should be an easy weeknight dish? No thanks. To make this restaurant dish at home, a little streamlining was definitely in order.

Some recipes that I found tried to cut down on pots by forgoing the roasting of the cauliflower and cooking it and the pasta in the same pan. Others called for steaming the florets in the same skillet that was used to cook the bacon and toast the bread crumbs. But without roasting, the texture and flavor of the vegetable was compromised. This is because raw cauliflower is more than 90 percent water, so when it is blanched or steamed, much of that water is retained—resulting in mushy florets that easily fade into the background.

Roasting the cauliflower seemed critical, since it would not only encourage moisture to escape but also create browning and enhance the nutty flavor of the florets. Wanting to avoid turning on my oven and using another pan, I tried browning the florets in batches in a skillet. But the sheer volume of florets (one head yields about 8 cups) meant that it took a long time to cook them all.

Generally we avoid crowding the pan because it causes the food to steam more than brown. But even in a crowded pan, I reasoned, some of the food will brown; maybe in this dish, that's all I'd need for an extra boost of flavor. Plus, if I kept the heat high enough, a lot of the water from the cauliflower would still evaporate. So the next time, instead of cooking the cauliflower in batches, I loaded up the skillet with the entire crop of florets and let it rip over medium-high heat. After about 10 minutes, a fair number of the florets were nicely browned and the whole lot was crisp-tender, too. Sold.

Now on to the last problem: When I stirred some of the pasta cooking water into the nearly finished dish to help create a sauce, I found that the pasta sucked most of it right up, and what little liquid was left was thin and unsatisfying. Restaurants don't have this problem. Their pasta cooking liquid is so viscous and superstarchy from boiling batch after batch in the same pot that it easily creates a creamy sauce when tossed with cooked pasta. The idea of adding starch to my finished dish seemed unappealing—but what if I just didn't throw any away? I switched cooking methods, adapting one usually reserved for making risotto, in which only the amount of liquid needed to cook the rice and create a starchy sauce is added to the pot and no more. This would mean that I wouldn't have to discard any water, and thus all the pasta starch would make it into the final dish.

I toasted some panko bread crumbs in a skillet, which I then wiped clean and used to brown my cauliflower in one heaping batch. In a Dutch oven, I crisped my bacon and then softened chopped onion and some thyme in the rendered fat. Then I added the pasta and a measured amount of water. As soon as the pasta was al dente and nearly all the water had been absorbed, I added the cauliflower and gave the mixture a stir. The resulting dish? Lush and well dressed. When I tried swapping in a mixture of wine and chicken broth for the water, tasters agreed: The flavor was even more complex.

It still tasted more bacon-y than I wanted, however, and the panko had become a bit soggy. I had a simple solution for that: Instead of cooking the pasta with the bacon, I made a bacon and bread-crumb garnish to sprinkle on the finished dish by cooking the bacon, toasting the bread crumbs in the bacon fat, and then mixing them with the bacon. A final addition of parsley and lemon juice enlivened the dish, and there it was: restaurant flavor at home—with only two pots.

—LAN LAM, *Cook's Illustrated*

Pasta with Cauliflower, Bacon, and Bread Crumbs

SERVES 4 TO 6

Farfalle, orecchiette, or gemelli can be substituted for the campanelle. If the pasta seems too dry, stir in up to ¼ cup of hot water.

- 3 slices bacon, cut into ¼-inch pieces
- ½ cup panko bread crumbs
  Salt and pepper
- 2 tablespoons vegetable oil
- 1 large head cauliflower (3 pounds), cored and cut into 1-inch florets
- 1 onion, chopped fine
- ½ teaspoon minced fresh thyme
- 1 pound campanelle
- 5½ cups chicken broth
- ½ cup dry white wine
- 3 tablespoons minced fresh parsley
- 1 teaspoon lemon juice, plus lemon wedges for serving

1. Cook bacon in 12-inch skillet over medium-high heat until crispy, 5 to 7 minutes. Add panko and ¼ teaspoon pepper and cook, stirring frequently, until panko is well browned, 2 to 4 minutes. Transfer panko mixture to bowl and wipe out skillet.

2. Heat 5 teaspoons oil in now-empty skillet over medium-high heat until shimmering. Add cauliflower and 1 teaspoon salt; cook, stirring occasionally, until cauliflower is crisp-tender and browned in spots, 10 to 12 minutes. Remove pan from heat and cover to keep warm.

3. Heat remaining 1 teaspoon oil in Dutch oven over medium heat until shimmering. Add onion, thyme, and ½ teaspoon salt; cook, stirring frequently, until onion has softened, 4 to 7 minutes. Increase heat to high, add pasta, broth, and wine, and bring to simmer. Cook pasta, stirring frequently, until most of liquid is absorbed and pasta is al dente, 8 to 10 minutes.

4. Remove pot from heat; stir in parsley, lemon juice, and cauliflower; and season with salt and pepper to taste. Serve, passing panko mixture and lemon wedges separately.

SLOW-COOKER SPICY MEATBALLS AND MARINARA

✔ WHY THIS RECIPE WORKS: Making meatballs in a slow cooker is hardly a new idea, so we wanted to up the ante on this satisfying Italian classic by adding some brightness and spice. Since slow cookers tend to dull flavors over the long cooking time, we took advantage of bold, zesty ingredients. For the meatballs, convenient meatloaf mix offered hearty flavor, and a panade (a mixture of bread crumbs and milk) kept them moist. Chopped pepperoncini and red pepper flakes delivered a solid punch of heat. To make sure the meatballs held together and to render some fat to prevent our sauce from becoming greasy, we microwaved the meatballs before transferring them to the slow cooker. For the sauce, a couple of cans of tomato puree provided the right consistency, while tomato paste, garlic, and oregano offered depth and a bit of sugar balanced the acidity of the tomatoes.

For me, meatballs and marinara sauce served over a generous portion of tender spaghetti and dusted with grated Parmesan cheese stirs up fond memories of family dinners. Although I love this familiar classic, sometimes I crave something a bit spicier. I wanted to take this essential comfort food and turn up the heat, and for convenience and ease, I opted to develop my spiced-up recipe in the slow cooker.

Slow-cooker recipes for spicy meatballs and marinara are plentiful but, judging by the ones I tried, generally underwhelming. Those that called for simply dumping raw meatballs and sauce ingredients into the slow cooker produced broken-down meatballs floating in flavorless, greasy marinaras. The ones that called for baking or searing the meatballs and simmering the sauce before adding everything to the appliance were better, but required so much prep that they defeated the whole point: convenience. I wanted to find a happy medium: thick, flavorful marinara; tender meatballs with a healthy dose of spiciness; and a reasonable amount of prep work.

Normally, marinara sauce gets complexity and heft from an hour-long simmer on the stove, which concentrates the flavors and texture. Slow cookers, however, don't allow for much evaporation, so my sauce would need to have a thick, hearty consistency from the start. To achieve this, I tried a range of tomato products. After a few test runs, I found that tasters liked the

SLOW-COOKER SPICY MEATBALLS AND MARINARA

pasta-coating abilities of tomato puree. While tomato puree is not usually among the test kitchen's favorite tomato products, it works well in long-simmered dishes where a smooth texture is desired. Tomato paste added depth without interrupting the smooth consistency of the sauce. A little bit of sugar amped up the flavor even more, but I kept the amount to just 1 teaspoon so the sauce wouldn't taste sweet. The classic additions of garlic and oregano rounded out the sauce and provided an aromatic backbone.

Happy with the texture and flavor of my sauce, I moved on to the meatballs. The test kitchen's stovetop recipe for meatballs uses Parmesan and some of the aromatics from the sauce to flavor the meatballs, so I followed suit. Using meatloaf mix as my base, I incorporated Parmesan, oregano, and garlic to give the meatballs hearty flavor. For a quick and easy boost of spiciness, I added red pepper flakes to the mix, but tasters found the heat one-dimensional. I cast about the pantry for other spicy additions, and came across a jar of pepperoncini. The slightly pickle-y, tangy flavor of the moderately spicy pepperoncini offset the rounder, deeper flavors in the meatballs, and added an extra hit of spice which quickly earned tasters' approval.

I hoped that a panade made from milk and sandwich bread would hold the meatballs together, since I didn't want to spend a lot of extra time baking the meatballs before I put them in the slow cooker. But the panade alone wasn't enough; after several hours in the slow cooker, my sauce looked like a meatball massacre. Swapping out the bread in the panade for slightly sturdier panko bread crumbs was a good start, but the meatballs still weren't holding their shape as much as I'd hoped.

Taking a cue from other test kitchen slow-cooker meatball recipes, I turned to the microwave. After only 5 minutes in the microwave, the meatballs firmed up enough to maintain their shape for the long cooking time; plus, I was able pour off the rendered fat to ensure the sauce wouldn't be greasy.

Finally, I boiled a pound of spaghetti and sat down to try my spicy meatballs and marinara. The punch of heat, hearty flavor, and tender meatballs came together perfectly to make a balanced dish with just the right amount of spice—and the right amount of prep work.

—STEPHANIE PIXLEY, *America's Test Kitchen Books*

Slow-Cooker Spicy Meatballs and Marinara

SERVES 4

This recipe is designed to work with 5½- to 7-quart slow cookers. Meatloaf mix is a prepackaged mix of ground beef, pork, and veal; if it's unavailable, use 8 ounces each of ground pork and 85 percent lean ground beef. This recipe will make about 8 meatballs and 5 cups of sauce, enough for 1 pound of pasta. Serve with spaghetti or your favorite long pasta.

- 1 **pound meatloaf mix**
- ½ **cup panko bread crumbs**
- ¼ **cup whole milk**
- ¼ **cup grated Parmesan cheese**
- ¼ **cup sliced pepperoncini, chopped fine**
- 6 **garlic cloves, minced**
- 2 **teaspoons dried oregano**
- ¾ **teaspoon red pepper flakes**
-    **Salt and pepper**
- 2 **(28-ounce) cans tomato puree**
- 2 **tablespoons tomato paste**
- 1 **teaspoon sugar, plus extra for seasoning**

1. Using your hands, mix meatloaf mix, panko, milk, Parmesan, pepperoncini, 1 tablespoon garlic, 1 teaspoon oregano, ½ teaspoon pepper flakes, ½ teaspoon salt,

NOTES FROM THE TEST KITCHEN

MICROWAVING MEATBALLS?

Many recipes recommend browning the meatballs in the oven or on the stovetop, but we skip this time-consuming step by using the microwave. Microwaving the meatballs for just five minutes set the exteriors, which kept them from falling apart in the slow cooker. The precooking also rendered some of the fat, minimizing the grease in our marinara sauce.

THE BEST TOMATO PUREE

Tomato puree, like tomato sauce, is cooked and strained to remove the tomato seeds, making it much smoother and thicker than other canned tomato products. But tomato puree has a slightly thicker consistency than tomato sauce, which is why we use it in our slow-cooker sauces—it helps us achieve the consistency of a stovetop sauce without the benefit of the reduction that comes with a long simmer in an uncovered pot or skillet. Our favorite brand is **Hunt's Tomato Puree**, which offers a nice, thick consistency and tomatoey flavor.

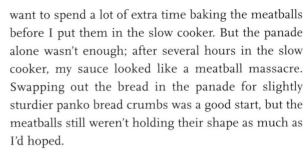

and ½ teaspoon pepper together in bowl until uniform. Pinch off and roll mixture into 2-inch meatballs (about 8 meatballs total) and arrange on large plate. Microwave meatballs until fat renders and meatballs are firm, about 5 minutes.

2. Combine tomato puree, tomato paste, sugar, ½ teaspoon salt, ½ teaspoon pepper, remaining 1 tablespoon garlic, and remaining 1 teaspoon oregano in slow cooker. Transfer microwaved meatballs to slow cooker, discarding rendered fat. Cover and cook until meatballs are tender, 4 to 5 hours on low.

3. Using large spoon, skim excess fat from surface of sauce. Season with salt, pepper, and extra sugar to taste, and serve.

PASTA ALLA NORCINA

✔ **WHY THIS RECIPE WORKS:** A specialty of a small Italian village in Umbria, *pasta alla norcina* is a unique pasta dish that showcases flavorful pork sausage in a light cream sauce. For an authentic-tasting version, we made our own sausage—a process which proved surprisingly simple. We streamlined our sausage by starting with store-bought ground pork which we mixed with a salty brine to soften the meat. To ensure the juiciest (and most flavorful) sausage, we added baking soda and seared the sausage in the form of a patty. We then chopped it into small pieces and gently finished it in a sauce of cream, white wine, earthy mushrooms, and a healthy handful of tangy grated Pecorino Romano. We added some last-minute brightness in the form of parsley and a squeeze of lemon juice.

In the Middle Ages, butchers in the Umbrian village of Norcia became so adept at cutting, salting, and curing pork that the products they produced—sausage, bacon, and prosciutto, to name a few—became legendary. Still named after the small town to this day, pork butcher shops throughout Italy are called *norcinerie*, and pork butchers bear the title of *norcino*. It's no surprise, then, that *pasta alla norcina*—featuring fresh sausage—is widely considered the ultimate pasta and sausage dish.

On a recent trip to the region, I sampled many versions, the best of which featured crumbled fresh sausage, juicy and tender as could be, napped in cream and tossed with a small, chunky pasta. While some plates were fancied up with black truffles or other garnishes,

sausage was always the focus. Made with the prized meat of Umbrian black pigs, the sausage tasted first and foremost of rich pork with hints of garlic and sometimes rosemary. I typically avoid trying to replicate dishes so deeply connected to their birthplace for fear that I won't do them justice, but my persistent cravings for this pasta dish won out. My goal was to come up with a version possessing all the virtues of the ones I'd savored in Italy.

Whipping up a cream-based sauce would be relatively easy, so I focused my efforts on getting the sausage just right. And here I ran into a predictable obstacle: Store-bought Italian sausage made a poor substitute for the true handmade Italian stuff. Depending on the brand, I found that the grind size and fat and salt contents varied considerably. Even more problematic was that the overwhelming majority of mild Italian sausage in this country is the fennel-spiked type, which was all wrong for this recipe. Undeterred, I decided to simply follow Norcian tradition: I would make my own sausage.

Making fresh sausage at home may sound daunting, but it's actually pretty easy. At its simplest, sausage is nothing more than a humble mixture of chopped or ground meat (in this case pork), fat, and salt. The typical procedure is to rub a tough cut like pork shoulder with salt and allow it to sit for at least a few hours, during which time the salt pulls water from the meat. The water then mixes with the salt and forms a shallow brine on the meat's surface. The brine is then reabsorbed by the flesh, and it starts to dissolve some of the protein fibers. Finally, the salted meat is ground with fat and then kneaded by hand or by machine. During kneading, the proteins cross-link and bind together, and a strong protein network develops—much like the gluten network that is created when bread dough is kneaded. This network traps moisture and fat and produces the satisfying snappy texture of a good sausage. Easy enough, but I wanted to find a way around the extended salting time, which seemed beyond the pale for what was basically a weeknight pasta dish.

Grinding my own meat was too much trouble, so I jumped straight to an 8-ounce package of preground pork. Luckily, store-bought ground pork already has the 4:1 ratio of meat to fat typically used for pork sausage. I mixed kosher salt into several different batches and let them sit for various lengths of time, hoping that the greater surface area of the preground pork would significantly reduce the salting time (from hours to just minutes) and allow me to start kneading right away.

Unfortunately, it took a full 30 minutes for the salt to dissolve, form a brine, and reabsorb. I needed to speed up the salting process. What if, instead of waiting for the salt to dissolve in the pork juices, I made the brine myself?

I did just that for my next batch, dissolving the salt in a spoonful of water and folding the solution into the pork. After 10 minutes, I could see the surface of the meat darken, a sure sign that the proteins were dissolving (as proteins dissolve they reflect light differently, causing a color shift). To this base, I added the simple flavorings I recalled from the sausage back in Norcia: minced garlic, ground black pepper, and chopped fresh rosemary. The pork was also quite soft; 10 seconds of mixing with a spoon efficiently brought the meat together into a thick, sticky mass, which meant that a strong protein network had developed.

I eagerly fried a small patty to check for seasoning. This stuff had the springy texture of well-made sausage, and it also tasted pretty good. My colleagues suggested adding a warm background spice, and a few tests proved that a little grated nutmeg accented the garlic and rosemary nicely. Still, for my imitation to compete with the real Umbrian sausage, I'd need to brown it well to develop as much meaty complexity as possible. And here I ran into another common problem: Thoroughly browning crumbled sausage deepens its flavor, but it practically guarantees tough, dry, meat. Was there a way to produce sausage that was well browned yet still moist?

Since ground pork sausage, like ground beef, has a tendency to dry out when crumbled and seared in a hot skillet, perhaps I needed to stop breaking it apart; instead, I'd try cooking it in one big piece, as I would a hamburger. I pressed the sausage into a 6-inch disk and browned it in a hot skillet slicked with oil. About 3 minutes per side was all it took to develop a crusty exterior, at which point the interior was still pink. I transferred the patty to a cutting board, chopped it into ⅛- to ¼-inch pieces, added the pieces back to the skillet, poured in some cream, and gently cooked them through. The good news: This sausage had terrific meaty flavor. The bad: It was still a bit drier than I would have liked. Could I do even better?

The test kitchen recently discovered the powerful effect that baking soda can have on moisture retention in meat, putting soda to good use in everything from pork stir-fries to turkey burgers. The alkaline soda raises the pH of the meat and dramatically improves its water-holding capacity by tenderizing its muscle fibers and giving them a looser structure. It was worth giving it a try in my sausage. I mixed up a few more batches of my recipe with increasing amounts of baking soda added to the brine. I then seared each batch on both sides, chopped them into rough bites, and simmered them for a few minutes in cream until they were no longer pink. With ¼ teaspoon of soda in the mix, the meat stayed incredibly juicy and tender—finally, American-made sausage was a reasonable facsimile of the Italian stuff.

With the sausage squared away, I focused on adding complementary flavors to the sauce. After chopping the browned sausage patty, I transferred it to a bowl with cream, where it could infuse its flavor, while I built the rest of the sauce (I would add the sausage-cream mixture back to the skillet later to cook the meat through). Super-pricey black truffles were out of the question, but I thought that a little background flavor from a much more common (and affordable) variety of fungi—cremini mushrooms—would be nice. I roughly chopped 8 ounces of cremini mushrooms and sautéed them in the skillet until they were nicely browned. Tasters liked the flavor but felt that the pieces of mushroom competed for attention with the sausage. Easy enough to fix: A quick spin in the food processor reduced them to a fine consistency that blended discreetly into the dish. To mirror the flavors in the sausage, I added garlic, black pepper, and rosemary to the mushrooms. Then, to balance the richness of the dish, I deglazed the skillet with white wine and stirred in the sausage and cream to finish cooking. As is tradition, I also stirred in a handful of grated Pecorino Romano.

After tossing the sausage-speckled sauce with al dente orecchiette—this cupped, ear-shaped pasta cradled the chunky sauce nicely—I sprinkled it with chopped parsley and a squeeze of lemon juice for a fresh-tasting finish. I'd finally met my objective: a true tribute to the dish that I'd eaten abroad, complete with the requisite homemade sausage.

—DAN SOUZA, *Cook's Illustrated*

Pasta alla Norcina

SERVES 6

White mushrooms may be substituted for the cremini, and short pasta such as mezzi rigatoni or shells for the orecchiette.

     Kosher salt and pepper
¼   **teaspoon baking soda**
8   **ounces ground pork**
3   **garlic cloves, minced**
1¼ **teaspoons minced fresh rosemary**
⅛   **teaspoon ground nutmeg**
8   **ounces cremini mushrooms, trimmed**
7   **teaspoons vegetable oil**
¾   **cup heavy cream**
1   **pound orecchiette**
½   **cup dry white wine**
1½ **ounces Pecorino Romano cheese, grated (¾ cup)**
3   **tablespoons minced fresh parsley**
1   **tablespoon lemon juice**

1. Grease large dinner plate with vegetable oil spray. Dissolve 1⅛ teaspoons salt and baking soda in 4 teaspoons water in medium bowl. Add pork and fold gently to combine; let stand for 10 minutes.

2. Add 1 teaspoon garlic, ¾ teaspoon rosemary, nutmeg, and ¾ teaspoon pepper to pork and smear with rubber spatula until well combined and tacky, 10 to 15 seconds. Transfer pork mixture to greased plate and form into rough 6-inch patty. Pulse mushrooms in food processor until finely chopped, 10 to 12 pulses.

3. Heat 2 teaspoons oil in 12-inch skillet over medium-high heat until just smoking. Add patty and cook without moving it until bottom is browned, 2 to 3 minutes. Flip patty and continue to cook until second side is well browned, 2 to 3 minutes longer (very center of patty will be raw). Remove pan from heat, transfer sausage to cutting board, and chop into ⅛- to ¼-inch pieces. Transfer sausage to bowl and add cream; set aside.

4. Bring 4 quarts water to boil in large pot. Add pasta and 2 tablespoons salt and cook, stirring often, until al dente. Reserve 1½ cups cooking water, then drain pasta and return it to pot.

5. While pasta cooks, return now-empty skillet to medium heat. Add 1 tablespoon oil, mushrooms, and

HOW TO MAKE JUICY, FLAVORFUL SAUSAGE

Store-bought Italian sausage didn't have the right flavors for this dish, so we made our own. Our unusual (but easy) approach produces meat that browns thoroughly on the outside and also stays tender and juicy within. To help the ground pork retain moisture and stay juicy, we brined it and added baking soda. Working in the seasonings with a rubber spatula gave the sausage its trademark springy texture, and browning the sausage in one large patty (as opposed to small, broken-up pieces) helped the meat stay tender while getting a good sear.

BROWN ONE LARGE PATTY
Patting the pork into a 6-inch "burger"
helps it withstand a hard sear.

DON'T GET STUCK

Orecchiette's cupped shape makes it perfect for pairing with chunky sauces, but it is prone to nest and stick when cooking. To keep the pieces separate, just stir—often.

⅛ teaspoon salt; cook, stirring frequently, until mushrooms are browned, 5 to 7 minutes. Stir in remaining 2 teaspoons oil, remaining garlic, remaining ½ teaspoon rosemary, and ½ teaspoon pepper; cook until fragrant, about 30 seconds. Stir in wine, scraping up any browned bits, and cook until completely evaporated, 1 to 2 minutes. Stir in sausage-cream mixture and ¾ cup reserved cooking water and simmer until meat is no longer pink, 1 to 3 minutes. Remove pan from heat and stir in Pecorino until smooth.

6. Add sauce, parsley, and lemon juice to pasta and toss well to coat. Before serving, adjust consistency with remaining reserved cooking water as needed and season with salt and pepper to taste.

RIGATONI WITH BEEF AND ONION RAGU

✔ **WHY THIS RECIPE WORKS:** This rich, supple meat sauce was born out of thrift in 16th-century Naples. *La Genovese* began as a combination of beef and aromatic vegetables that were cooked down to make two meals: a savory sauce for pasta and another, separate meal of cooked beef. Later, most of the vegetables took a backseat to the onions, which became the foundation of this deeply flavorful sauce. To make the ultrasavory recipe work in a modern context, we decided to turn all the elements into one substantial sauce by shredding the meat into the sauce. To eliminate the need for intermittent stirring and monitoring during cooking, we moved the process from the stovetop to the even heat of the oven. A surprising ingredient—water—proved essential to extracting maximum flavor from the onions. We also added tomato paste for an extra boost of flavor and color. To encourage the sauce to cling to the pasta, we vigorously stirred them together so that the starch from the pasta added body to the sauce. A bit of grated Pecorino Romano brought the flavors together and added a mild tang.

There are those who have the best of everything, and there are those who make the best of everything. The residents of 16th-century Naples fell into the latter category. Faced with a population explosion that caused severe food shortages, they created a thrifty yet supremely satisfying gravy of beef and aromatic vegetables known, ironically, as *la Genovese*. (The provenance of the name is unclear: Some theorize that Genovese cooks brought it to Naples; others believe that the name references the reputed frugality of the people of Genoa.)

Later in the 19th century, onions took center stage, and the dish became one of the region's most beloved. The classic preparation is straightforward: A piece of beef, usually from the round, is placed in a pot and covered with approximately twice its weight in sliced onions, along with chopped aromatic vegetables, salt, and perhaps some herbs. Then several cups of water and a bit of wine go into the pot, and the mixture is simmered for anywhere from 3 to 6 hours, until the liquid has evaporated, the beef is tender, and the onions have cooked down into a soft, pulpy mass.

Traditionally, frugal cooks served the beef-flavored onion gravy—notice that I didn't mention tomatoes; the dish predates the introduction of tomatoes to European kitchens—as a sauce for sturdy tubular pasta like rigatoni. (Incidentally, the sauce doesn't include garlic either.) The meat itself was typically reserved for a second meal, or at least a second course, with a vegetable. But in these comparatively prosperous times, the beef is more likely to be shredded and incorporated into the sauce for a substantial single dish—exactly the kind of pasta sauce I love to make in cold weather months.

I started with a very traditional recipe, but since I was making just one meal, not two, I immediately cut down the amount of beef and onions to a more practical size—1 pound of trimmed beef round and 2½ pounds of thinly sliced onions, which I hoped would produce six to eight servings. To those key players I added a finely chopped carrot and celery rib, plus some minced marjoram and salt, all of which I put in a Dutch oven with 8 cups of water and 1 cup of white wine (the meat is not usually seared). I let the pot bubble away for a good 2½ hours, giving it an occasional stir to keep the contents cooking evenly. By that point, the beef was fully cooked; I removed it to let it cool before chopping it (its texture was too tight to shred) and adding it back to the sauce. In the meantime I reduced the oniony cooking liquid.

Perhaps not surprisingly, this early version did not produce the succulent, deeply flavorful ragu I had envisioned. The lean round was not the best cut to be using in a moist heat environment; it lacks fat and collagen, which keep meat tasting tender and juicy, so it cooked up dry and tight. Also, reducing the sauce itself took too long—almost 40 minutes. Lastly, the color of the sauce was an unappealing beige.

What did impress me was the deeply savory flavor of the onions. They weren't sharp and sulfurous like fresh onions, nor did they have the sweetness of the caramelized kind. They were just plain beefy-tasting. In fact, one taster observed that the onions tasted beefier than the actual beef. I'd come back to this discovery once I'd nailed down the basics of the sauce—for starters, the meat.

Beef round's tight grain makes this cut a good candidate for slicing, but since I was in pursuit of more tender meat that I could shred and return to the sauce, I moved to our favorite braising cuts: short ribs, blade steaks, and chuck-eye roast. The latter won for its beefy flavor, tenderness, and (in homage to the thrifty nature of this dish) relatively low price tag. The only glitch? Cooked whole, it took upwards of 3½ hours to turn tender. Cutting it into four chunks reduced the cooking time to 2½ hours and allowed me to trim away intramuscular fat pockets. I also seasoned the roast with salt and pepper before cooking and moved the braising to a low (300-degree) oven, where the meat would cook more evenly.

And I cut way back on the water—down to 3 cups—hoping to drastically shorten the reduction time. But even with that little amount, it still took about a half-hour of stovetop reduction to turn the onions and cooking liquid saucy. I wondered: Did I have to add water at all?

In the next batch I omitted the water and simply nestled the beef in the onion mixture and sealed the pot tightly with foil (to lock in steam) and then the lid. This worked well; the meat braised to perfect tenderness in the released juices, and the sauce required less stovetop reduction time—just 10 minutes. But strangely, this version tasted less savory.

To ramp up meatiness, I turned to innovations that started to show up in later Genovese recipes: pancetta and salami (which I ground in the food processor) and tomato paste. They all made the ragu more savory, particularly the umami-rich tomato paste when I browned it in the pot before adding the onions. The tomato paste also warmed up the color of the formerly drab-looking finished sauce. But while this batch tasted meatier than the previous one, it still was not as savory as the first version. I was baffled. I had not only added meaty ingredients but also taken away the world's most neutral ingredient: water.

A consultation with our science editor solved the mystery. Astonishingly, it was the water that was the key to extracting the meaty flavor that was locked inside the onions. That meatiness is due to a water-soluble compound known as 3-mercapto-2-methylpentan-1-ol (MMP), the byproduct of a reaction that occurs when onions are cut and then heated in water.

By eliminating the water, I was severely limiting the development of savory flavors, so I added back 2 cups—just enough to cover the onions but not so much that the sauce's reduction time would be lengthy. I also switched from slicing the onions to chopping them in the food processor—a timesaving technique that would also lead to the creation of more MMP. This time the sauce regained the meatiness of the original batch, and then some, with the pancetta, salami, and tomato paste. Even better, I found that I could cook it in the oven with the lid off, which encouraged evaporation and saved

me some reducing time at the end. The sauce was a bit sweet, so I reserved half of the wine for adding at the end for extra brightness.

One last tweak: I found that when I vigorously mixed—instead of just lightly tossed—together the cooked pasta and sauce and a bit of cheese, the starch on the surface of the pasta pulled the components together, helping keep the liquid from separating out from the solids.

I had to hand it to those thrifty 16th-century Neapolitans. This was a true ragu—humble at its roots but as savory and satisfying as the meat-and-tomato-heavy versions that would follow. My 21st-century tweaks would make it a staple in my wintertime pasta sauce rotation.

—ANDREA GEARY, *Cook's Illustrated*

Rigatoni with Beef and Onion Ragu
SERVES 6 TO 8

If marjoram is unavailable, substitute an equal amount of oregano.

1	(1- to 1¼-pound) boneless beef chuck-eye roast, cut into 4 pieces and trimmed of large pieces of fat
	Kosher salt and pepper
2	ounces pancetta, cut into ½-inch pieces
2	ounces salami, cut into ½-inch pieces
1	small carrot, peeled and cut into ½-inch pieces
1	small celery rib, cut into ½-inch pieces
2½	pounds onions, halved and cut into 1-inch pieces
2	tablespoons tomato paste
1	cup dry white wine
2	tablespoons minced fresh marjoram
1	pound rigatoni
1	ounce Pecorino Romano cheese, grated (½ cup), plus extra for serving

1. Sprinkle beef with 1 teaspoon salt and ½ teaspoon pepper and set aside. Adjust oven rack to lower-middle position and heat oven to 300 degrees.

2. Process pancetta and salami in food processor until ground to paste, about 30 seconds, scraping down sides of bowl as needed. Add carrot and celery and process 30 seconds longer, scraping down sides of bowl as needed. Transfer paste to Dutch oven and set aside; do not clean out processor bowl. Pulse onions in processor in 2 batches, until ⅛- to ¼-inch pieces form, 8 to 10 pulses per batch.

3. Cook pancetta mixture over medium heat, stirring frequently, until fat is rendered and fond begins to form on bottom of pot, about 5 minutes. Add tomato paste and cook, stirring constantly, until browned, about 90 seconds. Stir in 2 cups water, scraping up any browned bits. Stir in onions and bring to boil. Stir in ½ cup wine and 1 tablespoon marjoram. Add beef and push into onions to ensure that it is submerged. Transfer to oven and cook, uncovered, until beef is fully tender, 2 to 2½ hours.

4. Transfer beef to carving board. Place pot over medium heat and cook, stirring frequently, until mixture is almost completely dry. Stir in remaining ½ cup wine and cook for 2 minutes, stirring occasionally. Using 2 forks, shred beef into bite-size pieces. Stir beef and remaining 1 tablespoon marjoram into sauce and season with salt and pepper to taste. Remove from heat, cover, and keep warm.

5. Bring 4 quarts water to boil in large pot. Add pasta and 2 tablespoons salt and cook, stirring often, until just al dente. Drain pasta and add to warm sauce. Add Pecorino and stir vigorously over low heat until sauce is slightly thickened and pasta is fully tender, 1 to 2 minutes. Serve, passing extra Pecorino separately.

NOTES FROM THE TEST KITCHEN

A SURPRISING FORMULA FOR MEATY FLAVOR

Believe it or not, much of the meaty flavor in our Genovese ragu actually comes from the 2½ pounds of onions in our recipe. Specifically, the flavor stems from a compound in onions called 3-mercapto-2-methylpentan-1-ol, or MMP for short. When an onion is cut, some of its sulfur compounds combine to form a new compound: propanethial-S-oxide—the stuff that makes your eyes tear. When heated, this compound turns into MMP. And what does MMP taste like? Meat broth.

To harness MMP's full savory power, we switched from slicing to finely chopping the onions in a food processor to create even more opportunities for sulfur compounds to be released and transformed into MMP. But there's a hitch: MMP's flavor is water-soluble, which means that to create it, water must be present. And the more water, the more beefy flavor that's extracted. By cooking the onions and meat in 2 cups of water (versus allowing them to simmer in their own juices), we were able to create a marked increase in meaty flavor.

LOTS OF ONIONS   **PROCESSED FINE**   **WATER**

ITALIAN EASTER PIE

✔ WHY THIS RECIPE WORKS: Made to feed a crowd, *torta rustica*, or Italian Easter pie, is a hefty construction of meats and cheeses wrapped in a pastry crust. To help the crust hold up to the considerable fillings, we reinforced the dough with eggs and kneaded it to develop structure. We used just two types of meat: hot capicola and Italian sausage, which offset some of the pie's richness with their subtle heat. We found that provolone provided creaminess while sharp, salty Pecorino Romano offered depth. Traditional ricotta, mixed with eggs, held the filling together. Sautéed broccoli rabe added a touch of bitterness along with a welcome freshness.

Torta rustica (or *pizza rustica*) is a very large, very rich, and very delicious Italian meat-and-cheese pie that's typically eaten in Italian American homes for Easter lunch. Among the recipes I looked at were one that made an 11-plus-pound pie and another that called for 3 pounds of cheese, 3½ pounds of meat (sausage, prosciutto, and *sopressata*), and 17 eggs. For a single pie.

When I lined up seven rustic, double-crusted pies on the test kitchen counter for us to sample, the elasticity of this folk recipe became clear. Ricotta was pretty much a constant, but other than that the fillings varied widely, encompassing all manner of Italian cold cuts, sausages, and cheeses. Some recipes called for stirring in vegetables. Crusts ranged from classic pie dough to yeast doughs to *pasta frolla*, a sweet, cookie-like Italian crust.

Since most Italian immigrants came to America to escape grinding poverty, who can blame them for loading up their tortas with as many delicious things as they could afford? But by today's standards, it was too much of a good thing. These tortas were rich to the point of dense, plus, they required that a home cook procure just about the entire contents of an Italian delicatessen. I would need to do some thoughtful pruning.

To begin with, rather than tussle with a large, cumbersome crust to fit a 13 by 9-inch casserole dish, as some recipes required, I'd make my torta in a deep cake pan. To help offset the rich cheeses and meat, I'd include vegetables. I sketched out a recipe and headed to the kitchen.

I began from the outside in—with the crust. Tasters damned pasta frolla with faint praise, calling it "interesting." I'd stick with a savory crust. A standard flaky pie crust proved flimsy for such a hefty torta, so I switched to an intriguing food processor crust from my first round of testing. It used eggs, which made it

ITALIAN EASTER PIE

elastic, and it called for kneading. Normally, kneading toughens pie crusts, but in this case it developed gluten, which gave the crust enough structure to hold the heavy filling. I used both butter, for flavor, and shortening, which made the dough pliable and easy to handle. With the crust settled, I turned to the filling.

Five different types of meat in one pie? Apparently, according to my first round of tests. In the interest of streamlining, I would limit myself to two. I went with hot Italian sausage and hot capicola; both are easy to find, plus their heat helped temper the rich torta. As for cheeses, along with provolone—sliced and available at any deli counter and a classic for Easter pie—I used creamy, milky ricotta for the base and lots of Pecorino Romano for its salty, sharp edge. I mixed the ricotta and Pecorino with two eggs; the provolone I'd simply layer in.

Greens brought much-needed lightness. Among the several greens I tried, broccoli rabe was the favorite. Its slight bitterness made it the perfect partner for the filling. I simply chopped it, sautéed it briefly with garlic and sausage to imbue it with garlicky, meaty flavor, and then layered it into the torta with the provolone, the capicola, and the ricotta mixture.

At this point in my testing, I'd baked more than 30 pies; coworkers were jokingly calling me *nonna*. But I'd managed to make a torta rustica that was in delicious balance. It was still big, rich, and celebratory, but now its cheesy creaminess was offset with a slight bitterness and heat, its heaviness relieved by greenery, and its sturdy crust a match for its heft. Finally, I had a torta rustica to call my own—and to share with you.

—DIANE UNGER, *Cook's Country*

Italian Easter Pie

SERVES 12

Use a cake pan that's at least 2 inches deep. If your pan is light-colored, increase baking time to 45 to 50 minutes.

DOUGH

- 3 large eggs
- 3 tablespoons cold water
- 3 cups (15 ounces) all-purpose flour
- 1¼ teaspoons salt
- 6 tablespoons unsalted butter, cut into ½-inch pieces and chilled
- 6 tablespoons vegetable shortening, cut into ½-inch pieces and chilled

FILLING

- 1 tablespoon olive oil
- 12 ounces broccoli rabe, trimmed and chopped
- 8 ounces hot Italian sausage, casings removed
- ¼ teaspoon salt
- 2 garlic cloves, minced
- 1 pound (2 cups) whole-milk ricotta cheese
- 4 ounces Pecorino Romano cheese, grated (2 cups)
- 2 large eggs
- 1 teaspoon pepper
- 8 ounces thinly sliced aged provolone cheese
- 6 ounces thinly sliced hot capicola

- 1 large egg yolk beaten with 1 tablespoon water

1. FOR THE DOUGH: Whisk eggs and cold water together in bowl; set aside. Process flour and salt in food processor until combined, about 3 seconds. Scatter butter and shortening over top and pulse until only pea-size pieces remain, about 10 pulses. Add egg mixture and pulse until dough ball forms, about 20 pulses. Turn out dough onto lightly floured counter and knead until smooth and elastic, about 20 turns. Divide dough into one 1-pound ball and one 10-ounce ball (roughly into two-thirds and one-third) and form each into 6-inch disk. Wrap disks tightly in plastic wrap and refrigerate for at least 1 hour or up to 24 hours.

2. FOR THE FILLING: Heat oil in 12-inch nonstick skillet over medium-high heat until shimmering. Add broccoli rabe, sausage, and salt and cook, breaking up sausage with spoon, until sausage is cooked through and broccoli rabe is tender, 5 to 7 minutes. Add garlic and cook until fragrant, about 30 seconds. Transfer to plate and let cool completely, about 15 minutes. Whisk ricotta, Pecorino, eggs, and pepper together in large bowl.

3. Adjust oven rack to middle position and heat oven to 375 degrees. Grease dark-colored 9-inch round cake pan. Roll 1-pound disk of dough into 14-inch circle on well-floured counter. Loosely roll dough around rolling pin and gently unroll it onto prepared pan, letting excess dough hang over edge. Ease dough into pan by gently lifting and supporting edge of dough with your hand while pressing into pan bottom and sides with your other hand. Leave overhanging dough in place.

4. Shingle half of provolone in bottom of dough-lined pan. Spread ricotta mixture over provolone. Scatter sausage mixture over ricotta mixture and press lightly into even layer. Shingle capicola over sausage mixture, followed by remaining provolone.

5. Roll remaining disk of dough into 10-inch circle on well-floured counter. Brush overhanging dough of bottom crust with egg wash. Loosely roll 10-inch circle around rolling pin and gently unroll it over filling. Trim overhanging top and bottom doughs to ½ inch beyond lip of pan and pinch firmly together. Fold overhanging dough inward so folded edge is flush with edge of pan. Crimp dough evenly around edge of pan with tines of fork.

6. Brush top of pie liberally with egg wash. Using paring knife, cut eight 1-inch vents in top of dough in circular pattern. Bake until filling registers 150 degrees halfway between edge and center of pie and crust is golden brown, 35 to 40 minutes. Transfer pie to wire rack and let cool for at least 4 hours before serving or cool and refrigerate for up to 2 days. Remove pie from pan, slice into wedges, and serve.

NOTES FROM THE TEST KITCHEN

ASSEMBLING ITALIAN EASTER PIE

1. Roll out first disk of dough. Gently press into pan, holding edge of dough with one hand while pressing with other hand.

2. Shingle half of provolone into pan, overlapping slices to cover bottom. Spread ricotta mixture over provolone. Spoon sausage mixture evenly over ricotta. Shingle capicola, then shingle remaining provolone.

3. After rolling and placing top crust, trim overhang to ½ inch beyond lip of pan. Pinch top and bottom crusts together, and fold overhang inward so folded edge is flush with pan. Crimp edge with fork.

PIZZA MONKEY BREAD

✔ **WHY THIS RECIPE WORKS:** Pizza monkey bread starts with balls of dough which are filled with classic pizza ingredients like cheese and pepperoni. Just like their sweet, cinnamon-sugar counterparts, the filled dough balls are baked into a crusty ring, meant for pulling apart and eating with your hands. For ease, we started off with store-bought pizza dough. Instead of shaping and filling each pizza-stuffed ball individually, we formed logs stuffed with the fillings and cut them into pieces. We found that string cheese was the perfect shape to roll up in the dough and had great mozzarella flavor. Microwaving the pepperoni before using it prevented greasy dough, and brushing a bit of the rendered oil onto the outside of the balls created a deeply browned crust. A simple tomato sauce for dipping completed our savory, fun-to-eat monkey bread.

Like the more typical sweet monkey bread, pizza monkey bread is knobs of dough baked in a Bundt pan to form a golden-brown ring that you pull apart and eat with your fingers. But instead of being tossed in cinnamon sugar, the knobs are stuffed with salty, gooey pepperoni pizza fixings to form a crunchy-chewy snack. Combining the salty-spicy appeal of pepperoni pizza with something that looks really neat and is fun to pick apart with your fingers sounded to me like the ultimate snack food.

Pizza monkey bread, it turns out, is an Internet sensation. After days of trying to get a handle on the more than 2.6 million search results, plus cookbook versions, I had identified the major variables and had a lineup of recipes to test. While we didn't find any superstars in the first round, we learned a few things: Store-bought pizza dough had better flavor and texture than more widely used store-bought biscuit dough; punchy Parmesan gave melty mozzarella a welcome flavor boost; and we loved the pepperoni but not the grease that dripped down our chins when we bit into the bread. As for the sauce, it was better served alongside for dipping than baked into the pieces of dough (which made the bread sodden).

These initial tests also gave me a few procedural leads: For instance, two short rising periods were a boon to texture, and brushing the outside of each dough ball with oil made the pieces easier to pull apart once baked. I found that the easiest batches to assemble were the least satisfying, while the ones with

PIZZA MONKEY BREAD

the crispiest crusts and best molten cheesy pockets included a painstaking process of individually rolling out, stuffing, and pinching closed about two dozen knobs of dough. For pizza monkey bread to live up to its reputation in the blogosphere as the best thing to happen to pizza since delivery, it would need to be not only delicious but also doable.

I cobbled together a recipe using what I'd learned, grabbed a stack of Bundt pans, and headed back into the kitchen. First, I tried taking a cue from ravioli: I rolled out two balls of store-bought pizza dough into large rectangles, arranged small piles of filling (shredded mozzarella, grated Parmesan, sliced pepperoni, and dried oregano) between the two sheets of dough, pressed to seal around each pile, and then cut between the piles. No dice. Unlike ravioli dough, pizza dough either came apart at the seams or the filling poked through its thin walls. I could roll out the dough thicker, but then I'd have too few bundles.

Undeterred, I rolled out the dough balls into two large rectangles again, but this time I had cinnamon roll construction in mind. After the dough rectangles had rested briefly, I arranged the cheese, pepperoni, and oregano in a line near the long edge of each rectangle. I rolled up each rectangle to form a log, pinched the long seams and ends, and then cut each log in half. I continued cutting and pinching until I had cut each log into 12 pieces. Some of the cheese had escaped or gotten stuck in the seams when I pinched the ends closed, but this method was definitely simpler and seemed promising. I brushed the pan with olive oil, laid a layer of dough pockets in the pan, brushed them with oil, and continued layering and brushing until I had used all the pieces. I let the bread rise for about 30 minutes. Then I baked it at 400 degrees until it was well browned. After turning it out, I saw that some cheese had leaked out, but otherwise the cheese was pleasantly gooey. The pepperoni was still greasy, but a colleague reminded me of a quick fix that we've used before: Microwave the pepperoni to render the grease and then drain it. It worked. Now I just had to devise a method to contain the cheese.

Shredded cheese spilled out when I cut the filled dough, so I tried cutting the cheese into batons. After rolling out the dough, I lined up the pepperoni, laid the batons end to end, and sprinkled the grated Parmesan

alongside. This time the cheese stayed put. But a colleague who'd been watching me thought all that cheese-cutting looked needlessly fussy. "Try string cheese," she suggested. "It comes precut and is made from mozzarella." I dashed off to the store—and streamlined my recipe.

Back in the kitchen, while I was microwaving the pepperoni, I had another thought: Why not enlist the rendered pepperoni oil in place of some of the olive oil that I was using to brush the dough? I gave it a try. While the bread was baking, I put together a quick tomato sauce and enjoyed the even more potent pepperoni pizza aroma that filled the kitchen. When I turned the bread out, we found that the pepperoni oil had given the crust a gorgeously bronze hue. We pinched off pieces and dipped them in sauce. Judging by the flurry of hands reaching for seconds, this recipe was living up to the legend.

—SARAH GABRIEL, *Cook's Country*

Pizza Monkey Bread

SERVES 6 TO 8

You will need all-purpose flour for dusting the counter. If the dough becomes slack or difficult to work with, refrigerate it for 10 minutes. Seal the open ends of the filled dough after each cut in order to keep the filling from leaking out. If your string cheese sticks are longer than 4½ inches, trim any overhang once you've placed the cheese on the dough.

MONKEY BREAD

- **2 (1-pound) balls pizza dough**
- **4 ounces sliced pepperoni**
- **3 tablespoons extra-virgin olive oil**
- **1½ ounces Parmesan cheese, grated (¾ cup)**
- **½ teaspoon dried oregano**
- **8 (4½-inch) sticks mozzarella string cheese**

TOMATO SAUCE

- **2 tablespoons extra-virgin olive oil**
- **4 garlic cloves, minced**
- **1 (28-ounce) can crushed tomatoes**
- **½ teaspoon dried oregano**
- **½ teaspoon salt**
- **½ teaspoon pepper**

1. FOR THE MONKEY BREAD: Line baking sheet with parchment paper and sprinkle with flour. Roll each dough ball into 10 by 6-inch rectangle on lightly floured counter, then transfer to prepared sheet. Cover with plastic wrap and let sit for 15 minutes.

2. Microwave pepperoni in bowl until fat is rendered, 60 to 90 seconds, stirring halfway through microwaving. Using tongs, transfer pepperoni to paper towel–lined plate, reserving pepperoni oil in bowl (you should have about 1 tablespoon). Pat pepperoni dry with paper towels. Stir olive oil into pepperoni oil. Brush 12-cup nonstick Bundt pan with 2 teaspoons oil mixture. Combine Parmesan and oregano in separate bowl.

3. Working with 1 dough rectangle at a time, return to lightly floured counter and roll into 18 by 9-inch rectangle with long edge parallel to counter edge, stretching corners as needed to make neat rectangle. Starting 2 inches from long edge of dough nearest you, shingle half of pepperoni parallel to long edge. Lay 4 mozzarella sticks end to end on top of pepperoni. Sprinkle half of Parmesan mixture alongside mozzarella. Fold bottom 2-inch section of dough over filling and roll tightly toward opposite edge. Pinch seam and ends to seal. Repeat with remaining dough rectangle, remaining pepperoni, remaining 4 mozzarella sticks, and remaining Parmesan mixture.

4. Cut each log in half and pinch open ends to seal. Cut each log in half again, pinching open ends to seal. Cut each log into thirds, pinching open ends closed as you go. Place single layer of stuffed dough balls (about 6) ½ inch apart in prepared pan and brush tops and sides with one-fourth of oil mixture. Layer remaining dough balls in pan, brushing tops and sides with remaining oil mixture as you go. Cover pan with plastic and let rise at room temperature until slightly puffed, about 30 minutes. Adjust oven rack to lower-middle position and heat oven to 400 degrees.

5. FOR THE TOMATO SAUCE: Meanwhile, heat oil in small saucepan over medium heat until shimmering. Add garlic and cook until beginning to brown, about 90 seconds. Add tomatoes, oregano, salt, and pepper and bring to boil. Reduce heat to medium-low and simmer until slightly thickened, about 10 minutes. Remove from heat, cover, and set aside.

6. Bake bread until well browned, about 40 minutes, rotating pan halfway through baking. Transfer pan to wire rack and let cool for 10 minutes. Place serving platter on top of pan and invert. Let cool 10 minutes longer. Reheat sauce and transfer to serving bowl. Serve monkey bread with sauce.

TO MAKE AHEAD: Monkey bread can be assembled, covered with plastic wrap, and refrigerated for up to 24 hours. Let sit on counter for 20 minutes before baking, increasing time by 5 to 10 minutes.

NOTES FROM THE TEST KITCHEN

CONSTRUCTING PIZZA MONKEY BREAD

1. ROLL OUT AND FILL:
Roll out each ball of pizza dough into a rectangle. Arrange pepperoni slices, mozzarella sticks, and seasoned Parmesan on dough.

2. ROLL UP AND SEAL:
Roll each rectangle into a log and pinch to seal the seam and ends.

3. DIVIDE INTO PIECES:
Cut each log into quarters, and quarters into thirds, for a total of 12 pieces per log. Seal open ends as you go.

4. FILL BUNDT PAN:
Layer the balls in a Bundt pan, brushing each layer with pepperoni oil for extra flavor and to make it easier to pull apart the baked bread.

GLUTEN-FREE PIZZA

✔ **WHY THIS RECIPE WORKS:** Gluten-free pizza crusts are often either dense and doughy or cracker-crunchy. We wanted a gluten-free pizza crust that could hold its own against any wheat-flour crust, with a crisp exterior, a tender interior, and just enough chew. First, we developed a gluten-free flour blend that mimicked many of the properties of wheat flour. To imitate the strength and structure that gluten provides in wheat flour, we used a small amount of ground psyllium husk. To create a tender, airy crumb, we significantly increased the water in the dough and added a generous amount of baking powder. We also added a small amount of almond flour to introduce richness and increase crispness without leaving the crust greasy. Since the added water made our dough sticky, we treated it like a batter and spread it onto a baking sheet with the help of a greased spatula. To ensure that the exterior of the crust didn't dry out before the interior had cooked through, we gently parbaked the crust at low heat before adding the toppings.

It made sense that I was asked to develop a gluten-free pizza crust. Baking bread has been my passion for nearly 30 years. But I've always embraced gluten as the magic ingredient in bread. It's the source of its structure and, as a result, much of its texture. So this was the bread baker's ultimate challenge: Develop a gluten-free pizza crust that everyone would want to eat, whether they were avoiding gluten or not.

My first forays into the world of gluten-free pizza were, in an odd way, encouraging. I sought out every pizza joint that sold a gluten-free pie, and every crust was awful. Some were rubbery and dense. Others were stiff and flavorless. And none bore any resemblance to the real thing, which needs to be—at the very least—crisp on the underside and airy and tender within. I also tried a handful of recipes from various gluten-free cookbooks and websites; the results were no better.

Clearly, the world of gluten-free pizza was so dismal that almost any improvement would be welcome. But I didn't want to settle for just passable; I wanted to make a crust with an airy texture and good chew, a crust that could hold its own against the wheat-flour versions.

The first thing I needed was a substitute for the wheat flour. This isn't an easy swap since there isn't a single wheat-free flour that can supply the same

characteristics as wheat flour's makeup of protein, starch, and fat. A blend was a must. Fortunately, some of my colleagues had just developed a multipurpose gluten-free blend for other gluten-free projects, so with the blend on hand, I got down to business.

Given the numerous flaws that I'd encountered in those early samples, I decided to start from the ground up. For two 12-inch pizzas, I figured that roughly 3 cups of the flour blend would be right. To this I added a teaspoon of instant yeast, 2 teaspoons of salt, and a teaspoon of xanthan gum.

Why xanthan gum? The gluten-free flour blend's protein network is weak in comparison with the gluten network of wheat flour, and xanthan gum (made by fermenting simple sugars using the microorganism Xanthomonas campestris) behaves like glue in many gluten-free baked goods, strengthening the weak network and improving elasticity. Some gluten-free recipes can work without its help (and recipes that do need it require varying amounts, which is why the test kitchen's blend didn't include it). But one of pizza dough's trademark qualities is its elasticity, which translates into a baked crust with an open crumb and a chewy texture. Some network reinforcement was going to be a must for my recipe; without it, the carbon dioxide produced by the yeast would simply pass through the dough and the resulting crust would be tough, dense, and squat. Xanthan gum appears most often in gluten-free recipes to perform this role, so I started there.

I placed my dry ingredients in the bowl of a stand mixer fitted with a dough hook, turned it on, and poured in 1½ cups of water and ¼ cup of oil (average amounts of both ingredients for standard pizza dough). I let the machine work the dough until it started to pull away from the sides of the bowl—the signal that there was decent structural development. (In a wheat-based dough you'd say "gluten development," but I was obviously dealing with a different protein network.) Then I put my dough in a lightly oiled bowl, covered it with plastic wrap, and waited for it to proof.

And waited. Even after 90 minutes, the dough showed no signs of expanding. When I cut into it, I found a network of tiny bubbles, but hardly the airy holes that I'd hoped for. But I forged ahead anyway, rolling out the dough (even with the xanthan gum, the dough was still too fragile to stretch like wheat-based pizza dough), topping the rounds with sauce and cheese, and baking them in a hot oven. The result? A crust that was dense and flat, with a tough underside and gummy interior. This was far from passable.

The obvious question to address was why the dough hadn't risen. In traditional yeasted doughs, the rise and the yeast tend to go hand in hand since yeast produces gas (as well as flavor compounds) as it ferments. So I tried adding more yeast in increasing amounts. But no matter how much I added, the dough refused to budge. In fact, the only noticeable difference was that in high amounts, the yeast gave the dough an overproofed, sour flavor.

Maybe the dough lacked the structure necessary to contain the gases; that pointed to the xanthan gum. For the next few tests, I added increasing amounts of xanthan gum, from 1½ teaspoons up to 3 tablespoons. While the greater amount increased the dough's ability to expand, it also gave the dough an unappealing rubbery consistency.

Could it be that xanthan gum wasn't the best choice? Maybe I should have been using one of the other two structural-reinforcement options that I'd seen called for: guar gum (produced by grinding the endosperm of Indian guar plant seeds) or powdered psyllium seed husks (most commonly used as a dietary fiber). The guar gum performed no better than the xanthan gum, and it also contributed an off-flavor. However, psyllium husk was a definite improvement. One and a half tablespoons delivered a dough that rose visibly during proofing and a final crust that had a more open crumb. Psyllium husk is far more effective at attracting and holding on to water molecules than the other gums are, which allows it to create a thick gel. This gel, combined with psyllium husk's insoluble fiber and protein, was providing strong structural reinforcement for my dough's protein network, making it capable of trapping lots of gas during proofing as well as steam during baking.

Nevertheless, the crust was far from perfect. The texture was better but still wasn't the light and airy crust that I'd set my sights on.

I'd been noticing something. While the dough now rose well during proofing, when I rolled it out to shape the crust, much of the gas was expelled. The dough never recovered like a wheat-flour dough, even if I tried letting it rise a second time post-shaping. If the crust couldn't hold on to gas as well as I needed it to, maybe I could give it a little boost. To this end I turned to an ingredient used in countless baked goods, though less often in yeasted ones: baking powder. Sure enough, 2½ teaspoons of the leavener, activated by the heat of the oven, gave the dough a bit more of the lift that it had been missing.

Still, it wasn't enough. Many traditional wheat-based pizza doughs can be rather stiff right after mixing yet end up open and airy, making it easy to stretch once fully proofed. This elasticity translates into a dough that can puff up with steam in the oven, and thus a crust that bakes up light and airy. But in the case of my gluten-free dough, the dough started out stiff and stayed stiff. Thinking about how, in the past, I've gotten some unworkably stiff wheat-based doughs to stretch more, I landed on water. Increasing the water in a wheat-based dough allows the protein network to be more fluid and thus more flexible and stretchable. Would the same rule apply to the network in my gluten-free pizza dough? To find out, I made a series of doughs using increasing amounts of water.

Even before I baked them off, I could tell that I was onto something: The more water the dough contained the more it rose during proofing. As it happened, my dough seemed to benefit from the additional water far more than I'd expected: The most tender crust and open crumb came when I'd added so much water that it went from being a dough to more of a thick batter.

Of course, this added liquid created some new problems. For one, mixing the dough with the dough hook was now ineffective: The dough was so wet that the hook just spun around. Switching to the paddle attachment was an easy fix. Second, the additional water made shaping the crust with a rolling pin, as I had been doing, impossible. Instead, I spread it out on a baking sheet with a rubber spatula into an 8-inch circle, much like spreading frosting on a cake, and then misted the dough with oil, covered it with a piece of plastic wrap, and pressed it into an even, large round with a properly thick edge around the perimeter. Last, and most important, while the final crust had the perfect tender texture and open, airy crumb around the outer edge, the added water had made it gummy toward the center, especially where the sauce met the crust.

To remove the excess water I tried parbaking the rounds without any topping in a hot oven just until they'd started to brown. This produced crusts that looked nice and dry on the exterior, but they were still gummy inside. To drive off enough water without over-baking the exterior, I tested incrementally lower oven temperatures and increased baking times. I finally got it just right when I started the crust in a cold oven, set the temperature to 325 degrees, and let it cook through slowly for about 45 minutes. I then sauced

THE BEST GLUTEN-FREE PIZZA

BUILDING OUR OWN BLEND

During testing, we found that store-bought gluten-free flour blends performed inconsistently, so we created our own.

When regular wheat flour is hydrated, starch granules in the flour swell. With the help of mixing or kneading, the proteins in the flour link up to form long elastic strands called gluten. These strands create a network that enables rise and a sturdy structure. Since no one gluten-free flour or starch performs in this way, a blend was a must. Multiple flours provided the right baseline of protein, starch, and flavor. Since different starches absorb water, swell, and gel at different temperatures and to different degrees, we enlisted multiple starches to create the right amount of chew and structure. We found that 3 parts total flour to 1 part total starch delivered the best results.

WHITE RICE FLOUR Provides a neutral-tasting, refined protein/starch base.

BROWN RICE FLOUR Rounds out the base with proteins that, along with those in the white rice flour, create a network that mimics gluten. Also provides a nutty, wheaty flavor.

POTATO STARCH Contributes large granules that gel at higher temperatures and set to a more extensive, open network when cool, thus providing tenderness.

TAPIOCA STARCH Provides smaller granules that gel at lower temperatures, forming a more compact network when cool, thus providing chew and elasticity.

MILK POWDER Contributes proteins that help improve structure and, along with its sugars, undergo the Maillard browning reaction, which leads to more complex flavor.

FORGET THE DOUGH, MAKE A BATTER

We more than double the hyradation level of a traditional pizza dough for a gluten-free dough that can stretch and rise. But because it is so wet, it can't be shaped like traditional dough.

1. Drop batter onto parchment-lined baking sheet, then spread it into rough circle with rubber spatula.

2. Cover with greased plastic wrap and press into even round with raised edge. To avoid gummy results, prebake crust, then top and bake to finish.

the parbaked crust, sprinkled it with mozzarella and a little Parmesan, and put it back in a 500-degree oven briefly to melt the cheese and finish browning the crust.

Now that I had a pizza crust with a light and airy (but not gummy) interior, there was only one obstacle: The underside of the crust was more tough than crispy. No problem, I thought: Adding more oil to the dough would get it to fry up a bit. Alas, while this did help it crisp, it also left the pizza greasy. Gluten-free flours, I learned, don't absorb fats as readily as wheat flour does, and clearly I'd gone over the maximum.

The solution turned out to be almond flour. Adding just 2½ ounces to the dough boosted the overall fat content and gave my crust the crispiness that it needed without causing any noticeable change in flavor. And because almonds (and nuts in general) don't shed all their oil when heated, the crust wasn't greasy.

As for the toppings, I like keeping it simple with just cheese and sauce, but I did find that additional toppings were fine as long as I limited them to no more than 6 ounces of vegetables and 4 ounces of meat per pie. (Thinly slice hearty vegetables, such as peppers and onions, and sauté them before using, and precook meats like pepperoni to drain them of fat.) Finally, I had a gluten-free pizza crust that I could serve proudly, even to those who didn't have to avoid gluten.

—ANDREW JANJIGIAN, *Cook's Illustrated*

The Best Gluten-Free Pizza

MAKES TWO 12-INCH PIZZAS

If you don't have almond flour, you can process 2½ ounces of blanched almonds in a food processor until finely ground, about 30 seconds. You can substitute 16 ounces (2⅔ cups plus ¼ cup) King Arthur Gluten-Free Multi-Purpose Flour or 16 ounces (2⅔ cups plus ½ cup) Bob's Red Mill GF All-Purpose Baking Flour for the ATK Blend. Pizza crust made with King Arthur will be slightly denser and not as chewy, and crust made with Bob's Red Mill will be thicker and more airy and will have a distinct bean flavor. This recipe requires letting the dough rise for 1½ hours and prebaking the crusts for about 45 minutes before topping and baking.

CRUST

16 ounces (3⅓ cups plus ¼ cup) America's Test Kitchen Gluten-Free Flour Blend

2½ ounces (½ cup plus 1 tablespoon) almond flour

1½ tablespoons powdered psyllium husk

2½ teaspoons baking powder

2 teaspoons salt

1 teaspoon instant or rapid-rise yeast

2½ cups warm water (100 degrees)

¼ cup vegetable oil

Vegetable oil spray

SAUCE

1 (28-ounce) can whole peeled tomatoes, drained

1 tablespoon extra-virgin olive oil

1 teaspoon red wine vinegar

1 garlic clove, minced

1 teaspoon dried oregano

½ teaspoon salt

¼ teaspoon pepper

CHEESE

1 ounce Parmesan cheese, grated fine (½ cup)

8 ounces whole-milk mozzarella cheese, shredded (2 cups)

1. FOR THE CRUST: Using stand mixer fitted with paddle, mix flour blend, almond flour, psyllium, baking powder, salt, and yeast on low speed until combined. Slowly add warm water and oil in steady stream until incorporated. Increase speed to medium and beat until dough is sticky and uniform, about 6 minutes. (Dough will resemble thick batter.)

2. Remove bowl from mixer, cover with plastic wrap, and let stand until inside of dough is bubbly (use large spoon to peer inside dough), about 1½ hours.

3. Adjust oven racks to middle and lower positions. Line 2 rimmed baking sheets with parchment paper and spray liberally with oil spray. Transfer half of dough to center of 1 prepared sheet. Using oil-sprayed rubber spatula, spread dough into 8-inch circle. Spray top of dough with oil spray, cover with large sheet of plastic, and, using your hands, press out dough to 11½-inch round, about ¼ inch thick, leaving outer ¼ inch slightly thicker than center; discard plastic. Repeat with remaining dough and second prepared sheet.

4. Place prepared sheets in oven and heat oven to 325 degrees. Bake dough until firm to touch, golden brown on underside, and just beginning to brown on top, 45 to 50 minutes, switching and rotating sheets halfway through baking. Transfer crusts to wire rack and let cool.

The America's Test Kitchen Gluten-Free Flour Blend

MAKES 42 OUNCES (ABOUT 9⅓ CUPS)

Be sure to use potato starch, not potato flour, with this recipe. Tapioca starch is also sold as tapioca flour; they are interchangeable. We strongly recommend that you use Bob's Red Mill white and brown rice flours. We also recommend that you weigh your ingredients; if you measure by volume, spoon each ingredient into the measuring cup (do not pack or tap) and scrape off excess.

24 ounces (4½ cups plus ⅓ cup) white rice flour

7½ ounces (1⅔ cups) brown rice flour

7 ounces (1⅓ cups) potato starch

3 ounces (¾ cup) tapioca starch

¾ ounce (¼ cup) nonfat dry milk powder

Whisk all ingredients in large bowl until well combined. Transfer to airtight container and refrigerate for up to 3 months.

5. FOR THE SAUCE: Process all ingredients in food processor until smooth, about 30 seconds. Transfer to bowl and refrigerate until ready to use.

6. One hour before baking pizza, adjust oven rack to upper-middle position, set baking stone on rack, and heat oven to 500 degrees.

7. TO ASSEMBLE PIZZA: Transfer 1 parbaked crust to pizza peel. Using back of spoon or ladle, spread ½ cup tomato sauce in thin layer over surface of crust, leaving ¼-inch border around edge. Sprinkle ¼ cup Parmesan evenly over sauce, followed by 1 cup mozzarella. Carefully slide crust onto stone and bake until crust is well browned and cheese is bubbly and beginning to brown, 10 to 12 minutes. Transfer pizza to wire rack and let cool for 5 minutes before slicing and serving. Repeat with second crust, ½ cup tomato sauce (you will have extra sauce), remaining ¼ cup Parmesan, and remaining 1 cup mozzarella.

TO MAKE AHEAD: Sauce can be refrigerated for up to 1 week or frozen for up to 1 month. Baked and cooled crusts can sit at room temperature for up to 4 hours. Completely cooled crusts can be wrapped with plastic wrap and then aluminum foil and frozen for up to 2 weeks. Frozen crusts can be topped and baked as directed without thawing.

GROWN-UP GRILLED CHEESE SANDWICHES

✓ **WHY THIS RECIPE WORKS:** Tired of tasteless American cheese in our grilled cheese sandwiches, we set out to create a version with more food appeal. We knew we wanted to use a cheese with more complex flavor, so we started our grilled cheese sandwiches with aged cheddar. To help the cheddar melt smoothly without becoming greasy, we added creamy, melty Brie and a splash of white wine. A bit of minced shallot incorporated seamlessly into the cheese, and increased the sandwiches' complexity without detracting from the cheese flavor. A smear of mustard butter gave the bread a subtle flavor enhancement.

The first bite of a grilled cheese sandwich is always the best one. The aroma of toasted butter is a familiar prelude to the crunch of crisp bread, which gives way to warm, gooey cheese. But the mystique fades quickly, mainly because the American cheese that is typically used has no taste. I crave a grilled cheese with potent flavor, which means taking several steps up from American. But whenever I try to build a sandwich with, say, aged cheddar and a white sandwich loaf (its delicate crust and fine crumb make it ideal for grilled cheese), I end up disappointed, since upscale cheeses tend to become grainy and leak fat as they melt.

Before attempting a fix, I did some reading and learned that how well a cheese melts depends partly on its moisture level, which decreases with age. When a young, moist cheese is heated, its casein matrix—casein is the primary protein in cheese—remains intact and holds on to fat. But as a cheese ages and dries out, its casein binds more tightly together, making it more difficult to liquefy. When the clumpy bonded structure finally does break down, it is unable to contain the fat, so it leaks out.

I would have to restore moisture to coax my cheddar into melting smoothly. I decided to try wine. After all, wine is a key ingredient in fondue, which is basically just melted cheese. I cubed 9 ounces of cheddar, pulled out a food processor, and whizzed the pieces along with 2 tablespoons of white wine. After smearing the cheese mixture onto bread coated with softened butter, I heated a nonstick skillet and slowly toasted the sandwich until the cheese had melted and the bread had browned. The good news: The wine in the cheese tasted terrific (no surprise there) and the added liquid meant that the cheese was not nearly as broken as in my previous attempts. The bad news: It was still a little greasy.

I thought back to fondue, which also contains flour. Could starch absorb some of the fat in the cheddar? Yes, but at a cost: If I added enough flour, I could produce a nongreasy filling, but the starch muted the taste of the cheese. My next strategy: Instead of trying to soak up the cheddar's excess oil, how about cutting back on the cheddar itself and replacing it with a moist, easy-melting cheese? I bought a block of Monterey Jack and a wedge of supermarket Brie and made batches of spread containing 7 ounces of cheddar and 2 ounces of one of these "melty" cheeses. Success: Using less cheddar and processing it with a smooth melter eliminated any trace of grease. I chose Brie over Jack since its buttery notes paired better with the sharp cheddar.

Now I just needed a little more depth of flavor. A few teaspoons of minced shallot did the trick, accenting the cheese with savory complexity.

To spice up the bread, I mixed a dollop of Dijon into the softened butter I had been slathering on the exterior of the sandwich. The result was a hit, smelling and tasting subtly of mustard. Emboldened by these results, I experimented and found that Asiago and dates on oatmeal bread, Comté and cornichon on rye, Gruyère and chives on rye, and Robiola and chipotle on oatmeal bread are fantastic combinations as well. Finally: I had a host of grilled cheese sandwiches engineered for adult tastes and good to the last bite.

—LAN LAM, *Cook's Illustrated*

Grown-Up Grilled Cheese Sandwiches with Cheddar and Shallot
SERVES 4

Look for a cheddar aged for about one year (avoid cheddar aged for longer; it won't melt well). To quickly bring the cheddar to room temperature, microwave the pieces until warm, about 30 seconds. The first two sandwiches can be held in a 200-degree oven on a wire rack set in a baking sheet.

- 7 ounces aged cheddar cheese, cut into 24 equal pieces, room temperature
- 2 ounces Brie cheese, rind removed
- 2 tablespoons dry white wine or vermouth
- 4 teaspoons minced shallot

3 tablespoons unsalted butter, softened

1 teaspoon Dijon mustard

8 slices hearty white sandwich bread

1. Process cheddar, Brie, and wine in food processor until smooth paste is formed, 20 to 30 seconds. Add shallot and pulse to combine, 3 to 5 pulses. Combine butter and mustard in small bowl.

2. Working on parchment paper–lined counter, spread mustard butter evenly over 1 side of slices of bread. Flip 4 slices of bread over and spread cheese mixture evenly over slices. Top with remaining 4 slices of bread, buttered sides up.

3. Preheat 12-inch nonstick skillet over medium heat for 2 minutes. (Droplets of water should just sizzle when flicked onto pan.) Place 2 sandwiches in skillet; reduce heat to medium-low; and cook until both sides are crisp and golden brown, 6 to 9 minutes per side, moving sandwiches to ensure even browning. Remove sandwiches from skillet and let stand for 2 minutes before serving. Repeat with remaining 2 sandwiches.

VARIATIONS

Grown-Up Grilled Cheese Sandwiches with Asiago and Dates

Substitute Asiago for cheddar, finely chopped pitted dates for shallot, and oatmeal sandwich bread for white sandwich bread.

Grown-Up Grilled Cheese Sandwiches with Comté and Cornichon

Substitute Comté for cheddar, minced cornichon for shallot, and rye sandwich bread for white sandwich bread.

Grown-Up Grilled Cheese Sandwiches with Gruyère and Chives

Substitute Gruyère for cheddar, chives for shallot, and rye sandwich bread for white sandwich bread.

Grown-Up Grilled Cheese Sandwiches with Robiola and Chipotle

Substitute Robiola for cheddar, ¼ teaspoon minced canned chipotle chile in adobo sauce for shallot, and oatmeal sandwich bread for white sandwich bread.

GRILLED PORTOBELLO BURGERS

WHY THIS RECIPE WORKS: Most portobello mushroom burgers are underwhelming at best. We wanted a portobello burger that we would gladly eat in place of a beef burger, full of meaty mushroom flavor and topped with plenty of complementary ingredients. We scraped out the gills of the mushrooms to prevent muddy flavor, and scored the caps to eliminate the tough outer skin and allow the flavorful marinade to penetrate. Stuffing the mushrooms with sun-dried tomatoes, roasted red peppers, and feta cheese gave them more great flavor, and a few rings of grilled onion and a handful of arugula provided a bit of crunchy bite. Sturdy kaiser rolls made a perfect base for our juicy, rich mushrooms.

I love portobellos, but most portobello "burgers" simply are not very good. Seeing no reason why that should be so, I set myself the goal of making portobello mushroom burgers that I would seek out—not just settle for.

Since smoke and char enhance any mushroom's meaty qualities, grilled recipes were my logical starting point. I found a few promising recipes for grilled portobello burgers. After firing up the grills, I assembled the sandwiches for my tasters. There were a couple of flavor-building tricks that we liked: marinating the portobello caps in a vinaigrette, and stuffing them with a savory filling. The biggest complaints were that most of the portobellos had a rubbery, tough "skin" on top, and they tasted muddy as opposed to pleasantly earthy.

I began with an established test kitchen technique for portobellos: scraping out the dark brown gills on the underside of the mushrooms to prevent funky and muddy flavors. Then I put the caps into a zipper-lock bag with a simple mixture of olive oil, vinegar, garlic, salt, and pepper and let them soak for 30 minutes before heading to the grill. A few trial runs led me to the best cooking method: I grilled the caps gill side up over a medium-hot fire until the tops were nicely charred and they had released their liquid. Then I flipped them over to let the liquid drain and sear the other side. These mushrooms were seasoned throughout and had great grill flavor. Unfortunately, the tops were still slightly tough. To fix this, I turned to a technique we use for meat: crosshatching. Cutting a shallow crosshatch pattern into the tops of the mushrooms created a textured surface and thus eliminated the chewy "skin" on

GRILLED PORTOBELLO BURGERS

the exterior. As an added bonus, the crosshatched caps soaked up even more marinade.

For the filling, I chose Mediterranean flavors to complement the simple marinade. I tried a variety of fillings, and finally landed on a combination of chopped roasted red peppers and sun-dried tomatoes, plus feta cheese for a briny kick. But when I stuffed the raw mushrooms, the filling tumbled out as the mushrooms softened, and there was no way to flip them. I found it best to grill them as before, add the filling, and place them back on the grill to warm through.

In keeping with the Mediterranean theme, I added chopped fresh basil to the mayonnaise. Peppery baby arugula was an upgrade from ordinary lettuce, and tasters loved grilled rounds of red onion (brushed with the mushroom marinade) until tender and sweet. Finally, I swapped out the squishy burger buns for more substantial kaiser rolls, which I toasted on the grill. I stacked a final batch of burgers and bit in; they were juicy and rich, yet bright and fresh. I'm not giving up on beef, but these portobello burgers are an amazing alternative that will convert even the biggest skeptics—like me.

—REBECCAH MARSTERS, *Cook's Country*

Grilled Portobello Burgers

SERVES 4

Our favorite feta cheese is Mt. Vikos Traditional Feta from Greece. If the mushrooms absorb all of the marinade, simply brush the onions with olive oil before grilling them in step 4.

- 4 portobello mushroom caps (4 to 5 inches in diameter), stems and gills removed
- ½ cup extra-virgin olive oil
- 3 tablespoons red wine vinegar
- 1 garlic clove, minced
  Salt and pepper
- 4 ounces feta cheese, crumbled (1 cup)
- ½ cup jarred roasted red peppers, patted dry and chopped
- ½ cup oil-packed sun-dried tomatoes, patted dry and chopped
- ½ cup mayonnaise
- ½ cup chopped fresh basil
- 4 (½-inch-thick) slices red onion
- 4 kaiser rolls, split
- 1 ounce (1 cup) baby arugula

1. Using tip of paring knife, cut ½-inch crosshatch pattern on tops of mushroom caps, 1/16-inch deep. Combine oil, vinegar, garlic, 1 teaspoon salt, and ½ teaspoon pepper in 1-gallon zipper-lock bag. Add mushrooms, seal bag, turn to coat, and let sit for at least 30 minutes or up to 1 hour.

2. Combine feta, red peppers, and sun-dried tomatoes in bowl. Whisk mayonnaise and basil together in separate bowl. Push 1 toothpick horizontally through each onion slice to keep rings intact while grilling.

3A. FOR A CHARCOAL GRILL: Open bottom vent completely. Light large chimney starter filled with charcoal briquettes (6 quarts). When top coals are partially covered with ash, pour evenly over grill. Set cooking grate in place, cover, and open lid vent completely. Heat grill until hot, about 5 minutes.

3B. FOR A GAS GRILL: Turn all burners to high, cover, and heat grill until hot, about 15 minutes. Turn all burners to medium-high.

4. Clean and oil cooking grate. Remove mushrooms from marinade, reserving excess. Brush onions all over with reserved mushroom marinade. Place onions and mushrooms, gill side up, on grill. Cook, covered for gas grill, until mushrooms have released their liquid and are charred on first side, 4 to 6 minutes. Flip mushrooms and onions and continue to cook (covered if using gas) until mushrooms are charred on second side, 3 to 5 minutes.

5. Transfer onions to platter; remove toothpicks. Transfer mushrooms to platter, gill side up, and divide feta mixture evenly among caps, packing down with hand. Return mushrooms to grill, feta side up, and cook, covered, until heated through, about 3 minutes.

6. Return mushrooms to platter, and tent with aluminum foil. Grill rolls cut sides down until lightly charred, about 1 minute. Spread basil-mayonnaise on bottom buns and top each with 1 mushroom and 1 onion slice. Divide arugula evenly among burgers, then cap with top buns. Serve.

NOTES FROM THE TEST KITCHEN

PREPARING PORTOBELLOS FOR THE GRILL

SCORE THE CAP: Cutting a shallow crosshatch into the top of each cap helps to minimize rubbery texture.

MEAT

CUBAN SHREDDED BEEF

✓ WHY THIS RECIPE WORKS: *Vaca frita* is a classic Cuban dish featuring beef that has been boiled, shredded, and fried so that the exterior develops a deep, golden-brown crust. But by the time we were able to achieve a crisp crust, the meat had dried out. We wanted to refine the recipe to develop optimal textural contrast: a crisp, crunchy exterior encasing juicy, tender meat. We started with collagen-rich chuck-eye roast, since the marbling made it less likely to dry out. We cut the roast into 1½-inch cubes to reduce the cooking time and gently simmered the pieces before pounding them flat to produce different-size shreds. To reinforce the beefy flavor, we fried the meat in the rendered beef fat. We found that a splash of orange juice added to the traditional flavorings of lime and garlic mellowed the lime's acidity while keeping the flavor bright and clean. Mixing the citrusy dressing into the meat after frying made for fresh, vibrant flavor.

Citrusy, garlicky pork roasts are a hallmark of Cuban cuisine, but the country is also home to a lesser-known beef dish with similarly bold, bright flavors. *Vaca frita*, which literally translates as "fried cow," consists of an evenly grained flat cut such as flank or skirt steak that's cooked twice: first boiled to tenderize it and then pulled into meaty shreds and pan-fried until the exterior develops a deep golden-brown crust. Along the way, the meat is seasoned with liberal doses of garlic and fresh lime as well as a touch of ground cumin. Finally, an onion is sliced thin, fried in the same pan, and stirred together with the beef. The mixture is usually served with lime wedges and generous helpings of rice and beans.

I'm addicted to the combination of lime, garlic, and beef—especially when the beef comes with crispy edges—but sometimes the dish isn't perfect. The beef can be so much about crispiness that after a few bites it starts to seem a little dry and stringy. My ideal version would showcase the dish's tangy, garlicky aspect while offering shreds of beef that were crispy and richly flavored at the edges but moist and succulent inside.

I figured that cuts more marbled and collagen-rich than flank steak might not dry out as much. When heated, collagen breaks down into gelatin, which retains water, while fat bastes the cooked meat and increases its perceived juiciness. So I rounded up flap meat, boneless short ribs, and a chuck roast, all of which are streaked with fat and collagen, and prepared them

according to a typical vaca frita recipe—but I made one notable change from the get-go. Instead of boiling the meats, I lowered the temperature of the cooking water to a simmer, knowing that the amount of moisture that meat loses during cooking is directly related to the temperature at which it cooks. To the water in each Dutch oven I added a portion of one of the various cuts of beef, a halved onion, several garlic cloves, and a couple of bay leaves, all per tradition. I then let the pots bubble until the meats were tender. Once they'd cooled, I shredded the meats and tossed the strips with minced garlic, lime juice, ground cumin, salt, and pepper. While those flavors absorbed, I thinly sliced another onion for each batch, grabbed some large skillets, and fried the pieces in about 1 tablespoon of oil per batch until they'd softened but still retained a little crunch. I removed the onions from the pan, added more oil, and seared the various cuts of beef, letting them sizzle until their edges were crisp and deeply brown.

Compared with the flank steak vaca frita that I'd tasted, all three alternatives cooked up moister, and my colleagues and I favored chuck for its bigger beef flavor. But there were a number of problems left to solve. The most glaring was the amount of time that it took to prepare the dish. Simmering the whole roast had taken almost 3 hours, so I cut it into 1½-inch cubes; that reduced the simmering time to less than 2 hours, making the extra knife work worth the time and effort. Cooking the beef in smaller chunks also allowed me to easily remove any large pockets of fat and connective tissue while I shredded the meat.

My other substantial cooking issue was rather obvious: If you fry uniformly shredded meat, you're going to have uniformly dry (albeit crispy) strips because the moisture evaporates so easily. I certainly wanted those crispy, delicate filigrees of beef, but some of the beef also needed to stay fairly intact if it was going to hang on to any moisture. In other words, I needed to shred the beef into different-size pieces.

That thought reminded me of a timesaving technique that I'd come across in a recipe from a food blog called Cuban in the Midwest: Rather than pull apart the beef with two forks, the blogger placed the cooked meat on a rimmed baking sheet, covered it with plastic wrap, and pounded it with a mallet. Turns out that flattening, not shredding, the beef is a brilliant shortcut. (Since I didn't have a mallet, I used a meat pounder plus aluminum foil.) Not only was this method faster but it also generated irregular pieces—some fine threads and some broken but intact chunks. Once they hit the hot oil, these now-flattened chunks needed less than 5 minutes to form a crisp crust, and the abbreviated frying time ensured that their insides remained moist and tender. Meanwhile, the finer threads contributed more fine shards of pure crispiness.

Having made progress with the meat's texture, I turned my focus to brightening the citrus flavor. Stripping zest off the lime and adding it to the juice didn't do enough, so I added more juice—which took the acidic bite too far and overwhelmed the beefy flavor. It wasn't until I thought about the flavors in Cuban roast pork that I realized I could supplement the lime juice with orange juice for bright (but not sharp) citrus flavor. Two tablespoons rounded out the fruity taste nicely and more subtly.

At the same time, the garlic element needed work, too. Three tablespoons of raw minced garlic wasn't just strong—it bit back. Instead, I treated it (and the cumin) as I would the aromatics in any sauté, pushing the browned meat to the sides of the skillet and quickly cooking the aromatics (with a little oil) in the center; after 30 seconds, the garlic's harshness had considerably softened and the cumin's flavor had bloomed. It was also time to test whether adding aromatics to the cooking water actually infused the meat with any noticeable flavor. I compared my working recipe with one in which I simmered the meat in plain salted water. It was impossible to tell which batch was which. Aromatics in the cooking water were out.

This change made me wonder whether I could make yet another one: Instead of simmering the meat in a big pot of water (which took a good 12 minutes to heat), what if I simply cooked it in a smaller amount of water in the skillet that I would then use to fry the beef? This way I could save time and reduce my dirty dish count. I threw a lid on the skillet while the beef simmered over low heat; when it was fully tender, I uncovered the pan and cranked the heat to medium so that any excess liquid would cook off. Once it had, only the beef fat was left—which gave me yet another idea. Rather than fry the onion and meat in vegetable oil, I'd reserve and use some of the rendered beef fat. One tablespoon turned out to be plenty. The trick ended up being more than thrifty; cooking in beef fat amped up the savory quality of the whole dish.

About the onion slices: I hadn't fiddled much with them, since my tasters and I liked how their faint crunch complemented the richer flavor and chew of the meat, but they were a tad on the sharp side. For due diligence, I tried bringing one batch to a caramelized stage, but their creamy, soft texture and deep sweetness just didn't mesh with the garlicky, tangy beef. Instead, I softened their sharp edge just a bit by deglazing the sautéed onion with a little dry sherry and water, knowing that the nutty fortified wine pairs naturally with onion.

The dish was finished when I added the onion slices back to the pan with the beef and tossed the whole mixture with the tangy citrus juices. Bright, garlicky, savory, and addictively crispy yet tender, vaca frita was well on its way to becoming one of my favorite beef preparations. And once I had scooped some beans and rice onto my plate, my vaca frita turned into one of the most satisfying meals I'd ever made.

—LAN LAM, *Cook's Illustrated*

Cuban Shredded Beef
SERVES 4 TO 6

The beef not only pairs well with rice and beans but also easily doubles as a filling for tacos, empanadas, or sandwiches. Use a well-marbled chuck-eye roast in this recipe. When trimming the beef, don't remove all visible fat—some of it will be used in lieu of oil later in the recipe. If you don't have enough reserved fat in step 3, use vegetable oil.

HOW CAN YOU MAKE BEEF BOTH TENDER AND CRISPY?

Unlike most versions of *vaca frita*, ours boasts a moist interior and a crispy crust—and comes together in just one pan.

1. SIMMER: Cook cubed beef at gentle simmer to help it retain moisture, then uncover and increase heat to burn off liquid.

2. POUND: Transfer beef to baking sheet (reserve fat) and flatten with meat pounder to produce mix of chunks and fine threads.

3. SAUTÉ ONION: Sauté onion slices in beef fat over high heat until golden, then deglaze with sherry and water. Transfer to bowl.

4. SEAR BEEF: Heat more reserved beef fat, then briefly sear meat until edges are dark brown and crisp.

5. BRIGHTEN: Clear center of pan; sauté minced garlic and cumin; then add orange juice, lime juice, and lime zest.

---

2 pounds boneless beef chuck-eye roast, pulled apart at seams, trimmed, and cut into 1½-inch cubes
  Kosher salt and pepper
3 garlic cloves, minced
1 teaspoon vegetable oil
¼ teaspoon ground cumin
2 tablespoons orange juice
1½ teaspoons grated lime zest plus 1 tablespoon juice, plus lime wedges for serving
1 onion, halved and sliced thin
2 tablespoons dry sherry

1. Bring beef, 2 cups water, and 1¼ teaspoons salt to boil in 12-inch nonstick skillet over medium-high heat. Reduce heat to low, cover, and gently simmer until beef is very tender, about 1 hour 45 minutes. (Check beef every 30 minutes, adding water so that bottom third of beef is submerged.) While beef simmers, combine garlic, oil, and cumin in bowl. Combine orange juice and lime zest and juice in second bowl.

2. Remove lid from skillet, increase heat to medium, and simmer until water evaporates and beef starts to sizzle, 3 to 8 minutes. Using slotted spoon, transfer beef to rimmed baking sheet. Pour off and reserve fat from skillet. Rinse skillet clean and dry with paper towels. Place sheet of aluminum foil over beef and, using meat pounder or heavy sauté pan, pound to flatten beef into ⅛-inch-thick pieces, discarding any large pieces of fat or connective tissue. (Some of beef should separate into shreds. Larger pieces that do not separate can be torn in half.)

3. Heat 1½ teaspoons reserved fat in now-empty skillet over high heat. When fat begins to sizzle, add onion and ¼ teaspoon salt. Cook, stirring occasionally, until onion is golden brown and charred in spots, 5 to 8 minutes. Add sherry and ¼ cup water and cook until liquid evaporates, about 2 minutes. Transfer onion to bowl. Return skillet to high heat, add 1½ teaspoons reserved fat, and heat until it begins to sizzle. Add beef and cook, stirring frequently, until dark golden brown and crusty, 2 to 4 minutes.

4. Reduce heat to low and push beef to sides of skillet. Add garlic mixture to center and cook, stirring frequently, until fragrant and golden brown, about 30 seconds. Remove pan from heat, add orange juice mixture and onion, and toss to combine. Season with pepper to taste. Serve immediately with lime wedges.

PRESSURE-COOKER POT ROAST

✓ **WHY THIS RECIPE WORKS:** Most pressure-cooker pot roast recipes produce overcooked vegetables, fatty meat, and bland, watery gravy. To improve this classic recipe, we made a few key adjustments. First we split the roast into two smaller pieces to speed cooking. A bit of baking soda encouraged browning and enhanced the flavor of the roast. We decreased the liquid in the pot to account for the lack of evaporation in the pressure cooker environment. Since the vegetables cooked differently depending on the pressure cooker model, we decided to purposefully overcook them and then puree them into the gravy to improve its flavor and consistency. A final reduction on the stove gave the sauce even better body, and some wine and added aromatics provided complexity and depth.

Recently, pressure cooking has made a comeback on the culinary scene. Sales of pressure cookers have grown by double digits in the past three years. Home cooks are rediscovering that with the pressure cooker's super-heated environment, meals with deep, slow-cooked flavor that would normally take hours to cook can be transformed into weeknight options.

Surprisingly, though, one of the most classic recipes to make in a pressure cooker, pot roast, isn't nearly as impressive as the appliance itself. At least that's what I found when I tried several different recipes. They all pretty much followed the same approach: Brown the roast, add liquid and vegetables, lock on the lid, bring to high pressure, and cook for the prescribed amount of time. The results were also the same: While the meat turned tender, it was also torn apart at the edges; the gravy was watery; and the vegetables were mushy.

Why would making pot roast in a pressure cooker be so likely to fail? I came up with a few good reasons. For one, the pot traps steam (this is how pressure is built), so sauces don't reduce and concentrate the way that they would in an open pot. Second, a pressure cooker doesn't lend itself to the staggered addition of ingredients. If you want to add something to the pot, you must depressurize before you can remove the lid, and then you have to bring the pot back up to pressure before continuing. But even hardy vegetables like carrots and potatoes can't handle the cooking time required to tenderize the meat. And finally, since a pressurized pot is a closed environment, there is no way to monitor cooking by sight or smell—timing is everything. With these issues in mind, I set about getting supertender, deeply flavorful pot roast on the table in half of its normal 4-hour cooking time.

Putting one of our established pot roast practices into action, I grabbed a 4-pound chuck-eye roast (the test kitchen's preferred cut for pot roast) and split it at its natural seam into two pieces. This allowed me to carve out the knobs of fat that would otherwise mar the interior slices. And more important, it would further speed cooking by creating two smaller roasts. While most of the recipes that I'd tried in my initial tests called for browning the meat on the stovetop, a few didn't. There was no noticeable flavor difference between these two approaches, so I decided to skip it. I simply seasoned both pieces of meat with salt and pepper and then set them aside while I built my cooking liquid. I melted some butter in the pot and stirred in thickly sliced onion and celery. After adding 2 cups of beef broth (about two-thirds of what a traditional recipe would use to account for the lack of reduction), I turned my attention to the main challenge: cooking the vegetables alongside the meat.

I asked our science editor if there are any tricks for keeping vegetables from falling apart during extended cooking, and it turns out that there is one. Certain vegetables (and fruits), including potatoes and carrots, contain an enzyme that enables them to remain firm during long cooking if given a low-temperature "pretreatment" first. When these vegetables are heated to between 130 and 140 degrees and held there for about 30 minutes, the enzyme alters the pectin in their cell walls, allowing it to cross-link with calcium ions to form a more durable structure. I experimented with the approach, bringing carrots and potatoes and a couple of quarts of water to 140 degrees and holding them there before draining the vegetables and proceeding with the recipe.

The results were impressive. Even after the hour of pressurized cooking that the meat required to turn tender, the carrots were intact and the potatoes were firm. But this pretreatment step was fussy and time-consuming. More important, I found after subsequent tests that this technique worked well only in some models of pressure cookers. When we tested pressure cookers last year, we found that the internal temperature of pots at high pressure varied as much as 23 degrees from one brand to the next. This isn't a big problem for long-cooked roasts since the window of doneness

PRESSURE-COOKER POT ROAST

is relatively wide, but it makes consistent timing nearly impossible for vegetables.

The other option was to cook the roasts on their own; depressurize the pot and set them aside; and then add the vegetables, repressurize, and cook until done. But this would add time—and hassle—to the process.

I resolved to go back to square one. I ditched the potatoes and, taking a cue from one of our traditional pot roast recipes, embraced the mushy veggies. After cooking the roast and a sliced carrot, celery rib, and onion together, I pureed the cooking liquid and vegetables in a blender into a thickened sauce. This eliminated my vegetable woes, and it also improved the body and flavor of the sauce. That said, the sauce still had a long way to go.

To help concentrate the flavor of the sauce, my next move was to cut back the amount of broth that I was adding to the pot to a single cup and to reduce the pureed sauce for just a few minutes back on the stovetop; at that point I also added a few pats of butter to improve body, along with a bit of red wine and a sprig of thyme for depth. When this wasn't enough, I called on one of the test kitchen's favorite umami boosters. A couple of teaspoons of soy sauce lent meatiness without making the sauce taste like a stir-fry. Things were definitely looking up, but I felt that I could do better still.

Even though I wasn't browning the meat at the outset, the roasts were still developing some browning, despite the wet environment inside the pot. This might sound confusing. After all, ordinarily you need to thoroughly dry meat before searing so that its surface will brown properly. But in those cases it's not so much the water itself that's the problem but rather its impact on temperature and the amount of cooking time that the meat requires. Browning can take place at temperatures as low as 160 degrees but only very,

very slowly. For something like a quick-cooking steak, browning needs to happen at a higher temperature (around 300 degrees) to ensure that the steak doesn't overcook before it browns.

With my pressure-cooker pot roast, the cooking time was fairly long, and the water and steam were reaching almost 250 degrees. So some browning of both the meat and the aromatics (and even the gravy) was in fact occurring. It just wasn't enough. In the past we've used baking soda to enable the Maillard reaction to work more rapidly. Could it help my pot roast recipe? When I added ¼ teaspoon of baking soda to the pot with my aromatics, I noticed almost immediately that the aromatics were softening and browning faster. But the real benefit wasn't clear until I tasted the final sauce, after the baking soda had had almost an hour of pressurized cooking time to do its work. This sauce was dark, rich, and incredibly meaty—a remarkable improvement for such a small ingredient change.

The last detail to address was how to release the pressure when the cooking time was up. Most recipes seemed to call for a quick release, and while this sped things up, I realized that the fast release of steam and pressure was causing the ultratender meat to fray at the edges, or even fall apart. For roasts that stayed intact and could be cut into neat slices, a gentler natural release, done by simply moving the pot off the heat and letting the pressure drop naturally, was the way to go.

Finally I had a pressure-cooker pot roast that held its own against the best of the traditional versions. Even better, it took less than 2 hours from start to finish.

—DAN SOUZA, *Cook's Illustrated*

NOTES FROM THE TEST KITCHEN

PROBLEMS UNDER PRESSURE
When we tested a dozen best-selling stovetop and electric pressure cookers, we made a key discovery: No two reached the same internal temperature. At high pressure, the temperatures (which should be 250 degrees) varied from as low as 230 degrees to as high as 253 degrees.

This variance can make a huge difference not only on the cooking time but also on the final results of a recipe. Usually, you'll need to do some trial and error before you get perfect results from your pot. (Note: In the test kitchen, we use the **Fagor Duo 8-Quart Stainless Steel Pressure Cooker**.)

Pressure-Cooker Pot Roast
SERVES 6 TO 8

If using an electric pressure cooker, turn off the cooker immediately after the pressurized cooking time and let the pressure release naturally for 10 minutes; do not let the cooker switch to the warm setting. To adjust for differences among pressure cookers, cook the roasts for the recommended time, check for doneness, and, if needed, repressurize and cook up to 10 minutes longer. A half teaspoon of red wine vinegar can be substituted for the wine.

1 (3½- to 4-pound) boneless beef chuck-eye roast, pulled into 2 pieces at natural seam and trimmed of large pieces of fat

Kosher salt and pepper
4 tablespoons unsalted butter, cut into 4 pieces
1 onion, sliced thick
1 celery rib, sliced thick
1 carrot, peeled and sliced thick
¼ teaspoon baking soda
1 cup beef broth
2 teaspoons soy sauce
2 bay leaves
1 tablespoon red wine
1 sprig fresh thyme

1. Using 3 pieces of kitchen twine per roast, tie each roast crosswise at equal intervals into loaf shape. Season roasts with salt and pepper and set aside.

2. Melt 2 tablespoons butter in pressure cooker over medium heat; refrigerate remaining 2 tablespoons butter. Add onion, celery, carrot, and baking soda to pot and cook until onion breaks down and liquid turns golden brown, about 5 minutes. Stir in broth, soy sauce, and bay leaves, scraping up any browned bits. Nestle roasts side by side on top of vegetables in cooker.

3. Lock lid in place and bring pot to high pressure over high heat, 3 to 8 minutes. As soon as indicator signals that pot has reached high pressure, reduce heat to medium-low and cook for 55 minutes, adjusting heat as needed to maintain high pressure.

4. Remove pot from heat and let pressure release naturally for 10 minutes. Quick-release any remaining pressure, then remove lid, allowing steam to escape away from you. Transfer roasts to carving board, tent loosely with aluminum foil, and let rest for 20 minutes.

5. Meanwhile, strain liquid through fine-mesh strainer into fat separator; discard bay leaves. Transfer vegetables in strainer to blender. Let liquid settle for 5 minutes, then pour defatted liquid into blender with vegetables. Blend until smooth, about 1 minute. Transfer sauce to medium saucepan. Add wine, thyme sprig, and 2 tablespoons chilled butter and bring to boil over high heat. Cook until sauce is thickened and measures 3 cups, 5 to 8 minutes.

6. Remove twine from roasts and slice against grain into ½-inch-thick slices. Transfer meat to serving platter and season with salt to taste. Remove thyme sprig from sauce and season sauce with salt and pepper to taste. Spoon half of sauce over meat. Serve, passing remaining sauce separately.

SLOW-COOKER CORNED BEEF AND CABBAGE

WHY THIS RECIPE WORKS: This traditional Irish boiled dinner often produces disappointing results: bland meat and overcooked vegetables. We knew we could improve this dish using the steady, gentle heat of the slow cooker to get moist, tender corned beef and perfectly cooked vegetables. We made a spiced braising liquid with chicken broth, peppercorns, allspice, and thyme, then gently simmered a corned beef brisket until it was tender and infused with the spices. Once the brisket was cooked, we put the flavorful cooking liquid to work, using it to microwave the cabbage, then pouring it over the meat to keep it moist and juicy. Small red potatoes and 3-inch pieces of carrots cooked to the perfect doneness along with the beef.

In the United States, corned beef and cabbage is rarely eaten outside of St. Patrick's Day—and maybe for good reason. When boiled, as is tradition, the meat often comes out salty and dry, and the vegetables are usually overcooked and bland. And if you rely on the packet of stale, listless seasonings that accompanies store-bought corned beef, you'll have to turn elsewhere for flavor—but don't look to the vegetables to find it. The classic pairing of cabbage and potatoes is more mush than flavor, glistening with grease from the beef. If ever a meal needed rescuing, this was it. Although the test kitchen has developed recipes for corned beef and cabbage before, I hoped that this time, the slow cooker would make a flavorful and convenient version that I would be able and willing to serve any day of the year.

I started with the meat. I knew I wanted to use a store-bought corned beef brisket; to "corn" my own beef, I'd need to salt it, weight it, and then wait seven days before I could even think about cooking it, with the unwieldy brisket hogging valuable refrigerator space all that time. Not going to happen. I would work with store-bought corned beef and throw away the seasoning packet.

But discarding the seasoning packet didn't mean I had to go without seasoning altogether. Why not infuse the beef with a flavorful cooking liquid of my own? I put a corned beef brisket in the slow cooker with some carrots, potatoes, and a few cups of store-bought beef broth, but found that the broth gave the meat and veggies a tinny off-flavor, which didn't disappear even when I replaced some of the broth with water. I opted for chicken broth instead, which I diluted with an equal amount of water so that it would taste savory but not chicken-y. It worked, but the flavor lacked depth. A bit of dried thyme, some black peppercorns, and a hint of allspice, along with the sweetness lent by the carrots, were enough to give the cooking liquid some complexity. (No salt necessary—the corned beef was salty enough already.) Although I played around with other aromatics, none seemed necessary, so I stuck with those three traditional options for the sake of simplicity. I let the corned beef cook for nearly 10 hours, sliced it thin, and tasted it. The beef was already tasting better, but the vegetables still needed help.

Since the dish was cooking all day, I wanted to avoid adding the vegetables in batches. No one wants to baby-sit a slow cooker, and having to prep and add ingredients at different times would detract from the simplicity of the recipe. I also knew I didn't want to eat cabbage that had been cooked for 10 hours—it would be nothing but mush. I left it for later, and turned my attention to the carrots and potatoes. I tried adding them to the cooking liquid and putting the brisket on top, hoping that the meat's juices would infuse the vegetables with flavor. No dice. The vegetables were overcooked by a mile. What if I used the brisket as a shield to protect the carrots and potatoes from the direct heat of the appliance? To further prevent overcooking, I cut the carrots into large, 3-inch-long chunks and left the small red potatoes whole. I piled the veggies on top of the brisket, put the slow cooker on low, and crossed my fingers. When I came back at the end of the cooking time, I not only had flavorful, tender meat, but also perfectly cooked carrots and potatoes.

Of course, the dish is called corned beef and cabbage, not corned beef and carrots and potatoes, so I turned my attention back to the namesake vegetable. While the meat rested, I cut the cabbage into wedges and microwaved them with some water until they were perfectly tender. I made up plates with beef, carrots, potatoes, and cabbage and called over my tasters. While everyone agreed that the cabbage was cooked well, it also seemed flat and flavorless next to the beef. Then it hit me—why not use the liquid I had used for the beef to cook the cabbage and infuse it with flavor? This fix worked perfectly.

I finally had a slow-cooker recipe for tender, moist corned beef that was so good, I didn't want to wait for St. Patrick's Day to make it.

—DAN ZUCCARELLO, *America's Test Kitchen Books*

Slow-Cooker Corned Beef and Cabbage
SERVES 6

This recipe is designed to work with 6½- to 7-quart oval slow cookers. Look for small red potatoes measuring 1 to 2 inches in diameter; if your potatoes are larger, cut them into 1-inch pieces to ensure that they cook through.

- 1 **(3-pound) corned beef brisket, rinsed and fat trimmed to ¼ inch**
- 2 **cups chicken broth**
- 2 **cups water**
- 1 **teaspoon dried thyme**
- ½ **teaspoon black peppercorns**
- ¼ **teaspoon allspice berries**
- 1½ **pounds small red potatoes, unpeeled**
- 1½ **pounds carrots, peeled, halved lengthwise, and cut into 3-inch lengths**
- 1 **head green cabbage (2 pounds), cut into 8 wedges**

1. Place corned beef, broth, water, thyme, peppercorns, and allspice in slow cooker. Place potatoes and carrots on top of brisket. Cover and cook until beef is tender, 9 to 10 hours on low or 6 to 7 hours on high.

2. Transfer vegetables to serving dish and cover tightly with aluminum foil. Transfer brisket to carving board, tent loosely with foil, and let rest for 15 minutes. Using large spoon, skim excess fat from surface of cooking liquid.

3. Microwave cabbage and ½ cup cooking liquid in covered bowl until leaves of cabbage are pliable and translucent, about 15 minutes; transfer to serving dish. Slice meat against grain into ¼-inch-thick slices and transfer to serving dish. Moisten corned beef and vegetables with cooking liquid as needed before serving.

NOTES FROM THE TEST KITCHEN

SERVING BEEF BRISKET

When serving brisket, it is important to slice it thin (we're talking about ¼ inch) and against the grain in order for the meat to taste tender. If the slices are cut too thick, the meat will have a tougher, chewy texture.

DEVILED BEEF SHORT RIBS

DEVILED BEEF SHORT RIBS

✓ **WHY THIS RECIPE WORKS:** We loved the idea of these spicy, crumb-crusted roasted short ribs, but none of the recipes we found hit the mark. To achieve perfectly rendered, ultratender ribs, we roasted them meat side down in a covered baking dish and lowered the oven temperature to 325 degrees. To boost the spiciness of the coating, we used a combination of traditional yellow mustard, cayenne, black pepper, and minced jalapeños. For depth of flavor, we added orange juice, lemon zest, and a bit of brown sugar. Browning panko bread crumbs in butter and then coating the short ribs with them at the end of cooking ensured that the crumb crust stayed crunchy.

When the cold weather hits, my friends start thinking about sipping wine by the fire. Me? I start thinking about braised short ribs. But at winter's midpoint—after I've braised a rodeo's worth of ribs—I'm ready for something other than the standard onion-wine-broth braise. And that's why I was so excited to stumble across deviled short ribs. This throwback recipe from the 1960s calls for roasting (not braising) the ribs after they've been "deviled" with either a rub of dry mustard, black pepper, and spices or a marinade of prepared yellow mustard, black pepper, and seasonings. Once tender, the ribs are sprinkled with bread crumbs and broiled until the crumbs are crispy. I was sold on the idea, but after cooking my way through nearly a dozen versions of this recipe, one thing was clear: The devil is in the details.

First, I needed to figure out how best to cook the ribs. Most recipes call for roasting the ribs, uncovered, in a moderate oven (anywhere from 350 to 425 degrees) for 3 to 5 hours, but I found this problematic, as the ribs never quite took on that silky quality that makes short ribs so appealing. Taking a cue from an old test kitchen technique, I turned down the oven to 325 degrees and roasted the ribs, meat side up, in a covered baking dish. The result was moist, tender, silky ribs in about 3 hours, though my tasters noted that a few pockets of fat remained. To make sure that the fat was fully rendered, I cooked the ribs meat side down so that the meat cooked in its own juices, resulting in ultratender ribs and completely rendered fat. With the cooking method settled, I could concentrate on making the flavor live up to its deviled name.

None of the initial recipes had been awful, but the seasonings were awfully meek: Maybe lots of mustard and black pepper were considered "devilish" 50 years ago, but they're not today. I decided I'd start by seasoning the ribs with just salt and pepper, roasting them, and then brushing them with an amped-up mixture of both prepared yellow mustard and dry mustard, a full tablespoon of black pepper, and a little cayenne near the end of cooking before sprinkling on the crumbs. This immediately improved the dish's flavor and kick, but these ribs needed more depth—and they weren't close to making anyone sweat.

I tested my working recipe with both Dijon and brown mustards, but my tasters preferred the clarity of traditional yellow mustard, so I'd have to add flavor in other ways. I tried all manner of citrus juices and zests, testing orange, lemon, and lime against each other and in combination. My tasters ended up liking the pairing of orange juice and lemon juice best. Some brown sugar added roundness, and a couple of minced jalapeños really brought the brimstone. Combining these ingredients in the food processor ensured that the heat was evenly incorporated and that the mixture was thick enough to hold the crumbs.

All that was left was brushing on the glaze, sprinkling on the bread crumbs (we liked panko for its superior crunch), and firing up the broiler. Unfortunately, the broiler was a no-go from the get-go. The crumbs on the exterior had a tendency to scorch, while those that were in contact with the glaze were gummy. Instead of using the broiler, I increased the oven temperature to 425 degrees. This browned the crumbs more evenly but didn't solve the gummy crumb problem. I hoped that I could fix this by brushing on the glaze and then roasting the ribs before coating them with the crumbs. It worked, and I found that I could actually glaze three times, for deeper flavor, before rolling the ribs in panko and roasting a final time to brown the crumbs.

I was almost there, but my tasters thought that the crumbs were unevenly browned and could use a little punching up. Changing course slightly, I opted to toast the crumbs in butter on the stovetop before coating the ribs and then serving them immediately. This allowed me to brown the crumbs perfectly while also adding a nutty sweetness from the butter and an herbal freshness from chopped parsley and lemon zest. Removed from the oven and rolled in the toasted crumbs before serving, these deviled beef short ribs definitely lived up to their name. And I didn't have to sell my soul to get them.

—JEREMY SAUER, *Cook's Country*

Deviled Beef Short Ribs

SERVES 4 TO 6

English-style short ribs contain a single rib bone. For a milder sauce, use only one jalapeño and discard the seeds.

- ⅔ cup yellow mustard
- ⅓ cup orange juice
- ⅓ cup packed light brown sugar
- 1–2 jalapeño chiles, stemmed, seeds reserved, and roughly chopped
- 4 teaspoons dry mustard
- 1 teaspoon grated lemon zest plus 1 tablespoon juice
- Salt and pepper
- ½ teaspoon cayenne pepper
- 5 pounds bone-in English-style short ribs, bones 4 to 5 inches long, 1 to 1½ inches of meat on top of bone, trimmed
- 2 tablespoons unsalted butter
- 1½ cups panko bread crumbs
- 1 tablespoon chopped fresh parsley

1. Adjust oven rack to middle position and heat oven to 325 degrees. Combine yellow mustard, orange juice, sugar, jalapeños and reserved seeds, dry mustard, lemon juice, and 2 teaspoons pepper in food processor and process until smooth, about 30 seconds; set aside. (Mustard mixture can be refrigerated for up to 1 week.)

2. Combine 1 tablespoon salt, 1 tablespoon pepper, and cayenne in bowl. Sprinkle ribs all over with spice mixture. Arrange ribs, meat side down, in 13 by 9-inch baking dish. Cover dish tightly with aluminum foil and roast until meat is nearly tender, about 3 hours.

3. Meanwhile, melt butter in 12-inch skillet over medium-high heat. Add panko and cook, stirring often,

---

NOTES FROM THE TEST KITCHEN

A ROASTING-BRAISING HYBRID METHOD
Most short rib recipes call for searing, then braising, and finally turning the braising liquid into a sauce. For Deviled Beef Short Ribs, we took a different road: We put the ribs in a baking dish, meat side down, and roasted them (covered) until tender, about 3 hours. The meat cooked in its own rendered fat and juices, giving us fully rendered, supertender short ribs without much hands-on work. To finish, we uncovered the ribs, brushed them with a glaze, roasted them meat side up, repeated, and then rolled them in toasted crumbs.

---

until golden brown, about 3 minutes. Off heat, stir in parsley and lemon zest and transfer to shallow dish.

4. Remove baking dish from oven and increase oven temperature to 425 degrees; transfer ribs to plate. Discard rendered fat and juices from dish. Brush meat (not bone) all over with one-fourth of mustard sauce and return ribs to dish, meat side up. Roast, uncovered, until beginning to brown, about 10 minutes. Brush meat again with one-third of remaining mustard sauce and continue to roast until well browned and completely tender, 10 to 15 minutes longer. Transfer ribs to serving platter, tent loosely with foil, and let rest for 15 minutes.

5. Brush meat once more with half of remaining mustard sauce and roll in panko mixture, taking care to entirely coat meat. Serve, passing remaining mustard sauce separately.

GRILLED CHUCK STEAKS

✅ **WHY THIS RECIPE WORKS:** A premium steak on the grill is a welcome treat, but we wondered whether we could also put a great, inexpensive steak dinner on the table. We started by narrowing down inexpensive cuts and landed on chuck-eye steak for its good beefy flavor. We found that buying a whole chuck-eye roast and cutting our own steaks ensured that the steaks were the same size and therefore cooked evenly. A half-grill fire worked to give the steaks perfectly cooked meat with nicely charred exteriors, and a little vegetable oil, brushed on before grilling, enhanced the charred crust. Slicing the meat thinly against the grain made the steak tender and minimized chewiness. A flavorful spice rub gave the meat extra punch.

Does a good steak dinner have to cost an arm and a leg? Hoping that the answer was no, I hit the meat counter looking for an inexpensive alternative to pricey strip, tenderloin, and rib-eye steaks. I talked to a butcher who recommended chuck steaks; he pointed to some in the case that were nicely marbled and looked pretty good. Chuck is cut from the hardworking shoulder of the steer, which means it's laden with both flavorful fat and tough connective tissue. Until now I'd always passed on buying chuck steaks, figuring that they could never become tender without long, slow cooking.

GRILLED CHUCK STEAKS

But recently I've been hearing from my chef buddies that chuck steaks can be great grilled, so I figured it was time to give chuck a chance.

I started my testing as we always do in the test kitchen: by gathering recipes. Most were frustratingly vague in that they called for "chuck steaks," which could mean any slab of meat from the chuck. (I knew from experience that the many different muscles of the chuck all cook—and eat—quite differently.)

A few recipes offered more direction, specifying blade, flat-iron, chuck-eye, and seven-bone steaks, all of which are cut from the chuck. Most of the recipes require seasoning the meat before cooking, via a marinade or a heavily spiced rub. All cooked for a short time over high heat—standard steak protocol.

I cooked off the steaks and called my tasters. I'll give it to you straight: The steaks were not very good. But these failures were instructive and helped me start to shape my recipe. Steaks that were marinated never achieved a good, hard, flavor-building sear (even when I patted them dry before grilling). We preferred the spice-rubbed steaks for their flavorful, well-browned crusts. More importantly, I figured out which cut of beef to use. The seven-bone and blade steaks were out because they were as tough as a dog's chew toy. Flat-iron steaks are hard to come by (I had to get them from a restaurant supplier), so those, too, were off the list. But my tasters did think that the chuck-eye steaks had some promise: While not melt-in-your-mouth tender, they were by far the least chewy of the bunch, and they had great beefy flavor.

Now that I'd decided on chuck-eye steaks, I needed to learn about them in more detail. With a little research, I discovered that the chuck eye comes from the intersection of the fifth and sixth ribs of the cow; this intersection is also the border between the chuck and the rib primal cuts. In other words, chuck-eye steaks come from the part of the cow closest to where rib eyes are cut from, which helps explain why they are more tender than other chuck cuts. I ordered more steaks to continue testing, but the steaks that came in from the market were inconsistent in size and shape, so they cooked at different rates. But there was a bigger problem: Even though everything I was getting was labeled "chuck-eye steaks," the steaks were so wildly different that I had to believe they were incorrectly marked.

To make sure that I was really getting chuck-eye steaks and that they would be consistent, I'd have to buy chuck-eye roasts and cut my own steaks. I ordered a few large chuck-eye roasts, which are basically two lobes of meat connected by a seam of fat that runs their length.

I removed the seam, making two smaller roasts, and then cut each smaller roast into two hefty steaks, creating four steaks that were a good 1 to 1½ inches thick (depending on the roast). Just as I had hoped, fabricating my own consistently sized steaks meant that they now cooked at the same rate.

As for the grilling, my first order of business was a good sear for flavor. First I tried the most straightforward approach—I grilled the steaks over a hot fire until they were charred on both sides, which took about 10 minutes total. But the steaks weren't yet cooked through. I had better luck creating hotter and cooler cooking areas: I could sear the steaks over the hotter part of the grill and then move them to the cooler area to cook through without burning the exterior. Brushing the steaks with a little vegetable oil right before cooking helped create even better char. Slicing the cooked meat thin against the grain, after a rest, of course (to let the juices redistribute), minimized the chewiness. Now all I had to do was perfect the spice rub.

I pieced together a working rub from the ones that we had liked best in the initial recipes, and then I tested and tweaked various iterations over the course of several days. Chipotle chile powder gave the rub a suitably assertive, complex base, and plenty of salt was an obvious addition. Garlic powder and coriander added complementary flavors, and an unexpected ingredient—cocoa powder—lent great depth, with brown sugar helping smooth out the bitter edges. The rub tasted good on the steaks, but the seasoning was superficial. There was an easy fix for this: time. I found that if I rubbed the steaks and refrigerated them for at least 6 (or up to 24) hours, the salt and spice flavor was much more pervasive.

I was curious but a little skeptical when I began testing. But as I chowed down on this relatively tender, definitely affordable steak, I realized I was ready to proselytize: Give chuck a chance!

—NICK IVERSON, *Cook's Country*

Grilled Chuck Steaks

SERVES 4

Choose a roast without too much fat at the natural seam.

- 1 tablespoon kosher salt
- 1 tablespoon chipotle chile powder
- 1 teaspoon unsweetened cocoa powder
- 1 teaspoon packed brown sugar
- ½ teaspoon ground coriander
- ½ teaspoon garlic powder
- 1 (2½- to 3-pound) boneless beef chuck-eye roast
- 2 tablespoons vegetable oil

1. Combine salt, chile powder, cocoa, sugar, coriander, and garlic powder in bowl. Separate roast into 2 pieces along natural seam. Turn each piece on its side and cut in half lengthwise against grain. Remove silverskin and trim

---

NOTES FROM THE TEST KITCHEN

CREATING CHUCK STEAKS AT HOME
We weren't satisfied with what we found labeled "chuck steaks" in stores, so we made our own. Start with a 2½- to 3-pound boneless beef chuck-eye roast and follow these simple steps to yield four steaks.

1. DIVIDE ROAST IN TWO: Use your hands to separate the roast at the natural seam.

2. CUT EACH HALF IN TWO: Turn each piece on its side and cut it in half lengthwise, against the grain.

3. TRIM EACH STEAK: Remove and discard the chewy silverskin and any excess fat.

---

fat to ¼-inch thickness. Pat steaks dry with paper towels and rub with spice mixture. Transfer steaks to zipper-lock bag and refrigerate for at least 6 hours or up to 24 hours.

2A. FOR A CHARCOAL GRILL: Open bottom vent halfway. Light large chimney starter filled with charcoal briquettes (6 quarts). When top coals are partially covered with ash, pour evenly over half of grill. Set cooking grate in place, cover, and open lid vent halfway. Heat grill until hot, about 5 minutes.

2B. FOR A GAS GRILL: Turn all burners to high, cover, and heat grill until hot, about 15 minutes. Turn primary burner to medium-high and secondary burner(s) to medium-low.

3. Clean and oil cooking grate. Brush steaks all over with oil. Place steaks over hotter side of grill and cook (covered if using gas) until well charred on both sides, about 5 minutes per side. Move steaks to cooler side of grill and continue to cook (covered if using gas) until steaks register 125 degrees (for medium-rare), 5 to 8 minutes.

4. Transfer steaks to carving board, tent loosely with aluminum foil, and let rest for 10 minutes. Slice steaks thin. Serve.

BARBECUED BURNT ENDS

✓ **WHY THIS RECIPE WORKS:** Barbecued burnt ends are usually made from generously-marbled point cut brisket, which is smoked for more than 12 hours until the exterior is almost black. The meat absorbs plenty of smoky flavor and becomes ultratender from the long cooking time. But for a home barbecue, we wanted to make these flavorful morsels using the more readily available (but much leaner) flat cut brisket. To maximize surface area for crunchy "bark," we cut the meat into 1½-inch-wide strips. Two hours in a brine solution kept the meat moist through cooking. A combined grill- and oven-smoked method provided the burnished exterior and tender meat characteristic of true burnt ends.

The best part of any slow-smoked barbecue, be it ribs, brisket, or pulled pork, is the bark—the dark, smoky, crusty, crispy exterior. So it stands to reason that burnt ends, the bark-iest kind of barbecue there is, are my absolute favorite. Professional pit masters make their burnt ends by rubbing huge whole briskets (which can weigh 15 pounds or more) with salt, pepper, and sugar and smoking them for up to 12 hours until tender. Then they divide each brisket into the point and flat cuts; the leaner flat cut is sliced and served, while the fattier point cut is put back into the smoker to further render, tenderize, absorb more smoke, and form more tasty bark. After several hours, the almost-black point-cut briskets are hauled out, chopped up, sometimes sauced, and enjoyed as burnt ends. They are, if I may say it, amazing.

But there are a few good reasons most home barbecuers don't make them: It's hard to find point cuts in supermarkets, and whole briskets are too big for most backyard grills and smokers. So my challenge was to try to make smoky, moist, tender burnt ends from lean flat-cut brisket on a backyard kettle grill.

After slow-smoking four briskets on my first day of testing, I learned that it's hard to get good bark on a smoked flat-cut brisket without drying out the meat because there is so little fat to render and provide moisture. So how could I get meat that had great bark but was still moist? I tested two of the test kitchen's favorite techniques to help keep lean meats moist: salting and brining. After a few days of testing various intervals, I found that both methods work, but brining is faster: 6 hours of brining got the same results as 12 hours of salting.

But the benefits of brining the briskets went only so far; when I smoked the briskets to tenderness (it took about 8 hours), cubed them, and put them back on the grill to get crusty and barky, the finished meat was dry. Was there a way to create the bark faster? Yes—cutting the brisket into long, 1½-inch-wide strips before brining exposed more surface area to "bark up" during the initial smoking. Cutting the meat into strips also cut the brining time from 6 hours to 2, a definite plus.

Some large problems remained. First of all, 8 hours of smoking meant refueling the charcoal grill several times, which was a pain. Luckily, the test kitchen has developed a hybrid grill-to-oven method for barbecued ribs that doesn't require any refueling—the meat stays on the grill only as long as one small pile of charcoal will throw heat, which is between 1 and 2 hours; water pans in the grill help moderate the temperature. I borrowed this technique and ended up with the following method: Cut the meat into strips, brine, smoke for roughly 2 hours, transfer the meat to a baking sheet, wrap tightly in foil to trap the steam, and bake at 275 degrees until tender, about 3 or 4 hours. Then I chopped the strips into chunks, tossed them with barbecue sauce (bottled for now), and called in my tasters.

"Pretty good . . . but not great" was the consensus. The problem was serious: The bark was too insubstantial. To fix it, I'd need to find a way to keep the strips of brisket on the grill longer without reloading the charcoal. I put my hopes on the Minion method, a barbecue circuit trick (named after the guy who came up with it, Jim Minion) where you place lit charcoal on a pile of unlit charcoal in your grill. After a few days of playing with the amounts and the timing, I was able to make it work by dumping 3 quarts of lit charcoal (plus a packet of soaked wood chips) on top of 3 quarts of unlit charcoal (and another packet of wood chips). This gave me a steady, smoky low heat for a full 3 hours. As a bonus, I could now shorten the succeeding oven time to 2 hours.

I made sure to rest the brisket, right in the foil-covered pan, for an hour after it came out of the oven to maximize juiciness. And I made a quick, tasty sauce by cooking a mixture of ketchup, brown sugar, cider vinegar, seasonings, and the defatted brisket juices. These burnt ends had it all: moist, beefy brisket with a burnished, crusty exterior and flavorful sauce. Are they as good as the barky ends served up by pit masters in brisket meccas like Austin and Kansas City? I think so, but why don't you judge for yourself?

—DIANE UNGER, *Cook's Country*

Barbecued Burnt Ends

SERVES 8 TO 10

Look for a brisket with a significant fat cap. This recipe takes about 8 hours to prepare. However, the meat can be brined ahead of time: After brining, transfer the meat to a zipper-lock bag, and refrigerate it for up to one day. If you don't have ½ cup of juices from the rested brisket, supplement with beef broth in step 6.

BRISKET AND RUB

- 2 cups plus 1 tablespoon kosher salt
- ½ cup granulated sugar
- 1 (5- to 6-pound) beef brisket, flat cut, untrimmed
- ¼ cup packed brown sugar
- 2 tablespoons pepper
- 4 cups wood chips
- 1 (13 by 9-inch) disposable aluminum roasting pan (if using charcoal) or 2 (8½- by 6-inch) disposable aluminum pans (if using gas)

BARBECUE SAUCE

- ¾ cup ketchup
- ¼ cup packed brown sugar
- 2 tablespoons cider vinegar
- 2 tablespoons Worcestershire sauce
- 2 teaspoons garlic powder
- ¼ teaspoon cayenne pepper

1. FOR THE BRISKET AND RUB: Dissolve 2 cups salt and granulated sugar in 4 quarts cold water in large container. Slice brisket with grain into 1½-inch-thick strips. Add brisket strips to brine, cover, and refrigerate for 2 hours. Remove brisket from brine and pat dry with paper towels.

2. Combine brown sugar, pepper, and remaining 1 tablespoon salt in bowl. Season brisket all over with rub. Just before grilling, soak wood chips in water for 15 minutes, then drain. Using 2 large pieces of heavy-duty aluminum foil, wrap soaked chips in 2 foil packets and cut several vent holes in tops.

3A. FOR A CHARCOAL GRILL: Open bottom vent halfway and place disposable pan filled with 2 quarts water on 1 side of grill, with long side of pan facing center of grill. Arrange 3 quarts unlit charcoal briquettes on opposite side of grill and place 1 wood chip packet on coals. Light large chimney starter halfway filled with charcoal briquettes (3 quarts). When top coals are partially covered with ash, pour evenly over unlit coals and wood chip packet. Place remaining wood chip packet on lit coals. Set cooking grate in place, cover, and open lid vent halfway. Heat grill until hot and wood chips are smoking, about 5 minutes.

3B. FOR A GAS GRILL: Add ½ cup ice cubes to 1 wood chip packet. Remove cooking grate and place both wood chip packets directly on primary burner; place disposable pans each filled with 2 cups water directly on secondary burner(s). Set grate in place, turn all burners to high, cover, and heat grill until hot and wood chips are smoking, about 15 minutes. Leave primary burner on high and turn off other burner(s). (Adjust primary burner as needed to maintain grill temperature of 275 to 300 degrees.)

4. Clean and oil cooking grate. Arrange brisket on cooler side of grill as far from heat source as possible. Cover (positioning lid vent over brisket for charcoal) and cook without opening for 3 hours.

5. Adjust oven rack to middle position and heat oven to 275 degrees. Remove brisket from grill and transfer to rimmed baking sheet. Cover sheet tightly with foil. Roast until fork slips easily in and out of meat and meat registers about 210 degrees, about 2 hours. Remove from oven, leave covered, and let rest for 1 hour. Remove foil, transfer brisket to carving board, and pour accumulated juices into fat separator.

6. FOR THE BARBECUE SAUCE: Combine ketchup, sugar, vinegar, Worcestershire, garlic powder, cayenne, and ½ cup defatted brisket juices in medium saucepan. Bring to simmer over medium heat and cook until slightly thickened, about 5 minutes.

7. Cut brisket strips crosswise into 1- to 2-inch chunks. Combine brisket chunks and barbecue sauce in large bowl and toss to combine. Serve.

GRILLED LAMB KOFTE

✔ WHY THIS RECIPE WORKS: *Kofte* are Middle Eastern spiced lamb patties which are typically grilled to enhance their rich character. Kofte's bold flavorings and slightly sausage-like texture appealed to us, but the finicky recipes we found needed tweaking to make them foolproof. We skipped the traditional hand-minced meat in favor of store-bought ground lamb, and replaced the bread panade with a little gelatin to keep our kofte moist after grilling. A surprising ingredient—ground pine nuts—added richness and kept the kofte from being too dense. A variety of warm spices and fresh herbs gave our kofte intense flavor, and a cool yogurt-based sauce proved a welcome contrast to the rich meat.

When I was growing up, my Armenian family had two basic meat-grilling modes for warm-weather events: skewered leg of lamb—shish kebab—or spiced ground lamb patties. Armenians call these *losh* kebabs, but they are known nearly everywhere else in the Middle East as *kofte*.

My family's version of kofte falls in line with some of the more common versions served in the Middle East, so when I set out to develop my own recipe, I used my father's as a baseline. He uses a mixture of hand-ground lamb, bread crumbs, grated onion, cumin, chiles, and whatever fresh herbs are available, kneading the ingredients together to disperse the fat and flavor and form an almost sausagelike springiness. His boldly spiced patties are quickly grilled over high heat on long metal skewers, making them tender and

GRILLED LAMB KOFTE

juicy on the inside and encased in a smoky, crunchy coating of char. To serve, he stuffs the kofte in pita and drizzles on a tangy yogurt-garlic sauce.

When I began my testing I quickly learned that the problem with kofte is that it's finicky. Because the patties are small, the meat easily overcooks and becomes dry. And since kofte is kneaded by hand in order to get the meat proteins to cross-link and take on a resilient texture, I found that it's easy to make it too springy—or not springy enough. I rounded up a handful of existing kofte recipes using a range of binders, spices, and kneading times, but I found that most of the results turned out dry and crumbly or were simply tough. I wanted my kofte to be warm and flavorful, with a cooling sauce; tender yet intact; and easy to boot. And I wanted to achieve this without needing years of practice.

Kofte is traditionally made by mincing meat—usually lamb—by hand with a cleaver. Unlike machine grinding, which roughs up the meat fibers to the point that they can't easily hold on to moisture upon cooking, hand mincing is far gentler and leads to kofte that is juicy and tender. But hand mincing is a lot of work—and therefore, for me, a nonstarter. I would stick with preground meat from the grocery store. And though I decided to go with lamb—its rich flavor pairs so well with earthy spices and smoky grill char—I wanted to develop a recipe that worked with ground beef, too.

After cobbling together a working recipe of ground lamb and grated onion, along with a little cumin, chile, and fresh parsley (knowing that I would return to deal with the spices later), I began trying to solve the moisture issue. In the test kitchen we usually turn to panades made from soaked bread or bread crumbs to keep ground meat patties moist when cooked through, since their starches help hold on to moisture released by the meat as it cooks. Many kofte recipes also use some form of binder, but when I tried bread crumbs, standard sandwich bread, torn-up pita bread, and all-purpose flour, these add-ins introduced some other problems. While my tasters found that all helped retain a bit of moisture and kept the kofte together, when enough was used to prevent drying out on the grill, the starchy panades gave the kofte an unwelcome pastiness, and they muted the flavor of the lamb. But what other options did I have?

I thought about meatballs, and, in particular, one of the test kitchen's past recipes for Italian meatballs. For this recipe, we used a panade along with powdered gelatin. Gelatin holds up to 10 times its weight in water, and the gel that forms when it hydrates is highly viscous (which is why sauces made from gelatin-rich reduced meat stocks are so silky smooth). And unlike starches, you need very tiny amounts of gelatin to see benefits, so it doesn't usually have negative effects on texture or flavor. Could gelatin work in my kofte? I tried adding a mere teaspoon per pound of lamb and then refrigerated the kofte to help the meat firm up, and I was pleased by the results: I now had nice, juicy kofte.

But I was still left with a problem. With the preground meat plus a solid 2 minutes of kneading, which was not only traditional but also necessary to help keep the kofte together on the grill, many of my finished products were so springy that they could practically bounce. I remembered a recipe I'd seen that had included bulgur. This coarse cracked wheat most likely wouldn't melt into the meat like bread crumbs but would instead keep the ground meat a bit separated and therefore less springy and more tender when cooked. But when I tried bulgur, adding a couple of tablespoons to the mix, I found that it only made the kofte gritty. I tried it again in smaller quantities, but the unpleasant texture remained.

The bulgur gave me an idea, though: What about incorporating something of a similar size but of a softer consistency? I'd seen a few kofte recipes containing ground pine nuts or pistachios, and I'd assumed that the nuts were used for flavor rather than texture. Coarsely ground nuts might be just the thing. So for my next test, I added a few tablespoons of ground pine nuts to the mixture. The results were even better than I'd hoped. The nuts helped prevent toughness in the kofte without adding their own texture. And best of all, thanks to the oil they contained, they gave the kofte a subtle but noticeable boost in richness.

Now all that remained was to sort out the flavorings and a sauce. Many kofte recipes contain *baharat*, a Middle Eastern spice blend that is a common seasoning

NOTES FROM THE TEST KITCHEN

THE BEST SKEWERS

We gathered six sets of innovative skewers, including our no-frills favorite from Norpro, and threaded them with chicken-vegetable kebabs, scallops, and *kofte*. Overall, we weren't impressed. One model's "heat-resistant" plastic slider melted. Double-pronged skewers splayed out awkwardly, and curved rods only let us turn food 180 degrees. We'll stick with our former champ, **Norpro's 12-Inch Stainless Steel Skewers**.

SKIP THE BURGER AND TRY THIS

These kebabs take only a little longer to throw together than burgers but boast far more complex flavors and textures. For sandwiches, serve in warm pita bread.

SPRINGY YET TENDER TEXTURE
Kneading the ground meat gives the *kofte* a sausagelike spring, while incorporating ground pine nuts ensures that it also stays tender.

WARM SPICES
Spices added to the meat, including hot smoked paprika, cumin, and cloves, contribute heat and depth.

TANGY SAUCE
Ours features traditional garlicky yogurt, plus a little tahini for added complexity.

FRESH HERBS
The bright, grassy flavors of two other mix-ins, parsley and mint, complement the kofte's richness.

---

for meat dishes. Recipes vary widely, but the common denominators are usually black pepper, cumin, coriander, and chile pepper. I came up with my own combination of these, with cumin as a dominant player and hot smoked paprika as the chile. To these I also added smaller amounts of ground cinnamon, nutmeg, and cloves. As for herbs, equal amounts of fresh parsley and mint did the trick. For the sauce, I borrowed an idea from a recipe I'd found in *Jerusalem*, the latest cookbook from British chefs Yotam Ottolenghi and Sami Tamimi: I added a small amount of tahini to the traditional mixture of crushed garlic, lemon juice, and yogurt usually served with kofte since this gave the sauce a depth to match that of the kofte itself.

With that, there was one last test to perform: Serve the kofte to my family. The result? My kofte was a big hit. Even my dad asked for the recipe.

—ANDREW JANJIGIAN, *Cook's Illustrated*

Grilled Lamb Kofte

SERVES 4 TO 6

Serve with rice pilaf or make sandwiches with warm pita bread, sliced red onion, and chopped fresh mint. You will need eight 12-inch metal skewers for this recipe.

YOGURT-GARLIC SAUCE

- 1 cup plain whole-milk yogurt
- 2 tablespoons lemon juice
- 2 tablespoons tahini
- 1 garlic clove, minced
- ½ teaspoon salt

KOFTE

- ½ cup pine nuts
- 4 garlic cloves, peeled
- 1½ teaspoons hot smoked paprika
- 1 teaspoon salt
- 1 teaspoon ground cumin
- ½ teaspoon pepper
- ¼ teaspoon ground coriander
- ¼ teaspoon ground cloves
- ⅛ teaspoon ground nutmeg
- ⅛ teaspoon ground cinnamon
- 1½ pounds ground lamb
- ½ cup grated onion, drained
- ⅓ cup minced fresh parsley
- ⅓ cup minced fresh mint
- 1½ teaspoons unflavored gelatin
- 1 large disposable aluminum roasting pan (if using charcoal)

1. FOR THE YOGURT-GARLIC SAUCE: Whisk all ingredients together in bowl. Set aside.

2. FOR THE KOFTE: Process pine nuts, garlic, paprika, salt, cumin, pepper, coriander, cloves, nutmeg, and cinnamon in food processor until coarse paste forms, 30 to 45 seconds. Transfer mixture to large bowl. Add lamb, onion, parsley, mint, and gelatin; knead with your hands until thoroughly combined and mixture feels slightly sticky, about 2 minutes. Divide mixture into 8 equal portions. Shape each portion into 5-inch-long cylinder about 1 inch in diameter. Using eight 12-inch metal skewers, thread 1 cylinder onto each skewer, pressing gently to adhere. Transfer skewers to lightly greased baking sheet, cover with plastic wrap, and refrigerate for at least 1 hour or up to 24 hours.

3A. FOR A CHARCOAL GRILL: Using skewer, poke 12 holes in bottom of disposable pan. Open bottom vent completely and place pan in center of grill. Light large chimney starter filled two-thirds with charcoal briquettes (4 quarts). When top coals are partially covered with ash, pour into pan. Set cooking grate in place, cover, and open lid vent completely. Heat grill until hot, about 5 minutes.

3B. FOR A GAS GRILL: Turn all burners to high, cover, and heat grill until hot, about 15 minutes. Leave all burners on high.

4. Clean and oil cooking grate. Place skewers on grill (directly over coals if using charcoal) at 45-degree angle to grate. Cook (covered if using gas) until browned and meat easily releases from grill, 4 to 7 minutes. Flip skewers and continue to cook until browned on second side and meat registers 160 degrees, about 6 minutes longer. Transfer skewers to platter and serve, passing yogurt-garlic sauce separately.

VARIATION
Grilled Beef Kofte

Substitute 80 percent lean ground beef for lamb. Increase garlic to 5 cloves, paprika to 2 teaspoons, and cumin to 2 teaspoons.

GRILLED GLAZED PORK TENDERLOIN ROAST

✔ **WHY THIS RECIPE WORKS:** Too often, delicate pork tenderloin turns out disappointing: The lean meat dries out easily, and it is plagued by uneven cooking because of its tapered shape. To make the pork cook more evenly and to create a more presentation-worthy roast, we tied two tenderloins together. Scraping the insides of the tenderloins with a fork created a sticky protein network which helped the tenderloins bind together. To ensure that our pork retained maximum juiciness, we brined the meat and cooked it mostly over indirect heat. Finally, we put together a few flavorful glazes. We made sure to use enough sugar (or ingredients containing sugar) to encourage browning, giving the pork a beautiful crust along with a flavor boost.

Pork tenderloin is wonderfully tender and versatile, it doesn't require much prep, and it's relatively inexpensive. But this cut also comes with a certain set of challenges. Because tenderloin is so lean, it's highly susceptible to drying out during cooking. Then there's its ungainly tapered shape: By the time the large end hits a perfect medium (140 degrees), the skinnier tail is guaranteed to be overdone. And while my favorite way to prepare mild meats like tenderloin is grilling (to develop a rich, meaty crust), extreme heat and natural fluctuations in temperature make this hard to do well. I wanted to find a way to make grilled pork tenderloin a bit more foolproof and at the same time elevate this cut above its "casual supper" status to something more special and elegant.

Keeping any meat juicy on the grill is a perennial challenge. In the test kitchen, we have a couple of tricks for addressing the problem, namely salting or brining. Both techniques introduce salt into the flesh, where it tenderizes the meat and increases water retention. Using our preferred type of pork, unenhanced (or natural)—meaning that it has not been injected with a salt solution—I ran a side-by-side test in which I salted and brined a few tenderloins, slicked them with oil, and grilled them. Tasters reported that the brined samples were the most succulent. So I moved on to another variable that affects juiciness: grill setup.

Many pork tenderloin recipes call for grilling the meat directly over a hot fire the entire time. The result? A well-browned exterior with a thick band of dry, overcooked meat below its surface—no thanks. A better approach, we've found, is to employ a combination high-low method: High heat provides great browning—which means great flavor—and low heat cooks meat evenly. And recently, we've favored cooking first over low heat followed by searing over high heat. During its initial stay on the cooler side of the grill, the meat's surface warms and dries, making for fast, efficient browning (and therefore precluding overcooking) when it hits the hotter part of the grate. Sure enough, when I gave this approach a try, I produced meat with rosy interiors surrounded by thin, flavorful crusts—at least at the thick ends. Unsurprisingly, the thin, tapered ends of the tenderloins (I was cooking two in order to serve six guests) were terribly overdone.

There was nothing I could do to the grill setup to make the unevenly shaped meat cook evenly, so what about altering the tenderloins themselves? I pounded and

GRILLED GLAZED PORK TENDERLOIN ROAST

portioned untold samples in search of a more uniform shape. Flattening the thicker end of the roast certainly made for more even cooking, but it also turned the cut into what looked like a gigantic, malformed pork chop. Slicing the tenderloin into medallions produced an awkward group of scallop-size pieces that were fussy to grill.

After a long, unsuccessful afternoon, I stood before the last two raw tenderloins on my cutting board. A light bulb went on: Why not tie them together? If I stacked the tenderloins with the thick end of one nestled against the thin end of the other, I'd produce a single, evenly shaped roast. I gave it a shot, fastening together my brined double-wide roast with lengths of kitchen twine and brushing it with oil before heading out to the hot grill. About 35 minutes later, I had a piece of meat that was perfectly cooked from one end to the other. This larger roast took longer to come up to temperature, but the added grill time was a boon to taste: More time over the fire meant more smoky grill flavor.

These successes aside, there was still an obstacle in my way. When I carved my impressive-looking roast, each slice inevitably flopped apart into two pieces. While this wasn't a deal breaker, I was eager to see if I could establish a more permanent bond between the tenderloins.

Trying to get meat to stick together might sound unorthodox, but it's something that happens naturally with ground meat. In sausages, burgers, meatballs, and meatloaf, tiny individual pieces of protein fuse together to form a cohesive whole. I wasn't working with ground meat, but maybe I could use it as inspiration.

It turns out that anytime meat is damaged (such as during grinding, slicing, or even pounding), sticky proteins are released. The proteins' gluey texture is what makes it possible to form a cohesive burger from nothing but ground beef. If salt is added—as it is to make sausage—the proteins become even tackier. When heated, the protein sets into a solid structure, effectively binding the meat together. To see if I could use this information for my tenderloins, I tried roughing up their surfaces in a variety of ways: lightly whacking them with a meat mallet, scraping them with a fork, and rubbing them vigorously with coarse salt. I tested these methods before brining, after brining, and both

before and after brining. Yes, my oddball experiments garnered plenty of strange looks from my colleagues. But I'll keep those skeptical glances in my memory as a point of pride because, in the end, I found my solution.

The key to getting two tenderloins to bind together? A few simple scrapes of a fork along the length of each one before brining, followed by a very thorough drying after brining. The scrapes, acting much like grinding, released plenty of sticky proteins, which the salty brine made even stickier. Finally, thorough drying ensured that moisture wouldn't interfere with this bond during cooking (the sticky mixture continued to exude from the meat even after I blotted off moisture). The technique is simple and, while not perfect (some slices had better cling than others), it provided me with a platter of attractive, mostly intact slices. Hurdle cleared, I turned my attention to flavoring the roast.

I wanted to dress up my beautifully browned pork tenderloin roast, and a bold, burnished glaze seemed like the ideal choice. Most glazes contain sugar, which caramelizes when exposed to heat, deepening flavor. But I wanted to add still more complexity—even meatiness. And I knew how to do it: by including glutamate-rich ingredients that enhance savory flavor. With this in mind, I combined glutamate-rich miso with sugar, mustard, mirin, and ginger. For my next version, I created a sweet and spicy glaze that benefited from the glutamates found in sweet and tangy hoisin sauce. When I tried out these new glazes on the pork, I was surprised by how much more flavor—and yes, meatiness—they contributed. It turns out that pork has a high concentration of nucleotides. When glutamates and nucleotides are combined, these compounds have a synergistic effect that magnifies meaty, savory flavor significantly more than glutamates alone do.

The only thing left was to refine how I applied the glaze. After slowly grilling my roast on the cooler side of the grill, I slid it to the hotter side to brown. I then glazed one side at a time, allowing the glaze to char before repeating the process with the other three sides. I also reserved some glaze to add an extra blast of flavor at the table. Time to get the party started.

—DAN SOUZA, *Cook's Illustrated*

Grilled Glazed Pork Tenderloin Roast

SERVES 6

Since brining is a key step in having the two tenderloins stick together, we don't recommend using enhanced pork in this recipe.

- 2 (1-pound) pork tenderloins, trimmed
- Salt and pepper
- Vegetable oil
- 1 recipe glaze (recipes follow)

1. Lay tenderloins on cutting board, flat side (side opposite where silverskin was) up. Holding thick end of 1 tenderloin with paper towels and using dinner fork, scrape flat side lengthwise from end to end 5 times, until surface is completely covered with shallow grooves. Repeat with second tenderloin. Dissolve 3 tablespoons salt in 1½ quarts cold water in large container. Submerge tenderloins in brine and let stand at room temperature for 1 hour.

2. Remove tenderloins from brine and pat completely dry with paper towels. Lay 1 tenderloin, scraped side up, on cutting board and lay second tenderloin, scraped side down, on top so that thick end of 1 tenderloin matches up with thin end of other. Spray five 14-inch lengths of kitchen twine thoroughly with vegetable oil spray; evenly space twine underneath tenderloins and tie. Brush roast with vegetable oil and season with pepper. Transfer ⅓ cup glaze to bowl for grilling; reserve remaining glaze for serving.

3A. FOR A CHARCOAL GRILL: Open bottom vent completely. Light large chimney starter filled with charcoal briquettes (6 quarts). When top coals are partially covered with ash, pour into steeply banked pile against side of grill. Set cooking grate in place, cover, and open lid vent completely. Heat grill until hot, about 5 minutes.

3B. FOR A GAS GRILL: Turn all burners to high, cover, and heat grill until hot, about 15 minutes. Leave primary burner on high and turn off other burner(s).

4. Clean and oil cooking grate. Place roast on cooler side of grill, cover, and cook until meat registers 115 degrees, 22 to 28 minutes, flipping and rotating halfway through cooking.

5. Slide roast to hotter part of grill and cook until lightly browned on all sides, 4 to 6 minutes. Brush top of roast with about 1 tablespoon glaze and grill, glaze side down, until glaze begins to char, 2 to 3 minutes; repeat glazing and grilling with remaining 3 sides of roast, until meat registers 140 degrees.

6. Transfer roast to carving board, tent loosely with aluminum foil, and let rest for 10 minutes. Carefully remove twine and slice roast into ½-inch-thick slices. Serve with remaining glaze.

NOTES FROM THE TEST KITCHEN

TURNING TWO TENDERLOINS INTO ONE
To get around the usual problems with grilling pork tenderloin, we "fused" two together and cooked them as a single roast.

1. ROUGH UP: Scrape flat sides of each tenderloin with fork until surface is covered with shallow grooves. This releases sticky proteins that will act as "glue."

2. TIE TOGETHER: Arrange tenderloins with scraped sides touching and thick end of one nestled against thin end of other. Tie tenderloins together.

Miso Glaze

MAKES ABOUT ¾ CUP

- 3 tablespoons sake
- 3 tablespoons mirin
- ⅓ cup white miso paste
- ¼ cup sugar
- 2 teaspoons Dijon mustard
- 1 teaspoon rice vinegar
- ¼ teaspoon grated fresh ginger
- ¼ teaspoon toasted sesame oil

Bring sake and mirin to boil in small saucepan over medium heat. Whisk in miso and sugar until smooth, about 30 seconds. Remove pan from heat and continue to whisk until sugar is dissolved, about 1 minute. Whisk in mustard, vinegar, ginger, and sesame oil until smooth.

MAKES ABOUT ¾ CUP

- 1 teaspoon vegetable oil
- 3 garlic cloves, minced
- 1 teaspoon grated fresh ginger
- ½ teaspoon red pepper flakes
- ½ cup hoisin sauce
- 2 tablespoons soy sauce
- 1 tablespoon rice vinegar

Heat oil in small saucepan over medium heat until shimmering. Add garlic, ginger, and pepper flakes; cook until fragrant, about 30 seconds. Whisk in hoisin and soy sauce until smooth. Remove pan from heat and stir in vinegar.

SLOW-COOKER CHINESE BARBECUED PORK

✓ **WHY THIS RECIPE WORKS:** Chinese barbecued pork isn't your standard barbecue: It's typically cooked in the oven with a sweet and savory glaze. We wanted to adapt this versatile recipe for the slow cooker. Although simply throwing the pork and sauce ingredients into the slow cooker was tempting, we found that the rendered fat and juice diluted the sauce. To solve this problem, we opted to use a dry spice rub on the pork; the juices from the meat combined with the spices to create a rich braising liquid. Five-spice powder was an easy shortcut to complex flavor. A final stint under the broiler was necessary to create the bronzed lacquer we were after.

If you've visited a Chinatown, you've seen glossy, red-tinged *char siu*—Chinese barbecued pork—hanging in the windows of takeout shops. This rich, lacquered, sweet and savory pork can be simply sliced and served with white rice and greens or used to fortify wonton soup, fried rice, or stir-fries. Unlike what we typically think of as barbecue, this dish is cooked neither on a grill nor in a smoker: It's cooked and then glazed in an oven. The test kitchen has an oven-to-broiler recipe for Chinese barbecued pork that is out of this world, so I decided to see if I could adapt it for the slow cooker.

Our recipe calls for cutting a boneless pork butt roast—the cut typically used for pulled pork—into strips, trimming some (but not all) of the fat, and marinating the meat in a mixture of sugar, soy sauce, garlic, ginger, and hoisin sauce. The marinated pork then goes through a three-step cooking process: First it's covered with foil and steamed; then it's uncovered and roasted; finally, it's glazed under the broiler on both sides with a sauce of some reserved marinade mixture cooked with ketchup and honey. The finished product is tender and flavorful, with a shiny, slightly charred exterior that tastes even better than it looks. My colleagues refer to it fondly as "meat candy."

Since much of the point of the slow cooker is to make life easier, I was hoping that I could eliminate the marinating step. I'd simply cook the trimmed pork strips with the sauce in the slow cooker. But when I tried it, I was reminded that pork butt has a lot of flavor in part because it has a lot of fat and connective tissue that melt out of the meat as it cooks. By the time the meat was tender, after about 5 hours on low, the sauce had been diluted by the rendered fat and pork juices. Sure, I could run this cooking liquid through a fat separator and then reduce it on the stovetop to use as a glaze when broiling, but I didn't want to work that hard for a slow-cooker recipe.

What about using only dry seasonings in the cooker? I made a Chinese-style rub using powdered garlic, ginger, coriander, star anise, fennel seeds, cinnamon, salt, and pepper; rubbed it on the strips of pork shoulder; arranged them in the slow cooker; and set the switch to "low." The meat rendered the same amount of fat and juices, but they combined with the spices to create a flavorful, more concentrated braising liquid for the meat, which now had deeper, richer flavor (I discarded the liquid when the slow cooking was done). I performed a few more tests and discovered that I could pare down my rub to just three ingredients—salt, pepper, and five-spice powder (the last handily collects five spices in one jar)—without sacrificing complexity.

To put the "char" in char siu and to properly lacquer the pork, I knew I'd have to finish it with sauce under the broiler, as we did in our original recipe. To streamline, though, I hoped that I wouldn't have to cook the sauce before brushing it on for the broiling step. After fiddling with various ratios of ingredients and testing the broiling mechanics, I found that I could use pretty much the same sauce as in our original recipe—without cooking it first—if I moved the oven rack up from the middle to about 4 inches from the broiler.

The stir-together sauce reduced into a sticky, clingy glaze right under the hot broiler. A little water in the pan prevented any sauce that dripped down from burning and smoking up the kitchen. With a slow cooker and this recipe, you're just a few hours away from incredibly tasty Chinese barbecued pork.

—DIANE UNGER, *Cook's Country*

Slow-Cooker Chinese Barbecued Pork

SERVES 8

This recipe is designed for 5½- to 7-quart oval slow cookers. Pork butt roast is often labeled Boston butt in the supermarket. Look for five-spice powder and hoisin sauce in the international aisle at your supermarket.

1½	teaspoons salt
1½	teaspoons five-spice powder
½	teaspoon pepper
1	(5- to 6-pound) boneless pork butt roast, trimmed and sliced crosswise into 1-inch-thick steaks
⅓	cup hoisin sauce
⅓	cup honey
¼	cup sugar
¼	cup soy sauce
¼	cup ketchup
2	tablespoons dry sherry
1	tablespoon toasted sesame oil
1	tablespoon grated fresh ginger
2	garlic cloves, minced

1. Combine salt, ¾ teaspoon five-spice powder, and pepper in bowl. Rub spice mixture all over pork and transfer to slow cooker. Cover and cook on low until pork is just tender, 5 to 6 hours.

2. When pork is nearly done, combine hoisin, honey, sugar, soy sauce, ketchup, sherry, oil, ginger, garlic, and remaining ¾ teaspoon five-spice powder in bowl. Set wire rack inside aluminum foil–lined rimmed baking sheet. Pour 1 cup water into sheet. Adjust oven rack 4 inches from broiler element and heat broiler.

3. Using tongs, transfer pork from slow cooker to prepared wire rack in single layer. Brush pork with one-third of hoisin mixture and broil until lightly caramelized, 5 to 7 minutes. Flip pork, brush with half of remaining hoisin mixture, and broil until lightly caramelized on second side, 5 to 7 minutes. Brush pork with remaining hoisin mixture and broil until deep mahogany and crisp around edges, about 3 minutes. Transfer to carving board and let rest for 10 minutes. Slice crosswise into thin strips. Serve.

STUFFED SPARERIBS

✔ **WHY THIS RECIPE WORKS:** We're used to barbecuing ribs here in the test kitchen, but in some circles, stuffing them like a Thanksgiving turkey is just as popular. We chose St. Louis spareribs for their manageable size and kept the flavors simple with a rub of salt, pepper, and brown sugar. As for the stuffing, bread cubes weren't cohesive and tumbled out of the ribs, but homemade bread crumbs—buttered and toasted to prevent sogginess—were the perfect choice. Tart apples, sweet prunes, and a handful of seasonings rounded out the stuffing. Sandwiched between two racks of ribs tied together with twine, the stuffing absorbed plenty of rich, porky flavor as the meat tenderized in the oven.

In my culinary career, I've stuffed chickens and turkeys. I've stuffed tomatoes and eggplant. I've even stuffed hamburgers and pizza. But spareribs? That was something completely new to me. But as I found out after just 10 minutes in the test kitchen's cookbook library, stuffed spareribs are a tried-and-true American recipe. I discovered a half-dozen such recipes, including ones from *Joy of Cooking*, James Beard, and Betty Crocker—a sure sign that the recipe was once well-known. The recipes all followed the same blueprint: Two racks of ribs (despite "sparerib" in the name, two recipes called for baby backs) are rubbed with spices (often warm spices like cinnamon and nutmeg), tied together around a pile of fruit-and-bread stuffing, and roasted for an hour or two. I chose six recipes that used a variety of stuffings and prepared them in the test kitchen. First, the good news: My tasters and I could tell that stuffed spareribs were a solid concept, as the stuffing readily absorbed the flavorful pork juices. And now the bad: The stuffings were mushy and dense, tasters didn't love the spice rubs, and the ribs were chewy and undercooked.

From these initial tests I learned that spareribs—and not baby backs—were the way to go because they were bigger (and thus held more stuffing) and had more meat. But which kind of spareribs? I pitted "full" spareribs against St. Louis–style ribs, which are trimmed of fat, bone, and meat into an evenly shaped rack. Not surprisingly, we liked the St. Louis–style spareribs because they were easier to eat. As for seasoning the ribs, I decided to keep the rub basic—just salt, pepper, and brown sugar—and make a superflavorful stuffing to compensate. Baking the rib bundles for about 3 hours in a 325-degree oven, instead of the 1½ to 2 hours called for in most recipes, solved the undercooking problem. (I did have to flip the rib bundles halfway through.)

I moved on to the stuffing. Most of the stuffed spareribs recipes I had found used store-bought bread crumbs mixed with sautéed onion and celery, plus apple chunks and/or dried fruit; prunes, dates, dried cranberries, and raisins were all in the mix. In the test kitchen, we usually prefer to make our own crumbs—it's hardly any work, and the flavor and texture are far superior to those of supermarket crumbs. But my homemade crumbs ended up soggy when roasted inside the ribs. I solved that problem by mixing the crumbs with butter and toasting them to golden brown in the oven before folding in the other ingredients. To be thorough, I tried making the stuffing with staled bread cubes (the kind you'd use for poultry stuffing), but the cubes kept falling out of the rib bundle.

We liked the two chopped apples in one of the recipes from my initial tests, so I kept the ingredient—choosing Granny Smiths for their assertive tartness—but doubled the amount for more impact and lost the comparatively bland celery. I tested all manner of dried fruit; in the end, we liked the complexity and richness of prunes. Fresh sage, minced garlic, and ground fennel rounded out the flavors, creating a sweet and savory stuffing that paired beautifully with the pork ribs.

My recipe was in the home stretch, but I wondered if I could skip the tying step and bake the two racks simply draped over a mound of stuffing. No can do: The stuffing burned on the baking sheet without the ribs to insulate it. When I tried moving the ribs to the bottom

and piling the stuffing on top, I couldn't flip the racks for even cooking, and the stuffing didn't absorb much meaty flavor. What I did learn in my testing was that the bundles were the most secure and held more stuffing when the concave (bony) sides faced the stuffing and when they were arranged with one wide end over one narrow end.

I'll forgive you if you think that stuffed spareribs sounds like a loony idea—I felt the same way when I first heard about the dish. But once we gave it a try, the combination of crusty, tender, savory ribs plus sweet-tart apples and earthy prunes won over even the most skeptical tasters. Beard wrote that stuffed spareribs were a "common dish . . . for over a century." Now I know why.

—NICK IVERSON, *Cook's Country*

Stuffed Spareribs

SERVES 6 TO 8

Try to buy racks of ribs of equal size for this recipe, and make sure they're St. Louis–style. If any stuffing falls onto the baking sheet as you tie the racks together or flip them during cooking, stuff the filling back inside the bundle.

- 10 slices hearty white sandwich bread, torn into 1-inch pieces
- 4 tablespoons unsalted butter
  Salt and pepper
- 4 Granny Smith apples, peeled, cored, and cut into ¼-inch pieces
- 1 onion, chopped
- 1 cup pitted prunes, chopped
- 2 tablespoons minced fresh sage
- 5 garlic cloves, minced
- 1 teaspoon ground fennel
- 3 tablespoons packed brown sugar
- 2 (2½- to 3-pound) racks St. Louis–style spareribs, trimmed and membrane removed

1. Adjust oven rack to middle position and heat oven to 325 degrees. Pulse half of bread, 1 tablespoon butter, ½ teaspoon salt, and ¼ teaspoon pepper in food processor until finely ground, 10 to 15 pulses. Transfer to rimmed baking sheet. Repeat with remaining bread,

STUFFED SPARERIBS

1 tablespoon butter, ½ teaspoon salt, and ¼ teaspoon pepper and add to sheet. Bake crumbs until golden brown, 15 to 20 minutes, stirring halfway through baking. Transfer to large bowl; set aside.

2. Meanwhile, melt remaining 2 tablespoons butter in 12-inch skillet over medium heat. Add apples, onion, 1 teaspoon salt, and ½ teaspoon pepper and cook until apples are soft and onion is translucent, 7 to 10 minutes. Add prunes, sage, garlic, and fennel and cook until fragrant, about 1 minute. Stir apple mixture into bread crumbs until well combined.

3. Line rimmed baking sheet with aluminum foil. Combine sugar, 1 tablespoon salt, and 1 tablespoon pepper in bowl. Pat ribs dry with paper towels and rub all over with sugar mixture. Lay five 20-inch-long pieces of kitchen twine about 3 inches apart crosswise on prepared sheet. Lay 1 rib rack, meat side down, across twine. Place stuffing mixture on top of rack and pack to uniform thickness. Place remaining rib rack, meat side up, on top of stuffing, arranging wider end of rack over tapered end of bottom rack to sandwich stuffing. Tie racks together and trim excess twine.

4. Roast ribs until tender and well browned, about 3 hours, flipping bundle halfway through roasting. Transfer ribs to carving board and let rest for 15 minutes. Cut ribs between bones, creating individual stuffed rib portions; discard twine. (Alternatively, discard twine and remove top rack of ribs. Transfer stuffing to platter. Cut ribs in between bones to separate and transfer to platter with stuffing.) Serve.

NOTES FROM THE TEST KITCHEN

STUFFED SPARERIBS? REALLY?

It sounds like an awkward operation, but our technique makes it easy.

Sandwich stuffing between two racks of ribs with bone sides facing each other, and tie with kitchen twine at 3-inch intervals. Make sure to position the racks wide end to tapered end.

SLOW-ROASTED BONE-IN PORK RIB ROAST

✅ **WHY THIS RECIPE WORKS:** Pork rib roast can be an impressive cut when it's done right, so we set out to create a celebration-worthy rib roast with big flavor and tender, moist meat. We cured the pork overnight with a salt and brown sugar rub, which had the double benefit of seasoning the meat and promoting flavorful browning, allowing us to skip tedious searing. Removing the bones before seasoning ensured that the meat was flavorful throughout, and tying the meat back onto the bones before roasting protected it from overcooking. Using a low oven ensured that the roast was evenly cooked from edge to center, and a final stint under the broiler crisped the fat nicely. To dress it up for a holiday feast, we paired the pork with an elegant and concentrated port wine and dried cherry beurre rouge sauce.

I have never understood why, aside from the ubiquitous Easter ham, pork isn't served more often at big-deal occasions. A center-cut pork rib roast, in particular, has a lot of potential. Its cylindrical, uniform loin muscle and long bones make this cut so appealing for serving that I've known butchers to call it the "pork equivalent of prime rib." Treated in a way that makes up for its slight shortcomings in the flavor department, it can be truly impressive: moist, tender, and full of rich, meaty taste. All this—and for far less money than a prime rib costs. This year, I was intent on featuring the cut as the focal point of my holiday spread.

To get my bearings, I cooked an initial roast following a standard approach: I sprinkled the meat with salt and pepper and seared it on all sides in a hot skillet. Next I placed the roast on a wire rack set in a baking sheet (to prevent the meat from steaming in its juices) and transferred it to a 375-degree oven. After about 90 minutes, it reached 145 degrees (the ideal doneness temperature for pork). I let the roast rest for 30 minutes and then sliced it up for evaluation. Not too surprisingly, tasters found its flavor so-so.

Pretreating the meat before cooking was definitely in order. Pork almost always benefits from the application of salt, whether the meat is soaked in a saltwater solution or rubbed with a coating of salt and left to sit in the refrigerator. Both techniques season the meat, which boosts flavor, and draw moisture into the flesh, helping keep it juicy.

Indeed, when I put the ideas into action, a simple salt brine produced a more flavorful roast that was very moist—but almost to a fault: It had a wet, almost spongy consistency, especially toward the exterior. The salt rub, which I left on for at least 6 hours, was far superior. It helped the meat hold on to just the right amount of moisture.

For the next go-round, I added brown sugar to the salt rub, thinking that its mild molasses notes would pair nicely with the pork. (I also sprinkled black pepper onto the meat right before roasting.) With sugar in the mix, the meat took on not just deeper flavor but also a gorgeous mahogany color, thanks to the Maillard reaction. In fact, the method worked so beautifully that I made a bold decision: I would skip the tedious task of searing the meat before roasting. Happily, tasters didn't miss the searing since the meat browned nicely in the oven. The only problem was that the oven wasn't hot enough to render the dense fat cap. But I had an easy fix for that: I simply scored deep crosshatch marks into the fat with a sharp knife to help it melt and baste the meat during roasting.

And yet in spite of these efforts, my roast wasn't quite centerpiece-worthy. Salting had improved its texture considerably, but the meat still had a tendency to over-cook and dry out toward the exterior. What's more, the meat closest to the bones wasn't nearly as well seasoned as the rest of the roast.

It seemed likely that bones were preventing the salt and sugar from penetrating into the meat. For my next test, I gave a boneless rib roast the usual application of salt and sugar. As I had expected, this meat was far better seasoned than a bone-in roast treated the same way, but I could hardly call the result an improvement: Without the bones to insulate the meat, much of the roast ended up dry.

I scrapped the boneless roast idea, racking my brain for other ways to improve a bone-in roast. Then it hit me: If this roast really was the pork equivalent of prime rib, why not cook it like prime rib? In a past test kitchen recipe for prime rib, we removed the bones from the beef in order to salt the meat on all sides, and then we nestled the meat back up against the bones and secured it with kitchen twine before transferring the assembly to the oven for roasting. I applied this idea to my pork roast and it worked perfectly: The meat was now seasoned throughout, and since heat travels more slowly through bone than through flesh, the bones helped keep the center of the roast moist. Another plus was that the finished roast, free of bones, was even easier to carve.

Thinking of my pork roast as prime rib also gave me a potential solution to the problem of an overcooked exterior: I could use a low-and-slow approach (our prime rib cooks at 200 degrees). In general, the lower the oven temperature and the longer the cooking time the more evenly cooked the meat will be. Here's why: With traditional high-heat cooking, the final temperature of the center of the roast (145 degrees for pork) will be a few hundred degrees lower than the oven temperature. This means that by the time the core of the roast is properly cooked, the outermost layers are well past the ideal temperature. Bring the oven temperature closer to the desired internal temperature and this differential mostly goes away.

To put the theory into practice, I cooked a series of roasts at temperatures from 200 to 375 degrees. Sure enough, the roasts cooked at the low end of the range were the most evenly cooked. But because pork is cooked to a higher final temperature than beef (145 versus 125), the pork cooked in a 200-degree oven required a whopping 6 hours. I knew that no one would want to wait that long. Thankfully, the 250-degree-oven roast clocked in at a more reasonable 3½ hours and was nearly as evenly cooked. As a final measure, I crisped up the fat by blasting the roast under the broiler for a couple of minutes just prior to serving.

With juicy, well-seasoned meat ready for the table, all that remained was to create an elegant sauce. In my mind, nothing is more luxurious than a classic French beurre rouge, a reduction of red wine and wine vinegar emulsified with butter. Pork loin is relatively lean, so I knew that it would benefit from this rich, concentrated sauce. To give the mixture real character, I traded the red wine for tawny port and the wine vinegar for balsamic. I also incorporated cream, minced shallots, fresh thyme, and a couple of handfuls of plump dried cherries.

This combination was a terrific match with my pork: The complex flavor with echoes of fruit and herbs balanced beautifully with the meaty roast. This was a dish that I'd be proud to serve at any special occasion. And only I would need to know how dead simple it was to prepare.

—ANDREW JANJIGIAN, *Cook's Illustrated*

Slow-Roasted Bone-In Pork Rib Roast

SERVES 6 TO 8

This recipe requires refrigerating the salted meat for at least 6 hours before cooking. For easier carving, ask the butcher to remove the chine bone. Monitoring the roast with an oven probe thermometer is best. If you use an instant-read thermometer, open the oven door as infrequently as possible and remove the roast from the oven while taking its temperature. The sauce may be prepared in advance or while the roast rests in step 3.

    1 (4- to 5-pound) center-cut bone-in pork rib roast,
       chine bone removed
    2 tablespoons packed dark brown sugar
    1 tablespoon kosher salt
    1½ teaspoons pepper
    1 recipe sauce (recipe follows)

1. Using sharp knife, remove roast from bones, running knife down length of bones and following contours as closely as possible. Reserve bones. Combine sugar and salt in small bowl. Pat roast dry with paper towels. If necessary, trim thick spots of surface fat layer to about ¼-inch thickness. Using sharp knife, cut slits, spaced 1 inch apart and in crosshatch pattern, in surface fat layer, being careful not to cut into meat. Rub roast evenly with sugar mixture. Wrap roast and ribs in plastic wrap and refrigerate for at least 6 hours or up to 24 hours.

2. Adjust oven rack to lower-middle position and heat oven to 250 degrees. Sprinkle roast evenly with pepper. Place roast back on ribs so bones fit where they were cut; tie roast to bones with lengths of kitchen twine between ribs. Transfer roast, fat side up, to wire rack set in rimmed baking sheet. Roast until meat registers 145 degrees, 3 to 4 hours.

BUTCHERING PORK "PRIME RIB"

Remove the rib bones from the pork so that it can be seasoned on all sides, but don't discard them: Since bone is a poor conductor of heat, tie them back onto the roast to guard against overcooking.

1. Using sharp knife, remove roast from bones, running knife down length of bones and closely following contours.

2. Trim surface fat to ¼ inch and score with crosshatch slits; rub roast with sugar mixture and refrigerate.

3. Sprinkle roast with pepper, then place roast back on ribs; using kitchen twine, tie roast to bones between ribs.

WHY ADD CREAM TO A BUTTER SAUCE?

To dress up our pork, we turned to a classic French preparation: beurre rouge. The beauty of this sauce, which translates as "red butter," is that at its most basic it requires just two components: butter and an acidic liquid. (Red wine and red wine vinegar for beurre rouge are traditional.) The preparation is equally simple: Just whisk cold butter into the reduced acidic liquid.

The problem is that butter sauces don't always stay emulsified. That's because the butter is highly temperature sensitive: If the sauce gets too hot (above 135 degrees), the butter will "break." If it gets too cold (below 85 degrees), the butterfat solidifies and forms crystals that clump together and separate when the sauce is reheated.

The key to foolproofing a butter sauce is thus stabilizing the butterfat so that it doesn't separate. We do this by whisking in the butter a little bit at a time, which keeps the temperature of the sauce relatively stable. Even more important, we also add cream. Cream surrounds and stabilizes the butterfat droplets so that they don't separate from the emulsion. Cream is such an effective stabilizer that our sauce can be made ahead, chilled, and gently reheated before serving.

3. Remove roast from oven (leave roast on sheet), tent loosely with aluminum foil, and let rest for 30 minutes.

4. Adjust oven rack 8 inches from broiler element and heat broiler. Return roast to oven and broil until top of roast is well browned and crisp, 2 to 6 minutes.

5. Transfer roast to carving board; cut twine and remove meat from ribs. Slice meat into ¾-inch-thick slices and serve, passing sauce separately.

Port Wine–Cherry Sauce

MAKES ABOUT 1¾ CUPS

2	cups tawny port
1	cup dried cherries
½	cup balsamic vinegar
4	sprigs fresh thyme, plus 2 teaspoons minced
2	shallots, minced
¼	cup heavy cream
16	tablespoons unsalted butter, cut into ½-inch pieces and chilled
1	teaspoon salt
½	teaspoon pepper

1. Combine port and cherries in bowl and microwave until steaming, 1 to 2 minutes. Cover and let stand until plump, about 10 minutes. Strain port through fine-mesh strainer into medium saucepan, reserving cherries.

2. Add vinegar, thyme sprigs, and shallots to port and bring to boil over high heat. Reduce heat to medium-high and reduce mixture until it measures ¾ cup, 14 to 16 minutes. Add cream and reduce again to ¾ cup, about 5 minutes. Discard thyme sprigs. Off heat, whisk in butter, few pieces at a time, until fully incorporated. Stir in cherries, minced thyme, salt, and pepper. Cover pan and hold, off heat, until serving. Alternatively, let sauce cool completely and refrigerate for up to 2 days. Reheat in small saucepan over medium-low heat, stirring frequently, until warm.

VARIATIONS

Cider–Golden Raisin Sauce

Substitute 2 cups apple cider for port and 1 cup golden raisins for cherries. In step 2, subsitute ½ cup cider vinegar for balsamic. Stir in 2 teaspoons cider vinegar and 1 tablespoon Calvados with the raisins and minced thyme.

Orange-Cranberry Sauce

Subsitute 2 cups white wine for port and 1 cup dried cranberries for cherries. In step 2, substitute ½ cup orange juice for balsamic and 4 fresh sage leaves for thyme sprigs. Omit minced thyme and stir in 1 tablespoon orange zest, 1 tablespoon Grand Marnier, and 2 teaspoons minced fresh sage with the cranberries.

PORK PERNIL

✓ **WHY THIS RECIPE WORKS:** Famous for its crispy skin, this Puerto Rican dish of long-cooked pork roast should result in flavorful meat along with the trademark crisp crust. We rubbed a picnic shoulder with a salty sofrito (a paste of aromatics and herbs) the day before roasting, which kept the meat moist and packed a flavor punch. We then roasted the pork skin-side down, covered, which helped transform tough collagen into gelatin. Next, we removed the foil cover to ensure that our pork didn't taste steamed, and then turned the roast skin side up on a V-rack to dry the skin to prepare it for the last step—a quick roast at very high heat.

Pernil is a much-loved Puerto Rican preparation of long-cooked, heavily seasoned pork roast that is chopped or shredded; it's often served at the holidays or at parties both on the island and in Puerto Rican communities in the States. As with American barbecue, aficionados love to debate the proper cut (fresh ham or picnic shoulder?), the proper seasonings (dry spices, a wet marinade, or a paste of aromatics and herbs called a *sofrito*?), and the best cooking method. I was easily sold on pernil—even before I heard about the crispy skin. For devotees, munching away on bits of crunchy, burnished skin glossed with salty, buttery fat is the kind of ecstatic experience that seems too good to be legal. I jumped at the chance to develop my own recipe for this classic dish.

Picnic shoulder is more widely available than fresh ham, so I'd use a bone-in, skin-on picnic shoulder. I collected and prepared six pernil recipes that represented different takes on the other variables. The good news? Every recipe that got the meat to 200 degrees yielded tender, flavorful meat. The bad? No matter the cooking time, oven temperature, or covering-uncovering regimen, crackling, crisp brown skin eluded me; the skin was either pale and rubbery or else dark and hard as ebony.

My plan was to fine-tune the seasonings and then tackle the issue of the skin. Bottled spice blends like Goya Sazón, which is common in modern pernil recipes, were too heavy on dehydrated onion and dusty spices. My tasters much preferred pork seasoned with a sofrito. After a bit of tinkering, I landed on a knockout sofrito by grinding onion, garlic, cilantro, cumin, dried oregano, kosher salt, and pepper in the food processor. By making the sofrito salty and rubbing it into the meat 12 to 24 hours before roasting, the salt had a chance to penetrate the pork and help keep it moist (as with a brine) when cooked.

I turned to the skin. I quickly learned that pork skin is finicky: It gets hard and dark if you cook it in a dry environment and pale and rubbery when cooked in a covered, moist environment. I hoped to split the difference with a hybrid method, cooking it covered for half of the time and uncovered for the remainder. I rubbed a 7-pound shoulder with the sofrito; let it sit overnight; and roasted it, skin side up, at 375 degrees, covered tightly with foil, for 3 hours. Then I uncovered it and continued to cook it until the meat reached 200 degrees, which took about 3 hours more. The juices started to burn off and smoke, so I added some water to the pan midway through cooking. This didn't work: In the end, the skin was too dark and too leathery to chew. The added water had created steam that prevented the skin from crisping. But without the water, the pernil smoked out the kitchen.

I continued to test different roasting variables over the course of several weeks; some tests were abject failures, while others offered glimpses of techniques that I thought might help me. As I tested and tested, the ideal method slowly took shape, and here is where I landed: First, for perfectly cooked pork, I roasted it, covered, skin side down for 90 minutes at 450 degrees. I made sure there was plenty of water in the pan to create lots of steam that would jump start the transformation of the roast's tough collagen into tender gelatin. Next I removed the foil and turned down the oven to 375 degrees for a good 2½ hours of roasting (if the roast was covered during this period, the meat would taste steamed). The prolonged braising of the skin—a technique that I borrowed from recipes for *chicharrón*

(deep-fried pork skin)—helped break down the skin's rubbery connective tissue so that it would hopefully crisp up later (with dry heat) without hardening.

At this point I elevated the roast, skin side up, on a V-rack and roasted it for another hour so that the now-softened skin could dry out while the meat cooked to 195 degrees, just shy of done. Finally, I moved the pork—still on the V-rack—to a clean, foil-lined baking sheet, turned up the oven to 500, and high-roasted for 15 to 30 minutes, until the skin was well-browned and perfectly crisp—finally. Letting the roast rest for 30 minutes before serving allowed the juices to redistribute and resulted in moist meat throughout. Normally we'd tent the meat with foil to keep it warm, but I found that the foil trapped steam that turned the crispy skin soggy.

I caught more than one taster crunching away at a big, crispy slab of mahogany pork skin, transfixed by the combination of potent seasoning, rich fat, and addictive crunch. But I had one last order of business: a quick sauce to dress the meat after I chopped it. Combining the pan drippings with lime juice, lime zest, and chopped cilantro couldn't be simpler, and the bright citrusy punch was an ideal foil for the rich and salty meat. After weeks of work—and more than 40 roasts—I finally had the enormously flavorful, crisp-skinned pernil I had set out to find.

—SARAH GABRIEL, *Cook's Country*

Pork Pernil

SERVES 8 TO 10

Depending on their size, you may need two bunches of cilantro. Crimp the foil tightly over the edges of the roasting pan in step 2 to minimize evaporation. Make sure to spray the V-rack in step 3.

1½ **cups chopped fresh cilantro leaves and stems**
1 **onion, chopped coarse**
¼ **cup kosher salt**
¼ **cup olive oil**
10 **garlic cloves, peeled**
2 **tablespoons pepper**
1 **tablespoon dried oregano**
1 **tablespoon ground cumin**
1 **(7-pound) bone-in pork picnic shoulder**
1 **tablespoon grated lime zest plus ⅓ cup juice (3 limes)**

1. Pulse 1 cup cilantro, onion, salt, oil, garlic, pepper, oregano, and cumin in food processor until finely ground, about 15 pulses, scraping down sides of bowl as needed. Pat pork dry with paper towels and rub sofrito all over. Wrap pork in plastic wrap and refrigerate for at least 12 hours or up to 24 hours.

2. Adjust oven rack to lower-middle position and heat oven to 450 degrees. Pour 8 cups water in large roasting pan. Unwrap pork and place skin side down in pan. Cover pan tightly with aluminum foil and roast for 90 minutes. Remove foil, reduce oven temperature to 375 degrees, and continue to roast for 2½ hours.

3. Remove pan from oven. Spray V-rack with vegetable oil spray. Gently slide metal spatula under pork to release skin from pan. Using folded dish towels, grasp ends of pork and transfer to V-rack, skin side up. Wipe skin dry with paper towels. Place V-rack with pork in roasting pan. If pan looks dry, add 1 cup water. Return to oven and roast until pork registers 195 degrees, about 1 hour. (Add water as needed to keep bottom of pan from drying out.)

4. Line rimmed baking sheet with foil. Remove pan from oven. Transfer V-rack and pork to prepared sheet and return to oven. Immediately increase oven temperature to 500 degrees. Cook until pork skin is well browned and crisp (when tapped lightly with tongs, skin will sound hollow), 15 to 30 minutes, rotating sheet halfway through cooking. Transfer pork to carving board and let rest for 30 minutes.

5. Meanwhile, pour juices from pan into fat separator. Let liquid settle for 5 minutes, then pour off 1 cup defatted juices into large bowl. (If juices measure less than 1 cup, make up difference with water.) Whisk remaining ½ cup cilantro and lime zest and juice into bowl.

6. Remove crispy skin from pork in 1 large piece. Coarsely chop skin into bite-size pieces and set aside.

NOTES FROM THE TEST KITCHEN

HOW TO COOK PERNIL

We start cooking the roast skin side down in a roasting pan, covered and with some water, to render the fat and soften the skin. Then we flip the roast skin side up and elevate it on a V-rack to finish cooking and crisp the flavorful skin.

Trim and discard excess fat from pork. Remove pork from bone and chop coarse. Transfer pork to bowl with cilantro-lime sauce and toss to combine. Serve pork, with crispy skin on side.

SLOW-ROASTED FRESH HAM

✔ **WHY THIS RECIPE WORKS:** Fresh ham is a meaty, uncured, unsmoked cut which turns tender and flavorful with slow-roasting. We wanted to figure out a foolproof way to cook the oddly shaped, thick-skinned shank-end ham. Removing the skin allowed the fat underneath to render, adding rich flavor to the meat. Cooking the ham in an oven bag kept in moisture for the necessary long cooking time. A simple glaze broiled on before serving made for a flavorful, impressive finish.

Quick: What color is ham? It's pink, right? Well, mostly. All cured ham is indeed pink, but there's another ham—fresh ham—that is uncured, unsmoked, and, when cooked, as pale as goose down. Fresh ham starts with the same cut as cured ham—the rear leg of the hog—so it's basically just a big, bone-in, skin-on pork roast. I decided that a fresh ham would be just the thing for my Easter table this year.

As I began cooking my way through recipes, my tasters were impressed by the tremendous meaty flavor of this cut. Every recipe I found called for shank-end hams, which are easier to carve than sirloin-end hams. But the problems with cooking shank-end hams quickly became evident. First, these hams are big—usually between 8 and 10 pounds—so it's hard to season the interior, especially with a thick, tough layer of skin covering much of the meat. Second, shank-end fresh hams are a strange, uneven shape—one taster thought that they looked like ski boots—so it's difficult to get them to cook evenly. That fresh hams are made up of different muscles (and lots of fat) that cook at different rates only compounds the problem. But the flavor payoff was so big that I was determined to figure out a foolproof way to cook fresh ham.

My first task was to establish the best way to season the ham. I tried brining it for a few days in a large plastic bucket. While the method did add seasoning and help keep the meat moist, the bucket took up a

SLOW-ROASTED FRESH HAM

lot of room—fine if you have a walk-in refrigerator as we do here in the test kitchen but not so fine for the home cook. Rubbing the roast with a salt mixture was a better approach: There's no bucket or sloshing brine, and—as long as you let the rubbed roast sit for at least 12 hours—the seasoning penetrates and, as with brining, helps the meat retain moisture during cooking. After several tests, I ended up using a mixture of kosher salt, brown sugar, fresh rosemary, and fresh thyme. To get the seasonings even deeper into the blocky ham, I cut a large pocket in the meaty end and rubbed the seasoning right into it. I had a good start, but I still needed to figure out how to cook the ham more evenly.

Most recipes agreed on a roasting temperature of around 325 degrees. Since these hams are between 8 and 10 pounds, a relatively low oven is necessary to cook them through without dehydrating or, worse, burning the exterior. I tried roasting the ham in all sorts of configurations: resting it on its flat bottom versus on its side; with water in the pan versus without; elevated versus simply sitting in the pan. I conducted these tests over the course of a week, and nothing was working: Most of the hams had some nicely cooked meat but also some that was over- or underdone. Most troublesome: I couldn't get the skin to render in the time required to cook the rest of the roast.

After more frustration than I care to admit, I made two decisions that saved this recipe (and my sanity): First, I removed the skin from the ham before cooking, leaving about ½ inch of fat (which I crosshatched so that it would render more efficiently) to add flavor to the ham. And second, I took a cue from some of the test kitchen's recipes for cured ham and cooked the fresh ham in an oven bag, elevated on a rack, until the meat reached 160 degrees. That took between 3½ and 5 hours, depending on the size of the ham. Then I let the ham rest, right in the bag, for an hour so that it could slowly finish cooking in the residual heat to perfect tenderness. Why do oven bags work? They create a moist environment that conducts heat more effectively than a dry oven does, so the ham reaches the cooking temperature more quickly and remains there longer. This helps break down fat and connective tissue into gelatin more efficiently, and gelatin helps keep meat moist. To get the ham to cook more evenly still, I tied kitchen twine around the widest part, forcing the ham into a more streamlined, regular shape.

All that was left was to develop a quick glaze that I could broil on the ham before serving. After I tried several combinations, my tasters liked a simple mixture of maple syrup, molasses, soy sauce, Dijon, and ground black pepper—and I liked that this glaze was an easy dump-and-stir affair.

Now that I had perfected the recipe in the test kitchen, I was excited to make it for my family. Once they got over their surprise that this "ham" was actually a roast, they were astonished at how good it tasted.

—DIANE UNGER, *Cook's Country*

Slow-Roasted Fresh Ham

SERVES 12 TO 14

Use a turkey-size oven bag for this recipe.

- 1 (8- to 10-pound) bone-in, shank-end fresh ham
- ⅓ cup packed brown sugar
- ⅓ cup kosher salt
- 3 tablespoons minced fresh rosemary
- 1 tablespoon minced fresh thyme
- 1 large oven bag
- 2 tablespoons maple syrup
- 2 tablespoons molasses
- 1 tablespoon soy sauce
- 1 tablespoon Dijon mustard
- 1 teaspoon pepper

1. Place ham flat side down on cutting board. Using sharp knife, remove skin, leaving ½- to ¼-inch layer of fat intact. Cut 1-inch diagonal crosshatch pattern in fat, being careful not to cut into meat. Place ham on its side. Cut one 4-inch horizontal pocket about 2 inches deep in center of flat side of ham, being careful not to poke through opposite side.

2. Combine sugar, salt, rosemary, and thyme in bowl. Rub half of sugar mixture in ham pocket. Tie 1 piece of kitchen twine tightly around base of ham. Rub exterior of ham with remaining sugar mixture. Wrap ham tightly in plastic wrap and refrigerate for at least 12 hours or up to 24 hours.

3. Adjust oven rack to lowest position and heat oven to 325 degrees. Set V-rack in large roasting pan. Unwrap ham and place in oven bag flat side down. Tie top of oven bag closed with kitchen twine. Place ham, flat side down, on V-rack and cut ½-inch slit in top of oven bag. Roast until thermometer inserted in center of ham, close to but not touching bone, registers 160 degrees, 3½ to 5 hours. Remove ham from oven and let rest in oven bag on V-rack for 1 hour. Heat oven to 450 degrees.

4. Whisk maple syrup, molasses, soy sauce, mustard, and pepper together in bowl. Cut off top of oven bag and push down with tongs, allowing accumulated juices to spill into roasting pan; discard oven bag. Leave ham sitting flat side down on V-rack.

5. Brush ham with half of glaze and roast for 10 minutes. Brush ham with remaining glaze, rotate pan, and roast until deep amber color, about 10 minutes longer. Move ham to carving board, flat side down, and let rest for 20 minutes. Pour pan juices into fat separator. Carve ham into ¼-inch-thick slices, arrange on platter, and moisten lightly with defatted pan juices. Serve, passing remaining pan juices separately.

NOTES FROM THE TEST KITCHEN

HOW TO SEASON DEEPLY AND COOK EVENLY
We found two tricks for deep seasoning and even cooking of a fresh ham.

1. Cut pocket in meaty end and rub ham all over (including in pocket) with seasoning mixture.

2. Tie twine around base to create more streamlined shape so ham cooks more evenly.

FRESH HAM
Fresh ham is a raw ham (the rear leg of the hog) that isn't cured, smoked, or aged. Basically, it's a big pork roast.

TOURTIÈRE

✓ WHY THIS RECIPE WORKS: This hearty French Canadian pork pie is traditionally served on Christmas Eve. The warm-spiced flavor profile had undeniable appeal, so we set out to create a foolproof recipe for this comforting holiday dish. Although some recipes included multiple meats, our tasters preferred pie made with just pork. A baking soda–salt solution mixed into the pork before cooking kept the meat moist. Grated potatoes proved a good binder for our filling, and a variety of warm spices, including cloves, allspice, cinnamon, and nutmeg provided deep background flavor. A simple pie crust made with sour cream and an egg gave us the perfect case for our rich filling.

Tourtière is a spiced pork pie that French Canadians eat at Christmas as part of a post–midnight mass feast. It's not known how tourtière made its way across the border, but a hearty pie of warm-spiced pork in buttery, flaky pastry is a Christmas dinner that everyone can get behind.

After a bit of recipe research, I began to understand the differences in style and technique that would set the parameters for my first few batches. Tourtière is always a double-crust pie flavored with warm spices, but many of the other details were up for debate: Should I use potato? If yes, should I dice or mash it? Did I need a starch to bind the filling? Should I use pork alone or combine it with beef, or veal? Heck, there were recipes for tourtière made with everything from moose meat to pigeon. The crust options ranged nearly as widely. The moose meat and game birds were out of the question, but the only way to settle the remaining debates was to eat some pie.

After we had worked our way through a tasting of six different pies, I had a good idea about how to proceed: For the filling, pork's mild sweetness edged out the combinations of meats, plus one meat was easier. But the fillings with pork were a little dry and crumbly; obviously, I'd need to fix that. Sautéed onion and garlic were easily voted in, while tomatoes were just as easily voted out. We found cinnamon, allspice, and nutmeg pleasantly warm, musky, and complex, and a pie that included 2 cups of mashed potato held together best.

After a few tries incorporating these choices, I thought that I had the flavor of the filling pretty well calibrated. I sautéed two chopped onions in butter, stirred in the spices, and then added the meat. I cooked the mixture until the pork had lost its pinkness, at which point I stirred in 2 cups of mashed potato. I let the mixture cool since I had found that warm filling makes the crust greasy. I lined a pie plate with our favorite store-bought crust, loaded it with the cooled filling, crimped on the top crust, and baked the pie on the lowest oven rack to get good browning on the bottom crust.

When it was done, I rounded up some tasters, including Gilles, our television crew's sound engineer—he's a Quebec native and Rhode Island resident who grew up with the dish. The verdict? The spice was almost right but needed a little more punch, the filling was too potato-y, and, as in the earlier versions, the meat had cooked—or rather overcooked—into tough, rubbery pellets. Clearly I still had some work to do.

The meat was both the main ingredient and the main problem, so I started there. None of the recipes that I'd found put raw meat in the pastry crust, and when I tried it as a solution to overcooking, I could see why: The meat baked into a solid slab, like a meatloaf in a pastry shell, which was definitely not true to the dish. For safety, I had to cook the meat completely before letting it cool and putting it in the pie, and then I had to bake the pie long enough to cook the crust, so less cooking wasn't an option. What I needed was a way to tenderize the meat despite all the cooking—and cooking at the relatively high temperature needed to brown a crust at that.

Luckily, this isn't the first time that we've seen this problem in the test kitchen: In previous dishes, we've used baking soda to tenderize sliced or ground meat. Cribbing from one of those recipes, I dissolved ¾ teaspoon of baking soda and some salt in a couple of tablespoons of water, and then I mixed the solution with the ground pork and let it sit for about 20 minutes. I cooked the filling and gave it a taste—so far so good. But would it survive being baked into the pie? It did. Unfortunately, though, now that the meat was tender, the mashed potato made the whole assemblage mushy.

Some of the first pies that I had baked used diced potato; one used grated. I'd gone with mashed because they bound the crumbly meat, but now that the meat was moist and tender, it was worth retesting the other options. I made three more pies, one each with mashed, diced, and grated potato. At the same time, I cut down on the amount of potato that I'd been using. I cooked both the diced and the grated potato in chicken broth until tender and then added the ground raw meat

right to the mixture; since I'd worked so hard to avoid overcooking it, I didn't brown it first.

The mashed potato was again pasty. And Gilles, the Quebecois audio engineer, frowned disapprovingly at the prominent chunks of diced potato. But the shreds of grated potato worked beautifully, keeping the meat in place as I sliced. Also, the grated potato had sloughed off enough starch during cooking to thicken the broth and the meat's juices, giving the impression that the pie was moistened with a bit of gravy. At Gilles's urging, I added a pinch of ground cloves. The filling had just the right texture and warm, spicy flavor; it was time to tackle the crust.

Luckily, I had a recipe in mind. A couple of years back, while working on our recipe for Moravian Chicken Pie, a colleague developed a tender, flaky, and easy to handle pie dough with sour cream and egg that I suspected might be exactly the thing for my tourtière.

It was. I put together one last pie using that dough recipe, and it drew raves from everybody, Canadian and otherwise. The tourtière was warming, stick-to-your-ribs food so delicious and surprising that I'm struggling for words to adequately capture it (maybe the French have some?). Within hours, people around the office who had never said a word about their heritage were chewing my ear off about French Canadian grandmothers. I figured that it was safe to put away my rolling pin and call it a day.

—SARAH GABRIEL, *Cook's Country*

Tourtière

SERVES 8

Both the pie dough and the filling need to chill for an hour or more before the pie can be assembled and baked. If time is short, use store-bought dough. Shred the potatoes on the large holes of a box grater just before cooking. Don't soak the shreds in water or their starch will wash away and the filling won't thicken properly. To cool the filling quickly, chill it in a large baking dish. Eat the pie when it's just slightly warm.

FILLING

　　Salt and pepper
¾　teaspoon baking soda
2　tablespoons water
2　pounds ground pork
2　tablespoons unsalted butter

2 onions, chopped fine

3 garlic cloves, minced

1 teaspoon minced fresh thyme

¼ teaspoon ground allspice

¼ teaspoon ground cinnamon

¼ teaspoon ground nutmeg

Pinch ground cloves

3 cups chicken broth

12 ounces russet potatoes, peeled and shredded

CRUST

½ cup sour cream, chilled

1 large egg, lightly beaten

2½ cups (12½ ounces) all-purpose flour

½ teaspoon salt

12 tablespoons unsalted butter, cut into ½-inch
pieces and chilled

1 large egg yolk lightly beaten with 2 tablespoons water

1. FOR THE FILLING: Dissolve 1¼ teaspoons salt and baking soda in water in medium bowl. Add pork and knead with your hands until thoroughly combined. Set aside until needed, at least 20 minutes.

2. Meanwhile, melt butter in Dutch oven over medium-high heat. Add onions and ¼ teaspoon salt and cook, stirring occasionally, until browned, 7 to 9 minutes. Add garlic, thyme, allspice, cinnamon, nutmeg, cloves, and 1 teaspoon pepper and cook until fragrant, about 1 minute. Add broth and potatoes, scraping up any browned bits, and bring to boil. Reduce heat to medium and simmer, stirring often, until potatoes are tender and rubber spatula leaves trail when dragged across bottom of pot, 15 to 20 minutes.

3. Add pork to pot, breaking up pieces with spoon, and cook until no longer pink, about 10 minutes. Transfer filling to 13 by 9-inch baking dish and refrigerate, uncovered, stirring occasionally, until completely cool, about 1 hour. (Cooled filling can be refrigerated, covered, for up to 24 hours before assembling pie.)

4. FOR THE CRUST: Combine sour cream and egg in bowl. Process flour and salt in food processor until combined, about 3 seconds. Add butter and pulse until only pea-size pieces remain, about 10 pulses. Add half of sour cream mixture and pulse until combined, about 5 pulses. Add remaining sour cream mixture and pulse until dough begins to form, about 10 pulses.

5. Transfer mixture to lightly floured counter and knead briefly until dough comes together. Divide dough

in half and form each half into 6-inch disk. Wrap disks tightly in plastic wrap and refrigerate for 1 hour. Let chilled dough sit on counter to soften slightly, about 10 minutes, before rolling.

6. Adjust oven rack to lowest position and heat oven to 450 degrees. Roll 1 disk of dough into 12-inch circle on lightly floured counter. Loosely roll dough around rolling pin and gently unroll it onto 9-inch pie plate, letting excess dough hang over edge. Ease dough into plate by gently lifting edge of dough with your hand while pressing into plate bottom with your other hand. Wrap dough-lined pie plate loosely in plastic and refrigerate until dough is firm, about 30 minutes. Trim overhang to ½ inch beyond lip of pie plate.

7. Pour filling into dough-lined pie plate. Roll other disk of dough into 12-inch circle on lightly floured counter. Loosely roll dough around rolling pin and gently unroll it onto filling. Trim overhang to ½ inch beyond lip of pie plate. Pinch edges of top and bottom crusts firmly together. Tuck overhang under itself; folded edge should be flush with edge of pie plate. Crimp dough evenly around edge of pie plate using your fingers. (If dough gets too soft to work with, refrigerate pie for 10 minutes, then continue.)

8. Cut four 1-inch slits in top of dough. Brush surface with egg wash. Bake until edges are light brown, about 15 minutes. Reduce oven temperature to 375 degrees and continue to bake until crust is deep golden brown and liquid bubbles up through vents, 15 to 20 minutes longer. Let pie cool on wire rack for 2 hours before serving.

TO MAKE AHEAD: Wrapped dough can be refrigerated for up to 2 days or frozen for up to 1 month. If frozen, let dough thaw completely on counter before rolling. Assembled pie (without egg wash) can be refrigerated for up to 24 hours before brushing with egg wash and baking.

NOTES FROM THE TEST KITCHEN

NOT JUST FOR BAKING
Most of the time baking soda lightens cakes, cookies, and pancakes, ensuring that they rise. It has a different function for our *tourtière*: We mix the ground raw pork with a little water, salt, and baking soda to keep the meat tender despite relatively long cooking.

PERFECT POACHED CHICKEN BREASTS

✓ **WHY THIS RECIPE WORKS:** Poaching can be a perfect way to gently cook delicate chicken breasts, but the standard approach can be fussy and it offers little in the way of flavor or pizzazz. To up the flavor ante, we added salt, soy sauce, garlic, and a small amount of sugar to the poaching liquid for meaty, rich-tasting chicken. We found that our salty poaching liquid could double as a quick brine, simplifying the recipe and infusing the chicken with flavor all the way through. To ensure that the chicken cooked evenly, we used plenty of water and raised the chicken off the bottom of the pot in a steamer basket. Taking the pot off the heat partway through cooking allowed the delicate meat to cook through using gentle, residual heat and prevented overcooking. A flavorful yogurt sauce made the perfect accompaniment to our tender, moist chicken.

I hear it all the time: Boneless, skinless chicken breasts are dry and stringy. I always reply that it's not the chickens' fault. Sure, modern chicken breasts are lean and mild. Yet we throw delicate chicken breasts onto a white-hot grill, sear them hard in a skillet, and even toss them under the broiler—all potential paths to leathery flesh. Meanwhile we ignore one of the most obvious methods for delivering tender, moist chicken: poaching.

This old-school technique has a reputation for being fussy—and it is. The traditional method calls for maintaining a pot of water just below a simmer (between 160 and 180 degrees); it's not exactly hands-free or foolproof since you have to be vigilant about keeping the heat level just so. Furthermore, it rarely does much for flavor.

That said, it has the potential to deliver meat that's exceptionally moist and succulent. If I could take away some of the fussiness and figure out how to use the method to boost flavor, I might just be able to kick-start a poaching renaissance.

I already had a head start: When we developed a chicken salad recipe a few years ago, we came up with an easier, more hands-free poaching method. Instead of heating water in a pot and then tossing in cold chicken breasts and fiddling constantly with the burner until the breasts are done, we combine the water and chicken from the beginning. Four boneless, skinless chicken breasts go into a Dutch oven with 6 cups of salted cold water; we heat the pot over medium heat until the water

temperature reaches 170 degrees; and then we remove the pot from the heat and allow it to sit, covered, until the breasts are cooked through.

The beauty of this technique is that it's incredibly gentle and mostly hands-off. It results in moist meat that's ready to be cubed and tossed with mayonnaise and seasonings for chicken salad. I adopted this basic approach as my starting point, hoping that a few adjustments would produce breasts with meatier, richer flavor and that were even more moist, if possible. I was after chicken breasts that could stand alone on a dinner plate with nothing more than a simple sauce.

The first change I made was increasing the water to 4 quarts. More water translates to a larger reserve of heat and thus better assurance that the breasts will hit the desired internal temperature of 160 degrees, even if you are using a thin pot or a poorly calibrated thermometer. And since the sides of the breasts in contact with the bottom of the pan could potentially cook faster, I also raised the breasts off the bottom of the pot—the additional liquid allowed me to put them in a steamer basket while still keeping them fully submerged. And finally, I used a meat mallet to lightly pound the thicker end of the breasts to promote more even cooking. These adjustments worked well, so I moved on to amping up flavor.

My primary goal was to add richer, more complex flavor to the breasts during cooking, but keep the flavors neutral enough that my chicken could still pair with a range of sauces for a versatile main course. Over the years we've learned that it's difficult for most flavorings to penetrate very far into a piece of poultry or meat. During marinating, brining, and even cooking, most flavors travel only a few millimeters into meat. There are, luckily, some exceptions. Many recipes, including my working one here, testify to the fact that given sufficient concentration and time, salt can penetrate much farther into the interior of a chicken breast. Sugar also works in this way, so I added a couple tablespoons to my salted poaching water. Tasters approved; the chicken didn't taste sweet—just a bit rounder and fuller.

I then looked to two other categories of ingredients for more flavor: alliums and foods rich in glutamate. The latter, a common amino acid, gives food a savory, meaty flavor. In addition to being found in ingredients like tomatoes, Parmesan cheese, and mushrooms, glutamates are in many fermented seasonings, such as miso, soy sauce, and fish sauce. I tried adding quantities of all three seasonings to my poaching liquid. Used in a relatively dilute concentration, the soy won out, adding meatiness and depth without giving itself away.

Alliums (such as onions, scallions, shallots, and garlic) not only offer potent flavor but, due to their solubility in water, can also move passively into meat along with water. I tried adding each of the aforementioned alliums to separate pots of poached chicken and asked tasters to pick a favorite. Garlic took first for the complex, sweet background flavor that it added; I smashed six cloves with the side of my knife, peeled away the skins, and tossed the cloves into the pot.

I was making good progress in the flavor department, and the salt was penetrating decently into each chicken breast, though not as much as I would have liked. Quantity and time are the key players in how far the salt could get, and the poaching time wasn't all that long. This got me thinking about brining and salting, two techniques that give salt time to diffuse deeper into pieces of meat or poultry. Salting is a longer process than brining, and it's a technique that we typically use when we want to develop browning and crisp skin on the meat—not something that I was going for here. But I'd just finished crafting the perfect salty, flavorful poaching liquid. Could it also serve as a brine? Our standard brine for boneless, skinless chicken breasts is ¼ cup salt to 2 quarts water. With ¼ cup salt and ½ cup soy sauce to 4 quarts water, my poaching solution was just below that ratio. My instinct was that it could serve as a gentle brine and double as the poaching liquid without making the chicken overly salty.

I gave it a shot, adding the chicken breasts to the poaching liquid and letting them sit for 30 minutes at room temperature, which allowed the breasts' internal temperature to slowly start to rise. Then I turned on the heat and proceeded with the recipe. Tasters declared this batch the most evenly seasoned and flavorful thus far, as well as the most juicy and tender. Those 30 minutes had given the salt time to dissolve some proteins in the chicken, resulting in a tenderizing effect. At the same time, the water, glutamate, and garlic flavor compounds had time to make their way deeper into the flesh. Even my skeptical "anti–white meat" colleagues had to admit that this was really good, flavorful chicken.

Now all I needed was a simple sauce that would complement the chicken's mild, meaty flavor and juicy, tender texture. I decided on a yogurt-based sauce with cumin, garlic, and fresh cilantro.

With a technique so easy, foolproof, and good, I bet that even the most skeptical of cooks will never again doubt the power of poaching.

—DAN SOUZA, *Cook's Illustrated*

Perfect Poached Chicken Breasts

SERVES 4

To ensure that the chicken cooks through, don't use breasts that weigh more than 8 ounces each. If desired, serve the chicken with Cumin-Cilantro Yogurt Sauce (recipe follows) or in a salad or sandwiches.

- 4 (6- to 8-ounce) boneless, skinless chicken breasts, trimmed
- ½ cup soy sauce
- ¼ cup salt
- 2 tablespoons sugar
- 6 garlic cloves, smashed and peeled

1. Cover chicken breasts with plastic wrap and pound thick ends gently with meat pounder until ¾ inch thick. Whisk 4 quarts water, soy sauce, salt, sugar, and garlic in Dutch oven until salt and sugar are dissolved. Arrange breasts, skinned side up, in steamer basket, making sure not to overlap them. Submerge steamer basket in brine and let sit at room temperature for 30 minutes.

2. Heat pot over medium heat, stirring liquid occasionally to even out hot spots, until water registers 175 degrees, 15 to 20 minutes. Turn off heat, cover pot, remove from burner, and let stand until meat registers 160 degrees, 17 to 22 minutes.

3. Transfer breasts to cutting board, cover tightly with aluminum foil, and let rest for 5 minutes. Slice each breast on bias into ¼-inch-thick slices, transfer to serving platter or individual plates, and serve.

Cumin-Cilantro Yogurt Sauce

MAKES ABOUT 1 CUP

Mint may be substituted for the cilantro. This sauce is prone to curdle and thus does not reheat well; prepare it just before serving.

- 2 tablespoons extra-virgin olive oil
- 1 shallot, minced
- 1 garlic clove, minced

1   teaspoon ground cumin

⅛   teaspoon red pepper flakes

½   cup plain whole-milk yogurt

⅓   cup water

1   teaspoon lime juice

    Salt and pepper

2   tablespoons chopped fresh cilantro

Heat 1 tablespoon oil in 8-inch skillet over medium heat until shimmering. Add shallot and cook until softened, about 2 minutes. Stir in garlic, cumin, and pepper flakes and cook until fragrant, about 30 seconds. Remove from heat and whisk in yogurt, water, lime juice, and remaining 1 tablespoon oil. Season with salt and pepper to taste and cover to keep warm. Stir in cilantro just before serving.

CHICKEN BAKED IN FOIL

✔ WHY THIS RECIPE WORKS: Chicken baked in foil packets can make a healthy, easy weeknight dinner, but the recipes we tried produced overcooked, flavorless chicken and mushy vegetables. To improve on this classic method, we started by salting the chicken, which seasoned the meat deeply. We chose sturdy, hardy vegetables like potatoes, carrots, and onion, and layered the potatoes under the chicken to insulate the meat and prevent overcooking. Leaving space at the top of each packet allowed heat to circulate evenly. Seasoning the chicken and vegetables with a few splashes of peppery olive oil, fresh thyme leaves, and red pepper flakes provided complexity and a bit of zing.

Recently I've been hearing a lot about chicken baked in foil, the latest wrinkle in the time-honored tradition of cooking food sealed in packets. Boneless chicken breasts and vegetables are sealed in foil pouches so that as they bake, the pouches trap steam and everything cooks in its own tasty juices. Each diner gets his or her own pouch, and when the pouches are opened, plumes of fragrant, appetite-stoking steam invite everyone to dig in.

This sounded like a great weeknight dinner to me, so I found a half-dozen recipes and prepared them. As the first batch went into the oven, I started to feel uneasy: As a trained cook, I'm used to gauging when meat is properly cooked by monitoring how it looks, sounds, feels, and smells throughout the process. All those cues went out the window here.

Nevertheless, I followed the recipes and called over my tasters. The mushy vegetables, overcooked chicken, and prevailing blandness did not impress them. In fact, these packets were not that much better than old-fashioned TV dinners, which is what many of us think of when the idea of "cooking in foil" is mentioned. But I knew that this idea held promise.

My first task was improving the bland, almost non-existent flavor. I knew right off that part of this fix would be adequate salting. I landed on sprinkling ⅛ teaspoon of salt over each side of each breast to guarantee thorough, even seasoning. I found that the chicken took on deeper seasoning the longer it sat with the salt on it; although refrigerating the assembled packets for an hour improved them markedly, overnight proved ideal.

Now I turned my attention to the vegetables. I learned that soft varieties, like spinach and tomatoes, cooked into mushy messes; my foil-pouch method required hardier sorts. After working my way through most of the usual suspects, I ultimately decided on potatoes, carrots, and onion, which were just sturdy enough, when properly sliced, to cook at the same rate as the chicken.

For the most even, foolproof cooking, I found it best to layer the potato slices under the chicken in the pouches and to bake the pouches on a rimmed baking sheet on the lower rack of a 475-degree oven for about 20 minutes. This way, the potatoes absorb the direct heat and help insulate the chicken. I also discovered that it was important to construct the pouches with plenty of headroom; this empty space at the top gave the steam room to circulate so that everything cooked at the same rate.

As for knowing when the chicken was properly cooked, at first I devised a method of placing one packet on an extra sheet of foil so I could open that packet, look at the chicken, and easily seal it again if need be. I then realized that this worked just as effectively as a way of plugging up the hole caused by sticking a thermometer through the foil to check the chicken's temperature, a much more reliable approach.

Now that I had the technique and cooking times down, I wanted to take the flavor even further, to make these packets seem like a special event rather than an

CHICKEN BAKED IN FOIL WITH SWEET POTATO AND RADISH

ordinary dinner. So before putting them in the packets, I seasoned the vegetables with olive oil that I infused with lots of garlic, red pepper flakes, and fresh thyme.

As I watched my tasters gobble up what was my final recipe test, I knew that chicken baked in foil was going to become a new weeknight staple in my house.

—DIANE UNGER, *Cook's Country*

Chicken Baked in Foil with Potatoes and Carrots

SERVES 4

To ensure even cooking, buy chicken breasts of the same size. If using table salt, use only ⅛ teaspoon for each entire breast. Refrigerate the pouches for at least 1 hour before cooking.

- 5 tablespoons extra-virgin olive oil
- 6 garlic cloves, sliced thin
- 1 teaspoon minced fresh thyme
- ¼ teaspoon red pepper flakes
- 12 ounces Yukon Gold potatoes, unpeeled, sliced ¼ inch thick
- 2 carrots, peeled, quartered lengthwise, and cut into 2-inch lengths
- ½ large red onion, sliced ½ inch thick, layers separated
   Kosher salt and pepper
- 4 (6-ounce) boneless, skinless chicken breasts, trimmed
- 2 tablespoons lemon juice
- 2 tablespoons minced fresh chives

1. Spray centers of four 20 by 12-inch sheets of heavy-duty aluminum foil with vegetable oil spray. Microwave oil, garlic, thyme, and pepper flakes in small bowl until garlic begins to brown, 1 to 1½ minutes. Combine potato slices, carrots, onion, 1 teaspoon salt, and garlic oil in large bowl.

2. Pat chicken dry with paper towels. Sprinkle ⅛ teaspoon salt evenly over each side of each chicken breast, then season with pepper. Position 1 piece of prepared foil with long side parallel to counter edge. In center of foil, arrange one-quarter of potato slices in 2 rows perpendicular to counter edge. Lay 1 chicken breast on top of potato slices. Place one-quarter of vegetables around chicken. Repeat with remaining foil, potato slices, chicken, and vegetables. Drizzle any remaining oil mixture from bowl over chicken.

3. Bring short sides of foil together and crimp to seal tightly. Crimp remaining open ends of packets, leaving as much headroom as possible inside packets. Place packets on large plate and refrigerate for at least 1 hour or up to 24 hours.

4. Adjust oven rack to lowest position and heat oven to 475 degrees. Arrange packets on rimmed baking sheet. Bake until chicken registers 160 degrees, 18 to 23 minutes. (To check temperature, poke thermometer through foil of 1 packet and into chicken.) Let chicken rest in packets for 3 minutes.

5. Transfer chicken packets to individual dinner plates, open carefully (steam will escape), and slide contents onto plates. Drizzle lemon juice over chicken and vegetables and sprinkle with chives. Serve.

VARIATION

Chicken Baked in Foil with Sweet Potato and Radish

Substitute 1 tablespoon grated fresh ginger for thyme; 12 ounces peeled sweet potato, sliced ¼ inch thick, for Yukon Gold potatoes; 2 celery ribs, quartered lengthwise and cut into 2-inch lengths, for carrots; rice vinegar for lemon juice; and minced fresh cilantro for chives. Add 4 radishes, trimmed and quartered, to vegetables in step 1.

NOTES FROM THE TEST KITCHEN

FOIL PACKET BLUEPRINT
We went through a lot of chicken—and foil—while figuring out the best way to construct our single-serving packets.

1. Place potato slices on bottom to insulate chicken. Arrange carrots and onion next to chicken.

2. Leave headroom (empty space) at top of packet to facilitate steam circulation.

CRISPY-SKINNED CHICKEN BREASTS

✓ **WHY THIS RECIPE WORKS:** Perfectly cooked chicken with shatteringly crispy, flavorful skin is a rare find, so we set out to develop a foolproof recipe that would work every time. Boning and pounding the chicken breasts was essential to creating a flat, even surface to maximize the skin's contact with the hot pan. We salted the chicken to both season the meat and dry out the skin; poking holes in the skin and the meat allowed the salt to penetrate deeply. Starting the chicken in a cold pan allowed time for the skin to crisp without overcooking the meat. Weighting the chicken for part of the cooking time with a heavy Dutch oven encouraged even contact with the hot pan for all-over crunchy skin. Finally, we created a silky, flavorful sauce with a bright, acidic finish, which provided the perfect foil to the skin's richness.

I'm always on the lookout for ways to get great skin on chicken. By that I mean skin that's paper-thin, deep golden brown, and so well crisped that it crackles when you take a bite. Such perfectly cooked skin, however, is actually a rarity. A good roast chicken may have patches of it, but the rotund shape of the bird means that uneven cooking is inevitable and that some of the skin will also cook up flabby and pale. And even on relatively flat chicken parts, there's the layer of fat beneath the skin to contend with: By the time it melts away during searing, the exterior often chars and the meat itself overcooks.

When I recently came across one of the best specimens of chicken I'd ever tasted at a restaurant in New York, I had to figure out how to re-create it myself. The tender meat and the tangy, spicy pickled cherry pepper sauce that was served with it had their own charms, but the chicken skin was incredible—a sheath so gorgeously bronzed and shatteringly crunchy that I'd swear it was deep-fried.

There were a number of hurdles to achieving the same chicken-skin nirvana at home, not the least of which was the cut of meat itself. The restaurant version served half of a chicken per person, removing all but the wing bones from the meat before searing it. For the sauce, the pickling liquid from the cherry peppers was reduced and then used to deglaze the pan.

The point of all that butchery is to flatten out the bird so that its entire surface makes direct, even contact with the pan—a must for producing thoroughly rendered, deeply crisped skin. But since few home cooks can do that kind of knife work confidently and quickly, I decided to keep things simple and work with only breast meat, which would eliminate more than half of the butchering. Removing the breast bones required just a few quick strokes of a sharp knife. Moreover, switching from half chickens to split breasts made for more reasonable portions. I would serve a pair of breasts—enough for two people—and keep things simple so that the dish would work as a weeknight meal.

Of course, the drawback to working with breast meat would be its tendency to overcook, particularly once I'd removed the bones—poor conductors of heat and, therefore, good insulators. My very basic initial cooking technique was placing the boned breasts skin side down in a hot, oiled skillet to crisp up their surface and then flipping the meat to let it color briefly on the other side. This gave me fairly crispy skin but meat that was dry and chalky. When I tried a slightly gentler approach, briefly pan-searing the chicken skin side down and then transferring the pan to the more even heat of a 450-degree oven until the breasts were cooked through, the meat was only somewhat more moist and tender. Clearly, some form of pretreatment was essential if I wanted the meat to be as succulent as the skin was crispy.

Brining was out, since it introduces additional water to the meat and inevitably leaves the skin slightly waterlogged. Salting would be the way to go. Besides seasoning the meat deeply and helping it retain moisture as it cooks, salt would assist in drying out the skin. To further encourage the skin's dehydration (as well as the salt's penetration), I used one of the test kitchen's favorite techniques for chicken: poking holes in both the skin and meat with a sharp knife before applying the salt.

Salting and slashing helped, but they got me only so far with the skin, which indicated that my simple searing technique needed further tweaking. Thus far, the best I'd accomplished was unevenly cooked skin, as I'd anticipated early on. What's more, the skin tended to shrink away from the edges of the breast as it cooked, which, apart from the unsightly appearance, also caused the now-exposed meat to brown and turn dry and leathery in the process. Finally, the thin end of the breast still cooked up a bit dry by the time the thick end had fully cooked.

Evening out the thickness of the meat was easy: I simply pounded the thick end of the breast gently so that the entire piece cooked at the same rate. As for evening out the browning of the skin, I adapted a classic Italian technique: pinning the bird to the cooking surface with bricks. I figured that I could mimic that technique by weighing down the chicken breasts with a heavy Dutch oven. (Since I had no interest in transferring the weighty duo of pans to the oven, I'd switch to cooking the breasts entirely on the stovetop.) After 10 minutes over medium heat, I removed the pot and surveyed the chicken skin, which, for the most part, was far crispier than ever before and not at all shrunken. But maddeningly, pockets of fat persisted under the surface at the center and along the edges. And the meat? It was way overcooked now that the lean meat was pressed hard against the hot surface.

Amid my frustration, I had noticed something curious: When I removed the Dutch oven, a puff of steam arose from the pan—moisture from the chicken that had been trapped beneath the pot. That moisture was thwarting my skin-crisping efforts, so I wondered if the weight was necessary for the entire duration of the cooking time or if I could remove it partway through to prevent moisture buildup.

I prepared another batch, this time letting the breasts cook in the preheated oiled skillet under the pot for just 5 minutes before uncovering them. As it continued to cook for another 2 to 4 minutes, the skin remained anchored to the pan, crisping up nicely without contracting in the least. Removing the pot early also allowed the meat to cook a bit more gently, as the heat that had been trapped around the chicken was released. But it wasn't quite gentle enough; dry meat still persisted.

The core problem—that it takes longer to render and crisp chicken skin than it does to cook the meat beneath it—had me feeling defeated until I realized a way to give the skin a head start: a "cold" pan. This is a classic French technique for cooking duck breasts— the ultimate example of delicate meat covered with a layer of fatty skin. Putting the meat skin side down in the oiled pan before turning on the heat allows more time for the skin to render out its fat layer before the temperature of the meat reaches its doneness point. I hoped this approach would apply to chicken.

Initially, I thought I'd hit a roadblock: The breasts were sticking to the skillet—a nonissue when adding proteins to a hot pan, which usually prevents sticking.

Fortunately, by the time the skin had rendered and fully crisped up, the breasts came away from the surface with just a gentle tug. Once the skin had achieved shattering crispiness, all it took was a few short minutes on the second side to finish cooking the meat.

Chicken with skin this bronzed and brittle was tasty enough as is, but to dress things up a bit, I set my sights on developing a few sauces.

My own rendition of the restaurant's sauce was nothing more than a reduction of pickled-pepper vinegar and chicken broth, thickened with a little flour and butter and garnished with a few chopped pickled peppers. Since it's the tanginess of that sauce that makes it the perfect accompaniment to the skin's ultrameaty flavor, I came up with a pair of variations on the same acid-based theme: lemon-rosemary and maple–sherry vinegar.

Satisfying my inner chicken skin perfectionist was gratifying in and of itself. But coming up with a quick and elegant way to dress up ordinary old chicken breasts? That was even better.

—ANDREW JANJIGIAN, *Cook's Illustrated*

Crispy-Skinned Chicken Breasts with Vinegar-Pepper Pan Sauce

SERVES 2

This recipe requires refrigerating the salted meat for at least 1 hour before cooking. Two 10- to 12-ounce chicken breasts are ideal, but three smaller ones can fit in the same pan; the skin will be slightly less crispy. A boning knife or sharp paring knife works best to remove the bones from the breasts. To maintain the crispy skin, spoon the sauce around, not over, the breasts when serving.

CHICKEN

- 2 (10- to 12-ounce) bone-in split chicken breasts
  Kosher salt and pepper
- 2 tablespoons vegetable oil

PAN SAUCE

- 1 shallot, minced
- 1 teaspoon all-purpose flour
- ½ cup chicken broth
- ¼ cup jarred hot cherry peppers, chopped, plus ¼ cup brine
- 1 tablespoon unsalted butter, chilled
- 1 teaspoon minced fresh thyme
  Salt and pepper

1. FOR THE CHICKEN: Place 1 chicken breast, skin side down, on cutting board, with ribs facing away from knife hand. Run tip of knife between breastbone and meat, working from thick end of breast toward thin end. Angling blade slightly and following rib cage, repeat cutting motion several times to remove ribs and breastbone from breast. Find short remnant of wishbone along top edge of breast and run tip of knife along both sides of bone to separate it from meat. Remove tenderloin (reserve for another use) and trim excess fat, taking care not to cut into skin. Repeat with second breast.

2. Using tip of paring knife, poke skin on each breast evenly 30 to 40 times. Turn breasts over and poke thickest half of each breast 5 to 6 times. Cover breasts with plastic wrap and pound thick ends gently with meat pounder until ½ inch thick. Evenly sprinkle each breast with ½ teaspoon salt. Place breasts, skin side up, on wire rack set in rimmed baking sheet, cover loosely with plastic, and refrigerate for 1 hour or up to 8 hours.

3. Pat breasts dry with paper towels and sprinkle each breast with ¼ teaspoon pepper. Pour oil in 12-inch skillet and swirl to coat. Place breasts, skin side down, in oil and place skillet over medium heat. Place heavy skillet or Dutch oven on top of breasts. Cook breasts until skin is beginning to brown and meat is beginning to turn opaque along edges, 7 to 9 minutes.

4. Remove weight and continue to cook until skin is well browned and very crispy, 6 to 8 minutes. Flip breasts, reduce heat to medium-low, and cook until second side is lightly browned and meat registers 160 degrees, 2 to 3 minutes. Transfer breasts to individual plates and let rest while preparing pan sauce.

5. FOR THE PAN SAUCE: Pour off all but 2 teaspoons oil from skillet. Return skillet to medium heat and add shallot; cook, stirring occasionally, until shallot is softened, about 2 minutes. Add flour and cook, stirring constantly, for 30 seconds. Increase heat to medium-high, add broth and brine, and bring to simmer, scraping up any browned bits. Simmer until thickened, 2 to 3 minutes. Stir in any accumulated chicken juices; return to simmer and cook for 30 seconds. Remove skillet from heat and whisk in peppers, butter, and thyme; season with salt and pepper to taste. Spoon sauce around breasts and serve.

VARIATIONS

Crispy-Skinned Chicken Breasts With Lemon-Rosemary Pan Sauce

In step 5, increase broth to ¾ cup and substitute 2 tablespoons lemon juice for brine. Omit peppers and substitute rosemary for thyme.

Crispy-Skinned Chicken Breasts With Maple–Sherry Vinegar Pan Sauce

In step 5, substitute 2 tablespoons sherry vinegar for brine, 1 tablespoon maple syrup for peppers, and sage for thyme.

NOTES FROM THE TEST KITCHEN

BONING A SPLIT CHICKEN BREAST

If you want to cook boneless breasts with skin, you'll have to do a little knife work. Removing the bones allows the entire surface of the meat to lie flat and even against the pan—a must for perfectly crispy skin.

1. With chicken breast skin side down, run tip of boning or sharp paring knife between breastbone and meat, working from thick end of breast toward thin end.

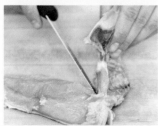

2. Angling blade slightly and following rib cage, repeat cutting motion several times to remove ribs and breastbone from breast.

3. Find short remnant of wishbone along top edge of breast and run tip of knife along both sides of bone to separate it from meat.

FRIED CHICKEN SANDWICHES

FRIED CHICKEN SANDWICHES

✓ **WHY THIS RECIPE WORKS:** Fried chicken sandwiches are a fast food staple, but we weren't satisfied with the soggy, flavorless offerings we found at roadside restaurants. To create a sandwich with all the crunchy appeal of fried chicken, we needed to start with the right piece of meat; boneless breasts halved crosswise proved to be ideal for their quick cook time and perfect sandwich size. We rubbed the chicken with salt and spices to deeply season the meat, and added baking powder to our craggy flour coating for the crunchiest crust. To make the coating adhere, we dipped the chicken in egg white. Letting the breaded chicken sit for 30 minutes before frying helped the coating set up and allowed the salt time to season the chicken throughout. A sturdy potato bun and a few simple toppings provided the perfect complements to our crunchy, flavorful chicken.

I'd been on the highway for 5 hours when I saw a sign for a fast-food place that's famous for its fried chicken sandwiches. Since fried chicken is just about my favorite food on the planet (and my stomach was rumbling), I decided to stop. As I sat and chewed, I wondered why this place was so popular—the sandwich in my hand had none of the crunchy, flavorful appeal of real fried chicken. What's more, the bun was spongy, the lettuce was wilted, and the gloppy sauce tasted of nothing but salt. That sandwich was an insult to fried chicken, and I knew that I could do better.

Back in the test kitchen, I started my recipe development. I wanted my recipe to make four sandwiches, so I started experimenting with exactly how big the pieces of chicken should be. Whole breasts were too thick, so the coating burned in the oil before the meat was cooked through. Cutlets had the opposite problem: The delicate white meat overcooked by the time the coating took on sufficient browning. After a few days of testing, I landed on using two chicken breasts (6 to 8 ounces each) that I cut in half crosswise and gently pounded to an even ½-inch thickness. These pieces were perfectly done by the time the coating was nicely browned, and they were just the right size for a sandwich. I found that a mere 1½ inches of oil—peanut and vegetable both work—was enough to fry in.

In the test kitchen, we like to brine bone-in chicken—either in salty water or salty buttermilk—before frying it to ensure deep seasoning and to keep the meat juicy. But would brining be necessary for boneless breasts? I tested water and buttermilk brines against a simple 30-minute salt, and my tasters couldn't taste much difference; to keep the recipe as simple as possible, I'd go with the salting. Since I was rubbing the breasts with salt, I figured that I might as well add more flavor at the same time. We liked a combination of paprika, pepper, garlic powder, thyme, sage, and a little cayenne added to the salt. It was time to move on to the coating.

I knew that I wanted a flavorful, craggy coating that stayed on the chicken and could hold its crunch in a sandwich. I took care of the "flavorful" part of it by stirring a tablespoon of the salt-spice mixture into the flour. Dredging chicken in seasoned flour makes for a smooth coating. To create a craggy surface (more surface area means more crunch), I added a few tablespoons of water to the flour so that it would clump a little and add mass to the coating. Since I wasn't brining, I needed something wet and sticky to help the coating adhere. Beaten egg tasted too, well, eggy, but egg whites held on to the coating without muddying the flavor. Finally, a teaspoon of baking powder mixed into the flour—a tried-and-true test kitchen trick that makes fried coatings supercrispy—gave the exterior extra crunch.

As for the buns—no small part of the sandwich experience—large Kaiser or onion rolls tasted good but were simply too big. Hamburger buns were OK, but they tend to be flavorless and squishy. I settled on potato rolls, which are flavorful, sturdy enough to hold a piece of hot chicken, and just the right size.

My fried chicken sandwiches were already way better than the fast-food versions, but I wasn't done yet. I found that it was best to refrigerate the breaded breasts for 30 to 60 minutes on a wire rack before frying. This gives the salt time to penetrate and also allows the coating to set up (because the chicken is elevated, the bottom won't get soggy) so that it adheres better. Plain mayonnaise was fine but not inspiring, so I created two easy, stir-together flavored mayos—one with dill pickles and mustard, the other with hot cherry peppers—to carry these sandwiches beyond good and into extraordinary.

The next time I'm tired and hungry on the highway, I'm going to step on the gas so that I can get home to make my own fried chicken sandwich.

—DIANE UNGER, *Cook's Country*

Fried Chicken Sandwiches

MAKES 4 SANDWICHES

Use a Dutch oven that holds 6 quarts or more. If desired, serve these sandwiches topped with shredded iceberg lettuce, sliced onion, and dill pickle chips and slathered with one of our flavored mayonnaises (recipes follow).

    1½ teaspoons kosher salt
    1   teaspoon paprika
    1   teaspoon pepper
    1   teaspoon garlic powder
    ½   teaspoon dried thyme
    ½   teaspoon dried sage
    ¼   teaspoon cayenne pepper
    2   (6- to 8-ounce) boneless, skinless chicken breasts, trimmed and halved crosswise
    1½ cups all-purpose flour
    1   teaspoon baking powder
    3   tablespoons water
    2   large egg whites, lightly beaten
    2   quarts peanut or vegetable oil
    4   potato sandwich rolls

1. Combine salt, paprika, pepper, garlic powder, thyme, sage, and cayenne in bowl. Measure out 1 tablespoon spice mixture and set aside. Pat chicken dry with paper towels. Using meat pounder, gently pound each chicken piece to even ½-inch thickness between 2 pieces of plastic wrap. Season chicken all over with remaining 2¾ teaspoons spice mixture.

2. Whisk flour, baking powder, and reserved 1 tablespoon spice mixture together in large bowl. Add water to flour mixture and rub together with your fingers until water is evenly incorporated and shaggy pieces form. Place egg whites in shallow dish.

3. Set wire rack in rimmed baking sheet. Working with 1 piece at a time, dip chicken in egg whites to thoroughly coat, letting excess drip back into dish, then dredge in flour mixture, pressing to adhere. Transfer chicken to prepared wire rack and refrigerate for at least 30 minutes or up to 1 hour.

4. Add oil to large Dutch oven until it measures about 1½ inches deep and heat over medium-high heat to 375 degrees. Add chicken to hot oil. Adjust burner, if necessary, to maintain oil temperature between 325 and 350 degrees. Fry, stirring gently to prevent pieces from sticking together, until chicken is golden brown and

registers 160 degrees, 4 to 5 minutes, flipping halfway through frying. Transfer to clean wire rack and let cool for 5 minutes. Serve on rolls.

Dill Pickle Mayonnaise

MAKES ABOUT 1 CUP

    ½   cup dill pickle chips, patted dry and chopped fine, plus 1 teaspoon pickle brine
    ½   cup mayonnaise
    1   tablespoon yellow mustard
    ½   teaspoon pepper

Combine all ingredients in bowl.

Hot Cherry Pepper Mayonnaise

MAKES ABOUT 1 CUP

    1   cup jarred hot cherry peppers, patted dry, stemmed, seeded, and chopped fine, plus 1 teaspoon brine
    ½   cup mayonnaise
    ½   teaspoon pepper

Combine all ingredients in bowl.

NOTES FROM THE TEST KITCHEN

CLUMPY FLOUR = CRUNCHIER COATING

Seasoned flour is the traditional coating for fried chicken. Adding a little liquid to the seasoned flour makes clumps, which adds texture—and extra crunch—to the fried coating.

PROBLEM: WHERE'S THE CRUNCH?

Dredging chicken in dry flour makes for a boring coating with minimal crunch.

SOLUTION: CLUMPY COATING

Moistening the dredging flour with water creates clumps that fry up extra-crunchy.

SLOW-COOKER GLAZED CHICKEN DRUMSTICKS

♥ **WHY THIS RECIPE WORKS:** Glazed drumsticks featuring tender chicken and a well-seasoned glaze make dinner a treat. And a slow cooker makes the process easy. To keep our glaze simple, we relied on fig preserves, which had great flavor and an ideal thick consistency; some balsamic vinegar and orange zest rounded out the flavor. To render fat from the drumsticks and make them meltingly tender, we took advantage of the moist heat of the slow cooker, seasoning the chicken simply with salt, pepper, and a bit of aromatic rosemary. We applied the glaze after the drumsticks came out of the slow cooker to ensure that the glaze maintained its thick consistency. A short stint under the broiler crisped the skin and helped achieve the deeply bronzed glaze we were after.

Drumsticks are one of the most versatile parts of a chicken: Their juicy, rich meat makes a perfect blank canvas for flavor. But this underused cut is most often slathered in barbecue sauce—delicious, yes, but not very interesting. I wanted to take advantage of the versatility of chicken drumsticks, and I wanted to use the slow cooker to do it.

I knew slow cooking would be a perfect way to cook the drumsticks. The appliance's gentle, moist heat renders fat and creates meltingly tender meat. I wanted to keep the recipe simple and streamlined, since much of the benefit of using the slow cooker is convenience. I started by choosing my flavorings. Part of the appeal of barbecue sauce is its tangy, slightly sweet profile, so I knew that I wanted to incorporate those elements into my sauce. Some drumstick recipes I had seen used an Italian-inspired fig-balsamic glaze, which sounded like just the thing: Fig would offer a bit of sweetness, which would be offset by the tangy balsamic vinegar. I wanted to avoid stovetop reduction time of the glaze, which seemed unnecessarily fussy for a slow-cooker recipe. For a thick glaze that would stick to the drumsticks, I opted to use fig preserves, which had a good consistency right out of the jar. I thinned the preserves slightly with balsamic vinegar, but found the flavor was a bit flat. I tried adding dimension with lemon zest, orange zest, and lime zest; lemon was overpowering and lime

simply tasted out of place. Tasters preferred orange for its subtle citrus notes. With only three ingredients and no reduction time needed, my glaze was ready.

Next, I needed to figure out the best way to approach the cooking. I tried coating the raw drumsticks with glaze and dumping them directly into the slow cooker, but after the long cooking time, the rendered fat and limited evaporation in the closed pot made my glaze a runny mess, and the skin on the drumsticks was pale and flabby. I tried again, this time browning the drumsticks in a pan on the stovetop before coating them in glaze; this gave the drumsticks a nice flavor boost, but didn't help the glaze adhere, and the crispness that the skin gained from browning was lost after hours in the slow cooker.

Could I apply the glaze after cooking? For my next test, I put the drumsticks in the slow cooker with just salt and pepper and let them cook to tender perfection. Once they were done, I stirred in the glaze. This didn't work either—the glaze tasted like an afterthought, and I missed the crisp skin and richer flavor of the browned chicken.

I was starting to realize that I couldn't rely solely on the slow cooker. I knew I would need to add the glaze after the drumsticks had cooked; I also wanted to brown the drumsticks to amp up savory flavor and achieve crisp skin. I hoped that a quick stint under the broiler would give me the perfect drumsticks I was after.

This time, I put all the drumsticks in the slow cooker and seasoned them with salt, pepper, and some rosemary for a hint of Italian-inspired herbal flavor, which I knew would be an earthy complement to my tangy glaze. When the fat was fully rendered and the drumsticks cooked through, I put them on a wire rack set in a baking sheet so that the heat of the oven could circulate evenly. A few minutes under the broiler gave them the crisp, browned skin I wanted. I painted on the glaze in batches, flipping the drumsticks as I brushed on more glaze for a perfect, evenly charred exterior. I reserved some glaze for the end to maintain some of the sticky tanginess that makes drumsticks so appealing.

With their slightly sweet, vinegary glaze; browned, crisp skin; moist, tender meat; and simple cooking method, I knew that these drumsticks would be a regular addition to my slow-cooker repertoire.

—STEPHANIE PIXLEY, *America's Test Kitchen Books*

Slow-Cooker Fig-Balsamic Glazed Chicken Drumsticks

SERVES 4 TO 6

This recipe is designed to work with 5½- to 7-quart slow cookers. Be sure to glaze the drumsticks generously.

    2 teaspoons dried rosemary
    4 pounds chicken drumsticks, trimmed
       Salt and pepper
    ¾ cup fig preserves
    3 tablespoons balsamic vinegar
    1½ teaspoons orange zest

1. Crumble rosemary into fine pieces. Season drumsticks with rosemary, salt, and pepper and place in slow cooker. Cover and cook until chicken is tender, 3 to 4 hours on low.

2. Adjust oven rack 10 inches from broiler element and heat broiler. Place wire rack in aluminum foil–lined rimmed baking sheet and spray with vegetable oil spray. Transfer drumsticks to prepared rack; discard cooking liquid. Broil until lightly charred and crisp, about 10 minutes, flipping halfway through cooking.

3. Meanwhile, combine preserves, vinegar, orange zest, 1 teaspoon pepper, and ½ teaspoon salt in bowl. Brush drumsticks with one-third of sauce and continue to broil until drumsticks are browned and sticky, about 10 more minutes, flipping and brushing drumsticks with more sauce halfway through cooking. Brush drumsticks with remaining sauce. Serve.

NOTES FROM THE TEST KITCHEN

THE BEST BALSAMIC VINEGAR
We were curious about the differences among the various brands of balsamic vinegar found at the supermarket. Right off the bat, we found that the sweetness and viscosity of the vinegars make a difference. A good balsamic vinegar must be sweet and thick, but it should also offer a bit of acidity. In the end, one vinegar—**Lucini Gran Riserva Balsamico**—impressed us with its nice balance of sweet and tangy.

GRILLED GLAZED BONELESS, SKINLESS CHICKEN BREASTS

✓ **WHY THIS RECIPE WORKS:** Grilled glazed chicken breasts are a quick and easy summer dinner, but too often the glaze burns or the chicken overcooks. To produce perfectly cooked chicken, we briefly brined the meat to season it and keep it moist during cooking, and used a two-level grill fire to prevent the glaze from singeing. Lightly coating the chicken with a surprising ingredient—milk powder—hastened browning during the quick cooking time. We developed a couple of sweet-savory glazes which complemented but didn't overpower the chicken. A small amount of corn syrup provided a mild sweetness and just enough viscosity to help the glaze cling to the meat.

Throwing a few boneless, skinless chicken breasts on the grill and painting them with barbecue sauce always sounds like a good idea. This lean cut is available everywhere, it cooks fast, and it makes a light, simple meal. The trouble is that the results are usually flawed. Because these disrobed specimens cook in a flash over coals, it's hard to get chicken that not only tastes grilled but also has a good glaze without overcooking it. Here's the dilemma: If you wait to apply the glaze until the meat is browned well, it's usually dry and leathery by the time you've lacquered on a few layers. (And you need a few layers to build anything more than a superficial skim of sauce.) But if you apply the glaze too soon, you don't give the chicken a chance to brown, a flavor boost that this bland cut badly needs. Plus, the sugary glaze is prone to burning before the chicken cooks through.

But the ease of throwing boneless, skinless breasts on the grill is too enticing to pass up. I decided to fiddle with the approach until I got it right: tender, juicy chicken with the smoky taste of the grill, glistening with a thick coating of glaze. While I was at it, I wanted to create glazes specifically designed to accentuate, not overwhelm, this lean cut's delicate flavors.

My first step was to brine the meat. I knew that a 30-minute saltwater soak would help keep the chicken juicy and well seasoned and could be accomplished while the grill was heating. I also opted for a two-level fire, which means that I piled two-thirds of the coals on one side of the kettle and just one-third on the other side. This would allow me to sear the breasts over the coals and then move them to the cooler side to avoid burning after I applied the glaze.

My real challenge was to figure out how to speed up browning, also known as the Maillard reaction, and the consequent formation of all those new flavor compounds that help meat taste rich and complex. If the chicken browned faster, it would leave me more time to build a thick glaze that would add even more flavor. My first thought was to enlist the aid of starch in absorbing some of the moisture on the exterior of the meat that normally would need to burn off before much browning could occur. First I tried dredging the breasts in flour, but this made them bready. Next I tried cornstarch, but this approach turned the breasts gummy. A technique we have employed when pan-searing chicken breasts—creating an artificial "skin" using a paste of cornstarch, flour, and melted butter—gave us better results. The starches (which break down into sugars) and the butter proteins helped achieve a browned surface more quickly, and the porous surface readily held a glaze. Unfortunately, the chicken still tasted more breaded than grilled.

Switching gears, I tried rubbing the surface of the chicken with baking soda. Baking soda increases the pH of the chicken, making it more alkaline, which in turn speeds up the Maillard reaction. Alas, while this did speed up browning, even small amounts left behind a mild soapy aftertaste.

I was unsure of what to do next. But then I remembered a really unlikely sounding test that one of my colleagues tried when attempting to expedite the browning of pork chops: dredging the meat in nonfat dry milk powder. While this strange coating did brown the meat more quickly, it made the chops taste too sweet. But might it be better suited for browning chicken? It was worth a try. After lightly dusting the breasts with milk powder (½ teaspoon per breast) and lightly spraying them with vegetable oil spray to help ensure that the powder stuck, I threw them on the grill. I was thrilled when the chicken was lightly browned and had nice grill marks in less than 2 minutes, or about half of the time of my most successful previous tests. Why was milk powder so effective? It turns out that dry milk contains about 36 percent protein. But it also contains about 50 percent lactose, a so-called reducing sugar. And the Maillard reaction takes place only after large proteins break down into amino acids and react with certain types of sugars—reducing sugars like glucose, fructose, and lactose. In sum, milk powder contained just the two components that I needed to speed things up.

But that wasn't the only reason milk powder was so successful in quickly triggering browning. Like starch, it's a dry substance that absorbs the excess moisture on the meat. This is helpful because moisture keeps the temperature too low for significant browning to take place until the wetness evaporates. There was yet one more benefit to using the milk powder: It created a thin, tacky surface that was perfect for holding on to the glaze. And now, with expedited browning in place, I had time to thoroughly lacquer my chicken with glaze by applying four solid coats before it finished cooking.

Next it was time to focus on perfecting the glaze itself. I started with flavor. Since I knew that I wanted to limit the amount of sweetness so as not to overpower the mild flavor of the chicken, I began by testing a host of ingredients that would be thick enough to serve as a clingy base but weren't sugary. I settled on coconut milk for one glaze and mustard for another. Then, in order to add balance and complexity, I introduced acidity in the form of citrus juice or vinegar, as well as a healthy dose of spices and aromatics, like red curry paste, fresh ginger, and ground fennel seeds.

My next step was to add a sweet (but not too sweet) element, which would provide further balance, promote browning, and give even more of a sticky cling to the glaze. Sweeteners like maple syrup, brown sugar, and fruit jams made the glazes saccharine. Corn syrup, which is about half as sweet as the other sweeteners, worked far better, giving the glaze just a goodly amount of stickiness while keeping the sweetness level under control. Two to 3 tablespoons, depending on the other ingredients, was just the right amount.

But all was not perfect: The glazes still had a tendency to become too loose when applied to the hot chicken after it browned. Whisking in a teaspoon or so of cornstarch helped.

At this point I was feeling pretty good. But many tasters wanted an even thicker glaze. This time I looked to adjust my cooking technique. My fix? I switched up the point at which I applied the glaze. Instead of brushing it on right before flipping the chicken, I began to apply the glaze immediately after it was flipped. This meant that less glaze stuck to the grill—and the glaze applied to the top of the chicken had time to dry out and cling. The result? Chicken breasts robed in a thick, lacquered glaze. My dinner was ready.

—KEITH DRESSER, *Cook's Illustrated*

Grilled Glazed Boneless, Skinless Chicken Breasts
SERVES 4

Our favorite chicken breasts are Bell & Evans Air Chilled Boneless Skinless Chicken Breasts.

- 3 tablespoons salt
- 3 tablespoons sugar
- 4 (6- to 8-ounce) boneless, skinless chicken breasts, trimmed
- 2 teaspoons nonfat dry milk powder
- ¼ teaspoon pepper
- Vegetable oil spray
- 1 recipe glaze (recipes follow)

1. Dissolve salt and sugar in 1½ quarts cold water. Submerge chicken in brine, cover, and refrigerate for at least 30 minutes or up to 1 hour. Remove chicken from brine and pat dry with paper towels. Combine milk powder and pepper in bowl.

2A. FOR A CHARCOAL GRILL: Open bottom vent completely. Light large chimney starter mounded with charcoal briquettes (7 quarts). When top coals are partially covered with ash, pour two-thirds evenly over half of grill, then pour remaining coals over other half of grill. Set cooking grate in place, cover, and open lid vent completely. Heat grill until hot, about 5 minutes.

2B. FOR A GAS GRILL: Turn all burners to high, cover, and heat grill until hot, about 15 minutes. Leave primary burner on high and turn other burner(s) to medium-high.

3. Clean and oil cooking grate. Sprinkle half of milk powder mixture over 1 side of chicken. Lightly spray coated side of chicken with oil spray until milk powder is moistened. Flip chicken and sprinkle remaining milk powder mixture over second side. Lightly spray with oil spray.

4. Place chicken, skinned side down, over hotter part of grill and cook until browned on first side, 2 to 2½ minutes. Flip chicken, brush with 2 tablespoons glaze, and cook until browned on second side, 2 to 2½ minutes. Flip chicken, move to cooler side of grill, brush with 2 tablespoons glaze, and cook for 2 minutes. Repeat flipping and brushing 2 more times, cooking for 2 minutes on each side. Flip chicken, brush with remaining glaze, and cook until chicken registers 160 degrees, 1 to 3 minutes. Transfer chicken to plate and let rest for 5 minutes before serving.

NOTES FROM THE TEST KITCHEN

WHERE GRILLING AND GLAZING GO WRONG
Here's what usually happens when you try for a deep sear and a substantial glaze.

BURNT GLAZE, BLAND MEAT
Layer on glaze from the get-go and it tends to burn. The chicken may be moist, but it lacks flavorful browning.

NICE GLAZE, DRY MEAT
If you wait to apply the sauce, you'll get good browning and a substantial glaze but dry, overcooked chicken.

Coconut Curry Glaze
MAKES ABOUT ⅔ CUP

- 2 tablespoons lime juice
- 1½ teaspoons cornstarch
- ⅓ cup canned coconut milk
- 3 tablespoons corn syrup
- 1 tablespoon fish sauce
- 1 tablespoon red curry paste
- 1 teaspoon grated fresh ginger
- ¼ teaspoon ground coriander

Whisk lime juice and cornstarch together in small saucepan until cornstarch has dissolved. Whisk in coconut milk, corn syrup, fish sauce, curry paste, ginger, and coriander. Bring mixture to boil over high heat. Cook, stirring constantly, until thickened, about 1 minute. Transfer glaze to bowl.

MAKES ABOUT ⅔ CUP

- 2 tablespoons cider vinegar
- 1 teaspoon cornstarch
- 3 tablespoons Dijon mustard
- 3 tablespoons honey
- 2 tablespoons corn syrup
- 1 garlic clove, minced
- ¼ teaspoon ground fennel seeds

Whisk vinegar and cornstarch together in small saucepan until cornstarch has dissolved. Whisk in mustard, honey, corn syrup, garlic, and fennel seeds. Bring mixture to boil over high heat. Cook, stirring constantly, until thickened, about 1 minute. Transfer glaze to bowl.

SLOW-COOKER WHOLE "ROAST" CHICKEN

✔ WHY THIS RECIPE WORKS: "Roasting" a chicken in a slow cooker may sound strange, but the moist, even heat of the appliance makes it an ideal way to cook temperamental whole chickens. To solve the problem of the light and dark meat cooking at different rates, we put the chicken in the slow cooker upside down, which allowed the juices from the dark meat to drip down and baste the delicate breast meat. To season the chicken, we opted for a fragrant, warm spice paste made of garam masala, chili powder, garlic, salt, and pepper; microwaving the spices with a little oil before rubbing them under and over the skin of the chicken bloomed their flavors. Keeping the slow cooker on low ensured that the chicken stayed moist and tender until it cooked through.

Famous chefs often boast about their ability to produce the perfect roast chicken. It's the new hallmark of a great chef, perhaps because roasting a chicken well is surprisingly difficult. Whole chickens suffer many problems, not the least of which is that by the time the dark meat cooks through, the breast meat is dry and overdone.

Of course, there is also something immensely comforting about roast chicken. The test kitchen has roast chicken recipes, but this time, I wanted to try something different: slow-cooker "roast" chicken that would require very little hands-on time, but would still offer all the flavor and comfort of an old-fashioned roast chicken.

As a jumping-off point, I used a test kitchen recipe for cooking chicken *en cocotte,* a French technique that uses the moist-heat environment of a covered pot to cook a chicken—similar to what I wanted to achieve with the slow cooker. In that recipe, we brown the chicken breast side down first, then flip it over and brown the other side before covering the pot tightly and cooking it in a low oven. To adapt this method, I got out a large pot, browned the chicken in a bit of oil, and then transferred it to the slow cooker. I knew from the chicken en cocotte recipe that adding vegetables to the pot would create too much moisture, which would make the chicken skin flabby and wash out the flavor of the meat. For now, I seasoned the chicken simply with salt, pepper, and a little bit of oil and put it in the slow cooker on low heat. When the chicken was done a few hours later, I was disappointed: The dark meat was decently moist, but the more delicate breast meat was dry and chalky.

I noticed, though, that there was a small pool of juices from the rendered dark meat in the bottom of the slow cooker, and I immediately started wondering how I could use that liquid to my advantage. Basting seemed out of the question—the chicken needed to spend several hours in the slow cooker, and having to constantly baste it would detract from the convenience of my recipe. What if I cooked the chicken upside down, so that the rendered fat from the flavorful dark meat would drip down and "baste" the white meat?

After a couple of tests, it was clear that this was the way to go. The breast meat was staying moist and tender, and the chicken was cooking more evenly.

I knew I would need to use plenty of aromatic ingredients to counteract the flavor-muting moisture of the slow cooker. I wanted warm spices that would create complex flavor for my simple chicken without overpowering it. I settled on chili powder, minced garlic, and garam masala, a multi-ingredient Indian seasoning that provided an easy shortcut to complex spice flavor. I made a quick paste with the spices, salt, pepper, and oil. I knew from past test kitchen experience that applying the paste only on top of the chicken skin would result in the spices (and the flavor) rolling right off the chicken and ending up in a pile on the bottom of the slow cooker. Gently loosening the chicken skin and rubbing the spices directly on the meat as well as on the skin gave the chicken more pronounced flavor.

When I called tasters to try this chicken, they agreed that the meat was tender and juicy but that the spices had a harsh, raw flavor, even after 4 hours in the slow cooker. Easy enough to fix. For the next test, I gave the spice mixture a short stint in the microwave, which bloomed the flavors of the aromatics and provided the rounded, warm spice flavor I had been after.

At this point, I started to wonder if I could skip the tedious step of browning the chicken before putting it in the slow cooker. After all, I wasn't trying to crisp skin in the slow cooker, so the browning was merely producing flavor. Would the seasonings alone give the meat enough depth? For my next test, I put my spice-rubbed chicken straight into the slow cooker and was happy to discover that the bloomed spices held their own, allowing me to save valuable time.

I finally had a recipe for a simple, comforting "roast" chicken right in my slow cooker that could rival any professional chef's.

—DAN ZUCCARELLO, *America's Test Kitchen Books*

Slow-Cooker Whole "Roast" Spice-Rubbed Chicken

SERVES 4

This recipe is designed to work with 5½- to 7-quart oval slow cookers. Note that garam masala is a boldly flavored spice blend; its potency will vary from brand to brand. Check the temperature of the chicken after 4 hours of cooking and continue to monitor until the breast registers 160 degrees and the thighs register 175 degrees.

- 2 tablespoons vegetable oil
- 1 tablespoon chili powder
- 1 tablespoon garam masala
- 3 garlic cloves, minced
  Salt and pepper
- 1 (4½- to 5-pound) whole chicken, giblets discarded

1. Microwave oil, chili powder, garam masala, garlic, 2 teaspoons salt, and 2 teaspoons pepper in bowl, stirring occasionally, until fragrant, about 1 minute; let cool slightly.

2. Use your fingers to gently loosen skin covering breast and thighs of chicken; place half of paste under skin, directly on meat of breast and thighs. Gently press

on skin to distribute paste over meat. Spread entire exterior surface of chicken with remaining paste and place chicken, breast side down, in slow cooker. Cover and cook until breast registers 160 degrees and thighs register 175 degrees, 4 to 5 hours on low.

3. Transfer chicken to carving board, tent loosely with aluminum foil, and let rest for 15 minutes. Carve chicken, discarding skin if desired. Serve.

THAI CHICKEN CURRY

✓ **WHY THIS RECIPE WORKS:** Warm-spiced, savory-sweet *massaman* curry is a Thai specialty, but it presents problems for the home cook with difficult-to-find ingredients and work-intensive processes. We set out to streamline the traditional recipe. To make a deeply flavorful curry paste, we toasted chiles and broiled garlic and shallots per tradition, but we replaced hard-to-find galangal with readily available ginger and traded out toasted, ground whole spices for preground five-spice powder. Coconut milk and lime juice rounded out the flavor of our curry. We stuck with the traditional potatoes, onion, chicken, and peanuts, simmered in the sauce until they were tender. A final garnish of lime zest and cilantro added a splash of color and brightness.

There are as many interpretations of Thai curries as there are cooks who prepare them, but the versions served in stateside restaurants tend to fit a similar profile: a coconut milk–based sauce that's flavored and thickened with a concentrated spice paste, filled out with meat or fish and vegetables, and served over plenty of steamed jasmine rice. Hot and tangy red and green curries are most familiar to Americans, along with curries tinted golden yellow by spices like turmeric. And then there's my favorite: a somewhat less well-known variety called *massaman*.

Unlike many Thai dishes that feature hot, sour, salty, and sweet elements, massaman curry trades on a warm, faintly sweet, and not overly spicy profile, thanks to the mix of warm spices like cinnamon, cloves, cardamom, and cumin, as well as roasted dried chiles and aromatics like shallots, garlic, and fresh galangal (a sweet-spicy cousin of ginger) that make up its paste. A last-minute

THAI CHICKEN CURRY WITH POTATOES AND PEANUTS

addition of either shrimp paste or fish sauce and a few teaspoons of tangy tamarind balance the rich sauce, which is typically paired with chicken (or beef), potato chunks, and roasted peanuts.

Massaman is a dish that presents challenges in an American kitchen. Ingredients like galangal and tamarind are hard to track down. Plus, precooking dried chiles and aromatic vegetables and toasting and grinding whole spices (another traditional step) make for one heck of a prep job—and that's just for the paste. I was determined to produce a massaman curry as fragrant and rich-tasting as any Thai restaurant's, but with less work.

Pulling together the curry at the end would be easy, so I skipped right to streamlining the paste. To see what would happen if I cut the precooking step for both the dried chiles and the aromatics, I compared the dish with two different batches of paste. The first I made the traditional way, using oven-toasted dried red chiles along with broiled skin-on shallots and garlic. In the second batch, the same ingredients (this time the alliums were peeled) went into the blender without precooking. Both pastes also got a knob of fresh ginger (the most obvious substitute for galangal), as well as a dash of fish sauce. As for the spices, some recipes I found called for up to a dozen different kinds, but to stick with my streamlining goal, I knocked down the list to whole cloves, cinnamon, cardamom, and cumin, all toasted and ground per tradition for now.

To finish both curries, I browned the pastes in a little oil to deepen their flavors, poured in chicken broth and coconut milk, and simmered the mixtures with Yukon Gold potatoes, onion, peanuts, and a little salt until the potatoes were tender. Finally I slipped in pieces of boneless, skinless chicken thighs. (Dark meat was a must for its rich flavor.)

My tasters declared the paste made with precooked chiles and alliums in a different league from its uncooked counterpart: richer-tasting, with rounder, more complex flavor, thanks to the caramelization of the sugars. I'd also discovered that there was a textural advantage to precooking: The heat had softened the vegetables, making them a bit easier to blend into a uniform paste, especially when I added a little water and several teaspoons of vegetable oil to the blender jar.

That meant that my only hope for a shortcut rested on the spices. Since they would end up blooming in oil, which also brings out their flavors, I wondered if toasting them beforehand was necessary—or if I could even sub in preground spices. Fortunately, this timesaver worked: The depth and intensity of the preground spice paste was a little less potent, but the basic effect I was going for—warmth with faint sweetness—came across just fine.

In fact, I wondered if I could take this streamlining one step further and use a commercial spice blend instead of measuring out individual spices. After trying pumpkin pie spice (too much cinnamon) and curry powder (too much turmeric), I landed on five-spice powder. Though not an exact match with the traditional massaman lineup, the generally warm, fragrant profile of this blend (which typically includes fennel, cinnamon, star anise, cloves, and either pepper or ginger) made a nice stand-in, and its flavor was potent enough that just a teaspoon got the job done. Some cumin and a little extra black pepper went into the mix, and I was done.

From there, I had only a couple of technique and flavor issues to work through. Traditional Thai curry recipes call for frying the paste in coconut cream (either skimmed from the top of a can of coconut milk or bought separately) that's first heated until its oil separates out, or "cracks." I pitted a batch of curry in which I had fried the paste in the skimmed, cracked cream against my working recipe, which called for simply frying the paste in vegetable oil. Admittedly, a few tasters picked up on the more concentrated flavor of the cracked cream curry, but most agreed that vegetable oil worked fine.

My colleagues were also clamoring for a bit of brightness, so I tried finishing the curry with a few teaspoons of lime juice—my best guess for a tamarind substitute. Alas, its effect was too sharp for massaman, and scaling back on the juice flattened its effect altogether.

What did work: changing *when* I added the lime juice rather than the amount. When I replaced some of the water in the paste with a few teaspoons of juice, the lime's acid mellowed as it cooked in the curry but didn't disappear. Finishing the curry with lime zest and cilantro freshened it even more.

Served with a heap of fragrant jasmine rice, my version of massaman curry captured everything I love about this dish: richness and depth from the roasted chiles and aromatics, warmth from the spices, crunch from the peanuts, and a touch of freshness from the lime and cilantro, all brought together in a manageable amount of time.

—LAN LAM, *Cook's Illustrated*

Thai Chicken Curry with Potatoes and Peanuts

SERVES 4 TO 6

Serve the curry with jasmine rice. The ingredients for the curry paste can be doubled to make extra for future use. Refrigerate the paste for up to one week or freeze it for up to two months.

CURRY PASTE

- 6 dried New Mexican chiles
- 4 shallots, unpeeled
- 7 garlic cloves, unpeeled
- ½ cup chopped fresh ginger
- ¼ cup water
- 4½ teaspoons lime juice
- 4½ teaspoons vegetable oil
- 1 tablespoon fish sauce
- 1 teaspoon five-spice powder
- ½ teaspoon ground cumin
- ½ teaspoon pepper

CURRY

- 1 teaspoon vegetable oil
- 1¼ cups chicken broth
- 1 (13.5-ounce) can coconut milk
- 1 pound Yukon Gold potatoes, unpeeled, cut into ¾-inch pieces
- 1 onion, cut into ¾-inch pieces
- ⅓ cup dry-roasted peanuts
- ¾ teaspoon salt
- 1 pound boneless, skinless chicken thighs, trimmed and cut into 1-inch pieces
- 2 teaspoons grated lime zest
- ¼ cup chopped fresh cilantro

1. FOR THE CURRY PASTE: Adjust oven rack to middle position and heat oven to 350 degrees. Line rimmed baking sheet with aluminum foil. Arrange chiles on prepared sheet and toast until puffed and fragrant, 4 to 6 minutes. Transfer chiles to large plate. Heat broiler.

2. Place shallots and garlic on foil-lined sheet and broil until softened and skin is charred, 6 to 9 minutes.

3. When cool enough to handle, stem and seed chiles and tear into 1½-inch pieces. Process chiles in blender until finely ground, about 1 minute. Peel shallots and garlic. Add shallots, garlic, ginger, water, lime juice, oil, fish sauce, five-spice powder, cumin, and pepper

to blender. Process to smooth paste, scraping down sides of blender jar as needed, 2 to 3 minutes. You should have 1 cup paste.

4. FOR THE CURRY: Heat oil in large saucepan over medium heat until shimmering. Add curry paste and cook, stirring constantly, until paste begins to brown, 2½ to 3 minutes. Stir in broth, coconut milk, potatoes, onion, peanuts, and salt, scraping up any browned bits. Bring to simmer and cook until potatoes are just tender, 12 to 14 minutes.

5. Stir in chicken and continue to simmer until chicken is cooked through, 10 to 12 minutes. Remove pan from heat and stir in lime zest. Serve, passing cilantro separately.

NOTES FROM THE TEST KITCHEN

THAI CURRY BY COLOR AND SPICE
Typical Thai curries are identifiable by their color—a reflection of the type and amount of chiles, aromatic vegetables, herbs, and spices in the curry paste. Massaman, a relative of yellow curry, is better known for its depth and fragrance from warm spices, which makes it stand out from other varieties.

RED
This curry, which has moderate salty sweetness, is fairly spicy and sour, thanks to lots of dried red chiles and a big hit of lime.

GREEN
A high ratio of fresh green chiles plus raw aromatics and very little sugar typically makes this variation the hottest and most pungent type of Thai curry.

YELLOW
Stateside versions tend to be mild, though authentic versions can be quite hot. All are heavy on turmeric—hence the color.

MASSAMAN
Though one of the mildest Thai curries, massaman is also one of the most complex. Traditionally, the paste combines cinnamon, star anise, cloves, cardamom, and cumin as well as dried chiles and aromatics. To cut down on ingredients, our recipe swaps some of the individual spices for five-spice powder.

THE BEST JASMINE RICE
Of the six jasmine rice products that we tasted, including a microwaveable rice and a pricey mail-order brand, top honors went to widely available **Dynasty Jasmine Rice** for its floral fragrance and separate, toothsome grains.

ROASTED CORNISH GAME HENS

ROASTED CORNISH GAME HENS

✓ **WHY THIS RECIPE WORKS:** Quick-cooking roasted Cornish game hens are an easy, elegant dinner option, but achieving crisp skin and tender meat in the short cooking time can be a challenge. Poking holes in the skin helped the fat to render quickly. To help the skin crisp up and brown, we used a baking powder rub and let the hens air-dry in the refrigerator overnight. To guarantee evenly golden skin, we butterflied the hens and started cooking them skin side down on a preheated baking sheet. Finally, we flipped them over for a final stint under the broiler. To season the meat inside and out, we added a light coating of kosher salt on the undersides of the birds.

Since they first appeared on American tables in the 1950s, Cornish game hens have typically been more of a special-occasion meal than a weeknight family dinner. But to me, these Lilliputian birds have attributes that make them appealing to serve any night of the week. For starters, they typically weigh about 1¼ to 1½ pounds, so they cook quickly—in less than 30 minutes. What's more, the exteriors of their smaller breasts aren't prone to dry out before the interiors cook through, a perennial hurdle when roasting regular chickens. The hens also boast a higher skin-to-meat ratio than regular chickens, which makes them both more forgiving and more flavorful. The skin shields the meat from the oven's heat, and its fatty underbelly bastes the meat throughout cooking, leaving not just the dark portions but the white meat juicy and rich in a way that the breast on a chicken rarely is. Finally, hens offer the benefit of elegant presentation: Everyone at the table gets an entire bird on his or her plate.

That's not to say that Cornish game hens don't come with challenges. In fact, their combination of small stature and abundant skin makes getting the exterior crisp and golden at the same time that the meat comes up to temperature even trickier than when working with a larger bird. In order for the skin to brown and crisp, it must first render its fat and moisture, a process that takes more time than the meat beneath it takes to cook through. With a regular chicken, the bird spends the better part of an hour in the oven (so it's doable though still a challenge); with a Cornish game hen, you're working with less than half of that time, which barely gives the skin a chance to render, much less

brown and crisp. With that in mind, I set my sights on roasting moist, juicy Cornish game hens with the same cracklingly crispy skin that I expect on larger birds.

The good news: In a past test kitchen recipe for roast chicken, we devised a few tricks that hasten the skin-crisping process and guarantee a bird with moist meat.

First, we attack the layer of fat under the skin before cooking, since fat can thwart crisping as much as moisture can. By loosening the skin and poking holes in the thickest pockets of fat, we essentially create channels through which the fat can drain.

Then we go after the skin's moisture: We rub the surface with a mixture of kosher salt and baking powder. Salt helps pull moisture to the skin's surface so that it can evaporate more quickly. And baking powder is slightly alkaline, which helps it break down the proteins in the skin to further promote crisping and browning. (For the hens, I also added a little vegetable oil to the salt before mixing in the powder, which helped the latter cling to the salt grains and, in turn, to the skin. Finally, we air-dry the salt-rubbed chicken uncovered in the fridge for a number of hours. This requires some forethought, but the results are worth it, as the naturally dry environment evaporates moisture from the skin.

I applied this three-pronged pretreatment to four hens, air-drying them for 4 hours, and compared them with another batch of birds that went straight from the package to the oven. The cooking method for both (which I adapted from that same roast chicken recipe) was simple: Roast the hens, breast side down on a cooling rack set in a rimmed baking sheet, in a 450-degree oven for 10 minutes; flip them and roast them 10 minutes longer; and then crank the heat to 500 degrees for the final 5 to 10 minutes of cooking, until the white and dark meat hit 160 and 175 degrees, respectively.

To my disappointment, the skin on the pretreated poultry was still far from ideal. Extending the air-drying time all the way to 24 hours (so that more moisture would evaporate) helped, but not enough, so I moved on to the cooking method. I thought that roasting the birds low and slow might give the skin time to render, at which point I could blast them under high heat to develop color. But when I dropped the heat to 300 degrees, not enough moisture evaporated from the skin and it didn't crisp. Plus, the birds took an hour to cook.

Next I took it to the opposite extreme. I tried roasting the hens really high, at 500 degrees, the entire time— and when that still didn't even out the skin color, I tried

GETTING CORNISH GAME HENS TO CRISP QUICKLY AND EVENLY

Because the meat on Cornish game hens finishes cooking long before their skin crisps, we devised a few tricks to accelerate the skin's progress.

1. SPATCHCOCK: Cutting out the backbones and flattening the birds promotes uniform browning.

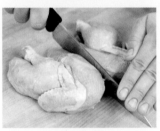

2. SPLIT: Halving the flattened hens (simple knife work with small birds) makes them easier to serve.

3. SEPARATE AND POKE: Loosening and poking holes in the skin allows the fat to drain during cooking, aiding crisping.

4. SALT AND AIR-DRY: Rubbing the birds with salt and baking powder and then chilling them wicks away moisture.

5. SEAR: Starting the birds skin side down on a preheated baking sheet effectively (and efficiently) crisps their skin.

pushing things even further. I left the birds in the oven past when the meat was up to temperature. My logic was that if there was all that extra fat and moisture, the meat might not suffer much if it was a little overcooked. That turned out to be true—to a point. The meat, including the breast, was still relatively juicy and tender at 180 degrees, but even then the skin was unimpressive. I continued to roast the hens until the skin was finally evenly browned, but by that point the meat was compromised.

What did get me closer was a blast under the broiler after the birds' initial 10-minute stint at 500 degrees. After about 5 minutes, their white and dark portions were up to temperature, the meat was juicy, and the skin was almost evenly burnished. Almost. The problem, I realized, was the birds' rotund shape, which was keeping some of the surface at a greater distance. A little knife work was in order.

Before pretreating my next batch, I removed the hens' backbones so that they could lie flat, giving their skin even exposure to the heating element. They looked really good now—golden from edge to edge. But the flattened birds spanned an entire dinner plate—not the elegant presentation I had in mind. Splitting them in half after removing the backbones made them more manageable to serve.

As a last-ditch move I went for the extreme and seared a couple of the halves skin side down in a skillet before transferring the pan to a 500-degree oven to finish cooking. At last, the skin was gorgeously brown and crisp. Of course, cooking four hens, two halves at a time, in a skillet was impractical, so I switched to using a baking sheet preheated in the oven. I spritzed the skin of each bird with vegetable oil spray and sprinkled it with pepper. Then I placed all the halves skin side down on the hot sheet and slid it into the oven. When I flipped the halves 10 minutes later, the skin looked almost as good as that on the batch I'd seared in the skillet. Blasting the birds skin side up under the broiler for 5 minutes easily finished the job.

All that remained to consider was flavor. The overnight salt rub was seasoning the tops of the birds; rubbing a bit more kosher salt on their undersides evened it out.

Now that I had a recipe for roasted poultry that guaranteed great meat and skin and, once pretreated, could be on the table in well under half an hour, Cornish game hens were looking more appealing than ever for any day of the week.

—ANDREW JANJIGIAN, *Cook's Illustrated*

Roasted Cornish Game Hens

SERVES 4

This recipe requires refrigerating the salted meat for at least 4 hours or up to 24 hours before cooking (a longer salting time is preferable). If your hens weigh 1½ to 2 pounds, cook three instead of four, and extend the initial cooking time in step 5 to 15 minutes. We prefer Bell & Evans Cornish Game Hens.

  4 **(1¼- to 1½-pound) Cornish game hens, giblets discarded**
    Kosher salt and pepper
 ¼ **teaspoon vegetable oil**
  1 **teaspoon baking powder**
    Vegetable oil spray

1. Using kitchen shears and working with 1 hen at a time, with hen breast side down, cut through bones on either side of backbone; discard backbone. Flatten hens and lay them breast side up on counter. Using sharp chef's knife, cut through center of breast to make 2 halves.

2. Using your fingers, carefully separate skin from breasts and thighs. Using metal skewer or tip of paring knife, poke 10 to 15 holes in fat deposits on top of breasts and thighs. Tuck wingtips underneath hens. Pat hens dry with paper towels.

3. Sprinkle 1 tablespoon salt on underside (bone side) of hens. Combine 1 tablespoon salt and oil in small bowl and stir until salt is evenly coated with oil. Add baking powder and stir until well combined. Turn hens skin side up and rub salt–baking powder mixture evenly over surface. Arrange hens skin side up and in single layer on large platter or plates and refrigerate, uncovered, for at least 4 hours or up to 24 hours.

4. Adjust oven racks to upper-middle and lower positions, place rimmed baking sheet on lower rack, and heat oven to 500 degrees.

5. Once oven is fully heated, spray skin side of hens with oil spray and season with pepper. Carefully transfer hens, skin side down, to preheated sheet and cook for 10 minutes.

6. Remove hens from oven and heat broiler. Flip hens skin side up. Transfer sheet to upper rack and broil until well browned and breasts register 160 degrees and drumsticks/thighs register 175 degrees, about 5 minutes, rotating sheet as needed to promote even browning. Transfer to platter or individual plates and serve.

JULIA CHILD'S STUFFED TURKEY, UPDATED

✔ WHY THIS RECIPE WORKS: In her 1989 cookbook, *The Way to Cook*, Julia Child separated a raw turkey into legs and breast to ensure that both white and dark meat were roasted to perfection. Julia's method made carving simpler, cooked faster than a whole turkey, and even included a small mound of rich sausage stuffing that tasted as though it had been roasted inside the bird. We loved the concept, but saw opportunities for improvement. We brined the breast to keep it juicy and flavorful. Jump-starting the cooking of the breast at 425 degrees decreased the overall cooking time, which also helped the meat retain moisture. For the stuffing, we made sure to thoroughly dry the bread cubes so the stuffing wouldn't be soggy. We also increased the amount of bread, and swapped the sausage for the brighter flavor of dried cranberries.

Anyone who has roasted a turkey knows the method has problems. Cooking takes forever, and breast and leg quarters cook at different rates, which makes delivering both perfectly cooked white and dark meat challenging. In the past, one way we've tackled these issues is by buying and roasting separate turkey parts rather than the whole bird. Parts cook more quickly and evenly, mostly because we are able to control the exact placement and timing of each piece. In the end, though, roasted turkey parts lack the celebratory grandeur of a whole bird. But in Julia Child's 1989 cookbook, *The Way to Cook*, she offers a way to achieve a turkey that is perfectly cooked *and* a gorgeous centerpiece.

Julia starts with a whole turkey that she turns into parts—first by using a cleaver and a rubber mallet to remove the turkey's backbone and then by lopping off the legs with a chef's knife. Next she bones the thighs and seasons their interiors with salt, pepper, and chopped fresh sage. The parts can be roasted separately, giving the breast a head start in a 325-degree oven before following with the leg quarters. Without the backbone (a poor conductor of heat) to slow things down, the bird cooks in about half of the time of a whole turkey. And her step of boning the thighs is a boon for carving: Some cooks remove the thighbones during carving in order to slice the meat against the grain for a more pleasing texture; with Julia's method the job is done upfront.

Julia also roasts her turkey breast atop a pile of stuffing—which results in stuffing that tastes as though it has been cooked in the bird. (Because this stuffing has greater exposure to heat than cooked-in-the-cavity stuffing does, it reaches a safe 165 degrees by the time the breast is done.) She then mounds the stuffing on a platter, props the breast on top, and rests a leg quarter on each side, camouflaging any gaps with garnishes so the parts look like a whole, intact (and celebratory) bird.

Quick, even cooking; idiotproof carving; and rich stuffing, all endorsed by Julia Child? I was sold.

I started by following Julia's recipe to a T. It turns out that dismantling a turkey with a cleaver and mallet isn't quite the carefree affair that Julia suggested. But with some experimenting, I figured out how to accomplish the task with just kitchen shears and a sharp knife: Happily, removing the legs and boning the thighs was a surprisingly simple operation. With the shears I followed the vertical line of fat where the breast meets the back and then, using two hands, bent back the breast to pop out the shoulder joint and cut away the back.

With my turkey prep complete, I continued to follow Julia's lead by whipping up a mound of her sausage and bread stuffing, which contains eggs, celery, and onions in addition to the namesake ingredients. I placed the breast on top of the stuffing, roasted it at 325 degrees, and then put the seasoned leg quarters in the oven 45 minutes later. After 2½ hours, all the parts were done.

How did it taste? Well, the legs and thighs were fantastic. My colleagues were also suitably impressed when I sliced the boned thighs crosswise. The stuffing, however, was a little too wet and there certainly wasn't enough of it—though it did have that irresistible savory taste of stuffing that's been cooked in the bird, something that I've missed in the years since we all stopped stuffing turkeys out of concern for food safety.

The breast was another story: Somewhat dry, tough, and underseasoned, it needed some serious attention.

To address the chalky, bland breast meat, I decided to employ our saltwater brining strategy. The meat would absorb some of the brine, allowing it to retain more moisture during cooking: Turkey breast, salt, water, fridge, 6 hours—done.

But when I roasted this first brined breast, it released its saltwater juices onto the stuffing, rendering it wet and inedibly salty. To address this problem, I started by adding 50 percent more bread in order to absorb the liquid. But before adding the bread cubes to the mix, I dried them out in the oven. We've used this technique many times for stuffing recipes, and even Julia calls for drying out the bread—just not for as long as we do. The key to a moist-but-not-too-moist stuffing cooked under a brined breast, I learned, was to dry the bread cubes for about 30 minutes at 300 degrees. The second tweak was to omit the sausage: Since all the turkey fat dripped into the stuffing, sausage was making the mixture overly rich and heavy, not to mention saltier. Third, I tossed in some dried cranberries along with the sautéed onions and celery that I'd retained from Julia's recipe, thinking that a sweet-tart note would be welcome. Finally, though stuffing recipes usually call for some added liquid, with all the turkey juices present, I introduced only eggs for a custardy richness.

When everything came out of the oven, this stuffing tasted great: It had just the right amount of moistness and was beautifully seasoned. But the breast, though now juicy, had pale, flabby skin. Plus the breast was taking too long to cook—about 2½ hours.

Some recipes call for jump-starting the turkey at a higher oven temperature to brown the skin and then finishing it at a lower temperature. I knew that would incinerate my stuffing. But who said the stuffing had to be part of the equation from the beginning?

For my next turkey, using the skillet in which I had softened the onions and celery for the stuffing, I arranged the breast skin side down to get a head start on browning. I blasted it in the oven at 425 degrees for 30 minutes while I set up my roasting pan with the stuffing and leg quarters. Then I arranged the breast, now skin side up, on top of the stuffing in the roasting pan and placed the whole assembly on the oven's upper-middle rack for even more browning. After another 30 minutes, I turned down the oven temperature to 350 degrees. Forty minutes later, my turkey was cooked through. I transferred the breast and legs to a carving board to rest for 30 minutes and stirred the stuffing to redistribute the juices before returning it to the now-off but still-warm oven. I sneaked a taste before summoning my colleagues to give the dish a try and sighed with relief—this golden-brown, juicy bird was the best of them all, and it had cooked in just an hour and 40 minutes.

At serving time, I reassembled my turkey by mounding the stuffing in the center of a platter, placing the breast on top, and resting a leg quarter on each side. This reconstructed bird was a showstopper indeed. And with that my turkey problems were solved, Julia-style.

—ANDREA GEARY, *Cook's Illustrated*

JULIA CHILD'S STUFFED TURKEY, UPDATED

Julia Child's Stuffed Turkey, Updated

SERVES 10 TO 12

If using a self-basting turkey (such as a frozen Butterball) or a kosher turkey, do not brine in step 3 and omit the salt in step 2. Remove any large pockets of fat from the neck cavity of the bird to ensure that the stuffing doesn't become greasy. The bottom of your roasting pan should be 7 to 8 inches from the top of the oven.

- 1 (12- to 15-pound) turkey, neck and giblets removed and reserved for gravy
- 1 teaspoon plus 2 tablespoons minced fresh sage
  Salt and pepper
  Wooden skewers
- 1½ pounds hearty white sandwich bread, cut into ½-inch cubes
- 1 tablespoon vegetable oil
- 3 tablespoons unsalted butter
- 3 onions, chopped fine
- 6 celery ribs, minced
- 1 cup dried cranberries
- 4 large eggs, beaten

1. With turkey breast side up, using boning or paring knife, cut through skin around leg quarter where it attaches to breast. Bend leg back to pop leg bone out of socket. Cut through joint to separate leg quarter. Repeat to remove second leg quarter. Working with 1 leg quarter at a time and with skin side down, use tip of knife to cut along sides of thighbone to expose bone, then slide knife under bone to free meat. Without severing skin, cut joint between thigh and leg and remove thighbone. Reserve thighbones for gravy.

2. Rub interior of each thigh with ½ teaspoon sage, ½ teaspoon salt, and ¼ teaspoon pepper. Truss each thigh closed using wooden skewers and kitchen twine. Place leg quarters on large plate, cover, and refrigerate for 6 to 12 hours.

3. Using kitchen shears, cut through ribs following vertical line of fat where breast meets back, from tapered end of breast to wing joint. Using your hands, bend back away from breast to pop shoulder joint out of socket. Cut through joint between bones to separate back from breast. Reserve back for gravy. Trim excess fat from breast. Dissolve ¾ cup salt in 6 quarts cold water in large container. Submerge breast in brine, cover, and refrigerate for 6 to 12 hours.

4. Adjust oven racks to upper-middle and lower-middle positions and heat oven to 300 degrees. Spread bread cubes in even layer on 2 rimmed baking sheets and bake until mostly dry and very lightly browned, 25 to 30 minutes, stirring occasionally during baking. Transfer dried bread to large bowl. Increase oven temperature to 425 degrees.

5. While bread dries, remove breast from brine and pat dry with paper towels (leave leg quarters in refrigerator). Tuck wings behind back. Brush surface with 2 teaspoons oil. Melt butter in 12-inch nonstick oven-safe skillet over medium heat. Add onions and cook, stirring occasionally, until softened, 10 to 12 minutes. Add celery, remaining 2 tablespoons sage, and 1½ teaspoons pepper; continue to cook until celery is slightly softened, 3 to 5 minutes longer. Transfer vegetables to bowl with bread and wipe out skillet with paper towels. Place turkey breast skin side down in skillet and roast on lower-middle rack for 30 minutes.

6. While breast roasts, add cranberries and eggs to bread mixture and toss to combine (mixture will be dry). Transfer stuffing to 16 by 13-inch roasting pan and, using rubber spatula, pat stuffing into level 12 by 10-inch rectangle.

7. Remove breast from oven and, using 2 wads of paper towels, flip breast and place over two-thirds of stuffing. Arrange leg quarters over remaining stuffing and brush with remaining 1 teaspoon oil. Lightly season breast and leg quarters with salt. Tuck any large sections of exposed stuffing under bird so most of stuffing is covered by turkey. Transfer pan to upper-middle rack and cook for 30 minutes.

8. Reduce oven temperature to 350 degrees. Continue to roast until thickest part of breast registers 160 degrees and thickest part of thigh registers 175 degrees, 40 minutes to 1 hour 20 minutes longer. Transfer breast and leg quarters to carving board and let rest for 30 minutes. While turkey rests, using metal spatula, stir stuffing well, scraping up any browned bits. Redistribute stuffing over bottom of roasting pan, return to oven, and turn off oven.

9. Before serving, season stuffing with salt and pepper to taste. Mound stuffing in center of platter. Place breast on top of stuffing with point of breast resting on highest part of mound. Remove skewers and twine from leg quarters and place on each side of breast. Carve and serve.

Turkey Gravy for Julia Child's Stuffed Turkey, Updated

MAKES ABOUT 4 CUPS

If you do not have ¼ cup of reserved turkey fat in step 4, supplement with unsalted butter.

> Reserved turkey giblets, neck, backbone, and thighbones, hacked into 2-inch pieces
> 2 onions, chopped coarse
> 1 carrot, peeled and cut into 1-inch pieces
> 1 celery rib, cut into 1-inch pieces
> 6 garlic cloves, unpeeled
> 1 tablespoon vegetable oil
> 3½ cups chicken broth
> 3 cups water
> 2 cups dry white wine
> 6 sprigs fresh thyme
> ¼ cup all-purpose flour
> Salt and pepper

1. Adjust oven rack to middle position and heat oven to 450 degrees. Place turkey parts, onions, carrot, celery, and garlic in large roasting pan. Drizzle with oil and toss to combine. Roast, stirring occasionally, until well browned, 40 to 50 minutes.

2. Remove pan from oven and place over high heat. Add broth and bring to boil, scraping up any browned bits. Transfer contents of pan to Dutch oven. Add water, wine, and thyme; bring to boil over high heat. Reduce heat to low and simmer until reduced by half, about 1½ hours.

3. Strain contents of pot through fine-mesh strainer set in large bowl. Press solids with back of spatula to extract as much liquid as possible. Discard solids. Transfer liquid to fat separator and let settle, 5 minutes.

4. Transfer ¼ cup fat to medium saucepan and heat over medium-high heat until bubbling. Whisk in flour and cook, whisking constantly, until combined and honey-colored, about 2 minutes. Gradually whisk in hot liquid and bring to boil. Reduce heat to medium-low and simmer, stirring occasionally, until thickened, about 5 minutes. Season with salt and pepper to taste. (Gravy can be refrigerated for up to 2 days.)

NOTES FROM THE TEST KITCHEN

CARVING THE TURKEY BEFORE COOKING
The beauty of Julia's recipe is that most of the butchery happens before the bird goes into the oven, minimizing the work at serving time. Here's our take on how to break down the turkey.

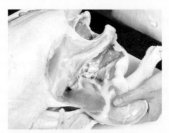

1. Using boning or paring knife, cut through skin around leg where it attaches to breast. Bend leg back to pop leg bone out of socket. Cut through joint to separate leg quarter.

2. With tip of knife, cut along sides of each thighbone to expose bone, then slide knife under bone to free meat. Without severing skin, cut joint between thigh and leg and remove thighbone.

3. Rub interior of each thigh with sage, salt, and pepper. Truss thighs closed with wooden skewers and kitchen twine.

4. Using kitchen shears, cut through ribs, following line of fat running from tapered end of breast to wing joint.

5. Using your hands, bend backbone away from breast to pop shoulder joint out of socket. Cut through shoulder joint to separate back from breast.

SEAFOOD

OVEN-STEAMED MUSSELS

✓ **WHY THIS RECIPE WORKS:** Briny-sweet mussels are surprisingly underutilized in home kitchens, so we set out to make them approachable and foolproof. First, we moved the cooking from the stovetop to the oven, where the even heat ensured they cooked through more gently. We traded the Dutch oven for a large roasting pan so they weren't crowded to further ensure even cooking. Covering the pan with aluminum foil trapped the moisture so the mussels didn't dry out. For a flavorful cooking liquid, we reduced white wine to concentrate its flavor and added thyme, garlic, and red pepper flakes for aromatic complexity. To streamline our recipe, we cooked the aromatics and wine on the stovetop in the roasting pan before tossing in our mussels and transferring the pan to the oven. A few pats of butter, stirred in at the end, gave the sauce richness and body.

I love cooking mussels. They're cheap and quick to prepare, with tender flesh and a briny-sweet, built-in broth created by the merging of the mussels and their steaming liquid.

So why don't more people make them? My friends all cite the same reasons: Mussels are hard to clean, and it seems a little dicey trying to figure out if they're safe to eat. Fortunately, these misconceptions are easy to dispel. Most mussels these days need very little cleaning. The vast majority are farmed, which leads to less sand and grit and fewer of the stringy beards that cling to the shell. As for figuring out whether a mussel is safe to cook, this couldn't be more straightforward. Your first clue is smell: A dead mussel smells very bad, whereas a live mussel should smell pleasantly briny, and its shell (if open) should close when tapped. That's it. If a mussel is alive before you cook it, it will be safe to eat when it's done.

The real problem with mussels is that they come in all different sizes, from pinky-finger small to almost palm-size large. Since they're generally sold in multi-pound bags, it's virtually impossible to select mussels that are all the same size and, therefore, will all cook at the same rate. This means that when steamed, a solid number of mussels will turn out perfectly, but inevitably some will remain closed (a sign that they're undercooked). If cooked until every one has opened, however, an equal number of mussels will turn out overdone. Could I figure out a way to get more of them to cook at the same rate?

First I needed a basic recipe. Most sources using the classic French method of steaming mussels, or *moules marinières*, follow this simple model: Sauté garlic and other aromatics in a Dutch oven, pour in wine and bring it to a boil, add the mussels, cover the pot, and cook for 10 minutes or so, until all the mussels have opened. Toss in a handful of herbs, stir, and serve with crusty bread to sop up the broth.

There were differences in the recipes I tried, of course. The more successful ones had you boil down the wine a bit before adding the mussels in order to take the edge off the alcohol and round out the flavors of the finished broth. Ditto for those recipes that added some sort of dairy as a thickener at the end of cooking to give the sauce body and help it cling to the mussels. Finally, a little aromatic complexity is a plus. In the end, I decided that red pepper flakes, thyme sprigs, and bay leaves (along with a generous amount of parsley) were just the right combination.

With a good basic recipe in hand, I moved on to the major mussel-cooking conundrum. I wondered if a more gentle approach would prevent those mussels that opened first from drying out before the others caught up. I cooked two batches of mussels on the stove—one at a simmer and the other at a rolling boil. Overall there wasn't a huge difference between the two approaches. If I waited for virtually every mussel to open, I was left with a fair number of tough, overcooked specimens.

But it was during this test that I realized another problem inherent in the traditional method of cooking mussels: the use of a big pot on the stove. With a relatively large number of mussels (at least a pound per person), my pot was nearly full to the brim, which made stirring to redistribute the mussels unwieldy. And if the mussels stay put, this only exacerbates the problem of uneven cooking, since the mussels at the bottom of the pot, whether small or large, are exposed to more heat. Cutting the amount of mussels in half so I could stir them more easily did make more of them cook at the same rate. But how could I mimic this result and still cook the quantity of mussels I wanted? A pot or pan with more surface area—or, better yet, a large roasting pan?

One way we've achieved more even cooking in recipes is by using the oven rather than the stove. In the oven, heat surrounds the food on all sides, leading to more even (and gentle) cooking. So for my next test, I preheated the oven to its highest setting. I placed 4 pounds

OVEN-STEAMED MUSSELS

SIX GOOD THINGS TO KNOW ABOUT MUSSELS

1. They're safe to eat. Mussels are routinely tested by state and local agencies for the presence of algae-derived toxins. The Monterey Bay Aquarium's Seafood Watch program calls them a "Best Choice" for environmental sustainability.

2. They need almost no cleaning. Most mussels are cultivated on long ropes suspended from rafts, which leaves them free of sand and grit—and for the most part, beards. In general, all they need is a quick rinse under the tap.

3. It's easy to tell when they're fresh. A live mussel will smell pleasantly briny. If open, its shell should close up when lightly tapped (but give it a moment; some mussels take longer than others to clam up).

4. It's equally easy to tell when they're not. A dead mussel deteriorates rapidly and will smell almost immediately. Also discard any mussel with a cracked or broken shell or a shell that won't close.

5. You can store mussels for up to three days. As soon as you bring them home, place them in a bowl, cover it with a wet paper towel, and store it in the fridge.

6. Unopened cooked mussels needn't be discarded. A mussel that's closed after cooking isn't unfit to eat. It's a sign that the mussel needs more cooking. To open a reluctant mussel, microwave it briefly (30 seconds or so).

"BEARDED"? DON'T WORRY.

Because of the way they're cultivated, most mussels these days are free of the fibrous strands, or "beards," that wild mussels use to hold on to rocks and other surfaces.

If your mussel has a beard, hold it and use the back of a paring knife to remove it with a stern yank.

of mussels in a large roasting pan, covered it tightly with foil, and set it on the middle oven rack. These mussels took a bit longer to cook (even at 500 degrees, the oven is more gentle than a direct flame), but when they were done, I breathed a sigh of relief: Only one or two hadn't opened and the others were moist and plump.

Once my friends discovered how unfounded their fears were and tried my method for oven steaming, I knew they'd be as hooked as I am on cooking mussels at home.

—ANDREW JANJIGIAN, *Cook's Illustrated*

Oven-Steamed Mussels

SERVES 2 TO 4

Discard any mussel with an unpleasant odor or with a cracked or broken shell or a shell that won't close.

- 1 tablespoon extra-virgin olive oil
- 3 garlic cloves, minced
  - Pinch red pepper flakes
- 1 cup dry white wine
- 3 sprigs fresh thyme
- 2 bay leaves
- 4 pounds mussels, scrubbed and debearded
- ¼ teaspoon salt
- 2 tablespoons unsalted butter, cut into 4 pieces
- 2 tablespoons minced fresh parsley

1. Adjust oven rack to lowest position and heat oven to 500 degrees. Heat oil, garlic, and pepper flakes in large roasting pan over medium heat; cook, stirring constantly, until fragrant, about 30 seconds. Add wine, thyme sprigs, and bay leaves and bring to boil. Cook until wine is slightly reduced, about 1 minute. Add mussels and salt. Cover pan tightly with aluminum foil and transfer to oven. Cook until most mussels have opened (a few may remain closed), 15 to 18 minutes.

2. Remove pan from oven. Push mussels to sides of pan. Add butter to center and whisk until melted. Discard thyme sprigs and bay leaves, sprinkle parsley over mussels, and toss to combine. Serve immediately.

VARIATIONS

Oven-Steamed Mussels with Hard Cider and Bacon

Omit garlic and red pepper flakes. Heat oil and 4 slices thick-cut bacon, cut into ½-inch pieces, in roasting pan until bacon has rendered and is starting to crisp, about 5 minutes. Proceed with recipe as directed, substituting dry hard cider for wine and ¼ cup heavy cream for butter.

Oven-Steamed Mussels with Leeks and Pernod

Omit red pepper flakes and increase oil to 3 tablespoons. Heat oil; 1 pound leeks, white and light green parts only, halved lengthwise, sliced thin, and washed thoroughly; and garlic in roasting pan until leeks are wilted, about 3 minutes. Proceed with recipe as directed, omitting thyme sprigs and substituting ½ cup Pernod and ¼ cup water for wine, ¼ cup crème fraîche for butter, and chives for parsley.

NEW ENGLAND LOBSTER ROLL

✓ **WHY THIS RECIPE WORKS:** Few New England traditions are as beloved as the lobster roll, but cooking lobster at home can be a daunting process. We wanted a foolproof way to achieve perfectly cooked lobster, whether we were putting it in a roll or not. We found that the best and safest way to cook the lobsters was to sedate them by placing them in the freezer for 30 minutes before dropping them in the pot. The lobsters were perfectly cooked when the tail reached 175 degrees. For our lobster roll, we mostly adhered to tradition: a top-loading supermarket hotdog bun, mayonnaise, and lots of lobster meat. We added a hint of fresh crunch with judicious amounts of lettuce and celery, and we added complementary brightness with lemon juice, cayenne, and chives.

Visitors to New England initially regard our beloved lobster roll with skepticism. After all, we're talking about coating pricey lobster meat with mayonnaise, piling it into a supermarket hot dog bun, and serving it with pickles and potato chips. It seems like a strangely cavalier treatment of a luxury foodstuff.

Such doubts vanish with the first bite. The simple mayo complements the richly flavored lobster without obscuring it, and the squishy bun molds like a custom-made cradle. The grilled sides of the top-loading bun provide a crisp, buttery frame for the cool salad within.

Because great seafood places are ubiquitous in these parts, New Englanders rarely make lobster rolls at home. But what if you live hundreds of miles from the Maine shore? Is it possible to re-create this classic in your own kitchen? Sure. But first you have to figure out a safe and foolproof way to cook a live and kicking lobster.

First decision: Would I be roasting, steaming, or boiling? Roasted lobster can be difficult to prepare because the slow heat of the oven causes proteins in the meat to adhere to the shell. Steaming required a steamer or a rack, and it left the lobsters slightly underseasoned.

Boiling in salt water was the way to go, but there was a problem: Every time I tried to maneuver a lobster into the pot, it thrashed its tail in protest, often sending a wave of boiling water across the stovetop. Surely there was an easier way—at least for the cook.

Many cooks advocate anesthetizing lobsters before cooking them. Some believe it is more humane, while others argue that gently handled lobsters are tastier.

Mostly I hoped it would make the little guys more manageable. The first few methods I tested ranged from grisly (slicing through the head) to quirky (soaking in a salt-water–clove oil bath), and—since they didn't sedate the lobster, didn't produce better flavor or texture, were too labor intensive, or all of the above—I quickly moved on.

In Harold McGee's *On Food and Cooking*, I discovered the most successful technique for sedating a lobster yet: immersing the lobster in an ice bath for 30 minutes before cooking. The chilled lobster seemed comatose as I transferred it from ice bath to pot, and its meat was properly cooked. However, chilling a single lobster in this manner required a 6-quart container and 2 quarts of ice, and chilling additional lobsters would have required more space and more ice, making it impractical for preparing multiple lobsters simultaneously.

Wondering if a simpler method might work, I placed four lobsters in a large bowl, which I then placed in the freezer while I brought a stockpot of salted water to a boil. After 30 minutes, I nudged them gently: nary a twitch. When I transferred the chilled lobsters to the pot, they were limp and unresponsive, and they sank to the bottom with just a few reassuring flutters that indicated that they were still alive. I had found the safest, easiest way to get the lobsters into the pot. Now to make the cooking method foolproof.

Most lobster recipes are accompanied by intimidating charts that tell you how long to boil based on your lobster's weight, whether it has a hard or soft shell, and how many are being cooked in the same pot. But why can't we simply take the temperature of a lobster the same way we do with other kinds of meat?

I discovered that we can do just that—but the target temperature turned out to be much higher than I expected. I usually cook fish to an internal temperature

NOTES FROM THE TEST KITCHEN

THE NEW BASICS OF COOKING LOBSTERS

Chilling lobsters in the freezer for 30 minutes induces a comalike state that makes it easier and safer to maneuver them into the pot. Cooking the tail to 175 degrees ensures perfectly cooked meat.

of 130 to 140 degrees, but when I pulled a lobster out at 135 (determined by a digital thermometer poked into the underside of the meaty tail), the meat was undercooked, translucent, and floppy. At 160 degrees it was still too soft. Eventually I landed at a tail temperature of 175 (after about 12 minutes of cooking), which guaranteed tender claws and knuckles and a pleasantly resilient tail.

Why the higher temperature? Fish muscle is composed of very short muscle fibers that require only mild heat to shrink them so that they firm up and turn from translucent to opaque. The muscle fibers in lobsters are much longer, especially in the tail section, so they require a higher temperature to attain that desirably firm, snappy texture. Now I was ready to build my roll.

There are as many "right" ways to prepare a lobster roll as there are people who eat them. Everything from the size of the lobster pieces and the inclusion of things like lettuce, herbs, and onions can differ from roll to roll. So I decided it would be my roll, my rules.

Traditionalists like to leave the lobster meat in generous hunks. The effect is one of impressive opulence, but it's darn hard to eat. Chunks are fine for the claws and knuckles because they're tender and, being smaller, well seasoned by the salted cooking water. But the tail is so meaty and dense that large pieces can seem undersalted and tough. So I bucked tradition and cut the tail into smaller pieces, making it easier to eat and giving it more surface area for the seasoned dressing to cling to.

For the vegetable additions, I opted for a single soft lettuce leaf in each roll and a bit of minced celery for unobtrusive crunch. A mere teaspoon of chives gave my salad a hint of bright herb flavor. A splash of lemon juice and a tiny pinch of cayenne pepper made a perfect counterpoint to the richly flavored meat and the buttery bun.

This was a New England lobster roll that would convince any skeptic. And now that I had a safe and foolproof way to cook lobster, I could enjoy it anytime.

—ANDREA GEARY, *Cook's Illustrated*

NOTES FROM THE TEST KITCHEN

THE BEST WAY TO EXTRACT LOBSTER MEAT

There's a lot more meat in a lobster than just the tail and claws—if you know how to get it. Here's our tried-and-true approach to extracting every last bit, no special tools needed. The method works for both hard- and soft-shell lobsters.

1. SEPARATE TAIL: Once cooked lobster is cool enough to handle, set it on cutting board. Grasp tail with one hand and body with other hand and twist to separate.

4. MOVE TO KNUCKLES: Twist "arms" to remove claws and attached "knuckles." Twist knuckles to remove from claws. Break knuckles at joint and use handle of teaspoon to push out meat.

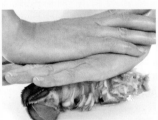

2. FLATTEN TAIL: Lay tail on its side on counter and use both hands to press down on tail until shell cracks.

5. REMOVE CLAW MEAT: Wiggle hinged portion of each claw to separate. If meat is stuck inside small part, remove it with skewer. Break open claws, cracking each side, and remove meat.

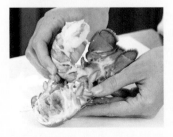

3. TAKE OUT TAIL MEAT: Hold tail, shell facing down. Pull back on sides to crack open shell, and remove meat. Rinse meat under water to remove green tomalley if you wish; pat meat dry with paper towels and remove dark vein.

6. FINISH WITH LEGS: Twist legs to remove and lay flat on counter. Using rolling pin, roll toward open end, pushing out meat. Stop rolling before reaching end of each leg; open tip of leg can crack and release pieces of shell.

Boiled Lobster

SERVES 4 OR YIELDS 1 POUND MEAT

To cook four lobsters at once, you will need a pot with a capacity of at least 3 gallons. If your pot is smaller, boil the lobsters in batches. Start timing the lobsters from the moment they go into the pot.

    4   (1¼-pound) live lobsters
    ⅓   cup salt

1. Place lobsters in large bowl and freeze for 30 minutes. Meanwhile, bring 2 gallons water to boil in large pot over high heat.

2. Add lobsters and salt to pot, arranging with tongs so that all lobsters are submerged. Cover pot, leaving lid slightly ajar, and adjust heat to maintain gentle boil. Cook for 12 minutes, until thickest part of tail registers 175 degrees (insert thermometer into underside of tail to take temperature). If temperature registers lower than 175 degrees, return lobster to pot for 2 minutes longer, until tail registers 175 degrees, using tongs to transfer lobster in and out of pot.

3. Serve immediately or transfer lobsters to rimmed baking sheet and set aside until cool enough to remove meat, about 10 minutes. (Lobster meat can be refrigerated for up to 24 hours.)

New England Lobster Roll

SERVES 6

This recipe is best when made with lobster you've cooked yourself. Use a very small pinch of cayenne pepper, as it should not make the dressing spicy.

    2   tablespoons mayonnaise
    2   tablespoons minced celery
    1½   teaspoons lemon juice
    1   teaspoon minced fresh chives
         Salt
         Pinch cayenne pepper
    1   pound lobster meat, tail meat cut into ½-inch pieces
         and claw meat cut into 1-inch pieces
    6   New England–style hot dog buns
    2   tablespoons unsalted butter, softened
    6   leaves Boston lettuce

1. Whisk mayonnaise, celery, lemon juice, chives, ⅛ teaspoon salt, and cayenne together in large bowl. Add lobster and gently toss to combine.

2. Place 12-inch nonstick skillet over low heat. Butter both sides of hot dog buns and sprinkle lightly with salt. Place buns in skillet, with 1 buttered side down; increase heat to medium-low; and cook until crisp and brown, 2 to 3 minutes. Flip and cook second side until crisp and brown, 2 to 3 minutes longer. Transfer buns to large platter. Line each bun with lettuce leaf. Spoon lobster salad into buns and serve immediately.

SHRIMP FRA DIAVOLO

✔ WHY THIS RECIPE WORKS: Ideally, shrimp fra diavolo is a lively, piquant dish full of briny, plump shrimp and juicy chunks of tomato, with pepper flakes and garlic providing an aromatic backbone. But too often, the shrimp are overcooked and the spice obliterates the other flavors, leaving the dish hot but one-dimensional. To highlight the sweet shrimp flavor in our spicy sauce, we browned the shrimp shells to make a stock. We also amped up the savory seafood flavor with minced anchovies. Poaching the shrimp directly in the sauce cooked them to succulent perfection. In addition, we intensified the heat and depth of the red pepper flakes by adding minced pepperoncini. A generous handful of chopped herbs, stirred in at the end, contributed freshness, while extra-virgin olive oil gave the dish a bright, peppery finish.

If the devil wanted to trick me into relinquishing my soul, I'd be insulted if he showed up for the occasion sporting a shiny red jumpsuit, pointy horns, and a slick goatee. I like to think that it would take a bit more subtlety and finesse to tempt me. Yet many dishes with "devilish" names are so in-your-face spicy and pungent and so obvious that they're about as suavely enticing as a cartoon Beelzebub.

Consider shrimp fra diavolo, the 20th-century Italian American combo of shrimp, tomatoes, garlic, and hot pepper, often served over spaghetti or with crusty bread. At its best, it's lively and piquant, the tangy tomatoes countering the sweet and briny shrimp, and the pepper and garlic providing a spirited kick. Unfortunately, the spice is often so heavy-handed that it completely overwhelms the other flavors.

SHRIMP FRA DIAVOLO

What's more, the fragile shrimp are often flambéed or pan-seared before being cooked further in the sauce, transforming them into chunks of overcooked, flavorless protein, identifiable only by their shape.

Simply taming the heat of shrimp fra diavolo would be as easy as cutting back on the red pepper flakes, but that would make it more like shrimp marinara. I intended to preserve the dish's fiery character and also heighten the other flavors so that they could stand up to the heat. And I'd make sure that those shrimp remained succulent.

I started with the simplest sauce recipe I could find: a goodly amount of both garlic and red pepper flakes and a bit of dried oregano—all sautéed in a few tablespoons of vegetable oil until fragrant—plus chopped canned whole tomatoes and their juice, cooked down for a few minutes until thickened. My question was how to cook the shrimp. Recipes that I found called for one of three techniques: sautéing the peeled shrimp (1½ pounds would yield four servings) along with the aromatics in oil before adding the sauce components; flambéing the sautéed shrimp by adding a few glugs of cognac to the pan and waving a lit match over the surface; and, the simplest method, slipping raw shrimp into the simmering tomato sauce, where they poached until just opaque and cooked through.

I hoped that by simply sautéing the shrimp I could coax out good briny flavor without overcooking them. Even more important, I hoped that the method would yield a valuable byproduct: the flavorful browned bits known as fond, which would serve as a rich shrimp base for the sauce. But alas, even browning the shrimp enough to develop fond had them teetering on the edge of overcooked, and stirring them back into the sauce before serving to meld their flavors sealed the deal.

Poaching, meanwhile, produced the tender shrimp that I was after, but the finished product tasted like what I was trying to avoid: spicy shrimp marinara. If only I could use this poaching method but along the way boost the flavor presence of the shrimp.

I considered sacrificing a small portion of the shrimp by searing them to build fond and then throwing them away. That way, I'd develop a rich seafood backbone for the sauce before gently poaching the remaining raw shrimp in the sauce. But then it occurred to me that I already had a flavor-building ingredient at my disposal.

Crustacean shells contain loads of proteins, sugars, and flavor-boosting compounds called glutamates and nucleotides that are ideal for building the flavorful browning known as the Maillard reaction. Searing these smaller shell-on shrimp would only overcook them, but browning the to-be-discarded shells as a foundation for the sauce was a possibility. The concept is a classic first step when making shrimp bisque.

I started a new batch, this time sautéing the shrimp shells in a little oil until they and the surface of the pan were spotty brown. Then I deglazed the pan with wine—another technique from seafood bisques. Next, I added the juice from a can of whole tomatoes (I'd add the solids later) and let the shells simmer, essentially creating a tomatoey shrimp "stock," which I strained from the shells about 5 minutes later. When I took a whiff of the cooking liquid, the intensity of its seafood aroma and the remarkably rich, savory flavor impressed me.

The rest of the sauce was quick to pull together. I wiped out the skillet and sautéed the garlic, pepper flakes, and oregano in a couple of tablespoons of oil until fragrant and then added the reserved tomato solids (which I pummeled with a potato masher to make a pulpy puree). In went the tomato stock. I cranked up the heat a bit and let the mixture simmer for about 5 minutes to let it thicken. Finally, I added the shrimp, turning them a few times to ensure that they cooked evenly, and finished the dish with handfuls of chopped basil and parsley and a drizzle of fruity extra-virgin olive oil.

I was almost satisfied: The shrimp were plump and juicy, and the sauce boasted true (but not overwhelming) heat. Searing the shells had paid off; there was more than a hint of rich shrimp flavor and brininess. And yet I hadn't nailed the intensity of either one of those flavors, so I pawed through the test kitchen pantry for something that might help.

Minutes later, I had an answer in each hand. The first: a jar of anchovies. Don't underestimate the potential of these little fish. Mincing a pair of fillets (rinsed first to reduce their saltiness) and browning them with the aromatics added remarkably savory, not fishy, depth. The second, more unexpected find was a jar of pepperoncini. When I stirred in two of these minced pickled peppers at the end with the herbs, the acidity—and heat—of the sauce perked up just a bit more. On a whim, I stirred in a teaspoon of the brine from the jar, too, which amplified the effect.

This version of shrimp fra diavolo had enough fire from the garlic and pepper to please the most daring of diners and a round, rich seafood flavor, too. Served with warm, crusty bread, it made a meal that would tempt the devil himself.

—ANDREA GEARY, *Cook's Illustrated*

Shrimp Fra Diavolo

SERVES 4

If the shrimp you are using have been treated with salt (check the bag's ingredient list), skip the salting in step 1 and add ¼ teaspoon of salt to the sauce in step 3. Adjust the amount of pepper flakes depending on how spicy you want the dish. Serve the shrimp with a salad and crusty bread or over spaghetti.

1½ pounds large shrimp (26 to 30 per pound), peeled and deveined, shells reserved

Salt

1 (28-ounce) can whole peeled tomatoes

NOTES FROM THE TEST KITCHEN

THE SECRET'S IN THE STOCK
To amp up savory shrimp flavor and brightness in our Shrimp Fra Diavolo, we eked out a shrimp stock by browning the shells—an ingredient we would have otherwise discarded. In just minutes, the shells give up remarkably rich flavor, which is balanced by the acidity from some white wine and juice from canned tomatoes.

FLAVOR FOUNDATION
Briefly simmering browned shrimp shells produces a surprisingly complex stock to bolster the flavor of the sauce.

3 tablespoons vegetable oil

1 cup dry white wine

4 garlic cloves, minced

½–1 teaspoon red pepper flakes

½ teaspoon dried oregano

2 anchovy fillets, rinsed, patted dry, and minced

¼ cup chopped fresh basil

¼ cup chopped fresh parsley

1½ teaspoons minced pepperoncini plus 1 teaspoon brine

2 tablespoons extra-virgin olive oil

1. Toss shrimp with ½ teaspoon salt and set aside. Pour tomatoes into colander set over large bowl. Pierce tomatoes with edge of rubber spatula and stir briefly to release juice. Transfer drained tomatoes to small bowl and reserve juice. Do not wash colander.

2. Heat 1 tablespoon vegetable oil in 12-inch skillet over high heat until shimmering. Add shrimp shells and cook, stirring frequently, until they begin to turn spotty brown and skillet starts to brown, 2 to 4 minutes. Remove skillet from heat and carefully add wine. When bubbling subsides, return skillet to heat and simmer until wine is reduced to about 2 tablespoons, 2 to 4 minutes. Add reserved tomato juice and simmer to meld flavors, 5 minutes. Pour contents of skillet into colander set over bowl. Discard shells and reserve liquid. Wipe out skillet with paper towels.

3. Heat remaining 2 tablespoons vegetable oil, garlic, pepper flakes, and oregano in now-empty skillet over medium heat, stirring occasionally, until garlic is straw-colored and fragrant, 1 to 2 minutes. Add anchovies and stir until fragrant, about 30 seconds. Remove from heat. Add drained tomatoes and mash with potato masher until coarsely pureed. Return to heat and stir in reserved tomato juice mixture. Increase heat to medium-high and simmer until mixture has thickened, about 5 minutes.

4. Add shrimp to skillet and simmer gently, stirring and turning shrimp frequently, until they are just cooked through, 4 to 5 minutes. Remove pan from heat. Stir in basil, parsley, and pepperoncini and brine and season with salt to taste. Drizzle with olive oil and serve.

CHARLESTON SHRIMP PERLOO

✓ **WHY THIS RECIPE WORKS:** We loved the simple concept behind *perloo*, a jambalaya-like traditional South Carolina one-pot meal of rice, vegetables, and meat (most traditionally shrimp) cooked in a flavorful stock. With so few elements, we knew that each one needed to be perfect. For our base we made a quick, deeply flavored shrimp stock by sautéing shrimp shells in butter with onion and celery. For the vegetables, we kept the flavor profile clean and simple with more onion and celery along with green bell pepper and canned tomatoes. Toasting the rice in butter helped the grains stay firm and separate—not mushy—when cooked. To avoid overcooking the shrimp, we stirred them in during the last few minutes of cooking, then took the pot off the stove and let the shrimp cook through in the gentle, residual heat. A touch of cayenne, garlic, and thyme gave our perloo an aromatic finish.

If you're not from Charleston, South Carolina, there's a good chance you've never heard of a *perloo* (pronounced "PUHR-low"). But it's a staple in South Carolina's Lowcountry, dating back to the 17th century. It's made by simmering long-grain white rice in broth with onions, celery, bell pepper, sometimes tomatoes, and meat—either chicken, game, or seafood. The rice soaks up the flavor of all the other ingredients as it cooks, making for an incredibly satisfying one-pot meal. The finished dish bears a strong resemblance to jambalaya, only less soupy, more tomatoey, and without the smoked sausage. It sounds straightforward enough, but I know that with these simple-seeming recipes, the devil is often lurking in the details. So I booked a plane ticket to Charleston to get some firsthand knowledge.

Down there, two amazing teachers walked me through the recipe. Chef Robert Stehling, of the famed Hominy Grill, made okra perloo in the oven, layering the ingredients in a roasting pan and then baking them for half an hour. My other guide was Mitchell Crosby, whom I'd found by nosing around Charleston's food community; if anyone can cook an authentic perloo, several people told me, it's Crosby. He cooked a shrimp perloo on the stovetop and made a point of resting the finished dish for 10 minutes, off heat. While the techniques were different, what both versions shared was tender, moist, just slightly sticky rice and fantastic flavor.

Back home in the test kitchen, I decided I'd tackle the recipe in three parts: broth, rice, and shrimp, in that order. And since I didn't need to make a roasting pan's worth, I'd stick with the stovetop.

Crosby's perloo, like many other modern ones, had used chicken broth. But after a couple of tests, I decided to go the classic route and make shrimp stock. I had the shells handy, and I knew from experience that shrimp stock is actually surprisingly easy to make. After peeling the shrimp, I sautéed the shells in butter with onions and celery until browned. Then I added water, bay leaves, peppercorns, and parsley and simmered for about 30 minutes. I strained out the solids and dipped in a spoon—excellent. I was off to a good start.

For the rice, I'd stick to the traditional flavors—the base of onions, celery, and bell pepper sautéed with garlic, thyme, and cayenne. I added a can of diced tomatoes (fresh tomatoes aren't reliable year-round), rice, and my shrimp stock. After everything had simmered, covered, for 20 minutes, I lifted the lid—and saw a pot of blown-out rice. I reviewed my notes and realized that I'd neglected a crucial step—Stehling had sautéed the rice before adding the stock to harden the grains' exterior starches and prevent mush.

Hoping that I'd identified the problem, I made another batch, adding the sautéing step. This batch was better but not perfect. Another test cook wondered if I'd failed to account for the liquid in the canned tomatoes. Rice is finicky to cook, and if you screw up the liquid-to-rice ratio, you're asking for trouble. I was using 2 cups of rice and 4 cups of shrimp stock. I tried again, this time using 3 cups of stock—bingo. The rice was tender, with separate grains.

And finally: the shrimp. These crustaceans are as finicky to cook as rice; one moment too long over the heat and they go from nicely firm to disastrously rubbery. Crosby had stressed the importance of the off-heat resting period, during which the residual heat inside the pot gently finishes the rice. I wondered if I could prevent rubbery shrimp by cooking them in that same gentle residual heat. I tried stirring in the shrimp as soon as I took the rice off the heat. They came out slightly underdone, so next I gently folded in the shrimp 5 minutes before turning off the rice and then let them rest, covered, as before. Perfect. This pot took me straight back to Charleston.

—NICK IVERSON, *Cook's Country*

Charleston Shrimp Perloo

SERVES 4 TO 6

After adding the shrimp to the pot, fold it in gently; stirring the rice too vigorously will make it mushy. Any extra stock can be refrigerated for three days or frozen for up to one month. Serve with hot sauce.

- 5 tablespoons unsalted butter
- 1½ pounds extra-large shrimp (21 to 25 per pound), peeled and deveined, shells reserved
- 2 onions, chopped
- 4 celery ribs, chopped
- Salt and pepper
- 4 cups water
- 1 tablespoon peppercorns
- 5 sprigs fresh parsley
- 2 bay leaves
- 1 green bell pepper, stemmed, seeded, and chopped
- 2 cups long-grain white rice
- 2 garlic cloves, minced
- 1 teaspoon minced fresh thyme
- ¼ teaspoon cayenne pepper
- 1 (14.5-ounce) can diced tomatoes

1. Melt 1 tablespoon butter in large saucepan over medium heat. Add shrimp shells, 1 cup onion, ½ cup celery, and 1 teaspoon salt and cook, stirring occasionally, until shells are spotty brown, about 10 minutes. Add water, peppercorns, parsley, and bay leaves. Increase heat to high and bring to boil. Reduce heat to low, cover, and simmer for 30 minutes. Strain shrimp stock through fine-mesh strainer set over large bowl, pressing on solids to extract as much liquid as possible; discard solids.

2. Melt remaining 4 tablespoons butter in Dutch oven over medium heat. Add bell pepper, remaining onion and celery, and ½ teaspoon salt and cook until vegetables are beginning to soften, 5 to 7 minutes. Add rice, garlic, thyme, and cayenne and cook until fragrant and rice is translucent, about 2 minutes. Stir in tomatoes and their juice and 3 cups shrimp stock (reserve remainder for another use) and bring to boil. Reduce heat to low, cover, and cook for 20 minutes.

3. Gently fold shrimp into rice until evenly distributed, cover, and continue to cook 5 minutes longer. Remove pot from heat and let sit, covered, until shrimp are cooked through and all liquid is absorbed, about 10 minutes. Serve.

CALIFORNIA FISH TACOS

✔ **WHY THIS RECIPE WORKS:** Simple, satisfying fish tacos from the West Coast combine fried fish, shredded cabbage, and a creamy mayo-based sauce in a soft corn tortilla. We wanted to keep our tacos simple and ensure a perfect balance of flavors and textures. An ultrathin beer batter using a combination of flour, cornstarch, and baking powder proved to be ideal for getting a light, crispy coating on the delicate white fish. Quick-pickled onions and jalapeños added tart spiciness, and tossing shredded cabbage with the pickling liquid just before serving added flavor without overcomplicating the dish. Lime juice and sour cream added tang to the traditional creamy sauce. Fresh cilantro added a lively finishing touch.

Named after the region in Mexico where they originated, Baja fish tacos have been making their way across the United States, gaining popularity as they go. It's easy to see the appeal of these tacos: The crispy fried whitefish, crunchy cabbage, and creamy white sauce, all piled onto a corn tortilla (or two), come together to deliver an irresistible combination of flavors and textures.

Determined to make a tasty version that was easy enough for a weeknight dinner, I weeded through a bevy of recipes for Baja tacos—rejecting those that called for "creative" ingredients like pineapple salsa—until I'd found several traditional versions to test.

After battering and frying what seemed like several schools' worth of fish, I called in my tasters. One takeaway was that less was more when it came to the batter coating. We liked the yeasty, slightly bitter flavor that beer imparted to the batter, but the texture was another story. Most coatings—even the beer batters—were thick and heavy, obscuring the delicate fish. Toppings ran the gamut from avocado *crema* to fried jalapeños, and while they were all good, there were just too many of them, and (once again) the fish got lost. I'd start simple—with just the essential crunchy cabbage and creamy white sauce.

Focusing on the fish, I started with cod—the whitefish that's most available here in the Northeast. After cutting the fish into 4 by 1-inch strips (the perfect size to fit inside a corn tortilla) and seasoning them, I mixed up my batter. Taking a cue from Japanese tempura batter—a super-thin batter that creates a crisp, light coating—I increased the ratio of beer to flour, thinning out the batter until it was just thick enough to coat the fish. As it turned out, equal parts flour and

CALIFORNIA-STYLE FISH TACOS

liquid was just right. Now I had good flavor and a thin coating—but still not enough crunch. To lighten the batter so it would fry up crispier, I used the test kitchen technique of replacing about a quarter of the flour with cornstarch. I was making progress, but I had another trick up my sleeve: baking powder. When the powder is activated, it produces carbon dioxide, which makes for a light coating. The combination of cornstarch and baking powder made my coating ethereally thin, light, and crispy. I found that I needed to fill my Dutch oven only ¾ inch deep to fry the fish.

With the batter and frying perfected, I moved on to the toppings. The cabbage I simply sliced thin. The white sauce served with these tacos is usually a mixture of mayonnaise and yogurt or sour cream thinned to drizzling consistency. We found that equal parts mayonnaise and sour cream supplied the right balance of tang and richness, that lime juice introduced brightness, and that a splash of milk thinned the sauce nicely.

Some of the initial test recipes went overboard on the toppings. But I had overcorrected. My fried fish and creamy sauce definitely needed something spicy and tart for contrast. A test recipe had called for topping the tacos with pickled onions; I took that idea and ran with it. To make a quick pickle, I heated vinegar, lime juice, sugar, and salt and poured the mixture over a sliced red onion. I added a couple of sliced jalapeños for heat, and after just 30 minutes for the flavors to meld, I had a third topping. But next to these flavorful homemade pickles, the naked shredded cabbage tasted lackluster. But I had an idea. Before assembling the tacos, I took ¼ cup of the pickling liquid from the onions and tossed it with the cabbage. This seasoned the cabbage and softened it slightly without taking away its crunch.

I laid out the toppings and fried a last batch of fish. I warmed a stack of corn tortillas, and set out a jar of green salsa and a bowl of cilantro leaves. These tacos were a happy tangle of crunchy, creamy, rich, bright, and fresh.

—REBECCAH MARSTERS, *Cook's Country*

NOTES FROM THE TEST KITCHEN

EASIER THAN IT LOOKS
Our recipe for California-Style Fish Tacos has several parts, but they come together faster than you might think.

QUICK PICKLED ONIONS: Just slice the onion and jalapeños, pour the vinegar mixture over, and let sit for at least 30 minutes. This can be done up to two days ahead.
NO-COOK CABBAGE: Simply shred the cabbage (by hand or in a food processor) and toss with the onion pickling liquid.
SIMPLE WHITE SAUCE: Measure ingredients and whisk together. This can be done up to two days ahead.

THE BEST JARRED GREEN SALSA
Mexican-style salsa verde is made from tomatillos, green chiles, onion, and cilantro. We rounded up five nationally available, shelf-stable products and tasted them plain and with tortilla chips. Flavor mattered more than either heat level or texture; bright, fresh-tasting salsas came out on top, but we also liked the complexity of roasted tomatillos. The nutrition labels showed us that we liked salsas with higher levels of vitamins A and C. The vitamins reveal which salsas have more and fresher fruits and vegetables processed at a lower temperature; these vitamins degrade in older produce and at higher temperatures. Our favorite salsa, **Frontera Tomatillo Salsa**, had neither preservatives nor stabilizers.

California-Style Fish Tacos
SERVES 6

Although this recipe looks involved, all the components are easy to execute and most can be made in advance. Light-bodied American lagers, such as Budweiser, work best here. Cut the fish on a slight bias if your fillets aren't quite 4 inches wide. You should end up with about 24 pieces of fish. Use a Dutch oven that holds 6 quarts or more. Serve with green salsa, if desired.

PICKLED ONIONS
- 1 small red onion, halved and sliced thin
- 2 jalapeño chiles, stemmed and sliced into thin rings
- 1 cup white wine vinegar
- 2 tablespoons lime juice
- 1 tablespoon sugar
- 1 teaspoon salt

CABBAGE
- 3 cups shredded green cabbage
- ¼ cup pickling liquid from pickled onions
- ½ teaspoon salt
- ½ teaspoon pepper

WHITE SAUCE
- ½ cup mayonnaise
- ½ cup sour cream
- 2 tablespoons lime juice
- 2 tablespoons milk

FISH

2	pounds skinless whitefish fillets, such as cod, haddock, or halibut, cut crosswise into 4 by 1-inch strips
	Salt and pepper
¾	cup all-purpose flour
¼	cup cornstarch
1	teaspoon baking powder
1	cup beer
1	quart peanut or vegetable oil
24	(6-inch) corn tortillas, warmed
1	cup fresh cilantro leaves

1. FOR THE PICKLED ONIONS: Combine onion and jalapeños in medium bowl. Bring vinegar, lime juice, sugar, and salt to boil in small saucepan. Pour vinegar mixture over onion mixture and let sit for at least 30 minutes. (Pickled onions can be made and refrigerated up to 2 days in advance.)

2. FOR THE CABBAGE: Toss all ingredients together in bowl.

3. FOR THE WHITE SAUCE: Whisk all ingredients together in bowl. (Sauce can be made and refrigerated up to 2 days in advance.)

4. FOR THE FISH: Adjust oven rack to middle position and heat oven to 200 degrees. Set wire rack inside rimmed baking sheet. Pat fish dry with paper towels and season with salt and pepper. Whisk flour, cornstarch, baking powder, and 1 teaspoon salt together in large bowl. Add beer and whisk until smooth. Transfer fish to batter and toss until evenly coated.

5. Add oil to large Dutch oven until it measures about ¾ inch deep and heat over medium-high heat to 350 degrees. Working with 5 to 6 pieces at a time, remove fish from batter, allowing excess to drip back into bowl, and add to hot oil, briefly dragging fish along surface of oil to prevent sticking. Adjust burner, if necessary, to maintain oil temperature between 325 and 350 degrees. Fry fish, stirring gently to prevent pieces from sticking together, until golden brown and crisp, about 2 minutes per side. Transfer fish to prepared wire rack and place in oven to keep warm. Return oil to 350 degrees and repeat with remaining fish.

6. Divide fish evenly among tortillas. Top with pickled onions, cabbage, white sauce, and cilantro. Serve.

FRIED CATFISH

✓ WHY THIS RECIPE WORKS: Fried catfish is a southern specialty: tender-firm fish encased in a crunchy cornmeal crust, generously seasoned with garlic and cayenne for zing. For a crunchy, not gritty, cornmeal crust, we found that it was best to process half of the cornmeal to a fine powder in a spice grinder. We seasoned the coating with plenty of salt, pepper, garlic, and cayenne to give the fish a flavorful bite. A dip in hot sauce–laced buttermilk helped the coating adhere and seasoned the fish even deeper. To maximize the crunchy exterior, we halved the fillets to make catfish "tenders." After only a few minutes in hot oil, the fish emerged crisp, golden brown, and perfectly seasoned. Spicy, Mississippi-style Comeback Sauce provided the perfect accompaniment to the fried fish.

Not too long ago, I was one of those northern naysayers who dismiss catfish as funny-looking, "pondy" tasting fish. Then I visited the Mississippi Delta. Mississippi is one of the biggest producers of farmed catfish in the United States. It's rare to visit a restaurant there that doesn't have fried catfish on the menu. The fish's firm texture and mild flavor give it broad appeal, but for most aficionados, deep-fried catfish is the only way to go. I was convinced of that when I tried it prepared this way at the famed Ajax Diner in Oxford, Mississippi, and at Taylor Grocery in the nearby hamlet of Taylor. Both versions exemplified the best in fried catfish: crispy, thin cornmeal crusts; perfectly cooked, sweet meat; and just enough spice to make it interesting.

I peppered both restaurant owners with questions about their techniques. While neither Ajax Diner owner Randy Yates nor Taylor Grocery owner Lynn Hewlett would give up his secret formula, both men were willing to talk to me about their general approach. Yates dips his catfish in a mixture of buttermilk and egg and then dredges it in a blend of cornmeal and all-purpose flour; the result is a delicate yet crispy coating with just a hint of seasonings. Hewlett soaks the fish in ice water (to firm up the meat) before breading. His coating is also cornmeal-based, but instead of flour, he adds cream meal—a very finely ground cornmeal—and his own blend of spices for a bit of kick. His crust is crunchy and deeply flavored, making me wish that it wasn't impolite to use my fingers to pick up every crumb.

When I returned to the test kitchen, I cobbled together my best approximations of the two Mississippi

FRIED CATFISH

versions that I'd tasted. Then, just to be sure that I was on the right track, I pitted these recipes against a few others that I found in our test kitchen library (including an all-cornmeal crust and one that called for "fish fry" coating). Tasters much preferred my Mississippi mock-ups: The Taylor Grocery coating came out ahead, while the Ajax Diner buttermilk wash scored big points for flavor. The all-cornmeal crust was too gritty. Fish fry, a packaged blend of corn flour and spices, had a decent texture, but tasters didn't love the seasoning, which inevitably varies from brand to brand. Better to stick with a more neutral base and select my own seasonings.

We loved the cornmeal–cream meal crust, but cream meal is difficult to come by outside the South. Scouring the test kitchen pantry for a substitute, I spied masa harina—the finely ground cornmeal product used to make tortillas. When I mixed masa harina with the coarse cornmeal, its texture resembled the Taylor Grocery coating. Unfortunately, masa harina is not exactly a pantry staple in many homes, and I hated to call for it, especially when I needed such a small amount. My working recipe used 1⅓ cups of cornmeal and ⅔ cup of masa harina, plus a few seasonings. I tried substituting an additional ⅔ cup of cornmeal, which I processed in a spice grinder, for the masa harina. After about 30 seconds, I had a pale yellow powder with the same lightness and grit as the masa harina. I continued to tinker with the ratios to find the best texture and crunch. We declared equal parts of the coarse and the ground cornmeal—1 cup of each—the winner.

Next I needed a balanced blend of spices. I knew from experience that Cajun seasoning brands vary widely, and the last thing I wanted was an overspiced, heavy-on-the-oregano blend. The fish that I had enjoyed most on my trip had plenty of salt and pepper, a hint of cayenne, and some garlic powder for backbone. After a few tries, I struck gold: 4 teaspoons of salt, 2 teaspoons each of pepper and garlic powder, and a teaspoon of cayenne.

At this point the coating had won over tasters with its piquant flavor and crunch—if it would just stay put. I tested buttermilk, whole milk, and ice water—with and without egg—to determine which was the best glue for the crust. We liked the slight tang that buttermilk imparted and its texture (thicker than milk) helped the crust adhere, even without an egg. To bump up the flavor, I added a teaspoon of hot sauce to the buttermilk, and I simply gave the fish a quick dunk in the mixture before dredging it in the seasoned cornmeal.

The fillets spent about 8 minutes in 2 quarts of 350-degree oil. They emerged moist and tender, with a supercrunchy crust—which we liked so much that we wanted more of it. I got it by halving the fillets lengthwise, which yielded more surface area for extra coating, thus extra crunch. Also, the smaller pieces were easier to manage both in and out of the pot. The catfish "tenders" fried slightly faster than the whole fillets—in about 5 minutes—making it a snap to cook the second batch while the first batch was still piping hot.

To top off the now-perfect fish, I developed a quick dipping sauce. In Mississippi, fried foods are often served with Comeback Sauce, a spicy mayo-based condiment that falls somewhere between a remoulade and Thousand Island dressing. I wanted to keep it simple, so I combined all the ingredients in a blender. Hot sauce, mustard, black pepper, paprika, and garlic gave it a kick. Ketchup and chili sauce (for sweetness), raw onion (for bite), Worcestershire (for savory depth), and lemon juice (for brightness) rounded out the spicy profile.

As I tucked into a piece of fish and heard the satisfying crunch, I thought that my newfound friends in the Delta would be pleased. Someday I'd like to make a return trip to this incredible area, but until then I can have a cornmeal-crusted reminder of my visit to Mississippi any time I want.

—CHRISTIE MORRISON, *Cook's Country*

Fried Catfish

SERVES 4 TO 6

Use a Dutch oven that holds 6 quarts or more. If your spice grinder is small, grind the cornmeal in batches or process it in a blender for 60 to 90 seconds. Serve with Comeback Sauce (recipe follows).

- 2 **cups buttermilk**
- 1 **teaspoon hot sauce**
- 2 **cups cornmeal**
- 4 **teaspoons salt**
- 2 **teaspoons pepper**
- 2 **teaspoons garlic powder**
- 1 **teaspoon cayenne pepper**
- 4 **(6- to 8-ounce) skinless catfish fillets, halved lengthwise along natural seam**
- 2 **quarts peanut or vegetable oil**
  Lemon wedges

1. Set wire rack in rimmed baking sheet and line half of rack with triple layer of paper towels. Whisk buttermilk and hot sauce together in shallow dish. Process 1 cup cornmeal in spice grinder to fine powder, 30 to 45 seconds. Whisk salt, pepper, granulated garlic, cayenne, remaining 1 cup cornmeal, and ground cornmeal together in second shallow dish.

2. Pat fish dry with paper towels. Working with 1 piece of fish at a time, dip fish in buttermilk mixture, letting excess drip back into dish. Dredge fish in cornmeal mixture, shaking off excess, and transfer to large plate.

3. Add oil to large Dutch oven until it measures about 1½ inches deep and heat over medium-high heat to 350 degrees. Working with 4 pieces of fish at a time, add fish to hot oil. Adjust burner, if necessary, to maintain oil temperature between 325 and 350 degrees. Fry fish until golden brown and crisp, about 5 minutes. Transfer fish to paper towel–lined side of prepared rack and let drain for 1 minute, then move to unlined side of rack. Return oil to 350 degrees and repeat with remaining fish. Serve with lemon wedges.

NOTES FROM THE TEST KITCHEN

HALVING CATFISH

Before coating and frying, we cut the catfish fillets in half along their natural seams. Smaller pieces cook faster and more evenly, and we get a better ratio of crunchy crust to flesh.

THE BEST CLIP-ON DIGITAL THERMOMETERS

In the test kitchen, we use hands-free clip-on digital thermometers to monitor temperatures when deep-frying food or making candy. We tested four models, evaluating the thermometers for accuracy, functionality, durability, and how well they fit a variety of pans. We liked two of the four models that we tested. The Polder Classic Digital Thermometer/Timer is our Best Buy. But while the **ThermoWorks ChefAlarm** is more expensive than the others, its accuracy, easy interface, and promise of longevity are well worth it.

MAKES ABOUT 1 CUP

Chili sauce, a condiment cousin of ketchup, has a sweet flavor and a subtle spicy kick; do not substitute Asian chili sauce.

- ½ cup mayonnaise
- ⅓ cup chopped onion
- 2 tablespoons vegetable oil
- 2 tablespoons chili sauce
- 1 tablespoon ketchup
- 2½ teaspoons Worcestershire sauce
- 2½ teaspoons hot sauce
- 1 teaspoon yellow mustard
- 1 teaspoon lemon juice
- 1 garlic clove, minced
- ¾ teaspoon pepper
- ⅛ teaspoon paprika

Process all ingredients in blender until smooth, about 30 seconds. (Sauce can be refrigerated for up to 5 days.)

SLOW-COOKER POACHED SALMON

✓ **WHY THIS RECIPE WORKS:** The success of poached salmon depends on proper technique, which can be tricky. Poach the fish too long or at too high a simmer and the fish turns chalky and dry. We wanted to make poaching salmon foolproof and thus turned to the gentle, moist heat of the slow cooker. Propping the fillets up on lemon slices added bright flavor and provided some insulation between the bottoms of the fillets and the slow cooker so the salmon steamed evenly and emerged tender and silky. To solve the problem of getting the salmon out of the slow cooker, we made a simple foil sling, which made it easy to lift the fillets out. A quick citrus relish offset the richness of the salmon and completed our fresh and easy meal.

When done right, poached salmon has an irresistibly supple, velvety texture. Add a simple sauce or relish and you have a healthy, flavorful meal. But poaching fish correctly can be elusive; most often the fish has a dry, chalky texture and washed-out taste that not even the best sauce can redeem.

The classic method for poaching salmon is to gently simmer an entire side of fish in a highly flavored broth. The salmon is often cooled and served cold, usually as part of a buffet. But I wasn't looking for a make-ahead method for cold salmon to serve a crowd. I wanted to produce perfectly cooked individual portions of hot salmon—and I wanted to do it in the slow cooker. Salmon, although less delicate than white fish, runs a high risk of overcooking and drying out. I wanted to use the gentle, moist heat of the slow cooker to develop flavor in my salmon and keep the fish moist. I also decided to make a fresh, light relish to go with the fillets to offset the salmon's natural richness.

My first objective would be to achieve great texture and flavor in the salmon itself; after that I would develop the relish to accompany it. Traditionally, poaching calls for gently simmering meat in a lot of water. Salmon, in particular, is often poached in a court-bouillon, an intensely flavored liquid that imparts lots of flavor to the fish. But making a court-bouillon for a slow-cooker recipe seemed unnecessarily work-intensive: A classic court-bouillon is made by filling a pot with water, wine, herbs, vegetables, and aromatics, then boiling it all very briefly. This would require not only a lot of prep work and measuring for a poaching liquid I was ultimately going to discard, it would also require me to get out my stockpot and dirty a lot of extra dishes. Not ideal. I decided to forgo the court-bouillon in favor of a simpler, more streamlined method. But poaching salmon in a lot of plain water would make the fish taste like just that—plain water. Could I poach the fillets in less water and use the power of steam instead, thereby keeping the flavor where it belonged—in the fish—and still achieve evenly cooked fillets?

I wanted to use skin-on salmon fillets, since I knew from past test kitchen recipes that the skin would help the fish hold together. I seasoned the fillets lightly with salt and pepper and placed them in the slow cooker with a small amount of lemon juice (for flavor) and water, so that only the bottom half of the fillets were immersed. Like all meat, salmon has a certain internal temperature range within which it is ideally cooked. The proteins in salmon begin coagulating at around 120 degrees, transforming it from translucent to opaque. At around 135 degrees, the flesh is completely firm. Any higher, and the salmon becomes dry as cardboard (like a well-done steak). Even though the thinner edges cook faster than the center, their higher fat content keeps these thinner parts moist until the center is done.

I monitored the internal temperature of the fillets carefully and took them out when the thick center reached 135 degrees—or at least, I attempted to take them out. The deep, straight sides of the slow cooker prevented me from getting my spatula neatly under the fish, and I ended up with broken, messy pieces of salmon. Luckily, the test kitchen has a simple fix for this problem: In my next test, I lined the slow cooker with a foil sling before laying down the salmon; that way, when the fish was done, I could pull out the whole sling, making it easy to maneuver the fillets without breaking them.

One problem remained though: Even though the top, sides, and center were now cooked just right (and the fillets were staying together), the bottom of the fish, which had been in direct contact with the heat, was overcooked and chalky.

Then I realized that I had the solution in my hand. Instead of squeezing lemon juice into the poaching liquid, I sliced the fruit into disks, which I laid in the bottom of the slow cooker. Then I arranged the salmon on top of the lemon slices. In this way, I was able to insulate the fish while simultaneously flavoring it. I added water up to the top of the lemon slices, and this time, the salmon came out evenly cooked all the way through.

For a fresh accompaniment to my salmon, I wanted a bright, citrusy relish that would complement the richness of the fish without overwhelming its delicate flavor. I tried making relishes with oranges, grapefruits, and mixtures of the two, but tasters preferred the slight bitterness of the grapefruit, declaring orange too sweet. I knew I also wanted an aromatic, herbal element to round out the bright grapefruit; I found my answer in a handful of chopped fresh basil and mild shallot. I brought all the elements together with a drizzle of olive oil and draped the relish over my tender, moist salmon. The salmon made for an elegant presentation—and no one but me needed to know that preparing it was so simple.

—ASHLEY MOORE, *America's Test Kitchen Books*

Slow-Cooker Poached Salmon with Grapefruit and Basil Relish

SERVES 4

This recipe is designed to work with 5½- to 7-quart oval slow cookers. Use salmon fillets of similar thickness so that they cook at the same rate, or buy a 1½- to 2-pound whole center-cut fillet and cut it into four equal pieces. Because delicate fish can easily overcook in the slow cooker, it requires some monitoring. Check the salmon's temperature after 1 hour of cooking and continue to monitor it until it registers 135 degrees.

1 lemon, sliced ¼ inch thick

4 (6- to 8-ounce) skin-on salmon fillets, about 1½ inches thick

Salt and pepper

2 red grapefruits

3 tablespoons chopped fresh basil

1 shallot, minced

2 tablespoons extra-virgin olive oil

1. Fold sheet of aluminum foil into 12 by 9-inch sling; press widthwise into slow cooker. Arrange lemon slices in single layer in bottom of prepared slow cooker. Pour water into slow cooker until it is even with lemon slices (about ½ cup water). Season fillets with salt and pepper; place skin-side down on top of lemon slices. Cover and cook until salmon is opaque throughout when checked with tip of paring knife and registers 135 degrees, 1 to 2 hours on low.

2. Meanwhile, cut away peel and pith from grapefruits. Cut grapefruits into 8 wedges, then slice each wedge crosswise into ½-inch-thick pieces. Combine grapefruit, basil, shallot, and oil in bowl and season with salt and pepper to taste.

3. Using sling, transfer fillets to baking sheet. Gently lift and tilt fillets with spatula to remove lemon slices and transfer to plates; discard poaching liquid. Serve with relish.

NOTES FROM THE TEST KITCHEN

REMOVING FISH FROM A SLOW COOKER
To easily remove salmon (and other delicate fish) from the slow cooker, we use a foil sling.

To form sling, fold sheet of aluminum foil into 12 by 9-inch rectangle and press widthwise into slow cooker. Before serving, use edges of sling as handles to lift fish out of slow cooker fully intact.

SESAME-CRUSTED SALMON

✓ **WHY THIS RECIPE WORKS:** Often, sesame-crusted salmon is a one-note affair in which rich salmon is coated with sesame seeds that provide little more than crunch. We wanted to highlight both the fish and the natural contrasts of these two elements and give them some bolder, brighter flavor. We brined the salmon fillets to ensure that each piece was thoroughly seasoned and remained moist after cooking. Giving the sesame seeds a dunk in the salmon brine and then toasting them brought out their deep, nutty flavor. To liven up the dish, we added minced scallion whites, lemon zest, grated fresh ginger, and a pinch of cayenne for zing. To make the flavorings and the sesame seeds adhere to the fish, we used rich tahini paste thickened with lemon juice.

The fish and sesame duo gets around, showing up in cuisines from Asia to California to the Middle East. The simplest approach is to coat fillets with the seeds and then pan-sear the fish. Tuna is often used, but so is less-expensive salmon—my preference for a weeknight meal. When I first tasted salmon prepared this way, I thought that only minor tweaks would be necessary to correct the ho-hum sesame flavor and slightly dry, unevenly cooked fish. But halfway through dinner, I realized that the problems ran deeper. Both salmon and sesame have a monotonous richness, so finishing a whole serving was a chore. I wanted a lively dish in which the salmon and sesame would be offset with bolder, brighter flavors.

Brining the fish for just 15 minutes took care of any dryness. It may seem odd to brine something that basically lived in a brine, but the saltwater soak seasons the flesh and subtly changes its protein structure, helping it retain moisture. I blotted the brined fillets with paper towels, applied the seeds to both sides, and eased the fillets into an oil-slicked nonstick skillet. When the seeds turned golden, I transferred the skillet to the oven for more gentle, even cooking. Flawlessly cooked, moist fish? Check.

On to the dull sesame flavor. A fellow cook mentioned Japanese *gomashio*. The term translates as "sesame salt" and at its most basic is just those two ingredients. To make the savory blend, you toast the seeds and then mix or grind them with salt.

Maybe salt and a little toasting were just what the seeds needed. But instead of grinding the toasted seeds with salt, I submerged the untoasted seeds in some of the brine that I had mixed up for the fish, drained them, and toasted them whole in a skillet. The brine woke up the nutty flavor of the seeds by infusing each one with salt. What's more, because the starch in the seeds absorbed water from the brine and then gelatinized during toasting, the seeds were now crisper than ever.

But I wanted an even more potent sesame punch. I experimented with cooking the fillets in sesame oil, but most of the oil's flavorful compounds vaporized in the hot skillet. I scanned the test kitchen pantry and spotted a Middle Eastern staple: tahini, which is basically ground sesame seeds. The only problem was its runny consistency—it would slide right off the slippery fillets. Before experimenting with thickeners, I decided to enliven the tahini with some lemon juice. I drizzled in the juice a little at a time, tasting after each addition. Oddly, the more juice I added the more viscous the tahini became. When I asked our science editor about this counterintuitive phenomenon, he told me that since much of tahini's makeup is carbohydrates, when a small amount of lemon juice (or any water-containing liquid) is added, a portion of each carbohydrate molecule is drawn to the water. As a result, clumps of carbohydrates appear. As the amount of water is increased, more clumps develop, causing the tahini to thicken overall. If you keep adding water, eventually you'll cross over the threshold of thickening it; enough water in the system will cause the tahini to loosen and thin out. In the end, two teaspoons of juice produced great tang and a misolike texture.

Happily, the thick paste was ideal for adhering other flavorful elements to the salmon, so I added minced scallion whites, lemon zest, grated fresh ginger, and a dash of cayenne. I smeared the flavor-packed mixture onto the fillets, pressed on the sesame seeds, seared the fish, and popped the pan into the oven. Now I had a real winner. The contrasting flavors shone through—and the last bite was as interesting as the first.

—LAN LAM, *Cook's Illustrated*

Sesame-Crusted Salmon with Lemon and Ginger

SERVES 4

For even cooking, purchase fillets that are about the same size and shape. If any of your fillets have a thin belly flap, fold it over to create a more even thickness.

    Salt
¾ cup sesame seeds
4 (6- to 8-ounce) skinless salmon fillets
2 scallions, white parts minced, green parts sliced thin
1 tablespoon grated lemon zest plus 2 teaspoons juice
4 teaspoons tahini
2 teaspoons grated fresh ginger
⅛ teaspoon cayenne pepper
1 teaspoon vegetable oil

1. Adjust oven rack to middle position and heat oven to 325 degrees. Dissolve 5 tablespoons salt in 2 quarts water. Transfer 1 cup brine to bowl, stir in sesame seeds, and let stand at room temperature for 5 minutes. Submerge fillets in remaining brine and let stand at room temperature for 15 minutes.

2. Drain seeds and place in 12-inch nonstick skillet. Cook seeds over medium heat, stirring constantly, until golden brown, 2 to 4 minutes. Transfer seeds to pie plate and wipe out skillet with paper towels. Remove fillets from brine and pat dry.

3. Place scallion whites and lemon zest on cutting board and chop until whites and zest are finely minced and well combined. Transfer scallion-zest mixture to bowl and stir in lemon juice, tahini, ginger, cayenne, and ⅛ teaspoon salt.

4. Evenly distribute half of paste over bottoms (skinned sides) of fillets. Press coated sides of fillets in seeds and transfer, seed side down, to plate. Evenly distribute remaining paste over tops of fillets and coat with remaining seeds.

5. Heat oil in now-empty skillet over medium heat until shimmering. Place fillets in skillet, skinned side up, and reduce heat to medium-low. Cook until seeds begin to brown, 1 to 2 minutes. Remove skillet from heat and, using 2 spatulas, carefully flip fillets over. Transfer skillet to oven. Bake until center of salmon is translucent when checked with tip of paring knife and registers 125 degrees, 10 to 15 minutes. Transfer to serving platter and let rest for 5 minutes. Sprinkle with scallion greens and serve.

VARIATION

Sesame-Crusted Salmon with Lime and Coriander
Substitute 4 teaspoons lime zest for lemon zest, lime juice for lemon juice, and ¼ teaspoon ground coriander for cayenne.

CHAPTER 8

BREAKFAST, BRUNCH, AND BREADS

PERFECT FRIED EGGS

PERFECT FRIED EGGS

✓ WHY THIS RECIPE WORKS: Achieving diner-style eggs at home—with tender whites, perfectly runny yolks, and lightly browned, crisp edges—is a balancing act: The whites must cook through before the yolks set up. Cracking the eggs into bowls before sliding them into the pan, (rather than cracking them one at a time into the hot pan) helped all of the eggs cook at the same rate. Heating the oil slowly ensured that it heated evenly, and some butter added just before the eggs provided rich flavor and promoted browning. Once in the pan, we covered the eggs right away and removed the pan from the stovetop after 1 minute, so that the eggs would be enveloped by gentle, residual heat.

To me, a fried egg should be fried. I'm talking about the sort you find at the best diners: sunny-side up and crisp on its underside and edges, with a tender and opaque white and a perfectly runny yolk.

Ideally, I'd whip up this diner-style breakfast in my own kitchen, but the fried egg recipes I'd tried had failed to produce the results I wanted. My home-cooked sunny-side up eggs either suffered from undercooked whites (specifically, a slippery, transparent ring of white surrounding the yolk) or overcooked yolk (often it was fluid on top but cooked solid on the underside).

These faults are due to a predicament that plagues most types of egg cookery: Yolks and whites set at different temperatures. This means that yolks, which start to solidify at around 158 degrees, are inevitably overcooked by the time the whites, which set up at 180 degrees, are opaque. My objective, then, was to get the whites to cook through before the yolks did. I also wanted whites with beautifully bronzed, crisp edges. I had my work cut out for me.

There are two basic approaches for tackling an egg's disparate doneness temperatures: Cook low and slow or hot and fast. The former calls for breaking the egg into a warm, greased nonstick skillet and letting it gradually come to temperature over low heat, which can take 5 or more minutes. If the flame is low enough, the heat will firm up the white before the yolk sets. The downside: This technique doesn't add browning or crispness. Raising the heat toward the end of cooking only overcooks the entire egg.

The opposite method blasts the egg with fierce heat from the start in an attempt to cook the white so quickly that it is out of the pan before the yolk even considers setting up. The best example that I've tried comes from Spanish chef José Andrés, who calls for shallow-frying an egg in a tilted skillet containing an inch or so of very hot olive oil. Within seconds, the bottom of the white bubbles and browns, and as you continuously baste the egg with hot oil, the top of the white cooks through as well. The whole process happens so quickly (just 30 seconds or so) that the yolk can't possibly overcook, and the result—a filigree of browned, crispy egg surrounding a tender white and a runny yolk—is just what I wanted.

And yet, there were drawbacks. The flavor of the egg wasn't quite what I had in mind. Olive oil gave it a great savory taste, but it lacked the buttery richness of a diner-style egg. What's more, the sputtering oil made a mess of my stovetop and threatened to burn my forearms. The method also required cooking only one egg at a time. Sure, they cooked quickly, but I wanted to produce two or four eggs at one time. Could I use high heat and far less oil and be able to feed two people breakfast in one go?

I reviewed what I had learned: First, it was difficult to get the eggs to cook evenly when I broke them one by one into the pan. Breaking the eggs into small bowls ahead of time so that all I had to do was slide them into the pan saved time—and went a long way in a recipe in which mere seconds make a difference. Plus, it worked equally well with two or four eggs. Second, it was important to let the pan fully preheat low and slow. A quick blast of high heat can cause hot spots to form and, thus, the eggs to cook at different rates. I got the best results by adding a teaspoon of vegetable oil to the skillet and setting it over low heat for a full 5 minutes. You also need a pan roomy enough for the eggs to spread out but not so much that large areas of the pan remain empty, which could cause the fat to burn. A 12- or 14-inch pan works best for four eggs, an 8- or 9-inch pan for two. Finally, adding a couple of pats of butter to the pan right before slipping in the eggs resulted in great flavor and browning due to the butter's milk proteins.

I fried a few rounds of eggs on medium-high heat after preheating the skillet on low. The butter and oil sizzled nicely and the eggs started to brown almost immediately. But things digressed from there, with the whites undercooking or the yolks overcooking, depending on when I reached for my spatula. Lowering the heat once the whites were browned at the edges did let them solidify before the yolks set up, but that process took so long that the whites, in effect, oversolidified, turning tough and rubbery.

FLAWLESS FRIED EGGS: IT'S ALL IN THE DETAILS

1. PREHEAT THE PAN: Preheating your pan on low heat for 5 full minutes guarantees that there will be no hot spots in the skillet that could lead to unevenly cooked eggs.

2. USE TWO FATS: We use vegetable oil, with its high smoke point, while preheating the pan. Butter, added just before the eggs, imparts a diner-style richness.

3. ADD EGGS ALL AT ONCE: Cracking the eggs into small bowls makes it possible to add them to the skillet simultaneously so they cook at the same rate.

4. COVER IT UP AND FINISH OFF HEAT: A lid traps heat so the egg cooks from above as well as below. Moving the pan off the heat after 1 minute allows the whites to gently finish cooking while keeping the yolks liquid.

For a moment I was stumped—until I thought back to the key to Andrés's shallow-fried eggs: basting. Basting the eggs with hot fat helped quickly cook the white before the yolk could set up. I wasn't up for basting due to its accompanying splatter, but I could think of another way to generate heat from above: a lid. The reflected heat and steam trapped by a lid might just work.

For my next test, I covered the pan as soon as the eggs were in place. Ninety seconds later, I lifted the lid for a peek, fingers crossed, before using a spatula to quickly remove my specimens. The good news was that the ring of jiggly, uncooked white around the yolk was

gone, and the white was perfectly tender, with a nicely browned underside and edges. But the lid had trapped too much heat: The yolk was now a bit overcooked.

Instead, I slid the covered skillet off the burner entirely, hoping the gentle residual heat of the pan would firm up the white but not the yolk. It took a few dozen more eggs to get the timing just right but— stopwatch in hand—I finally nailed down the proper intervals: One minute over medium-high heat followed by an additional 15 to 45 seconds off heat produced beautifully bronzed edges; just-set, opaque whites; and fluid yolks every time.

Mission accomplished: perfect diner-style fried eggs—no diner necessary.

—ANDREW JANJIGIAN, *Cook's Illustrated*

Perfect Fried Eggs

SERVES 2

When checking the eggs for doneness, lift the lid just a crack to prevent loss of steam should they need further cooking. When cooked, the thin layer of white surrounding the yolk will turn opaque, but the yolk should remain runny. To cook two eggs, use an 8- or 9-inch nonstick skillet and halve the amounts of oil and butter. You can use this method with extra-large or jumbo eggs without altering the timing.

- 2 teaspoons vegetable oil
- 4 large eggs
  Salt and pepper
- 2 teaspoons unsalted butter, cut into
  4 pieces and chilled

1. Heat oil in 12- or 14-inch nonstick skillet over low heat for 5 minutes. Meanwhile, crack 2 eggs into small bowl and season with salt and pepper. Repeat with remaining 2 eggs and second small bowl.

2. Increase heat to medium-high and heat until oil is shimmering. Add butter to skillet and quickly swirl to coat pan. Working quickly, pour 1 bowl of eggs in 1 side of pan and second bowl of eggs in other side. Cover and cook for 1 minute. Remove skillet from burner and let stand, covered, 15 to 45 seconds for runny yolks (white around edge of yolk will be barely opaque), 45 to 60 seconds for soft but set yolks, and about 2 minutes for medium-set yolks. Slide eggs onto plates and serve.

FEATHERBED EGGS

✓ **WHY THIS RECIPE WORKS:** Most recipes for this cornbread-based strata call for making homemade cornbread, cutting it into cubes, and drying it in the oven before proceeding with the usual strata protocol—mixing the bread with custard and letting it sit overnight. To speed up the process, we baked our cornbread on a rimmed baking sheet, creating a thin, quick-cooking layer of cornbread. The increased surface area also meant that we could eliminate the extra oven-drying step, and simply break the cornbread into pieces with our hands. To prevent the spices from clumping in the custard, we added them to the cornbread batter instead. Eggs, milk, cheddar cheese, and scallions made a rich, flavorful base for this impressive make-ahead brunch dish.

Leafing through an old breakfast cookbook, I came across a recipe for featherbed eggs. The name was so enchanting that I did some more research. After a search in our cookbook library, I found that featherbed eggs is simply a name sometimes given to strata, a favorite brunch standby. Strata is a casserole of eggs, milk or cream, bread, and cheese that is assembled and stored in the refrigerator overnight to let the custard permeate the bread (sometimes, heavy cans are placed on top of the wrapped strata to further encourage absorption). Recipes for classic strata usually call for white sandwich bread or French bread, which don't add much in either flavor or texture. But the recipes that really piqued my interest used cornbread.

Changing up the add-ins can spruce up an old strata recipe, but swapping the bread would give me a completely new base flavor; I selected half a dozen recipes that used cornbread. A few called for store-bought cornbread, while the rest called for making cornbread and letting it cool before continuing with the standard strata procedure of slicing or dicing the bread; oven-drying or staling it; and then mixing it with cheese, add-ins, and the custard. We found the store-bought cornbread too sweet and otherwise inconsistent, but homemade cornbread, while delicious, required significantly more work. I needed to whittle this down.

Rather than reinvent the wheel, I started with a simple dump-and-stir test kitchen cornbread recipe. To see if I could just skip the drying and staling routine, I baked and cooled a batch of cornbread, cut it up, and mixed it with shredded cheddar and sliced scallions in a baking dish. Then I poured in a working custard of six eggs and 4½ cups of milk and sprinkled more cheese over the top. After covering the dish with plastic wrap, I weighed it down and set it in the fridge overnight. In the morning, I baked it until it puffed up ever so slightly and the custard set. The pepper and cayenne had clumped in the custard and ended up in one spot, but that was the least of my problems. The cornbread had disintegrated and become slimy. I tried again with less custard; now the dish was denser, but the slimy bread persisted. Skipping the drying step was not an option.

So I needed dry bread—but I wanted an easy way to get it. I tried turning down the oven and baking the bread low and slow, essentially overcooking it on purpose to dry it out in just one trip through the oven. With this process the cornbread took an hour to bake and 45 minutes to cool. Only then could I cut it up to assemble the casserole. In other words, it took fewer steps but much more time. Maybe, I thought, I could decrease the cooking time by increasing the surface area. I spread the same amount of batter that I had been baking in an 8-inch square pan over an entire rimmed baking sheet. The batter, now only about ¼ inch deep in the pan, browned and pulled away from the edges of the pan in less than 20 minutes, and in just 10 more minutes it was almost completely cool. As an added advantage, this flat sheet of cornbread was easy to tear into pieces—no more slicing or dicing. I mixed the bread with the cheese and scallions, poured on the custard, covered the casserole, and weighed it down. The next morning, I baked it for about an hour. Ah, success.

Well, mostly. My baking sheet cornbread was dry enough to soak up the custard and remain intact so the texture of the strata was custardy, not slimy, but the spices still weren't evenly distributed. As I was mixing up the dry ingredients for the cornbread, I got an idea that I thought might solve my clumping-spice problem: Put the cayenne and pepper in the cornbread instead of in the custard. The bread came out nicely speckled and made an evenly seasoned batch of featherbed eggs. At last, I had a new brunch dish worth getting out of bed for.

—SARAH GABRIEL, *Cook's Country*

Featherbed Eggs

SERVES 10 TO 12

To weigh down the assembled strata so the custard permeates the bread, fill two 1-quart zipper-lock bags with rice or sugar and lay them side by side over the plastic-covered surface. Serve the strata with hot sauce.

CORNBREAD

1	cup (5 ounces) cornmeal
1	cup (5 ounces) all-purpose flour
2	teaspoons baking powder
½	teaspoon baking soda
1½	teaspoons pepper
½	teaspoon salt
¼	teaspoon cayenne pepper
1⅓	cups whole milk
2	large eggs, lightly beaten

CUSTARD

10	ounces sharp cheddar cheese, shredded (2½ cups)
6	scallions, sliced thin
4½	cups whole milk
6	large eggs, lightly beaten
2	teaspoons salt

1. FOR THE CORNBREAD: Adjust oven rack to middle position and heat oven to 400 degrees. Line rimmed baking sheet with parchment paper and spray with vegetable oil spray.

2. Whisk cornmeal, flour, baking powder, baking soda, pepper, salt, and cayenne together in bowl. Whisk milk and eggs together in separate bowl. Whisk milk-egg mixture into cornmeal mixture until just combined. Pour batter into prepared sheet and spread to cover entire sheet. Bake until lightly browned and edges of cornbread pull away from sides of sheet, 17 to 19 minutes. Let cornbread cool in sheet on wire rack for 10 minutes.

3. FOR THE CUSTARD: Spray 13 by 9-inch baking dish with oil spray. Tear cornbread into 1-inch pieces and place in prepared dish. Add 1½ cups cheddar and scallions to cornbread and toss to combine. Whisk milk, eggs, and salt in bowl; pour custard over cornbread mixture. Top casserole with remaining 1 cup cheddar. Cover with plastic wrap, weigh down, and refrigerate for 6 to 24 hours.

4. Adjust oven rack to middle position and heat oven to 325 degrees. Remove weights from casserole and discard plastic. Bake until lightly browned and center registers 170 degrees, 50 to 60 minutes. Let rest for 15 minutes. Serve.

VARIATION

Maple-Sausage Featherbed Eggs

Bake 1 pound breakfast sausage links on middle rack of 400-degree oven until 165 degrees, about 10 minutes. Slice sausages into ½-inch pieces. Add sausage to cornbread pieces with cheddar and scallions. For custard, substitute ½ cup maple syrup for ½ cup milk and reduce salt to 1 teaspoon. Drizzle 1 tablespoon maple syrup over casserole just before baking.

CHEESE SOUFFLÉ

✔ **WHY THIS RECIPE WORKS:** Making a truly great cheese soufflé is like finding the holy grail for most cooks—unattainable. But this classic French dish doesn't have to be relegated to the realm of professional chefs. We wanted a cheese soufflé with bold cheese flavor, good stature, and a light but not-too-airy texture—all without the fussiness of most recipes. To bump up the cheese flavor without weighing down the soufflé, we added lightweight-but-flavorful Parmesan cheese to the traditional Gruyère. Reducing the amount of butter and flour also amplified the cheese flavor. Filling the soufflé dish to an inch below the rim allowed ample room for the soufflé to rise high. To get the texture just right while keeping the preparation simple, we beat egg whites to stiff peaks, and then—rather than carefully folding them into the cheese sauce—added the sauce right to the stand mixer, and beat everything until uniform. When the center reached 170 degrees, our soufflé had a perfect luscious creamy center and lightly bronzed edges.

Soufflé *au fromage*—ethereally light eggs and nutty, tangy Gruyère cheese combined and lifted to startlingly tall heights—can't help but impress. So why don't many people make it anymore?

Maybe because most people assume that it's a dish fraught with disaster, ready to collapse with the slightest disturbance. Classic French cookbooks intimidate with pages upon pages devoted to how to perfectly whip and fold in egg whites and precisely time the dish for your guests. Then there's the matter of fashioning a parchment collar around the dish to contain the batter as it rises, not to mention the mystery of determining when the soufflé is done—more concerns that make soufflé seem like a dish best left to the experts.

As I tried out a few recipes, I realized the truth: Soufflés are neither complicated nor finicky. In fact, a cheese soufflé is nothing more than a sauce that's transformed into dinner through the addition of egg whites and air. The sauce, typically a béchamel made of milk thickened with a paste (or roux) of equal parts butter and flour, provides the soufflé with stability. Grated cheese is added for flavor, and egg yolks introduce richness and a silky texture. Stop here and you'd have something that might dress up steamed broccoli or poached chicken. But fold in stiffly beaten egg whites and the dish stands on its own, literally and figuratively. After this batter is poured into a round, straight-sided soufflé dish and baked in a hot oven, the water in the mixture rapidly turns to steam, inflating air bubbles and raising the soufflé to high heights.

But that doesn't mean all recipes for soufflés lead to optimal results. Some of the recipes I tried turned out soufflés that were overly heavy and dense; others were so light and ethereal that they were hardly substantial enough for a meal. Still others had negligible cheese flavor. I wanted a cheese soufflé boasting not only stature but also enough substance to serve as a main course. It needed a balanced but distinctive cheese flavor and contrasting textures in the form of a crisp, nicely browned crust and a moist, almost custardy center.

I cobbled together a basic recipe—six eggs, 6 tablespoons each of butter and flour, a little more than a cup of milk, and 4 ounces of grated Gruyère (the classic choice)—and got down to testing. The resulting soufflé wasn't terrible, but it had a long way to go. It didn't have loads of cheese flavor; its texture was closer to that of a quiche than that of a soufflé; and it rose only about an inch or so above the lip of the dish.

I wondered if the béchamel might be the cause of multiple problems. Flour has a tendency to mute flavors, and its thickening power, while essential to providing the soufflé with stability, can also weigh things down. When I dialed back the amounts of butter and flour to 4 tablespoons each (anything less than that and the soufflé verged on soupy), the flavor of the cheese came through more clearly and the texture lightened up. This gave me enough wiggle room to add

more cheese. But beyond a certain point (6 ounces) the texture began to suffer and my soufflé turned out squat. In order to increase the cheese flavor without causing damage, I turned to more intensely flavored yet feathery grated Parmesan. Adding 5 tablespoons, along with the 6 ounces of Gruyère, gave the soufflé the cheese flavor that it needed without the weight. I also dusted the sides and bottom of the soufflé dish and the top of the batter with a few more tablespoons of Parmesan.

As for baking temperature, recipes that I consulted varied from 300 degrees to 400 degrees. I wanted a soufflé with a crisp mahogany crust; nicely set edges; and a moist, barely set core. When the soufflé was cooked at too-low temperatures, the crust resisted browning and the interior set too evenly. Excessively high temperatures, on the other hand, cooked it too fast: When the crust was nicely browned, the interior was still soupy. I found that 350 degrees worked best. Another key discovery: Rather than deal with the fussy step of greasing a parchment collar and securing it around the lip of the dish to create a taller soufflé and also prevent overflow as the soufflé rises, I simply left about 1 inch of headspace between the top of the batter and the lip of the dish.

Knowing when the soufflé was done turned out to be very straightforward. Some recipes tell you that it should be "slightly jiggly" at the center, while others say to insert a skewer (or knitting needle) and look for a moist but not wet batter. I liked using two spoons to pry open the middle of the soufflé to check that it looked barely set but not soupy. Even better, though, was using an instant-read thermometer. I found that when inserted into the soufflé's core, the thermometer should reach about 170 degrees.

I was making progress, but the interior consistency of the soufflé was still not exactly where I wanted it to be. The soufflé was rising nearly 3 inches when cooked, making it a bit too light and delicate. I already knew that more cheese wasn't the answer (plus I already had the cheese flavor down), so what could I do to create a soufflé that was light but not featherweight?

Up until now I'd been following soufflé convention and whipping the egg whites to stiff peaks in order to create maximum volume. I wondered whether I could dial back the lightness by not working them so hard. For my next test, I whipped the whites to soft peaks instead. While the resulting soufflé had a denser consistency, it was a little too dense and squat. Here was my

THE BEST SOUFFLÉ DISH

A round, straight-sided ceramic soufflé dish elegantly launches a soufflé—that's its raison d'être. Sweet as well as savory soufflés rose reliably in each of the three classic soufflé dishes, priced from about $10 to $42, that we selected for testing. Differences came down to two factors: the actual (versus stated) capacity of each dish and the thickness of each dish's walls. With its straight, not-too-thick sides and just the right capacity, our winning dish produced perfect, evenly cooked soufflés. At about $15, the **HIC 64 Ounce Soufflé** baked soufflés that did us proud.

ACHIEVING LIFTOFF
The HIC 64 Ounce Soufflé produced sweet and savory soufflés that baked perfectly.

SOUFFLÉ MYTHS DEBUNKED

MYTH: The soufflé will collapse from loud noises or sudden movements.
REALITY: Steam will keep a hot soufflé fully inflated. No loud noise or slamming of the oven door can change that.

MYTH: The egg whites must be gently folded into the base.
REALITY: Egg whites whipped to stiff peaks will have ample structure to handle aggressive beating, even in a stand mixer.

MYTH: Prodding to check doneness will make it collapse.
REALITY: A soufflé is not a balloon; it's a matrix of very fine bubbles. No tool can pop enough of them to cause it to fall.

MYTH: You can't make a fallen soufflé rise again.
REALITY: Yes, your soufflé will fall after it's been out of the oven for about 5 minutes. But returning it to a 350-degree oven will convert the water back into steam and reinflate it (it will lose about ½ inch of height).

FALLEN FROM GRACE   **RETURNED TO GLORY**

Goldilocks moment: Stiff peaks provided a bit too much lift and airiness, and soft peaks provided not quite enough. "Medium" peaks would probably be perfect—if I only knew of a way to call for such a thing. Soft peaks retain some shape but droop slowly from the end of a whisk, while stiff peaks are glossy and firm and hold their shape entirely. But the midway point between the two is a nebulous thing; there just isn't a good visual indicator for such a stage.

But maybe there was another way. Most recipes insist that you fold the whites gradually and gently into the cheese-béchamel mixture to ensure that the soufflé rises properly. I wondered if that was really important. Next time around, I whipped the whites to stiff peaks and then stirred them vigorously rather than folded them into the cheese mixture. I didn't hold back: I hoped that I could break down some of the structure by whipping out just enough air from the whites. I worried that such manhandling might be overkill and ruin the soufflé completely, but it seemed to have plenty of volume going into the oven. And it baked up better than ever. The soufflé had risen beautifully (if not quite as high as before), and its consistency was perfect: light and airy but with the extra heft that it had been missing. I did one more test to see if I could streamline things even further and found that I could simply whip the cheese mixture into the whites right in the stand mixer.

Before wrapping things up, I wanted to find out if other cheeses could stand in for the Gruyère. Softer or milder cheeses, like goat, blue, and mild cheddar, were not good alternatives, since they either added too much moisture to the soufflé or were simply not potent enough. But cheeses with a similar depth of flavor, consistency, and meltability, like Comté, sharp cheddar, and gouda, made equally great-tasting soufflés.

At last, I had a richly flavored, entrée-worthy cheese soufflé that was as easy to prepare as it was impressive.
—ANDREW JANJIGIAN, *Cook's Illustrated*

Cheese Soufflé

SERVES 4 TO 6

Serve this soufflé with a green salad for a light dinner or as a brunch centerpiece. Comté, sharp cheddar, or gouda cheese can be substituted for the Gruyère. To prevent the soufflé from overflowing the soufflé dish, leave at least 1 inch of space between the top of the batter and the rim of the dish; any excess batter should be discarded. The most foolproof way to test for doneness is with an instant-read thermometer. To judge doneness without an instant-read thermometer, use two large spoons to pry open the soufflé so that you can peer inside it; the center should appear thick and creamy but not soupy.

1	ounce Parmesan cheese, grated (½ cup)
¼	cup (1¼ ounces) all-purpose flour
¼	teaspoon paprika
¼	teaspoon salt
⅛	teaspoon cayenne pepper
⅛	teaspoon white pepper
	Pinch ground nutmeg
4	tablespoons unsalted butter
1⅓	cups whole milk
6	ounces Gruyère cheese, shredded (1½ cups)
6	large eggs, separated
2	teaspoons minced fresh parsley
¼	teaspoon cream of tartar

1. Adjust oven rack to middle position and heat oven to 350 degrees. Spray 8-inch round (2-quart) soufflé dish with vegetable oil spray, then sprinkle with 2 tablespoons Parmesan.

2. Combine flour, paprika, salt, cayenne, white pepper, and nutmeg in bowl. Melt butter in small saucepan over medium heat. Stir in flour mixture and cook for 1 minute. Slowly whisk in milk and bring to simmer. Cook, whisking constantly, until mixture is thickened and smooth, about 1 minute. Remove pan from heat and whisk in Gruyère and 5 tablespoons Parmesan until melted and smooth. Let cool for 10 minutes, then whisk in egg yolks and 1½ teaspoons parsley.

3. Using stand mixer fitted with whisk, whip egg whites and cream of tartar on medium-low speed until foamy, about 1 minute. Increase speed to medium-high and whip until stiff peaks form, 3 to 4 minutes. Add cheese mixture and continue to whip until fully combined, about 15 seconds.

4. Pour mixture into prepared dish and sprinkle with remaining 1 tablespoon Parmesan. Bake until risen above rim, top is deep golden brown, and interior registers 170 degrees, 30 to 35 minutes. Sprinkle with remaining ½ teaspoon parsley and serve immediately.

CURRANT SCONES

✔ WHY THIS RECIPE WORKS: Compared to American scones, British scones are lighter, fluffier, and less sweet; perfect for serving with butter and jam. Rather than leaving pieces of cold butter in the dry ingredients as we would with American scones, we thoroughly worked in softened butter until it was fully integrated. This protected some of the flour granules from moisture, which in turn limited gluten development and kept the crumb tender and cakey. For a higher rise, we added more than the usual amount of leavening and started the scones in a 500-degree oven to boost their lift before turning the temperature down. We brushed some reserved milk and egg on top for enhanced browning, and added currants for tiny bursts of fruit flavor throughout.

"This is fantastic. But it's not a scone." The setting was a café in Cambridge, Massachusetts, and the speaker was an English customer who was emphatically brandishing a pastry that I had made. It was a large, rustic triangle with a craggy, sugary exterior and a buttery, fruit-studded middle. At the time, I naively believed it to be a scone.

Years later, on a visit to the United Kingdom, I understood what he meant—mine were American, not British, scones. Though they share the same name and a lot of the same characteristics, they are, as the Brits might say, as different as chalk and cheese.

Proper British scones are round and tall, with a light, cakelike crumb and a soft, tender crust. They're not as sweet or as rich as American scones, but that's because they're usually split in half, lavishly spread with butter or clotted cream, and piled high with jam at teatime.

While I love American-style scones, that cozy British teatime ritual holds tremendous appeal. I resolved to develop a recipe for light, fluffy, British-style scones.

Here's how I've made American scones for almost two decades: I combine all-purpose flour, sugar, baking powder, and salt in a bowl; then I rub in a very generous amount of cold butter until it is distributed throughout the dry ingredients in thin, broad flakes. I whisk together milk and eggs and gently stir that mixture into my dry ingredients to form a shaggy dough. At that point I add some flavorings (fresh or dried fruit, nuts, chocolate chips, spices, maple syrup—the sky's the limit), and then, working gently and quickly, I form the dough into disks, which I cut into wedges. A bit of egg wash, maybe a sprinkling of coarse sugar, and the scones go into the oven. They emerge somewhat crumbly, squat, and whimsical in shape, but they have a buttery charm that has ensured their spot in my baking repertoire.

The recipes that I collected for British scones featured the same basic ingredients as mine, minus all the add-ins and with two key differences. First, British recipes call for self-raising flour, which is like American all-purpose flour with a leavening agent already added. (Don't confuse it with American self-rising flour, which is lower in protein and has added salt.) It's ubiquitous in the United Kingdom but harder to find here. For authenticity's sake, I tracked down a couple of bags locally, knowing that I would devise a substitution later.

The second difference was more clear-cut: British recipes call for about one-third of the amount of butter that my recipe requires. So I lowered the butter content in my recipe, and I also cut back on the sugar to make my scones more jam-compatible. I followed my trusty mixing method, but instead of forming the dough into wedges, I used a cookie cutter to make round scones. No egg wash, no sugar—just straight into a 425-degree oven. The result looked familiar. In fact, here in America we have a special name for such a thing: a biscuit. These scones tasted great, but they lacked the tender, cakelike crumb of British scones. Yet they were made with the same ingredients and in the same ratios. How had I ended up with a bready biscuit?

Realizing that the difference had to be in the methods, I compared them closely to see what didn't line up. I quickly realized that the butter was the problem.

I was still working the cold, hard fat quickly into the dry ingredients, leaving noticeable bits of butter in the mixture. But a close reading of traditional British scone recipes reveals a significant difference in technique: The butter is completely rubbed into the dry ingredients so that it is no longer visible. In fact, British cooks often use soft, room-temperature butter to make the process even easier, quicker, and more thorough. This approach promises a finer, more even and tender crumb because the structure is not disrupted by those large pieces of fat. With more of the flour particles coated with fat, and thus protected from the wet ingredients, a lot of the proteins in the flour are prevented from linking up to form gluten. The result is a fine-textured scone, much more cakelike than biscuitlike.

For my next batch, I thoroughly worked softened butter into the dry ingredients before mixing the dough

lightly. (I also switched to using a food processor to blend in the butter, which many cooks prefer to using their hands.) This subtle change worked to give me the cakelike texture I was after.

This discovery led to another equally compelling one. My method called for rolling out the dough once, cutting eight scones from it, and then rerolling the scraps to make four more scones. I noticed that the scones from the second roll consistently rose a bit higher in the oven than those from the first roll, which seems counterintuitive when you consider all those warnings about overmixing that are so often a feature of baking recipes. The fear in those cases is that the gluten network will overdevelop and become tighter if it is overworked, leading to tougher texture and a hampered rise. But in this case, so much of the flour was coated in fat that it was effectively waterproofed, making it harder for gluten bonds to form. This meant that working the dough a bit more was actually beneficial since it offered those proteins still available (i.e., from any uncoated flour) a chance to link together, giving the scones a little more structure to support more lift. With this in mind, I upped the number of times that I kneaded the dough from a dozen to 25 to 30 and rerolled the scraps with no qualms.

I was encouraged by my progress, but my scones still lacked impressive height. I knew that I could do better.

It was time to find a substitute for that self-raising flour. I had seen recommendations for adding anywhere from 1 to 2 teaspoons of baking powder per cup of all-purpose flour to approximate the lift of self-raising, and most British scone recipes go on to boost the lift even more with additional baking powder, which varied in amount from recipe to recipe as well.

In search of maximum lift and no leavening flavor, I made five more batches, starting with 3 tablespoons of baking powder and decreasing it by 1 teaspoon per batch and tracking scone height and negative flavor comments. I found my sweet spot at 2 tablespoons.

Next I considered the oven temperature. Yeast-leavened breads often start in an extremely hot oven to maximize "oven spring," the growth spurt that happens when water vaporizes into steam and the air in the dough heats up and expands. Then the heat is lowered to ensure that the crust does not burn before the interior is cooked through. When I tried this method—preheating my oven to 500 degrees and then turning it down to 425 degrees after putting in the scones—I got the lightest, fluffiest batch yet.

BRITISH-STYLE CURRANT SCONES

A couple more tweaks brought my scones to the level of those that I had enjoyed in England. I added currants rather than raisins because their smaller size meant better distribution within each scone, and they seemed more appropriate. And I reserved a small amount of the milk and egg mixture to brush on top of the scones before baking. It helped the scones brown a bit more, and gave them the soft, tender crust that I wanted.

The words "stately" and "fluffy" are rarely used together, but they both described my scones perfectly. And while they looked quite impressive piled on a plate, they really came into their own when split and topped with plenty of butter—or clotted cream—and jam, served alongside a mug of tea. If I ever meet another Englishman who's keen to talk scones, I'm confident that I'll be able to hold my own in both English and American.

—ANDREA GEARY, *Cook's Illustrated*

NOTES FROM THE TEST KITCHEN

WHEN A SECOND ROLL DOESN'T PRODUCE SECOND-BEST

For many baked goods that require rolling out the dough (biscuits, pie dough), rerolling scraps produces a tougher, more squat result. This is because just as with kneading, the action of rolling creates a stronger, tighter gluten network—and too much gluten can negatively influence texture and rise. But our British-style scones offer more leeway. The butter is worked into the flour so thoroughly that it prevents many of the proteins from ever linking up to form gluten in the first place. Far from being a hazard, rerolling the second batch of dough merely encourages more of the proteins to link together, leading to a bit more structure and more lift in the oven.

A TALE OF TWO SCONES

While rich, dense American scones are no-holds-barred, cakelike British scones show restraint.

THE AMERICAN		THE BRIT
1½ cups, chilled	BUTTER	½ cup, softened
1 tablespoon of baking powder	LEAVENER	2 tablespoons of baking powder
The more the better	ADD-INS	A smattering of currants
Egg wash and lots of coarse sugar	TOPPING	Light milk-and-egg wash

British-Style Currant Scones
MAKES 12 SCONES

We prefer whole milk in this recipe, but low-fat milk can be used. The dough will be quite soft and wet; dust your work surface and your hands liberally with flour. For a tall, even rise, use a sharp-edged biscuit cutter and push straight down; do not twist the cutter. Serve with jam as well as salted butter or clotted cream.

- 3 cups (15 ounces) all-purpose flour
- ⅓ cup (2⅓ ounces) sugar
- 2 tablespoons baking powder
- ½ teaspoon salt
- 8 tablespoons unsalted butter, cut into ½-inch pieces and softened
- ¾ cup dried currants
- 1 cup whole milk
- 2 large eggs

1. Adjust oven rack to upper-middle position and heat oven to 500 degrees. Line rimmed baking sheet with parchment paper. Pulse flour, sugar, baking powder, and salt in food processor until combined, about 5 pulses. Add butter and pulse until fully incorporated and mixture looks like very fine crumbs with no visible butter, about 20 pulses. Transfer mixture to large bowl and stir in currants.

2. Whisk milk and eggs together in second bowl. Set aside 2 tablespoons milk mixture. Add remaining milk mixture to flour mixture and, using rubber spatula, fold together until almost no dry bits of flour remain.

3. Transfer dough to well-floured counter and gather into ball. With floured hands, knead until surface is smooth and free of cracks, 25 to 30 times. Press gently to form disk. Using floured rolling pin, roll disk into 9-inch round, about 1 inch thick. Using floured 2½-inch round cutter, stamp out 8 rounds, recoating cutter with flour if it begins to stick. Arrange scones on prepared sheet. Gather dough scraps, form into ball, and knead gently until surface is smooth. Roll dough to 1-inch thickness and stamp out 4 rounds. Discard remaining dough.

4. Brush tops of scones with reserved milk mixture. Reduce oven temperature to 425 degrees and bake scones until risen and golden brown, 10 to 12 minutes, rotating sheet halfway through baking. Transfer scones to wire rack and let cool for at least 10 minutes. Serve scones warm or at room temperature.

RHODE ISLAND JOHNNYCAKES

✔ **WHY THIS RECIPE WORKS:** Johnnycakes are unleavened corn pancakes that are native to Rhode Island. At their best, they have golden, crispy crusts and creamy, soft interiors with plenty of corn flavor, but many versions turn out dull, gritty, and crumbly. Traditionally, boiling water is poured over a mixture of cornmeal, salt and sugar, but we found that the texture of the cakes improved dramatically if we poured the dry ingredients into the boiling water instead. Increasing the water-to-cornmeal ratio and letting the batter rest eliminated grittiness. Finally, we perfected the cooking method by making sure to let the johnnycakes cook completely on one side before flipping and flattening them slightly. A quick homemade maple butter made the perfect, slightly sweet accompaniment to the johnnycakes.

Being from New England, I had of course heard about Rhode Island johnnycakes. But these unleavened corn pancakes never seemed worth seeking out: They're made from nothing but the stone-ground white cap flint corn that is native to Rhode Island (this tough corn is used for cornmeal) mixed with water or milk, salt, and a bit of sugar. And the technique seems clunky: Mix cornmeal with salt and sugar, pour boiling liquid over it, stir, form, and cook. I didn't see where the deliciousness would come from.

But that idea changed completely when I attended the annual Johnny Cake Festival in West Kingston, Rhode Island. At the Kenyon's Grist Mill booth, cooks were flipping johnnycakes by the dozens on well-seasoned flat-top griddles the size of banquet tables. The cakes they piled on my plate were golden brown and crispy on the outside, creamy on the inside, and just thick enough that you got the perfect ratio of crisp exterior to soft, delicate, corn-flavored interior. Served with creamy maple butter, they were better than I had ever imagined.

Previously, I had sampled versions from all over Rhode Island. Some, from the East Bay area, were thin and lacy; others, from the West Bay, were more like pancakes. I had preferred the thick ones because the thin ones ate more like crêpes and had little corn flavor. But even the thicker versions resembled disks of dried-out cornbread.

But now that I had tasted johnnycake greatness, I was determined to achieve it at home. I stocked up on a case of johnnycake meal at the Mill's quaint little store and made the drive back to Boston. I searched out a handful of recipes, both old and new, including the one on the box of Kenyon's Johnny Cake Corn Meal. I was thrilled because I assumed I'd soon be eating cakes as excellent as those I'd enjoyed at the festival.

The technique used by virtually every recipe I found was as simple as the ingredient list: Whisk together the dry ingredients, then pour boiling water over the top, mix again, and ladle out small dollops of batter onto a lightly greased griddle. Unfortunately, following these instructions resulted in johnnycakes that were nothing like the ones I was trying to re-create. Instead, I got a succession of cakes that were either gritty or sandy and either fell apart when I tried to turn them or ended up with the consistency of wet cardboard. After a few frustrating attempts, I asked several other test cooks to also make the Kenyon's recipe. Not only were the textures of each of their cakes as unpleasant as mine but each was different.

What was the problem? I tried to recall exactly how the cooks at that stand back in Rhode Island had made their johnnycakes, and one factor did occur to me: I remembered that the texture of their batter as it dropped onto the griddle looked different from mine. I went back over the photos I had taken, and sure enough, I found a picture of their batter in a saucepan, looking very much like mashed potatoes. Mine was much thinner. I figured I could probably get this texture if I used a different approach. Rather than pouring boiling water over the dry ingredients, what if I whisked the dry ingredients into the boiling water?

This turned out to be the key. When I switched to this method, I got consistent results every time and ended up with johnnycakes with a much smoother texture, without a hint of grittiness. It actually made perfect sense. This approach resulted in cornmeal that was more thoroughly cooked before it went on the griddle, which got rid of the gritty or sandy qualities that resulted from batters with less fully cooked cornmeal. This approach gave me consistent cakes from batch to batch, and I also got very similar results even when I tested it with other brands of stone-ground cornmeal.

I had overcome a major hurdle, but I wasn't home free yet. I still was having problems with the thickness of the batter. The cooking method I was now using tended to make the batter too thick, since the cornmeal was cooking and therefore absorbing more water before it went on the griddle. Once again, I found the solution to this problem by ignoring the package instructions, which called for about equal parts cornmeal and water. I made batches with increasing amounts of water until I got a batter that cooked up into the proper creamy consistency: 2¾ cups water to 1 cup cornmeal. If I cooked this for about 30 seconds after whisking in the cornmeal and then let it sit for 15 minutes so the cornmeal absorbed even more water, it had the perfect consistency, like ploppable mashed potatoes. (I also found that, since this batter did thicken as it sat, I had to add a couple of tablespoons more water to the second batch in order to achieve the right consistency.)

Now I was almost there. But my johnnycakes were still not perfect, since they too often fell apart as I turned them. Like standing in line, this was a matter of patience. Attempting to cook johnnycakes as you would a standard flour pancake didn't work. Because the batter has no leavener, eggs, or flour, as regular pancake batter does, getting it to hold together is all about the cooking technique. The cakes need to be cooked for at least 6 minutes, and often as long as 8 minutes on the first side, so they form a crust that will hold the cake together when flipped. When you start to see a golden-brown crust forming around the edge of the pancake, then and only then is it time to flip. In addition, after flipping the cakes, you need to gently flatten them to about ¼ inch, at which height they will cook through by the time the second side has properly browned.

Now I had real johnnycakes—or at least the kind of cakes I had been working toward since that day at the festival. They were perfect just as is for a side dish, but for breakfast they needed a little something. Maple butter, made by simply mixing well-softened butter with pure maple syrup, was the easiest and best route to this final goal.

And you know what? The next time I called the tasters to try my johnnycakes topped with maple butter, they were very happy to stand in line for them.

—DIANE UNGER, *Cook's Country*

Rhode Island Johnnycakes

MAKES 12 JOHNNYCAKES

Johnnycakes are best served warm with maple butter for breakfast (recipe follows), or as a side dish for soups and stews. For authentic Rhode Island johnnycakes, we recommend using Kenyon's Johnny Cake Corn Meal, available by mail order. Do not try to turn the johnnycakes

too soon or they will fall apart. If you prefer crisper johnnycakes, press the pancakes thinner in step 5.

1 cup (5 ounces) johnnycake meal or stone-ground cornmeal
2 teaspoons sugar
¾ teaspoon salt
2¾ cups water, plus extra hot water for thinning batter
2 tablespoons unsalted butter
2 tablespoons vegetable oil

1. Adjust oven rack to middle position and heat oven to 200 degrees. Set wire rack in rimmed baking sheet.

2. Whisk johnnycake meal, sugar, and salt together in bowl. Bring water to boil in large saucepan. Slowly whisk johnnycake meal mixture into boiling water until no lumps remain; continue to cook until thickened, about 30 seconds. Off heat, whisk in butter. Scrape batter into bowl, cover with plastic wrap, and let sit until slightly firm, about 15 minutes.

3. Rewhisk batter until smooth. Batter should be consistency of ploppable mashed potatoes; if not, thin with 1 to 2 tablespoons extra hot water until mixture is able to drop easily from spoon.

4. Heat 1 tablespoon oil in 12-inch nonstick skillet over medium heat until shimmering. (Or heat nonstick griddle to 400 degrees.) Using greased ¼-cup dry measuring cup, drop 6 evenly spaced scoops of batter

---

NOTES FROM THE TEST KITCHEN

SHAPING JOHNNYCAKES

1. Use greased ¼-cup measuring cup to carefully portion six mounds of batter into hot pan.

2. When edges are crisp and brown, carefully flip cakes and gently flatten with spatula.

into skillet, using spoon to help release batter from cup as needed. Cook johnnycakes, without moving them, until edges appear crisp and golden brown, 6 to 8 minutes.

5. Carefully flip johnnycakes and press with spatula to flatten into 2½- to 3-inch-diameter pancakes. Continue to cook until well browned on second side, 5 to 7 minutes. Transfer johnnycakes to prepared wire rack and place in oven to keep warm. Whisk 2 to 4 tablespoons extra hot water into remaining batter to return to correct consistency. Repeat cooking with remaining 1 tablespoon oil and remaining batter. Serve.

Maple Butter
MAKES ¼ CUP

Maple butter will keep, covered and refrigerated, for one week. Try it on roasted vegetables, corn bread, or pork chops, as well as johnnycakes.

- **4** tablespoons unsalted butter, softened
- **1** tablespoon pure maple syrup
- ¼ teaspoon salt

Whisk butter, maple syrup, and salt together in bowl until combined.

LEMON RICOTTA PANCAKES

✓ **WHY THIS RECIPE WORKS:** Light, fluffy ricotta pancakes are sophisticated enough for special occasions, but getting the balance of ingredients just right is essential for pancakes that are puffy and tender, not dense and wet. To compensate for the extra weight of the ricotta, we decreased the amount of flour and stirred four whipped egg whites into the batter. Baking soda provided extra rise and aided with browning. Bright, tangy lemon juice complemented the rich, creamy ricotta, and lemon zest enhanced the citrus flavor without watering down the batter. A touch of vanilla extract brought depth and subtle sweetness. For a company-worthy finishing touch, we draped the pancakes with a warm fruit compote.

I've always liked pancakes, but until recently I'd never been wowed by them. That all changed when I stole a forkful of ricotta pancakes from a friend's stack at brunch. I'd been seeing this style of pancake on upscale restaurant menus around town, but with a signature ingredient like ricotta, I'd always imagined them to be somewhat heavy and damp. These cakes were anything but. They had a remarkably light, tender, pillowy texture and a sweet, milky flavor that made them more intriguing than the usual griddle cakes. I could easily imagine dressing up these pancakes with confectioners' sugar or fresh fruit toppings and serving them to company.

I gathered a handful of recipes, which by and large looked like variations on a typical pancake formula. Mostly it was the cheese content that varied; some batters were enriched with just a few spoonfuls of ricotta while others were loaded with a 2:1 ratio of cheese to flour. Predictably, the recipes that called for a conservative amount of cheese were fluffy, but with so little cheese in the mix, the results hardly earned their ricotta name. Meanwhile, the cheese-laden recipes confirmed that ricotta cakes could indeed be wet and heavy.

The obvious solution was to go down the middle, so I started with a moderate 1¼ cups of ricotta, which I stirred together with two eggs, a couple of tablespoons of melted butter, ⅓ cup of milk, and a little sugar and vanilla. Separately, I whisked ¾ cup of flour with ½ teaspoon each of baking powder and salt and then combined the wet and dry and ladled the batter onto a hot griddle, where the pancakes cooked until golden on each side. It was a decent start, I thought, noticing the ricotta's rich, creamy presence when I took a bite. But texturewise, I had a ways to go: The pancakes had none of the billowy lightness of the ones I'd tasted at brunch.

Several recipes I'd found called for incorporating whipped egg whites into the batter as you would for a soufflé. I gave the technique a go, separating the two eggs in my working recipe and then beating the whites with the sugar and whisking just the yolks with the ricotta and milk before adding them to the dry ingredients. But it turns out that there's only so much heavy lifting two whipped whites and a little baking powder can do. The pancakes weren't exactly dense, but they'd maintained that somewhat starchy, conventional pancake texture.

I realized that if I wanted more soufflé-like pancakes, I'd have to cut back on the "bready" element: the flour. I took it down to ⅔ cup, and for a few minutes it seemed that my work was done. The cakes rose beautifully, but then they completely deflated when they hit the plate. It occurred to me that I might get better results if I added a second leavener, so ½ teaspoon of baking soda went into the mix. Of course, baking soda requires an acid in order to react, so I squeezed a few teaspoons of lemon juice into the batter as well and hoped that its brightness would complement the cheese. As it turned out, the lemon-ricotta flavor match was great—so I bolstered it with some lemon zest—and the hotcakes rose high on the griddle. Two leaveners seemed to be the answer—until the pancakes again fell flat on the plate.

At this point I either had to cut back on the cheese or call in reinforcements. Hedging my bets, I did a bit of both. I trimmed back the cheese to 1 cup and, invoking the "many hands make light work" principle, whipped two more whites. This, finally, was the combination I was looking for: The lift from the leavener combined with the four whipped egg whites made for the lightest pancakes ever. I started to wonder if all three leavening sources—baking soda, baking powder, and a large amount of egg foam—were really necessary, so I made one more batch and ditched the baking powder (ditching the baking soda was out of the question since the lemon juice was a keeper). Happily, nobody missed it.

There was another bonus to switching to baking soda: The cakes were browning a little more deeply and evenly. While I was pleased by this effect, which boosted flavor, I was also a little surprised. Alkaline baking soda can enhance browning by raising the pH of a food, but I'd assumed that with a pure acid like lemon juice in the mix, its effect would be neutralized. But our science editor explained that there were two other acid neutralizers in the batter: egg whites, which contribute alkalinity, and cheese, which contains casein proteins that buffer the action of the acid. As a result, the batter's pH was more than high enough to allow for rapid browning.

These exquisitely light, tender, and golden-brown pancakes were so good that I found myself eating them straight from the pan without even a dusting of powdered sugar. But to dress them up for company, I threw together a couple of quick fruit toppings: one made with apples, cranberries, and nutmeg; another with pears, blackberries, and cardamom. Conveniently, I was able to soften the fruits (with a little sugar) in the microwave while the pancakes cooked.

With pancakes this easy and this good, I might never go back to ordinary flapjacks.

—ANDREA GEARY, *Cook's Illustrated*

Lemon Ricotta Pancakes

MAKES TWELVE 4-INCH PANCAKES; SERVES 3 TO 4

An electric griddle set at 325 degrees can also be used to cook the pancakes. We prefer the flavor of whole-milk ricotta, but part-skim will work, too; avoid nonfat ricotta. The pancakes are exceptionally rich and tender if you use homemade ricotta (recipe follows). Serve pancakes with honey, confectioners' sugar, or one of our fruit toppings.

⅔ cup (3⅓ ounces) all-purpose flour
½ teaspoon baking soda
½ teaspoon salt
8 ounces (1 cup) whole-milk ricotta cheese
2 large eggs, separated, plus 2 large whites
⅓ cup whole milk
1 teaspoon grated lemon zest plus 4 teaspoons juice
½ teaspoon vanilla extract
2 tablespoons unsalted butter, melted
¼ cup (1¾ ounces) sugar
1–2 teaspoons vegetable oil

1. Adjust oven rack to middle position and heat oven to 200 degrees. Spray wire rack set in rimmed baking sheet with vegetable oil spray and place in oven. Whisk flour, baking soda, and salt together in medium bowl and make well in center. Add ricotta, egg yolks, milk, lemon zest and juice, and vanilla and whisk until just combined. Gently stir in melted butter.

2. Using stand mixer fitted with whisk, whip egg whites on medium-low speed until foamy, about 1 minute. Increase speed to medium-high and whip whites to soft, billowy mounds, about 1 minute. Gradually add sugar and whip until glossy, soft peaks form, 1 to 2 minutes. Transfer one-third of whipped egg whites to batter and whisk gently until mixture is lightened. Using rubber spatula, gently fold remaining egg whites into batter.

3. Heat 1 teaspoon oil in 12-inch nonstick skillet over medium heat until shimmering. Using paper towels, wipe out oil, leaving thin film on bottom and sides of pan. Using ¼-cup measure or 2-ounce ladle, portion batter into pan in 3 places, leaving 2 inches between portions. Gently spread each portion into 4-inch round. Cook until edges are set and first side is deep golden brown, 2 to 3 minutes. Using thin, wide spatula, flip pancakes and continue to cook until second side is golden brown, 2 to 3 minutes longer. Serve pancakes immediately or transfer to prepared wire rack in preheated oven. Repeat with remaining batter, using remaining oil as needed.

Homemade Ricotta Cheese

MAKES ABOUT 2 POUNDS (4 CUPS)

For best results, don't stir the milk too hard, and be very gentle with the curds once they form.

⅓   cup lemon juice (2 lemons)
¼   cup distilled white vinegar, plus extra as needed
1   gallon pasteurized (not ultrapasteurized or UHT) whole milk
2   teaspoons salt

1. Line colander with butter muslin or triple layer of cheesecloth and place in sink. Combine lemon juice and vinegar in liquid measuring cup; set aside. Heat milk and salt in Dutch oven over medium-high heat, stirring frequently with rubber spatula to prevent scorching, until milk registers 185 degrees.

2. Remove pot from heat, slowly stir in lemon juice mixture until fully incorporated and mixture curdles, about 15 seconds. Let sit undisturbed until mixture fully separates into solid curds and translucent whey, 5 to 10 minutes. If curds do not fully separate and there is still milky whey in pot, stir in extra vinegar, 1 tablespoon at a time, and let sit another 2 to 3 minutes, until curds separate.

NOTES FROM THE TEST KITCHEN

WHY SO LIGHT?
Here's how we keep the wet, milky ricotta from weighing down the pancakes.

LOTS OF WHIPPED WHITES Just as when making soufflés, we whip the egg whites—in this case, four of them—which creates an egg foam that lightens the batter.

NOT TOO MUCH FLOUR A moderate ⅔ cup of flour adds enough starch to shore up the egg foam's structure but not so much that the pancakes become bready.

AN ACID PLUS A BASE Lemon juice not only contributes tangy flavor but also reacts with the alkaline baking soda to produce carbon dioxide that inflates the egg foam.

---

3. Gently pour mixture into prepared colander. Let sit, undisturbed, until whey has drained from edges of cheese but center is still very moist, about 8 minutes. Working quickly, gently transfer cheese to large bowl, retaining as much whey in center of cheese as possible. Stir well to break up large curds and incorporate whey. Refrigerate ricotta until cold, about 2 hours. Stir cheese before using. Ricotta can be refrigerated for up to 5 days.

Apple-Cranberry Pancake Topping

MAKES 2½ CUPS

Golden Delicious apples are a good year-round choice for this topping, but other seasonal varieties of apples can be used. Just make sure to choose an apple that will retain its shape when cooked.

3   Golden Delicious apples, peeled, cored, halved, and cut into ¼-inch pieces
¼   cup dried cranberries
1   tablespoon sugar
1   teaspoon cornstarch
    Pinch salt
    Pinch ground nutmeg

Combine all ingredients in bowl and microwave, covered, until apples are softened but not mushy and juices are slightly thickened, 4 to 6 minutes, stirring once halfway through microwaving. Stir before serving.

Pear-Blackberry Pancake Topping

MAKES 3 CUPS

3   ripe pears, peeled, halved, cored, and cut into ¼-inch pieces
1   tablespoon sugar
1   teaspoon cornstarch
    Pinch salt
    Pinch ground cardamom
5   ounces (1 cup) blackberries

Combine pears, sugar, cornstarch, salt, and cardamom in bowl and microwave, covered, until pears are softened but not mushy and juices are slightly thickened, 4 to 6 minutes, stirring once halfway through microwaving. Stir in blackberries before serving.

QUICKER CINNAMON BUNS

QUICKER CINNAMON BUNS

✓ **WHY THIS RECIPE WORKS:** Rich, gooey, homemade cinnamon buns can take upwards of 3 hours to prepare. We wanted the same tender, yeasty results in half the time. For a quicker rise, we supplemented the yeast (which we proofed in warm milk for extra speed) with baking powder. A mere 2 minutes of hand-kneading and a single 30-minute rise were enough to give us the flavor and texture we were looking for. We used a cooler-than-normal oven to give the yeast time to rise and develop flavor before the tops of the buns set. Brown sugar and butter in the filling and a touch of vanilla in our tangy cream cheese glaze made these buns ultra-rich and indulgent.

Cinnamon buns should be big and gooey, tender, and over-the-top sweet. And did I mention the requisite sweet, shiny glaze? Naturally, we have a recipe at America's Test Kitchen that produces just such a cinnamon bun. It's irresistible. So what's the problem? We rarely have time to make it. Between mixing, kneading, rising, shaping, rising again, and baking, these buns take more than 3 hours out of our overscheduled lives. I wanted to make cinnamon buns in half the time.

I found plenty of recipes that claimed to deliver quick cinnamon buns. I made a half-dozen or so. They were delicious—but they weren't cinnamon buns. Instead, they were more like frosted cinnamon biscuits. No surprise, since these recipes called for taking ordinary biscuit dough (leavened with baking powder and/or soda), rolling it out in a rectangle, brushing it with butter, sprinkling it with cinnamon sugar, rolling it up, and slicing it into individual biscuits, which were then baked and glazed. Good as they were, they lacked the unmistakable yeasty flavor and sweet bread texture of a real cinnamon bun. I decided to take a "cinnamon biscuit" recipe, retain as much of its efficiency as possible, and try to restore the yeasted cinnamon bun taste and texture.

Taking the best of the biscuit recipes from my initial test (a basic buttermilk biscuit with a cream-cheese-and-butter glaze), I began its transformation. Almost all baked items are leavened, either by yeast (think bread or Danish) or by the chemical leaveners baking soda and baking powder (think cookies and cakes). But I had an idea based on an unusual Southern recipe known as angel biscuits. To get their famously light and fluffy texture, these biscuits pull out all the stops, incorporating baking powder, baking soda, *and* yeast. Similarly,

I'd take my cinnamon "biscuit" dough and try adding back the yeast of a cinnamon bun.

My working recipe, which used 1¼ teaspoons of baking powder and ½ teaspoon of baking soda for 2¾ cups of flour, made eight buns. I tried the recipe with gradually increasing amounts of yeast, from 2¼ teaspoons (the amount in a single envelope of yeast) up to 2 tablespoons. I hit the sweet spot at 4 teaspoons; we liked the flavor that it gave these cinnamon buns, plus the amount—quite a bit relative to the amount of flour—produced lots of carbon dioxide gas fast. That meant that the buns, helped along by the two other leaveners, would rise quickly in the oven. To further speed along the yeast, I first dissolved it in warm milk with a little sugar. Once upon a time, this step, which is known as proofing the yeast, was part of every recipe calling for yeast. With instant yeast, which I was using, it isn't necessary. But I did it anyway, since proofing accelerates rise and flavor development, and speed was my mantra.

Now that I was making a yeast dough, albeit an unusual one, two things came into play that don't with biscuit dough: kneading and rising. Our classic recipe for cinnamon buns calls for about 10 minutes of kneading in the mixer, followed by two rises, totaling 3 long hours, both before and after shaping the dough into buns. Where was the line between cinnamon bun qualities (tender, yeasty, breadlike) and my desired cinnamon bun timetable? It took many tests to figure that out—not that I heard much complaining from coworkers, who cheerfully lined up to "evaluate" bun after bun. Eventually, I found the perfect compromise between time, taste, and texture: a mere 2 minutes of kneading by hand and—after the dough was rolled out, filled, and cut into buns—a single 30-minute rise.

But I still had a problem. Despite the leaveners, the kneading, and the rise time, the buns remained somewhat squat; they didn't spring up in the oven, as they should. All along, I'd been baking them at 425 degrees—a standard oven temperature for biscuits. But with my hybrid biscuit bun, this high temperature worked against me: The golden-brown tops set before the combined leaveners had time to lift. In several tests, I turned down the oven in 25-degree increments. At 350 degrees, these quicker cinnamon buns reached their full height potential. Our science editor mentioned a second benefit to the cooler oven: Because the yeast was killed more slowly (yeast dies at 140 degrees), it had more time to multiply, ergo there was more flavor development.

The hard work was done. Now I tweaked the filling and the glaze, adding more brown sugar and butter to the former and a little vanilla to the latter. I retained the cream cheese in the glaze from the original biscuit recipe; its tang brought balance to these sugary buns. I was writing up the recipe when I spotted a chance to simplify. Could I switch from buttermilk to more convenient milk? Yep. And without acidic buttermilk, it turned out that I didn't need baking soda either. I wrote it out of the recipe, increasing the baking powder accordingly and making my cinnamon bun recipe shorter and simpler.

It would be an exaggeration to call these cinnamon buns "quick." If you count prepping, shaping, rising, and baking, they still take about 1½ hours. But that's less than half of the time needed to make ordinary cinnamon buns—for the same tender, oozy, and deliciously indulgent reward.

—DIANE UNGER, *Cook's Country*

NOTES FROM THE TEST KITCHEN

LIGHT PANS MAKE UNDERDONE BUNS

We've long known that dark cake pans produce more deeply browned cakes, but it wasn't until we tested our Quicker Cinnamon Buns recipe in both light and dark cake pans that we understood how great the difference can be. We developed our recipe using a dark cake pan, which absorbs heat more efficiently. Made in a light-colored pan, the same recipe yielded doughy, pale, and sunken buns.

BAKED IN A LIGHT PAN
No dark pan? Increase the time and temperature, or your buns will be pale like these.

TWICE THE POWER, HALF THE TIME

By adding a lot of yeast to an ordinary biscuit dough, we combine some of the speed of biscuit-making with the flavor and texture of sweet yeast dough. With both yeast and baking powder, our Quicker Cinnamon Buns take just 2 minutes to knead and 30 minutes to rise.

Quicker Cinnamon Buns
MAKES 8 BUNS

Since the filling, dough, and glaze all require melted butter, it's easier to melt all 10 tablespoons in a liquid measuring cup and divvy it up as needed. We developed this recipe using a dark cake pan, which produces deeply caramelized buns. If your cake pan is light-colored, adjust the oven rack to the lowest position, heat the oven to 375 degrees, and increase the baking time to 29 to 32 minutes.

FILLING
- ¾ cup packed (5¼ ounces) light brown sugar
- ¼ cup (1¾ ounces) granulated sugar
- 1 tablespoon ground cinnamon
- ⅛ teaspoon salt
- 2 tablespoons unsalted butter, melted
- 1 teaspoon vanilla extract

DOUGH
- 1¼ cups whole milk, room temperature
- 4 teaspoons instant or rapid-rise yeast
- 2 tablespoons granulated sugar
- 2¾ cups (13¾ ounces) all-purpose flour
- 2½ teaspoons baking powder
- ¾ teaspoon salt
- 6 tablespoons unsalted butter, melted

GLAZE
- 3 ounces cream cheese, softened
- 2 tablespoons unsalted butter, melted
- 2 tablespoons whole milk
- ½ teaspoon vanilla extract
- ⅛ teaspoon salt
- 1 cup (4 ounces) confectioners' sugar, sifted

1. FOR THE FILLING: Combine brown sugar, granulated sugar, cinnamon, and salt in bowl. Stir in melted butter and vanilla until mixture resembles wet sand; set aside.

2. FOR THE DOUGH: Grease dark 9-inch round cake pan, line with parchment paper, and grease parchment. Pour ¼ cup milk in small bowl and microwave until 110 degrees, 15 to 20 seconds. Stir in yeast and 1 teaspoon sugar and let sit until mixture is bubbly, about 5 minutes.

3. Whisk flour, baking powder, salt, and remaining 5 teaspoons sugar together in large bowl. Stir in 2 tablespoons butter, yeast mixture, and remaining

1 cup milk until dough forms (dough will be sticky). Transfer dough to well-floured counter and knead until smooth ball forms, about 2 minutes.

4. Roll dough into 12 by 9-inch rectangle, with long side parallel to counter edge. Brush dough all over with 2 tablespoons butter, leaving ½-inch border on far edge. Sprinkle dough evenly with filling, then press filling firmly into dough. Using bench scraper or metal spatula, loosen dough from counter. Roll dough away from you into tight log and pinch seam to seal.

5. Roll log seam side down and cut into 8 equal pieces. Stand buns on end and gently re-form ends that were pinched during cutting. Place 1 bun in center of prepared pan and others around perimeter of pan, seam sides facing in. Brush tops of buns with remaining 2 tablespoons butter. Cover buns loosely with plastic wrap and let rise for 30 minutes. Adjust oven rack to middle position and heat oven to 350 degrees.

6. Discard plastic and bake buns until edges are well browned, 23 to 25 minutes. Loosen buns from sides of pan with paring knife and let cool for 5 minutes. Invert large plate over cake pan. Using potholders, flip plate and pan upside down; remove pan and parchment. Reinvert buns onto wire rack, set wire rack inside parchment-lined rimmed baking sheet, and let cool for 5 minutes.

7. FOR THE GLAZE: Place cream cheese in large bowl and whisk in butter, milk, vanilla, and salt until smooth. Whisk in sugar until smooth. Pour glaze evenly over tops of buns, spreading with spatula to cover. Serve.

FRESH CORN CORNBREAD

WHY THIS RECIPE WORKS: We love lightly sweet, Northern-style cornbread, but the finished product rarely tastes like corn. We wanted to make cornbread that really tasted like its namesake. We started with stone-ground cornmeal, which had more corn flavor than fine-ground. We pureed fresh corn kernels to make a "corn butter," which gave our cornbread intense corn flavor. Buttermilk added tang, and baking the cornbread in a buttered skillet ensured a beautifully crisp, well-browned crust.

Cornbread falls into two main styles: the sweet, cakey Northern type and the crusty, savory kind more often found in Southern kitchens. Each has its die-hard fans, but—let's face the facts—neither tastes much like corn. This is because most cornbreads are made with cornmeal alone, and no fresh corn at all. Furthermore, the so-called "field" or "dent" corn used to make cornmeal is far starchier (read: less flavorful) than the sweet corn grown to eat off the cob.

So what would it take to get real corn flavor in cornbread? Simply tossing fresh-cut kernels into the batter didn't work. When I tried, I found that I needed to add at least 2 whole cups of kernels for the corn flavor to really shine, and that created a slew of problems. Since fresh kernels are full of moisture, the crumb of the cornbread was now riddled with unpleasant gummy pockets. What's more, the kernels turned chewy and tough as the bread baked. But there had to be a way to get true sweet corn flavor in cornbread, and I was determined to figure it out.

I decided to work on the cornbread base first. In my earlier tests, tasters found that the little bit of sweetener added to the Northern-style versions helped fresh corn flavor break through, so I settled on that cornbread archetype. For my working recipe, I used slightly more cornmeal than flour and decided to abandon fine-ground cornmeal in favor of the stone-ground type, which contains both the hull and the oil-rich germ of the corn kernel. The upshot: a more rustic texture and fuller flavor. For sweetness, honey, maple syrup, and brown sugar all masked the fresh corn taste, but 2 tablespoons of regular granulated sugar fell neatly in line. For the liquid component, I would stick with traditional tangy buttermilk. Three tablespoons of melted butter and two eggs provided richness, and baking the cornbread in a cast-iron skillet allowed it to develop a brown, crisp crust.

With the batter figured out, I turned back to the fresh corn. I wondered if I could get rid of the unpleasantly steamed, chewy texture of the kernels by soaking them in a solution of water and baking soda before adding them to the batter. The alkaline environment provided by the baking soda helps soften the hulls of the kernels. Sure enough, the kernels were tender, but once they were baked in the bread, the heat toughened them right back up. And I still had those wet, gummy pockets.

I was nearly out of ideas when I came across a recipe for "corn butter" made by pureeing fresh kernels and then reducing the mixture on the stove until thick. I tried it using three large ears of corn and found that the puree thickened and turned deep yellow in minutes, transforming into a "butter" packed with concentrated corn flavor. While the recipes I found used the corn butter as a spread, I had another idea: I added the reduced puree to a batch of batter, baked it—and rejoiced. For the first time, my cornbread tasted like real corn—and without any distracting chewiness.

This method offered another benefit: Since cooking the corn puree drove off moisture, my bread no longer had gummy pockets surrounding the kernels. In fact, the bread was almost too dry and even a little crumbly—a result of the large amount of natural cornstarch (released by pureeing the kernels) that was now absorbing surrounding moisture in the batter. Happily, this problem was easy to solve by simply adding an extra egg yolk and 2 more tablespoons of butter to the batter. I had one more tweak: I melted a pat of butter in the skillet before adding the batter, which gave the bread a more crisp and buttery-tasting bottom crust.

Moist, tender, and bursting with corn flavor, my cornbread tasted like a bite of corn on the cob.

—BRIDGET LANCASTER, *Cook's Illustrated*

Fresh Corn Cornbread

SERVES 6 TO 8

We prefer to use a well-seasoned cast-iron skillet in this recipe, but an ovensafe 10-inch skillet can be used in its place. Alternatively, in step 4 you can add 1 tablespoon of butter to a 9-inch cake pan and place it in the oven until the butter melts, about 3 minutes.

1⅓	cups (6⅔ ounces) stone-ground cornmeal
1	cup (5 ounces) all-purpose flour
2	tablespoons sugar
1½	teaspoons baking powder
¼	teaspoon baking soda
1¼	teaspoons salt
3	ears corn, kernels cut from cobs (2¼ cups)
6	tablespoons unsalted butter, cut into 6 pieces
1	cup buttermilk
2	large eggs plus 1 large yolk

1. Adjust oven rack to middle position and heat oven to 400 degrees. Whisk cornmeal, flour, sugar, baking powder, baking soda, and salt together in large bowl.

2. Process corn kernels in blender until very smooth, about 2 minutes. Transfer puree to medium saucepan (you should have about 1½ cups). Cook puree over medium heat, stirring constantly, until very thick and deep yellow and it measures ¾ cup, 5 to 8 minutes.

3. Remove pan from heat. Add 5 tablespoons butter and whisk until melted and incorporated. Add buttermilk and whisk until incorporated. Add eggs and yolk and whisk until incorporated. Transfer corn mixture to bowl with cornmeal mixture and, using rubber spatula, fold together until just combined.

4. Melt remaining 1 tablespoon butter in 10-inch cast-iron skillet over medium heat. Scrape batter into skillet and spread into even layer. Bake until top is golden brown and toothpick inserted in center comes out clean, 23 to 28 minutes. Let cool on wire rack for 5 minutes. Remove cornbread from skillet and let cool for 20 minutes before cutting into wedges and serving.

EASY SANDWICH BREAD

✔ **WHY THIS RECIPE WORKS:** Hastily made yeast breads can often lack the structure necessary for a satisfactory domed top, and their interiors are often wet and bland. Our goal was to make a soft, well-risen, even-crumbed loaf of bread in less than 2 hours. To encourage a strong gluten structure, we used plenty of warm water, and used high-protein bread flour instead of all-purpose flour. We also added some whole-wheat flour for nutty flavor. A small amount of honey added extra complexity and promoted browning. We withheld the salt until the second mix, which gave our bread more time to develop spring and lift. Switching our mixer's dough hook for the paddle attachment and increasing the speed to medium not only shortened our mixing time but also gave our dough enough structure to rise into a high dome. To give our bread some presentation-worthy appeal, we painted on a shiny egg wash before baking and then brushed the baked loaf with a thin coat of melted butter.

A freshly baked loaf of bread is one of life's great pleasures. But these days, most people don't have 4 hours to devote to mixing dough, waiting for it to rise—twice—plus kneading (even if it's the stand mixer approach), shaping, and baking. While I can appreciate the classic bread-making process, I wondered: Could I find a way to make a yeasted loaf of bread in about half of the time? And could I possibly shortcut some of the work?

I began by scouring cookbooks and websites for clever bread-making tricks and came across an old-fashioned type of loaf: batter bread. As its name implies, the yeasted

EASY SANDWICH BREAD

loaf begins with a fluid batter (not a thick dough) that's made of all-purpose flour, yeast, salt, sugar, and quite a bit of water. Since its hydration level is so high (80 to 85 percent), the batter is beaten with a paddle instead of a dough hook (usually for about 5 minutes) and is transferred straight from the mixing bowl to a prepared loaf pan, no shaping required. And some recipes call for only one rise rather than the two needed to make most traditional loaves. They all promised tender loaves with great flavor—homemade sandwich bread without all the work. Was it too good to be true?

Well, yes and no. The few batter bread recipes I tried featured quick and easy aspects—less time being kneaded in the mixer (some even relied on just a wooden spoon and bowl), abbreviated or fewer proofs, and no shaping—that met my requirements. But that speed and simplicity came at a price. The loaves were generally squat and dumpy-looking, with bumpy, sunken tops instead of smooth, tender domes. Slicing revealed damp, fragile interiors that were exceedingly yeasty but otherwise bland. I wanted great-tasting bread with a soft, uniform crumb sturdy enough to support sandwich fillings. To get a loaf that justified even a modest effort, I'd have to make some serious modifications.

I decided to solve the easiest problem first: that single-note yeast flavor. For quick rising, all the batter bread recipes that I found rely on more than twice as much yeast as traditional artisanal loaf recipes do: 2¼ teaspoons versus 1 teaspoon. But all that yeast was giving the breads an overly yeasty, not "bready," flavor. Nevertheless, I was committed to sticking with the large amount since it made such a huge time savings.

My elementary but effective strategy was to cover up part of the yeastiness by working in some more flavorful ingredients. Adding a few tablespoons of melted butter was a good start toward a tastier loaf, and substituting whole-wheat flour for a portion of the all-purpose flour provided nutty, wheaty depth. I also traded 1 tablespoon of honey for the sugar, which was a twofer: It contributed complexity, and because heat causes honey to break down into simple sugars that encourage browning, it also gave the crust a bit more color.

Next up: building that complexity. In traditional bread, complexity develops by way of fermentation, which happens during the first and second rises. In these two proofing stages (each of which takes about an hour) the yeast consumes the sugars that are created

as the starches in the flour break down, producing the gases essential for making the dough rise. Along the way, a multitude of flavorful byproducts are generated: sugars, acids, and alcohol. Knowing this, I decided that there was no way that I could get by with just one rise. Two 20-minute proofs—one after mixing the batter and one after transferring it to the pan—would allow for at least some flavor development.

My bread, which was coming together in about 90 minutes, now had quite a bit more depth, and the yeast flavor was much less noticeable than in previous versions. But it still wasn't winning points for its damp, fragile texture or sunken appearance.

Yeasted breads derive their light, airy structure from gluten, a stretchy protein network that forms only when wheat flour is combined with water. That network traps the gases given off by the yeast, inflating the dough and causing it to rise. (If the gluten structure is weak, the network can't hold enough gas and the bread will collapse in the heat of the oven.) When a dough is initially mixed, the proteins that form the network are weak and disorganized. They need to align in order to link up and acquire strength. Given enough time, they will line up on their own, or they can be physically encouraged to do so by kneading.

You'd think that my bread would have had a mighty strong gluten network since I had been beating the batter in the mixer for 5 minutes. Yet the loaf's inadequate volume, sunken top, and fragile crumb suggested otherwise.

Before launching an in-depth investigation into the disappointing structure and crumb, I made a quick adjustment: I swapped the all-purpose flour for higher-protein bread flour. More gluten-forming proteins in the bread-flour dough would surely result in a more robust structure. This switch was a step in the right direction, but my loaf still had a long way to go.

My batter had so much water in it that the loaf was damp. Maybe that was too much liquid? I knew that the hydration level of a dough (or batter, in this case) affects gluten strength: Generally, the more water, the stronger and more extensible the gluten strands are and the better able they are to provide support. That translates into a sturdier, airier bread. But there's a tipping point: Unless you are planning on a long fermentation—which I wasn't—too much water can actually inhibit the formation of gluten. I had been using

1¾ cups warm water (using warm, rather than room-temperature, water helps jump-start the yeast's activity, ensuring a faster rise). Guessing that my existing batter was too wet, I reduced the water in my next batch to 1¼ cups. I hoped that the resulting loaf would have a slightly drier crumb and that the gluten framework would be sturdier.

I attached the paddle to the mixer, beat the batter for 5 minutes on medium speed, and then set it aside to rise. (The hydration level was still notably high—the dough was still pourable.) After 20 minutes, I transferred the mixture to a greased loaf pan, smoothed the top with a spatula, and let it rise again briefly before baking it for 40 minutes. After the loaf cooled, I evaluated it for signs of improvement. It had a better top: not quite domed, but at least it wasn't lumpy or sunken. When I sliced it, I found a crumb that was not as damp as those of my earlier versions, but it was still fragile. I had made modest progress but not enough.

I thought back to other test kitchen bread recipes in which we have waited to add the salt until later in the mixing process. Why? Salt inhibits both the ability of flour to absorb water and the activity of the enzymes that break down proteins to begin the process of forming gluten. By delaying the addition of salt, I hoped that my bread would be able to develop a stronger gluten network. I mixed the flours, yeast, honey, water, and butter until everything was evenly combined and let the batter rise for 20 minutes. Then I added the salt (dissolved in 2 tablespoons of water for even distribution) and proceeded with mixing, rising, and so on.

At last I had a complete success. The resulting loaf was crowned with a rounded top, and the crumb was more resilient and no longer wet. I had a flavorful sandwich bread that could be made start to finish in about 90 minutes. But I had to admit that its parched surface was not really showcasing my success. To highlight my crowning achievement, I brushed the risen loaf with a shine-enhancing egg wash before baking. As a finishing touch, I brushed the warm loaf with melted butter after turning it out on the cooling rack, which augmented the sheen and made the thin crust even more tender and delicious.

This bread is so easy and quick that fitting it into my weekly schedule will be no problem. But considering how quickly it disappears, I think I'd better make it twice a week.

—ANDREA GEARY, *Cook's Illustrated*

Easy Sandwich Bread

MAKES 1 LOAF

The test kitchen's preferred loaf pan measures 8½ by 4½ inches; if using a 9 by 5-inch pan, check for doneness 5 minutes early. To prevent the loaf from deflating as it rises, do not let the batter come in contact with the plastic wrap.

- 2 cups (11 ounces) bread flour
- 6 tablespoons (2 ounces) whole-wheat flour
- 2¼ teaspoons instant or rapid-rise yeast
- 1¼ cups plus 2 tablespoons warm water (120 degrees)
- 3 tablespoons unsalted butter, melted
- 1 tablespoon honey
- ¾ teaspoon salt
- 1 large egg, lightly beaten with 1 teaspoon water and pinch salt

1. In bowl of stand mixer, whisk bread flour, whole-wheat flour, and yeast together. Add 1¼ cups warm water, 2 tablespoons melted butter, and honey. Fit stand mixer with paddle and mix on low speed for 1 minute. Increase speed to medium and mix for 2 minutes. Scrape down bowl and paddle with greased rubber spatula. Continue to mix 2 minutes longer. Remove bowl and paddle from mixer. Scrape down bowl and paddle, leaving paddle in batter. Cover with plastic wrap and let batter rise in warm place until doubled in size, about 20 minutes.

2. Adjust oven rack to lower-middle position and heat oven to 375 degrees. Spray 8½ by 4½-inch loaf pan with vegetable oil spray. Dissolve salt in remaining 2 tablespoons warm water. When batter has doubled, attach bowl and paddle to mixer. Add salt-water mixture and mix on low speed until water is mostly incorporated, about 40 seconds. Increase speed to medium and mix until thoroughly combined, about 1 minute, scraping down paddle if necessary. Transfer batter to prepared pan and smooth surface with greased rubber spatula. Cover with plastic and leave in warm place until batter reaches ½ inch below edge of pan, 15 to 20 minutes. Uncover and let rise until center of batter is level with edge of pan, 5 to 10 minutes longer.

3. Gently brush top of risen loaf with egg mixture. Bake until deep golden brown and loaf registers 208 to 210 degrees, 40 to 45 minutes. Using dish towels, carefully invert bread onto wire rack. Reinvert loaf and brush top and sides with remaining 1 tablespoon melted butter. Let cool completely before slicing.

FLORENTINE LACE COOKIES

✓ **WHY THIS RECIPE WORKS:** Wafer-thin almond Florentines have a reputation for being fussy and unpredictable, but these elegant, confectionlike cookies have undeniable appeal. To make our recipe foolproof, we ground the almonds and decreased the flour to allow the cookies to spread more. Instead of getting out a thermometer to make the caramel-like base of the dough, we removed the pan from the heat when the sugar mixture thickened and began to brown. Substituting orange marmalade for the usual candied orange peel and corn syrup produced a more concentrated, complex citrus flavor. A drizzle of faux-tempered chocolate completed the professional pastry shop effect.

You may think you don't know what Florentine cookies are, but chances are that you do. Remember those slim, lacy disks of ground almonds bound with buttery caramel and gilded with bittersweet chocolate that you see in upscale pastry shops? The ones that you probably eat first whenever they appear on a cookie platter? Those are Florentines. Any lack of familiarity with the name probably derives from the fact that most people don't make them at home, so the name doesn't get repeated much.

That's because Florentines have a reputation for being fussier and more unpredictable than the average cookie. They start out like candy: Butter, sugar, cream, and either honey or corn syrup are cooked in a saucepan until the mixture reaches 238 degrees, the temperature at which most of the water has evaporated. Then they veer into cookie territory, as flour, almonds, candied citrus, and sometimes dried fruit are stirred in to form a loose, slippery dough. Spoonfuls of dough are then deposited on baking sheets and baked until each forms a crisp, thin, perfectly browned disk—or, if things don't go well, a mottled, chewy, amoebalike blob. Factor in the uncertainty of whether the chocolate is going to set up firm and shiny or remain sticky and dull, and it's no wonder that most people leave this cookie to the pros.

But here's the thing about Florentines: While producing bakery-quality specimens does require a careful formula, they're actually less work to make than many more conventional cookies because the dough doesn't require beating in a stand mixer—just a brief stir in a saucepan. Plus, these confectionlike cookies are stylish and keep well for several days, making them ideal for holiday baking. As for coming up with a careful formula, that would be my job.

Setting aside the chocolate issue for the moment, I concentrated on the cookie itself. Following a typical method, I melted butter with cream, sugar, and corn syrup (which I chose over honey for its more neutral flavor) in a saucepan and cooked the mixture for 6 to 8 minutes, until it reached 238 degrees. I admit that I wasn't keen on breaking out my thermometer for cookie making, so as the caramel mixture cooked, I kept my eye out for visual indicators that might allow me to leave the device in its drawer. Happily, I noticed that the mixture turned a distinctive creamy beige color and started to catch on the bottom of the pan just as the temperature approached 238 degrees—exactly the kind of cue I had been hoping for. (No need for that thermometer after all.) After I took the mixture off the heat, I stirred in chopped almonds, flour, a bit of vanilla, and a good amount of candied orange peel to give the cookies a citrusy brightness to offset their richness. I scooped 1-tablespoon portions of dough onto baking sheets and baked them for 12 minutes.

This early batch was, in a word, disappointing. The cookies hadn't spread sufficiently, so they were chunky instead of thin and delicate, and their surfaces sported tight fissures instead of the fine, lacy holes that are characteristic of Florentines. Their texture was also tough and a bit chewy. Finally, instead of enhancing flavor, the candied peel didn't taste like much of anything.

It occurred to me that finely grinding, rather than chopping, the almonds might give the cookies a flatter profile, and upping the cream might encourage them to spread more. Those changes did indeed move me toward a thinner Florentine, but I didn't produce the crispness and delicate filigreed appearance of bakery-quality cookies until I had made a few more adjustments. Three extra minutes in the oven allowed the cookies to crisp and turn deeply golden brown from edge to edge, and a touch less flour helped them spread even thinner. Since more spreading also encouraged my neat rounds to bleed into amorphous shapes, I took a minute to pat each mound of dough into a flat circle. Bingo: These thin, round, crispy wafers looked like prime pastry shop offerings. If only there was a way to boost that backbone of orange flavor.

Swapping the candied orange peel for freshly grated orange zest (and adding a bit of salt) helped, but it wasn't enough. Adding more zest wasn't an option—the little bits became too noticeable. But there was one bakery cookie that I'd tasted as part of my research that I knew had exactly the orange profile I was after. It came from the Lakota Bakery in Arlington, Massachusetts, and proprietor Barbara Weniger generously divulged her secret: orange marmalade.

When I added ¼ cup of marmalade to my working recipe (swapping it for the corn syrup, which contributed similar viscosity), the difference was incredible. Thanks to the marmalade's concentrated flavor, my Florentines finally had the bright, citrusy, and faintly bitter taste that I wanted, and the jam provided a contrast to the rich, sweet caramel base. Satisfied with my thin, crispy, orangey cookie, I moved on to the final hurdle: the chocolate.

The classic Florentine has a thin, smooth coat of bittersweet chocolate on its underside, an elegant effect achieved by dipping the entire bottom surface of each cookie into a large container of melted chocolate. This approach presents two problems for the home cook: First, you wind up with loads of leftover chocolate. Second, to ensure that the chocolate retains an attractive sheen, you have to either temper it (a painstaking process of melting and cooling the chocolate to ensure that it stays within the optimal temperature range) or get your hands on special coating chocolate, which contains a small amount of a highly saturated vegetable fat that extends the temperature range at which the chocolate can safely melt. I needed to come up with an easier, more practical alternative.

After some trial and error, I devised a great faux-tempering method that involved melting part of the chocolate at 50 percent power in the microwave and then stirring in the remainder—a very gentle approach that kept the chocolate glossy when it resolidified. To apply the method to the cookies, I tried spreading a small bit of chocolate onto their undersides with a spatula, but that looked messy. The chocolate seeped through those lacy holes that I had worked so hard for, and it was difficult to get the skim coat that I wanted, which meant that the chocolate flavor overwhelmed the delicate cookies. In the end, I took a different but not uncommon approach: piping decorative zigzags over the top of each cookie. (In lieu of a pastry bag, which not all home cooks have, I poured the melted chocolate into a zipper-lock bag and snipped off the corner.)

With Florentines as crisp, flavorful, and elegant as these, I know exactly what I'll be giving for holiday gifts this year.

—ANDREA GEARY, *Cook's Illustrated*

THE BEST FRENCH PRESS COFFEE MAKER

The French press (or *cafetière à piston*, as the French call it) uses a piston-like mechanism to force ground coffee through hot water, sending the spent grounds to the bottom of the pot and leaving a full-bodied brew on top. But there are potential drawbacks: The mass of steeped coffee creates pressure, making it hard to push down the filter, sometimes shattering glass pots. Also, heat escapes glass pots quickly. Some people dislike suspended coffee particles in their brew. And wet, compressed grounds can be hard to dislodge.

Several new models promised to address these issues, so we rounded up six 8-cup pots priced from $26.43 to $119.95. In the end, our top pick was the insulated stainless-steel **Bodum Columbia French Press Coffee Maker, Double Wall** ($79.95). It delivers hot, full-bodied coffee and is dishwasher-safe.

DON'T LOSE YOUR TEMPER

Tempering is a complex process that involves carefully heating and cooling chocolate to prevent its fat crystals from dissolving and reforming into less stable crystals; if this happens (a common occurrence when chocolate gets too warm), the chocolate's surface will turn soft, grainy, and dull—fine for incorporating into cake batter and cookie dough, but not suitable for decorating. For an equally gentle but less fussy way to keep chocolate in temper, we microwave most of the chocolate at 50 percent power until mostly melted, then stir in the remainder of the chocolate until all of it is fully melted.

IT'S A SNAP
Chocolate that's been tempered is glossy and breaks cleanly if snapped.

LOST ITS TEMPER
Chocolate that is melted and cooled without tempering will look dull and bend instead of breaking.

Florentine Lace Cookies

MAKES 24 COOKIES

It's important to cook the cream mixture in the saucepan until it is thick and starting to brown at the edges; undercooking will result in a dough that is too runny to portion. Do not be concerned if some butter separates from the dough while you're portioning the cookies. For the most uniform cookies, use the flattest baking sheets you have. When melting the chocolate, pause the microwave and stir the chocolate often to ensure that it doesn't get much warmer than body temperature.

- 2 cups slivered almonds
- ¾ cup heavy cream
- 4 tablespoons unsalted butter, cut into 4 pieces
- ½ cup (3½ ounces) sugar
- ¼ cup orange marmalade
- 3 tablespoons all-purpose flour
- 1 teaspoon vanilla extract
- ¼ teaspoon grated orange zest
- ¼ teaspoon salt
- 4 ounces bittersweet chocolate, chopped fine

1. Adjust oven racks to upper-middle and lower-middle positions and heat oven to 350 degrees. Line 2 baking sheets with parchment paper. Process almonds in food processor until they resemble coarse sand, about 30 seconds.

2. Bring cream, butter, and sugar to boil in medium saucepan over medium-high heat. Cook, stirring frequently, until mixture begins to thicken, 5 to 6 minutes. Continue to cook, stirring constantly, until mixture begins to brown at edges and is thick enough to leave trail that doesn't immediately fill in when spatula is scraped along pan bottom, 1 to 2 minutes longer (it's OK if some darker speckles appear in mixture). Remove pan from heat and stir in almonds, marmalade, flour, vanilla, orange zest, and salt until combined.

3. Drop 6 level tablespoons dough at least 3½ inches apart on each prepared sheet. When cool enough to handle, use damp fingers to press each portion into 2½-inch circle.

4. Bake until deep brown from edge to edge, 15 to 17 minutes, switching and rotating sheets halfway through baking. Transfer cookies, still on parchment, to wire racks and let cool. Let baking sheets cool for 10 minutes, line with fresh parchment, and repeat portioning and baking remaining dough.

5. Microwave 3 ounces chocolate in bowl at 50 percent power, stirring frequently, until about two-thirds melted, 1 to 2 minutes. Remove bowl from microwave, add remaining 1 ounce chocolate, and stir until melted, returning to microwave for no more than 5 seconds at a time to complete melting if necessary. Transfer chocolate

NOTES FROM THE TEST KITCHEN

HOW CONFECTION AND COOKIE BECOME ONE

1. MAKE CARAMEL, THEN DOUGH: Boil cream, butter, and sugar in saucepan until thick and brown at edges. Off heat, stir in ground almonds, marmalade, flour, vanilla, orange zest, and salt.

2. DROP AND SHAPE: Spoon dough onto parchment paper–lined baking sheets and press into circles.

3. BAKE AND COOL: Bake cookies until uniformly brown; transfer on parchment paper to cooling racks. Let sheets cool for 10 minutes; repeat.

4. "TEMPER" CHOCOLATE: Microwave some chocolate at 50 percent power, stirring frequently, until two-thirds melted. Stir in remaining chocolate.

5. PIPE AND CHILL: Pour chocolate into zipper-lock bag, snip off corner, and pipe onto cookies. Refrigerate for 30 minutes to set chocolate.

to small zipper-lock bag and snip off corner, making hole no larger than 1/16 inch.

6. Transfer cooled cookies directly to wire racks. Pipe zigzag of chocolate over each cookie, distributing chocolate evenly among all cookies. Refrigerate until chocolate is set, about 30 minutes, before serving. (Cookies can be stored at cool room temperature for up to 4 days.)

GLUTEN-FREE CHOCOLATE CHIP COOKIES

✓ **WHY THIS RECIPE WORKS:** Chocolate chip cookies are a classic favorite, but most gluten-free versions turn out crumbly, gritty, and greasy. Using the test kitchen's gluten-free flour blend, we set out to create a gluten-free cookie that would be as good as the original version. Cutting back on butter helped to minimize greasiness. Melting the butter, rather than creaming (as called for in traditional recipes), gave the cookies a chewier texture. Some xanthan gum helped give the cookies structure, allowing them to hold together. To alleviate grittiness, we added more liquid in the form of milk and let the dough rest for 30 minutes so that the starches had time to hydrate and soften. Upping the ratio of brown sugar to granulated sugar made our cookies crisp on the edges and chewy in the center, and also gave the cookies more complex, toffee-like flavor.

When it comes to cookies, chocolate chip ranks high on the list of universal favorites. But even with the abundance of gluten-free baked goods available now, I had yet to come across a gluten-free chocolate chip cookie that came anywhere close to the classic original. The gluten-free versions I had tried were too cakey or had an odd, gritty texture. I wanted to make a gluten-free chocolate chip cookie with the toffee-like flavor, crisp exterior, and tender interior of a cookie made with wheat flour.

I set to work, mixing up a batch of the gluten-free flour blend that the test kitchen had just developed (see more information on page 104). To start my cookie recipe, I simply swapped in the blend for the all-purpose flour in a standard Toll House cookie recipe. Unsurprisingly, these cookies had problems:

They were flat, sandy, greasy, and nothing like what a chocolate chip cookie should be.

First, I decided to address the structural issues. Because starches are liquid when hot and don't set up until cool, and because the bonds between the proteins in gluten-free flour blends are weak and few in number, gluten-free cookies don't have the ability to hold their shape like traditional cookies. To prevent the cookies from spreading all over the baking sheet, I needed to add something to reinforce the weak structure of the gluten-free flour. Just a small amount of xanthan gum did the trick.

Next, I worked on the greasiness problem. I knew from colleagues' testing of other gluten-free recipes that gluten-free flours behave differently than wheat flour. Our gluten-free flour blend contains more starch and less protein than all-purpose flour, and it's the proteins that are compatible with fat. The 12 tablespoons of butter found in traditional chocolate chip cookie recipes weren't being properly absorbed by the gluten-free blend, making the cookies greasy. I made several more batches, decreasing the butter by a tablespoon each time. I found that 8 tablespoons of butter was the most that the cookies could manage. I also realized that creaming the butter and sugar was aerating the butter, which made the cookies too cakey. Melting the butter got me closer to the texture I was after.

But because I had decreased the amount of butter, the dough now had very little liquid to hydrate the flour (butter is about 18 percent water) and my cookies were noticeably gritty. To solve this problem, I added a small amount of liquid in the form of milk. I also knew that a brief rest would give the starches enough time to absorb the liquid. Two tablespoons of milk and a 30-minute rest hydrated the dough just enough to eliminate grittiness. Resting the dough also helped stiffen it, which further improved structure and prevented spread.

Finally, I moved on to texture and flavor. I wanted a cookie that was chewy in the center and slightly crisp on the outside. The Toll House cookie recipe calls for equal amounts of granulated sugar and brown sugar. Granulated sugar contributes to a caramelized, crisp texture and provides structure, while brown sugar adds moisture and rich caramel notes. I decided to increase the brown sugar and decrease the granulated sugar to achieve a perfectly chewy center with crisp edges. Using more brown sugar than white also had the added benefit of enhancing the rich, toffee-like flavor that I expect in a cookie like this.

I baked up a final batch and called in my tasters. When my non-gluten-free colleagues started reaching for seconds, I knew I had done something right.

—MEAGHEN WALSH, *America's Test Kitchen Books*

Gluten-Free Chocolate Chip Cookies

MAKES ABOUT 24 COOKIES

Not all brands of chocolate chips are processed in a gluten-free facility, so read labels carefully. We highly recommend you weigh the ingredients for this recipe, rather than rely on cup measurements. You can substitute 8 ounces (¾ cup plus ⅔ cup) King Arthur Gluten-Free Multi-Purpose Flour or 8 ounces (1½ cups plus 2 tablespoons) Bob's Red Mill GF All-Purpose Baking Flour for the ATK Blend. Note that cookies made with King Arthur will spread more and be more delicate, while cookies made with Bob's Red Mill will spread more and have a distinct bean flavor.

8	ounces (1¾ cups) ATK Gluten-Free Flour Blend (page 105)
1	teaspoon baking soda
¾	teaspoon xanthan gum
½	teaspoon salt
8	tablespoons unsalted butter, melted
5¼	ounces (¾ cup packed) light brown sugar
2⅓	ounces (⅓ cup) granulated sugar
1	large egg
2	tablespoons milk
1	tablespoon vanilla extract
7½	ounces (1¼ cups) semisweet chocolate chips

1. Whisk flour blend, baking soda, xanthan gum, and salt together in medium bowl; set aside. Whisk melted butter, brown sugar, and granulated sugar together in large bowl until well combined and smooth. Whisk in egg, milk, and vanilla and continue to whisk until smooth. Stir in flour mixture with rubber spatula and mix until soft, homogeneous dough forms. Fold in chocolate chips. Cover bowl with plastic wrap and let dough rest for 30 minutes. (Dough will be sticky and soft.)

NOTES FROM THE TEST KITCHEN

STORING COOKIES

Once cooled, most cookies can be stored in an airtight container at room temperature for about 3 days. When storing decorated cookies, like our Florentine Lace Cookies (page 232), slip sheets of waxed or parchment paper between layers of cookies to keep decorations or fillings intact.

Gluten-free cookies have a shorter shelf life than cookies made with all-purpose flour, so they are best eaten the day they are made. Gluten-free flour blends have a higher starch content, and that starch is very good at absorbing moisture. It continues to absorb the moisture in the cookies over time, making them taste drier and crumble more easily.

We have also found that freezing unbaked cookie dough can be a good option for both gluten-free and regular cookies. You can freeze portioned and shaped cookie dough, then bake off cookies straight from the freezer as you want them. To bake frozen cookie dough, arrange the dough balls (do not thaw) on a parchment-lined baking sheet and bake as directed, increasing baking time as necessary.

1. To freeze unbaked cookie dough, portion and shape dough according to recipe. Arrange unbaked dough balls on baking sheet and place in freezer.

2. Freeze dough until completely firm, 2 to 3 hours, then transfer dough balls to zipper-lock freezer bag and freeze for up to 2 weeks.

2. Adjust oven rack to middle position and heat oven to 350 degrees. Line 2 baking sheets with parchment paper. Using 2 soupspoons and working with about 1½ tablespoons of dough at a time, portion dough and space 2 inches apart on prepared sheets. Bake cookies, 1 sheet at a time, until golden brown and edges have begun to set but centers are still soft, 11 to 13 minutes, rotating sheet halfway through baking.

3. Let cookies cool on sheet for 5 minutes, then transfer to wire rack. Serve warm or at room temperature. (Cookies are best eaten on day they are baked, but they can be cooled and placed immediately in airtight container and stored at room temperature for up to 1 day.)

ALMOND CAKE

🗸 **WHY THIS RECIPE WORKS:** Simple, rich almond cake makes a sophisticated dessert, but traditional European versions can be heavy and dense. For a slightly cakier version with plenty of nutty flavor, we swapped out traditional almond paste for toasted blanched sliced almonds and added a bit of almond extract for extra depth. Lemon zest in the batter provided citrusy brightness. For a lighter crumb, we increased the flour slightly and added baking powder. Making the batter in a food processor ensured that the cake had just the right amount of structure. We swapped some butter for oil and lowered the oven temperature to produce an evenly baked, moist cake. For a crunchy finishing touch, we topped the cake with sliced almonds and a sprinkle of lemon zest–infused sugar.

Almond cake is elegantly simple, consisting of a single layer so rich in flavor that it requires no frosting. That nearly every European country has a version of the cake—from Sweden's visiting cake to Italy's *torta di mandorle* to Spain's *tarta de Santiago* (which harks back to the Middle Ages)—is a testament to its appeal.

In addition to its great taste, a reason for the cake's popularity in Europe may be that it's almost impossible to screw up. Putting one together is a straightforward matter. First you cream almond paste or ground almonds with sugar and then butter. Eggs go into the bowl next, followed by a small amount of flour, a bit of salt, and perhaps some almond extract. The batter is poured into a prepared pan and baked, and the dessert is ready to eat as soon as it's cool.

Since recipes for almond cake typically call for little flour and rarely include a leavening agent, the texture of the cake is usually quite dense—the opposite of a fluffy American yellow cake. And when almond paste is used instead of ground almonds, the cake becomes even more solid, bearing a particularly smooth, almost fudgelike consistency. While this is exactly what European cooks intend, I've always found this style a bit too heavy to nibble with tea or to enjoy after a rich dinner. I didn't want an ultrafluffy crumb, but I did want a dessert that was more cake than confection—without sacrificing the trademark rich almond flavor and simplicity of the original.

My first decision was to nix the almond paste. Store-bought almond paste is usually made up of a 1:1 ratio of ground almonds to sugar, along with a binding agent, such as glucose syrup. But its high sugar content is at least partially responsible for the candylike texture that I wanted to eliminate. That said, commercial almond paste does have one thing going for it: great nutty flavor. Could I replace the almond paste without losing that?

Using a basic recipe calling for 1¼ cups of sugar, 10 tablespoons of butter, four eggs, and ½ cup of flour, I tried the most convenient substitute first: store-bought almond flour (which is just very finely ground blanched almonds), which I added to the batter with the other dry ingredients. Unfortunately, almond flour's only benefit was accessibility: The cake that it produced had weak almond flavor, plus the flour was so finely milled that the crumb was still quite dense. Since nuts are commonly toasted to improve their taste, I whipped up one more cake using almond flour that I'd browned in a skillet, but it was tricky to get the small particles to toast evenly, and the browning did nothing to help the textural issue.

Next up: toasted whole almonds ground in a food processor. The flavor of this cake was miles ahead of the almond-flour cake, but the pulverized skins of the nuts tasted somewhat bitter, so I switched to blanched almonds. For depth, I stirred in a drizzle of almond extract. This cake had the concentrated almond flavor of an almond-paste cake, and though it was still rather dense, it was now dotted with tiny nut particles that at least broke up the crumb a little. With the almonds settled, I went on to find other ways to lighten the cake.

I considered the flour first. When butter and sugar are creamed, the airy mixture can help give a cake lift—but only if the batter contains enough gluten to support air pockets. My cake had so little flour (and therefore so little gluten development) that it was unable to hold on to air, hence its short, dense form. I tried substituting higher-protein bread flour for all-purpose flour, hoping that I could stick with ½ cup and still produce a cake with a strong structure. The bread flour created structure all right—so much that the crumb turned tough and chewy. The best option turned out to be a simple one: adding an extra ¼ cup of all-purpose flour (for a total of ¾ cup), which helped my cake rise a bit higher. Another obvious consideration was leavener, so I stirred a bit of baking powder into my next batch. Just ¼ teaspoon helped inflate the air pockets, resulting in a taller rise. But the cake needed even more lift.

I knew that whipped eggs can give a cake—particularly a low-flour cake like this one—great structure since their protein network can trap air, so I gave it a shot. Using a stand mixer, I whipped the four eggs and

BEST ALMOND CAKE

1¼ cups of sugar for 2 minutes. I lit up when the pale yellow mixture nearly tripled in volume. With high hopes, I added the butter (melted so it would be easy to incorporate) and then the remaining dry ingredients, poured the batter into a prepared pan, and slid the pan into a 325-degree oven. Sure enough, this was the tallest cake yet. In fact, it was even loftier than I had intended: Now it was on the high end of the fluffiness spectrum, with the domed top and superlight, aerated crumb typical of an American layer cake. Using fewer eggs wasn't the answer; a two-egg cake was squat and dense.

Feeling as though I was at the end of my rope, I decided to take a break from ingredient testing to consider the equipment. Given that this was a cake known for its simplicity, I wasn't happy calling for two large kitchen appliances—a food processor and a stand mixer. The food processor was a must, as there was no way my stand mixer was going to grind almonds. But what would happen if I tried to whip my ingredients in the food processor instead of in the mixer?

I cracked my eggs into the food processor, added the sugar, and hit the on button. I was excited to see the mixture turn pale and gain some height in the bowl. But when I turned off the machine, the foam partially deflated. Still, I pressed on, adding the melted butter and finally the flour, ground almonds, salt, and baking powder to the food processor bowl. I put the cake in the oven, worried that I'd wasted my time and ingredients. But when I pulled out the finished cake, things were looking up. The unwanted doming hadn't happened, leaving the nicely level top that I was looking for. The crumb was no longer reminiscent of an American layer cake. Instead, it was rich and rustic—neither too fluffy nor too dense. Even better, I had used only one appliance to make the cake.

It turns out that a mixer gently unfolds the protein strands of eggs, creating a strong foam that holds on to air. The sharp blade of a food processor is more damaging to protein strands, so the foam that it creates is less sturdy. Lucky for me, this meant that I got exactly the moderately risen crumb and elegant level top that I was looking for.

Now for a few tweaks. The perimeter of the cake was baking through before the middle was set, resulting in slightly dry edges. Knocking down the oven temperature by 25 degrees and substituting vegetable oil for half of the butter solved the problem. The lower oven temperature allowed the cake to bake more slowly, so it cooked more

evenly, and since oil, unlike butter, contains no water that evaporates during baking, it produced a moister crumb.

But the lower oven temperature created a new problem. Now the cake wasn't browning as well, emerging pale instead of golden brown. Once again, a seemingly small change had a dramatic impact. Just ⅛ teaspoon of baking soda, which encourages browning reactions, brought back the color without noticeably altering the crumb.

Finally, I wanted to create a crunchy, flavorful topping with a hint of citrus to play off of the great almond flavor. In keeping with the nearly effortless adornment of traditional almond cakes (usually just a dusting of confectioners' sugar), I decided on a sprinkling of sliced almonds and lemon-infused granulated sugar. To echo the lemony flavor of my topping, I also added some lemon zest to the cake batter itself. These easy additions produced a delicate crunch and a pop of citrus flavor. And for those who really want to dress up the dessert, I also developed an orange-spiked crème fraîche.

With its rich taste, lighter texture, and lovely flat top, my almond cake had all the great flavor of the European version with a texture more suited to my American palate.

—SARAH MULLINS, *Cook's Illustrated*

Best Almond Cake
SERVES 8 TO 10

If you can't find blanched sliced almonds, grind slivered almonds for the batter and use unblanched sliced almonds for the topping. Serve plain or with Orange Crème Fraîche (recipe follows).

- 1½ cups plus ⅓ cup blanched sliced almonds, toasted
- ¾ cup (3¾ ounces) all-purpose flour
- ¾ teaspoon salt
- ¼ teaspoon baking powder
- ⅛ teaspoon baking soda
- 4 large eggs
- 1¼ cups (8¾ ounces) plus 2 tablespoons sugar

NOTES FROM THE TEST KITCHEN

EGG FOAMS: MIXER VERSUS FOOD PROCESSOR
The goal when mixing most cake batters is to incorporate a lot of air into the eggs so that the cake will bake up light and tall, and a mixer is usually the best tool to get the job done. For our Best Almond Cake, however, we wanted a flat, level top; just a moderate rise; and a texture that was neither too fluffy nor too dense. Ditching the mixer in favor of a food processor did the trick. Here's why: When eggs and sugar are whipped in a mixer, the whisk gently unfolds the protein strands in the eggs while incorporating lots of air, producing a foam with a strong network that holds on to that air. The outcome? A tall, well-risen, domed cake. A food processor, with its high rpm and very sharp blade, similarly unravels the eggs' protein strands and incorporates air, but it also damages some strands along the way. The result is just what we were after: a flatter, slightly denser cake.

MIXER
Tall and domed.

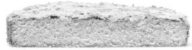

FOOD PROCESSOR
Perfectly flat.

- 1 tablespoon plus ½ teaspoon grated lemon zest (2 lemons)
- ¾ teaspoon almond extract
- 5 tablespoons unsalted butter, melted
- ⅓ cup vegetable oil

1. Adjust oven rack to middle position and heat oven to 300 degrees. Grease 9-inch round cake pan and line with parchment paper. Pulse 1½ cups almonds, flour, salt, baking powder, and baking soda in food processor until almonds are finely ground, 5 to 10 pulses. Transfer almond mixture to bowl.

2. Process eggs, 1¼ cups sugar, 1 tablespoon lemon zest, and almond extract in now-empty processor until very pale yellow, about 2 minutes. With processor running, add melted butter and oil in steady stream, until incorporated. Add almond mixture and pulse to combine, 4 to 5 pulses. Transfer batter to prepared pan.

3. Using your fingers, combine remaining 2 tablespoons sugar and remaining ½ teaspoon lemon zest in small bowl until fragrant, 5 to 10 seconds. Sprinkle top of cake evenly with remaining ⅓ cup almonds followed by sugar-zest mixture.

4. Bake until center of cake is set and bounces back when gently pressed and toothpick inserted in center comes out clean, 55 to 65 minutes, rotating pan after 40 minutes. Let cake cool in pan on wire rack for 15 minutes. Run paring knife around sides of pan. Invert cake onto greased wire rack, discard parchment, and reinvert cake onto second wire rack. Let cake cool, about 2 hours. Cut into wedges and serve. (Cake can be stored in plastic wrap at room temperature for up to 3 days.)

Orange Crème Fraîche
MAKES ABOUT 2 CUPS

- 2 oranges
- 1 cup crème fraîche
- 2 tablespoons sugar
- ⅛ teaspoon salt

Remove 1 teaspoon zest from 1 orange. Cut away peel and pith from oranges. Slice between membranes to release segments and cut segments into ¼-inch pieces. Combine orange pieces and zest, crème fraîche, sugar, and salt in bowl and mix well. Refrigerate for 1 hour before serving.

ORANGE KISS-ME CAKE

✓ **WHY THIS RECIPE WORKS:** This snack cake, created in the 1950s, called for putting a whole orange in a blender—pith, peel, and all—and then mixing it into a simple cake batter. We were intrigued by the concept, but the recipe was fussy, and the cake was too sweet and a bit gummy. Reducing the amount of sugar helped with sweetness, and upping the amount of walnuts ensured that the cake had a tender texture. To streamline the recipe, we eliminated the mixer and used only a food processor. We amped up orange flavor by using a second orange to make a fresh, flavorful glaze to drizzle over our finished cake.

In 1950, one Lily Wuebel took home $25,000 in the Pillsbury Bake-Off for her unusual grand prize–winning Orange Kiss-Me Cake. She stuck an entire orange—peel, pulp, and all—in the blender with raisins and walnuts and then mixed the fruity paste into a simple cake batter. More than 60 years after its triumph, Orange Kiss-Me Cake still struck me as a fresh and unique recipe—a definite must-try.

Following the original recipe, I squeezed ⅓ cup of juice from the orange for drizzling over the baked cake. I ground up the rest of the orange in the blender as prescribed. I put together the basic batter (flour, sugar, baking soda, milk, butter, and eggs) in a mixer, stirred in the orange paste, and scooped the mixture into a baking dish. Some 40 minutes later, I drizzled the hot baked cake with the squeezed juice and sprinkled it with cinnamon sugar and walnuts. Like many snack cakes, this one had a humble appearance, but the intensely orangey aroma had me standing over the cooling cake, shifting from one foot to the other with impatience.

When we tasted it, we were amazed that the orange peel, with all that usually bitter white pith attached, had produced such delicious results. We loved the marmalade-like flavor, while the moist fruit and ground-up nuts made the cake uncommonly tender. I concluded that while the recipe could benefit from some adjustments, on the whole, Lily Wuebel knew what she was about. On my list to tweak: Temper the sweetness, curb a mild gumminess, and bump up the orange flavor of the finishing drizzle/sprinkle. Also, I hoped to streamline the method.

Reducing the amount of sugar in the batter brought both sweetness and gumminess under control. The drop in sugar made the cake slightly less tender, but I simply added extra ground walnuts and restored the texture. So far so good.

Next I took on the sugar-and-chopped-walnut topping. Cutting back on cinnamon and adding orange zest proved a modest improvement, but for real orange flavor, I took drastic action: I added a second orange. I used its juice to double the amount that I was drizzling on the warm cake, which did bolster the flavor but also made the cake soggy. For my next try, I cooked down the juice from both oranges, thus doubling the flavor without adding extra liquid. To intensify the flavor further, I added strips of zest to the simmering juice, and a little sugar transformed it from juice into syrup. Now the cake was moist, tender, and saturated with orange. If I could only simplify the process.

The original recipe called for grinding the fruit and nuts in the blender and then making the batter separately in a mixer. In addition, the topping required finely chopped walnuts—did I have to chop them by hand? To begin, I switched from the blender to the food processor, hoping that it could handle all the cake-making tasks. After a few tries, I figured out that the most efficient method was to coarsely grind the sugar and nuts for both batter and topping in the processor. I removed ⅓ cup and mixed it with the orange zest and cinnamon to make the topping. I then added the orange pulp and peel and the raisins to the processor, followed by softened butter, the eggs and milk, and, finally, the dry ingredients.

Go ahead—kiss the cook. Now Orange Kiss-Me Cake is as easy to put together as it is delicious.

—SARAH GABRIEL, *Cook's Country*

Orange Kiss-Me Cake

SERVES 10 TO 12

To prevent overbrowning, use a glass or ceramic baking dish.

- 2 oranges
- 2 cups (10 ounces) all-purpose flour
- 1¼ teaspoons salt
- 1 teaspoon baking soda

1 cup (7 ounces) plus 2 tablespoons sugar

¾ cup walnuts, toasted

¼ teaspoon ground cinnamon

1 cup golden raisins

8 tablespoons unsalted butter, softened

1 cup milk

2 large eggs

1. Adjust oven rack to middle position and heat oven to 350 degrees. Spray 13 by 9-inch baking dish with vegetable oil spray. Grate ½ teaspoon zest from 1 orange into small bowl. Remove three 2-inch strips zest from same orange with vegetable peeler; set aside.

2. Halve zested orange and squeeze juice into liquid measuring cup. Discard spent halves. Halve and squeeze second orange into same measuring cup, removing any seeds (you should have about ⅔ cup juice total). Set aside spent second orange halves for cake batter.

3. Whisk flour, salt, and baking soda together in bowl. Pulse 1 cup sugar and walnuts in food processor until walnuts are coarsely ground, about 10 pulses. Transfer ⅓ cup walnut mixture to bowl with grated zest, add cinnamon, and stir to combine; set aside.

4. Add raisins and reserved spent orange halves to remaining walnut mixture in food processor and process until paste forms, about 30 seconds. Add butter and process until combined, about 10 seconds. Add milk and eggs and process until combined, about 10 seconds, scraping down sides of bowl as needed. Add flour mixture and pulse until just combined, about 5 pulses.

5. Pour batter into prepared dish and smooth top with rubber spatula. Bake until toothpick inserted in center comes out clean, 30 to 35 minutes, rotating dish halfway through baking.

6. Meanwhile, combine reserved orange zest strips, orange juice, and remaining 2 tablespoons sugar in small saucepan. Bring to strong simmer over medium heat, stirring occasionally, and cook until syrupy and reduced to ¼ cup, 8 to 12 minutes; discard zest strips.

7. Immediately after removing cake from oven, drizzle with orange syrup, spreading evenly with rubber spatula. Let cake sit for 5 minutes to absorb syrup, then sprinkle with walnut-zest mixture. Let cake cool completely in dish on wire rack, about 2 hours. Serve.

LEMON PUDDING CAKES

✔ **WHY THIS RECIPE WORKS:** Despite the appeal of a single batter that produces two texturally distinct layers, lemon pudding cake can be unpredictable, sporting underbaked cake or grainy pudding. We wanted lots of lemon flavor, tender cake, and rich, creamy pudding. Whipping the egg whites to soft peaks and decreasing the amount of flour gave us the best ratio of pudding to cake. Baking powder gave the cake layer some lift, while also producing a golden top. Using a cold water bath in a large roasting pan prevented the pudding from curdling while still allowing the cake to cook through. By infusing the milk and cream with lemon zest, we achieved maximum lemon flavor without a disruption in the smooth texture of the dessert. We finished off the cakes with a sweet, fruity blueberry compote to complement the tart lemon flavor.

Pudding cakes have been around, in one form or another, since the 1700s. Part of the dessert's appeal is its seemingly magical transformation during baking: A single batter goes into the oven but comes out as a twofer—an airy, soufflélike cake resting on top of a silky lemon pudding. Of course, that's assuming it's executed correctly. The reality is that most of the lemon pudding cakes I've sampled have been subpar, often featuring wet, underbaked cake or grainy, curdled pudding, or both. What would it take to fix the problems associated with this dessert?

I got my bearings by preparing a fairly typical recipe, whisking together ¾ cup of sugar, two egg yolks, fresh lemon juice and zest, and ½ cup of flour. Next I stirred in 1 cup of whole milk plus ½ cup of cream for richness and then gradually folded in four egg whites whipped with a bit more sugar. Finally, I poured the batter into six ramekins. (Baking the pudding in a single dish is more typical, but individual ramekins would be more elegant.) This dessert always bakes in a water bath, which helps insulate the pudding layer from the heat of the oven and helps prevent it from curdling. Following the test kitchen's approach, I arranged a folded dish towel in the bottom of a roasting pan as an anchor and then nestled the ramekins into the towel. I poured boiling water into the pan and transferred the assembly to a 350-degree oven. Once baked, the batter separated into distinct tiers of cake and pudding. So what causes the batter to do its trademark split? The answer is surprisingly straightforward: The whipped egg whites

LEMON PUDDING CAKES

are less dense than the other ingredients and thus rise to the top of the dessert during baking, taking some of the flour with them. The egg white proteins coagulate and set to a "solid" cakelike structure, while the denser ingredients settle to the bottom of the baking dish, where they thicken into a pudding.

Simple enough, but I wanted to better understand the role that the egg whites play. I made two desserts, one in which I whipped my egg whites only very slightly and another in which I beat them to firm, dry peaks that stood up on my whisk. As it turned out, this affected the end result quite a bit. Though the pudding layers were unsurprisingly near identical, the cake layers had stark differences. The barely whipped whites produced a dense, rubbery cake that was less than ¼ inch tall. The stiff whites, on the other hand, produced a firm, almost tough layer that rose higher than an inch. I now knew that the height of the cake was directly related to the amount of air in the whites. I wanted a tender cake with moderate lift, so I would whip my whites to the midway point between loose and stiff: soft, glossy peaks.

Next up: the flour. Since pudding cakes contain so little flour, I wondered if adjusting the quantity might shed even more light on the mechanics of this dessert. Sure enough, when I doubled the amount of flour to 1 cup, the pudding disappeared entirely. On the other hand, when I tried ¼ cup of flour instead of the ½ cup I had been using, the amount of pudding increased, producing a 1:4 pudding to cake ratio that my tasters thought was ideal.

There were two big problems remaining. First, the cake lacked structure. Second, the pudding cooked faster than the cake, and even with the water bath, it was still curdling by the time the cake was done.

I decided to tackle the texture of the cake first. Though somewhat unconventional for lemon pudding cake, using baking powder to create and expand gas pockets might give the top layer a little more lift and make it seem more cakelike. When I added various amounts to my batter, tasters agreed that ½ teaspoon of baking powder did the trick. As an added bonus, the baking powder also helped produce a gorgeous golden top.

Now what could I do to prevent the pudding layer from cooking more quickly than the cake and curdling? Reducing the oven temperature from 350 to 325 degrees helped a little bit, but not enough.

What about the water bath? In most recipes that use the technique, the water added to the pan is boiling. I wondered if I could slow things down with a cool bath instead of a hot one. I baked pudding cakes in pans filled with cold water, ice water, and (as a control) boiling water. I poured the water only one-third of the way up the sides of the ramekins, so the water insulated only the pudding portion, giving the slow-baking cake a little extra exposure to the heat. As it had been doing, the pudding in the boiling-water bath continued to curdle. However, the desserts baked in cold and ice water boasted smooth pudding. Since it took longer to bake, the cake layer could now fully cook without risk of overdone pudding. Because cold and ice water produced nearly identical results, I chose to use cold since it baked the desserts a little faster.

The size of the water bath also made a difference. By using probes to record the temperatures of the baths, I learned that the cake layers in a smaller bath baked in 40 minutes (at which point the water was 186 degrees), but the puddings curdled. The cakes in a larger pan required 53 minutes of baking and their puddings were as silky as could be. I checked the final temperature of this water bath: 179 degrees. Going back to my data, I found that the smaller water bath had reached the same temperature a whole half-hour earlier, at 23 minutes. The bigger bath was better, delivering a gentler cooking environment so that the layers finished in tandem.

With the consistency of the dessert right where I wanted it, I was ready to focus on the lemon flavor. After some tinkering, I determined that ½ cup of lemon juice and 3 tablespoons of zest struck just the right balance. The only problem was that the zest ruined the texture of the silky pudding, riddling it with tiny, gritty threads.

Seeking to capture the flavor of the zest but not its abrasive texture, I instead infused it into the warmed milk-cream mixture for 15 minutes and then strained out the solids.

My last move was to embellish the dessert with a colorful, flavorful garnish. Taking a classic, simple approach, I whipped up a quick blueberry compote that meshed well with the dessert's tart notes.

With a few tweaks, I'd turned a rather humble classic into a dessert that consistently delivered a smooth, silky pudding and a light cake every time.

—SARAH MULLINS, *Cook's Illustrated*

Lemon Pudding Cakes

SERVES 6

To take the temperature of the pudding layer, touch the probe tip to the bottom of the ramekin and pull it up ¼ inch. The batter can also be baked in an 8-inch square glass baking dish. We like this dessert served at room temperature, but it can also be served chilled (the texture will be firmer). Spoon Blueberry Compote (recipe follows) over the top of each ramekin or simply dust with confectioners' sugar.

  1 cup whole milk
  ½ cup heavy cream
  3 tablespoons grated lemon zest plus ½ cup juice
     (3 lemons)
  1 cup (7 ounces) sugar
  ¼ cup (1¼ ounces) all-purpose flour
  ½ teaspoon baking powder
  ⅛ teaspoon salt
  2 large eggs, separated, plus 2 large whites
  ½ teaspoon vanilla extract

1. Adjust oven rack to middle position and heat oven to 325 degrees. Bring milk and cream to simmer in medium saucepan over medium-high heat. Remove pan from heat, whisk in lemon zest, cover pan, and let stand for 15 minutes. Meanwhile, fold dish towel in half and place in bottom of large roasting pan. Place six 6-ounce ramekins on top of towel and set aside pan.

2. Strain milk mixture through fine-mesh strainer into bowl, pressing on lemon zest to extract liquid; discard lemon zest. Whisk ¾ cup sugar, flour, baking powder, and salt in second bowl until combined. Add egg yolks, vanilla, lemon juice, and milk mixture and whisk until combined. (Batter will have consistency of milk.)

3. Using stand mixer fitted with whisk, whip egg whites on medium-low speed until foamy, about 1 minute. Increase speed to medium-high and whip whites to soft, billowy mounds, about 1 minute. Gradually add remaining ¼ cup sugar and whip until glossy, soft peaks form, 1 to 2 minutes.

4. Whisk one-quarter of whites into batter to lighten. With rubber spatula, gently fold in remaining whites until no clumps or streaks remain. Ladle batter into ramekins (ramekins should be nearly full). Pour enough cold water into pan to come one-third of way up sides of ramekins. Bake until cake is set and pale golden brown and pudding layer registers 172 to 175 degrees at center, 50 to 55 minutes.

5. Remove pan from oven and let ramekins stand in water bath for 10 minutes. Transfer ramekins to wire rack and let cool completely. Serve.

Blueberry Compote

MAKES ABOUT 1 CUP

To use fresh blueberries, crush one-third of them against the side of the saucepan with a wooden spoon after adding them to the butter and then proceed as directed.

  1   tablespoon unsalted butter
  10 ounces (2 cups) frozen blueberries
  2   tablespoons sugar, plus extra for seasoning
      Pinch salt
  ½   teaspoon lemon juice

Melt butter in small saucepan over medium heat. Add blueberries, 2 tablespoons sugar, and salt; bring to boil. Lower heat and simmer, stirring occasionally, until thickened and about one-quarter of juice remains, 8 to 10 minutes. Remove pan from heat and stir in lemon juice. Season with extra sugar to taste.

NOTES FROM THE TEST KITCHEN

MAXIMIZING CITRUS FLAVOR

To produce bold citrus flavor in our pudding without marring its silky-smooth texture with pieces of lemon zest, we steep the zest in liquid (and then strain it out). Some of the flavor compounds in the zest are fat-soluble, such as d-limonene. Others, like citric acid, are water-soluble. To extract the most flavor, we infuse the zest into a mixture of two liquids that we use in our batter—milk and heavy cream—that together contain goodly amounts of both water and fat.

A COLD BATH

Water baths insulate food from the heat of the oven, helping custards and other delicate desserts cook more slowly. Typically, the bath gets filled with boiling water. Because the bottom pudding layer in this dessert cooks more quickly than the cake layer, we found that cold water works better, allowing the pudding to set slowly and without curdling, giving the cake time to bake through.

FRESH STRAWBERRY MOUSSE

FRESH STRAWBERRY MOUSSE

✓ **WHY THIS RECIPE WORKS:** There's a good reason that strawberry mousse recipes aren't very prevalent: The berries contain lots of juice that can easily ruin the texture of a mousse that should be creamy and rich. Plus, the fruit flavor produced by most strawberry mousse recipes is too subtle. To achieve a creamy yet firm texture without losing the strawberry flavor, we replaced some of the cream with cream cheese. We processed the berries into small pieces and macerated them with sugar and a little salt to draw out their juice. We then reduced the released liquid to a syrup before adding it to the mousse, which standardized the amount of moisture in the dessert and also concentrated the berry flavor. Fully pureeing the juiced berries contributed bright, fresh berry flavor. A dollop of lemon whipped cream made for a tangy finish.

When it comes to mousse desserts, recipes for the chocolate kind—or even citrus versions—abound. But it's not often that you see recipes for mousses that feature strawberries—which, in my opinion, is a sad omission. The berry's bright, sweet flavor is a natural fit in other creamy desserts and would surely make a light and refreshing variation. Plus, mousse is great for warm-weather entertaining: It doesn't require turning on the oven, it looks elegant once it's portioned into bowls and dressed up with a simple garnish, and it's entirely make-ahead.

With a little digging, I managed to find a few recipes for strawberry mousse. Most followed the same simple steps: Puree fresh berries, strain the mixture, add sugar and a stabilizer (most often gelatin), and then fold the puree into whipped cream and allow it to set in the refrigerator. But once I tried these recipes, I realized why this type of mousse isn't more common: Not one of the resulting mousses tasted much like strawberries. The reason wasn't hard to determine. Even in season, the average supermarket strawberry is watery and just doesn't have a lot of flavor. Cooking the berries to drive off some of their moisture and concentrate flavor, as a few recipes suggest, wasn't the answer. While these mousses had more discernible strawberry flavor, they also tasted cooked and jamlike. Meanwhile, those recipes that didn't call for cooking down the fruit also suffered textural problems: The large amount of juice given up by the berries made these desserts loose and runny.

A strawberry mousse that lived up to the name would need to have a lush yet light texture and the sweet flavor of the best fresh summer berries. My strategy would be to get the flavor of the mousse tasting genuinely like fresh strawberries and then figure out how to deal with what would inevitably be an overly wet, soft texture.

Because this was strawberry season, I indulged myself with one quick test, splurging on the best farmers' market berries I could find. This batch did taste brighter and sweeter, but it was a predictably impractical solution. Besides the high price and limited availability of the fruit, the texture of the dessert was a disaster. Thanks to these superjuicy berries, the dessert was more akin to melted ice cream than mousse.

I went back to supermarket berries, figuring I'd ramp up the amount of puree until I had something that tasted sufficiently fruity. I started by softening 1¾ teaspoons of gelatin in a few tablespoons of water. Then I pulsed 2 pounds of strawberries—nearly twice the amount called for in most recipes—to create about 2 cups of puree. I strained out the seeds and added the softened gelatin and ½ cup of sugar. I folded the fruit mixture into 1 cup of heavy cream that I'd whipped to stiff peaks, portioned it into serving bowls, and let the mousse chill for about 4 hours to set up.

Frustratingly, this puree-heavy mousse wanted for still more concentrated fruit flavor. And the texture was worse than I thought—so loose that it practically dribbled off the spoon.

Putting the flavor issue on hold, I reviewed my options for tightening up the texture. My recipe already contained gelatin, which acts as a stabilizer by forming a gel network that traps liquid. Adding more only made the mousse go from soupy to so overly set that it jiggled like Jell-O. I tried other common mousse stabilizers: pectin, whipped egg whites, and even white chocolate.

Pectin was a quick strikeout. It acts like gelatin when exposed to heat, its molecules linking up and forming a water-trapping matrix, and it made the mousse springy. Also a fail were whipped egg whites, as we disliked their eggy flavor and foamy texture. Melted white chocolate made the mousse taste chalky, and its rich flavor overpowered the delicate taste of the strawberries.

What if I replaced some of the whipped cream with another dairy product that contributed thicker body? Sour cream, mascarpone, and cream cheese came to mind, and after another round of tests, I settled on the latter. The soft but dense cream cheese (I swapped in

GETTING THE MOST OUT OF SUPERMARKET STRAWBERRIES

Supermarket strawberries rarely deliver the bright flavor and concentrated sweetness that you find in farmers' market specimens. By macerating the finely chopped berries and then using both fresh and cooked forms of the fruit, we were able to capture the bright, deep strawberry flavor that we wanted.

A LITTLE CONCENTRATED JUICE
By reducing the shed berry juice (about ⅔ cup) to just 3 tablespoons, we were able to deepen its flavor and control the amount of liquid we're adding to the mousse.

A LOT OF FRESH PUREE
Pureeing and straining the macerated chopped berries yields about 1⅔ cups of puree—enough for a punch of bright, fresh berry flavor.

4 ounces for ½ cup of heavy cream) was a big step in the right direction. It firmed up the mousse's texture and didn't mask strawberry flavor.

And yet the mousse was still softer than I liked. It also lacked depth—an important part of great strawberry flavor. Cooking the berries would only destroy that brightness, but there was an approach that could allow me to keep the fresh berry taste while still concentrating its flavor: macerating the berries and then reducing their shed liquid to a fixed amount. This would also allow me to limit the amount of juice going into the mousse without wasting it.

Instead of immediately pureeing the berries for my next batch, I pulsed them just a bit (to produce small pieces with lots of surface area) and then tossed them with sugar and a pinch of salt. After 45 minutes, I strained them, which left me with an impressive ⅔ cup of juice. I then pureed the drained berries and strained the resulting pulp to get rid of the seeds. From there I reduced the juice until it measured about 3 tablespoons—I'd essentially made a berry syrup—and then I whisked in the softened gelatin until it was dissolved, followed by the softened cream cheese and the berry puree. I folded the enriched fruit puree into the whipped cream and chilled it.

This batch was wonderfully rich and creamy and not runny in the least, and the strawberry flavor was the best yet. Thanks to the tandem effect of the berry syrup and the fresh puree, my mousse tasted both bright and concentrated (but not "cooked"). Happily, the results were

just as good when I made the mousse with frozen berries, which turned this into a year-round dessert. (Frozen berries actually have a perk of their own: Freezing causes them to naturally exude quite a bit of moisture, so the macerating step is unnecessary.)

I made just two more adjustments. Instead of softening the gelatin in water, I dissolved it in a little of the drained strawberry juice—a tweak that enhanced the berry flavor a bit more. (I still reduced the remaining liquid to 3 tablespoons.) Replacing berry juice with strawberry (or raspberry) liqueur, a colleague's suggestion, was a great option for when I wanted even more complex berry flavor.

The other adjustment addressed a lingering complaint from my tasters: The mousse had always been a bit streaky—that is, folding the fruit mixture into the cream with a spatula didn't thoroughly marry the two components. Using a whisk to more thoroughly combine the cream with the puree–cream cheese mixture gave the mousse uniform flavor and color.

Finally, to make this dessert more elegant and give it one more boost of fresh berry flavor, I scattered extra diced fresh strawberries over the top. And since frozen strawberries don't make for a pretty garnish, I also came up with a topping that would work whether you're using fresh or frozen fruit: a lemon-zest-and-juice-spiked whipped cream, which underscored the bright, lightly tangy flavor in the berries.

—SARAH MULLINS, *Cook's Illustrated*

Fresh Strawberry Mousse

SERVES 4 TO 6

This recipe works well with supermarket strawberries and farmers' market strawberries. In step 1, be careful not to overprocess the berries. If you like, substitute 1½ pounds (5¼ cups) of thawed frozen strawberries for fresh strawberries. If using frozen strawberries skip step 1 (do not process berries). Proceed with the recipe, adding the ½ cup of sugar and the salt to the whipped cream in step 4. For more complex berry flavor, replace the 3 tablespoons of raw strawberry juice in step 2 with strawberry or raspberry liqueur. In addition to the diced berries, or if you're using frozen strawberries, you can serve the mousse with Lemon Whipped Cream (recipe follows).

- 2 **pounds strawberries, hulled (6½ cups)**
- ½ **cup (3½ ounces) sugar**
- **Pinch salt**
- 1¾ **teaspoons unflavored gelatin**
- 4 **ounces cream cheese, cut into 8 pieces and softened**
- ½ **cup heavy cream, chilled**

1. Cut enough strawberries into ¼-inch dice to measure 1 cup; refrigerate until ready to garnish. Pulse remaining strawberries in food processor in 2 batches until most pieces are ¼ to ½ inch thick (some larger pieces are fine), 6 to 10 pulses. Transfer strawberries to bowl and toss with ¼ cup sugar and salt. (Do not clean processor.) Cover bowl and let strawberries stand for 45 minutes, stirring occasionally.

2. Strain processed strawberries through fine-mesh strainer into bowl (you should have about ⅔ cup juice). Measure out 3 tablespoons juice into small bowl, sprinkle gelatin over juice, and let sit until gelatin softens, about 5 minutes. Place remaining juice in small saucepan and cook over medium-high heat until reduced to 3 tablespoons, about 10 minutes. Remove pan from heat, add softened gelatin mixture, and stir until gelatin has dissolved. Add cream cheese and whisk until smooth. Transfer mixture to large bowl.

3. While juice is reducing, return strawberries to now-empty processor and process until smooth, 15 to 20 seconds. Strain puree through fine-mesh strainer into medium bowl, pressing on solids to remove seeds and pulp (you should have about 1⅔ cups puree). Discard any solids in strainer. Add strawberry puree to juice-gelatin mixture and whisk until incorporated.

4. Using stand mixer fitted with whisk, whip cream on medium-low speed until foamy, about 1 minute. Increase speed to high and whip until soft peaks form, 1 to 3 minutes. Gradually add remaining ¼ cup sugar and whip until stiff peaks form, 1 to 2 minutes. Whisk whipped cream into strawberry mixture until no white streaks remain. Portion into dessert dishes and chill for at least 4 hours or up to 2 days. (If chilled longer than 6 hours, let mousse sit at room temperature for 15 minutes before serving.) Serve, garnishing with reserved diced strawberries.

Lemon Whipped Cream

MAKES ABOUT 1 CUP

If preferred, you can replace the lemon with lime.

- ½ **cup heavy cream**
- 2 **tablespoons sugar**
- 1 **teaspoon finely grated lemon zest plus**
  1 tablespoon juice

Using stand mixer fitted with whisk, whip cream on medium-low speed until foamy, about 1 minute. Add sugar and lemon zest and juice, increase speed to medium-high, and whip until soft peaks form, 1 to 3 minutes.

NOTES FROM THE TEST KITCHEN

CREAM CHEESE FOR CONSISTENCY

In addition to using whipped cream and gelatin, we fortify our Fresh Strawberry Mousse with an unusual ingredient: cream cheese. The rich, soft-but-dense texture of the cultured dairy lends the mousse just enough body and a bit of subtle tang.

BODY BUILDER
Cream cheese gives mousse a thick, creamy
texture without turning it dense.

BLITZ TORTE

✔ WHY THIS RECIPE WORKS: Blitz torte was developed by German immigrants who wanted to recreate elaborate German cakes but expedite the process. Traditionally, this impressive five-layer cake is made by baking the meringue and cake layers together, then stacking them with a fruit and cream filling. But the recipes we tried produced underbaked meringue, overdone, tough cake, and oozy filling. We started by scaling back the test kitchen's yellow cake recipe, and replaced the egg whites in the batter with milk so we could use the whites in the meringue. Almost an hour in a 325-degree oven baked both the cake and the meringue perfectly. For a light, bright filling, we simply mixed lemon curd into whipped cream and stabilized the mixture with a bit of gelatin. A layer of raspberries, macerated with orange liqueur and sugar, offered a fresh final touch.

Blitz torte—a big, gorgeous, many-layered dessert composed of cake, meringue, whipped cream (or custard), and fruit—is thought to be the invention of German immigrants to America: They wanted to duplicate the sort of elaborate cakes that they knew from their homeland, but with less time and effort. They named their creation *blitz*, or "lightning" in German, to imply that it could be made at lightning speed (admitted, some hyperbole here). I can't understand why the torte is so seldom seen today, but if you know where to look, you can find recipes in Junior League cookbooks, community cookbooks, and even a James Beard cookbook.

The beauty of blitz torte is that you get five impressive layers—cake, meringue, fruit-and-cream filling, more cake, and more meringue—plus a sprinkle of nuts for about the same amount of work required by an ordinary two-layer cake. That's because the recipe is so clever: Each meringue layer is baked directly atop the yellow cake batter instead of as a separate component. Also, the recipe is pleasingly symmetrical: The egg yolks go into the cake, while the whites go into the meringue. I chose five blitz torte recipes and headed to the kitchen.

Lined up on the counter, these cakes looked fabulous, and everybody oohed and ahhed. But while their promise was obvious, the execution was problematic. The tortes shared some common faults—timing, for one. Typically, meringues bake in a low oven, about 250 degrees, for almost 2 hours (plus more time to cool in the turned-off oven), whereas yellow layer cakes bake at 350 degrees for 20 to 25 minutes. Getting both

to come out right when baked together was a challenge, and judging by these samples, either the cake overbaked or the meringue underbaked. Next problem: The cakes were neither as tender nor as flavorful as a favorite test kitchen yellow cake recipe, which, as far as I'm concerned, is the gold standard. Also, a few of the yellow cakes domed, which caused the meringue layers to bulge and crimp and ultimately made the cakes harder to stack. Lastly, the fillings oozed out when I cut slices, turning showstoppers into sloppy heaps.

Rather than waste time repairing the yellow cake part of the torte, I'd use the test kitchen's recipe. We employ a technique that's known as reverse creaming: The dry ingredients (cake flour, sugar, baking powder, and salt) are mixed with butter before the wet ingredients (milk and eggs) are added. Coating the flour with fat before the liquid is introduced minimizes gluten development, which makes for an amazingly velvety, tender crumb. Reverse creaming also limits the amount of air that gets incorporated into the batter, producing flatter cakes that are perfect for layering. How? Less air means less expansion of gases in the cake, making it less likely that the center will be pushed up before the cake's structure sets.

Unfortunately, our yellow cake recipe uses whole eggs, which means that I'd need to crack extra eggs for the meringue layers in blitz torte, and I'd be stuck with leftover yolks. After several tests, I figured out a solution: I removed the egg whites from the batter (to use for the meringue) and made up the difference with extra milk. The milk kept the batter loose enough to spread and the cake itself nice and moist. Our recipe for yellow cake produces tall, beautiful layers. That's normally a good thing, but as I got to thinking about the meringue, I realized that I'd need to scale back the cake batter to make room for it. Reducing the cake batter by a third gave me layers of just the right height.

For the meringue, I whipped the egg whites that I'd set aside with cream of tartar (for stability), sugar, and vanilla. Once they were glossy and voluminous, I spread them over the cake batter that I'd already divided between the pans, sprinkled on sliced almonds (whole nuts deflated the delicate meringue, as I learned the hard way), and baked the cakes at 350 degrees for about 20 minutes, as our yellow cake recipe instructs. No good: When the cake was ready, the meringue was still wet in the center. I made the cake again and again, playing with time and temperature before the two components met in the middle—325 degrees and nearly an hour in the oven.

Much as we'd liked the custard fillings during my initial tests, in the end I couldn't justify the extra work for this easy (or at least easier-than-it-looks) torte. I'd use whipped cream. But to mimic custard's rich egginess and to perk up the filling, I got the idea to fold store-bought lemon curd into the whipped cream. This tasted beyond fantastic, but as before, slicing the cake caused a major collapse. To stabilize my curd-cream filling, I added unflavored gelatin. Though it sounds complicated, it took less than 5 minutes to make the creamy, lemony filling and, once it set up, it made neat slices of cake.

Most blitz torte recipes call for adding berries to the whipped cream. I settled on raspberries, which I macerated briefly with sugar and orange liqueur. After draining their juices, I tried simply folding the berries into the cream, but it turned a frightening shade of pink. Instead, I sandwiched the berries between two layers of whipped cream. As I assembled one last blitz torte, my tasters assembled, too (never a shortage of those for this torte). "Blitz torte?" said one taster as she set down her empty plate. "Bliss torte is more like it."

—REBECCAH MARSTERS, *Cook's Country*

NOTES FROM THE TEST KITCHEN

HOW THE LAYERS COME TOGETHER
This multilayered, European-style cake is easier to make than it looks, in part because several of the components are combined.

TWO LAYERS BAKE AS ONE: The meringue gets spread over the raw cake batter, and the two bake together.

A RICH FILLING: We fortify the standard whipped cream filling with lemon curd and gelatin, and we layer it with raspberries.

Blitz Torte
SERVES 8 TO 10

We developed this recipe using light-colored cake pans, which we prefer for baking cakes. If your pans are dark, reduce the baking time in step 6 to 30 to 35 minutes. In step 1, be sure to whip the heavy cream–gelatin mixture to firm, stiff peaks, and let the filling set up in the refrigerator for at least 1½ hours before assembling the cake.

FILLING
- 1 teaspoon unflavored gelatin
- 2 tablespoons water
- 1 cup heavy cream, chilled
- 1 teaspoon vanilla extract
- ½ cup lemon curd
- 10 ounces (2 cups) raspberries
- 2 tablespoons orange liqueur
- 1 tablespoon sugar

CAKE
- ½ cup whole milk
- 4 large egg yolks
- 1½ teaspoons vanilla extract
- 1¼ cups (5 ounces) cake flour
- 1 cup (7 ounces) sugar
- 1½ teaspoons baking powder
- ½ teaspoon salt
- 12 tablespoons unsalted butter, cut into 12 pieces and softened

MERINGUE
- 4 large egg whites
- ¼ teaspoon cream of tartar
- ¾ cup (5¼ ounces) sugar
- ½ teaspoon vanilla extract
- ½ cup sliced almonds

1. FOR THE FILLING: Sprinkle gelatin over water in small bowl and let sit until gelatin softens, about 5 minutes. Microwave until mixture is bubbling around edges and gelatin dissolves, 15 to 30 seconds. Using stand mixer fitted with whisk, whip cream and vanilla on medium-low speed until foamy, about 1 minute. Increase speed to medium-high and whip until soft peaks form, about 2 minutes. Add gelatin mixture and whip until stiff peaks form, about 1 minute.

2. Whisk lemon curd in large metal bowl to loosen. Gently fold whipped cream mixture into lemon curd.

Refrigerate whipped cream filling for at least 1½ hours or up to 3 hours. (Filling may look slightly curdled before assembling cake.)

3. FOR THE CAKE: Meanwhile, adjust oven rack to middle position and heat oven to 325 degrees. Grease 2 light-colored 9-inch round cake pans, line with parchment paper, grease parchment, and flour pans.

4. Beat milk, yolks, and vanilla together with fork in 2-cup liquid measuring cup. Using stand mixer fitted with paddle, mix flour, sugar, baking powder, and salt on low speed until combined, about 5 seconds. Add butter, 1 piece at a time, and mix until only pea-size pieces remain, about 1 minute. Add half of milk mixture, increase speed to medium-high, and beat until light and fluffy, about 1 minute. Reduce speed to medium-low, add remaining milk mixture, and beat until incorporated, about 30 seconds (mixture may look curdled). Give batter final stir by hand. Divide batter evenly between prepared pans and spread into even layer using small offset spatula.

5. FOR THE MERINGUE: Using clean, dry mixer bowl and whisk, whip egg whites and cream of tartar on medium-low speed until foamy, about 1 minute. Increase speed to medium-high and whip whites to soft, billowy mounds, 1 to 3 minutes. Gradually add sugar and whip until glossy, stiff peaks form, 3 to 5 minutes. Add vanilla and whip until incorporated.

6. Divide meringue evenly between cake pans and spread evenly over cake batter to edges of pan. Use back of spoon to create peaks in meringue. Sprinkle meringue with almonds. Bake cakes until meringue is golden and has pulled away from sides of pan, 50 to 55 minutes, switching and rotating pans halfway through baking. Let cakes cool completely in pans on wire rack. (Cakes can be baked up to 24 hours in advance and stored, uncovered, in pans at room temperature.)

7. To finish filling, 10 minutes before assembling cake, combine raspberries, liqueur, and sugar in bowl and let sit, stirring occasionally.

8. Gently remove cakes from pans, discarding parchment. Place 1 cake layer on platter, meringue side up. Spread half of whipped cream filling evenly over top of meringue. Using slotted spoon, spoon raspberries evenly over filling, leaving juice in bowl. Gently spread remaining whipped cream filling over raspberries, covering raspberries completely. Top with second cake layer, meringue side up. Serve cake within 2 hours of assembly.

HUMMINGBIRD CAKE

✓ **WHY THIS RECIPE WORKS:** This classic Southern cake full of banana, pineapple, and pecans needed some revamping—its namesake may be lighter than air, but the original cake was heavy and greasy. Reducing the oil was the first step, and using both baking powder and baking soda helped create tall, attractive layers. Mashing the bananas proved a better approach than simply stirring in chunks, and toasting the pecans gave them deeper, more pronounced flavor. To amp up the wan pineapple flavor, we more than doubled the amount of fruit and boiled down the juices to concentrate flavor and prevent leaden layers. Finally, a tangy cream cheese frosting balanced the sweet cake.

In 1978, a reader of *Southern Living* submitted a recipe to the magazine for a moist, three-layer, mildly spiced pineapple-banana cake slathered with cream cheese frosting and dotted with pecans. She called it "hummingbird cake," and it struck an immediate chord. The cake continued a grand tradition of very sweet, larger-than-life Southern layer cakes, and it went on to win blue ribbons, show up in countless bakery cases, and earn the devotion of home bakers from the Carolinas to Texas.

We tested the *Southern Living* recipe and several other versions—most of them not much different from that one. As we expected, hummingbird cake is very easy to put together and tasted fine. That said, with four entire bananas, an 8-ounce can of pineapple, and 1½ cups of vegetable oil in the batter, the cake was heavy and greasy. Tasters bolted the first few bites, but not many could finish a slice. Plus, despite all that pineapple, the pineapple flavor was faint. The pecans didn't contribute much either. Finally, the big chunks of banana in the original recipe turned mushy in the baked cake and the banana flavor was limited: It was there when you bit into a chunk but nonexistent otherwise. These flaws seemed decidedly fixable, though, so I went into the test kitchen aiming to turn a good cake into a great one.

I began by changing the cake's dimensions, shifting from three 8-inch layers to two 9-inch ones. Two layers meant one less pan to prep (grease, fit with parchment, grease again, and flour) and wash. I knocked a couple of the other easy problems out of the way right at the start as well. To bring out the flavor of the pecans, I toasted them—a small change but a big improvement. And for better distribution, I mashed the (very ripe) bananas, as though I were making banana bread, and stirred the

HUMMINGBIRD CAKE

mash, rather than the chunks, into the batter. Now the banana flavor was present in every bite.

Next I turned to amplifying the pineapple. The original recipe called for one 8-ounce can of crushed pineapple, including the juice. I tried straining out the juice (about ⅓ cup) and concentrating it by boiling it down and then adding the concentrated juice plus the pineapple solids to the cake batter. The pineapple flavor was better, but it took a happy accident to really get it where I wanted it.

One afternoon, all I could find in the test kitchen pantry was a 20-ounce can of pineapple, so I measured my ⅓ cup of juice and weighed my 8 ounces of pineapple solids. The cake I made that day tasted truly, deeply tropical, but where had all that flavor come from? It doesn't take a genius to figure it out: The 8-ounce can of pineapple that I'd been using didn't actually contain 8 ounces of fruit solids. When I measured it out later, I discovered that an 8-ounce can has just 3.6 ounces of pineapple solids; the rest is juice. By using a full 8 ounces of fruit, I'd inadvertently more than doubled the amount in the cake. Could I sneak in extra pineapple juice, too? I boiled down ⅔ cup of juice (the amount from two 8-ounce cans, from which I'd also get my fruit) and stirred it into the batter. The flavor of this cake was the most delicious yet.

But while the extra pineapple bolstered the flavor, it made the cake heavier and denser than ever. Turning to the oil to fix both faults, I cut back 1 tablespoon at a time. Eight test cakes later, I was using one-third less oil than at the start, and the cake was moist yet no longer greasy.

To further lighten my cake, I took a look at the leavener. The original cake called for 1 teaspoon of baking soda. I knew from experience that too much soda produces baked goods with a metallic taste and, counterintuitively, less rise; introducing more wasn't an option. Instead, I'd try adding baking powder. I spent several days testing my cake with varying ratios of the two. Finally, with 1 teaspoon of baking soda and 2 teaspoons of powder, my cake was light, tall, and beautiful.

Turning to the frosting, I borrowed an unusual test kitchen method: In the past we've found that if you beat together softened cream cheese and butter, the frosting is soft and squishy, making the cake difficult to slice unless you chill it for many hours. Instead, I beat together the softened butter and the confectioners' sugar, adding the chilled cream cheese last, bit by bit; this way, the frosting was firmer and didn't squish out between the layers.

Now that we were tasting the frosted cake, we realized that the extra pineapple had pushed an already sweet cake over the edge. After a few frosting tests, I restored balance with a tangier cream cheese frosting— a simple matter of using less confectioners' sugar.

When my colleagues started to hover like hummingbirds whenever I was baking, I knew that my cake was ready to fly.

—DIANE UNGER, *Cook's Country*

Hummingbird Cake

SERVES 12 TO 16

Toast a total of 2 cups of pecans to divide between the cake and the frosting. The cake will slice more cleanly if you refrigerate it for at least 1 hour.

CAKE

     2 (8-ounce) cans crushed pineapple in juice
     3 cups (15 ounces) all-purpose flour
     2 teaspoons baking powder
     1 teaspoon baking soda
     1 teaspoon ground cinnamon
     1 teaspoon salt
     2 cups (14 ounces) granulated sugar
     3 large eggs
     1 cup vegetable oil
     4 very ripe large bananas, peeled and mashed (2 cups)
  1½ cups pecans, toasted and chopped
     2 teaspoons vanilla extract

FROSTING

    20 tablespoons (2½ sticks) unsalted butter, softened
     5 cups (20 ounces) confectioners' sugar
  2½ teaspoons vanilla extract
     ½ teaspoon salt
    20 ounces cream cheese, chilled and cut into
           20 equal pieces
     ½ cup pecans, toasted and chopped

1. FOR THE CAKE: Adjust oven rack to middle position and heat oven to 350 degrees. Grease 2 light-colored 9-inch round cake pans, line with parchment paper, grease parchment, and flour pans. Drain pineapple in fine-mesh strainer set over bowl, pressing to remove juice. Pour juice into small saucepan and cook over medium heat until reduced to ⅓ cup, about 5 minutes; set aside.

2. Whisk flour, baking powder, baking soda, cinnamon, and salt together in bowl. Whisk sugar and eggs together in separate large bowl; whisk in oil. Stir in bananas, pecans, vanilla, drained pineapple, and reduced pineapple juice. Stir in flour mixture until just combined.

3. Divide batter evenly between prepared pans and smooth tops with rubber spatula. Bake until dark golden brown on top and toothpick inserted in center comes out clean, 50 to 55 minutes, rotating pans halfway through baking. Let cakes cool in pans on wire rack for 20 minutes. Remove cakes from pans, discarding parchment, and let cool completely on rack, about 2 hours.

4. FOR THE FROSTING: Using stand mixer fitted with paddle, beat butter, sugar, vanilla, and salt together on low speed until smooth; continue to mix for 2 minutes, scraping down bowl as needed. Increase speed to medium-low, add cream cheese 1 piece at a time, and mix until smooth; continue to mix for 2 minutes.

5. Place 1 cake layer on platter. Spread 2 cups frosting evenly over top, right to edge of cake. Top with second cake layer, press lightly to adhere, then spread 2 cups frosting evenly over top. Spread remaining frosting evenly over sides of cake. To smooth frosting, run edge of offset spatula around cake sides and over top. Sprinkle top of cake with pecans. Refrigerate cake for at least 1 hour before serving. (Cake can be refrigerated for up to 2 days.)

NOTES FROM THE TEST KITCHEN

THE BEST CANNED CRUSHED PINEAPPLE

Our Hummingbird Cake relies on canned crushed pineapple for intense tropical flavor. But are there noticeable differences from product to product? We tested three national products packed in pineapple juice (which we prefer to sugary syrup).

Our verdict: Brand matters. Our favorite product had small, even chunks that tasted "almost like fresh" and gave the cake textural interest. Our least favorite product had a texture like that of "baby food." Experts we spoke with said that variety, processing, harvesting time, and postharvest storage and handling all affect flavor and texture.

In the end, **Dole Crushed Pineapple in 100% Pineapple Juice**, the least expensive product in our lineup, was lightly sweet yet tart, with recognizable pineapple chunks—just right for our baking and cooking needs.

SLOW-COOKER CHOCOLATE CHEESECAKE

✔ **WHY THIS RECIPE WORKS:** Chocolate cheesecake represents the ultimate in decadence, but making it doesn't have to be complicated. To mimic the environment of a water bath without the hassle, we turned to the moist heat of the slow cooker. Raising the pan off the bottom of the slow cooker using a foil rack and putting a bit of water in the bottom of the insert ensured that the moist heat cooked the cake evenly all the way through. We added two forms of chocolate—melted semisweet chocolate and cocoa powder—to our creamy cheesecake for intense chocolate flavor. Swapping traditional graham crackers for chocolate sandwich cookies ensured a flavorful crust.

I love chocolate cheesecake. At its best, it has a thick, satiny, and creamy core, and velvety cake-like edges. The flavor should be tangy, sweet, and rich, with plenty of intense chocolate flavor. But this impressive dessert is notoriously fussy to make at home—it has to cook in a water bath, and if everything doesn't go just right the top cracks, or the cake turns out leaden, pasty, or overly fluffy.

Often, cheesecake bakes in a water bath to ensure gentle, even cooking. The water creates a moist heat environment so that the cheesecake doesn't develop cracks on top. But this method is plagued by leaking pans, an excess of aluminum foil, and having to transport a large pan full of boiling water into and out of the oven. But there is a way to re-create the even heat created by a water bath without having to turn on the oven: a slow cooker. The slow cooker uses moist heat to cook foods gently—perfect for my chocolate cheesecake.

First, I needed to determine how best to "bake" the cheesecake in the slow cooker. I would still need to use a springform pan in order to get the cheesecake out of the slow cooker. Using a basic test kitchen recipe for cheesecake (minus the chocolate—I would figure that out later), I got to work. I knew that the doneness of cheesecake can be determined by temperature—150 degrees is ideal. Cooking the cake on low took too long, and the resulting cake never had the right consistency; the center stayed loose even after chilling. Cooking on high was better, though the cheesecake was still cooking unevenly, since the bottom of the pan was in direct contact with the heat source. I was able to solve this problem by raising the cheesecake off the bottom using a simple foil rack. I also put about ½ inch of water in the bottom of the insert, which supplemented the moisture and ensured that my cake baked uniformly. But even with these fixes, the cheesecake had a tendency to overcook in the constant high heat. I remembered that many cheesecake recipes rely on baking at a high temperature followed by a lower temperature. I realized that rather than turning the slow cooker to low, I could simply turn it off after its initial stint on high heat. The residual heat finished cooking the cheesecake gently, producing a perfectly textured, evenly cooked cake.

Next, I needed to work on the cake itself. I started from the outside in—with the crust. I wanted my crust to emphasize and accentuate the chocolate flavor, and chocolate sandwich cookies proved the perfect solution. Ground to crumbs in the food processor and mixed with melted butter, they provided a sturdy, flavorful crust.

As for the cake itself, I wanted big chocolate flavor. I started by adding melted chocolate to my basic cheesecake recipe, using the food processor to make sure everything was well combined and perfectly smooth. Although this cake looked super-chocolaty, the chocolate flavor was lacking. I found that a couple of tablespoons of unsweetened cocoa powder heightened the chocolate flavor without sacrificing the creamy texture of the cake.

Garnished with some chocolate shavings, my cheesecake looked impressive enough for company, but the recipe was so simple, I didn't need to wait for a special occasion to make it.

—DAN ZUCCARELLO, *America's Test Kitchen Books*

Slow-Cooker Chocolate Cheesecake

SERVES 8

This recipe is designed to work with 5½- to 7-quart slow cookers. Any brand of chocolate sandwich cookies will work well here, but avoid any "double-filled" cookies because the crust won't set properly. Check the temperature of the cheesecake after 1½ hours of cooking and continue to monitor until it registers 150 degrees. To make neat slices, dip the knife blade into hot water and wipe it clean with a dish towel after each cut. Serve with chocolate shavings, if desired.

1   aluminum foil rack (see photo)

4   ounces semisweet chocolate, chopped

8   chocolate sandwich cookies

2   tablespoons unsalted butter, melted and cooled

18   ounces cream cheese, softened

⅔   cup (4⅔ ounces) sugar

¼   teaspoon salt

¼   cup sour cream

2   large eggs, room temperature

2   tablespoons unsweetened cocoa powder

1   teaspoon vanilla extract

1. Fill slow cooker with ½ inch water (about 2 cups) and place foil rack in bottom. Microwave chocolate in bowl at 50 percent power, stirring occasionally, until melted, 1 to 2 minutes; let cool slightly.

2. Pulse cookies in food processor to fine crumbs, about 20 pulses. Combine crumbs and melted butter in bowl until evenly moistened. Transfer crumbs to 6-inch springform pan and, using bottom of dry measuring cup, press crumbs evenly into pan bottom. Wipe out processor bowl.

3. Process cream cheese, sugar, and salt in now-empty food processor until combined, about 15 seconds, scraping down sides of bowl as needed. Add cooled chocolate, sour cream, eggs, cocoa, and vanilla and process until just incorporated, about 15 seconds; do not overmix. Pour filling into prepared pan and smooth top. Set cheesecake on prepared rack, cover, and cook until cake registers 150 degrees, 1½ to 2½ hours on high. Turn off slow cooker and let cheesecake sit for 1 hour (keeping slow cooker covered).

4. Transfer cheesecake to wire rack. Run small knife around edge of cake; gently blot away condensation using paper towels. Let cool in pan to room temperature, about 1 hour. Cover with plastic wrap; refrigerate until well chilled, at least 3 hours or up to 3 days.

5. About 30 minutes before serving, run small knife around edge of cheesecake, then remove sides of pan. Slide thin metal spatula between crust and pan bottom to loosen, then slide cheesecake onto serving dish. Serve.

NOTES FROM THE TEST KITCHEN

MAKING A FOIL RACK

To make an aluminum foil rack, loosely roll a 24 by 12-inch piece of foil into a 1-inch cylinder. Then bend the sides in to form an oval ring that measures 8 inches long by 5 inches wide.

GLUTEN-FREE BIRTHDAY CUPCAKES

✓ **WHY THIS RECIPE WORKS:** Most gluten-free cupcakes are overly sweet, dense, and greasy. We knew we could do better. For perfect, tender cupcakes with a slightly domed top and a light, open crumb, we used the easiest mixing method (combining everything in a bowl), which made the cupcakes more compact and less crumbly than using an electric mixer. Adding xanthan gum and reducing the amount of baking powder also helped with structure. We swapped traditional butter for oil, and used sour cream and melted white chocolate to provide moisture and richness. A dollop of creamy frosting completed our cupcakes.

A good yellow cupcake should be melt-in-your-mouth tender, with buttery vanilla flavor. But many of the gluten-free cupcake recipes I've tried produce overly sweet, dense, gummy, and even greasy cupcakes. Could I devise a recipe that would not only solve these problems, but also produce cupcakes that would be as good as any made with wheat flour?

I started with the test kitchen's recently developed gluten-free flour blend (see more information on page 104). I knew that the high starch content in the flour blend meant that it wouldn't absorb fat (in the case of traditional cupcakes, butter) in the same way that all-purpose flour would. So I cut way down on the amount of butter, using only 6 tablespoons instead of two sticks. But now the cupcakes were dry and lean-tasting. I needed another source of moisture and richness to replace the butter. Buttermilk is often used in traditional yellow cakes for moisture and flavor, but when I used enough buttermilk to properly hydrate the starches in the flour blend, it made the batter too loose and ended up making the cupcakes denser. Instead, I used sour cream, which gave me a thicker batter that baked up with a much more tender crumb.

My cupcakes were better, but still a bit too dry. I wondered if I could borrow a technique often used in chocolate cakes: adding melted chocolate. But rather than using bittersweet chocolate, I turned to white chocolate. This worked like a charm, boosting richness without making the cupcakes greasy. Plus, the sweetness of the white chocolate was balanced by the tang of the sour cream.

Although the flavor was coming along, the cupcakes were coming out of the oven with extremely domed tops that made them difficult to frost. Up to this point,

I had been whipping the egg whites for extra lift (a technique employed in other gluten-free recipes), and using both baking powder and baking soda. I needed the baking soda to aid with browning and tenderness, but could I reduce the amount of baking powder? Cutting back on the baking powder did help a bit, but it turned out that adjusting my mixing method helped even more: By not separating the eggs and whisking, rather than beating, the ingredients together, I introduced less air and therefore, less rise. A bit of xanthan gum helped the now perfectly shaped cupcakes hold together (without making them dense).

But the mixing method had created a new problem: Without the power of the mixer, the butter wasn't being emulsified into the batter. Swapping it out for an equal amount of vegetable oil made the batter more cohesive.

My cupcakes were nearly perfect: The crumb was tender and fluffy, and I had curbed the intense sweetness and greasiness. Finally, I devised two recipes for creamy frostings that made the perfect accompaniment to my gluten-free cupcakes. Frosted and finished, these were cupcakes I could bring to any birthday party—whether there were gluten-free guests or not.

—DANIELLE DESIATO-HALLMAN,
America's Test Kitchen Books

Gluten-Free Birthday Cupcakes
MAKES 12 CUPCAKES

We highly recommend you weigh the ingredients for this recipe, rather than rely on cup measurements. You can substitute 6½ ounces (⅔ cup plus ½ cup) King Arthur Gluten-Free Multi-Purpose Flour or 6½ ounces (1⅓ cups) Bob's Red Mill GF All-Purpose Baking Flour for the ATK Blend. Note that cupcakes made with King Arthur will not rise as well and will taste slightly pasty, and cupcakes made with Bob's Red Mill will have a coarser crumb and a distinct bean flavor. Once frosted, serve the cupcakes within a few hours.

- 4 **ounces white chocolate, chopped**
- 6 **tablespoons vegetable oil**
- 6½ **ounces (¾ cup plus ⅔ cup) ATK Gluten-Free Flour Blend (page 105)**
- 1 **teaspoon baking powder**
- ⅛ **teaspoon baking soda**
- ½ **teaspoon xanthan gum**
- ½ **teaspoon salt**

GLUTEN-FREE BIRTHDAY CUPCAKES

2   large eggs

2   teaspoons vanilla extract

3½ ounces (½ cup) sugar

⅓   cup sour cream

1   recipe frosting (recipes follow)

1. Adjust oven rack to middle position and heat oven to 325 degrees. Line 12-cup muffin tin with paper or foil liners.

2. Microwave white chocolate and oil together in bowl at 50 percent power, stirring occasionally, until melted, about 2 minutes. Whisk mixture until smooth, then set aside to cool slightly. In separate bowl, whisk flour blend, baking powder, baking soda, xanthan gum, and salt together.

3. In large bowl, whisk eggs and vanilla together. Whisk in sugar until well combined. Whisk in cooled chocolate mixture and sour cream until combined. Whisk in flour blend mixture until batter is thoroughly combined and smooth.

4. Using ice cream scoop or large spoon, portion batter evenly into prepared muffin tin. Bake until cupcakes are set on top and spring back when pressed lightly, 20 to 22 minutes, rotating muffin tin halfway through baking. Let cupcakes cool in muffin tin on wire rack for 10 minutes. Remove cupcakes from tin and let cool completely, about 1 hour. (Unfrosted cupcakes can be stored in airtight container at room temperature for up to 24 hours.)

5. Spread or pipe frosting over top of cupcakes and serve.

NOTES FROM THE TEST KITCHEN

PIPING FROSTING ONTO CUPCAKES
Frosting cupcakes with a small icing spatula or butter knife is certainly easy, but for an extra-special presentation consider using a pastry bag fitted with a large star tip.

Swirl frosting into tall pile on top of cupcake, starting at outer edge of cupcake and working toward center.

Easy Vanilla Frosting
MAKES 2 CUPS

Even if you omit the added salt, salted butter will ruin this recipe. The heavy cream is a simple refinement that gives this fast frosting a silky quality—don't omit it.

12 tablespoons unsalted butter, cut into 12 pieces and softened

1½ tablespoons heavy cream

1¼ teaspoons vanilla extract

⅛   teaspoon salt

1½ cups (6 ounces) confectioners' sugar

1. Using stand mixer fitted with whisk, whip butter, cream, vanilla, and salt together on medium-high speed until smooth, 1 to 2 minutes. Reduce mixer speed to medium-low, slowly add sugar, and whip until incorporated and smooth, 1 to 2 minutes.

2. Increase speed to medium-high and whip frosting until light and fluffy, 3 to 5 minutes.

Creamy Chocolate Frosting
MAKES 2 CUPS

Cool the chocolate to between 85 and 100 degrees before adding it as the final step in this recipe.

⅓   cup (2⅓ ounces) sugar

2   large egg whites

    Pinch salt

12 tablespoons unsalted butter, cut into 12 pieces and softened

6   ounces bittersweet chocolate, melted and cooled

½   teaspoon vanilla extract

1. Combine sugar, egg whites, and salt in bowl of stand mixer; place bowl over pan of simmering water. Whisking gently but constantly, heat mixture until slightly thickened and foamy and it registers 150 degrees, 2 to 3 minutes.

2. Place bowl in stand mixer fitted with whisk. Whip mixture on medium speed until it has consistency of shaving cream and has cooled slightly, about 5 minutes. Add butter, 1 piece at a time, until smooth and creamy. (Frosting may look curdled after half of butter has been added; it will smooth out with additional butter.)

3. Once all butter is added, add cooled melted chocolate and vanilla and mix until combined. Increase speed to medium-high and beat until light and fluffy, about 30 seconds, scraping beater and sides of bowl with rubber spatula as necessary. If frosting seems too soft after adding chocolate, chill it briefly in refrigerator, then rewhip until creamy.

FRESH PEACH PIE

✓ **WHY THIS RECIPE WORKS:** Juicy summer peaches often produce soupy peach pies, and the amount of moisture changes from pie to pie. To control the moisture level, we macerated the peaches to draw out some of their juices and then added a measured amount back to the filling. A combination of cornstarch and pectin helped hold the filling together without making it gluey or bouncy, and mashing some of the peaches helped make neat, attractive slices. A buttery, tender lattice-top crust allowed moisture to evaporate in the oven and made for an impressive presentation.

While the almost-impossible juiciness of a ripe peach is the source of the fruit's magnificence, it's also the reason that fresh peaches can be tricky to use in pies. The hallmark of any fresh fruit pie is fresh fruit flavor, but ripe peaches exude so much juice that they require an excess of flavor-dampening binders to create a filling that isn't soup. Fresh peaches can also differ dramatically in water content, so figuring out how much thickener to add can be a guessing game from one pie to the next. Finally, ripe peaches are delicate, easily disintegrating into mush when baked. In my book, a perfect slice of peach pie is a clean slice of pie, with fruit that's tender yet intact.

In the past, we've had some success in perfecting a filling by using potato starch, but this ingredient isn't always readily available. Furthermore, it still leaves the filling a little looser than I'd like. I wanted to make a peach pie with a filling that holds the slices in place without being the least bit gluey, grainy, or cloudy or preventing any of the fresh peach flavor from shining through.

But before I could nail down the filling, I'd need a reliable crust. Experimenting with a few recipes taught me one thing: The fillings in pies with lattice-top crusts had far better consistency than those in pies with solid tops, since the crosshatch allows moisture to evaporate during cooking. Moreover, lattices served as windows into the pies' interiors, making it easy to

know when the filling was bubbly at the center, a sure sign that it was fully cooked.

When making a lattice, it's actually helpful to have a dough with a little more structure than the usual flaky pastry. Luckily, we have such a dough in our archives. It calls for a few more tablespoons of water than usual and a little less fat, both of which help create a sturdy dough that can withstand the extra handling involved in making a lattice. Just as important, this dough still manages to bake up tender and taste rich and buttery.

With the choice of crust settled, I moved on to thinking about the mechanics of building the lattice itself. It takes practice (not to mention patience) to create neat, professional-looking lattice-top pies. I wanted a lattice that a novice baker could do perfectly. The best approach I found came from the test kitchen's Linzertorte, which skips the weaving in favor of simply laying one strip over the previous one in a pattern that allows some of the strips to appear woven. Even with less handling, I still found it helpful to freeze the strips for 30 minutes before creating the lattice. Done.

Now it was time to get down to the fruit. Most recipes I'd tested called for tossing thinly sliced peaches with sugar and spices before throwing them into the pie crust and then putting the pie into the oven. But I'd noted that the peaches handled this way shed a lot of moisture before they even reached the oven, thanks to the sugar's osmotic action on the slices. Sugar is hygroscopic—meaning it easily attracts water to itself—making it superbly capable of pulling juice out of the peaches' cells. If I was going to gain control over the consistency of the filling, that's where I'd need to start. Since osmosis occurs on the surface, one obvious tweak would be to make the peach slices relatively large to minimize total surface area. So instead of slicing the peaches thin, I cut them into quarters and then cut each of these into thick—but still bite-size—1-inch chunks.

Another quick fix was to let the sugared peaches macerate for a bit and then drain off the juice before tossing the fruit into the pie, adding back only enough juice to moisten—not flood—the filling. This would allow me to control how much liquid the peaches contributed from batch to batch. I tossed 3 pounds of peaches with ½ cup of sugar, 1 tablespoon of lemon juice, and a pinch of salt. When I drained the peaches 30 minutes later, they yielded more than ½ cup of juice. I settled on using exactly ½ cup—the right amount to moisten the filling. To this I added just enough cinnamon and

FRESH PEACH PIE

nutmeg to accent the flavor of the peaches without overshadowing it.

Now it was time to experiment with thickeners that would tighten up the fruit and juice while maintaining the illusion that nothing was in the pie but fresh peaches. Flour left the filling grainy and cloudy, while tapioca pearls never completely dispersed, leaving visible beads of gel behind. (Grinding the rock-hard tapioca pearls into finer grains helped but was a pain.) Potato starch and cornstarch each worked admirably up to a point, but after that they did not eliminate further runniness so much as turn the filling murky and gluey. More important, all these starches dulled the flavor of the peaches.

Maybe adding starch was not the best approach. I thought about apple pie, which barely needs any thickener to create a filling that slices cleanly. Apples are less juicy than peaches, but they also contain lots of pectin, which helps them hold on to their moisture and remain intact during baking. Peaches, on the other hand, contain much less pectin. For my next test I stirred some pectin (I used the low-sugar kind since I wanted to keep sweeteners to a minimum) into my reserved peach juice, heated the mixture briefly on the stove, and then folded it into the peach chunks. This filling turned out smooth and clear and tasted brightly of peaches. But it was still runnier than I wanted. Adding more pectin wasn't the solution; a hair too much and the filling turned bouncy. Then I thought back to our recipe for Fresh Strawberry Pie, which used a combination of pectin and cornstarch. When we had added cornstarch alone, it left the pie gluey but still fluid. But could I find the sweet spot using both thickeners? Yes: Two tablespoons of pectin and 1 tablespoon of cornstarch left me with a filling that was smooth, clear, and moist from edge to center without being soupy.

One problem remained: a tendency for the peach chunks to fall out of the pie slices—because of the chunks' irregular shapes, they never fit together perfectly. I tried mashing a small amount of the macerated peaches to a coarse pulp with a fork and used it as a form of mortar to eliminate gaps and stabilize the filling. Happily, it worked.

At last, I had a fresh peach pie that looked perfect, tasted of fresh peaches, and sliced neatly.

—ANDREW JANJIGIAN, *Cook's Illustrated*

Fresh Peach Pie

SERVES 8

If your peaches are too soft to withstand the pressure of a peeler, cut a shallow X in the bottom of the fruit, blanch them in a pot of simmering water for 15 seconds, and then shock them in a bowl of ice water before peeling. For fruit pectin we recommend both Sure-Jell for Less or No Sugar Needed Recipes and Ball RealFruit Low or No-Sugar Needed Pectin.

3	pounds peaches, peeled, quartered, and pitted, each quarter cut into thirds
½	cup (3½ ounces) plus 3 tablespoons sugar
1	teaspoon grated lemon zest plus 1 tablespoon juice
⅛	teaspoon salt
2	tablespoons low- or no-sugar-needed fruit pectin
¼	teaspoon ground cinnamon
	Pinch ground nutmeg
1	recipe Pie Dough for Lattice-Top Pie (recipe follows)
1	tablespoon cornstarch

1. Toss peaches, ½ cup sugar, lemon zest and juice, and salt in medium bowl. Let stand at room temperature for at least 30 minutes or up to 1 hour. Combine pectin, cinnamon, nutmeg, and 2 tablespoons sugar in small bowl and set aside.

2. Remove dough from refrigerator. Let chilled dough sit on counter to soften slightly, about 10 minutes. Roll 1 disk of dough into 12-inch circle on lightly floured counter. Transfer to parchment paper–lined baking sheet. With pizza wheel, fluted pastry wheel, or paring knife, cut round into ten 1¼-inch-wide strips. Freeze strips on sheet until firm, about 30 minutes.

3. Adjust oven rack to lowest position, place rimmed baking sheet on rack, and heat oven to 425 degrees. Roll other disk of dough into 12-inch circle on lightly floured counter. Loosely roll dough around rolling pin and gently unroll it onto 9-inch pie plate, letting excess dough hang over edge. Ease dough into plate by gently lifting edge of dough with your hand while pressing into plate bottom with your other hand. Leave any dough that overhangs plate in place. Wrap dough-lined pie plate loosely in plastic wrap and refrigerate until dough is firm, about 30 minutes.

4. Meanwhile, transfer 1 cup peach mixture to small bowl and mash with fork until coarse paste forms. Drain remaining peach mixture through colander set in large bowl. Transfer peach juice to liquid measuring cup (you should have about ½ cup liquid; if liquid measures more than ½ cup, discard remainder). Return peach pieces to bowl and toss with cornstarch. Transfer peach juice to 12-inch skillet, add pectin mixture, and whisk until combined. Cook over medium heat, stirring occasionally, until slightly thickened and pectin is dissolved (liquid should become less cloudy), 3 to 5 minutes. Remove skillet from heat, add peach pieces and peach paste, and toss to combine.

5. Transfer peach mixture to dough-lined pie plate. Remove dough strips from freezer; if too stiff to be workable, let stand at room temperature until malleable and softened slightly but still very cold. Lay 2 longest strips across center of pie perpendicular to each other. Using 4 shortest strips, lay 2 strips across pie parallel to 1 center strip and 2 strips parallel to other center strip, near edges of pie; you should have 6 strips in place. Using remaining 4 strips, lay each one across pie parallel and equidistant from center and edge strips. If dough becomes too soft to work with, refrigerate pie and dough strips until dough firms up.

6. Trim overhang to ½ inch beyond lip of pie plate. Press edges of bottom crust and lattice strips together and fold under. Folded edge should be flush with edge of pie plate. Crimp dough evenly around edge of pie using your fingers. Using spray bottle, evenly mist lattice with water and sprinkle with remaining 1 tablespoon sugar.

7. Place pie on preheated sheet and bake until crust is set and begins to brown, about 25 minutes. Rotate pie and reduce oven temperature to 375 degrees; continue to bake until crust is deep golden brown and filling is bubbly at center, 25 to 30 minutes longer. Let cool on wire rack for 3 hours before serving.

Pie Dough For Lattice-Top Pie
FOR ONE 9-INCH LATTICE-TOP PIE

3	cups (15 ounces) all-purpose flour
2	tablespoons sugar
1	teaspoon salt
7	tablespoons vegetable shortening, cut into ½-inch pieces and chilled
10	tablespoons unsalted butter, cut into ¼-inch pieces and frozen for 30 minutes
10–12	tablespoons ice water

1. Process flour, sugar, and salt in food processor until combined, about 5 seconds. Scatter shortening over top and process until mixture resembles coarse cornmeal, about 10 seconds. Scatter butter over top and pulse until mixture resembles coarse crumbs, about 10 pulses. Transfer to bowl.

2. Sprinkle 5 tablespoons ice water over flour mixture. With rubber spatula, use folding motion to evenly combine water and flour mixture. Sprinkle 5 tablespoons ice water over mixture and continue using folding motion to combine until small portion of dough holds together when squeezed in palm of your hand, adding up to 2 tablespoons remaining ice water if necessary. (Dough should feel quite moist.) Turn out dough onto clean, dry counter and gently press together into cohesive ball. Divide dough in half and form each half into 4-inch disk. Wrap disks tightly in plastic wrap and refrigerate for 1 hour. (Wrapped dough can be refrigerated for up to 2 days or frozen for up to 1 month. If frozen, let dough thaw completely on counter before rolling.)

NOTES FROM THE TEST KITCHEN

BUILDING A "NO-WEAVE" LATTICE TOP

1. Roll dough into 12-inch circle, transfer to parchment paper–lined baking sheet, and cut into ten 1¼-inch-wide strips with a fluted pastry wheel, pizza wheel, or paring knife. Freeze for 30 minutes.

2. Lay 2 longest strips perpendicular to each other across center of pie to form cross. Place 4 shorter strips along edges of pie, parallel to center strips.

3. Lay 4 remaining strips between each edge strip and center strip. Trim off excess lattice ends, press edges of bottom crust and lattice strips together, and fold under.

APPLE PIE WITH CHEDDAR CHEESE CRUST

✓ **WHY THIS RECIPE WORKS:** A wedge of cheddar is the perfect savory foil to a slice of warm, sweet apple pie, so we decided to bake the cheddar right into the crust. For ample cheese flavor, we found that we had to cut back a bit on butter or the crust would crumble. We were able to load 2 cups of cheese into the crust—extra-sharp packed the most punch—and two unlikely ingredients boosted the cheese flavor even more: dry mustard and cayenne. As for the apples, cooking them down before filling the pie prevented a gap under the top crust, and a combination of Granny Smith and Golden Delicious provided the right texture and sweet-tart balance.

Across New England, you very often find a slice of cheddar cheese included with a wedge of warm apple pie on restaurant and diner menus. It's a powerful sweet-savory combination. And if a nibble of cheese eaten with a forkful of pie could be so satisfying, wouldn't it be even better if the cheese were baked right into the crust? I decided to find out.

I tracked down recipes and baked a few pies. Expecting assertive cheese flavor, I was disappointed that most of these pies came up short. Crusts that had decent cheese flavor were tough or greasy; the bottom crusts looked as though they had fried, rather than baked, in all the extra fat. And the pies with better texture tasted only faintly of cheese. The apple fillings were fairly standard, so for now I would use a simple recipe from the test kitchen's archive while I figured out the crust.

I took the best crust of the previous lot and gave it a closer look: The recipe called for 6 ounces (1½ cups) of cheddar, 12 tablespoons of butter, and 2½ cups of flour, and it relied on a food processor for ease. The crust was reasonably flaky, but the cheese flavor was underwhelming. Replacing the regular cheddar with extra-sharp helped, but not enough, so I decided to investigate how much cheese I could add before compromising the crust's structure and texture. I tested my working recipe with eight, 10, and 12 ounces (a full 3 cups) of extra-sharp cheddar. The more I added, the stronger the cheese flavor; alas, the pastry crust couldn't handle the onslaught. Though cheesy, the crust was now tough, crumbly, nearly impossible to roll, and once baked, it was greasy.

A good pie crust is all about balance: fat to flour to liquid. Since I was adding fat to the crust in the form of cheese, did I need to cut back on the butter? I couldn't ever make 3 cups of cheese work, so I retested the crust with 2 cups and 2½ cups, at the same time reducing the butter from 12 tablespoons to as few as four. I found the right balance at 2 cups of cheese plus 8 tablespoons of butter. Not quite as flaky as a traditional pastry crust, this cheddar crust was tender but denser, with a mottled brown top from flecks of cheese and a noticeable cheddar flavor. For an even bigger impact, I borrowed an idea from—of all things—a test kitchen recipe for mac and cheese, adding a teaspoon of dry mustard. Odd for a pie, perhaps, but the spice added a complex, savory quality that really underlined the crust's cheese flavor. Similarly, we've found that a touch of cayenne—even in sweets—can cut through richness and make flavors stand at attention. Just a smidgen did the job here without adding detectable heat.

Next, I moved on to the filling, using a past test kitchen recipe as a jumping-off point. One problem with double-crust pies is the gap that forms between the top crust and the fruit. It develops as the apples break down while baking—at the same time that steam pushes the crust up. We solve this by precooking the apples. I cooked 4 pounds of sliced apples—both tart and sweet—with sugar, salt, cinnamon, and lemon zest until the apples were just tender, adding lemon juice at the end.

It's a mistake to pour hot filling into a chilled crust, as the butter in the crust must be cold to promote flakiness. I'd need to let the apples cool first. For even, efficient cooling, I spread the apple mixture on a baking sheet and let it sit. After about 30 minutes, I assembled the pie.

I put the pie on a baking sheet, placed it on the bottom rack of a 425-degree oven, and set the timer for about 45 minutes (our usual protocol). When I checked the pie after about 25 minutes, the crust was beginning to burn around the edges, since the milk solids in cheese contain natural sugars that caramelize (or burn) at high temperatures. Reducing the heat to 375 degrees kept the edges from burning, but the bottom crust didn't brown. So I split the difference, baking the pie at 425 degrees for 20 minutes to set the bottom crust and then lowering the heat to 375 degrees for the last 35 to 45 minutes.

This time the bottom crust was nicely browned and properly cooked, the top crust flush against the fruit, and both were properly flaky. The filling was moist, with a sweet-tart flavor that complemented the cheese crust. My recipe was in apple pie order.

—CHRISTIE MORRISON, *Cook's Country*

Apple Pie with Cheddar Cheese Crust

SERVES 8

For the best flavor, be sure to use extra-sharp cheddar here. Freezing the butter for 15 minutes promotes flakiness in the crust—do not skip this step.

CRUST

2½ cups (12½ ounces) all-purpose flour
1 tablespoon granulated sugar
1 teaspoon salt
1 teaspoon dry mustard
⅛ teaspoon cayenne pepper
8 ounces extra-sharp cheddar cheese, shredded (2 cups)
8 tablespoons unsalted butter, cut into ¼-inch pieces and frozen for 15 minutes
⅓ cup ice water, plus extra as needed

FILLING

2 pounds Granny Smith, Empire, or Cortland apples, peeled, cored, halved, and sliced ¼ inch thick
2 pounds Golden Delicious, Jonagold, or Braeburn apples, peeled, cored, halved, and sliced ¼ inch thick
6 tablespoons (2⅔ ounces) granulated sugar
¼ cup packed (1¾ ounces) light brown sugar
½ teaspoon grated lemon zest plus 1 tablespoon juice
¼ teaspoon salt
⅛ teaspoon ground cinnamon

1. FOR THE CRUST: Process flour, sugar, salt, mustard, and cayenne in food processor until combined, about 5 seconds. Scatter cheddar and butter over top and pulse until butter is size of large peas, about 10 pulses.

2. Pour half of ice water over flour mixture and pulse until incorporated, about 3 pulses. Repeat with remaining ice water. Pinch dough with your fingers; if dough feels dry and does not hold together, sprinkle 1 to 2 tablespoons extra ice water over mixture and pulse until dough forms large clumps and no dry flour remains, 3 to 5 pulses.

3. Divide dough in half and form each half into 4-inch disk. Wrap disks tightly in plastic wrap and refrigerate for 1 hour. Let chilled dough sit on counter to soften slightly, about 10 minutes, before rolling. (Wrapped dough can be refrigerated for up to 2 days or frozen for up to 1 month. If frozen, let dough thaw completely on counter before rolling.)

4. FOR THE FILLING: Stir apples, granulated sugar, brown sugar, lemon zest, salt, and cinnamon together in Dutch oven. Cover and cook over medium heat, stirring frequently, until apples are just tender but still hold their shape, 10 to 15 minutes. Off heat, stir in lemon juice. Spread apple mixture on rimmed baking sheet and let cool completely, about 30 minutes. (Filling can be refrigerated for up to 24 hours.)

5. Roll 1 disk of dough into 12-inch circle between 2 sheets of parchment paper or plastic. Loosely roll dough around rolling pin and gently unroll it onto 9-inch pie plate, letting excess dough hang over edge. Ease dough into plate by gently lifting edge of dough with your hand while pressing into plate bottom with your other hand. Trim overhang to ½ inch beyond lip of pie plate. Wrap dough-lined pie plate loosely in plastic and refrigerate until dough is firm, about 15 minutes.

6. Adjust oven rack to lowest position and heat oven to 425 degrees. Fill pie shell with apple mixture. Roll other disk of dough into 12-inch circle between 2 sheets of parchment or plastic. Loosely roll dough around rolling pin and gently unroll it onto filling.

7. Trim overhang to ½ inch beyond lip of pie plate. Pinch edges of top and bottom crusts firmly together. Tuck overhang under itself; folded edge should be flush with edge of pie plate. Crimp dough around edge of pie plate using your fingers. Cut four 2-inch slits in top of dough.

8. Set pie on foil- or parchment-lined baking sheet and bake for 20 minutes. Reduce oven temperature to 375 degrees and continue to bake until crust is deep golden brown and filling is bubbling, 35 to 45 minutes. Transfer pie to wire rack and let cool for at least 1½ hours. Serve.

NOTES FROM THE TEST KITCHEN

RAPID COOLING

The hot apple filling must cool before it goes into the crust. If left to cool in the Dutch oven, some of the apples will overcook. We dump the filling onto a rimmed baking sheet, where the heat can quickly dissipate.

PEANUT BUTTER PIE

✓ **WHY THIS RECIPE WORKS:** For a pie with the intense, nutty flavor of peanut butter but not its dense texture, we whipped smooth peanut butter with confectioners' sugar, a touch of cream, and cream cheese (for tang and sliceability) until the mixture was light and fluffy. Folding in more whipped cream lightened it even further. To enhance our basic graham cracker pie shell, we swapped out granulated sugar for brown sugar—its caramel notes complemented the peanut flavor. We sprinkled the baked crust with candied peanuts before layering in the filling and then topped the pie with more whipped cream before chilling. A second dose of crunchy peanuts provided a perfect finishing touch.

With its smooth, creamy texture and robust peanut flavor, it's no surprise that peanut butter was pressed into service as a pie filling by some nameless Southern cook back in the early 1970s. Since then, peanut butter pie—a mousselike peanut butter filling nestled in a crumb crust and topped with whipped cream or chocolate sauce—has gone on to become a fixture on picnic tables all over the country. Some recipes call for cooking the peanut butter with eggs, dairy, and sweeteners to create a pudding-style filling, while others take the even easier (and more popular) route of simply combining peanut butter with cream cheese and confectioners' sugar in a no-bake filling.

For my initial testing, I tried both styles of pie. Tasters appreciated the relatively light texture of the ones with pudding-style fillings, but the pies lacked rich peanut butter flavor and were often so loose that they were unsliceable. The no-cook fillings, on the other hand, had good peanut butter flavor, but they were too dense and either too sweet or too tangy.

Given the stronger peanut butter flavor of the no-cook fillings, I decided to go that route with my pie. I started out with a relatively standard version, mixing together 6 ounces of cream cheese, ½ cup of peanut butter, and ¾ cup of confectioners' sugar in a stand mixer until well combined and then folding in ¾ cup of whipped cream for lightness. It wasn't a bad start, since the whipped cream was helping lighten the otherwise thick texture, but the flavor of the cream cheese obscured the big peanut flavor I was looking for. After several days spent testing various ratios, I finally landed on an additional ¼ cup of peanut butter. This was a significant enough jump in the amount of peanut butter that its flavor was in the forefront, but not so much that it obliterated the slight tang of the cream cheese.

Now I turned to the filling's texture. The problem with combining cream cheese and peanut butter is that, independently, each feels rather thick and heavy in the mouth; put them together and that effect is compounded. Though the whipped cream did lighten the texture of the filling somewhat, the filling was still too heavy. But what if I added some cream to the initial mixture and turned up the mixer speed so that it would aerate more during mixing? (Having a more liquid initial mixture would also make it easier to fold in the whipped cream later, so less aeration would be lost.) I lined up several pies for tasting, each with a different amount of cream added to the initial mixture, and waited. Tasters preferred the pie with 3 tablespoons of cream, which had a lighter, more mousselike texture than previous versions did.

Satisfied with the filling, I moved on to the crust. I had all kinds of suggestions from coworkers, including, "Did you try a pretzel crust?" The pretzel crusts I tried were either sandy and falling apart or required so much butter to stay together that they were too rich for this pie. After many tests and much discussion, I opted to stick with an already proven test kitchen recipe: the graham cracker crumb crust. But to enhance the peanut butter flavor, I swapped out the granulated sugar that's typical in graham cracker crumb crusts for brown sugar; its caramel notes played off the peanut butter beautifully.

Now for the fun part: the toppings. Chocolate sauce was a real contender, but it turned out that it distracted too much from the peanut butter flavor I had worked so hard to bring to the fore. Instead, I went with a whipped cream topping, since it added some textural lightness without introducing a distracting flavor. I decided to play up the salty-sweet peanut taste even more by scattering honey-roasted peanuts over both the baked crust and the top of the chilled pie. (Despite the time it takes to make them, homemade candied peanuts were preferred by tasters who thought the honey-roasted nuts were a little too salty. A recipe for candied peanuts follows.)

Now I had it: With its creamy and light filling, whipped cream topping, crunchy candied peanuts, and graham cracker crumb crust, this was a fully grown-up, fully delicious dessert.

—CRISTIN WALSH, *Cook's Country*

Peanut Butter Pie

SERVES 8

All-natural peanut butters will work in this recipe. You can use our Homemade Candied Peanuts (recipe follows) in place of the honey-roasted peanuts.

  9 whole graham crackers, broken into 1-inch pieces
  3 tablespoons packed light brown sugar
  5 tablespoons unsalted butter, melted
  ½ cup honey-roasted peanuts, chopped
  ¾ cup (3 ounces) plus 2 tablespoons confectioners' sugar
  ¾ cup creamy peanut butter
  6 ounces cream cheese, softened
  1¾ cups heavy cream
  1 teaspoon vanilla extract

1. Adjust oven rack to middle position and heat oven to 325 degrees. Grease 9-inch pie plate. Process graham crackers and brown sugar in food processor until finely ground, about 30 seconds. Add melted butter and pulse until combined, about 8 pulses.

2. Transfer crumbs to prepared plate. Using bottom of dry measuring cup, press crumbs into bottom and up sides of plate. Bake until crust is fragrant and beginning to brown, 12 to 14 minutes, rotating plate halfway through baking. Let crust cool completely on wire rack, about 30 minutes. Spread ⅓ cup peanuts evenly over bottom of cooled crust.

3. Using stand mixer fitted with whisk, mix ¾ cup confectioners' sugar, peanut butter, cream cheese, and 3 tablespoons cream on low speed until combined, about 1 minute. Increase speed to medium-high and whip until fluffy, about 1 minute. Transfer to large bowl; set aside.

4. In now-empty mixer bowl, whip ¾ cup cream on medium-low speed until foamy, about 1 minute. Increase speed to high and whip until stiff peaks form, 1 to 3 minutes. Gently fold whipped cream into peanut butter mixture in 2 additions until no white streaks remain. Spoon filling into crust and spread into even layer.

5. In now-empty mixer bowl, whip vanilla, remaining cream, and remaining 2 tablespoons confectioners' sugar on medium-low speed until foamy, about 1 minute. Increase speed to high and whip until stiff peaks form, 1 to 3 minutes. Spread whipped cream evenly over filling. Refrigerate until set, about 2 hours. Sprinkle with remaining peanuts. Serve.

VARIATION

Peanut Butter Pie with Chocolate Graham Crust

In step 1, substitute chocolate graham crackers for graham crackers.

Homemade Candied Peanuts

MAKES ABOUT ½ CUP

  ½ cup dry-roasted peanuts
  2 tablespoons granulated sugar
  2 tablespoons water
  ¼ teaspoon salt

1. Line baking sheet with parchment paper. Bring all ingredients to boil in medium saucepan over medium heat. Cook, stirring constantly, until water evaporates and sugar appears dry, opaque, and somewhat crystallized and evenly coats peanuts, about 5 minutes.

2. Reduce heat to low and continue to stir peanuts until sugar turns amber color, about 2 minutes longer. Transfer peanuts to prepared sheet and spread in even layer. Let cool completely, about 10 minutes.

FUDGY TAR HEEL PIE

✓ **WHY THIS RECIPE WORKS:** This popular Southern brownie pie calls for pouring brownie batter into a pie shell. We loved the idea, but many recipes produced cloyingly sweet pies with little chocolate flavor. To correct the sweetness without sacrificing fudgy flavor, we replaced the granulated sugar with dark brown sugar, which introduced depth and molasses undertones. Upping the vanilla and salt and adding cocoa powder rounded out the fudgy flavor. To make the pie gooey but not runny, we reduced the flour to just ¼ cup, and used both butter and oil to create a softer, chewier crumb. Prebaking the pie crust and toasting the nuts before adding them to the batter ensured that both stayed crisp.

I first encountered Tar Heel pie in a pie cookbook, and I wondered if it was widely known. When I dug deeper into old food magazines and Southern community cookbooks, I found my answer: There are hundreds—if not thousands—of (very similar) recipes for this pie.

FUDGY TAR HEEL PIE

Melt a stick of butter with 1 cup of semisweet chocolate chips; whisk in ½ cup each of brown and granulated sugars, ½ cup of flour, a pinch of salt, and a cup of chopped pecans; pour the batter into an uncooked pie shell; and bake it until the edges brown and the filling sets. One version included shredded coconut and a few called for adding chocolate chunks, but by and large the recipes were nearly identical.

Along the way, I learned that the pie dates back to at least the 1950s, although this particular name came into being only a few decades ago. The story goes that a secretary at a postcard company in North Carolina dubbed "brownie pie" Tar Heel pie. A postcard with a picture of the pie was distributed, and the new name stuck.

I made a few pies—whatever they're called—with and without added coconut and chocolate chunks, and after the team tasted each one, I tallied up the pros and cons. Combine pie and brownie and you should get doubly delicious results, right? Apparently not. The filling was far too sweet, as well as gloppy rather than fudgy, plus the chocolate flavor was wimpy; the underdone crust was more pasty than pastry; and the nuts were mealy.

Some of our problems with the pie (pasty, raw crust and mealy nuts), while significant, were hardly mysterious. None of the recipes that I had found called for a parbaked pie shell or toasted pecans. Buried in wet batter, neither had a chance of crisping up. I'd try starting with a parbaked shell and toasted nuts. Using the filling recipe from the first round with a parbaked shell and toasted pecans, I baked a new pie at 325 degrees until it was set but still moist, about 35 minutes. The filling was still too sweet and lackluster in the chocolate flavor department, but the crust was flaky and the pecans were crunchy.

Encouraged by these early successes, I pressed on. Could curbing the cloying sweetness be as simple as using less sugar? Well, yes and no. When I eliminated 2 tablespoons each of granulated sugar and brown sugar, the sweetness level was correct, but the pie was bland and no longer fudgy. Sugar behaves like a wet ingredient in baked goods, dissolving in the oven and making the finished product moister. I returned to the original amounts and tried replacing the semisweet chocolate with unsweetened. This pie was dry and brittle, like unsweetened chocolate itself. I circled back to semisweet chocolate. Brown sugar is moister

than granulated, so maybe I could rein in the sweetness without harming the texture by switching to all brown sugar and using less of it. At last, real progress: ¾ cup of brown sugar did just that, plus its molasses undertones bolstered the chocolate flavor.

Adding cocoa powder gave the chocolate flavor an extra push, and doubling the salt and the vanilla extract filled out the background tastes. Since the flavor and the texture were so entangled, I wondered if I could take them both one step further by exchanging the light brown sugar for dark. Flavor, check: The pie now tasted delicious. While conducting these tests, I discovered something interesting: If I mixed the eggs separately with the sugar, the pie developed a crackly, shiny, attractive top.

Nice, but otherwise, the texture still needed work. Going for gooey, I decided to try backing down from the ½ cup of flour. Reducing it by half definitely upped the fudgy factor, but any less and this would be a custard pie. I'd leave the flour at ¼ cup and try to find another way to further tenderize the filling.

Fat can tenderize baked goods, but I was already using a stick of butter; would more be overkill? As I was putting the second stick of butter back in the fridge, I got an idea. Maybe it wasn't more fat I needed but a softer fat—a liquid fat, to be exact. Chewy boxed brownies call for vegetable oil rather than butter, and

---

NOTES FROM THE TEST KITCHEN

MAKING THE MOST OF PECANS

1. For better flavor and to ensure that the pecans don't get soggy, toast them in a 350-degree oven for about 5 minutes.

2. Sprinkle the nuts in the bottom of the prebaked pie shell; don't mix them into the filling. This way, the pie shell won't get soggy and the pie will be easy to slice.

a few years back a colleague cracked the code to chewy homemade brownies by using a combo of butter and vegetable oil. I made my pie again, this time using 4 tablespoons each of butter and oil. Now the crust wasn't just an extra. For people who like brownies so fudgy and barely cooked that they are too messy to eat out of hand, this pie is a must.

—SARAH GABRIEL, *Cook's Country*

Fudgy Tar Heel Pie

SERVES 8

Serve with ice cream.

CRUST

1¼ cups (6¼ ounces) all-purpose flour
1 tablespoon granulated sugar
½ teaspoon salt
4 tablespoons vegetable shortening, cut into ½-inch pieces and chilled
6 tablespoons unsalted butter, cut into ¼-inch pieces and chilled
3–4 tablespoons ice water

FILLING

1 cup (6 ounces) semisweet chocolate chips
4 tablespoons unsalted butter
¼ cup vegetable oil
2 tablespoons unsweetened cocoa powder
¾ cup packed (5¼ ounces) dark brown sugar
2 large eggs
1 tablespoon vanilla extract
¾ teaspoon salt
¼ cup (1¼ ounces) all-purpose flour
1¼ cups pecans, toasted and chopped coarse

1. FOR THE CRUST: Process flour, sugar, and salt in food processor until combined, about 5 seconds. Scatter shortening over top and process until mixture resembles coarse cornmeal, about 10 seconds. Scatter butter over top and pulse until mixture resembles coarse crumbs, about 10 pulses.

2. Transfer mixture to medium bowl. Sprinkle 3 tablespoons ice water over mixture. Stir and press dough together, using stiff rubber spatula, until dough sticks together. If dough does not come together, stir in remaining ice water, 1 teaspoon at time, until it does.

3. Form dough into 4-inch disk, wrap tightly in plastic wrap and refrigerate for 1 hour. Let chilled dough sit on counter to soften slightly, about 10 minutes. (Wrapped dough can be refrigerated for up to 2 days or frozen for up to 1 month. If frozen, let dough thaw completely on counter before rolling.)

4. Adjust oven rack to lower-middle position and heat oven to 375 degrees. Roll dough into 12-inch circle on lightly floured counter. Loosely roll dough around rolling pin and gently unroll it onto 9-inch pie plate, letting excess dough hang over edge. Ease dough into plate by gently lifting edge of dough with your hand while pressing into plate bottom with your other hand. Trim overhang to ½ inch beyond lip of pie plate. Tuck overhang under itself; folded edge should be flush with edge of pie plate. Crimp dough evenly around edge of pie using your fingers. Wrap dough-lined pie plate loosely in plastic and freeze until dough is fully chilled and firm, about 15 minutes.

5. Line chilled pie shell with two 12-inch squares of parchment paper, letting parchment lie over edges of dough, and fill with pie weights. Bake until lightly golden around edges, 18 to 25 minutes. Carefully remove parchment and weights, rotate pie shell, and continue to bake until center begins to look opaque and slightly drier, 3 to 6 minutes. Let cool completely.

6. FOR THE FILLING: Reduce oven temperature to 325 degrees. Combine ⅔ cup chocolate chips and butter in bowl and microwave at 50 percent power, stirring often, until melted, about 90 seconds. Whisk in oil and cocoa until smooth.

7. In separate bowl, whisk sugar, eggs, vanilla, and salt together until smooth. Whisk chocolate mixture into sugar mixture until incorporated. Stir in flour and remaining ⅓ cup chocolate chips until just combined.

8. Spread pecans in bottom of pie shell, then pour batter over top, using spatula to level. Bake pie until toothpick inserted in center comes out with thin coating of batter attached, 30 to 35 minutes. Let pie cool on wire rack until barely warm, about 1½ hours. Serve. (Pie can be reheated, uncovered, in a 300-degree oven until warm throughout, 10 to 15 minutes.)

FRENCH APPLE TART

✔ **WHY THIS RECIPE WORKS:** Classically elegant French apple tart is little more than apples and pastry, but such simplicity means that imperfections like tough or mushy apples, unbalanced flavor, and sodden crust are hard to hide. We wanted a foolproof way to achieve tender apples and a flavorful, buttery crust. We parbaked our quick pat-in-pan dough for a cookie-like texture that gave the tart a sturdy base. For intense fruit flavor, we packed the tart with a whopping 5 pounds of Golden Delicious apples. We cooked half into a concentrated puree, which we made more luxurious with butter and apricot preserves. For textural contrast, we sliced and par-cooked the remaining apples and used them to adorn the top. A thin coat of preserves and a final stint under the broiler provided an attractively caramelized finish.

The word "elegant" is usually used to describe something that's exquisite and special occasion–worthy, like hand-cut crystal. But it can also refer to something that's ingeniously simple yet effective, like a mathematical proof. Both applications of the word fit the classic French apple tart, a visually stunning dessert that has intense fruit flavor and diverse textures, yet is made with just a few basic ingredients.

Some variations feature extras like almonds or custard, but in its simplest form *tarte aux pommes* has a crisp pastry shell that's filled with a concentrated apple puree and then topped with a spiraling fan of paper-thin apple slices. It's usually finished with a delicate glaze, which caramelizes during baking, providing an extra layer of flavor and a distinctly European flair.

But dazzling looks quickly lose their appeal when there's no integrity backing them up, and poor structure is the fatal flaw of many a handsome apple tart. If the apple slices on top are tough, they resist the knife and the soft puree beneath squirts out under the pressure. That layer of puree also tends to make the crust sodden and mushy. And the dessert's overall flavor can be a bit one-dimensional.

Still, I was drawn to the idea of a showstopper dessert that could be made with a short list of pantry staples. My challenge would be perfecting each component to produce a tart with lively, intense apple flavor and a crust that stayed crisp. And I was unwilling to sacrifice integrity for beauty; I wanted both.

To find the best dough for the job, I started by preparing three classic French pastry options and filling each with a placeholder puree: five peeled and cored Golden Delicious apples (widely available, and good quality year round), cooked with a splash of water until soft, mashed, and reduced until thick. (I'd deal with the apple slices on top later).

My first attempt was with frozen puff pastry, which is essentially many alternating layers of lean dough and butter. I lined the 10-inch tart pan with a sheet of the dough that I had rolled very thin, parbaked it to dry it out and firm it up, and then filled it with the puree. But it was a flop—literally. Despite the parbaking, the dough shrank, and its initially crisp texture softened beneath the wet puree. On to the next option.

Following a classic recipe for *pâte brisée* (essentially the French equivalent of flaky American pie dough), I buzzed 1⅓ cups of flour in the food processor with a touch each of salt and sugar and then pulsed 11 tablespoons of cold butter until the mixture formed a coarse meal strewn with lumps of butter. I drizzled in 5 tablespoons of water, pulsed the mixture until the dough formed a solid mass, chilled it, and then moved through a series of prebaking steps known as blind-baking: I rolled out the chilled dough, fitted it into the tart pan, chilled it again, lined the dough with parchment, weighed it down with pie weights, parbaked it, removed the parchment and weights, and baked it until it was crisp.

The purpose of all that upfront work is to keep the dough from shrinking; this shell held its shape nicely. But the puree still turned the pastry soggy.

Lastly, I tried a *pâte sucrée* (also called *pâte sablée*). This pastry typically contains more sugar than the previous doughs, but the most significant difference is the degree to which the butter gets incorporated. Whereas most of the butter in pâte brisée is left in small chunks, here the butter is thoroughly worked into the flour, which limits the development of gluten—the strong elastic network that forms when flour proteins are moistened with water. Less gluten translates to pastry that is less prone to shrinking and that bakes up with a finer, "shorter" crumb.

I worked the butter into the dry ingredients until the mixture looked like sand, and then I bound it with an egg (typical in pâte sucrée recipes). I chilled, rolled, chilled, and baked.

This crust baked up plenty sturdy, even without the pie weights. Even better, it didn't sog out when I filled it with the puree. Its texture was, however, a tad puffy, like a sugar cookie. And, frankly, all that chilling and rolling was tiresome. Maybe there was an easier way to get the dough into the pan.

I suspected that the cookie-like lift had something to do with the egg, so I eliminated it. But without the egg's moisture, how would I bind the dry ingredients with the cold butter?

I didn't want to add water, milk, or cream, since they would create gluten. But what if I turned the butter (which contains very little water) into a liquid by melting it?

Using melted butter produced a cohesive, Play-Doh-like mass—so far so good. Plus, its consistency was so malleable, it didn't need rolling; I could simply press it into the pan. Then I chilled and baked it.

This was by far the easiest pastry I'd ever made. The crust baked up perfectly sturdy and, without the egg, was no longer puffed up like a sugar cookie, but crisp and delicate like shortbread. When I filled it with the puree, cut a slice, and heard a promising crunch as the knife passed through the still-crisp crust, I knew that this ultrasimple pastry was a game changer.

But it got even better: Subsequent streamlining tests showed that I didn't even have to chill this modified pâte sucrée before baking; the sides of the tart pan were shallow enough that the pastry didn't slump. Now to improve that placeholder puree.

My apple filling had to meet two criteria: concentrated fruit flavor and enough body to not require a spoon.

NOTES FROM THE TEST KITCHEN

ARRANGING APPLES IN A ROSETTE

1. Starting at edges and working toward center, arrange most of the cooled sautéed apple slices in tightly overlapping concentric circles.

2. Bend remaining slices to fit in center.

The latter goal I'd almost met by cooking down the puree until it measured about 2 cups. The texture, and actually the flavor, was something of a cross between applesauce and more-concentrated apple butter. The only change I made was to move this operation from a saucepan to a covered skillet, the wide surface of which helped water from the fruit evaporate faster.

But for that European flair, I wanted the flavor to be more distinctive. I found just what I was looking for in Julia Child's recipe for tarte aux pommes, in which she adds butter and apricot preserves to her puree. I did the same and found that adding a few tablespoons of butter and ½ cup of the tangy fruit preserves to the pot along with the apples yielded a richer, brighter-tasting puree. (A dash of salt boosted that flavor.) The preserves also contributed pectin, which helped the filling firm up.

I'm a forbearing cook, but painstakingly shingling thin-sliced apples (for ease, I'd stick with Golden Delicious on the top as well) over the entire surface almost drove me 'round the bend. The outer ring looked uniform, but placement of the slices became more difficult and looked increasingly amateurish as I proceeded toward the center.

Hoping the tart would look better in its fully baked state, I briefly turned my attention to making a glaze. The apricot preserves I was already using would add bright flavor and a dazzling sheen, so I microwaved them to make them fluid, sieved them, gingerly painted a few tablespoons over the tart's surface (tricky, because the slightest drag of the brush could dislodge the delicate apples), and baked it.

What I pulled out of the oven 30 minutes later looked OK, if a bit pale. The bigger problem was that the apple slices never became tender enough for me to cut the tart without them resisting and becoming dislodged. I made a series of attempts to soften the fruit—baking the tart longer, brushing the slices with water or melted butter, covering the tart with foil for part of the baking time so the slices might soften in the trapped steam—none of which made much of a difference.

In the end, I swapped the wafer-thin apple slices for more generous slices and (since I was already using a skillet to make the apple puree) sautéed them briefly to jump-start the softening before placing them on the tart. As for the spiral shingling, I decided to forgo this fussy tradition and devise a more easygoing, but still elegant, alternative. What I came up with: a rosette pattern made by placing the apple slices in concentric circles. The parcooking had made the slices conveniently pliable, so I could simply bend the pieces and slip them into place.

Encouragingly, these sturdier pieces stayed put when I brushed them with the glaze, leaving me hopeful as I placed the tart in the oven. Then I briefly ran the tart under the broiler to get the burnished finish that characterizes this French showpiece.

The rosette-like design of this tart made it look a bit different from the classic French apple tart, but it was every bit as elegant. And thanks to the now-tender apple slices, the rich puree, and the crisp—not to mention utterly simple and foolproof—crust, every slice of the tart that I cut was picture-perfect, too.

—ANDREA GEARY, *Cook's Illustrated*

French Apple Tart

SERVES 8

You may have extra apple slices after topping the tart in step 6. If you don't have a potato masher, you can puree the applesauce in a food processor. For the best flavor and texture, be sure to bake the crust thoroughly. To ensure that the outer ring of the pan releases easily from the tart, avoid getting apricot glaze on the crust. The tart is best served the day it is assembled.

CRUST

- 1⅓ cups (6⅔ ounces) all-purpose flour
- 5 tablespoons (2¼ ounces) sugar
- ½ teaspoon salt
- 10 tablespoons unsalted butter, melted

FILLING

- 10 Golden Delicious apples (8 ounces each), peeled and cored
- 3 tablespoons unsalted butter
- 1 tablespoon water
- ½ cup apricot preserves
- ¼ teaspoon salt

1. FOR THE CRUST: Adjust 1 oven rack to lowest position and second rack 5 to 6 inches from broiler element. Heat oven to 350 degrees. Whisk flour, sugar, and salt together in bowl. Add melted butter and stir until dough forms. Using your hands, press two-thirds of dough into bottom of 9-inch tart pan with removable bottom. Press remaining dough into fluted sides of pan. Press and smooth dough with your hands to even thickness. Place pan on wire rack set in rimmed baking sheet and bake on lowest rack, until crust is deep golden brown and firm to touch, 30 to 35 minutes, rotating pan halfway through baking. Set aside until ready to fill.

2. FOR THE FILLING: Cut 5 apples lengthwise into quarters and cut each quarter lengthwise into 4 slices. Melt 1 tablespoon butter in 12-inch skillet over medium heat. Add apple slices and water and toss to combine. Cover and cook, stirring occasionally, until apples begin to turn translucent and are slightly pliable, 3 to 5 minutes. Transfer apples to large plate, spread into single layer, and set aside to cool. Do not clean skillet.

3. While apples cook, microwave apricot preserves until fluid, about 30 seconds. Strain preserves through fine-mesh strainer into small bowl, reserving solids. Set aside 3 tablespoons strained preserves for brushing tart.

4. Cut remaining 5 apples into ½-inch-thick wedges. Melt remaining 2 tablespoons butter in now-empty skillet over medium heat. Add remaining apricot preserves, reserved apricot solids, apple wedges, and salt. Cover and cook, stirring occasionally, until apples are very soft, about 10 minutes.

5. Mash apples to puree with potato masher. Continue to cook, stirring occasionally, until puree is reduced to 2 cups, about 5 minutes.

6. Transfer apple puree to baked tart shell and smooth surface. Select 5 thinnest slices of sautéed apple and set aside. Starting at outer edge of tart, arrange remaining slices, tightly overlapping in concentric circles. Bend reserved slices to fit in center. Bake tart, still on wire rack in sheet, on lowest rack, for 30 minutes. Remove tart from oven and heat broiler.

7. While broiler heats, warm reserved preserves in microwave until fluid, about 20 seconds. Brush evenly over surface of apples, avoiding tart crust. Broil tart, checking every 30 seconds and turning as necessary, until apples are attractively caramelized, 1 to 3 minutes. Let tart cool for at least 1½ hours. Remove outer metal ring of tart pan, slide thin metal spatula between tart and pan bottom, and carefully slide tart onto serving platter. Cut into wedges and serve.

TO MAKE AHEAD: The baked crust, apple slices, and apple puree can be made up to 24 hours in advance. Apple slices and puree should be refrigerated separately. Assemble tart with refrigerated apple slices and puree and bake as directed, adding 5 minutes to baking time.

TEST KITCHEN RESOURCES

Every product tested may not be listed in these pages. Please visit CooksIllustrated.com to find complete listings and information on all products tested and reviewed.

BEST KITCHEN QUICK TIPS

ROUNDING OUT PIE DOUGH

Instead of trimming dough after she has placed it in the pie pan, Laurie Martin of Sweet Home, Ore., likes to create as perfect a circle as possible before it goes in the pan. Here's how she does it.

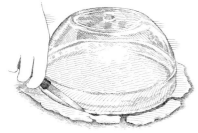

1. Roll the dough into an 11-inch round. Place a 10-inch-wide bowl on top and trim around the edge.

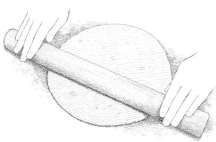

2. Finish rolling the circle into the desired size (the dough will be thin but sturdy enough to transfer to a pie plate).

TWIST-TIE TEPEE

Transporting frosted cakes or cream pies without a cake carrier means covering the dessert with plastic wrap, but if the plastic is not propped up, it will smudge the topping. Toothpicks keep the plastic at bay—if their sharp points don't poke through it. Instead, Anne Walbridge of Sausalito, Calif., creates a blunt-edged prop by folding twist ties in half. Just before serving, she touches up the topping.

PEELING JUST ONE TOMATO

Blanching tomatoes (or peaches) in a pot of boiling water is a great way to remove their peels, but when she needs to peel just a single piece of fruit, Monique Verrier of Healdsburg, Calif., takes a shortcut. She microwaves 1⅓ cups of water in a 2-cup liquid measuring cup for 1 to 2 minutes until simmering. Then she cuts a shallow X into the bottom of the fruit, drops it into the hot water for 30 seconds, and then transfers it to ice water for 30 seconds. The peel pulls right off.

CLEVER CONDIMENT CUPS

When serving condiments at her backyard barbecues, Penny Senouci of Denver, Colo., uses a jumbo muffin tin to contain condiments like ketchup, mustard, relish, and chopped onion. The toppings stay together and she has only one container to clean at the end of the party. (A popover pan also works.)

ALUMINUM FOIL SCRUBBER

When she runs out of steel wool but needs to get tough, baked-on food off glass baking pans or her oven rack, Allison Brown of San Francisco, Calif., uses dishwashing liquid and a crumpled-up ball of aluminum foil. The craggy foil is more abrasive than a sponge and is a great way to recycle used—but still clean—sheets of foil.

BRUSHING OFF BEET STAINS

No matter how hard you scrub your hands, simple soap and water do little to remove red beet stains. Lisa Morrison of West Tisbury, Mass., has discovered that rubbing a dab of whitening toothpaste with peroxide over the area helps erase the stains.

BREAKING UP ROCK-HARD BROWN SUGAR

If Joyce Goldberg of Montvale, N.J., discovers that her brown sugar has dried out and formed rock-hard clumps, she uses her coffee grinder to quickly break up what she needs so that she can proceed with her recipe.

FUSS-FREE POLENTA

To keep polenta from clumping, most recipes suggest pouring cornmeal in a thin stream into boiling water and whisking vigorously—a somewhat finicky process. But Ray Nazzai of Herndon, Va., has discovered that adding the cornmeal to cold water and stirring a bit to break up clumps before heating delivers the same creamy results. (The method works for coarse and fine cornmeals, as well as farina.)

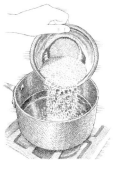

PERFECTING THE PROOF

In the winter, the kitchen of Mark Carrara of Tucumcari, N.M., gets too chilly (less than 70 degrees) to proof bread dough. Expanding on a reader's idea for an improvised microwave proof box, he uses his cooler and this method for larger batches.

1. Heat 1½ cups of water in a measuring cup in a microwave for 1 minute or until nearly simmering.

2. Place the cup of hot water and the dough in an insulated cooler. Close the lid and let the dough rise. (The hot water will keep the interior warm for up to 2 hours.) Remove the dough once it has doubled in size or reached the desired volume.

MESS-FREE MUFFIN MAKING

Instead of portioning batter into a muffin tin using a spoon or a measuring cup—both of which tend to dribble batter on the counter—Diane Merkel of Fallbrook, Calif., employs an unusual tool: a canning funnel. The gadget neatly fits into each cup and allows her to deposit batter without any drips.

A PEELING IDEA

Hard-cooked eggs can be difficult to peel, which is why Judy Puckett of Seattle, Wash., uses this technique.

1. Tap the surface of a cooked egg with the back of a teaspoon to crack the shell.

2. Slip the edge of the spoon under the shell at the egg's base to loosen it. Then continue to move along the curve of the egg to remove the rest of the shell.

HOMEMADE BENCH SCRAPER

Bench scrapers make easy work of removing scraps of sticky dough from the counter or lifting chopped ingredients into a bowl or pan. Harry Lipman of Brooklyn, N.Y., found a way to fashion the tool from an old plastic cutting mat. After cleaning it well, he cut the flexible mat into 4 by 3-inch rectangles.

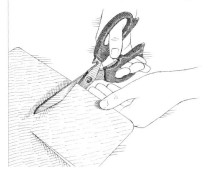

STORING EXTRA EGGS

It's not uncommon for Ken Burnham of Marco Island, Fla., to purchase a new carton of eggs before he's used up the old one. To save fridge space, he places the newer carton upside down on a shelf and sets the older eggs in the now-inverted cups on the bottom of the carton.

ALTERNATIVE BISCUIT CUTTER

Unable to find a biscuit cutter while in the midst of baking one day, Lindsay Westley of South Hero, Vt., reached for a canning jar ring. While its edge is slightly duller than that of the traditional tool, it easily stamps through dough and creates a perfect circle every time.

BEST KITCHEN QUICK TIPS

CUPCAKE TOPPER

Cupcakes topped with swirled frosting may look like the work of a pro, but Robert Casillas of Los Angeles, Calif., has found a way to bring the method home.

1. Spoon a line of colored frosting down the center of a piece of plastic wrap and then spoon a second color alongside it. Fold the plastic in half lengthwise.

2. Roll the frosting into a log, twisting and knotting one end of the plastic.

3. Insert the open end of the log into a pastry bag and pull it through the piping tip.

4. Pull the plastic wrap tightly through the tip and snip off the excess plastic. Pipe the frosting onto cupcakes as usual.

(SPLATTER) SCREEN TEST

When frying bacon, splatter screens prevent the hot grease from making a mess of the stovetop. But Carla Wheeler of Live Oak, Fla., also found that the perforated flat surfaces can double as platters to hold cooked slices. After removing the screen to retrieve cooked bacon from the pan, replace it and lay the strips on top while other slices finish cooking. The cooked bacon not only drains excess fat (blot it further before serving, if desired) but also stays warm.

POPPING DIFFICULT LIDS

When Kate Chuprevich of Chestnut Hill, Mass., has trouble opening a stubborn jar, she reaches for a thin metal spoon. Using the spoon as a lever, she slides its tip between the lid and the jar—avoiding the lid's notches—and gently presses down on the handle until the seal releases.

KEEPING TABS ON TEA BAGS

When brewing iced tea in a pitcher, Dan McCoy of Brooklyn, N.Y., found that the weight of the tea bags often pulled the attached short strings and tabs into the hot water. Fed up with fishing out the bags, he now crimps the strings' tabs to fit through the holes of a slotted spoon and props it across the opening while the tea steeps. The strings aren't pulled in, and removing the bags is as simple as lifting the spoon.

RACKING UP MEASURING CUPS

Wendy Nicholls of San Francisco, Calif., has found the perfect way to store her metal measuring cups: on a magnetic knife strip. Not only are the cups easy to access but each measurement is also in view, as opposed to when the cups are nested together in a stack.

BROKEN-CUPCAKE PARFAIT

Even the best bakers sometimes end up with a couple of broken cupcakes. Instead of panicking if her cupcakes stick, Sally McQuail of Downington, Pa., makes use of the crumbly pieces by alternating cake and frosting to fill individual plastic cups.

KEEPING SALAD GREENS FRESHER

We've verified that blowing into a bag of salad greens (thereby increasing the carbon dioxide level) keeps the contents fresh longer, but we don't recommend this method for sanitary reasons. Looking for another carbon dioxide source, David Griffith of Somerville, Mass., turned to his seltzer maker. A few puffs before he seals the bag do the trick.

DIGITAL DISPLAY

Mary Aman of Melbourne, Fla., often uses her tablet computer to view recipes while cooking, but its flat design means that it doesn't stand on its own. Rather than invest in a tablet stand, she puts her plate stand to use. The easel-like tool secures the tablet and keeps it upright for easy reading. (The stand also works for cookbooks.)

IMPROMPTU CUTLERY CARRIER

When Mary Liz Towne of Sheboygan, Wis., needs to transport a knife, she takes care to sheathe the sharp blade. Because she doesn't own a guard for each knife in her set, she uses this unlikely alternative: lint roller tape. She unrolls the sheet to accommodate the length of her blade and folds it in half to cover the blade. (Trim any excess width, if necessary.)

SECOND LINERS

While in the middle of baking cupcakes, Leila Rieder of Providence, R.I., ran out of liners. Thinking quickly, she devised an easy substitute.

1. Cut 5-inch squares from a sheet of parchment paper and firmly press them over the base of an inverted drinking glass to shape them.

2. Place the shaped liners into the muffin cups. Fill and bake as directed.

BETTER OVEN-FRIED BACON

Many cooks line their baking sheets with aluminum foil when oven-frying bacon to simplify cleanup. Betty Pfeifer of Bay Village, Ohio, takes this idea a step further: She fashions a makeshift rack by crimping the foil at 1-inch intervals before placing the bacon horizontally across the crimps. This technique makes cleanup a snap and elevates the strips so that grease drips into the foil crevices during cooking, ensuring a crispier result.

REHEATING LEFTOVER RICE

For leftover rice that tastes just as fluffy and moist as a fresh-made pot, Jim Smith of Rockville, Md., uses this method.

1. Fill a saucepan with ½ inch of water. Place a steamer basket lined with a damp coffee filter in the pan.

2. Add chilled rice; cover and cook until heated through, about 5 minutes. Fluff with a fork and serve.

EASIER FRENCH PRESS CLEANING

French presses are hard to clean as the spent grounds cling to the bottom of the carafe. To easily get rid of all the grounds without having any go down her disposal (usually considered inadvisable), Janet Lazrow of Philadelphia, Pa., fills the carafe with water, pours its contents into a fine-mesh strainer over the sink, and dumps the grounds into the trash.

HOMEMADE SPECIALTY COFFEE

Combining his love of flavored coffee and his stash of spent vanilla beans, Gregory Rubino of Lake Charles, la., makes his own vanilla-flavored brew. After air-drying empty vanilla bean pods for two to three days, he adds half of a pod to a coffee grinder full of enough coffee beans for a pot and processes it before brewing as usual.

EVERYDAY STIR-FRYING

The beauty of stir-frying is that you can do it quickly with just about anything in your fridge—but it's not a free-for-all. Here's how to do it well.

CHOOSE YOUR INGREDIENTS

The best stir-fries feature a variety of textures and colors, which is largely determined by the vegetable choices. We recommend limiting yourself to two or three different types of produce; otherwise, the medley can become cluttered. Amounts mentioned yield four servings.

PROTEIN

Use ¾ to 1 pound of one of the following tender cuts (best for stir-frying because they soften quickly).

BEEF: Flank steaks, sirloin tip steaks, blade steaks
- Prep: Cut the meat against the grain and on the bias into ¼-inch-thick slices.

CHICKEN: Boneless, skinless breasts
- Prep: Remove the tenderloins if attached. Cut each breast against the grain into ¼-inch-thick slices.

PORK: Tenderloin
- Prep: Cut crosswise into ¼-inch-thick slices and then cut each slice into ¼-inch-thick strips.

SHRIMP: Extra-large (21 to 25 shrimp per pound)
- Prep: Thaw (if frozen), peel, devein, and remove the tails.

CHILL MEAT BEFORE SLICING

Briefly freezing meat before cutting firms it up so that it is easier to slice. Freeze chicken breasts and steaks for 20 to 30 minutes, pork tenderloin for 30 to 45 minutes.

VEGETABLES

Mix and match your vegetables using a total of 1 to 1½ pounds.

LONG COOKING 3 to 7 minutes	MEDIUM COOKING 1 to 3 minutes	FAST COOKING 30 to 60 seconds
Broccoli	Asparagus	Bean sprouts
Carrots	Bell pepper	Bok choy greens
Cauliflower	Bok choy stalks	Celery
Green beans	Eggplant	Frozen peas
Green or red cabbage	Frozen shelled edamame	Napa cabbage
Snap peas	Mushrooms	Scallion greens
	Onions	Tender greens
	Scallion whites	Tomatoes
	Snow peas	Water chestnuts

SAUCE

Prefab stir-fry sauces are usually too sweet or too salty, and making your own takes just minutes. For each recipe, whisk the ingredients in a medium bowl.

CLASSIC STIR-FRY SAUCE

Combine ½ cup chicken broth, ¼ cup dry sherry, 3 tablespoons hoisin sauce or oyster sauce, 1 tablespoon soy sauce, 2 teaspoons cornstarch, and 1 teaspoon toasted sesame oil.

SWEET AND SOUR SAUCE

Combine 6 tablespoons red wine vinegar, 6 tablespoons orange juice, 6 tablespoons sugar, 3 tablespoons ketchup, 1 teaspoon cornstarch, and ½ teaspoon salt.

COCONUT–RED CURRY SAUCE

Combine 1 cup coconut milk, 1 tablespoon fish sauce, 2 teaspoons Thai red curry paste, 1 teaspoon packed brown sugar, and 1 teaspoon cornstarch.

PRETREAT YOUR PROTEIN

Don't skip these quick soaking steps. They help the meat cook up flavorful and tender.

PROTECT CHICKEN AND PORK WITH BAKING SODA BEFORE MARINATING

Soaking lean meat slices in a baking soda solution before marinating softens them and helps them stay juicy during cooking. Don't soak meat longer than 15 minutes or it will break down too much. Be sure to rinse off the solution before marinating.

Soak meat for 15 minutes in 1 teaspoon baking soda dissolved in 2 tablespoons water.

MARINATE CHICKEN, PORK, AND BEEF IN A SALTY LIQUID

Salty liquids like soy sauce or fish sauce not only boost meat's savory flavor but also act as a brine, helping the meat retain moisture during cooking. Drain the meat well before cooking; removing excess moisture will ensure good browning.

Soak meat in 2 tablespoons soy or fish sauce for 15 minutes.

SOAK SHRIMP IN OIL

Salty marinades overwhelm the delicate flavor of shrimp, so we came up with a subtler soak: a mixture of oil, minced garlic, and salt. The salt seasons the shrimp and helps it retain moisture and draws out flavor from the garlic. Oil distributes those flavors evenly over the flesh.

Soak shrimp in 3 tablespoons vegetable oil, 6 cloves minced garlic, and ½ teaspoon salt for 30 minutes.

FOLLOW THIS SEQUENCE

It's easy to fail at stir-frying because the cooking happens so quickly. Being prepared—we even line up ingredients in the order in which they go into the pan—and sticking to this order of operations will guarantee success.

1. HEAT OIL: Measure 1½ teaspoons oil into 12-inch nonstick skillet set over high heat and heat until just smoking. Repeat every time you add food to pan.

- Peanut, vegetable, and canola oils are best for stir-frying because they're neutral and won't burn before the pan is hot enough for browning. However, any oil will burn if you don't start cooking as soon as it smokes. If the oil scorches, wipe out the pan and start over with fresh oil.

2. SEAR PROTEIN: Cook marinated protein in 2 batches, breaking up clumps, until browned. Transfer to bowl; cover to keep warm.

- Don't sear shrimp; their lean flesh overcooks quickly. Instead, add them to the pan after searing the vegetables and aromatics and stir-fry them over medium-low heat.

3. SEAR VEGETABLES: Cook vegetables sequentially according to chart, starting with longer-cooking items.

- Dry rinsed vegetables thoroughly to prevent them from steaming. To wick away trapped moisture, dry leafy vegetables in a salad spinner.

4. ADD AROMATICS: Clear center of pan and add 3 minced garlic cloves and 1 tablespoon grated ginger mixed with 1 teaspoon vegetable oil. Mash mixture until fragrant, 15 to 30 seconds, and stir into vegetables.

- Mixing aromatics with a little vegetable oil before adding them to the hot pan helps prevent them from burning.

5. COMBINE; ADD SAUCE: Return protein to pan. Whisk sauce to recombine, then add to skillet and toss constantly until liquid is thickened, about 30 seconds.

- If desired, garnish stir-fry with sliced scallions, toasted sesame seeds, chopped toasted nuts, or chopped cilantro; drizzle with toasted sesame and/or chile oil.

BREAK YOUR BAD HABITS

Some of the most common stir-fry practices are also the wrong ones.

DON'T USE A WOK: The broad surface of a large (12-inch) nonstick skillet makes more contact with flat Western burners than a round-bottomed wok, making it a better choice for browning. Don't use a smaller pan.

DON'T CROWD THE PAN: Adding all the ingredients at once will cause the food to steam rather than sear. Cook in batches in even layers and leave space between pieces of meat so that they brown well.

DON'T ADD AROMATICS TOO SOON: Waiting to add ginger and garlic until after the protein and vegetables are cooked prevents them from scorching over the high heat.

DON'T STIR TOO MUCH: Nomenclature aside, it's best to stir your stir-fry infrequently. Western-style burners have a relatively low heat output, so stirring food infrequently during cooking allows for proper browning.

DON'T COOK FULLY WHEN SEARING: Remove meat and vegetables from the pan when they're just shy of being done. They will finish cooking when added back to the pan with the sauce.

COMMON COOKING MYTHS, DEBUNKED

We believed some of them, too—until our testing proved us wrong.

SALT MAKES WATER BOIL FASTER.

FACT: Salt will increase the time it takes water to reach a boil—but only if you add a whole lot of it. When we conducted an experiment—bringing 4 quarts of water to a boil with and without 1 tablespoon of salt—we found that salted and unsalted water came to a boil in the same amount of time: 17½ minutes. A whopping 1½ tablespoons of salt per quart of water is required to raise the boiling point by just 1 degree, thus slightly increasing the time it takes the water to reach a boil. Those proportions yield a super-salty solution, one that we wouldn't use to cook with anyway.

4 quarts water — 1 TB SALT = 17½ minutes to boil = 4 quarts water — NO SALT

A SLAMMED DOOR WILL RUIN A SOUFFLÉ OR CAKE.

FACT: Slamming won't make a difference.
Soufflés and cakes rise as tiny air bubbles in the batter expand in the heat of the oven. To find out if slamming the door shut would interrupt the process enough to spell disaster, we mixed batters for muffins, yellow cake, angel food cake, and cheese soufflé and loaded them into hot ovens. Just before each item reached its maximum height, we opened the oven door and gave it a hard slam. The muffins emerged unharmed, as did the yellow cake. Even the notoriously fragile angel food cake and the soufflé survived. A properly developed foam is pretty resilient.

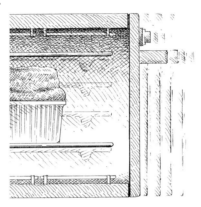

COLD EGGS WILL RUIN BAKED GOODS.

FACT: In most cases you can use eggs of any temperature. We conducted a blind tasting of two yellow cakes: one made with room-temperature eggs, the other with eggs pulled from the refrigerator. The cake made with room-temperature eggs had a slightly finer, more even crumb. The cold-egg cake produced a thicker batter and took 5 minutes longer to bake than the room-temperature-egg cake but was entirely acceptable. So it's fine to use cold eggs in most basic cake recipes. But do be sure to use room-temperature eggs when making finicky cakes like angel food and chiffon, which rely on air incorporated into the beaten eggs as a primary means of leavening. In these cases, we found that cold eggs didn't whip nearly as well and the cakes didn't rise properly.

ROOM TEMPERATURE
Best for recipes in which whites are whipped.

FROM THE FRIDGE
Fine for everything else.

BREAD STALES BECAUSE IT LOSES MOISTURE.

FACT: Bread stales because starch molecules absorb moisture. Once exposed to air, bread starch undergoes a process called retrogradation: The starch molecules begin to crystallize and absorb moisture, turning the bread hard and crumbly. This is why for certain recipes (like stuffing), you should dry bread in the oven (to drive out moisture) instead of letting it go stale.

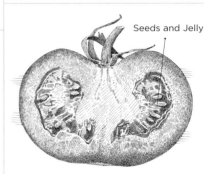

Seeds and Jelly

THE BEST PART OF A TOMATO IS THE FLESH.

FACT: The seeds and jelly contain the most flavor. Many believe it imperative to remove the seeds and jelly of tomatoes because they detract from the texture of your dish. That may be, but they affect flavor, too. The seeds and jelly actually contain three times the amount of flavor-enhancing glutamic acid as the flesh. (Also called glutamate, this is the compound that supplies the savory quality known as umami in many foods.) Sometimes removing seeds may be necessary, but it should be a last resort.

COOKING WINE REMOVES ALL ITS ALCOHOL.

FACT: Cooking reduces the alcohol content but rarely eliminates it. When alcohol and water mix, they form an azeotrope—a mixture of two different liquids that behaves as if it were a single compound. This means that even though alcohol evaporates at a lower temperature than water, the vapors coming from an alcohol-water azeotrope will contain both alcohol and water until the entire mixture is gone. In sum, about 5 percent of the initial alcohol content will remain no matter how long you simmer the mixture.

COOKING IN LIQUID KEEPS MEAT MOISTER.

FACT: Despite the wet conditions, braising adds no moisture. We simulated braising by placing samples of beef chuck, along with measured amounts of broth, in individual vacuum-sealed bags. We submerged the bags in water held at 190 degrees (the temperature of a typical braise) for 90 minutes. The weight of the meat decreased an average of 12.5 percent during cooking while the volume of liquid increased, demonstrating that moisture had been pulled from the meat into the surrounding liquid, not the other way around. Braised meat seems moist not because of the moisture surrounding the meat but because of the temperature at which the meat cooks. Gentle cooking is one way to help break down the meat's connective tissue and collagen, which lubricate and tenderize its fibers.

WASHING MUSHROOMS MAKES THEM ABSORB WATER.

FACT: Soaking will, but a quick rinse won't. When we learned that mushrooms were more than 80 percent water, we began to question their ability to absorb yet more liquid. We weighed whole mushrooms before and after soaking them in water for 5 minutes and found that 6 ounces of mushrooms gained only 1½ teaspoons of water. But, to entirely prevent absorption, we wash mushrooms the same way we wash other vegetables: by rinsing them under cold water. However, if you will be using the mushrooms raw, rinse them just before serving or avoid rinsing altogether, since the surfaces of wet mushrooms turn slimy when exposed to air for more than 5 minutes.

POTATOES CAN MAKE A DISH LESS SPICY.

FACT: You need fat or sugar to reduce the heat. We tried adding potatoes to foods to tame spiciness, but it simply doesn't work. There is another solution: Add ingredients from the opposite end of the flavor spectrum to balance things out. Depending on the recipe, you can add a fat (such as butter, cream, sour cream, cheese, or oil) or a sweetener (such as sugar, honey, or maple syrup) to counteract the offending ingredient. Obviously, it wouldn't make sense to add cheese to a too-spicy Thai beef stir-fry, so use your best judgment.

OIL AND VINEGAR DON'T MIX.

FACT: They can—and do—when properly emulsified. An emulsion is a combination of two liquids that don't ordinarily mix, whisked strenuously until one breaks down into droplets so tiny that they remain separated by the other liquid. The addition of an emulsifying agent (like mayonnaise or mustard) helps the two liquids stay together in a unified sauce. We made vinaigrettes with each emulsifier and found that the mayo sample lasted 1½ hours while the mustard dressing broke after 30 minutes. A sample with no emulsifier began to break immediately.

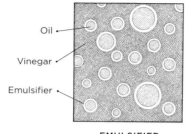

Oil
Vinegar
Emulsifier

EMULSIFIED
Mayonnaise keeps oil and vinegar suspended together in a sauce.

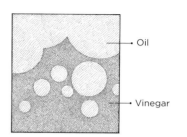

Oil

Vinegar

SEPARATING
With no emulsifier, vinegar and oil won't stay mixed.

ALL PARTS OF A CHILE ARE EQUALLY HOT.

FACT: The pith contains the real spicy stuff. All chiles get their heat from a group of chemical compounds called capsaicinoids, the best known being capsaicin. It's often thought that the seeds have more heat than the flesh, but they are essentially guilty—or hot—by association. Most of the capsaicin is concentrated in the inner whitish pith, with progressively smaller amounts in the seeds and the flesh. For example, there are just 5 milligrams of capsaicin per kilogram of green jalapeño flesh, 73 milligrams per kilogram in the seeds, and 512 milligrams per kilogram in the pith.

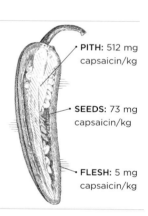

PITH: 512 mg capsaicin/kg

SEEDS: 73 mg capsaicin/kg

FLESH: 5 mg capsaicin/kg

SEARING MEAT SEALS IN JUICES.

FACT: Searing just creates a crusty layer of flavor. We cooked two batches of rib-eye steaks, searing the first batch in a skillet over high heat and then cooking the steaks in a 250-degree oven until they reached 125 degrees. For the second batch we reversed the order, first baking the steaks until they reached 110 degrees and then searing them until a crust developed and their interiors hit 125 degrees. We weighed the steaks before and after cooking and found that both sets had lost around 22 percent of their weight. If searing truly seals in juices, the steaks seared first (while raw) would have had more moisture trapped inside them (and thus less weight loss) than the steaks seared after cooking in the oven.

ACIDIC MARINADES TENDERIZE MEAT.

FACT: In actuality, they can make meat mushy. To tenderize meat, you have to break down muscle fiber and collagen, the connective tissue that makes meat tough. While acidic ingredients do weaken collagen, their impact is confined to the meat's surface—and if left too long, acids turn the outermost layer of meat mushy, not tender. To minimize mushiness, we use acidic components sparingly and only for short marinating times. Truly tender meat comes down to the cut, cooking time, method, and temperature. Highly salted marinades can also act as brines, helping meat retain moisture and cook up more tender.

SECRETS TO FOOLPROOF PIZZA AT HOME

Producing a perfect parlor-style pizza is almost entirely about getting the dough right. We take you inside the recipe to show you why ours works every time.

Thin-Crust Pizza
MAKES TWO 13-INCH PIZZAS

- 3 cups (16½ ounces) bread flour
- 2 tablespoons sugar
- ½ teaspoon instant or rapid-rise yeast
- 1⅓ cups ice water
- 1 tablespoon vegetable oil
- 1½ teaspoons salt
- 1 cup tomato pizza sauce
- 1 ounce Parmesan cheese, grated fine (½ cup)
- 8 ounces whole-milk mozzarella cheese, shredded (2 cups)

1. In food processor fitted with dough blade, pulse flour, sugar, and yeast until combined, about 5 pulses. With food processor running, slowly add ice water; process until dough is just combined and no dry flour remains, about 10 seconds. Let dough sit for 10 minutes.

2. Add oil and salt to dough and process until dough forms satiny, sticky ball that clears sides of bowl, 30 to 60 seconds. Transfer dough to lightly oiled counter and knead briefly by hand until smooth, about 1 minute. Shape dough into tight ball and place in large, lightly oiled bowl. Cover bowl tightly with plastic wrap and refrigerate for at least 24 hours or up to 3 days.

3. One hour before baking, adjust oven rack 4 to 5 inches from broiler element, set baking stone on rack, and heat oven to 500 degrees. Transfer dough to clean counter and divide in half. With cupped palms, form each half into smooth, tight ball. Place balls of dough on lightly greased baking sheet, spacing them at least 3 inches apart; cover loosely with greased plastic and let sit at room temperature for 1 hour.

4. Coat 1 ball of dough generously with flour and place on well-floured counter (keep other ball covered). Use your fingertips to gently flatten dough into 8-inch disk, leaving 1 inch of outer edge slightly thicker than center. Using your hands, gently stretch disk into 12-inch round, working along edges and giving disk quarter turns as you stretch. Transfer dough to well-floured pizza peel and stretch into 13-inch round. Using back of spoon or ladle, spread ½ cup sauce in thin layer over surface of dough, leaving ¼-inch border around edge. Sprinkle ¼ cup Parmesan evenly over sauce, followed by 1 cup mozzarella. Slide pizza carefully onto baking stone and bake until crust is well browned and cheese is bubbly and beginning to brown, 10 to 12 minutes, rotating pizza halfway through baking. Transfer pizza to wire rack and let cool for 5 minutes before slicing and serving.

5. Repeat step 4 to shape, top, and bake second pizza.

WHY THE FORMULA WORKS

Here's a behind-the-scenes look at why each ingredient and step adds up to the ideal parlor-quality crust, which is thin, crisp, and spottily charred on the exterior and tender yet chewy inside.

WHY BREAD FLOUR?
Bread flour contains 12 to 14 percent protein by weight (our favorite, from King Arthur, contains 12.7 percent protein), compared with 10.5 to 11.9 percent for all-purpose flour. The more protein in a flour the more readily the individual proteins link together to form gluten, leading to a denser, chewy crust.

WHAT ABOUT OIL?
Just a tablespoon of oil coats some of the gluten strands, allowing them to stretch and slide past one another, ensuring that the crust, while chewy, isn't too tough.

KNEAD IN A FOOD PROCESSOR
A food processor kneads dough in about a minute, while a stand mixer takes 8 to 10 minutes. Besides saving time, this limits the dough's exposure to air, and curbing oxidation adds up to better flavor.

HOW SUGAR HELPS
The browning temperatures of sugars are as much as 100 degrees lower than those of the starches and proteins in flours. We found that a recipe with 4 percent sugar, or 2 teaspoons per cup of flour, guaranteed quick browning in the time that it took the crust to cook through without adding noticeable sweetness.

REST BEFORE ADDING SALT
After processing the dough just until it comes together, we give it a 10-minute rest and then add the salt (and oil). This rest is called an autolyse, and it gives enzymes in the wheat time to snip into smaller pieces the long strands of gluten that have initially formed. These shorter chains more readily link together to form a stronger gluten network with subsequent processing. Because salt inhibits the enzymes that make autolyse possible, we hold off on adding it until after the dough has rested.

USE ENOUGH WATER—AND MAKE IT ICED
The hydration level of the dough—or the weight of the water in relation to the weight of the flour—affects how easy the dough is to work with as well as its final texture. We use 65 percent hydration (10.66 ounces of water to 16.5 ounces of flour), for a dough that is neither too stiff nor too sticky and retains moisture in a hot oven. Why ice water? It prevents the dough from heating up in the food processor, which would cause it to ferment too quickly and produce overly strong flavors.

24 HOURS IN THE FRIDGE
Resting pizza dough in the fridge instead of at room temperature slows fermentation, which creates more complex flavor compounds. The chilled dough also bakes up with a finer, less bready crumb.

GETTING A HANDLE ON HANDLING DOUGH

Shaping pizza dough can be a cinch—if it doesn't snap back. Following these tips will make it easy.

TO STRETCH DOUGH EVENLY, USE COUNTER INTELLIGENCE

This draping method uses gravity to pull the dough into a perfectly round shape.

 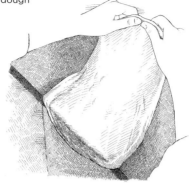

1. Drape dough (pressed into 8-inch round with outer inch left thicker to create a "handle") over edge of counter. Lift up top half, with hands at 10 and 2 o'clock.

2. Rotate dough clockwise, using left hand to feed dough to right hand, meeting at 12 o'clock. Continue until gravity has pulled dough to 12-inch diameter.

IF DOUGH CONTRACTS, RELAX

Our cold-fermentation method creates a more relaxed dough. But if yours still retracts when flattened into a disk, give it a 5-minute rest on the counter to help it relax.

SHAKE BEFORE YOU BAKE

After placing the dough on the peel, give the peel a quick shake over the counter. A quick swipe of the bench scraper under the dough will release any sticky spots. Also, be sure that the peel is dry—dollops of sauce could cause sticking.

HOW TO FREEZE DOUGH

FREEZE EXTRA DOUGH BEFORE SHAPING

Our recipe yields enough dough for two 13-inch pies. Although the dough is best used fresh, you can freeze whatever you don't choose to bake right away. Follow the recipe as directed, letting the dough proof in the refrigerator for at least 24 hours. Then, instead of shaping it, wrap it in plastic wrap coated with vegetable oil spray, place it in a zipper-lock freezer bag, and freeze it. Thaw the dough in the refrigerator for 24 to 48 hours before dividing and shaping.

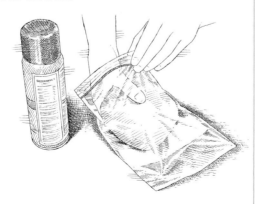

BEST BAKING STRATEGIES

Pizza parlor ovens have a distinct advantage over home ranges: blazing heat. Here's how we improvise.

SUPERHEAT THE STONE

Preheating the baking stone for a full hour at 500 degrees may sound like overkill, but it's not. In tests, we found that 30 minutes of preheating produced an anemic-looking bottom crust, and even 45 minutes wasn't sufficient to produce the ultracrisp, well-browned bottom crust created by an hour of preheating.

AIM (THE STONE) HIGH

Placing the baking stone as close to the ceiling of the oven as possible—instead of its usual orientation on the lowest rack—means that heat will hit the top of the pie and brown the toppings before the crust overcooks.

WHAT IF YOU DON'T HAVE A PIZZA STONE?

Use an inverted baking sheet. You'll still need to preheat it, but 30 minutes in a 500-degree oven is ample time for its lesser mass.

ESSENTIAL TOOLS

Here are our favorite tools for making perfect pizza.

PIZZA WHEEL

OXO Good Grips 4" Pizza Wheel for Non-Stick Pans ($12.99) and OXO Good Grips 4" Pizza Wheel ($11.99)

BAKING PEEL

Super Peel by EXO Products, Inc. ($55)

BAKING STONE

Old Stone Oven Pizza Baking Stone ($38.69)

ESSENTIAL GUIDE TO OIL

Just because supermarket shelves are crammed with dozens of different oils doesn't mean you need them all. For most of our cooking needs, we rely on just three.

❶ VEGETABLE OIL BLEND

Vegetable oil should have a neutral taste that highlights (rather than masks) the flavors of other ingredients. Some varieties, such as corn and canola, take on subtle but distinct flavors in certain applications, so we make a point of avoiding them and go for a blend instead; that way, no one flavor will dominate.

FAVORITE: Crisco Natural Blend Oil ($6.89 for 48 oz) A mix of canola, sunflower, and soybean oils, this oil tastes "very clean" even in high-heat applications.

❷ EVERYDAY EXTRA-VIRGIN OLIVE OIL

In recent tests we've found that the flavors of extra-virgin olive oil (or EVOO) are driven off more thoroughly—and rapidly— by heat than we ever knew. So for cooking Mediterranean dishes like tomato sauce, moussaka, and paella in which olive oil is traditional, we stock the cheapest bottle we can find.

❸ PREMIUM EXTRA-VIRGIN OLIVE OIL

The hallmark of a truly superior-quality EVOO is a pronounced flavor profile that can range from richly fruity, to grassy, to peppery and sharp. We reserve this good stuff for cold applications like dressings and for drizzling on food after cooking.

FAVORITES: Columela Extra Virgin Olive Oil ($15.90 for 17 oz) and **California Olive Ranch Arbequina** ($16.69 for 500 ml)

SHOPPING TIPS: If you can't buy one of our recommended premium extra-virgin olive oils, prioritize freshness. Look for a harvest date on the label; try to buy oils from only this year's crop. Alternatively, look for a "best by" date as far away as possible. (Unopened olive oil is good for up to 18 months from the time it was bottled.)

DOES IT PAY TO COOK WITH EXTRA-VIRGIN OLIVE OIL?

In Mediterranean countries, good olive oil has historically been plentiful and cheap and so used for almost everything. The health benefits of cooking with extra-virgin olive oil are well documented, but how much flavor does it add to a dish once it has been heated? And does high-end EVOO keep more of its flavor than cheaper EVOO?

TASTE TESTS: We had 10 of our top tasters sample three oils straight out of the bottle: Crisco Natural Blend Oil, our favorite premium EVOO from Columela, and a much more affordable EVOO from Filippo Berio. We then had these same tasters try the oils again after we'd heated them to 350 degrees for 10 minutes. Finally, we had tasters sample potatoes tossed in the oils and then roasted.

RESULTS: Tasters were easily able to distinguish the bold fruity and grassy flavors of both EVOOs compared with vegetable oil in the raw tasting. These differences lessened once the oils were heated. Some tasters were able to detect a peppery finish in the EVOOs but little else. The three oils were indistinguishable from one another in roasted potatoes.

BOTTOM LINE: Cooking with EVOO may be healthy, but don't expect even a premium EVOO to add much flavor once it's heated.

UNDERSTUDY OILS

These two oils are also worth keeping on hand.

TOASTED SESAME OIL: We drizzle this nutty-tasting Asian oil over everything from dumplings to stir-fries to noodles and soups.

PEANUT OIL: Though not a must, this neutral-flavored oil has a high smoke point, which means that it's able to withstand prolonged heating without breaking down. Its high smoke point makes it an excellent choice for deep frying.

STORING OIL

Store all oils in a cool, dark place. Store nut and seed oils in the refrigerator to help stave off rancidity, but avoid refrigerating olive oil. Repeatedly chilling olive oil and rewarming it to room temperature can create condensation in the bottle that degrades the flavor.

CHECKING FOR FRESHNESS

Properly stored, vegetable oil should last six months once opened and EVOO at least three months. If you're unsure whether an oil is past its prime, heat a few tablespoons in a skillet. If vegetable oil smells anything other than neutral— and if olive oil smells musty rather than fruity—discard it.

SAUTÉING TIPS

We use a vegetable oil blend for nearly all our sautéing needs.

GET A COLD START

Cooks debate whether oil should be added to the pan before or after the pan is preheated. We strongly prefer adding oil to the cold (unheated) pan for a couple of reasons: Hot oil gives visual cues about when it's time to add food to the pan. And heating an empty nonstick pan can damage its coating and emit fumes.

LET OIL SHIMMER, THEN SAUTÉ

For proper browning, the oil must be moderately hot before you add food to the pan. To know when it's ready, use the visual cue of "shimmering." When the oil starts to ripple, start cooking.

MIND SMOKING MORE THAN SMOKE POINTS

Most sautéing falls below an oil's smoke point, so you won't see smoke unless the pan gets too hot. (An exception: When searing food in a very hot skillet, wisps of smoke indicate that it's time to cook.) It's more important to be vigilant of vigorous smoking—if you see it, immediately remove the pan from the heat and let it cool. Dispose of the oil, wipe the pan clean, and start again.

BAKING BENEFITS

Butter is traditional in baking, but in many applications, oil can improve flavor and texture.

TENDERNESS: Oil is better than butter at preventing too much gluten development. Many recipes that require tenderness but not added flavor, such as quick breads, rely on vegetable oil.

MOISTURE: When butter's high water content evaporates in the oven, it can leave baked goods dry. A combination of butter and vegetable oil makes some items, like cakes, moister than using all butter.

CLEAN TASTE: While butter adds its own rich flavor, neutral-tasting oil allows other flavors to come to the fore.

FRYING KNOW-HOW

When deep-frying food in batches in which the oil will be heated for longer than 15 minutes, we may seek out peanut oil. But for shallow frying, which happens at a lower temperature, vegetable oil blend is our go-to.

SHALLOW VERSUS DEEP FRYING

We reserve shallow frying, in which the oil reaches only partway up the food, for bulky items like breaded cutlets or bone-in chicken pieces. These foods cook slowly enough that they can be browned in the oil one side at a time without risk of overcooking. With deep frying, food is completely submerged in the oil, which enables smaller, quick-cooking items like French fries to brown on all sides simultaneously.

OIL AMOUNT

When shallow-frying, make sure the oil reaches halfway up the sides of the food; otherwise, you'll end up with a pale band around the exterior. When deep-frying, you'll need at least 1 quart of oil to completely cover the food—but don't fill the pot more than half full to avoid splattering.

SHALLOW FRYING

DEEP FRYING

MONITOR THE TEMPERATURE

When deep-frying, use a clip-on candy/deep-fry thermometer to guarantee that the oil reaches—and remains at—the target temperature. Don't let the thermometer touch the bottom or sides of the pot; if it does, you may get a false reading.

INCLUDE SOME "RECYCLED" OIL

When deep-frying, the first batch is often paler and less crisp than those that follow. But by mixing strained, previously used frying oil into fresh oil, you can get golden, crispy results from the start. Why? Oil that's already been exposed to heat produces surfactants that can penetrate the water barrier that surrounds food as it fries. This increased contact promotes browning and a nice crust. We use a 1:5 ratio of used oil to fresh.

DRESSING GUIDELINES

A premium extra-virgin olive oil is typically our first choice in vinaigrettes.

GET THE RATIO RIGHT

For a vibrant but balanced dressing, we prefer a 3:1 ratio of oil to vinegar.

AVOID MOTORIZED MIXING

Never emulsify extra-virgin olive oil in a blender or food processor. The whirring blades will break the oil into very small droplets, releasing bitter-tasting compounds into the mix. (Note: In recipes that contain lots of other robust flavors, such as pesto, we have found that any bitter taste goes unnoticed.)

MIX IN A LITTLE MAYO OR MUSTARD

Mayonnaise and mustard both contain emulsifying agents that keep dressing stable for longer. Add ½ teaspoon of mayonnaise or mustard for every 3 tablespoons of oil and 1 tablespoon of vinegar.

ESSENTIAL SAUCES FOR THE MODERN COOK

There's a reason certain sauces never go out of style. A great sauce can transform a dish, adding intense flavor and pulling all the elements into balance. Here's how we updated some of the classics.

Red Wine Pan Sauce
MAKES ½ CUP

The beauty of a pan sauce is that it needs only a few ingredients and a little bit of time to taste deeply savory. The key is incorporating the browned bits (or fond) left in the pan after searing the protein by dissolving them with wine. Red wine pan sauce's best mates are steaks and chops.

WHAT CAN GO WRONG: The wine can make the sauce taste harsh and boozy.

HOW WE FIXED IT: We reduce the wine separately from the broth. Wine and broth reduced together had as much as eight times more alcohol than wine reduced on its own. Less booziness allows more complex flavors to come to the fore. A medium-bodied fruity blend, such as a Côtes du Rhône, works well here.

1 **large shallot, minced**
½ **cup red wine**
¾ **cup chicken broth**
2 **teaspoons packed brown sugar**
3 **tablespoons unsalted butter, cut into 3 pieces and chilled**
1 **teaspoon minced fresh rosemary**
¼ **teaspoon balsamic vinegar**
Salt and pepper

Pour off all but 2 teaspoons fat from pan used to cook meat. Add shallot to pan and cook over medium-high heat, stirring frequently, until softened, 1 to 2 minutes. Add wine and simmer rapidly, scraping up any browned bits, until liquid is reduced to glaze, about 30 seconds. Stir in broth and sugar and simmer until reduced to ⅓ cup, 4 to 6 minutes. Stir in any accumulated meat juices. Off heat, whisk in butter, 1 piece at a time, until melted and sauce is thickened and glossy. Stir in rosemary and vinegar. Season with salt and pepper to taste, spoon over meat, and serve.

White Wine Pan Sauce
MAKES ½ CUP

Lighter and brighter than its red wine sibling, white wine pan sauce makes plain pan-seared chicken breasts or pork tenderloin seem special.

WHAT CAN GO WRONG: As with red wine pan sauce, it can taste boozy and flat.

HOW WE FIXED IT: We use our Red Wine Pan Sauce method, reducing the wine before we add the broth. Sauvignon Blanc is best for this sauce, but dry vermouth is a close second—and it has a longer shelf life.

1 **large shallot, minced**
2 **garlic cloves, minced**
½ **cup dry white wine**
¾ **cup chicken broth**
3 **tablespoons unsalted butter, cut into 3 pieces and chilled**
1 **teaspoon minced fresh thyme**
¼ **teaspoon white wine vinegar**
Salt and pepper

Pour off all but 2 teaspoons fat from pan used to cook meat. Add shallot and garlic to pan and cook over medium heat, stirring frequently, until softened, 1 to 2 minutes. Add wine and simmer rapidly, scraping up any browned bits, until liquid is reduced to glaze, about 30 seconds. Stir in broth and simmer until reduced to ⅓ cup, 4 to 6 minutes. Stir in any accumulated meat juices. Off heat, whisk in butter, 1 piece at a time, until melted and sauce is thickened and glossy. Stir in thyme and vinegar. Season with salt and pepper to taste, spoon over meat, and serve.

Choose the right wine.

Reduce it separately.

Combine yolks and butter first.

Hollandaise
MAKES ABOUT 2 CUPS

This lush, lemony butter sauce isn't just for eggs Benedict. It also works well with steamed vegetables, steak, crab cakes, and roasted potatoes.

WHAT CAN GO WRONG: Hollandaise is prone to break quickly. This is because its emulsion—the dispersal of tiny fat droplets in water, held in place by the yolks—is weak.

HOW WE FIXED IT: We rearranged the usual order of operations. Instead of combining the egg yolks with water from the start, we whisk the yolks with butter and then introduce water. The resulting sauce is so stable, it can be chilled and reheated.

12 **tablespoons unsalted butter, softened**
6 **large egg yolks**
½ **cup boiling water**
2 **teaspoons lemon juice**
⅛ **teaspoon cayenne pepper**
Salt

Whisk butter and egg yolks together in large heatproof bowl set over medium saucepan filled with ½ inch barely simmering water, making sure that water does not touch bottom of bowl. Slowly add boiling water (for accuracy, bring 1 cup to a boil and then measure ½ cup) and cook, whisking constantly, until thickened and sauce registers 160 degrees, 7 to 10 minutes. Off heat, stir in lemon juice and cayenne. Season with salt to taste. Serve.

TO MAKE AHEAD: Hollandaise can be refrigerated for up to 3 days. Microwave at 50 percent power, stirring every 10 seconds, until heated through, about 1 minute.

Beurre Blanc
MAKES ABOUT ⅔ CUP

Use this delicately flavored butter sauce to add richness to simply prepared fish, shellfish, chicken, and vegetables.

WHAT CAN GO WRONG: Beurre blanc is a water-in-fat emulsion that breaks easily.

HOW WE FIXED IT: We add cream to stabilize the emulsion.

3 tablespoons dry white wine

2 tablespoons white wine vinegar

1 small shallot, minced

   Pinch salt

1 tablespoon heavy cream

8 tablespoons unsalted butter, cut into 8 pieces and chilled

Bring wine, vinegar, shallot, and salt to boil in small saucepan over medium-high heat. Reduce heat to medium-low and simmer until reduced by two-thirds, about 5 minutes. Whisk in cream. Add butter, 1 piece at a time, whisking vigorously after each addition until butter is incorporated and forms thick, pale yellow sauce, 30 to 60 seconds. Remove pan from heat and serve.

Aïoli
MAKES ABOUT ¾ CUP

This garlicky mayonnaise adds kick to sandwiches, vegetables, and seafood.

WHAT CAN GO WRONG: The sauce can taste overly harsh and bitter.

HOW WE FIXED IT: We minced the garlic to a paste for full, even garlic flavor. A mix of oils leads to clean flavor.

2 large egg yolks

4 teaspoons lemon juice

1 garlic clove, minced to paste

   Salt and white pepper

⅛ teaspoon sugar

½ cup vegetable oil

¼ cup extra-virgin olive oil

In large bowl, combine egg yolks, lemon juice, garlic, ¼ teaspoon salt, and sugar. Whisking constantly, very slowly drizzle oils into egg mixture until thick and creamy. Season with salt and pepper to taste.

TO MAKE AHEAD: Aïoli can be refrigerated for up to 3 days.

Basil Pesto
MAKES ¾ CUP; ENOUGH FOR 1 POUND PASTA

Pesto's most familiar application is dressing pasta, but its bright, nutty flavor can enliven soups and stews, chicken, sandwiches, and steamed potatoes.

WHAT CAN GO WRONG: The sharpness of raw garlic can overpower more delicate, aromatic basil. The basil also quickly turns a drab, unappealing dark green.

HOW WE FIXED IT: To mellow the garlic's flavor, we toast the whole, unpeeled cloves in a dry skillet. A small amount of parsley helps keep the pesto green. Pounding the herbs before pureeing them releases more of their flavorful oils so that they can stand up to the garlic.

3 garlic cloves, unpeeled

2 cups fresh basil leaves

2 tablespoons fresh parsley leaves

7 tablespoons extra-virgin olive oil

¼ cup pine nuts, toasted

   Salt and pepper

¼ cup finely grated Parmesan or Pecorino Romano cheese

1. Toast garlic in a heavy 8-inch skillet over medium heat, shaking pan occasionally, until fragrant and color of cloves deepens slightly, about 7 minutes. Let garlic cool slightly, then peel and chop.

2. Place basil and parsley in heavy-duty 1-gallon zipper-lock bag. Pound bag with flat side of meat pounder or rolling pin until all leaves are bruised.

3. Process oil, pine nuts, ½ teaspoon salt, garlic, and herbs in food processor until smooth, scraping down sides of bowl as needed, about 1 minute. Stir in Parmesan and season with salt and pepper to taste.

TO MAKE AHEAD: Pesto can be covered with thin layer of oil (1 to 2 tablespoons) and refrigerated for up to 4 days or frozen for up to 1 month.

Toast garlic; add parsley.

Process sauce with toasted bread.

Salsa Verde
MAKES 1½ CUPS

This green sauce boasts a fresh grassy taste along with tangy, garlicky, flavor. Use it on steak, chicken, pork, or shrimp.

WHAT CAN GO WRONG: With so many assertive flavors in the mix, the sauce can come on too strong, and it separates easily.

HOW WE FIXED IT: We add an unusual ingredient—bread—and process it with the oil and lemon juice before adding the other ingredients. Bread mellows the assertive flavors and its starches stabilize the emulsified sauce by increasing its viscosity as well as absorbing the lemon juice so it doesn't separate from the oil.

2 slices hearty white sandwich bread

1 cup extra-virgin olive oil

¼ cup lemon juice (2 lemons)

4 cups fresh parsley leaves

4 anchovy fillets, rinsed

4 tablespoons capers, rinsed

1 garlic clove, minced

¼ teaspoon salt

Toast bread in toaster at lowest setting until surface is dry but not browned, about 15 seconds. Remove crusts and cut bread into rough ½-inch pieces (you should have about 1½ cups). Process bread pieces, oil, and lemon juice in food processor until smooth, about 10 seconds. Add parsley, anchovies, capers, garlic, and salt. Pulse until mixture is finely chopped (mixture should not be smooth), about 5 pulses, scraping down sides of bowl with rubber spatula after 3 pulses. Transfer mixture to small bowl before serving.

TO MAKE AHEAD: Salsa verde can be refrigerated for up to 2 days. Bring to room temperature and stir to recombine before serving.

HOW TO GRILL A GREAT STEAK

Knowing a few methods for pretreating steaks—and a universal grilling technique—will allow you to produce great results from a variety of cuts.

SAVVY SHOPPING

INSPECT THE MEAT

- Buy bright red or pink steaks with fine streaks (not clumps) of pure white intramuscular fat. Dark red/purple meat indicates an older, tougher animal.

- Juices should be in the meat, not in the package. The latter, known as purge, may be a sign of botched freezing, and the meat will cook up dry and cottony.

"ORGANIC" MEANS SOMETHING; "NATURAL" DOESN'T

- Organic is a government term that means the meat is antibiotic-free, has no added hormones, and that the animal ate an organic diet. Natural is simply advertising.

GRASS-FED MAY NOT BE WORTH THE MONEY

- Grass-fed steaks can cost at least twice as much as the same grain-fed cuts, but when we tasted the two styles in strip and rib-eye steaks, we generally found the flavor differences between them to be negligible. Save your money for premium cuts.

PREMIUM STEAKS

STRIP STEAK

ALTERNATIVE NAMES: Top loin, shell, sirloin strip, Kansas City strip, New York strip

TENDERNESS: ★★★

FLAVOR: ★★★

RIB EYE

ALTERNATIVE NAMES: Spencer steak (West Coast), Delmonico steak (East Coast)

TENDERNESS: ★★★

FLAVOR: ★★★

T-BONE

TENDERNESS: ★★★

FLAVOR: ★★★

BEFORE GRILLING: SEASON AND THEN REST OR FREEZE

Inherently flavorful and tender, premium cuts need little more than salt and pepper. That said, applying either of these simple techniques will make a great steak even better.

WHEN TIME ALLOWS: SALT AND REST

Prolonged salting will tenderize, season, and dry out the meat's surface to encourage better browning.

Two hours before grilling, pat the steaks dry, season them with 1½ teaspoons of kosher salt per pound of meat, and let them rest in the fridge.

WHEN TIME IS SHORT: RUB AND FREEZE

Coating steaks with a mixture of cornstarch and salt and freezing them briefly helps evaporate surface moisture—crucial for achieving a substantial crust.

For every pound of steak, combine 1½ teaspoons of kosher salt and ¾ teaspoon of cornstarch. Apply a thin coat of the rub all over the steaks' exteriors. Freeze the meat on a wire rack set in a rimmed baking sheet for 30 minutes.

EVERYDAY STEAKS

FLANK STEAK

ALTERNATIVE NAME: Jiffy steak

TENDERNESS: ★

FLAVOR: ★★★

FLAP MEAT SIRLOIN STEAK

ALTERNATIVE NAMES: Sirloin tips, flap meat, steak tips

TENDERNESS: ★★

FLAVOR: ★★★

BONELESS SHELL SIRLOIN

ALTERNATIVE NAMES: Top butt, butt steak, top sirloin butt, top sirloin steak, center-cut roast

TENDERNESS: ★★

FLAVOR: ★★

BEFORE GRILLING: MARINATE OR RUB

Applied properly, a marinade or spice rub will boost flavor and tenderness in less expensive cuts. Using plenty of salt (or a salty liquid like soy sauce) increases juiciness by pulling moisture into the meat.

SCORE MEAT BEFORE MARINATING OR RUBBING

Cutting crosshatch slits (1/16 inch deep) on both sides of the meat allows seasonings to penetrate faster and gives marinades or rubs a strong foothold.

MIX UP AN EFFECTIVE MARINADE

Prepare a soy-based marinade, reserving ¼ cup. Marinate scored steaks in a 1-gallon zipper-lock bag for 1 hour in the refrigerator, flipping them after 30 minutes. Discard the bag and the marinade, pat the steaks dry, and grill. Slice the grilled, rested steaks and toss the slices in the reserved marinade to further boost their flavor.

APPLY A SALTY SPICE RUB

Briefly toast whole spices (use 2 to 3 tablespoons per pound of meat) in a dry skillet. Grind spices, add 1½ teaspoons of kosher salt per pound of meat, and press the rub onto dry, scored steaks. Refrigerate the steaks for 2 hours. Just before grilling, mist the steaks with vegetable oil spray to help the rub cling and encourage the spices' fat-soluble compounds to "bloom" on the grill.

BUILD A HALF-GRILL FIRE

Any steak can be grilled by creating a hotter side for quickly developing the crust and, if needed, a cooler side to finish cooking over gentle radiating heat.

CHARCOAL SETUP

Open bottom vent completely. Light large chimney starter filled with charcoal briquettes (6 quarts). When top coals are partially covered with ash, pour evenly over half of grill. Set cooking grate in place, cover, and open lid vent completely. Heat grill until hot, about 5 minutes.

GAS SETUP

Turn all burners to high, cover, and heat grill until hot, about 15 minutes. Leave primary burner on high and turn off other burner(s).

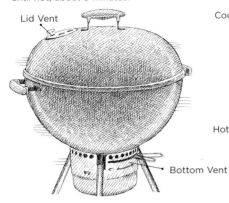

Lid Vent

Bottom Vent

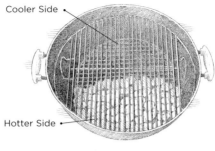

Cooler Side

Hotter Side

Clean and oil the cooking grates for both charcoal and gas grills after the grill is hot but before placing the steaks.

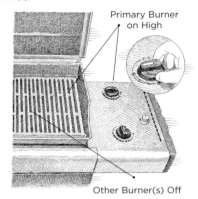

Primary Burner on High

Other Burner(s) Off

FOOLPROOF GRILLING METHOD

1. SEAR AND FLIP: Grill steaks over hotter side, without moving them, for 2 to 4 minutes. Once first side is well browned, flip steaks and cook 2 to 4 minutes longer.

2. TAKE TEMPERATURE: Lift each steak off grill and insert thermometer through its side to check for desired doneness: rare (120 degrees), medium-rare (125 degrees), or medium (135 degrees).

3. TRANSFER IF NECESSARY: Drag any unfinished steaks to cooler side of grill to finish cooking.

TIP: Steaks less than 1 inch thick may cook to the desired temperature during the initial sear.

4. REST: To allow some expelled juices to move back in to the meat, let steaks rest on wire rack set in rimmed baking sheet (to keep crust dry) loosely covered with aluminum foil for about 10 minutes.

5. SLICE: Using sharp chef's knife, slice tougher steaks (flank, sirloin steak tips, and boneless shell sirloin) against grain into thin pieces to make them seem more tender.

TOPPINGS FOR TOP STEAKS

Premium steaks don't need much adornment. Try a sprinkle of flake sea salt (such as Maldon), the large crystals of which add a delicate crunch to the meat's crust. We also like the Tuscan tradition of finishing grilled T-bone or porterhouse steaks with a drizzle of high-quality extra-virgin olive oil and a squeeze of fresh lemon juice. Alternatively, you can add richness and more assertive flavor to any type of plain grilled steak by topping it with a compound butter.

SHALLOT-HERB BUTTER

MAKES ABOUT ½ CUP; ENOUGH FOR 3 POUNDS STEAK

- 4 **tablespoons unsalted butter, softened**
- 2 **tablespoons minced shallot**
- 2 **tablespoons minced fresh parsley**
- 1 **garlic clove, minced**
- ¼ **teaspoon salt**
- ¼ **teaspoon pepper**

Combine all ingredients in medium bowl. Divide butter evenly among steaks and serve.

SUPERIOR STEAK KNIVES

Our favorite steak knives, the six-piece **Victorinox Rosewood Straight Edge Steak Knife Set** ($109.99), feature 4¾-inch blades that are exceptionally sharp and nimble, not to mention comfortable (and handsome) wood handles.

BEST BLADES
Supersharp straight-edge steak knives from Victorinox slice through even tough cuts with ease.

CHICKEN BROTH

Chicken broth is an ultraversatile ingredient in savory dishes: we use it daily in the test kitchen. When homemade broth isn't an option, store-bought broth can be an easy, reliable alternative. We chose 10 widely available broths (eight liquids and two concentrates) with sodium levels between 400 mg and 700 mg: any less makes for a bland broth, any more and it becomes too salty when reduced. We tasted each broth plain, in risotto, and in gravy. Surprisingly, higher protein content (and therefore a higher ratio of meat to water) didn't mean better chicken flavor. In fact, one of our favorite broths was a concentrate with only 1 g of protein per cup, which relied on a combination of glutamates and nucleotides to create savory qualities. Our top choice, however, was a boxed liquid, which tasters praised for its rich, meaty flavor. Chicken broths are listed in order of preference.

RECOMMENDED

SWANSON Chicken Stock
PRICE: $3.19 for 3 cups ($1.06 per cup)
SODIUM: 510 mg PROTEIN: 4 g
INGREDIENTS: Chicken stock; contains less than 2%: sea salt, dextrose, carrots, cabbage, onions, celery, celery leaves, salt, parsley
COMMENTS: Unlike most of the other liquid broths in our lineup, this one achieved "rich," "meaty" flavor, and did so the old-fashioned way—with a relatively high percentage of meat-based protein. The only problem: Some tasters thought it came across as "beefy" or even "mushroomy," not chicken-y.

BETTER THAN BOUILLON Chicken Base
PRICE: $5.99 for 8-oz jar that makes 38 cups ($0.16 per cup) BEST BUY
SODIUM: 680 mg PROTEIN: 1 g
INGREDIENTS: Chicken meat including natural chicken juices, salt, sugar, corn syrup solids, chicken fat, hydrolyzed soy protein, dried whey (milk), flavoring, disodium inosinate, guanylate, turmeric
COMMENTS: By adding nucleotides to its glutamate-rich base, this brand produced a remarkably "savory" broth, despite the fact that it contains very little protein. It's also by far the cheapest broth we tasted, and once opened it lasts for two years in the fridge. However, this product's high sodium content pushed our upper limits for saltiness, so we had to dial back the company's prescribed ratio of concentrate to water.

RECOMMENDED WITH RESERVATIONS

KNORR Homestyle Stock Reduced Sodium Chicken
PRICE: $3.99 for 4 tubs that make 3.5 cups each, 14 cups total ($0.29 per cup)
SODIUM: 600 mg PROTEIN: 0 g
INGREDIENTS: Water, maltodextrin (corn), salt, palm oil, autolyzed yeast extract, sea salt, sugar, carrots, lactic acid, chicken fat, leeks, potato starch, xanthan gum, garlic, chicken powder (with rosemary extract to protect quality), parsley, natural flavor, malic acid, locust bean gum, thiamin hydrochloride, disodium guanylate, disodium inosinate, disodium phosphate, glycerin, ascorbic acid, caramel color, succinic acid, spice, mustard oil, beta carotene (for color), coconut oil, sulfur dioxide (used to protect quality)
COMMENTS: This concentrate's "meaty" depth is built on the same flavor-boosting combination of glutamates and nucleotides as Better Than Bouillon—and it fared quite well as straight broth. But 32 ingredients later, this concentrate fell short on actual chicken flavor. It was also sweet like "canned pumpkin" when reduced.

RECOMMENDED WITH RESERVATIONS *(continued)*

SWANSON Natural Goodness Chicken Broth
PRICE: $2.99 for 4 cups ($0.75 per cup)
SODIUM: 570 mg PROTEIN: 2 g
INGREDIENTS: Chicken stock; contains less than 2%: salt, flavoring, yeast extract, carrot juice concentrate, celery juice concentrate, onion juice concentrate
COMMENTS: This broth was "not super-meaty;" it was like "sweet squash" when reduced in gravy. No surprise: It was average for salt and contains the most sugar per serving, carrot juice being the likely culprit.

PROGRESSO Reduced Sodium Chicken Broth
PRICE: $2.79 for 4 cups ($0.70 per cup)
SODIUM: 560 mg PROTEIN: 3 g
INGREDIENTS: Chicken broth, salt, sugar, natural flavor, carrot puree, yeast extract
COMMENTS: Off-notes detracted from the otherwise "good chicken flavor" of this broth. Some of us called out a "sour" lemony taste, while others fingered "sweet," "floral," "gingery," and even "minty" flavors that were out of place in chicken broth.

NOT RECOMMENDED

COLLEGE INN Light & Fat Free Chicken Broth, 50% Less Sodium
PRICE: $2.59 for 4 cups ($0.65 per cup)
SODIUM: 450 mg PROTEIN: 1 g
INGREDIENTS: Chicken broth, salt, dextrose, natural flavor, yeast extract, onion juice concentrate, carrot and carrot juice concentrate
COMMENTS: This "weak" broth "could be dishwater," according to one taster. "Chicken of any kind is a stretch," wrote another. This makes sense considering that the broth has very little protein, which suggests that not much chicken was used in production. Instead, "vegetal" flavors came to the forefront. This product has the second lowest amount of sodium and low glutamate levels. At press time, we learned that the company was in the process of repackaging this product.

PACIFIC Organic Free Range Chicken Broth
PRICE: $4.59 for 4 cups ($1.15 per cup)
SODIUM: 570 mg PROTEIN: 1 g
INGREDIENTS: Organic chicken broth, organic chicken flavor, sea salt, organic cane sugar, organic onion powder, organic turmeric extract, organic rosemary extract
COMMENTS: This was some seriously funky broth. For one thing, its taste was "not chicken-y . . . or meaty at all." Worse, "sour, vegetal" notes dominated, not to mention other "really odd" flavors reminiscent of "old Chinese buffet."

SUPERMARKET BACON

Good bacon is meaty, smoky without tasting like an ashtray, salty without imitating a salt lick, and sweet without being cloying—what industry experts call "balanced bacon flavor." We rounded up thick-cut and traditional slices of nationally available supermarket bacons. Tasters took off points for strips that were too fatty, and panned the brand that used vaporized smoke instead of traditional smoking techniques. Thick strips with high ratios of protein to fat, which contributed to more complex flavor, consistently topped tasters' rankings. Their "substantial," "crisp" texture also won us over. Bacons are listed in order of preference.

HIGHLY RECOMMENDED

FARMLAND Thick Sliced Bacon
PRICE: $7.99 for 1½ lb ($0.33 per oz)
THICKNESS: ⅛ in SALT: 2.17 g PROTEIN: 11.36 g FAT: 36.88 g

COMMENTS: This thick strip was also one of the meatiest, with saltiness offset by sweetness, all combining to deliver bacon balance. Tasters described it as "a good meaty slice" that was "sweet," "smoky, porky, and salty."

PLUMROSE Premium Thick Sliced Bacon
PRICE: $5.99 for 1 lb ($0.37 per oz)
THICKNESS: ⅛ in SALT: 1.95 g PROTEIN: 13.96 g FAT: 30.48 g

COMMENTS: With one of the highest amounts of protein, this "substantially meaty" bacon was "pleasantly smoky," "with very little fat." Plumrose is the only brand cured with brown sugar, which contributed to its "deeply browned, Maillard flavor."

RECOMMENDED

WRIGHT Naturally Hickory Smoked Bacon
PRICE: $7.48 for 1½ lb ($0.31 per oz)
THICKNESS: ⅛ in SALT: 1.28 g PROTEIN: 11.42 g FAT: 35.37 g

COMMENTS: This thick-cut bacon was "good all around," delivering "great smoky flavor with enough salt and sweet." Other tasters rated it the smokiest in the lineup and also praised its "meaty" taste and "substantial" texture.

WELLSHIRE FARMS Black Forest Dry Rubbed Salt Cured Bacon
PRICE: $8.99 for 18 oz ($0.50 per oz)
THICKNESS: ⅛ in SALT: 1.2 g PROTEIN: 11.45 g FAT: 41.92 g

COMMENTS: This "substantial" thick-cut slice, the only bacon we tasted that was dry cured, was "smoky, sweet, salty, meaty—the four basic bacon food groups!" Others compared its sweetness with "barbecued brisket" or "burnt ends," with its "porky, sweet-but-not-too-sweet" taste.

OSCAR MAYER Naturally Hardwood Smoked Thick Cut Bacon
PRICE: $7.49 for 1 lb ($0.47 per oz)
THICKNESS: ⅛ in SALT: 1.67 g PROTEIN: 12.86 g FAT: 38.28 g

COMMENTS: The thick version of classic Oscar Mayer bacon ranked in the middle of the pack for smokiness, just ahead of its thinner companion product. It was "deeply porky" and "meaty"—"a very nice, satisfying slice."

RECOMMENDED (continued)

OSCAR MAYER Naturally Hardwood Smoked Bacon
PRICE: $7.49 for 1 lb ($0.47 per oz)
THICKNESS: ⅒ in SALT: 1.60 g PROTEIN: 13.24 g FAT: 37.86 g

COMMENTS: With "a nice ratio of fat to lean meat," this regular-sliced strip cooked up "smoky" and "sweet," and tasted "not bad for thin bacon," as one taster deemed it. "Perfect in terms of crispness," summed up another.

HORMEL Black Label Bacon
PRICE: $6.99 for 1 lb ($0.44 per oz)
THICKNESS: ⅟₁₁ in SALT: 1.58 g PROTEIN: 10.85 g FAT: 43.39 g

COMMENTS: Some found this bacon—one of two in our lineup that was sprayed with vaporized liquid smoke rather than dry smoked—"leathery" and "not very smoky." Others deemed it "good" and "decently meaty."

RECOMMENDED WITH RESERVATIONS

HORMEL Black Label Thick Cut Bacon
PRICE: $6.99 for 1 lb ($0.44 per oz)
THICKNESS: ⅛ in SALT: 2.13 g PROTEIN: 10.49 g FAT: 47.43 g

COMMENTS: Ranked low for smokiness (applied as vaporized liquid smoke) and sweetness, this "fatty" thick-cut bacon tasted "grilled rather than smoky." A few tasters praised its "good pork flavor," but most said that it lacked taste and was "chewy" rather than crisp.

NOT RECOMMENDED

PLUMROSE Premium Sliced Bacon
PRICE: $5.49 for 1 lb ($0.34 per oz)
THICKNESS: ⅟₁₅ in SALT: 2.07 g PROTEIN: 12.44 g FAT: 32.16 g

COMMENTS: Sliced considerably thinner than most of the other regular-sliced strips, this "blah" bacon had so little smoke flavor that one taster likened its taste to that of "lunch meat." At best, its flavor was "middle-of-the-road."

DARK CHOCOLATE

Finding a great snacking chocolate is easy, but when cooking, the type of chocolate can make or break a dessert. To find an everyday chocolate that would work for all purposes, we gathered nine bars that contained at least 35 percent cacao (the FDA standard for the "bittersweet" or "semisweet" label). We tasted each bar plain, in brownies, and in pots de crème. Products with more than 50 percent sugar sank to the bottom of the ratings for their barely-there chocolate flavor, while bars with high levels of cocoa solids earned accolades from tasters for their intensity and complexity. There was a tipping point though: bars with the highest percentage of cocoa solids fared less well in creamy applications. Chocolates are listed in order of preference.

HIGHLY RECOMMENDED

GHIRARDELLI 60 Percent Cacao Bittersweet Chocolate Premium Baking Bar
PRICE: $2.99 for 4 oz ($0.75 per oz)
CACAO PERCENTAGE: about 60% COCOA SOLIDS: about 22%
SUGAR: 16 g (38%) FAT: 16 g (38%)

COMMENTS: This bar rated the highest for eating plain, with a complex flavor that combined the tart fruitiness of cherries and wine with a slight smokiness. Its high—but not too high—level of cocoa solids made this bar easy to work with in creamy desserts, turning out exceptionally "satiny, gorgeous" pots de crème with "dark, bold" flavor that "screams chocolate."

CALLEBAUT Intense Dark Chocolate, L-60-40NV
PRICE: $8.39 for 1.05 lb ($0.50 per oz)
CACAO PERCENTAGE: about 60% COCOA SOLIDS: about 30%
SUGAR: 15.12 g (36%) FAT: 12.6 g (30%)

COMMENTS: Our previous winner was again "rich," "intense," and "earthy," with notes of "coffee," "a balanced bitterness," and "just the right amount of sweetness"—attributes that made their way into the brownies. With a high level of cocoa solids, this product sometimes made pots de crème that were a bit grainy.

RECOMMENDED

DOVE Silky Smooth Dark Chocolate
PRICE: $3.20 for 3.3 oz ($0.97 per oz)
CACAO PERCENTAGE: about 55% COCOA SOLIDS: about 22%
SUGAR: 19 g (45%) FAT: 14 g (33%)

COMMENTS: This fudgy mass-market bar lacked bitterness but still offered pleasing complexity: boozy notes of Kahlúa and rum with a "nutty, mocha flavor." But a few tasters found it too sweet in desserts—more "like a candy bar" than like baking chocolate. It was notably smooth, with tasters calling it "lush" and "melt-in-your-mouth."

SCHARFFEN BERGER Semisweet Fine Artisan Dark Chocolate
PRICE: $4.29 for 3 oz ($1.43 per oz)
CACAO PERCENTAGE: about 62% COCOA SOLIDS: about 25%
SUGAR: 15.6 g (37%) FAT: 15.6 g (37%)

COMMENTS: Many detected "intense" grown-up flavors in this chocolate, which boasted hints of berry and a "background smokiness." Others found it "pleasant but generic," impressions that carried over to brownies and pots de crème.

RECOMMENDED WITH RESERVATIONS

BAKER'S Bittersweet Baking Chocolate Squares
PRICE: $4.99 for 6 oz ($0.83 per oz)
CACAO PERCENTAGE: about 66% COCOA SOLIDS: about 30%
SUGAR: 15 g (36%) FAT: 15 g (36%)

COMMENTS: In both the plain and the brownie tastings, this basic supermarket product was a hit with tasters, earning praise for a "rich," "intense" chocolate flavor that had notes of coconut and coffee. But with high levels of cocoa solids, it consistently made "gritty" pots de crème.

GHIRARDELLI Semi-Sweet Chocolate Premium Baking Bar
PRICE: $2.99 for 4 oz ($0.75 per oz)
CACAO PERCENTAGE: about 52% COCOA SOLIDS: about 19%
SUGAR: 20 g (48%) FAT: 14 g (33%)

COMMENTS: The pleasing bitter and dried fruit flavors in this bar were muted by a milky sweetness. This product was "enjoyable" in brownies, but with low cocoa solids, it made loose pots de crème.

NOT RECOMMENDED

HERSHEY'S Semi-Sweet Chocolate Baking Bar
PRICE: $2.49 for 4 oz ($0.62 per oz)
CACAO PERCENTAGE: about 42% COCOA SOLIDS: about 13%
SUGAR: 24 g (57%) FAT: 12 g (29%)
COMMENTS: Far too sweet and milky, this high-sugar, very low

cocoa solids bar was "like a Tootsie Roll." Its strong notes of caramel and butterscotch overwhelmed its feeble chocolate flavor; the brownies "might as well be blondies," one taster said. The pots de crème were runny.

HERSHEY'S Special Dark Chocolate Bar
PRICE: $2.19 for 4.25 oz ($0.52 per oz)
CACAO PERCENTAGE: about 45% COCOA SOLIDS: about 14%
SUGAR: 21 g (50%) FAT: 13.2 g (31%)
COMMENTS: Despite its name, this bar was too much like milk chocolate, a "cream bomb" with just a touch of caramel and

roasted nuts. Texturally, it was "bendy," with "no snap." It made "loose and runny" pots de crème and its brownies rated "on the bland side."

NESTLÉ Semi-Sweet Baking Chocolate Bar
PRICE: $3.31 for 4 oz ($0.83 per oz)
CACAO PERCENTAGE: about 43% COCOA SOLIDS: about 14%
SUGAR: 24 g (57%) FAT: 12 g (29%)

COMMENTS: Sampled plain, this bar was flat-out sweet, like "cheap Halloween candy." Brownies were its best application, though it was still overly sugary and weak on chocolate flavor. In pots de crème it was "runny, like bad pudding."

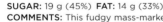

SWISS CHEESE

A pockmarked wedge of Swiss may be instantly recognizable as the icon of "cheese," but it's rarely celebrated for its flavor—at least here in the U.S. But genuine Swiss cheese, also known as Emmentaler, can boast nuanced, nutty flavors. We sampled cheeses from a wide spectrum of price points and presentations (sliced or in wedges) and tasted them plain and in grilled cheese sandwiches. Served plain at room temperature, tasters preferred the savory flavors of long-aged cheeses over the rubbery, bland younger cheeses. But in grilled cheese sandwiches, tasters panned the longest-aged wedges for their unpleasant flavors. However, heat improved the younger cheeses: Not only did most of them melt beautifully but several young cheeses suddenly boasted "nutty tang." We recommend shopping for Swiss with a purpose: For heated applications, some younger cheeses are excellent options. For cheese plates, go for aged raw-milk cheeses. Cheeses are listed in order of preference.

HIGHLY RECOMMENDED FOR CHEESE PLATE ONLY

EDELWEISS CREAMERY Emmentaler Switzerland Swiss Cheese
PRICE: $12.99 for 1¼ lb ($0.65 per oz)
AGED: Up to 12 months
STYLE: Raw milk, American-made
SODIUM: 60 mg per oz
COMMENTS: We think that Wisconsin-based Edelweiss Creamery, which emulates traditional Swiss methods including the use of copper vats for flavor development, makes a better Swiss cheese than the Swiss—and for a lot less money. This cheese's "grassy" nuttiness makes it worth mail-ordering, but don't melt it. Those flavors turned "funky" in grilled cheese.

EMMI Kaltbach Cave-Aged Emmentaler Switzerland AOC
PRICE: $12.99 for 8 oz ($1.62 per oz)
AGED: 12 to 18 months
STYLE: Raw milk, Swiss import
SODIUM: 50 mg per oz
COMMENTS: The rich "savory," "almost gamy" flavors that make this cave-aged raw-milk Swiss import eminently worthy of a cheese plate (and command a high price tag) also render it unsuitable for melting. It made for an "oily" grilled cheese with a "lingering metallic taste."

RECOMMENDED FOR CHEESE PLATE AND COOKING

EMMI Emmentaler Cheese AOC
PRICE: $18.99 for 1 lb ($1.19 per oz)
AGED: 120 days (4 months)
STYLE: Raw milk, Swiss import
SODIUM: 50 mg per oz
COMMENTS: Thanks to its relative youth and raw-milk base, this Swiss import offered the best of both worlds: a texture that turned "creamy" when melted in a grilled cheese and enough "pleasantly pungent" character for eating out of hand.

RECOMMENDED FOR COOKING ONLY

BOAR'S HEAD Gold Label Switzerland Swiss Cheese
PRICE: $9.75 for 1 lb ($0.61 per oz)
AGED: More than 120 days
STYLE: Pasteurized milk, Swiss import
SODIUM: 60 mg per oz
COMMENTS: Its "mild nutty flavor" made tasters dub this product a "generic Swiss" straight out of the package, but it soared to the top of the heap in grilled cheese, where it boasted a "great mineral" taste in addition to a "smooth" texture.

NORSELAND Jarlsberg
PRICE: $6.99 for 1 lb ($0.44 per oz)
AGED: 60 days
STYLE: Pasteurized milk, Norwegian import
SODIUM: 180 mg per oz
COMMENTS: This Norwegian version of Swiss shared the relatively bland flavor profile of many of the other cheeses in the lineup, but heat drew out its "nicely salty" flavor (Jarlsberg typically contains more sodium than other Swiss-style cheeses) and also turned it pleasantly "gooey."

NOT RECOMMENDED

KRAFT Natural Cheese Big Slice Swiss
PRICE: $2.68 for 8 oz ($0.34 per oz)
AGED: 0 days
STYLE: Pasteurized milk, American-made
SODIUM: 49 mg per oz
COMMENTS: Without raw milk or any aging at all, this cheese couldn't help tasting like "bland city." Though it developed "some nutty tang" when melted, its texture was also unappealingly "chewy."

SARGENTO Natural Aged Swiss Deli Style Sliced Swiss Cheese
PRICE: $4.29 for 7 oz ($0.61 per oz)
AGED: 60 days or longer
STYLE: Pasteurized milk, American-made
SODIUM: 55 mg per oz
COMMENTS: "Kids' cheese," "generic," "plasticky"—pick your descriptor. This cheese was downright "bland" when eaten plain. Warming it in grilled cheese made it "extremely melty and oozy," but the flavor was still "Blandsville."

ORANGE JUICE

Orange juice is America's most popular juice, a breakfast staple with a sunny, wholesome image. Package labels tempt us with phrases like "fresh squeezed" and "grove to glass," but can the contents live up to the promises on the cartons? To find out, we built a tasting lineup consisting of five nationally available refrigerated orange juices, two frozen concentrates, and two lower-calorie juices. The juices were evaluated for freshness, flavor, texture, and overall appeal. Fresh flavor was of top importance to our tasters. Our top juice was minimally processed, while the juices that ranked just below our favorite used relatively high quantities of ethyl butyrate, a compound that occurs naturally in oranges and that is added back to most commercial orange juice to make its flavor seem fresher. Juices are listed in order of preference.

RECOMMENDED

NATALIE'S 100% Florida Orange Juice, Gourmet Pasteurized
PRICE: $5.99 for 64 oz ($0.09 per fl oz)
ETHYL BUTYRATE: 1.01 mg per liter
COMMENTS: Because Natalie's squeezes its juice within 24 hours of shipping it and doesn't manipulate its flavor, the juice tasted "super-fresh." Less processing also made its flavor more variable; tasters found notes of guava and mango in the batch we sampled.

SIMPLY ORANGE Not from Concentrate 100% Pure Squeezed Pasteurized Orange Juice, Medium Pulp
PRICE: $3.99 for 59 oz ($0.07 per fl oz)
ETHYL BUTYRATE: 3.22 mg per liter
COMMENTS: This juice nailed an appealing balance of flavors. A generous amount of ethyl butyrate helped it taste "fresh squeezed," and its "intensely sweet" orange flavor was tempered by a "bright," "mildly sour" tang.

MINUTE MAID Pure Squeezed Never from Concentrate Pasteurized 100% Orange Juice, Some Pulp
PRICE: $3.79 for 59 oz ($0.06 per fl oz)
ETHYL BUTYRATE: 3.7 mg per liter
COMMENTS: Tasters liked the "full, round" flavor of this juice, which was "very orangey" and "fresh." Tasters' only complaint was that this juice carried "more tartness" than they wanted.

MINUTE MAID Original Frozen Concentrated Orange Juice
PRICE: $2.99 for 64 oz ($0.05 per fl oz)
ETHYL BUTYRATE: 0.92 mg per liter
COMMENTS: With "vibrant," "balanced" flavor and only "a hint of bitterness," this product challenged frozen concentrate's bad rap. That it has a shelf life of three to five years and a lower price point than ready-to-serve juices is also a plus.

FLORIDA'S NATURAL 100% Pure Florida Orange Juice, with Pulp
PRICE: $3.79 for 59 oz ($0.06 per fl oz)
ETHYL BUTYRATE: 4.92 mg per liter
COMMENTS: This juice had a "fragrant," "blossoming orange" aroma, but some tasters picked up on a "processed" taste, suggesting that its flavor wasn't quite as fresh. The juice was big on pulp, which some likened to fresh squeezed, though others found it too thick.

RECOMMENDED (continued)

TROPICANA 100% Frozen Concentrated Orange Juice
PRICE: $1.89 for 48 oz reconstituted ($0.04 per fl oz)
ETHYL BUTYRATE: None detected
COMMENTS: Some tasters called out this frozen concentrate for its "bitter," "metallic" flavor, while others found it sweet without being "cloying." Its "perfect amount of pulp" was also a draw that made it seem "close to freshly squeezed OJ," and we can't argue with its rock-bottom price.

RECOMMENDED WITH RESERVATIONS

TROPICANA Pure Premium Orange Juice, Homestyle
PRICE: $3.99 for 59 oz ($0.07 per fl oz)
ETHYL BUTYRATE: 1.71 mg per liter
COMMENTS: Tropicana's flagship juice (and our previous winner) tasted "slightly sweet" and "reasonably fresh" but comparatively acidic (lab results confirmed that it was the most acidic juice we tasted), with "tart" flavor that was "bitter, like grapefruit."

NOT RECOMMENDED

MINUTE MAID Pure Squeezed Light Orange Juice Beverage
PRICE: $3.39 for 59 oz ($0.06 per fl oz)
ETHYL BUTYRATE: 8.53 mg per liter
COMMENTS: "Tang or Sunny D, right?" guessed one taster. Others suggested "Pez." No wonder: This low-cal juice was cut with water and sweetened with stevia. That not only made it downright "sugary" but also overwhelmed the fresh-tasting effect of a high dose of ethyl butyrate.

TROPICANA Trop50 Orange Juice Beverage
PRICE: $3.99 for 59 oz ($0.07 per fl oz)
ETHYL BUTYRATE: None detected
COMMENTS: Another "sugar bomb," this stevia-sweetened low-calorie juice was "abrasively sweet," "cloying," and "artificial." More important: "It doesn't taste like it was made from oranges." It was also "watery" and "thin."

WHITE BEANS

The creamy texture and mildly nutty flavor of cannellini beans round out soups, casseroles, pasta dishes, and salads, and they make appealing dips. We've always appreciated the convenience of canned beans for use in quick recipes, but we've also always been a little prejudiced in favor of dried beans, considering their flavor and texture superior. We included five brands each of canned and dried beans, including two dried "heirloom" varieties. We held six blind tastings, serving two rounds each of the beans plain, in dip, and in soup. We didn't tell participants whether the beans they were evaluating were canned or dried. Surprisingly, top scores for canned beans actually edged out top scores for dried beans. In both canned and dried varieties, tasters liked beans that were firm and intact, with meltingly tender skins, creamy texture, and clean bean flavor. In dried beans, calcium levels determined how well the beans held their shape during cooking, and moisture content (indicative of storage techniques) between 10 and 18 percent made for the best flavor and most even cooking. Beans are listed in order of preference.

CANNED WHITE BEANS

RECOMMENDED

GOYA Cannellini
PRICE: $1.49 for 15.5 oz ($0.10 per oz)
SODIUM: 416 mg per ½ cup serving
COMMENTS: Tasters' favorite canned beans were "well seasoned" (they had the highest sodium level of the lineup), as well as "big and meaty," with both "earthy sweetness" and "savory flavor." Their texture was consistently "ultracreamy and smooth," with a "nice firm bite"—all evidence of carefully calibrated processing.

BUSH'S BEST Cannellini Beans White Kidney Beans
PRICE: $1.19 for 15.5 oz ($0.08 per oz)
SODIUM: 270 mg per ½ cup serving
COMMENTS: "Creamy and firm," these beans were "smooth and intact," with a nutty, clean flavor. In soup, the beans kept their creamy texture and "hearty" flavor. But these beans lost a few points because they tasted less seasoned than our winner did and had a slightly chalkier texture in the dip.

RECOMMENDED WITH RESERVATIONS

PROGRESSO Cannellini White Kidney Beans
PRICE: $1.59 for 19 oz ($0.08 per oz)
SODIUM: 340 mg per ½ cup serving
COMMENTS: With a "mild, vegetal" flavor, these beans were also "a bit mealy." "Almost every bean is broken, with tough skins and grainy flesh," noted one taster. A few tasters detected a "slight sharp, canned/metallic finish." Their softness helped make the dip "richer and creamier," but "bits of skin" got in the way.

NOT RECOMMENDED

EDEN ORGANIC Cannellini White Kidney Beans, No Salt Added
PRICE: $2.19 for 15 oz ($0.15 cents per ounce)
SODIUM: 40 mg per ½ cup serving
COMMENTS: Tasters hated these beans, which have no added salt, calcium chloride, or preservatives, rejecting them in every tasting. We found them "very sour," and "watery" with "grainy interiors" and "tough skins." At best, they were "inedibly bland." Even with fresh lemon, parsley, garlic, and olive oil, the dip tasted like "chalk dip."

DRIED WHITE BEANS

RECOMMENDED

RANCHO GORDO Classic Cassoulet Bean
PRICE: $5.95 for 1 lb ($0.37 per oz), plus shipping
MOISTURE: 10.5% CALCIUM: 362 mg per 100 g
COMMENTS: Although this heirloom bean purveyor was sold out of cannellini beans, the company suggested a variety grown in California from French Tarbais beans. Our tasters found them "creamy and smooth, nutty and sweet," with a "fresh, clean" taste and a "lovely texture and appearance."

RECOMMENDED WITH RESERVATIONS

ZÜRSUN IDAHO Heirloom Beans, Cannellini
PRICE: $8 for 1½ lb ($0.33 per oz), plus shipping
MOISTURE: 8.67% CALCIUM: 204 mg per 100 g
COMMENTS: An heirloom variety grown in Idaho's Snake River Canyon region, these beans were "buttery"-tasting, both plain and in dip; tasters found them "fresh," with a texture that "melts in the mouth but still has a slight bite." But they lost points in soup for "tough skins" and "lots of blowouts."

BOB'S RED MILL Cannellini Beans, Premium Quality
PRICE: $8.08 for 1½ lb ($0.34 per oz)
MOISTURE: 9.25% CALCIUM: 176 mg per 100 g
COMMENTS: These were "big, intact, smooth beans; all identical; sweet and nutty," with a "slightly grassy" taste. The "substantial" beans struck tasters as "fresh." They lost points for textural issues, with tasters noting that they were a bit "grainy" and "dry," both plain and in dip.

GOYA White Kidney Beans Cannellini, No. 1 Grade
PRICE: $1.99 for 1 lb ($0.12 per oz)
MOISTURE: 9.36% CALCIUM: 168 mg per 100 g
COMMENTS: The dried version of our winning canned bean was disappointing. Goya said the identical variety of beans is sold in both canned and dried form. But the dried beans cooked up "uneven" with "tough skins" and "lots of blowouts." In dip, the skins remained "too chewy." Still, tasters appreciated their "solid" flavor, finding it "earthy and comforting."

JARRED MEDIUM SALSA

In an ideal world, we'd always make homemade salsa. In the real world, when we're pressed for time, we rely on the open-the-jar convenience of store-bought. But the sheer number of products and variations is daunting. Which tastes best? We focused on the red Tex-Mex style, which dominates U.S. sales, and on a medium level of heat. We tasted each one plain and with tortilla chips. While many of the salsas were marred by mushy, slimy vegetables with no textural contrast, our top pick included firm, crunchy, evenly diced vegetables. Moreover, where other salsas were out of whack—overdoing the tomatoes or hot peppers or onions—our favorite got the ratios right. The heat level mattered, too. We preferred medium heat from chile peppers, specifically the jalapeño chiles that our top three products used. The better salsas also derived their complexity from naturally sweet tomatoes, rather than added sugar. Salsas are listed in order of preference.

RECOMMENDED

CHI-CHI'S Medium Thick and Chunky Salsa
PRICE: $2.50 for 16 oz ($0.16 per oz)
SUGAR: 2 g per 2-tablespoon serving
PEPPERS: Jalapeño
COMMENTS: This salsa was balanced, vibrant, and "bright with acidity." Tasters found it "spicy, fresh, and tomatoey," with "plenty of heat" that was "pleasant, not overpowering." It also had a "good texture" that was "not too thin or thick," placing it squarely "in between [the] stewed and the crunchiest" salsas. In sum: It offered a "good dipping consistency."

RECOMMENDED WITH RESERVATIONS

TOSTITOS Chunky Salsa, Medium
PRICE: $3 for 15.5 oz ($0.19 per oz)
SUGAR: 2 g per 2-tablespoon serving
PEPPERS: Jalapeño
COMMENTS: Familiar, mild, and sweet, this salsa had big chunks of peppers and onions and a kid-friendly flavor. Tasters described it as "classic jarred salsa": "pleasant" but "not very spicy or complex," with a rich red sauce and a vinegary kick. Some found it too salty when eaten with chips, plus it tasted cooked, not fresh.

PACE Chunky Salsa, Medium
PRICE: $2.49 for 16 oz ($0.16 per oz)
SUGAR: 2 g per 2-tablespoon serving
PEPPERS: Jalapeño
COMMENTS: Tasters liked the "nice lingering heat" of this salsa, as well as its "smoky, heavy on the chiles" flavor. But it was somewhat "vinegar-heavy." While we appreciated "very firm" vegetable chunks, the surrounding liquid was "too runny" and "doesn't stay on the chip."

ORTEGA Original Salsa, Medium
PRICE: $2.50 for 16 oz ($0.16 per oz)
SUGAR: 1 g per 2-tablespoon serving
PEPPERS: Red bell, green bell, chili pepper puree, jalapeño
COMMENTS: Though this salsa had a "nice, thick texture," with big chunks of sweet peppers in thick sauce, tasters found it off balance: The "heat took over all other flavor." With two kinds of hot peppers and not enough sugar to balance it, this salsa also registered as salty, "bitter," and "tinny."

NOT RECOMMENDED

NEWMAN'S OWN Medium Salsa
PRICE: $2.50 for 16 oz ($0.16 per oz)
SUGAR: 1 g per 2-tablespoon serving
PEPPERS: Green chili, green bell, red jalapeño, red bell
COMMENTS: This salsa was nice and chunky with crunchy contrast. Unfortunately, the appealing texture couldn't make up for the nasty flavor. With too much black pepper and a slew of dusty dried herbs, it didn't taste fresh. Plus the seasonings were strange: "Too sweet," tasters said, and oddly "Italian American," with oregano and basil.

LA VICTORIA Thick'n Chunky Salsa, Medium
PRICE: $3.60 for 16 oz ($0.23 per oz)
SUGAR: 1 g per 2-tablespoon serving
PEPPERS: Jalapeño, green chiles
COMMENTS: This underseasoned salsa tasted like cooked tomatoes and not much else. Tasters compared it to "mild tomato puree," "tomato soup," and "marinara sauce." The vegetables were "mushy." Diced too fine, they disappeared into the puree, leaving the salsa "soupy," "like ketchup."

HERDEZ Salsa Casera, Medium
PRICE: $2.69 for 16 oz ($0.17 per oz)
SUGAR: 1 g per 2-tablespoon serving
PEPPERS: Serrano
COMMENTS: Serranos are usually hotter than jalapeños—not here. "Where's the HEAT?" tasters demanded. These particular chiles were either too few or on the mild end of the heat spectrum. This sample tasted like "bad gazpacho," with "mushy" vegetables in "thin tomato water." It had the second highest level of sodium among the salsas we tasted, with no balancing vinegar or heat.

EGG NOODLES

Egg noodles are the starchy soul of many of our favorite comfort foods. The best versions should taste lightly wheaty, like traditional pasta, but have a richer flavor that comes from eggs in the pasta dough. We sampled seven brands of egg noodles, both plain and in soup. Rich, eggy flavor was a huge plus, but tasters also favored noodles made with semolina flour, which gave the noodles a firm yet tender bite. Our favorite noodles used the most yolks (and, therefore, had the highest fat content) of any of the products, which gave the noodles a gentle egg flavor that was just rich enough. Their wide, corkscrew shape worked well in both soup and pasta. Noodles are listed in order of preference.

RECOMMENDED

PENNSYLVANIA DUTCH Wide Egg Noodles
PRICE: $1.99 for 12 oz ($0.17 per oz)
FAT: 3 g **FLOUR:** Semolina, durum flour
COMMENTS: Our winning egg noodles had the most flavor, thanks to a higher ratio of yolks, which gave the pasta a "gentle egg flavor" that was "just rich enough." This product's high semolina content gave noodles a firm yet tender bite with a "nice, subtle chew." The wide, corkscrew shape worked in both soup and pasta.

DE CECCO Egg Pappardelle
PRICE: $4.46 for 8.8 oz ($0.51 per oz)
FAT: 2 g **FLOUR:** Semolina
COMMENTS: These imported, expensive Italian noodles were "mildly eggy," with long, broad pappardelle-like planks that were "thin" and "delicate" but "not too soft." Their semolina content helped them remain "al dente," so they "held up" in soup. Their shape was great as pasta, but some tasters found them too long for soup, slithering off spoons.

LIGHT 'N FLUFFY Egg Noodles, Wide
PRICE: $1.99 for 12 oz ($0.17 per oz)
FAT: 2.5 g **FLOUR:** Durum flour
COMMENTS: This product won our previous taste test, and we liked it again for its "classic," "light," "neutral" flavor, which was more wheaty than eggy. The "soft" noodles lacked the al dente bite of our winner but were perfectly passable and came in our preferred short, fat corkscrew shape.

BIONATURAE Traditional Egg Pasta Pappardelle
PRICE: $3.53 for 8.8 oz ($0.40 per oz)
FAT: 2 g **FLOUR:** Organic semolina
COMMENTS: These wide planks were mild, "gentle," "neutral," and "clean," with "no off-flavors." They had "pleasant chew," with "thick" noodles that stayed "firm" but were best as pasta; in soup the shape was hard to eat, prompting one taster to dub them "the Chuck Norris of noodles. These are so big they kicked my chicken off the spoon!"

RECOMMENDED (continued)

MANISCHEWITZ Wide Premium Enriched Egg Noodles
PRICE: $2.79 for 12 oz ($0.23 per oz)
FAT: 2.5 g **FLOUR:** Durum flour
COMMENTS: These noodles were "a bit on the starchy side," with a "subtle" flavor that was "suitable" but "nothing to write home about." They were "softer" yet "didn't sog out" and had a versatile, short, fat corkscrew shape that was "spoon-friendly."

RECOMMENDED WITH RESERVATIONS

NO YOLKS Cholesterol Free Egg White Pasta, Broad
PRICE: $2.39 for 12 oz ($0.20 per oz)
FAT: 1 g **FLOUR:** Durum flour, corn flour
COMMENTS: These noodles used egg whites but no yolks; tasters found them "very plain," and it was "hard to discern any flavor," but they were still "acceptable" and "neutral." (And to be fair, these noodles are marketed to people who are watching their fat and cholesterol intake.) It was the only noodle in our lineup to include corn flour, which according to the company is employed for its yellow color, firming texture, and smooth taste. The noodles' thin corkscrew shape was harder to scoop up: They were "a bit slippery."

NOT RECOMMENDED

REAMES Homestyle Egg Noodles
PRICE: $4.25 for 24 oz ($0.18 per oz)
FAT: 1.9 g **FLOUR:** Bleached enriched wheat flour
COMMENTS: While they're sold as egg noodles, these frozen noodles were a very different sort from the rest in our lineup; they were short, thick planks that resembled dumplings. Also, they are made from all-purpose flour, not the more usual durum or semolina. No wonder tasters found them "bland," "floury," and "dense."

BREAD CRUMBS

Good bread crumbs should be mildly wheaty but otherwise neutral in flavor. What really matters is that they be ultracrunchy and have excellent coating abilities. We gathered seven best-selling national bread-crumb products—five panko and two traditional—and put them in the ring in an East-meets-West bread-crumb battle royal. We tasted our lineup deep-fried as a coating for chicken nuggets, shallow-fried as a coating for pork cutlets, baked as a coating for chicken breasts, and used in a panade (a paste of bread crumbs and milk) for meatballs. The winner was clear: The panko delivered craggy texture and excellent crunch in coatings, crushing the traditional crumbs. Our top-rated panko's combination of small and medium-size particles hit the sweet spot: small enough for great coverage and big enough for crunch, yet not so big that the crumbs sloughed off. The panko also worked well in our panade. The traditional crumbs failed to adhere tightly to food and made floppy, wan, soggy coatings. Bread crumbs are listed in order of preference.

HIGHLY RECOMMENDED

IAN'S Panko Breadcrumbs, Original Style
PRICE: $4.69 for 9 oz ($0.52 per oz)
PARTICLE SIZE: 75 percent large, 25 percent small
COMMENTS: Although the competition has grown, Ian's—our previous favorite—won again. The crumbs were "crunchy" and "substantial," with particles big enough to stay crisp yet on the smaller end of the panko spectrum. The medium grain "allows for an even coating" and "great cling factor."

RECOMMENDED

KIKKOMAN Panko Japanese Style Bread Crumbs
PRICE: $1.99 for 8 oz ($0.25 per oz)
PARTICLE SIZE: 92 percent large, 8 percent small
COMMENTS: Tasters liked these bread crumbs for their "good neutral flavor," "slight" sweetness, and "big" crunch. As one taster put it, "Holy crunch, Batman!" But the large and porous crumbs sometimes absorbed too much oil, making "greasy" chicken nuggets.

PROGRESSO Panko Crispy Bread Crumbs, Plain
PRICE: $2.99 for 8 oz ($0.37 per oz)
PARTICLE SIZE: 86 percent large, 14 percent small
COMMENTS: These bread crumbs "tasted fresh, not stale," our tasters said, and had a "definite crunch" from "big," "chunky" particles. A few tasters faulted them for ho-hum adhesion, but overall they were passable: "Didn't knock my socks off but seemed like a workhorse."

4C Bread Crumbs Japanese Style Panko, Plain
PRICE: $2.19 for 8 oz ($0.27 per oz)
PARTICLE SIZE: 89 percent large, 11 percent small
COMMENTS: These bread crumbs were "a little yeasty, like fresh bread," with a "crispy, crunchy, and jagged" bite. They were serviceable, but their larger particle size meant that they produced greasier food and left bare spots on meat.

RECOMMENDED (continued)

DYNASTY Panko Japanese-Style Bread Crumbs
PRICE: $2.95 for 8 oz ($0.37 per oz)
PARTICLE SIZE: 92 percent large, 8 percent small
COMMENTS: These bread crumbs reminded tasters of "lightly toasted toast"; they were a "pleasant" complement to chicken. They were crispy and "super-light," but with the largest crumb size of all the products we tested, the crumbs were sometimes soggy, and they coated unevenly.

NOT RECOMMENDED

4C Bread Crumbs, Plain
PRICE: $2.99 for 24 oz ($0.12 per oz)
PARTICLE SIZE: 100 percent small
COMMENTS: These traditional-style "sandy" bread crumbs were too small for proper crunch. They stuck together to form a limp crust, which then failed to stick to the chicken nuggets. Among the seven products we tasted, only this one elicited complaints about the salt; this product has five times the sodium per gram as our winning product.

PROGRESSO Bread Crumbs, Plain
PRICE: $3.29 for 24 oz ($0.14 per oz)
PARTICLE SIZE: 100 percent small
COMMENTS: Tasters likened these traditional-style bread crumbs to cardboard, describing them as "musty" and "dusty." They made a "powdery" coating that "separated from the nuggets" and was soggy in some spots yet "way too sandy and grainy" in others. In sum, "needs more crunch and cling."

CORN TORTILLAS

While we love homemade corn tortillas, we usually rely on the convenience of store-bought. Good corn tortillas should be soft and pliable, with a fresh, light corn flavor. We compared the tortillas in two blind taste tests, first assessing them warmed in an oven and served plain, and then pitting the top four products against one another in enchiladas. We asked tasters to judge both taste and texture. Tasters faulted many of the tortillas for being either too sweet or too bland. Our winning product has 2½ to 13 times more salt than any other in our lineup, which adds flavor but didn't make the tortillas taste salty. Our winner is also the only product to add wheat gluten, which ups the protein content of the tortilla dough and makes it more cohesive and elastic, which in turn creates a softer, stronger tortilla. Tortillas are listed in order of preference.

RECOMMENDED

MARIA AND RICARDO'S Handmade Style Soft Corn Tortillas, Yellow
PRICE: $2.99 for 8 tortillas, 11.57 oz ($0.37 per tortilla)
SODIUM: 120.5 mg PROTEIN: 6.3 g
SUGAR: 0 g
COMMENTS: These winning "tender yet substantial" tortillas wrapped enchilada fillings securely with the help of wheat gluten that kept them soft and pliable. "Clean" and "mellow," the tortillas had a light, cornlike sweetness with a hint of nuttiness, perhaps from the griddle marks that speckled each tortilla.

RECOMMENDED WITH RESERVATIONS

MISSION White Corn Tortillas, Restaurant Style
PRICE: $1.89 for 12 tortillas, 10 oz ($0.16 per tortilla)
SODIUM: 11 mg PROTEIN: 2.2 g
SUGAR: 2.2 g
COMMENTS: These "mildly sweet" runner-up tortillas were "earthy," with good corn flavor and a drier yet more traditional texture (there is no added wheat gluten). Their "faint, stone-ground grit" was "pleasant," though some tasters complained that the tortillas were crumbly and disintegrated in the enchiladas.

GUERRERO White Corn Tortillas
PRICE: $1.79 for 30 tortillas, 25 oz ($0.06 per tortilla)
SODIUM: 11 mg PROTEIN: 2.2 g
SUGAR: 2.2 g
COMMENTS: These tortillas had "more corn taste" than others, with a light "tang" and a sweetness that was like "fresh corn" to some tasters and like "raw pancake" to others. Tasters described the tortillas as a bit dry, with relatively thin sheets that could be "gritty."

LA BANDERITA Corn Tortillas, White (also sold as Olé)
PRICE: $2.49 for 30 tortillas, 27.5 oz ($0.08 per tortilla)
SODIUM: 35 mg PROTEIN: 2 g
SUGAR: 1 g (natural sugars and dextrose)
COMMENTS: These tortillas separated into distinct layers—a quality that separated our tasters. Some found them "tender and flaky," whereas one groused, "Separates into sheets like toilet paper!" The cornlike sweetness also split tasters: One camp approved; the other judged the tortillas too sweet (this product adds dextrose).

NOT RECOMMENDED

LA BANDERITA Corn Tortillas, Yellow (also sold as Olé)
PRICE: $2.49 for 36 tortillas, 33 oz ($0.07 per tortilla)
SODIUM: 35 mg PROTEIN: 2 g
SUGAR: 1 g (natural sugars and dextrose)
COMMENTS: Like their white-corn counterparts, these fragile tortillas flaked apart. Moreover, tasters found them "weirdly sweet" (maybe the added dextrose is to blame) and compared their flavor to "Pepto-Bismol" and "cough syrup."

MISSION White Corn Tortillas
PRICE: $1.99 for 10 tortillas, 6.92 oz ($0.20 per tortilla)
SODIUM: 9 mg PROTEIN: 2.7 g
SUGAR: 2.7 g
COMMENTS: With a mere 9 milligrams of sodium per serving, these tortillas were "quite bland." Worse, we detected "metallic notes" and a "weird, off sweetness" (this product has the most sugar per serving of any in our lineup). The texture—"rubbery"—was also unappealing.

MARIA AND RICARDO'S Corn Tortillas
PRICE: $1.99 for 12 tortillas, 11 oz ($0.17 per tortilla)
SODIUM: 15 mg PROTEIN: 2 g
SUGAR: 0 g
COMMENTS: These "bland," "boring" siblings of our winning product "didn't taste like corn"—or much else. They were dry, and they cracked when we rolled them up because they lack the tenderizers or gluten used by other corn tortilla brands.

BROWN MUSTARD

When it comes to mustard, yellow tends to hog all the glory. But here at the test kitchen we like brown mustard, too, for its spicy, robust flavor. To find the best brown mustard, 21 test kitchen editors and cooks sampled nationally available products in three blind taste tests: plain, in deviled eggs, and with boiled hot dogs. In every taste test, hotter mustards scored higher. We measured each mustard's acidity and found that more acidic products, usually those with more vinegar, rated lowest in our taste tests because vinegar slows the formation of mustard oil, which gives mustard its characteristic bite. Our tasters also demanded mustards that were smooth and creamy and adhered well to hot dogs. Mustards that were gritty, chunky, or runny got lower scores. In cooked applications like deviled eggs, however, differences nearly disappeared. Mustards are listed in order of preference.

RECOMMENDED

GULDEN'S Spicy Brown Mustard
PRICE: $1.99 for 12 oz ($0.17 per oz)
INGREDIENTS: Vinegar, mustard seed, salt, spices, turmeric
ACIDITY: 2.84%
MUSTARD OIL: 0.014%
COMMENTS: We liked Gulden's "bright," "classic" and familiar taste. On hot dogs, it was "complex" and "balanced" with a "smooth" texture that "goes great with the meat." As one taster summarized, it's "what brown mustard should taste like."

FRENCH'S Spicy Brown Mustard
PRICE: $2.19 for 12 oz ($0.18 per oz)
INGREDIENTS: Distilled vinegar, #1 grade mustard seed, water, salt, spices, turmeric and natural flavors
ACIDITY: 3.1%
MUSTARD OIL: 0.02%
COMMENTS: "Tastes like what I grew up with," said one taster. With "lots of bite" and "bold," "complex" flavors, French's earned high marks for its "full-frontal spiciness" and "punch of mustard heat." It led the pack on hot dogs, where we liked its "thick" and "creamy" texture.

BEAVER Deli Mustard
PRICE: $3.50 for 12.5 oz ($0.28 per oz)
INGREDIENTS: Water, mustard seed, vinegars (white distilled, white wine and red wine), soybean oil, sugar, salt, white wine, grated horseradish roots, garlic, eggs, spices, xanthan and cellulose gums, sodium benzoate (preservative), citric acid, turmeric, high fructose corn syrup, lemon juice, calcium disodium EDTA (retains product freshness), artificial and natural flavors, annatto, red chili peppers, ginger
ACIDITY: 2.6%
MUSTARD OIL: 0.029%
COMMENTS: A curveball in our lineup, Beaver was the only mustard we tested with whole seeds and an unusual ingredient list, full of additions like eggs, corn syrup, artificial flavors, and xanthan gum. Because of these characteristics, some of our tasters felt that this product was "a different animal." But most loved the "pleasant pop" of seeds in this "full-flavored," "well-balanced," "sweet and savory" mustard.

RECOMMENDED (continued)

KOOPS' Spicy Brown Mustard
PRICE: $3.39 for 12 oz ($0.28 per oz)
INGREDIENTS: Vinegar, water, mustard seed, salt, turmeric
ACIDITY: 2.72%
MUSTARD OIL: 0.009%
COMMENTS: Koops' "smooth," "uniform" texture won many fans, and most tasters favorably likened its "mild" and "light" flavor to that of yellow mustard; it was similar to "what you would expect at any hot dog stand." However, a few tasters faulted its "simple" taste for being "barely there."

RECOMMENDED WITH RESERVATIONS

HEINZ Spicy Brown Mustard
PRICE: $1.80 for 17.5 oz ($0.10 per oz)
INGREDIENTS: Distilled white vinegar, mustard seed, mustard bran, salt, spices, xanthan gum, turmeric, natural flavoring
ACIDITY: 4.35%
MUSTARD OIL: 0.007%
COMMENTS: We picked up on an unusual array of flavors in this mustard, from "warm baking spices" like clove, allspice, and nutmeg to "curry," "minerals," and "berry flavors." While we've nothing against these flavors, per se, our tasters did find them out of place in a mustard.

NOT RECOMMENDED

EDEN FOODS Organic Brown Mustard
PRICE: $2.78 for 9 oz ($0.31 per oz)
INGREDIENTS: Organic whole mustard seed, Eden organic apple cider vinegar, water, Eden sea salt
ACIDITY: 3.23%
MUSTARD OIL: 0.017%
COMMENTS: "I'm not sure I'd know this was mustard without seeing it." "Whoa—vinegar superoverload!" With relatively high acidity and wimpy heat, this mustard tasted out of balance. While a few testers favorably compared its consistency to that of "stone-ground," most found it "mealy," "sandy," and "gritty."

LEMONADE

Few images are more iconic of American can-do spirit than the childhood lemonade stand. There's good reason why these budding entrepreneurs always sell lemonade: it's very simple to make. So why is it so hard to find a supermarket version that tastes great? We tasted a variety of nationally available brands chosen from the frozen, refrigerated, and bottled soft drink sections of the supermarket. Tasters gave high scores to tart lemonades, which had higher acidity from higher percentages of real lemon juice. Tasters also universally preferred lemonades sweetened with sugar over those made with corn syrup; products made with sugar were crisper and more refreshing. Our top choices also had shorter ingredient lists and contained no preservatives or artificial additives, letting the lemon flavor shine. Lemonades are listed in order of preference.

RECOMMENDED

NATALIE'S Natural Lemonade
PRICE: $3.25 for 64 fl oz ($0.05 per fl oz)
CATEGORY: Refrigerated
PERCENTAGE LEMON JUICE: 20%
ACIDITY: .88 SUGAR PER 8 OZ SERVING: 33 g
COMMENTS: Tasters loved the "super tart," "fresh lemon" flavor of this small-batch lemonade, which contains 20 percent lemon juice—far more than any other in our lineup. It was "tangy" and "refreshing."

SIMPLY LEMONADE
PRICE: $3.49 for 59 fl oz ($0.06 per fl oz)
CATEGORY: Refrigerated
PERCENTAGE LEMON JUICE: 11%
ACIDITY: .62 SUGAR PER 8 OZ SERVING: 28 g
COMMENTS: "Tastes like childhood," remarked one happy taster. This lemonade was "clean" and "bright," with a "good balance of sweet and tart."

MINUTE MAID Premium Frozen Lemonade Concentrate
PRICE: $1.89 for 12 fl oz ($0.03 per fl oz)
CATEGORY: Frozen
PERCENTAGE LEMON JUICE: 15%
ACIDITY: .69 SUGAR PER 8 OZ SERVING: 27 g
COMMENTS: Tasters favorably compared this "bright," "lemony" frozen concentrated lemonade to "fresh-squeezed," though a few found it "a little watery." "Simple, tried, and true," said one taster.

RECOMMENDED WITH RESERVATIONS

NEWMAN'S OWN Organic Virgin Lemonade
PRICE: $2.99 for 59 fl oz ($0.05 per fl oz)
CATEGORY: Refrigerated
PERCENTAGE LEMON JUICE: 15%
ACIDITY: .66 SUGAR PER 8 OZ SERVING: 27 g
COMMENTS: Tasters praised our previous winner for its "balanced" flavor and visible pulp, but some were turned off by a lingering "metallic," "bitter" aftertaste.

NOT RECOMMENDED

MINUTE MAID Lemonade
PRICE: $2.19 for 67.6 fl oz ($0.03 cents per fl oz)
CATEGORY: Shelf-stable
PERCENTAGE LEMON JUICE: 3%
ACIDITY: .47 SUGAR PER 8 OZ SERVING: 27 g
COMMENTS: "Bland city" and "weak" were among the ways tasters described this "watered down" and "cloyingly sweet" bottled lemonade. To us, it tasted more "engineered" and "cheap" than its frozen counterpart.

COUNTRY TIME Lemonade
PRICE: $1.50 for 67.6 fl oz ($0.02 per fl oz)
CATEGORY: Shelf-stable
PERCENTAGE LEMON JUICE: 0%
ACIDITY: .62 SUGAR PER 8 OZ SERVING: 24 g
COMMENTS: "I wouldn't drink this if I was stranded in the desert," one taster said. Others picked up on a "fake" flavor and strong "chemical aroma," which isn't surprising: this brand contains citric acid but no lemon juice.

TURKEY HILL Lemonade
PRICE: $1.89 for 64 fl oz ($0.03 per fl oz)
CATEGORY: Refrigerated
PERCENTAGE LEMON JUICE: 10%
ACIDITY: .35 SUGAR PER 8 OZ SERVING: 26 g
COMMENTS: With the lowest acidity in our rankings, this lemonade was a "sugar overload" for our tasters who compared its "sick, sticky sweetness" to "lemon frosting."

INNOVATIVE COOKWARE

From heat-spreading fins on the bottoms of stockpots to ceramic nonstick coatings on skillets, innovations in cookware are everywhere. Whether these innovations actually work is another story. To see if any new designs could do more—or better—than our long-standing favorite pots and pans, we rounded up three contenders in each of three major cookware categories: Dutch ovens (or stockpots), large (roughly 12-inch) nonstick skillets, and saucepans. While we're not planning on trading in our favorite stand-bys anytime soon, a few of the innovations were promising. The chart below compares our favorite traditional products to their most comparable innovative counterpart.

CONVENTIONAL COOKWARE	INNOVATIVE COOKWARE		
FAVORITE DUTCH OVEN	**RECOMMENDED**	**PERFORMANCE**	**TESTERS' COMMENTS**

| | | **DOES IT WORK?** Yes
STEW: ★★★
FRIES: ★★
RICE: ★★★ | This large, sturdy pot has a thick, multilayer base that encloses a silicone oil chamber designed to spread heat slowly and evenly. It browned meat uniformly and helped reduce stew to the ideal velvety thickness. We let a big batch of chili bubble away for an hour without stirring, and it didn't scorch at all. The only drawback was its mammoth size. Heavy and broad, it needed well over 3 quarts of oil to cook French fries, and its temperature recovery was a bit slow. |

LE CREUSET 7¼-Quart Round French Oven
MODEL: LS2501-28 PRICE: $249.95
This gold standard of Dutch ovens puts a "gorgeous, golden crust" on meat and creates great fond. Stew, braises, and rice cook up perfectly.

PAULI COOKWARE Never Burn Sauce Pot, 10 Quart
MODEL: 1001 PRICE: $229.99
COOKING SURFACE: 10.5 in WEIGHT: 11.9 lb
INNOVATION: Silicone oil chamber in base to provide slow, even heating and prevent scorching

	RECOMMENDED		
FAVORITE NONSTICK FRY PAN	**WITH RESERVATIONS**	**PERFORMANCE**	**TESTERS' COMMENTS**

| | | **DOES IT WORK?** Partly
COOKING: ★★★
DESIGN: ★
COATING DURABILITY: ★★½ | This lightweight pan fried 77 eggs without fat before the coating began to wear off—almost as many as our favorite nonstick skillet. We liked its smooth interior and low flared sides; it nicely browned beef for stir-fry and wiped out easily throughout testing. But the handle loosened and was impossible to fix. The pan is also oven-safe to only 350 degrees (our winner is oven-safe to 450 degrees). A heat indicator spot on the handle stopped working. With these flaws, it's a hard sell. |

T-FAL Professional Non-Stick Fry Pan, 12.5 Inches
MODEL: E9380864 PRICE: $25.27
This inexpensive pan has a slick, durable nonstick coating that released food perfectly throughout testing. It is lightweight and has a generous cooking surface.

MONETA Padella Whitech Frypan, 28 Cm (11 inches)
MODEL: 3820128 PRICE: $110
COOKING SURFACE: 9 in
OVEN-SAFE TEMPERATURE: 350°
INNOVATION: Aluminum pan with ceramic interior, enamel exterior

	RECOMMENDED		
FAVORITE SAUCEPAN	**WITH RESERVATIONS**	**PERFORMANCE**	**TESTERS' COMMENTS**

| | | **DOES IT WORK?** No
COOKING: ★★
DESIGN: ★ | With its white ceramic coating and wooden lid that doubles as a trivet, this pan is designed to go elegantly from stovetop to table. But the removable tong-like handle, the clamp of which is wrapped in rubber to affix to the pan's walls, required near-constant squeezing to stay secure, which hurt our hands. The pan made great rice pilaf, but the very thin aluminum scorched onions and broke our pastry cream. Overall, the innovation didn't seem worth the trouble. |

ALL-CLAD Stainless 4-Quart Saucepan with Lid and Loop
MODEL: 4204 PRICE: $224.95
Our longtime champ heats slowly and evenly enough to prevent onions from scorching and pastry cream and rice from overcooking.

ABCT Low Casserole with Universal Handle and Mahogany Lid
MODEL: AB10324; handle AB200; lid AB10024
PRICE: $158 (pan $72; handle $40; lid $46)
CAPACITY: 2 qt COOKING SURFACE: 9 in
WEIGHT: 1.45 lb
INNOVATION: Removable handle, lid doubles as trivet

INEXPENSIVE CHEF'S KNIVES

A good chef's knife is a kitchen workhorse, so we wanted to find one that could perform a variety of tasks while maintaining a sharp cutting edge and a comfortable grip. We sought out 8-inch chef's knives (the most all-purpose size) which cost $50 or less, and found 10 models which met our criteria. We enlisted testers of varying skill levels and hand sizes to put the knives through their paces, cutting up whole chickens, squash, onions, and herbs. Our least favorite knives were uncomfortable at best and unsafe at worst. Our top performer had the most basic handle, which was comfortable for all our testers. Its sharp edge also stayed sharp for longer than any other knife we tested, largely a result of the manufacturing process. Certain elements, such as carbon and vanadium, increase a steel's hardness so that it can hold its edge and resist chipping, denting, and folding over. Additionally, each of our top three knives was factory-sharpened to a slim 15-degree edge, an angle that once mainly defined Asian knives and is increasingly found on Western knives. Knives are listed in order of preference.

HIGHLY RECOMMENDED	PERFORMANCE	TESTERS' COMMENTS
VICTORINOX 8" Swiss Army Fibrox Chef's Knife MODEL: 47520 PRICE: $39.95 BLADE ANGLE: 15 degrees STEEL TYPE: x50CrMoV15	BLADE DESIGN: ★★★ HANDLE: ★★★ KITCHEN TASKS: ★★★ EDGE RETENTION: ★★★	Still the best—and a bargain—after 20 years, this knife's "super-sharp" blade was "silent" and "smooth," even as it cut through tough squash, and it retained its edge after weeks of testing.

RECOMMENDED		
VICTORINOX Swiss Army Swiss Classic 8" Chef's Knife MODEL: 6.8063.20US1 PRICE: $37.62 BLADE ANGLE: 15 degrees STEEL TYPE: x50CrMoV15	BLADE DESIGN: ★★★ HANDLE: ★★ KITCHEN TASKS: ★★★ EDGE RETENTION: ★★★	Marketed as the consumer version of the Fibrox with an identical blade, this sibling made equally sharp, agile cuts. The downside was the handle. Testers complained that they were forced to grip "too far back," resulting in less comfort and control.
MERCER Renaissance Forged Riveted 8" Chef's Knife MODEL: M23510 PRICE: $31.99 BLADE ANGLE: 15 degrees STEEL TYPE: x50CrMoV15	BLADE DESIGN: ★★½ HANDLE: ★★ KITCHEN TASKS: ★★½ EDGE RETENTION: ★★	This knife's blade was "sturdy" and "plenty sharp." However, we deducted minor points for a semisharp spine that dug into a few testers' hands. Some testers liked that the "heavier handle" felt "solid" and "nicely balanced"; others did not prefer the "heft."

RECOMMENDED WITH RESERVATIONS		
MESSERMEISTER Four Seasons 8-Inch Chef's Knife MODEL: 5025-8 PRICE: $42 BLADE ANGLE: 20 degrees STEEL TYPE: x55CrMoV14	BLADE DESIGN: ★½ HANDLE: ★★ KITCHEN TASKS: ★★ EDGE RETENTION: ★★	"Chunky" and "fat" is how testers described this blade—the thickest and broadest that we tested. As a result, it "wedged" through squash instead of slicing it, but it made for a "solid butchering knife."

NOT RECOMMENDED		
HENCKELS INTERNATIONAL Classic 8-Inch Chef's Knife MODEL: 31161-201 PRICE: $49.95 BLADE ANGLE: 17.5 degrees STEEL TYPE: x55CrMoV15	BLADE DESIGN: ★½ HANDLE: ★ KITCHEN TASKS: ★½ EDGE RETENTION: ★★½	This model produced the thinnest peels and the least amount of waste, but we often needed to go over patches again to finish the job. Many testers found the thick handle fatiguing and clunky. Its low bridge clogged frequently.
WÜSTHOF Silverpoint II 8-Inch Cook's Knife MODEL: 4561/20 PRICE: $38.72 BLADE ANGLE: 14 degrees STEEL TYPE: modified 420	BLADE DESIGN: ★½ HANDLE: ★ KITCHEN TASKS: ★½ EDGE RETENTION: ★★	This knife features a "thin," "lightweight" blade attached to a "skinny," "super-cheap" handle. Most testers found the knife "agile" but lamented that the blade felt "flimsy" and "wobbly" when cutting dense squash.
OXO PROFESSIONAL 8" CHEF'S KNIFE MODEL: 1064648 PRICE: $19.99 BLADE ANGLE: 15 degrees STEEL TYPE: 420	BLADE DESIGN: ★ HANDLE: ★ KITCHEN TASKS: ★ EDGE RETENTION: ★	Brand-new copies of this blade struggled to slice paper. It was "flimsy"; cutting chicken and squash felt "unsafe." OXO's usual grippy handle was "comfortable" when dry but became super slick when held by wet hands.

STAND MIXERS

Given the dizzying range of features and still considerable cost of stand mixers, we shop carefully—and test exhaustively—before we commit. To find a model that would muscle through stiff bread dough as confidently as it creamed butter and sugar, we ordered nine models, ranging in price from about $230 to a whopping $849. The highest marks went to the machines that could quickly and easily handle all tasks, and were intuitive to set up, use, and clean. Some machines lost points for attachments which did not reach the entire surface of the bowl. We found that the torque, or rotational force, of each machine mattered more than horsepower. Our top two models, although the horsepower was the same as or less than other models', could handle everything from whipping egg whites to kneading heavy bagel dough, which we think makes them a worthwhile investment. Products are listed in order of preference.

HIGHLY RECOMMENDED		PERFORMANCE	TESTERS' COMMENTS

KITCHENAID Pro Line Series 7-Qt Bowl Lift Stand Mixer
MODEL: KSM7586P   PRICE: $549.95
STATED CAPACITY: 7 qt
ACTUAL CAPACITY: 5¾ qt
WEIGHT: 27 lb
HORSEPOWER: 1.3   STYLE: Bowl-lift

WHIPPING: ★★★
CREAMING: ★★★
KNEADING: ★★★
DESIGN: ★★★
EASE OF USE: ★★★

This powerful, smartly designed machine made quick work of large and small volumes of food. The bent tines of its whisk fit the bowl's shape perfectly, and the model handled batches of stiff dough without flinching. Testers liked the bowl-lift design and large bowl handle that aided pouring.

RECOMMENDED

KITCHENAID Classic Plus Series 4.5-Quart Tilt-Head Stand Mixer `BEST BUY`
MODEL: KSM75WH   PRICE: $229.99
STATED CAPACITY: 4½ qt
ACTUAL CAPACITY: 3¼ qt
WEIGHT: 21.5 lb
HORSEPOWER: 0.37   STYLE: Tilt-head

WHIPPING: ★★★
CREAMING: ★★★
KNEADING: ★★★
DESIGN: ★★½
EASE OF USE: ★★★

This basic, compact, heavy machine's across-the-board performance knocked out many competitors that were bigger and much more costly. We wish that its bowl had a handle, and a bowl-lift (rather than a tilt-head) design would have been nice, but those are small concessions given its affordable price.

KITCHENAID Professional 600 Series 6-Quart Bowl-Lift Stand Mixer
MODEL: KP26M1X   PRICE: $449.95
STATED CAPACITY: 6 qt
ACTUAL CAPACITY: 5¼ qt
WEIGHT: 25.4 lb
HORSEPOWER: 0.8   STYLE: Bowl-lift

WHIPPING: ★★½
CREAMING: ★★★
KNEADING: ★★½
DESIGN: ★★½
EASE OF USE: ★★½

Compared with its siblings, our former favorite stand mixer wasn't quite as impressive. It was relatively noisy, and as it jerked slightly on tough kneading tasks, the bowl briefly popped out of place. But the results were nonetheless excellent.

RECOMMENDED WITH RESERVATIONS

CUISINART 5.5 Quart Stand Mixer
MODEL: SM-55   PRICE: $349
STATED CAPACITY: 5½ qt
ACTUAL CAPACITY: 3 qt
WEIGHT: 17.8 lb
HORSEPOWER: 1.07   STYLE: Tilt-head

WHIPPING: ★★
CREAMING: ★★
KNEADING: ★★★
DESIGN: ★½
EASE OF USE: ★½

Our former cowinner was outmatched by the competition. Its loose speed dial made it hard to pinpoint settings and its small bowl handles made pouring awkward. It produced fine dough, but cookie dough repeatedly stuck in its Z-shaped paddle.

NOT RECOMMENDED

VOLLRATH 7-Quart Countertop Commercial Mixer
MODEL: 40755   PRICE: $849
STATED CAPACITY: 7 qt
ACTUAL CAPACITY: 5¼ qt
WEIGHT: 43.9 lb
HORSEPOWER: 0.87   STYLE: Bowl-lift

WHIPPING: ★★
CREAMING: ★★★
KNEADING: ★★★
DESIGN: ½
EASE OF USE: ★

We struggled to move this 43.9-pound behemoth, and its 19.5-inch-tall body didn't fit under our cupboards. Cake batter and larger volumes of cream and egg whites were no problem, but the ill-designed bowl and attachments meant that it struggled with smaller amounts of food. The attached bowl guard began to separate from the bowl by the end of heavy kneading (and doesn't detach for cleaning).

BREVILLE Scraper Mixer Pro
MODEL: BEM800XL   PRICE: $280.95
STATED CAPACITY: 5 qt
ACTUAL CAPACITY: 3¾ qt
WEIGHT: 16.5 lb
HORSEPOWER: 0.74   STYLE: Tilt-head

WHIPPING: ★★★
CREAMING: ★★★
KNEADING: zero
DESIGN: ★★
EASE OF USE: ★★★

This model's fast, quiet whipping and creaming and user-friendly features (scraper paddle and timer) advanced it to the lead—until it utterly choked during kneading. A second copy also failed. We can't justify spending nearly $300 on a machine that's no better than a hand mixer.

13 BY 9-INCH METAL BAKING PANS

We can't think of a piece of cookware that's more basic than the 13 by 9-inch metal baking pan, but we also can't think of one that's more essential. We tested eight pans with straight sides and 90-degree corners, since this shape provides the most even cooking surface, and used them to make brownies, sticky buns, and cornbread. We assessed each pan on its performance, design, cleanup, and ability to withstand scratches. Pans that were too dark left some of our baked goods nearly burnt, while lighter finishes produced more even browning. We also preferred pans with a nonstick coating, as they released baked goods easily (even gooey sticky buns) and cleaned up nicely. Products are listed in order of preference.

HIGHLY RECOMMENDED	PERFORMANCE	TESTERS' COMMENTS

WILLIAMS-SONOMA Goldtouch Nonstick Rectangular Cake Pan, 9" x 13"
MODEL: 1984723 PRICE: $32.95
MATERIAL: Aluminized steel
NONSTICK COATING: Yes
DISHWASHER-SAFE:
Yes, but hand washing recommended

PERFORMANCE: ★★★
DESIGN: ★★★
CLEANUP: ★★★
SCRATCHING: ★★

Producing the most evenly cooked, professional-looking baked goods of all the pans we tested, this model made brownies that were level and moist from center to edge and cornbread that was deeply golden and uniformly browned. Not even sticky bun glaze stuck to the pan. Its surface released perfectly and was easy to clean.

RECOMMENDED

USA PAN Rectangular Cake Pan
MODEL: 1110RC PRICE: $19.99
MATERIAL: Aluminized steel
NONSTICK COATING: Yes
DISHWASHER-SAFE: No

PERFORMANCE: ★★★
DESIGN: ★★
CLEANUP: ★★★
SCRATCHING: ★★½

This pan was a strong performer in all tests, though its corrugated-looking bottom ridges were controversial: They left marks that some testers found unappealing on baked goods, but the ridges helped minimize scratches. The pan's nonstick coating released flawlessly.

RECOMMENDED WITH RESERVATIONS

FAT DADDIO'S 9- by 13- by 2-Inch Sheet Cake Pan
MODEL: POB-9132 PRICE: $12.94
MATERIAL: 14-gauge anodized aluminum
NONSTICK COATING: No
DISHWASHER-SAFE: No

PERFORMANCE: ★★
DESIGN: ★★★
CLEANUP: ★½
SCRATCHING: ★½

The large rolled lip on this pan made it extra-easy to handle. It baked evenly, but the lack of nonstick coating was problematic for gooey sticky bun recipes. The surface showed every scratch, and the pan is not dishwasher-safe.

NOT RECOMMENDED

CHICAGO METALLIC Non-Stick Bake & Roast Pan
MODEL: 16945 PRICE: $13.49
MATERIAL: Aluminized steel
NONSTICK COATING: Yes
DISHWASHER-SAFE:
Yes, but hand washing recommended

PERFORMANCE: ★
DESIGN: ★★
CLEANUP: ★★★
SCRATCHING: ★

The darkest pan in the testing produced the deepest browning, which gave us a flavorful crust on cornbread but created a challenge with other recipes. We had to check for doneness early. The pan's coating released well, but the knife scratched it deeply, and tiny pieces of coating chipped off.

FAT DADDIO'S Anodized Aluminum Sheet Cheesecake Pan with Removable Bottom
MODEL: POBCC-9133 PRICE: $23.79
MATERIAL: 14-gauge anodized aluminum
NONSTICK COATING: No
DISHWASHER-SAFE: No

PERFORMANCE: ★
DESIGN: ★★
CLEANUP: ★
SCRATCHING: ★

We had high hopes for this pan with a removable bottom (like a tart pan), looking forward to not having to flip out a cake. But sticky bun glaze leaked and burned, and cornbread batter oozed under and baked the removable bottom right into the bread. The surface scratched deeply.

FOCUS FOODSERVICE Aluminum Sheet Pan Extender, Quarter Size
MODEL: FSPA811 PRICE: $9.99
MATERIAL: Aluminum
NONSTICK COATING: No
DISHWASHER-SAFE: No

PERFORMANCE: ★
DESIGN: ★
CLEANUP: ★
SCRATCHING: N/A

For bakeries, this product may be a great way to get another use out of a rimmed baking sheet, but it was a flop for us: Sticky glaze leaked all over the oven and burned, and cornbread rose on both sides of the extender and glued it to the sheet.

COLANDERS

Italian chefs on TV dip their tongs into pots of boiling water to retrieve strands of pasta. The rest of us drain our pasta like mere mortals: in a colander. To find the best one, we ordered 16 colanders, ranging in design and price. Right off the bat we eliminated eight models that were so fundamentally flawed that we didn't consider them worthy contenders—collapsible models in particular. The annoying tendency of these supposedly innovative colanders to come unclipped or tip over and dump pasta all over the sink canceled out their flat storage appeal. The other eight colanders were put through a battery of tests. Colanders with large holes lost points for letting orzo slip through. Colanders with small or wire-mesh holes performed much better, keeping all of the food in the colander, and they drained more efficiently. We also preferred colanders with some kind of base to keep food out of the range of the sink floor (and unsanitary backwash). Being able to put the colander in the dishwasher was another big plus, but some silicone models came out looking dingy. Products are listed in order of preference.

HIGHLY RECOMMENDED		PERFORMANCE	TESTERS' COMMENTS
RSVP INTERNATIONAL Endurance Precision Pierced 5 Qt. Colander MODEL: PUNCH-5 PRICE: $25.99 MATERIAL: Stainless steel HOLE SIZE: 2.28 mm DISHWASHER-SAFE: Yes		PERFORMANCE: ★★★ DESIGN: ★★★ CLEANUP: ★★★	With all-over tiny perforations that don't allow small foods to escape, our longtime favorite colander remains unmatched. Its 1⅛ inches of ground clearance was enough to keep nearly all the drained pasta from getting hit with backwash. The model cleans up nicely in the dishwasher, and its handles are slim but still substantial enough to grip easily.

RECOMMENDED

		PERFORMANCE	TESTERS' COMMENTS
OXO Good Grips 5-Quart Stainless Steel Colander MODEL: 1134700 PRICE: $29.99 MATERIAL: Stainless steel; nonslip plastic rim and feet HOLE SIZE: 2.28 mm DISHWASHER-SAFE: Yes		PERFORMANCE: ★★★ DESIGN: ★★½ CLEANUP: ★★★	Testers appreciated this colander's beefy rim, its point at the center of the base to drive liquid down and out, and its nonskid feet, though we wish they raised the bowl more than ⅜ inch off the sink floor to combat the backwash effect.
CUISINOX 24 Cm Footed Colander MODEL: COL-2 PRICE: $19.90 MATERIAL: Stainless steel HOLE SIZE: 2.98 to 3.58 mm DISHWASHER-SAFE: Yes		PERFORMANCE: ★★½ DESIGN: ★★½ CLEANUP: ★★★	Though its larger perforations allowed some food to escape, this reasonably priced colander had other redeeming traits—namely, a deep bowl and large, easy-to-grip handles. But it felt a bit chintzy, which made us worry about long-term durability.

RECOMMENDED WITH RESERVATIONS

		PERFORMANCE	TESTERS' COMMENTS
EXCEL STEEL Cook Pro Stainless Steel Mesh Colanders with Silicone Handles, Set of 3 MODEL: 29030 PRICE: $39.95 MATERIAL: Steel mesh, with silicone-covered handles HOLE SIZE: 1.90 mm DISHWASHER-SAFE: Yes		PERFORMANCE: ★★★ DESIGN: ★★ CLEANUP: ★★	Each of the fine-mesh colanders in this set of three drained just as efficiently as our winner but lacked its sturdy frame: Their delicate walls dented easily. Orzo grains became lodged between the mesh and the frame.
NORPRO Krona Stainless Steel 9.5" Deep Colander MODEL: 227 PRICE: $32.27 MATERIAL: Stainless steel HOLE SIZE: 2.72 to 4.18 mm DISHWASHER-SAFE: No		PERFORMANCE: ★★½ DESIGN: ★★½ CLEANUP: ★★	No strand pasta slipped through the holes on this deep colander, but 2 tablespoons of orzo did. Its clusters of holes didn't allow water to drain as easily as other models. The deep bowl cleaned up readily with a soapy sponge—but it isn't dishwasher-safe.

NOT RECOMMENDED

		PERFORMANCE	TESTERS' COMMENTS
RESTON LLOYD Calypso Basics 5-Quart Colander MODEL: 88100 PRICE: $25.99 MATERIAL: Enameled steel HOLE SIZE: 5.59 to 7 mm DISHWASHER-SAFE: No		PERFORMANCE: ★ DESIGN: ★★ CLEANUP: ★★	This model's only perk: its 1¾-inch base, which raised it high off the sink floor. But since it allowed a whopping ½ cup of orzo to escape, was not dishwasher-safe, and required vigorous scrubbing to remove stuck-on bits of pasta, we'll pass.

MANDOLINES

You don't have to be a restaurant chef to appreciate a good mandoline. These tools can thin-slice, julienne, and (in some cases) waffle-cut produce far faster than a skilled cook wielding a sharp knife can, and with utter precision. That uniformity is at least as valuable as the time savings—and not just for cosmetic reasons. When cuts are uneven, so is cooking. But for a mandoline to be truly useful in a home kitchen, it must be easy to set up, clean, and store. And given that you're working with sharp blades, it must also be as safe to use as it is efficient. We selected seven models under $50 each and cut firm russet potatoes and soft ripe tomatoes with all available slice thicknesses. We julienned potatoes and carrots, sliced zucchini lengthwise, and made wavy/waffle slices when available. We liked built-in blades, which felt safer than having to manually switch out the blades, and models that were intuitive to assemble and contained storage. Long, wide, smooth platforms also earned points. The best models also had sharp blades which produced even, clean edges, even on soft tomatoes. Products are listed in order of preference.

HIGHLY RECOMMENDED		PERFORMANCE	TESTERS' COMMENTS
SWISSMAR Börner Original V-Slicer Plus Mandoline MODEL: V-1001 PRICE: $29.99 CUTS: 2 slices, 2 juliennes		EASE OF USE: ★★★ SAFETY: ★★★ CLEANUP: ★★★ PERFORMANCE: ★★★	This simple device made cuts effortlessly with stunningly precise results. Its hat-shaped guard protects well; cleanup and storage is a breeze, thanks to its compact vertical caddy.
KYOCERA Adjustable Slicer with Handguard MODEL: CSN-202-RD PRICE: $24.95 CUTS: 4 slices		EASE OF USE: ★★★ SAFETY: ★★ CLEANUP: ★★★ PERFORMANCE: ★★★	This paddle continues to be a terrific choice for cooks looking only for fast, precise slicing (it doesn't julienne). Changing the thickness requires no blade handling, and it stows in a drawer.

RECOMMENDED			
PROGRESSIVE PREPWORKS Julienne and Slicer MODEL: HG-53 PRICE: $22.25 CUTS: 3 slices, 1 julienne (3 thicknesses)		EASE OF USE: ★★½ SAFETY: ★★ CLEANUP: ★★★ PERFORMANCE: ★★½	A built-in julienne blade and slice adjustment settings make this paddle efficient, compact, and easy to use. One quibble: The thinnest slice setting was almost flush with the platform and worked best with firm foods.
OXO Good Grips V-Blade Mandoline Slicer MODEL: 1155700V2 PRICE: $39.99 CUTS: 4 slices, 2 juliennes, 1 wavy/waffle		EASE OF USE: ★★ SAFETY: ★★★ CLEANUP: ★½ PERFORMANCE: ★★★	Our former favorite adjusts slice thickness with a dial, includes a broad hand guard, and makes crisp cuts. But stored blades get dirty during cutting, forcing us to clean and reassemble them—a tricky task.

RECOMMENDED WITH RESERVATIONS			
NORPRO Mandoline Slicer/Grater with Guard MODEL: 306 PRICE: $24.25 CUTS: slices adjustable up to 7 mm, 2 juliennes, 2 graters, 1 shredder, 1 wavy/waffle, 1 citrus juicer		EASE OF USE: ★★ SAFETY: ★★½ CLEANUP: ★★ PERFORMANCE: ★★½	A dial adjusts slice thickness—no blade handling required—but gauging thickness requires a ruler. Though it slices and juliennes well, other nonessential "bonus" attachments proved disappointing. The lock switch to change blades also jams when the slicer is wet.

NOT RECOMMENDED			
KUHN RIKON Thick & Thin Mandoline MODEL: 22339 PRICE: $25 CUTS: 2 slices		EASE OF USE: ★ SAFETY: ★★½ CLEANUP: ★★ PERFORMANCE: ★	Two blades—one thick, one thin—built into this slicer's platform were set too close together to allow for long slices. The skinny platform forced us to trim down a potato and squeeze in a tomato. Its mini hat-shaped hand guard was ineffective.
MICROPLANE Adjustable Slicer with Julienne Blade MODEL: 34040 PRICE: $29.95 CUTS: 3 slices, 1 julienne (3 thicknesses)		EASE OF USE: ★ SAFETY: ★ CLEANUP: ★½ PERFORMANCE: ★	Handling this paddle's julienne blade felt dicey. An ill-placed support bar broke long slices. Long spikes on the guard mangled food. Slicing firm potatoes was fine, but softer tomatoes turned to mush.

SMALL SLOW COOKERS

We used to turn to our slow cooker only when we were cooking for a crowd or making a big batch of stew meant to last for several meals (our favorite model holds 6 quarts). But these days, many manufacturers are selling smaller models, too, offering the same set-it-and-forget-it convenience for small families—or for small kitchens. To assess these smaller versions, we bought eight 4-quart models priced from about $25 to $130. We looked for a model that would heat up quickly to get food into the safe zone and then maintain a simmer; according to the U.S. Food and Drug Administration, the meat's internal temperature must reach at least 140 degrees within 2 hours. A good slow cooker should also produce perfect results on both low and high settings, and in recipes with lots of sauce or very little. We tested each model by making chicken thighs in tomato sauce, braised smothered steaks, and sticky ribs—recipes which require varying amounts of liquid. Our favorite models brought the meat to safe temperature quickly, then cooked the food gently to tenderness, and performed equally well in all three applications. Digital programmable timers allowed us to set the slow cooker and walk away. Dishwasher-safe inserts and easy-to-grip handles also earned points. Products are listed in order of preference.

RECOMMENDED		PERFORMANCE	TESTERS' COMMENTS
CUISINART 4-Quart Cook Central 3-in-1 Multicooker MODEL: MSC-400 PRICE: $129.95 SOURCE: cuisinart.com CONTROLS: Digital programmable MAXIMUM TEMPERATURE: 198 degrees on low, 195 degrees on high		COOKING: ★★★ DESIGN: ★★★	This "multicooker"—a slow cooker that can also saute and steam food—produced perfect chicken, steaks, and ribs. Its programmable timer can be set to cook for up to 24 hours. We liked its lightweight, easy-to-clean metal insert with extra-large, comfy handles, and its oval shape, clear lid, and intuitive controls.
HAMILTON BEACH Stay or Go 4-Quart Slow Cooker `BEST BUY` MODEL: 33246T PRICE: $26.99 SOURCE: hamiltonbeach.com CONTROLS: Manual MAXIMUM TEMPERATURE: 191 degrees on low, 206 degrees on high		COOKING: ★★★ DESIGN: ★★	This cooker performed well. A gasket and clips on the lid let you take your cooker to a potluck without risking spills. It's comparatively low-tech: The "off," "low," "high," and "warm" settings are on a manual dial—which is its drawback.

RECOMMENDED WITH RESERVATIONS

		PERFORMANCE	TESTERS' COMMENTS
WEST BEND 4 Qt. Oval Crockery Cooker MODEL: 84384 PRICE: $29.99 CONTROLS: Manual MAXIMUM TEMPERATURE: 209 degrees on low, 212 degrees on high		COOKING: ★★ DESIGN: ★★	This model performed fine with chicken Provençal. It cooked steak to tenderness (although the sauce scorched slightly). But ribs developed a tough leathery crust wherever they touched the hot bottom of the insert. The model is manually controlled, which means you must switch off the cooker to stop cooking.
BREVILLE the Risotto Plus MODEL: BRC600XL PRICE: $129.99 CONTROLS: Digital programmable MAXIMUM TEMPERATURE: 212 degrees on low, 212 degrees on high		COOKING: ★★ DESIGN: ★½	This 4-quart model is a slow cooker, rice cooker, and risotto maker. It works OK, as long as you don't cook low-moisture recipes. The insert lacks handles and is the only insert that isn't dishwasher-safe.

NOT RECOMMENDED

		PERFORMANCE	TESTERS' COMMENTS
CROCK-POT Manual Slow Cooker MODEL: SCV401-TR PRICE: $24.99 CONTROLS: Manual MAXIMUM TEMPERATURE: 189 degrees on low, 204 degrees on high		COOKING: ½ DESIGN: ★½	Chicken thighs never reached a safe temperature. The water-temperature performance was inconsistent, and cooking results reflected that. We retested the model by ordering other copies, but we had the same problems. While manual controls were our only design gripe, this model's cooking was fatally flawed.

ROUND CAKE PANS

Why don't your homemade layer cakes ever look as good as those from a bakery? Your cake pans could be at fault. A bad cake pan—flimsy, warped, worn out—makes lumpy, irregularly browned layers that stick, cling, and crack. A good cake pan is a baker's best friend. We wanted a cake pan that was at least 2 inches deep with straight sides. We gathered seven pans priced from $9.85 to $16.99 apiece (remember, you need two pans to make a layer cake) with a variety of finishes. We tested each pan with yellow layer cake, and found that the darker the pan, the darker the cake. The darker pans also made domed layer cakes, which indicates uneven baking. Lighter pans produced taller, more level layers. However, in recipes that required deep browning, such as cinnamon buns, the darker pans were preferable. Though nonstick coating didn't matter much for cakes, it did make a difference in other applications, such as Pepperoni Pan Pizza, which fused irreparably to the pans without nonstick coatings. In the end, we chose a light-colored pan as our winner, but we'll keep a dark-colored pan on hand for recipes that require browning. Products are listed in order of preference.

HIGHLY RECOMMENDED		PERFORMANCE	TESTERS' COMMENTS
NORDIC WARE NATURALS Nonstick 9-Inch Round Cake Pan MODEL: 46950 PRICE: $14.32 SOURCE: amazon.com NONSTICK/COLOR: Yes, light MATERIAL: Aluminum, with galvanized steel–reinforced rim		CAKE: ★★★ PIZZA: ★★½	Solidly built, with light gold nonstick coating, this pan produced tall, fluffy, level cakes. Layers shaped up perfectly, no matter how the pan was greased. Upside-down cake and pizza released and browned well, but cinnamon buns were too pale.

RECOMMENDED			
USA PAN 9" Round Cake Pan MODEL: 1070LC PRICE: $14.99 SOURCE: amazon.com NONSTICK/COLOR: Yes, light silver MATERIAL: Aluminized steel		CAKE: ★★½ PIZZA: ★★½	This sturdy light-toned pan with a corrugated bottom browned consistently and produced level, tall cake layers, though they weren't quite as tall as those baked in our winner. Pan pizza browned well but not as deeply as it did in darker pans.
CHICAGO METALLIC Non-Stick 9" Round Cake Pan MODEL: 16629 PRICE: $10.97 SOURCE: amazon.com NONSTICK/COLOR: Yes, dark MATERIAL: Aluminized steel		CAKE: ★½ PIZZA: ★★★	This pan released perfectly but its dark finish radiated a lot of heat, setting the edges of the cake too quickly, which let the center rise to a dome. Layers were slightly less attractive when we used baking spray. But the dark finish browned pizza and cinnamon buns nicely.

RECOMMENDED WITH RESERVATIONS			
FAT DADDIO'S Professional Series Round Cake Pan Solid Bottom, 9" x 2" MODEL: PRD-92 PRICE: $9.99 NONSTICK/COLOR: No, light MATERIAL: Anodized aluminum		CAKE: ★★½ PIZZA: ★	This thick, sturdy pan with a light, uncoated, matte finish produced mostly uniform cake layers with only slightly sloping edges. Cakes released fine, but with pizza, the lack of a nonstick coating was a big problem: Testers could hardly hack the pizza out of the pan.

NOT RECOMMENDED			
CALPHALON Nonstick Bakeware 9-Inch Round Cake Pan MODEL: 1826052 PRICE: $16.99 NONSTICK/COLOR: Yes, dark MATERIAL: Steel		CAKE: ★ PIZZA: ★★	The cakes baked in this dark pan were some of the darkest and least risen among all the pans we tested, and their edges shrank from the sides, making them slope. The manufacturer does not recommend baking spray, so we used shortening, which overcrisped the edges. Grease and flour are imperatives.

ROASTING PANS

Cookware companies are constantly coming out with new roasting pans. But what really makes a good roasting pan? Our search turned up seven contenders, costing $18 and up, including a $200 model that we tested to see if spending more meant better performance. Materials ranged from all aluminum to enamel-coated steel, plain stainless steel, and a tri-ply construction of stainless steel sandwiching a core of aluminum. All models were at least 12 inches wide and 16 inches long and came with racks. We roasted potatoes, pork loins, and turkeys in each pan. We found that the combination of stainless steel and aluminum provided the most even, deep browning (without burning). Though these tri-ply pans were heavier to maneuver, they heated steadily on the stovetop, never warping or buckling, leaving golden-brown crusts on pork roasts—ditto the anodized all-aluminum pan. The tri-ply pans' lighter finish also provided golden-brown fond that worked perfectly for gravy. Pans with big handles facing upward gave us a sure grip with potholders and helped us transfer the pan steadily, and those with snug-fitting racks earned extra points for easy maneuverability. Products are listed in order of preference.

HIGHLY RECOMMENDED

	PERFORMANCE	TESTERS' COMMENTS

CALPHALON Contemporary Stainless Roasting Pan with Rack
MODEL: LRS1805P   PRICE: $99.99
SOURCE: cookwareking.net
DIMENSIONS: 16 by 13.5 in; 5 lb, 12.5 oz
MATERIAL: 18/10 stainless steel surrounding aluminum core; dishwasher-safe

PERFORMANCE: ★★★
DESIGN AND HANDLING: ★★★

This reasonably priced pan wins again. The tri-ply construction made it sturdy and reliable for stovetop searing and delivered even, consistent browning. The handles were roomy and secure, even with potholders. The U-shaped rack was slightly loose in the pan—a minor drawback.

RECOMMENDED

CUISINART MultiClad Pro Stainless 16" Roasting Pan with Rack
MODEL: MCP117-16BR   PRICE: $129.95
SOURCE: cutleryandmore.com
DIMENSIONS: 16 by 12.25 in; 6 lb, 9 oz
MATERIAL: Stainless steel surrounding aluminum core; dishwasher-safe

PERFORMANCE: ★★★
DESIGN AND HANDLING: ★★½

This pan vied closely with our winner, searing pork loin nicely without buckling or burning and putting an even, golden-brown crust on potatoes. It held a 19-pound turkey easily and its flat bottom aided deglazing. The rack fit snugly, but its handles line up with the pan's, making it tricky for unloading.

CALPHALON Commercial Hard-Anodized Roasting Pan with Nonstick Rack   `BEST BUY`
MODEL: GR1805P   PRICE: $59.99
SOURCE: cooking.com
DIMENSIONS: 16.5 by 13 in; 3 lb, 8 oz
MATERIAL: Anodized aluminum; not dishwasher-safe

PERFORMANCE: ★★½
DESIGN AND HANDLING: ★★½

A great choice at about half of the price of our winner. This anodized aluminum pan browned potatoes quickly and made dark fond (so we had to watch it closely). It withstood stovetop heat without buckling, and its completely flat bottom was great for deglazing. The only drawback: Its handles flare inward.

RECOMMENDED WITH RESERVATIONS

LE CREUSET 17" x 13¾" Roasting Set
MODEL: SSC8512-40P   PRICE: $199.99
DIMENSIONS: 17 by 13.75 in; 7 lb, 3 oz
MATERIAL: Stainless steel surrounding aluminum core; dishwasher-safe

PERFORMANCE: ★★★
DESIGN AND HANDLING: ★

Though it browned evenly and made great fond, this pricey pan was big, heavy, and boxy, making it awkward and tricky for pouring off drippings. Its rack slid in every direction as we moved the pan.

NOT RECOMMENDED

CUISINART Chef's Classic 16" Roasting Pan with Rack
MODEL: 7117-16UR   PRICE: $61.29
DIMENSIONS: 16.75 by 13 in; 3 lb, 8 oz
MATERIAL: Stainless steel; dishwasher-safe

PERFORMANCE: ★
DESIGN AND HANDLING: ★½

This all-steel pan was hotter on the edges and cooler in the middle, browning potatoes unevenly and rendering little fond from roasting turkey. It was roomy but flimsy, and it blackened on the stovetop.

RACHAEL RAY 16.5 Inch Roaster with Rack
MODEL: 54929   PRICE: $49.99
DIMENSIONS: 16.5 by 12.5 in; 3 lb, 12 oz
MATERIAL: Enamel on steel; not dishwasher-safe

PERFORMANCE: ★½
DESIGN AND HANDLING: ★

This thin, lightweight pan buckled on the stove, and enamel pieces sheared off. Channels on the bottom impeded gravy making. The pan's low enamel handles were impossible to grab. Potatoes roasted unevenly, and fond from turkey was too dark.

DISH TOWELS

Whether we're using it to dry a dish, soak up a spill, or wring water from frozen spinach, a dish towel must be absorbent, maneuverable, and sturdy. We tested a wide variety of towels (even including cloth diapers, which one of our test cooks swears by). We dunked the towels in buckets of water to test absorbency, used them to dry delicate champagne glasses to test maneuverability, squeezed 10 ounces of defrosted spinach dry, and used each one to pull hot dishes from the oven. We also put them through 26 wash cycles. All the towels became more absorbent after several washes. The best towels had thinner areas that transported water and thicker spongelike zones that held on to it. Our favorite ones, which accomplished each task easily, were thin- to medium-weight cotton towels.

HIGHLY RECOMMENDED

	PERFORMANCE	TESTERS' COMMENTS
WILLIAMS-SONOMA Striped Towels, Set of 4 MODEL: 29-8845570 PRICE: $19.95 ($4.99 per towel) SOURCE: williams-sonoma.com SIZE (AFTER WASHING): 26 by 18.5 in (3.34 sq ft) MATERIAL: Cotton, alternating strips of basket and flat weave 	ABSORPTION: ★★★ HANDLING: ★★★ DURABILITY: ★★★	Goldilocks would like this towel: It's not too thick or too thin, too big or too small. Its fabric tightened, toughened, and grew more absorbent the more we used and washed it. Stripes camouflaged stains until they washed out and kept this sturdy towel looking fresh.
NOW DESIGNS Ripple Kitchen Towel, Set of 2 MODEL: 197545a PRICE: $16 ($8 per towel) SOURCE: amazon.com SIZE (AFTER WASHING): 25 by 18.25 in (3.17 sq ft) MATERIAL: Cotton, ribbed weave	ABSORPTION: ★★★ HANDLING: ★★ DURABILITY: ★★★	Our previous winner still impressed with its streak-free drying, soft fabric, and excellent absorption. We'd heard complaints about unraveling but couldn't reproduce this in testing. One quibble: All that fluffy ribbing makes for a snug fit when drying tight corners.

RECOMMENDED WITH RESERVATIONS

	PERFORMANCE	TESTERS' COMMENTS
AUNT MARTHA'S Flour Sack Dish Towels, Set of 7 MODEL: TTS28 (28 x 28) PRICE: $15.99 ($2.28 per towel) SIZE (AFTER WASHING): 26.25 by 26.25 in (4.79 sq ft) MATERIAL: Cotton flour sack, flat weave	ABSORPTION: ★★ HANDLING: ★★ DURABILITY: ★★★	This traditional flour-sack towel was big but thin, fitting neatly inside a champagne flute. It dried without leaving behind lint. It was terrific for squeezing spinach. However, big spills overwhelmed its flat weave, it was mediocre as an oven mitt, and shadowy stains persisted.
KUSHIES Washable Flat Diapers, Set of 6 MODEL: D-1026 PRICE: $19.99 ($3.33 per towel) SIZE (AFTER WASHING): 28 by 24 in (4.67 sq ft) MATERIAL: Cotton, flat weave 	ABSORPTION: ★★½ HANDLING: ★★ DURABILITY: ★½	This cloth diaper was great for drying dishes, for squeezing vegetables, and as a potholder, but after washing, it felt like a baby blanket—flannel and fuzzy. At nearly 5 square feet, it was an awkward size for kitchen work.

NOT RECOMMENDED

	PERFORMANCE	TESTERS' COMMENTS
COTTON CRAFT Terry Waffle Weave Kitchen Towels, Set of 2 MODEL: X000D02AKH PRICE: $5.99 ($3 per towel) SIZE (AFTER WASHING): 26.75 by 15.25 in (2.83 sq ft) MATERIAL: Cotton, lattice weave 	ABSORPTION: ★½ HANDLING: ★½ DURABILITY: ★½	Although its absorption improved after several washes, when new, this towel repelled liquid. Its thick lattice texture absorbed water where it touched rather than transporting liquid through the towel. Its label banned bleach and insisted that the towel be washed separately in cold water.
NOUVELLE LEGENDE Microfiber Kitchen Towels, Set of 2 MODEL: NL-MT-R-N-2 PRICE: $7.95 ($3.98 per towel) SIZE (AFTER WASHING): 27.25 by 16 in (3.03 sq ft) MATERIAL: Microfiber, ribbed weave 	ABSORPTION: ★★★ HANDLING: zero DURABILITY: ★	This superabsorbent microfiber towel did many things well. But it turned from ivory to pea green after laundering, and testers hated its static feel. When pressed into service as a potholder, it smelled bad and felt alarmingly hot. It just doesn't seem like a dish towel to us.
KEEBLE OUTLETS Premium Dish Towels, 24-Ounce, Set of 12 MODEL: 24-ounce PRICE: $23.99 ($2 per towel) SIZE (AFTER WASHING): 22.25 by 14 in (2.16 sq ft) MATERIAL: Cotton, herringbone weave 	ABSORPTION: ★½ HANDLING: ★ DURABILITY: ★	This ultrathin restaurant towel is cheap, but its crisp appearance quickly went downhill, and its performance was underwhelming in every category. Small, floppy, and skimpy, the towel was gray, stained, and covered in lint by the end of testing.

LIQUID DISH SOAP

As much as we love our dishwashers, when washing delicate china, wood cutting boards, sharp knives, and pots and pans, we still rely on soap and sponge. We tested seven dish soaps to find the best one. We included three products designed for people who scrub dishes under a running tap rather than fill the sink with soapy water: two with pumps that foam straight from the bottle, and one with a special motion-sensor system for germ-free dispensing. We also found a dishwasher detergent/dish soap hybrid. To test the soaps, we burned skillets with measured portions of hard-to-clean foods like béchamel sauce and chicken teriyaki. Controlling for the amount of soap, water temperature, and type of sponge, we washed the pans using both the fill-sink method and the rinse method, counting the strokes needed to get each pan clean. Our best soaps required fewer than 70 strokes, while others needed anywhere from 85 to 100. The strength of each soap was largely determined by the strength of the surfactants, chemicals that encourage water and fat to mix by lowering the surface tension of water. Testers also preferred lightly scented soaps. All but one of our soaps performed reasonably well. Our recommended soaps worked no matter how we washed with them. Products are listed in order of preference.

HIGHLY RECOMMENDED		PERFORMANCE	TESTERS' COMMENTS
MRS. MEYER'S Clean Day Liquid Dish Soap, Lavender PRICE: $3.99 for 16 oz ($0.25 per oz) STRENGTH: 4.1 times more effective than water		STRENGTH OF SURFACTANTS: ★★★ CLEANING PERFORMANCE: ★★★ SCENT: ★★★	This "97% naturally-derived" dish soap cut through caked-on grime quickly and effortlessly. It cleaned burnt-on chicken teriyaki more than two times faster than other soaps that we tested, and testers loved its "clean," "herbal" lavender scent.

RECOMMENDED			
LYSOL No-Touch Kitchen System, Shimmering Berry PRICE: $10.39 for starter pack, including dispenser, batteries, and 8.5 oz of soap (starter pack: $1.22 per oz; soap refill: $0.47 per oz) STRENGTH: 4.6 times more effective than water		STRENGTH OF SURFACTANTS: ★★★ CLEANING PERFORMANCE: ★★★ SCENT: ★½	Most testers weren't fond of this self-dispensing soap's "strong" berry scent. But its cleaning prowess was undeniable. The motion sensor base unit works cleanly and quickly and is particularly useful for those who prefer to wash dishes under running water.
DAWN Platinum Erasing Dish Foam, Fresh Rapids PRICE: $3.27 for 10.1 oz ($0.32 per oz) STRENGTH: 2.8 times more effective than water		STRENGTH OF SURFACTANTS: ★★ CLEANING PERFORMANCE: ★★½ SCENT: ★★★	A concentrated dish liquid that foams straight out of the pump, this soap scrubbed away burnt-on béchamel effortlessly. Testers compared its "pleasant" scent to "freshly cleaned laundry."
DAWN Ultra, Original Scent PRICE: $2.97 for 24 oz ($0.12 per oz) STRENGTH: 3.6 times more effective than water		STRENGTH OF SURFACTANTS: ★★½ CLEANING PERFORMANCE: ★★ SCENT: ★★	The nation's top-selling dish soap product, this traditional liquid soap worked reliably through all our tests, performing particularly well when we soaked dirty dishes in a sinkful of its soapy water.

RECOMMENDED WITH RESERVATIONS			
METHOD Power Foam Dish Soap, French Lavender PRICE: $4 for 16 oz ($0.25 per oz) STRENGTH: 3.2 times more effective than water		STRENGTH OF SURFACTANTS: ★★ CLEANING PERFORMANCE: ★½ SCENT: ★	Testers were split on this innovative dish soap, designed for spraying directly onto dirty dishes. It washed well but needed double the soap to get the job done, and some found it awkward to use.

NOT RECOMMENDED			
EARTH FRIENDLY PRODUCTS DuoDish, Organic Lavender PRICE: $4.49 for 25 oz ($0.18 per oz) STRENGTH: 1.1 times more effective than water		STRENGTH OF SURFACTANTS: ★ CLEANING PERFORMANCE: ★ SCENT: ★★	We had high hopes for this all-natural soap meant for use in the dishwasher and the sink, but the product proved adept at neither.

GRILL SPATULAS

Grill spatulas are long-handled turners designed to keep your hands away from the flames while grilling. In our lineup of eight models priced from $10 to almost $41, we hoped that at least one would perform all our tests—turning large swordfish steaks, grilled pizzas, and closely packed hamburgers—with assurance, proving to be comfortable, secure, and maneuverable enough for any job. Spatulas with heads of medium width, roughly 4 inches, offered the best compromise of support and dexterity. Rounded grips without any edges were universally comfortable, and everyone favored plastic and wood over metal. Testers were also unanimous in their enthusiasm for the one spatula with an offset handle. The handle was set 45 degrees above the head, providing extra clearance between the griller's hand and the grill. Products are listed in order of preference.

RECOMMENDED	PERFORMANCE	TESTERS' COMMENTS
WEBER Original Stainless Steel Spatula MODEL: 306620 PRICE: $9.99 SOURCE: weber.com WEIGHT: 7 oz **HANDLE GRIP LENGTH:** 7⅞ in OVERALL HANDLE LENGTH: 13 in (including offset) HEAD WIDTH: 3¾ in	PERFORMANCE: ★★½ EASE OF USE: ★★★	Testers of all sizes loved this spatula's slim, rounded, offset handle, remarking on the agility, sense of control, and confidence that it inspired. Particularly when the grill is really packed, this is your spatula. Its relatively small head was also able to lift and move large swordfish steaks.
OXO Good Grips BBQ Turner MODEL: 19091 PRICE: $10.99 SOURCE: oxo.com WEIGHT: 7⅝ oz **HANDLE GRIP LENGTH:** 8⅞ in OVERALL HANDLE LENGTH: 12¾ in HEAD WIDTH: 3⅜ in	PERFORMANCE: ★★½ EASE OF USE: ★★½	This spatula's slim, rounded, soft-grip handle worked well for all testers, many of whom noted that it allowed their hands to "get closer to the food for more control." Because the handle extended almost straight out from the head, it wasn't quite as maneuverable as the Weber.

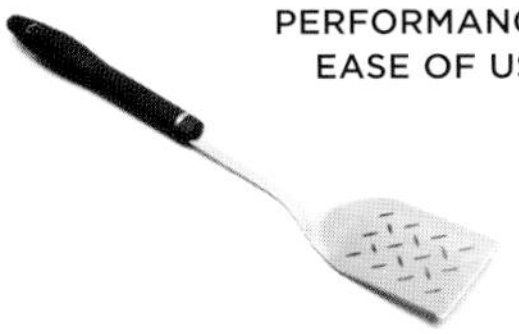

RECOMMENDED WITH RESERVATIONS

CHARCOAL COMPANION Big Head Spatula MODEL: CC1032 PRICE: $17.47 WEIGHT: 12¼ oz **HANDLE GRIP LENGTH:** 13¾ in OVERALL HANDLE LENGTH: 13¾ in HEAD WIDTH: 5 in	PERFORMANCE: ★★½ EASE OF USE: ★★	This spatula's wide head offered good support for swordfish and pizza but wasn't well suited to a crowded grill, forcing testers to work mostly with the corners. Opinion about the wood handle was divided.
STEVEN RAICHLEN Best of Barbecue Stainless Steel Spatula MODEL: SR8110 PRICE: $17.09 WEIGHT: 17 oz **HANDLE GRIP LENGTH:** 5¾ in OVERALL HANDLE LENGTH: 12¾ in (excluding bottle opener) HEAD WIDTH: 5⅛ in	PERFORMANCE: ★★½ EASE OF USE: ★★	The large head offered great support for swordfish and pizza, but it struck smaller testers as heavy, and in tandem with the short handle grip made this spatula feel unbalanced. It was also the heaviest model we tested. Its large head also pushed burgers on a crowded grill every which way.

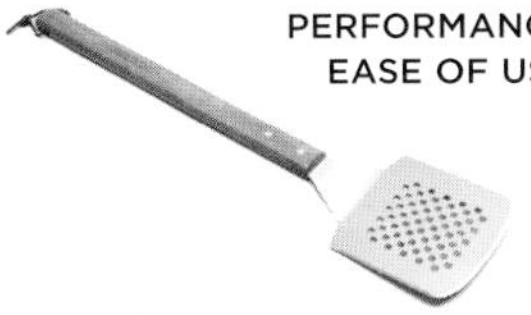

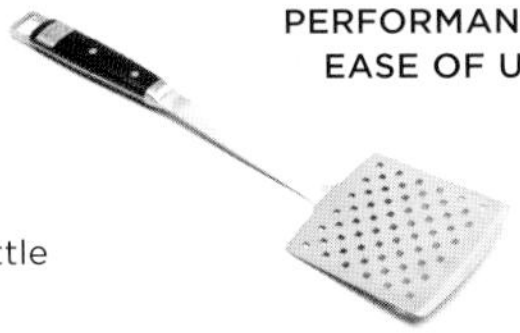

NOT RECOMMENDED

RÖSLE Barbecue Turner MODEL: 12365 PRICE: $40.95 WEIGHT: 13⅞ oz **HANDLE GRIP LENGTH:** 5½ in OVERALL HANDLE LENGTH: 11 in HEAD WIDTH: 4¼ in	PERFORMANCE: ★★ EASE OF USE: ★½	This expensive tool (at twice the price of most others) was flawed. The weighty head and short handle grip felt out of balance, especially to smaller testers. The handle grip, which was metal, got hot if we accidentally left it too close to the grill body.
GRILL DADDY Heat Shield Pro Spatula MODEL: GQ52611WB PRICE: $19.99 WEIGHT: 16 oz **HANDLE GRIP LENGTH:** 6¼ in OVERALL HANDLE LENGTH: 19 in (fully extended) HEAD WIDTH: 4 in	PERFORMANCE: ★★ EASE OF USE: ★	The quality was poor and the extra features were silly. The head (which is interchangeable with other components, available separately at extra cost) wobbled like crazy. The handle grip felt bulky to smaller testers, and its loose, swiveling "heat shield" was far more nuisance than help.

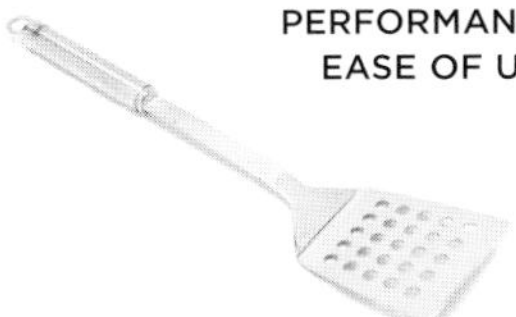

CONVERSIONS & EQUIVALENCIES

SOME SAY COOKING IS A SCIENCE AND AN ART. We would say that geography has a hand in it, too. Flour milled in the United Kingdom and elsewhere will feel and taste different from flour milled in the United States. So, while we cannot promise that the loaf of bread you bake in Canada or England will taste the same as a loaf baked in the States, we can offer guidelines for converting weights and measures. We also recommend that you rely on your instincts when making our recipes. Refer to the visual cues provided. If the bread dough hasn't "come together in a ball,"

as described, you may need to add more flour—even if the recipe doesn't tell you so. You be the judge.

The recipes in this book were developed using standard U.S. measures following U.S. government guidelines. The charts below offer equivalents for U.S., metric, and imperial (U.K.) measures. All conversions are approximate and have been rounded up or down to the nearest whole number. For example:

1 teaspoon = 4.929 milliliters, rounded up to 5 milliliters
1 ounce = 28.349 grams, rounded down to 28 grams

VOLUME CONVERSIONS

U.S.	METRIC
1 teaspoon	5 milliliters
2 teaspoons	10 milliliters
1 tablespoon	15 milliliters
2 tablespoons	30 milliliters
¼ cup	59 milliliters
⅓ cup	79 milliliters
½ cup	118 milliliters
¾ cup	177 milliliters
1 cup	237 milliliters
1¼ cups	296 milliliters
1½ cups	355 milliliters
2 cups	473 milliliters
2½ cups	591 milliliters
3 cups	710 milliliters
4 cups (1 quart)	0.946 liter
1.06 quarts	1 liter
4 quarts (1 gallon)	3.8 liters

WEIGHT CONVERSIONS

OUNCES	GRAMS
½	14
¾	21
1	28
1½	43
2	57
2½	71
3	85
3½	99
4	113
4½	128
5	142
6	170
7	198
8	227
9	255
10	283
12	340
16 (1 pound)	454

CONVERSIONS FOR INGREDIENTS COMMONLY USED IN BAKING

Baking is an exacting science. Because measuring by weight is far more accurate than measuring by volume, and thus more likely to achieve reliable results, in our recipes we provide ounce measures in addition to cup measures for many ingredients. Refer to the chart below to convert these measures into grams.

INGREDIENT	OUNCES	GRAMS
Flour		
1 cup all-purpose flour*	5	142
1 cup cake flour	4	113
1 cup whole-wheat flour	5½	156
Sugar		
1 cup granulated (white) sugar	7	198
1 cup packed brown sugar (light or dark)	7	198
1 cup confectioners' sugar	4	113
Cocoa Powder		
1 cup cocoa powder	3	85
Butter†		
4 tablespoons (½ stick, or ¼ cup)	2	57
8 tablespoons (1 stick, or ½ cup)	4	113
16 tablespoons (2 sticks, or 1 cup)	8	227

* U.S. all-purpose flour, the most frequently used flour in this book, does not contain leaveners, as some European flours do. These leavened flours are called self-rising or self-raising. If you are using self-rising flour, take this into consideration before adding leavening to a recipe.

† In the United States, butter is sold both salted and unsalted. We generally recommend unsalted butter. If you are using salted butter, take this into consideration before adding salt to a recipe.

OVEN TEMPERATURES

FAHRENHEIT	CELSIUS	GAS MARK (imperial)
225	105	¼
250	120	½
275	135	1
300	150	2
325	165	3
350	180	4
375	190	5
400	200	6
425	220	7
450	230	8
475	245	9

CONVERTING TEMPERATURES FROM AN INSTANT-READ THERMOMETER

We include doneness temperatures in many of our recipes, such as those for poultry, meat, and bread. We recommend an instant-read thermometer for the job. Refer to the table above to convert Fahrenheit degrees to Celsius. Or, for temperatures not represented in the chart, use this simple formula:

Subtract 32 degrees from the Fahrenheit reading, then divide the result by 1.8 to find the Celsius reading.

EXAMPLE:

"Roast chicken until thighs register 175 degrees." To convert:

$175° \text{ F} - 32 = 143°$

$143° \div 1.8 = 79.44°\text{C}$, rounded down to $79°\text{C}$

INDEX

D

E

F